STATE AND LOCAL GOVERNMENT:
POLITICS AND PROCESSES

STATE AND LOCAL GOVERNMENT:

POLITICS AND PROCESSES

by G. THEODORE MITAU
James Wallace Professor of Political Science
MACALESTER COLLEGE

CHARLES SCRIBNER'S SONS · NEW YORK

To Charlotte

CONTENTS

INCLUDING TABLES AND FIGURES

✓ *PREFACE*

THIS book has a point of view. It is dedicated to the conviction that governmental units physically closest to us represent vast and intriguing laboratories which can yield meaningful insights into the operations of government and politics as such and can provide a heightened appreciation for the perplexing dilemmas that inhere in the making of public policy and in the choice of candidates and party.

*

Some of the most convulsive changes in American federalism are now occurring in state and local governmental levels as the system struggles with the problems of taxation and education, of reapportionment and political realignment, of budgets and welfare, of the exploding metropolis and the urban sprawl, of civil rights and public order. These changes affect the lives of millions throughout every state and region of this country.

*

Many of the men and women now in our political science classes will not be satisfied with being mere passive bystanders but will want to have a part in directing these changes and in their institutional implementation. To be effective leaders and followers, they must know how state and local governments really operate—how power is held in city and state and how it is exercised, how laws and ordinances are passed and blocked—how the state's political forces and influences shape the concepts of the public good, and why some groups favor localism over federalism and some conservatism over liberalism.

To help readers become doers, each chapter includes a set of practical problems which are structured to invite various solutions based on realistic sets of assumptions. With the aid of the text, the sources cited in the footnotes, the chapter bibliographies (which do not duplicate the footnote sources), and the general bibliography along with other community resources and the methods of survey research, these problems will challenge those who learn by role-taking to defend their decisions in terms of the politically possible, in terms of having found "proximate solutions to insoluble problems."

*

Writers of textbooks are deeply grateful to the professional contributions of their colleagues without which their books could not have been written. This writer's indebtedness to the scholarly efforts of others is no exception. Nor can he ever sufficiently acknowledge the inspiration he gained from his students— their questions, their magnificent persistence in searching for the real and for the unadorned. Whatever this book's errors of omission or commission, of fact or judgment, only the author can be held responsible.

Special appreciation is due Mr. Ronald E. Weber for his invaluable assistance in the preparation of this manuscript.

G. THEODORE MITAU

STATE AND LOCAL GOVERNMENT:
POLITICS AND PROCESSES

Chapter I

POWER, POLITICS, AND THE DECISION-MAKING PROCESS

STATE and local governments constitute political systems within which rules are made, policies formulated, laws interpreted, programs administered, and political accommodations arranged. In these systems individuals and groups compete with each other for political power—for influence in the making of decisions and in their implementation. Control over these processes enables the influential to attain the goals which either they or the groups whom they represent consider important for the preservation or strengthening of their interests in the political system. No one group within these systems is ordinarily strong enough in its financial, leadership, or organizational resources to accomplish its objective single-handedly. Therefore, it is imperative for the various interest groups to enter into coalitions of expedience for the purpose of building the necessary electoral, legislative, executive, or judicial support without which they could not hope to maximize their political power. Bargaining between these groups is carried on by skilled negotiators, by politicians—professionals in intergroup communication who can blunt the conflicts, reconcile the nearly irreconcilable, and articulate the consensus. Such political processes are obviously not carried on in a vacuum. The nature of the strategies that a successful politician will wish to adopt and the range of choices available to him or to the interest group will be profoundly influenced by the nature of the political system. The purpose of this introductory section, then, is to describe briefly some of the major qualities which have given American state and local government its peculiar character and complexities.

CONSTITUTIONALISM

In systems of state and local politics, constitutions cannot be viewed merely as describing the structures and divisions of government, as defining the powers and duties of officeholders, or as cataloguing the rights and privileges of the individual citizen. Though legally superior to ordinary statutory law, these constitutional arrangements were certainly not made in heaven. The framers of state constitutions represented concrete political

I

interests and reflected distinct political views which can still be clearly identified and discerned. Thus, much of contemporary state politics is still forced to operate in a constitutional climate which favors rural over urban interests, agriculture over industry, and a governmental consensus over exact majority rule.

The political ethos of America's state constitutions is frankly antagonistic to social engineering. It emphasizes minimal government and defines freedom in the traditional norms of laissez-faire. Property rights are held sacred, and taxation is regarded as inherently hostile to private enterprise. Government is to be distrusted—even government of, by, and for the people, because the men who guide government seem so easily corrupted by public power. Such constitutions speak of elections but not of politics, of candidates but not of parties, of the objectivity of law, but not of the forces behind the law.

Socio-economic interests that wish to resist change find their political resources greatly enhanced by basic charters which provide for a highly decentralized executive and judiciary, for short tenures of office, and for detailed restrictions on the powers of governors, legislatures, and local governments. Outdated but constitutionally frozen apportionment formulas also proved helpful in that they protected rural minorities against urban majorities and constitutionally anchored limitations on public revenues and expenditures. Legal frameworks which can dull the thrust of political initiative and leadership reinforce the status quo. This has meant that the restrictive provisions and diffusions of political power characteristic of nearly all of this country's fifty constitutions must, therefore, be credited with considerable success in frustrating or delaying the efforts of political coalitions which have been seeking more positive governmental action. The public services which rapidly growing populations demanded from units of government physically closest to them were not forthcoming. Failure to respond to these pressures for services encouraged interest groups formerly active in the state system to revise their political tactics and turn to Washington for federal intervention, assistance, or control.

THE HOBBLED EXECUTIVE

Other conservative qualities of this country's state and local governmental systems are the many constitutional, political, and legal obstacles which have been placed in the path of executive leadership. In fact, there is much to prevent governors from governing. Short terms of office, the direct election rather than gubernatorial appointment of major officials (legislative and judicial), and popular distrust of executive power and discretion—all of these factors have made their contribution towards impotency in the governor's office.

Under the principles and practices of separation of powers, conflicts between executives and legislatures are the planned and deliberate outcomes of divided government. The rules of the game clearly prefer leadership patterns of slow and cautious bargaining and compromise rather than of inspired stewardship or charismatic momentum. The underlying norms of the system evidently favor caution in place of efficiency, inaction in place of action, and accommodation in place of innovation.

Unlike the presidency, governorships generally lack the professional staffs, patronage, budgetary powers, and administrative controls which are indispensable for maximum influence. Also, governors rarely, if ever, stand at the focus of world or domestic crises where a decisive and dramatic act may yield the kind of public confidence and support from which the batteries of presidential powers can be readily recharged.

What is all the more remarkable, in view of the system's obvious preference for caution and continuity, is the fact that quite a few governors did actually manage to become strong governors and leaders of major reforms. These were the men who discovered and successfully applied the handful of power levers that were still available to them. How they rewarded their friends and punished their enemies and what tactics they employed to persuade recalcitrant legislators to support this or oppose that measure are matters that will be discussed in later chapters. Important now, however, is the point that the governorship (as well as the men who occupy it) constitutes a critical center of power within the system. In the decision-making process on the state level some groups will be attracted to the governorship, others will be repelled by it; some will attempt to capture the office in order to restrain executive leadership, others in order to urge its expansion; some will wish to have the governor adopt a more conservative stance, others will insist on more liberal positions. Few groups, indeed, can ever be neutral in their attitude about the disposition of executive power.

LEGISLATURES—THE HAMMERING OUT OF CONSENT

There are probably no interests within a state that remain unaffected by the over 35,000 laws enacted during regular and special legislative sessions. In the name of protecting or furthering the health, welfare, order, and peace of the community nearly 8,000 lawmakers throughout fifty states make decisions that profoundly affect the rights and privileges of property and persons, of groups and corporate enterprises. The legislature, then, is the arena where the major battles are waged, the outcome of which will determine who must bear what share of the cost of maintaining the commonwealth and who may do what with his person or property. Thus every tax law or welfare measure represents a point on a map which marks with some accuracy the advances and retreats that the legislative combatants were forced to make as they contended for positions of advantage or strength. In such a struggle every law represents at best a transitory truce or an experimental design which results in different consequences for the various areas and segments of the community. How each of the plural interests will fare in such encounters depends largely on how much political power each is able to generate at the critical stages of the legislative process.

Power in a legislature assumes many forms. Its manifestations include: strategic positions of influence (committee chairmanships, speakers, and floor leaders); control over rules and calendar; expertise in legislative procedures; technical knowledge of legislative subject matter, including the ability to marshal evidence and skillful lobbyists; and favorable votes in committees and on the floor. In a setting where party discipline is ordinarily weak and leadership divided among competing legislative blocs, where rules are complex and conducive to the delay and derailment of bills, where power is in the hands of the senior members of the chamber, where the public lacks information, understanding, or interest, the business of lawmaking calls for inordinate resources of patience and persistence. There is rarely anything smooth or automatic as a bill inches its way towards passage. Underlying most legislative victories are the successful tactics of the professionals who succeeded somehow in putting together a winning coalition from interests often diverse and occasionally even contradictory. Legislative politics thus places a high premium on skillful bargaining and on the careful applications of the art and science of the possible.

POLITICS IN THE SYSTEM—IDEOLOGY IS MINIMIZED BUT NOT ABSENT

Ever since *Conscience of a Conservative* was published and later with the candidacy of its author for the presidency of the United States, the whole issue of whether American politics should or could become more ideologically oriented has received wide public attention. Senator Goldwater's defeat in November of 1964 in no way stilled the debate. Contenders for leadership within the Republican party have so far been unable to resolve this enormously complicated question. Whatever the outcome of the struggle for power presently wrenching the GOP and irrespective of the consequences that will confront the Democrats as a result of a possible realignment of parties and politicians, the relative absence of delineated political ideologies has long been a fundamental quality of American politics. This is not to say that prior to 1964 the politics of this country operated in an ideological vacuum or that political positions or practices were devoid of all normative implications. Regardless of party predilictions, however, the vast majority of the American people shared the consensus that the basic constitutional framework was sound, that the Founding Fathers were men of wisdom and goodness, that the doctrine of separation of powers was well conceived and continuously relevant, that the geographic division of power (federalism) was this country's most unique contribution to the science of government, and that the Declaration of Independence and the federal Constitution contained the central premises of America's democratic faith.

What has divided America's national parties and politics, especially since the days of the Great Depression, are disagreements about the role of government within the framework of the overriding consensus. How much federal intervention and control is desirable? Should the federal government be urged to assume major responsibilities for full employment, for social welfare and security, for the support of public education, for the smoother operation of labor-management relations, for the more rapid emancipation of the American Negro, for the expansion of public power and urban renewal, for the management of the investment market and the rate of economic growth? Fairly consistently, a majority of Northern Democrats can be found voting on one side of these questions, a majority of Republicans on the other. When the role of the presidency itself, however, is at issue, party lines often crumble. Liberals within both political camps seem to look for presidential leadership, while conservatives (Republicans and Democrats) prefer to place their faith in the Congress.

Compared with American national politics, parties and candidates on state and local levels appear even more assiduous in minimizing or avoiding ideological commitments and alignments. This is, of course, more easily accomplished in some areas of decision-making than in others. Liberal-conservative ideological divisions are probably less readily discernible in votes on liquor control, highway construction, adoption of daylight saving time, the coloring of oleomargarine, lifting limitations on bonded indebtedness on local school districts, extension of governmental immunity to tort liability, administrative reorganization, or revision of home-rule provisions. On the other hand, such divisive issues as taxation, workmen's compensation, loyalty oaths, right-to-work statutes, and welfare benefits tend to produce voting alliances in which the politically more liberal find themselves opposed fairly consistently by the politically more conservative and in which considerations of ideology do in fact play a major role.

In general, however, the business of state and local government is influenced much more directly by power struggles between urban and rural interests, between core city and suburb, labor unions and employers' associations, agriculture and industry, between regions of the state, factions within parties, and those loyally attached to particular candidates and localities. While confrontations of this kind necessarily involve decisions often based on significantly differing value judgments and preferences, the tactics of practicing politicians operating in the system are aimed frankly at submerging or clouding philosophical symmetry in favor of the more mundane pragmatic adjustments which stress flexibility and moderation.

Those in search of meaningful generalizations about the ideological content of state and local politics must be cautioned not to equate the minimization of an explicit ideology with an easy assumption that pragmatic adjustments occur in a value void. On the contrary, the failure to articulate the philosophical standards underlying a particular political decision and its contemplated social consequences, may in itself say a great deal about the nature of the consensus among the participants in the system. A majority of individuals and groups, leaders and followers, politicians and electorates seems largely content to work out its compromises in a climate that favors stability and continuity and that expects no radical change in the distribution of political power and privilege.

A POLITICAL SYSTEM WITHOUT CLEARLY IDENTIFIABLE RULING ELITES

For some years now, the professional literature of American political science and sociology has dealt with the question as to whether or not the decision-makers of a particular community can be scientifically shown to comprise a relatively closed group of "rulers" whose decisions are transmitted downward through a hierarchically ordered power structure. Floyd Hunter and his team of researchers, employing a highly complex series of interviews (the "reputational method" and a "cross section of 'judges' in determining leadership rank"), purported to identify empirically a group of forty white and mostly upper-class persons who could be designated as the ruling elite of "Regional City," a metropolitan community of 500,000 (Atlanta, Georgia). These were the men who made the major decisions that affected the lives and welfare of the entire population.

> The top group of the power hierarchy has been isolated and defined as comprised of policy-makers. These men are drawn largely from the businessmen's class in Regional City. They form cliques or crowds, as the term is more often used in the community, which formulate policy. Committees for formulation of policy are commonplace, and on community-wide issues policy is channeled by a "fluid committee structure" down to institutional, associational groupings through a lower-level bureaucracy which executes policy . . . the structure is held together by common interests, mutual obligations, money, habit, delegated responsibilities, and in some cases by coercion and force.[1]

The theoretical framework of the class-stratification approach to the study of community power used by Hunter and others has come under severe criticism from a group of political scientists who follow the research strategies of pluralism as employed by David B. Truman, Robert A. Dahl, Nelson W. Polsby, and Herbert Kaufman.[2] "The first and perhaps most basic presupposition of the pluralist approach," emphasizes Polsby, "is that nothing categorical can be assumed about power in any community."

> It rejects the stratification thesis that *some* group necessarily dominates a community. If anything, there seems to be an unspoken notion among pluralist

[1] Floyd Hunter, *Community Power Structure, A Study of Decision Makers* (Chapel Hill, 1953), p. 113.
[2] David B. Truman, *The Governmental Process* (New York, 1953); Robert A. Dahl, *A Preface to Democratic Theory* (Chicago, 1956), "The Concept of Power," *Behavioral Science*, July, 1957, and *Who Governs? Democracy and Power in an American City* (New Haven, 1961); Nelson W. Polsby, *Community Power and Political Theory* (New Haven, 1963); Herbert Kaufman and V. Jones, "The Mystery of Power," *Public Administration Review*, Summer, 1954.

researchers that at bottom *nobody* dominates in a town, so that their first question to a local informant is likely to be not "Who runs this community?" but rather "Does anyone at all run this community?"

Pluralists hold that power may be tied to issues, and issues can be fleeting or persistent, provoking coalitions among interested groups and citizens ranking in their duration from momentary to semipermanent.

Pluralists . . . see American society as fractured into congeries of hundreds of small special interest groups, with incompletely overlapping memberships, widely differing power bases, and a multitude of techniques for exercising influence on decisions salient to them. . . . (They) are not surprised at the low priority Americans give to their class memberships as bases of social action.[3]

Pluralists thus neither assume a hierarchical power structure within a particular community nor do they categorically deny the possibility of its existence.

By describing and specifying leadership roles in concrete situations, pluralists are in a position to determine the extent to which a power structure exists. High degrees of overlap in decision-making personnel among issue-areas, or high degrees of institutionalization in the bases of power in specified issue-areas, or high degrees of regularity in the procedure of decision-making—any of these situations, if found to exist, could conceivably justify an empirical conclusion that some kind of power structure exists.[4]

As new research evidence continues to cast considerable doubt on the notion that cities are governed by power elites, the pluralistic hypothesis receives increased professional recognition as the most rewarding and reliable investigative strategy for an understanding of the decision-making process in local government. As long, however, as local community studies find it difficult to identify empirically single groups of "rulers," efforts to discern the ruling elite of an entire state political system must necessarily prove even more difficult. This is so for at least two reasons. (1) American government is clearly not a composite of three delineated and distinct systems of government—national, state, and local. To approach it as a three-layer arrangement would be to ignore a fabric of constitutional, legal, fiscal, and political interrelationships which sets very definite limits to the range of decision-making for all governmental components and for all political interests that operate within the national and state systems. (2) It becomes increasingly apparent that the major policies and decisions which affect this country's highways, public health, taxation, education, labor, agriculture, business, housing, social welfare, urban renewal, and legislative apportionment tend to blur as well as bridge federal, state, and local jurisdictions and autonomies. Such a federalism of interdependence and mutual accommodation continues to shrink drastically the areas of public policy that comprise strictly local or statewide concern.

Neither one of these qualities of American government makes it easier

[3] Polsby, pp. 113, 115, and 118.
[4] *Ibid.*, p. 119.

for the scholar to describe the centers of power or to identify the men who make the critical decisions. But then the task of governing far transcends considerations of academic convenience or simplicity, of clarity or certainty. In the meantime, those who wish to acquire a reasonably satisfactory understanding of the political behavior predominant in the systems of state and local government will be well advised to concentrate their attention on the interactions of political institutions with issues and interest groups. The emerging political compromises, their substance and direction, will then provide the observer with the clues from which new and rewarding hypotheses can be structured that relate to the degree of "overlap in decision-making personnel among issue-areas."

SELECTED BIBLIOGRAPHY

T. J. ANTON, "Power, Pluralism, and Local Politics," *Administrative Science Quarterly*, March, 1963, pp. 423–457.

P. BACHRACH and M. BARATZ, "Two Faces of Power," *American Political Science Review*, December, 1962, pp. 947–952.

EDWARD C. BANFIELD, *Political Influence* (Glencoe, Ill., 1961).

ERNEST A. T. BARTH, "Community Influence Systems: Structure and Change," *Social Forces*, October, 1961, pp. 58–63.

C. M. BONJEAN, "Community Leadership: A Case Study and Conceptual Refinement," *American Journal of Sociology*, May, 1963, pp. 672–681.

HOWARD J. EHRLICH, "The Reputational Approach to the Study of Community Power," *American Sociological Review*, December, 1961, pp. 926–927.

WILLIAM H. FORM and WARREN L. SAUER, "Organized Labor's Image of Community Power Structure," *Social Forces*, May, 1960, pp. 332–341.

L. FREEMAN, *Local Community Leadership* (Syracuse, 1960).

L. J. R. HERSON, "In the Footsteps of Community Power," *American Political Science Review*, December, 1961, pp. 817–830.

MORRIS JANOWITZ (ed.), *Community Political Systems* (Glencoe, Ill., 1960).

ORRIN E. KLAPP and L. VINCENT PADGETT, "Power Structure and Decision-making in a Mexican Border City," *American Journal of Sociology*, January, 1960, pp. 400–406.

SEYMOUR MARTIN LIPSET, *Political Man: The Social Bases of Politics* (Garden City, 1960).

ROBERT V. PRESTHUS, *Men At The Top, A Study in Community Power* (New York, 1964).

PETER H. ROSSI, "Power and Community Structure," *Midwest Journal of Political Science*, November, 1960, pp. 390–401.

PETER H. ROSSI and ROBERT A. DENTLER, *The Politics of Urban Renewal* (New York, 1961).

RICHARD A. SCHERMERHORN, *Society and Power* (New York, 1961).

TED C. SMITH, "The Structuring of Power in a Surburban Community," *Pacific Sociological Review*, Fall, 1960, pp. 83–88.

CAROL ESTES THOMETZ, *The Decision-Makers* (Dallas, 1963).

BENJAMIN WALTER, "Political Decision-making in North Carolina Cities," *PROD*, May, 1960, pp. 18–21.

AARON B. WILDAVSKY, *Dixon-Yates: A Study in Power Politics* (New Haven, 1962).

AARON B. WILDAVSKY, *Leadership in a Small Town* (Totawa, N. J., 1964).

OLIVER P. WILLIAMS and CHARLES R. ADRIAN, *Four Cities, A Study in Comparative Policy-Making* (Philadelphia, 1963).

RAYMOND E. WOLFINGER, "Reputation and Reality in the Study of Community Power," *American Sociological Review*, October, 1960, pp. 636–644.

✔ *Chapter II*

STATE
CONSTITUTIONS

Why are state constitutions so much longer, so much more detailed, and so much more restrictive than the federal Constitution?

Why has it been so difficult to write and adopt new state constitutions which would reflect more accurately the needs of present-day urban America?

MUCH unlike the Ten Commandments in brevity, directness, or authorship, American state constitutions are crowded with amendments, burdened with contradictions, and couched in cumbersome syntax; nonetheless, they are extraordinarily significant charters of government. In fact, there are few if any problems in modern American state and local government for which suggested solutions will not sooner or later run headlong into constitutional prohibitions, restrictions, or obstructions.

Should a newly-elected governor wish to appoint to key offices individuals committed to supporting an agreed-upon executive program, nearly all the state constitutions as now framed would make such appointments impossible. With the exception of Alaska, Hawaii, New Jersey, and Pennsylvania, such "cabinet" positions as attorney general, secretary of state, and treasurer are defined in state constitutions as separate elective offices with specific terms, qualifications, and duties and thereby removed by express design and intent from either gubernatorial direction or control.

If, for example, cities or towns cannot effectively respond to the challenges created by the "population explosion," if the dedication or freezing of tax sources prevents a legislature from developing an integrated budget, if a legislature cannot successfully be forced to reapportion, if highways cannot be relocated, if executive departments cannot be consolidated, or if the state's tax structures cannot be modernized, it is in the nature and language of state constitutions where much of the explanation can be found.

Thirty-eight constitutions were written during the eighteenth and nineteenth centuries for a very different America—an essentially rural society with little industry, with wide open frontiers, with slow means of transportation, and with few people. Government then was viewed with much distrust and fear, and constitutions were framed with the explicit purpose of further restricting the power of the elected officials—elected, particularly after the Jacksonian era, for short terms and for clearly limited duties.

Unlike the federal Constitution which through its remarkable brevity and general language made interpretation and growth fairly easy and thus adaptable to the ever-changing social and economic conditions, the framers of state constitutions insisted on spelling out their views in great detail. Some of these details were so obviously restrictive on governors, legislators, and city councils that a number of state governments would not have been able to operate at all under the impact of the revolutions in industry and communications and the ensuing social changes unless these restrictions were either ignored or rendered flexible through court interpretation and custom. Judicial and practical ingenuity offered solutions where the road to formal constitutional amendment or convention was blocked by the delaying requirements of submission and ratification. When amendment did occur, new details were added to repeal old details, new clauses repealed old clauses. Not unlike the atolls of the Pacific, these constitutional manipulations resulted in islands which were to prove hazardous to the unwary and expensive to the people. Thus, constitutions were first bent and twisted and then amended and re-amended as rapid urbanization around the turn of the century called for the development of public utilities and public mass transportation. Private industrial and railroad corporations demanded constitutional protection and special charters for their operations; farm and labor groups demanded public regulation and certification of these new business giants; and improved standards of safety, health, and service called for more elaborate administrative machinery and supervision. New technologies created new social problems, and the politically-conscious segments of the electorate had no hesitancy in demanding positive government from city hall and courthouse, from state Capitol, and even from the nation itself when the Great Depression underscored fiscal limitations of the more immediate levels of government.

Since World War II the pressure for more formal constitutional change has again increased. State and local governments are now faced with major population increases and shifts not merely from farm to city but from city to suburb and with rapidly increasing costs for educational and welfare services on all levels and for all units of government. Heavy expenditures are needed for building and expanding highways, airports, water and sewage disposal plants, schools, universities, and other types of public institutions; yet local and state governments find their fiscal powers severely restricted in charters and constitutions.

Failure to reapportion shackles the will of the states as urban legislators continue to be outvoted by rural majorities, the latter increasingly apprehensive of losing power, and as governors head diffused and disjointed executive branches preventing responsible leadership despite popular demand and expectation. How then to adapt state constitutions to make possible responsible state and local government in the second half of the twentieth century for an America that insists on both "majority rule" and "minority rights" is certainly one of the issues with which this chapter must deal.

A CLOSER LOOK AT THE FIFTY STATE CONSTITUTIONS

All of the states have formal constitutions (see Table 1). Spelled out in varying degrees of detail and frequently with an overly zealous concern for obtuse legalisms, are the customary provisions for three branches of

TABLE 1. GENERAL INFORMATION ON STATE CONSTITUTIONS

State or other jurisdiction	Number of constitutions	Dates of adoption	Effective date of present constitution	Estimated length (number of words)	Number of amendments Proposed	Number of amendments Adopted
Alabama	6	1819; 1861; 1865; 1868; 1875; 1901	1901	80,000	367	212
Alaska	1	1956	1959	12,000	—	—
Arizona	1	1912	1912	15,000	108	50
Arkansas	5	1836; 1861; 1864; 1868; 1874	1874	21,500	(a)	59
California	2	1849; 1879	1879	70,000	600	350
Colorado	1	1876	1876	15,000	(a)	64
Connecticut	1	1818(b)	1818	6,750	(a)	57(c)
Delaware	4	1776; 1792; 1831; 1897	1897	20,000	(a)	80(d)
Florida	5	1839; 1861; 1865; 1868; 1887	1887	14,500	176	117
Georgia	8	1777; 1789; 1798; 1861; 1865; 1868; 1877; 1945	1945	30,000	85	26
Hawaii	1	1950	1959	14,670	8	5(e)
Idaho	1	1889	1890	14,000	102	68
Illinois	3	1818; 1848; 1870	1870	15,000	30	13
Indiana	2	1816; 1851	1851	7,816	47	20
Iowa	2	1846; 1857	1857	11,000	(a)	21
Kansas	1	1859	1861	8,052	73	45(f)
Kentucky	4	1792; 1799; 1850; 1891	1891	21,500	40	18
Louisiana	10	1812; 1845; 1852; 1861; 1864; 1868; 1879; 1898; 1913; 1921	1921	227,000	566	439
Maine	1	1820	1820	12,438	107	89
Maryland	4	1776; 1851; 1864; 1867	1867	15,445	133	108
Massachusetts	1	1780	1780	11,361	98	81
Michigan	4	1835; 1850; 1908; 1963	1964	19,203	—	—
Minnesota	1	1858	1858	14,986	178	90
Mississippi	4	1817; 1832; 1869; 1890	1890	15,302	104	35
Missouri	4	1820; 1865; 1875; 1945	1945	40,000	26	13
Montana	1	1889	1889	22,000	46	30
Nebraska	2	1866; 1875	1875	16,550	147	94
Nevada	1	1864	1864	15,840	97	56
New Hampshire	2	1776; 1784(g)	1784	8,700	105	41(g)
New Jersey	3	1776; 1844; 1947	1947	12,500	9	6
New Mexico	1	1911	1912	22,400	130	55
New York	6	1777; 1801; 1821; 1846; 1868; 1894	1894	45,000	174	133
North Carolina	2	1776; 1868	1868	14,000	(a)	(a)
North Dakota	1	1889	1889	20,000	(a)	76
Ohio	2	1802; 1851	1851	10,700	162	88
Oklahoma	1	1907	1907	36,412	135	49
Oregon	1	1859	1859	21,982	249	111
Pennsylvania	4	1776; 1790; 1838; 1873	1873	15,092	92	62
Puerto Rico	1	1952	1952	9,000	5	5
Rhode Island	1	1843(b)	1843	6,780	70	36
South Carolina	6	1776; 1778; 1790; 1865; 1868; 1895	1895	30,000	364	251
South Dakota	1	1889	1889	25,000	132	71
Tennessee	3	1796; 1835; 1870	1870	8,220	24	10

TABLE 1   (continued)

State or other jurisdiction	Number of constitutions	Dates of adoption	Effective date of present constitution	Estimated length (number of words)	Number of amendments	
					Proposed	Adopted
Texas_____	5	1845; 1861; 1866; 1869; 1876	1876	35,000	247	154
Utah_____	1	1896	1896	20,500	(a)	33
Vermont_____	3	1777; 1786; 1793	1793	4,840	193	44
Virginia_____	5	1776; 1830; 1851; 1868; 1902	1902	23,101	98	92
Washington_____	1	1889	1889	28,235	(a)	39
West Virginia_____	2	1863; 1872	1872	22,000	61	36
Wisconsin_____	1	1848	1848	10,717	99	66(h)
Wyoming_____	1	1890	1890	15,000	48	25

(a) Data not available.
(b) Colonial Charters with some alterations, in Connecticut (1662) and Rhode Island (1663), served as the first constitutions for these states.
(c) In 1955, 47 earlier amendments were recodified and incorporated in the constitution. Amendment I, adopted prior to 1955, was incorporated in the constitution in 1961. Nine amendments have been adopted since 1955.
(d) Figure does not include amendments of a local nature.
(e) Three amendments adopted in June, 1959 in accordance with Public Law 86–3, 86th Congress, providing for Hawaii's admission.
(f) If a single proposition amends more than one section of the constitution, it may not be counted as more than a single amendment.
(g) The constitution of 1784 was extensively amended, rearranged and clarified in 1793. Figures show proposals and adoptions since 1793.
(h) Including two amendments subsequently held invalid by the Wisconsin Supreme Court.
SOURCE: *Book of the States, 1964–1965*, p. 12.

government—executive, legislative and judicial; functions and powers of the major administrative offices of state; basic rights presumed to inhere in the electorate; relationship between the state and its local units; rules governing the disposition of the public domain and natural resources; procedures and ratios that are to be applied in tax assessment; collection and distribution of public funds; and methods by which amendments may be added to the constitution or by which an entirely new constitution might be adopted. Beyond this, nearly all the constitutions have additional provisions or separate articles dealing with such topics as education, highways, banks, corporations, municipalities and elections. This list of articles and subject matter is neither complete nor identical from state to state.

PREOCCUPATION WITH CONSTITUTIONAL DETAIL—
A FEW ILLUSTRATIONS

Constitutions are obviously not written as an exercise in correct syntax. Therefore, the extent to which constitutional provisions become "unwarranted detail" and to what extent they merely constitute "legitimate" restrictions upon broad grants of power inserted for "the safety of the Republic" is less often a matter of inadequate design or accident. More often these "woodchunks" represent the crowning achievements of interest groups in search of special consideration or the unmistakable evidence of the community's dominant group enshrining its basic political views.

Some constitutional provisions may illustrate the framers' basic lack of faith in the political judgment or self-discipline of elected officials. Thus, lest legislators forget to quit and go home, sixteen states have imbedded into their constitutions the precise number of days that they may meet in their regular sessions, and twenty-four states have fixed their salaries either at specific dollar figures per diem or per session.

Concern for caution and an unhurried legislative process led framers of the constitutions of Alabama, California, Mississippi, and Oklahoma to go to such lengths as to include the procedural requirement that there must be a *full reading* of all bills at least on final passage, while those who authored the constitutions of Arkansas, Illinois, Kentucky, Ohio, Pennsylvania, and West Virginia went further to insist on this requirement at each of the three separate readings of the bill (unless the rules be suspended). In Pennsylvania the full reading requirement appears constitutionally unqualified. The impossibility of living up to these requirements is not difficult to understand in view of the hundreds of bills—some of them book length—with which legislatures are confronted each year. And yet this is what the basic law still formally stipulates.

Concern for economic interests as reflected in constitutional tax exemptions may be illustrated variously. For example, Illinois, Missouri, Montana, Nebraska, and South Dakota exempt property held by agricultural and horticultural societies; growing crops may be exempted in California, Kentucky, Louisiana, Oklahoma, Tennessee, Texas, and West Virginia. Delaware exempts capital stock of corporations; natural gas facilities can by law be exempted in Louisiana; grapevines under age of three years from the time of planting are exempt in California; art works, in Georgia; and athletic clubs, in Louisiana.

The preceding is but a small, a very small, sample of a wide variety of classifications designed to provide protection, encouragement, or advantage to particular economic and social interests for diverse reasons and justifications.

Nor is this solely a matter of the past. Within the last fifteen years businessmen were able to include the famous "right-to-work principle" in the constitutions of Arizona, Arkansas, Florida, Kansas, Mississippi, Nebraska, and South Dakota, while organized labor was able to give constitutional expression to the right of workers to bargain collectively and join trade unions of their own choosing in Hawaii, Missouri, New Jersey, and New York.

Some detail, however, seems to be plainly unnecessary detail. Louisiana, for example, uses over two hundred and fifty words to spell out the power of parish police juries to create garbage districts;[1] Oklahoma devotes seventeen

[1] For a discussion of unnecessary constitutional detail, see Kimbrough Owen, "The Need for Constitutional Revision in Louisiana," *Louisiana Law Review*, November, 1947.

pages to the division of the state into counties and their boundaries; South Carolina's constitution "expounds" in six lines on the meaning of a durable hard surface for streets in the city of Greenville; and Minnesota until 1956 defined the precise points of beginning and ending for the seventy major roads in its trunk highway system. Numerous additional examples could be given where detail deflects from the central task of constitutions to deal with the fundamental in place of the incidental.

AGE AND LENGTH OF CONSTITUTIONS

Is there much of a difference between the older and the newer constitutions in terms of the number of amendments added?

Table 2 shows a total of 597 amendments added, making an average of 59 amendments for each of the ten oldest constitutions. If Louisiana is deleted from Table 3, the average for the newer constitutions would come to 50. Thus,

TABLE 2. THE TEN OLDEST CONSTITUTIONS

State	Effective year of present constitution	Number of amendments
Massachusetts	1780	81
Vermont	1793	44
New Hampshire	1793	41
Connecticut	1818	57
Maine	1820	89
Wisconsin	1848	66
Indiana	1851	20
Ohio	1851	88
Iowa	1857	21
Minnesota	1858	90
	Total number of amendments	597

TABLE 3. THE TEN NEWEST CONSTITUTIONS *

State	Effective year of present constitution	Number of amendments
Michigan	1963	0
New Jersey	1947	6
Missouri	1945	13
Georgia	1945	26
Louisiana	1921	439
New Mexico	1912	55
Arizona	1912	50
Oklahoma	1907	49
Virginia	1902	92
Alabama	1901	212
	Total number of amendments	942
	—Louisiana	439
		503

* Excepting Alaska and Hawaii.

speaking in terms of averages, the state constitutions of twentieth-century America have not yet demonstrated any significant superiority over their predecessors in their capacities for adjustment through inherent flexibility rather than through formal amendment.

Aside from Louisiana which obviously confused regular legislative lawmaking with the framing of a more basic constitutional document setting forth principles rather than operational details, population and size appear to be the substantial factor of distinction between the states in Tables 4 and 5.

TABLE 4. THE TEN LONGEST CONSTITUTIONS

State	Effective year of present constitution	Estimated length (Number of words)
Louisiana	1921	227,000
Alabama	1901	80,000
California	1879	70,000
New York	1894	45,000
Missouri	1945	40,000
Oklahoma	1907	36,412
Texas	1876	35,000
Florida	1886	30,000
Georgia	1945	30,000
Washington	1889	28,235

TABLE 5. THE TEN SHORTEST CONSTITUTIONS

State	Effective year of present constitution	Estimated length (Number of words)
Vermont	1793	4,840
Connecticut	1818	6,750
Rhode Island	1843	6,780
Indiana	1851	7,816
Kansas	1858	8,052
Tennessee	1870	8,220
New Hampshire	1784	8,700
Ohio	1851	10,700
Wisconsin	1848	10,717
Iowa	1857	11,000

Not unrelated to size, of course, is the fact that among the ten with the shortest constitutions not one of the states lies west of the Great Plains.

What is rather remarkable is that despite the enormous changes in the growth of this country, seventeen states have had but one constitution, and that one in each case was written before 1900. Massachusetts, New Hampshire, and Vermont with much pride still retain their eighteenth-century documents. On the other end of the distribution, for historical reasons, Louisiana leads with 10; Georgia–8; Alabama, New York, and South Carolina–6; Arkansas, Florida, Texas, and Virginia–5; Delaware, Kentucky, Maryland, Michigan, Mississippi, Missouri, and Pennsylvania–4.

Manifestly more important than a constitution's age, length, or number of amendments is its content and structure. And what has happened to these essentials particularly in recent years indicates something of the direction that may be taken by American state and local government in the second half of the twentieth century.

PREAMBLES

The framers of state constitutions wished to leave no doubt as to the source of political power or of its ultimate sanction. Thirty-seven of the fifty constitutions begin with "We, the people" and in thirty-one of these introductory statements of purpose explicit reference is made to divine authority for safeguarding liberty and for achieving the highest standards of citizenship. Here are a few of the typical preambles: "We, the people of the state of Arizona, grateful to Almighty God for our liberties do ordain this constitution"; "We, the people of Colorado, with profound reverence for the Supreme Ruler of the Universe, in order to form a more independent and perfect government . . ."; "We, the people of the state of New Jersey, grateful to Almighty God for the civil and religious liberty which He hath so long permitted us to enjoy. . . ."

In clear contradiction to the express terms of the First Amendment of the federal Constitution, Massachusetts goes beyond this to insist that "all persons should worship the Supreme Being"; Delaware, that "all persons should assemble for public worship"; and eight states prohibit the nonbeliever from holding public office. In six of these eight states—Arkansas, Maryland, Mississippi, North Carolina, South Carolina, and Texas—a person cannot hold office if he denies the existence or "being of Almighty God." In Pennsylvania and Tennessee a person, to hold office, must believe in God as well as a "future state of rewards and punishments."

Whereas the framers of the Tennessee constitution needed over four hundred words to retell in great detail the story of their various conventions, the preamble of the Texas document is brief and to the point: "Humbly invoking the blessing of Almighty God, the people of the state of Texas do ordain and establish this constitution." The latest addition to the Union, Hawaii, sensitive of its unique position and role, added a new dimension to the great American experiment in constitution making: ". . . mindful of our Hawaiian heritage, . . . and with an understanding heart toward all the peoples of the earth, we do hereby ordain and establish this constitution for the State of Hawaii."

BILL OF RIGHTS

Every state has a bill of rights, and all but one of them assert the basic freedoms of speech, press, worship, and peaceful assembly. Besides these substantive rights, there is frequent reference made to such basic procedural safeguards as the writ of habeas corpus, trial by jury, protection against double jeopardy and self-incrimination in criminal trials, prohibitions against ex post facto laws, imprisonment for debt, and excessive bail.

Table 6 offers a summary of the subject matter included in the bills of rights of the fifty states. Its subjects fall into three major categories: procedural rights, substantive rights, and the basic political rights upon which all exercise of governmental power must ultimately rest.[2]

What this table does not show is the extent to which material is obsolete or in some instances in direct conflict with express federal law, thus crowding these bills of rights and contributing greatly to their ineffectiveness as well as to their unnecessary length.

Maryland's Declaration of Rights, for example, provides that compensa-

TABLE 6. SUBJECT MATTER IN BILLS OF RIGHTS

Subject	Number of states
Excessive bail	48
Freedom of assembly and petition	50
Freedom of religion	49
Freedom of speech and press	50
Imprisonment for debt	33
Military authority subordinate to civil authority	39
Natural rights	35
Political power in the people	47
Power of eminent domain	50
Protection against double jeopardy	38
Quartering of troops	31
Right to bear arms	35
Saving clause "those enumerated are not all"	50
Security against searches and seizures	48
Speedy trial	39
Suspension of the writ of habeas corpus	50
Treason	32
Trial by jury	50

SOURCE: W. Brooke Graves (ed.), *Major Problems in State Constitutional Revision* (Chicago, 1960), p. 162.

tion for the abolition of slavery "is due from the United States"; North Carolina stipulates that the state is "never to assume or pay . . . any claim for loss or emancipation of any slave," and that no hereditary rights "ought to be granted"; and the honorable art of dueling still comes in for constitutional attention in Alabama, Arkansas, Kentucky, South Carolina, Tennessee, and Wisconsin. References to feudal land tenure can be found in New York; land leases in excess of twenty years are out in Iowa; English must be taught in the public, private, and parochial schools of Nebraska; and the religious views of a witness shall not affect the weight given to his testimony in Oregon and Washington. In Minnesota a farmer "may sell or peddle the products of the farm . . . occupied and cultivated by him without obtaining a license

[2] Two recent studies on state bills of rights of exceptional merit are the following: Robert S. Rankin, *State Constitutions: Bill of Rights* (New York, 1960) and Charles Shull, *The Declaration of Rights in the Michigan Constitution* (Lansing, 1961).

therefor"; the right to fish is guaranteed in California; and the right of private clubs or fraternal organizations to sell alcoholic liquors is specifically enumerated in the Oregon bill.

Recent and much more significant developments in the area of civil rights and labor affairs have not failed to leave their impact on these bills of rights. Florida, one of the states that has incorporated "right-to-work" provisions into its constitution, considered this matter sufficiently important to have it inserted in its declaration of rights. In the New York bill, labor is defined as not being a commodity nor an article of commerce. Explicit provisions against discrimination in the state's military forces because of religion, race, or ancestry are now found in Hawaii, Missouri, New Jersey, and New York, and Alaska insists that all persons should be entitled "to fair and just treatment in the course of legislative and executive investigations."

Despite the widespread acceptance of a more positive role for government in certain fields of economic and social life, it is still true that the general tenor of bills of rights now as in the past represents a deeply held preference for limited government and a maximum realm of personal immunities.

FEDERAL RIGHTS AND STATE RIGHTS

"No State shall make or enforce any law which shall abridge the privileges or immunities of citizens of the United States; nor shall any State deprive any person of life, liberty, or property, without due process of law; nor deny to any person . . . the equal protection of the laws." Is there, in view of this language of the Fourteenth Amendment, any further need for state bills of rights to have state assurances of a citizen's basic freedoms and procedural rights or are they but redundant propositions of interest to historians only? Despite powerful dissents by such leading members of the Supreme Court as Justices Harlan, Brewer, Field, Cardozo, and Black who have sought to interpret the key clauses of the Fourteenth Amendment ("due process of law," "privileges or immunities," and "equal protection of laws") as enabling the uniform application of the entire federal bill of rights to the states, the majority of the Court has so far been unwilling to accept this interpretation and has generally rejected the "incorporation theory." This has not prevented the Court, however, during the last half century from admitting "some of the federal list." At the top of the list are the freedoms of speech, press, religion, and assembly. Justice Cardozo, in *Palko* v. *Connecticut* (1937),[3] then writing for the majority, called them "the matrix, the indispensable condition, of nearly every other form of freedom." Federal procedural safeguards have not until very recently fared so well. Mr. Justice William J. Brennan in his James Madison Lecture for 1961 at the New York University Law Center,[4] was able

[3] 302 U. S. 319 (1937).

[4] William J. Brennan, Jr., "The Bill of Rights and the States," *New York University Law Review*, April, 1961, pp. 761–778.

to find only three federal procedural guarantees applicable to the states by "due process of law": (1) "States are required to see to it that 'just compensation' shall be paid for private property taken for public use" (Fifth Amendment). (2) Counsel must "be appointed for an accused charged with an offense punishable by death" (Sixth Amendment). (3) There cannot be "unreasonable searches and seizures" (Fourth Amendment). Since then the Supreme Court has extended further provisions of the Fifth and Sixth Amendments to state court proceedings. In *Gideon* v. *Wainwright* (1963) [5] the Court ruled that states must guarantee defendants counsel even if they cannot afford to employ one for themselves. In *Malloy* v. *Hogan* (1964) [6] the Court said that the Fifth Amendment protection against self-incrimination applies in state as well as federal court proceedings.

Thus, given the present construction of the federal bill of rights, should a citizen wish to enjoy the right to a "speedy and public trial by an impartial jury," to "be confronted with the witness against him," to have "compulsory process for obtaining witnesses in his favor," and to be protected against "excessive bail or fines," he would have to find these rights and guarantees in the constitution of his particular state. And if they are found there, the interpretation and implementation of these rights is and remains in the hands of state law enforcement agencies, subject to removal into a federal jurisdiction only upon proof of the most blatant and arbitrary of discriminations.

DISTRIBUTION OF GOVERNMENTAL POWERS

In American political thought, the doctrine of separation of powers solidly anchored in a written constitution has always been considered an indispensable element in the fabric of a government designed to insure freedom under law. At least forty states have separate or section articles in their constitutions that give effect to that doctrine. Virginia's provision is typical: "Legislative, executive and judicial departments are to be separate and distinct so that neither exercises power of more than one at the same time."

Actually Virginia and all the other states have discovered that it is much easier to lay down the principle that there should be rigid separation of powers than to operate a government on such basis. In nearly every instance an act of government must necessarily involve the interplay and to some extent the cooperation of all three—the lawmaking, the law enforcing, and the law adjudicating functions of the state. The framers of the New Hampshire constitution must have had this in mind when they wrote that the three "essential powers . . . ought to be kept as separate from, and independent of, each other, as the nature of a free government will admit, or as consistent with that chain of connection that binds the whole fabric of the Constitution in one indissoluble bond of unity and amity." Two recent constitutions, those

[5] 372 U. S. 335 (1963).   [6] 378 U. S. 1 (1964).

of Hawaii and Alaska, omit any specific references to the mutual exclusiveness of the three branches.[7]

One of the objectives of the framers of constitutions was undoubtedly the desire to protect the interests of the minority by blocking or slowing down unwise and hurried actions by a transitory majority. Not only transitory but genuine majorities as well were soon to testify to the successful attainment of this objective. Had another objective been a wish to facilitate an orderly arrangement of all legislative activity within the legislative branch and all executive business within the executive branch, there would have been much disappointment among the founding fathers, for subsequent developments through amendment and law were to work nearly always in the opposite direction. This caused one authority to conclude that as the trademark of American constitutions, separation of powers is "one of their least successful concepts."[8]

THE LEGISLATIVE ARTICLE

Nearly all of the constitutions begin this article with a general statement to the effect that the "legislative power of the state shall be vested in a legislature. . . ." Then they go on with varying degrees of detail to provide for the composition and organization of the upper and lower houses (except for Nebraska which has the country's only unicameral legislature), for rules governing the passage of legislation, for the qualification, election, tenure, and privileges of legislators, and for such special subjects as quorums, impeachments, special sessions, gubernatorial veto, and reapportionment.[9]

Since the lawmaking power of the typical American state legislature is truly immense, a vast number of constitutional provisions center on the limitations placed on the exercise of such powers. There are at least four major categories:

A. Prohibitions against special, private, or local laws on any matters and in all situations which can be covered by general law.

B. Delineation in the constitution of subjects or situations which cannot be dealt with by special or local laws.

C. A requirement that all general laws be uniform in their operations throughout the state.

[7] For appraisals of these documents, see J. S. Hellenthal, "Alaska's Heralded Constitution: The 49th State Sets an Example," *American Bar Association Journal,* December, 1958; P. A. Dionisopoulos, "Indiana 1851, Alaska 1956: A Century of Difference in State Constitutions," *Indiana Law Journal,* Fall, 1958; and P. C. Bartholomew and R. M. Kamins, "Hawaiian Constitution: A Structure for Good Government," *American Bar Association Journal,* November, 1959.

[8] Harvey Walker, "Myth and Reality in State Constitutional Development," in W. Brooke Graves (ed.), *Major Problems in State Constitutional Revision* (Chicago, 1960), p. 5.

[9] For a recent study of state constitutional provisions for legislatures, see Herbert Garfinkel, *The Constitution and The Legislature* (Lansing, 1961).

D. The establishment of a special procedure for public notice before legislation affecting one locality may be considered by the legislature and for local referendum before the enactment takes effect.

Due to the nature of American federalism there is still another, a fifth, limitation. The "supremacy clause" of the United States Constitution declares federal law "made in pursuance" of the United States Constitution or "under its authority" to be supreme—binding all judges to its support—"anything in the constitution or laws of any state to the contrary notwithstanding."

Fortunately, in view of extremely heavy work loads, constitutional developments in recent years have actually tended to strengthen rather than further restrict legislatures, especially in terms of their internal organization. For example, legislatures are now considered to be in continuous session or are empowered to meet annually instead of biennially in Alaska, Arizona, California, Colorado, Delaware, Georgia, Hawaii, Kansas, Louisiana, Maryland, Massachusetts, Michigan, New Jersey, New York, Pennsylvania, Rhode Island, South Carolina, South Dakota, and West Virginia. The 1963 sessions of the Illinois, New Mexico, and Nevada legislatures approved the proposition of an annual session and submitted it to the electorate for ratification in 1964.

Most constitutions still do not allow a legislature to call itself into special session (without gubernatorial initiation). So far only a dozen states have been willing to adopt this procedure.

Even less progress than that can be recorded in removing one of the major obstacles to making legislative chambers more effective and responsible—constitutional provisions on reapportionment and redistricting. In too many instances such provisions prevent legislatures from acknowledging the growth and concern of America's cities. "It is safe to conclude," noted a study completed only two years before the United States Supreme Court signalled major federal intervention in this field, "that at least two dozen of the 99 total state legislative bodies are effectively placed outside the sphere of reapportionment or redistricting except by constitutional amendment." [10] Nor is this tendency to "freeze" legislative districts exclusively a matter of the past. Strong anti-urban bias has continued to find expression in senatorial districts constitutionally "frozen" in Arkansas (1952), in Hawaii (1959) (where Oahu with 70 per cent of the population was given 40 per cent of the voting power in the Senate), in Alaska (1961), in Colorado (1963), in Illinois (1955), in North Dakota (1963), and in Maryland (1962). At least eleven states—Arizona, California, Connecticut, Delaware, Idaho, Montana, Nevada, New Jersey, New Mexico, South Carolina, and Vermont—have, in their constitutions, specified counties or towns as the basis upon which Senate or House seats are to be allocated.

What has happened to urban areas when such governmental units are so designated can be seen from a few illustrations.

In New Jersey, 19 per cent of the voters now elect a majority of the Senate. In California, a recent study pointed out that three mountain

[10] Gordon E. Baker, *State Constitutions: Reapportionment* (New York, 1960), p. 14.

counties—Alpine, Mono, and Inyo, with a total population of 14,294—have the same representation in the Senate as Los Angeles County which has over six million people. The four most populous counties—Los Angeles, San Francisco, Alameda, and San Diego—with more than eight million people, or about 60 per cent of the state, have four senators, while four other senatorial districts with a combined population of only 116,956, or less than one per cent of the state, have the same representation in the Senate. In Connecticut two seats in the state House are given to Hartford, population 162,000; and two, to the city of Colebrook, population 791. In Delaware no constitutional changes were made between 1894 and 1963 when New Castle County (Wilmington) with 69 per cent of the state's population received only one-third of the Senate seats.

Most of the state constitutions do provide for some form of periodic reapportionment or redistricting following a state or federal census. The failure of American state legislatures to live up to these constitutional duties prior to the *Baker* v. *Carr* (1962) decision represents one of the most difficult practices to correct.[11] Attempts to force legislatures through judicial procedures to live up to their constitutional mandates were until 1962 largely unsuccessful. Courts in general were unwilling to assume jurisdiction on the grounds that their actions would constitute entering into "political questions" thus violating the doctrine of separation of powers or on the grounds that recourse to the ballot would best correct the inequities. Among the most promising recent constitutional developments have been those in Alaska, Arkansas, Arizona (House), Delaware, Hawaii, Maryland (House), Michigan, Missouri, and Ohio where a legislative failure to reapportion can then be followed by taking the matter of reapportionment entirely out of its hands and placing it in the hands of the governor, or an executive commission, or the county boards, or the secretary of state. In other states—California, Illinois, Maine, North Dakota, Oregon, South Dakota, and Texas—reapportionment may be accomplished by an executive commission, or the secretary of state, or the state supreme court if the legislature fails to reapportion itself. Two of the three most recent constitutions—those of Alaska and Hawaii —go into considerable detail to assure periodic reapportioning. To further strengthen these provisions, any qualified voter may force the governor to perform his reapportioning duties through application for a writ of mandamus, and the state supreme court itself is additionally authorized to review, and if necessary, correct such reapportionment.

How successful these newer provisions have been in forcing legislatures to reflect the strength of shifts to urban and suburban areas cannot now be ascertained. Nearly all these constitutions still retain the requirement that "area" has to be represented in one chamber. Qualifications are set for the redrawing of districts. Even the mandate for reapportionment itself can be significantly circumvented, in purpose at least, by making only minor revi-

---

[11] For a study of the apportionment problem in Michigan previous to *Baker* v. *Carr*, see Herbert Garfinkel and Charles Shull, *Legislative Apportionment in Michigan* (Lansing, 1961).

sions or by merely shuffling districts. Here as in so many other constitutional issues, the root of the problem is neither simply legal nor procedural but mostly political.

THE EXECUTIVE ARTICLE

Provisions of this article deal with the powers, duties, terms, qualifications, and, in six states, the salaries of such major constitutional offices as governor, lieutenant governor, attorney general, secretary of state, treasurer, and auditor and the procedures that are to be followed in filling vacancies for such positions.

Then, there are separate sections for topics such as these: veto power, martial law, pardons and reprieves, removal of local officials, messages to the legislature, budget, impeachment, and special sessions.

As was true in connection with the legislative article, governors also are initially given sweeping grants of power. They are to take care "that the laws are faithfully executed," they are to "transact all executive business," or they are to be the "Conservators of Peace" (Georgia, Missouri, and Oklahoma). But one need not read much further to discover that these constitutional grants must not be taken too literally, for important phases of executive power are in fact and in law located in a diverse number of constitutionally and legislatively defined executive officials, boards, and commissions.

To give an example, in 1959–1960, Michigan's executive branch in addition to six key elected officials included twenty-three executive departments, six ex-officio boards and commissions, sixty-four appointed boards and commissions, four elected boards, and five retirement boards.[12] The new Michigan constitution, which went into effect January 1, 1964, reduces the number of elective officials to four and provides that all administrative offices must be reorganized into not more than twenty principal departments. In Minnesota there were thirty-seven administrative departments and boards besides twenty-nine policy, advisory, and "miscellaneous boards and commissions" along with such elective officials as the attorney general, secretary of state, treasurer, lieutenant governor, and auditor. To speak of the governor as transacting all executive business under those circumstances or to hold him accountable for executive leadership for policy and administration of his branch of government appears somewhat unrealistic. While there is undoubtedly disagreement on how many executive agencies there should be or whether it is desirable or possible to fix a particular maximum, most of the recent and some of the older constitutions have attempted to do just this. Alaska, Hawaii, Massachusetts, New Jersey, and New York put the limit at twenty; and Missouri, at fourteen major departments.

Alaska goes beyond, insisting that "all executive and administrative offices, departments, and agencies of the state government . . . shall be allocated by law among and within not more than 20 principal depart-

12 Robert H. Pealy (ed.), *The Voter and the Michigan Constitution* (Ann Arbor, 1960), p. 28.

ments. . . ." It even gives to the governor (in line with the federal pattern) the power to make changes "in the organization of the executive branch or in the assignment of functions among its units which he considers necessary for efficient administration." These changes become law unless the legislature disapproves of the executive orders within sixty days.

Alaska's provisions are certainly not typical. Expressions of deep distrust of a strong governor, with broad powers of appointment and removal heading up an executive branch pyramidically arranged with clear lines of direction and accountability, run deep in nearly all of America's state constitutions. Presently a truly short executive ballot is possible only in Alaska, Hawaii, and New Jersey. In Alaska in addition to the governor, the secretary of state is the only other statewide elective executive officer, and in Hawaii it is the lieutenant governor. In New Jersey the governor is the only elected executive official. By way of contrast, superintendents or commissioners of education are still on the ballot in twenty-two states, and insurance commissioners are on the ballot in Delaware, Kansas, Louisiana, Mississippi, North Carolina, North Dakota, Oklahoma, and Washington.

How little the voter may know about these elective officials and how ineffective public accountability may become from such Jacksonian practices may be illustrated. "Even when the questions were limited to the one elective office with which the voter said he was most familiar," a Michigan study noted some years ago, "73% could not name the incumbent secretary of state, 75% could not name the highway commissioner, 77% could not name the superintendent of public instruction, 81% could not name the attorney general, and 96% could not name the treasurer, who had been in office longer than any other official on the list." [13]

Thirty-six states now have a four-year term for the governorship, but in fifteen of these—with the exception of Oklahoma and Missouri, all of them east of the Mississippi—the governor may not succeed himself, and in Alaska, Delaware, Maryland, New Jersey, New Mexico, Oregon, and South Dakota, he is limited by the constitution to two successive terms. Massachusetts adopted the four-year term for its executive officers in 1964.

A constitutional pattern—now partially emerging as evidenced in Alaska, Hawaii, Michigan, New Jersey, and New York—which envisages a stronger governorship would have to include four key elements:

A. Adopting the four-year term of office.
B. Removal of inability provisions precluding a governor's reelection.
C. Ceding to the legislature determination of such matters as salaries, residence requirements, and age.
D. Increasing the governor's power of appointment, removal, and administrative reorganization.

Nor is much of this novel. "The ingredients which constitute energy in the Executive," argued Alexander Hamilton nearly two hundred years ago, "are

[13] Coleman B. Ransone, Jr., *The Office of Governor in the United States* (University, Ala., 1956), p. 376.

first, unity; secondly, duration; thirdly, an adequate provision for its support; fourthly, competent powers." [14] Whether or not a stronger governorship is desirable is, of course, a matter of policy. The political implications of this issue will be explored in Chapter V.

THE JUDICIAL ARTICLE

A survey of fifty state constitutions reveals, underneath a tremendous variety of detail and terminology, elements of a judicial order common to all. There are:

A. Provisions establishing a court system based on jurisdiction comprising:
  1. Courts of limited jurisdiction such as probate courts, county courts, municipal courts, justice of the peace courts, police courts, municipal courts, juvenile courts, domestic relations courts, etc.
  2. Major trial courts such as chancery courts, circuit courts, district courts or courts of record.
  3. Appellate courts including courts of last resort usually called state supreme courts—in some of the larger and more populous states—intermediate appellate courts.
B. Provisions governing the qualification, tenure, election, appointment, terms, filling of vacancies, retirement, and removal of judicial personnel.
C. Provisions with regard to the location of judicial rule-making power affecting practice and procedure.
D. Provisions governing the internal administration of the courts.

Excessive details, multiplicity of courts, overlapping jurisdictions, diverse rules of practice within different divisions of the same court, overcrowded dockets in one judicial district with explicit constitutional prohibition against transferring non-resident judges from a neighboring but less busy district, unrealistically low salaries—these are some of the reasons for the very large number of amendments proposed to state judiciary articles in recent years. Between 1946 and 1957 alone some 160 amendments were submitted in thirty-two states.[15]

And while these certainly did not purport to cure all of the states' judicial ills, they did make possible establishing or strengthening municipal courts in California, Louisiana, and Virginia; juvenile courts in Florida, Louisiana, and Wyoming; traffic courts in Georgia and Louisiana; more prompt filling of judicial vacancies in Alabama, California, Georgia, Louisiana, Maryland, New York, and Pennsylvania; and judicial salary increases in Michigan, New Mexico, Ohio, Utah, and Wyoming.

In the last twenty years more basic judicial reforms centered, however, around selection procedures for justices of the major state courts, tightening up of judicial administration, and integrating state courts into a single unified

---

[14] *The Federalist*, No. 70.
[15] W. Brooke Graves, "Use of Amending Procedure Since World War II," in Graves, p. 118; for a recent study of one state's judicial system, see Charles W. Joiner, *The Michigan Constitution and the Judiciary* (Lansing, 1961).

judicial system with uniform qualifications, longer terms, and legislatively determined salaries for the judges. Many of these developments required changes in constitutional authority. Constitutional amendments approved by voters in Colorado, Illinois, and North Carolina in 1962 gave the state supreme courts administrative power over the lower courts of the three states.

Under provisions now operative in Missouri and in California, members of the more important courts are appointed by the governor with the assistance of special nonpartisan nominating commissions. In Missouri the plan calls for the governor to pick his candidates from a list submitted to him by the commission; while in California it works the other way around, in that the commission in order to validate the governor's nominations must approve or ratify his choice.

The most comprehensively integrated judicial system is probably contained in the constitutions of Alaska, Hawaii, and New Jersey. In broad outline the governor appoints the state judges (with the advice and consent of the Senate); the minimum basic term is no less than six years and continued tenure is greatly facilitated; the judicial power of the state is vested in one supreme court, courts of general jurisdiction and in such inferior courts (courts of local jurisdiction) "as the legislature may from time to time establish"; a compulsory retirement age of 70 is provided; and the supreme court is given broad rule-making power for the entire system.

There are, of course, a few important variations. Alaska establishes a seven-member judicial council with powers "to conduct studies for the improvement of the administration of justice" and to notify the governor when necessary "that a supreme court justice appears to be so incapacitated as substantially to prevent him from performing his judicial duties."

New Jersey goes beyond this and includes the judges of the superior and county courts as eligible for such forced retirement by the governor but substitutes the supreme court for the Alaskan judicial council as certifying the "incapacity." Hawaii does not mention a particular certifying agency but authorizes the legislature to establish such a commission by law.

To assist the state supreme court with the considerable administrative duties assigned to it as head of the unified court system, Alaska empowers the chief justice to appoint with the approval of the supreme court "an administrative director to serve at his pleasure and to supervise the administrative operations of the judicial system." Hawaii and New Jersey along with twenty-two other states have authorized such or similar administrative directors simply through appropriate legislative action.

The new Michigan constitution provides for a five-tiered unified court system. All judges are elected on a nonpartisan basis for terms of eight (supreme court justices) and six (all other judges) years. The supreme court is given rule-making and administrative powers over the lower courts.

With amazing unanimity leading spokesmen for the American and state bar associations, constitutional experts, law professors, political leaders, and reform-minded citizens have viewed the integrated court system and the associated improvements in judicial administration as among the most significant institutional prerequisites for raising judicial standards. Citizens could thus be afforded the kind of competent, fair, efficient, and reliable justice they have a right to expect from a responsible democratic government.

ARTICLE ON SUFFRAGE AND ELECTIONS

Often forgotten by many but politically never to be ignored for an understanding of United States federalism is the legal fact that most of the rules and regulations affecting a person's right to vote are formulated by the states for the electorate of the state. Although all fifty states have provisions regarding who may or may not vote and who may or may not hold office, no two agree on any major provision and only the constitutions of Alaska, Hawaii, and Michigan have been able to reduce most relevant subject matter into a single article.[16]

History as well as obsolescence weighs heavily in many of the constitutions. California, Mississippi, Nevada, Texas, and Wisconsin make fighting, challenging, or siding in dueling a basis for lawful disenfranchisement. Betting is similarly classed in Florida, New York, and Wisconsin; "quiet and peaceable behavior" is required in Vermont; "paupers" are prohibited from voting in Delaware, Maine, Massachusetts, Rhode Island, South Carolina, Texas, Virginia, and West Virginia; property requirements may be constitutionally imposed on voters for local elections creating "indebtedness" in Idaho, Montana, Rhode Island, South Carolina, and Utah. A "good character" and one "embracing the duties and obligations of citizenship" is demanded in Alabama, Connecticut, and Georgia. As a condition for voting, the ability to read and write articles of the United States and state constitutions is stipulated in considerable detail in Alabama, Georgia, Mississippi, North Carolina, Oklahoma, and South Carolina. Poll taxes were specifically authorized in Alabama, Arkansas, Florida, Louisiana, Massachusetts, Mississippi, Nevada, Texas, and Virginia. (These provisions have been nullified by Amendment XXIV to the United States Constitution.) Officeholders in Maryland and Texas must believe in God or a Supreme Being and in Massachusetts they should be possessed with "piety, justice, moderation, temperance, industry, and frugality."

Still this catalogue of electoral idiosyncracies is far from complete. Going on from the more atypical to the more typical, nearly all constitutions now set out three basic voting requirements: age (18 in Georgia and Kentucky, 19 in Alaska, and 21 in all other jurisdictions); United States citizenship; and residence, the norm being one year in the state, thirty days to six months in the precinct and four to six months in the county.

---

16 For a recent discussion of constitutional provisions on suffrage and elections, see John P. White, *The Elective Franchise and the Michigan Constitution* (Lansing, 1961).

Qualifications for voting and officeholding constitute only a part of the constitutional material in this article. A recent survey noted that fifteen state constitutions contain mandatory provisions for voter registration, eight include references to primaries, fourteen call for a secret ballot, nineteen states authorize absentee voting, twelve permit the use of voting machines; and thirteen states—all but one of them Western—make some form of provision for voters to hold "recall" elections for different classes of public officials.[17] Elective officials are specifically made subject to the possibility of "recall" in Alaska, Arizona, California, Colorado, Idaho, Kansas, Louisiana, Michigan, Nevada, North Dakota, Washington, and Wisconsin; elective judicial officials are exempted in Alaska, Idaho, Louisiana, Michigan, and Washington; three states, Kansas, Nevada, and Oregon make the "recall" applicable to all public officials, elective or appointive.

Again it is in the constitutions of Hawaii and Alaska where a successful effort has been made to avoid the inclusion of unnecessary detail. Description of the election operations, vote canvassing, settling of contests, certification of winners (or losers) or the naming of election officials are wisely left to the legislature. By so doing, Hawaii, for example, was able to reduce to a total of 222 words its entire article on suffrage and elections. The five basic sections of the article encompass all that is really necessary. They set out simply and with an economy of words all the needed fundamentals pertaining to voting qualifications and conduct of elections.

TAXATION AND FINANCE ARTICLE

"Limitation" is the key concept overshadowing all others in the thousands of words dedicated to the delineation of state and local governmental revenue expenditures and debt systems.

Were it not for these express limitations or restrictions, state legislatures and their local subdivisions would have the inherent power to raise and spend all the money they consider necessary for legitimate purposes not otherwise restricted in either state or national constitutions. Federal restrictions are essentially twofold: states may not tax an instrumentality of the federal government employed by it "in the execution of its powers," and states may not use their powers of taxation to interfere with or obstruct the exercise of powers delegated to the national government.

State constitutional restrictions are much more numerous and much more complex.[18] Taxes may only be levied and collected for a public purpose. Taxation shall be uniform and equal upon the same class of subjects. The

---

[17] O. Douglas Weeks, "Popular Control of Government: Suffrage and Elections," in Graves, pp. 179–182.

[18] For a recent study of constitutional provisions on taxation and finance, see Raleigh Barlowe, *Taxation and Fiscal Policy in the Michigan Constitution* (Lansing, 1961) and the Illinois Legislative Council study entitled *Constitutional Mandates for Uniformity of Taxation* (Springfield, 1959).

power of taxation shall not be surrendered by the legislature, but municipalities may be vested with the authority to assess and collect taxes for certain types of purposes. Certain classes of property may be exempted by special constitutional direction: state or local government bonds, cemeteries, municipal public property, homesteads, forests, improvements on land, libraries, new industries, public utilities, and property devoted to religious, educational, or charitable purposes. [19]

Then there are limitations upon the power of taxation in the form of "earmarking" state revenues for the support of selected programs. Approximately half of all state revenues cannot be used for other than enumerated purposes. In the mid-1950's, the per cent of earmarked revenue ranged from none at all in Delaware to 89 per cent in Alabama with nearly half of the states earmarking gasoline, motor vehicle registration, or operator's license taxes to the support of their state highway systems.

Some states, for example, have constitutionally pegged a particular tax rate: Alabama, Arkansas, Louisiana, and North Carolina have done this to their income tax; Michigan, to its sales tax; Minnesota, to its gross earnings tax on railroads; Louisiana, to certain severance taxes on natural resources; and nearly all of the poll tax states authorized their legislatures to fix the rates within or up to certain specific dollar limits. Michigan prohibits the levying of a graduated income tax.

Debt limitation represents another form of restriction on the state's fiscal powers. All but five states have constitutional prohibitions against the unlimited contracting of debts. While at least eighteen states have resounding prohibitions against the incurring of public debts in general, and thirteen states fix some specific debt limits in terms of a dollar or in terms of a percentage of the value of property in the state, some exceptions nevertheless are permitted. Debts may be incurred or debt limits may be exceeded in about eighteen states to repel invasion, suppress insurrection, and defend the state in military operations. Also, exceptions may be made in thirteen states to supply deficiencies of revenues for appropriations already made. Long-term obligations for major capital construction or improvement may be authorized by a referendum vote or an amendment to the restrictive constitutional section, thereby providing added flexibility in some of these states. The largest proposal of this kind—a $1.75 billion California water bond issue—was narrowly passed by the voters of that state in November, 1960. An unmistakable design for greater flexibility characterizes the taxation and finance articles of the constitutions of Alaska and Hawaii.

The Alaskan legislature may determine such matters as assessment standards for the appraisal of all property assessed by the state or by its political subdivisions; tax exemptions (in addition to property used exclusively for non-profit religious, charitable, cemetery, or education purposes); and interim borrowing. Taxes or revenues may be dedicated (except when

[19] For a discussion of exemptions in state constitutions, see Robert E. Childs, *State Constitutional Provisions on Exemptions* (Lansing, 1961).

required by the federal government and except those already committed at the time of ratification of the constitution).

Hawaii fixes a debt limit of $60 million but provides that this may be exceeded "when authorized by a two-thirds vote of all the members" of the legislature and provided that such total indebtedness would not exceed "a sum equal to fifteen per cent of the total of assessed values for tax rate purposes of real property in the State. . . ."

Also authorized but not considered part of the state debt are instruments of indebtedness or bonds "to meet appropriations for any fiscal period in anticipation of the collection of revenues for such period" as well as for some other purposes. Local governments are also permitted to use instruments of indebtedness and are given a debt limit of 10 per cent of their assessed valuations.

Both states also provide in their articles on finance and taxation for the so-called executive budget under which the governor submits an integrated budget to the legislature along with his detailed recommendations and plan for revenues and expenditures; Hawaii along with several other states calls for an auditor elected by and responsible to the legislature who shall "conduct post-audits of all transactions and of accounts kept by or for all departments."

LOCAL GOVERNMENT ARTICLE

The fact that all local governmental units are legally only creatures of the state is the central constitutional theme in all of the states. Powers are delegated to them, expanded, contracted, or circumscribed by legislatures operating within constitutional frameworks characterized until fairly recently by much built-in hostility to local independence and local experimentation.[20] These restrictions may take the form of detailed provisions for the structural organization of counties, towns, cities, school districts, or special districts— garbage, fire, hospital, ditch, harbor, road, or mosquito and pollution control.

They may establish tax, debt and borrowing limits, define the types of revenues collectable, and prescribe the division of funds between city, county, and state.

The quest for the extension of home rule and for the consolidation of units intensified as population increased and shifted and as the fiscal and organizational bases of local government proved increasingly inadequate to cope with twentieth century social service expectations. Long ballots and overlapping jurisdictions accentuated the problems by helping to confuse the voter, confound the administrator, and increase the costs of the rapidly expanding governmental services.

Something had to be done and various constitutional patterns did emerge. Beginning with Missouri (1875), California (1879), Washington

---

[20] For a recent study of local government provisions in one state, see Louis L. Freidland, *Local Government and the Michigan Constitution* (Lansing, 1961).

(1889), and Minnesota (1896), nearly half of the states now permit their cities and villages to draw up their own governmental charters thus removing from their internal organizational affairs constant legislative intervention and plain meddling. A certain amount of experimentation was even permitted with different types of city governmental structures (city-manager).

New York developed the "optional charter" system under which cities could select from various types of charters the one most appropriate which would be submitted to the voters for approval. In New Jersey and Minnesota despite home-rule charters the legislature still has the specific power to legislate on local matters provided the city—its governing board or its voters through a referendum—will have an opportunity to pass on the proposal before it goes into effect.

Florida (with the exception of Dade County [Miami]) and about half a dozen other states still use the system of issuing home-rule charters in the form of special acts which the legislature may then continue to amend. Thirteen states have extended the concept of home rule to all or to some of their counties,[21] and in California eleven out of fifty-eight counties have actually adopted such charters.

The post-World War II population movement from core city to suburb intensified local government problems. Suburban needs for new educational and recreational facilities, new highways, airports, and improved mass transportation systems became more acute, and as these metropolitan areas grew in size and significance, all of these developments helped to bring into constitutional focus the possibilities of allowing city-county patterns of cooperation or even city-county consolidation. Officials in the more urban counties watch with much interest governmental performance in certain phases of joint actions by city and county as now carried on in Dade County, Florida; Erie County, New York; and Los Angeles County, California.

Alaska has probably gone further than any other state in allowing its local governmental authorities maximum autonomy. "The purpose of this article," the constitution asserts, "is to provide maximum local self-government with a minimum of local government units, and to prevent duplication of tax levying jurisdictions. A liberal construction shall be given to the power of local government units." Using "boroughs" instead of counties, Alaska gives to such units and to cities "all local powers"; home-rule charters may be adopted, amended, or repealed by cities or boroughs in a manner provided by law; all charters shall be submitted to the qualified voters of the borough or city; home-rule boroughs or cities may exercise all legislative powers not prohibited by law or by charter; borough assemblies include representatives from the cities in the borough and from voters resident outside such cities; borough assemblies shall have the power to establish special service areas but no new service area or district shall be established "if the new service can be provided by an existing service area, by incorporation as a city, or by annexation to a

21 Graves, pp. 244–246.

city"; and each borough (organized or unorganized) "shall embrace an area and population with common interests to the maximum degree possible." Left to legislative determination are methods of establishing the boroughs, services that may be rendered by the state to unorganized boroughs, and procedures by which cities are to incorporate. To assist and advise these local governmental units, the constitution provides for the establishment of a special agency in the executive branch.

Although the Hawaiian constitution does not emphasize local action quite as much, provision is made for each political subdivision to have the "power to frame and adopt a charter for its own self-government."

ARTICLES ON EDUCATION, HIGHWAYS, NATURAL RESOURCES, AND CORPORATIONS

EDUCATION

The desirability of a statewide system of free public education is reflected in all fifty state constitutions. As to religion and education, sixteen states have explicit provisions against sectarian influences and controls as to race; fourteen states still retain the now obsolete requirements for complete segregation.

Typical constitutional provisions deal with primary, secondary, higher, and vocational education in separate sections—each filled with enormous detail as to curricula, administration, and financial management.[22] The legislature is given the right to provide for public transportation of school children, to manage current and permanent school funds, to dispose of school lands, and to set the pattern of control over state universities, schools of agriculture, and the other technical institutions of higher learning. Deemed weighty enough for constitutional attention are such positions as county and state superintendents of schools and school board members. Even their terms, professional qualifications for office, salaries, and method of election or appointment are itemized. About three hundred words are needed in Oklahoma to state the composition of the board of regents and its voting procedures and in Louisiana to describe how parish (county) funds for public elementary and secondary schools are to be collected and controlled.

Similarly detailed in a number of states are curricular directions. For example, the metric system is to be taught in Utah; North Dakota insists that "instruction is to be given to inculcate the vital importance of truthfulness, temperance, purity, public spirit, and respect for honest labor of every kind"; California stipulates the length of time for which textbooks may be used; and

---

[22] For a recent discussion of constitutional provisions for education in one state, see Donald J. Leu, *Elementary and Secondary Education and the Michigan Constitution* (Lansing, 1961).

all instruction is to be given in the English language in Arizona and New Mexico.

All such details are avoided in Alaska and Hawaii. Both clearly set out their basic policies: a statewide system of public schools free from sectarian control shall be supported; funds may not be appropriated for the "support or benefit of any sectarian, or private educational institutions; there shall be no segregation in public educational institutions because of race, religion or ancestry" (Hawaii). Both call for the establishment of a state university, for a board of regents appointed by the governor, and Hawaii specifies a state board of education with a membership similarly appointed. All other matters are left to the legislature.

HIGHWAYS

Concern for the economic and social life-giving power of roads and highways finds its expression in two major respects. Legislatures are forbidden to alter the course of highways by special or local laws and most of the taxes paid by highway users may not be diverted to any other purposes than that of constructing, maintaining, and expanding the system. Arkansas, Louisiana, Oklahoma, Missouri, and New Mexico provide for a state highway commission and for the terms, qualifications, powers, and duties of its membership. There is no reference to highways or roads in the constitutions of Hawaii and Alaska.

NATURAL RESOURCES

In the majority of the states constitutional policies regarding the conservation and disposition of natural resources will not be found in a single integrated article. To discover what the legislature may or may not do by way of natural resources management, separate sections on minerals, soil, water, land, forests, wildlife, etc. must be consulted.

Most of the sections relate to the terms and conditions upon which leases may be obtained for the use and development of state-owned lands or resources and for the administrative arrangements that the legislature may wish to provide. Western constitutions reflect the concern for water distribution and water rights. In Colorado the "water of every natural stream not heretofore appropriated . . . is property of the public . . . and dedicated to the use of the people"; provisions stressing the public use of water can be found in Arizona, California, Colorado, Idaho, Montana, New Mexico, North Dakota, Washington, and Wyoming. Specific legislative authority to set aside areas for wildlife conservation and management can be found in Alaska, California, Hawaii, Massachusetts, New York, Ohio, Tennessee, and Texas, and state expenditures for major internal improvements may be constitutionally made in North Dakota and South Dakota or through special improvement districts in Oklahoma, Tennessee, Texas, and Wyoming. In 1960 the voters of New York approved an amendment which permitted the state to issue $75 million in bonds to acquire land for the development of state and local parks. Specific authorization for public airport financing, construction, and operation is given in Alabama, Louisiana, Michigan, Minnesota, North Dakota, Pennsylvania, Wisconsin, and Wyoming.

Similarly, state financial assistance to public housing has come in for constitutional notice—largely a result of the population explosion of the postwar years. Alabama, California, Georgia, Hawaii, Maryland, Massachusetts, Missouri, New Jersey, New York, and Rhode Island now have constitutionally empowered their legislatures to aid municipalities and other local governmental units in projects involving slum clearance, redevelopment of blighted areas, and low-cost public housing.

Another relatively recent development in removing internal improvement restrictions or possible legal doubt about legislative rights has been the addition of amendments authorizing the legislatures to help counties or cities to establish industrial parks for purposes of attracting and encouraging business, or to permit the creation of industrial development commissions with powers to make loans. In 1960 voters approved amendments to such effect in Georgia, Maryland, and Nebraska.

Alaska's article on natural resources, the longest of all recent constitutions, stresses the duty of the legislature to provide for "the utilization, development, and conservation of all natural resources belonging to the State, including land and waters, for the maximum benefit of its people." The legislature is also empowered to acquire "sites, objects, and areas of natural beauty or of historical, cultural, recreational, or scientific value." Mineral rights are made subject to discovery and to appropriation and the "continuation of these rights shall depend upon the performance of annual labor, or the payment of fees, rents, or royalties, or upon other requirements" of law.

CORPORATIONS

The growth during the late nineteenth century of the business corporation and certain other types of enterprises clearly concerned with the public interest—banks, mines, railroads, electric power, gas, pipe lines, telegraph and telephone companies, express companies, common carriers, etc.—caused some states to incorporate into their constitutions various provisions for their legislative treatment and supervision.[23] The most numerous prohibitions present in about thirty-five states are against creating special laws for corporations, while in about a dozen states the legislature is given the power (actually inherent in them without such grants) to create certain regulatory

---

[23] For a recent treatment of constitutional provisions for corporations in one state, see Alfred J. Conrad, Richard W. Ogden, and Timothy J. Scanlon, *Corporations and the Michigan Constitution* (Lansing, 1961).

commissions with powers to issue franchises, to fix reasonable maximum rates, to hold hearings, and to make periodic reports of the findings.

ARTICLES ON AMENDMENT AND CONVENTION

Constitutions can be revised formally through documentary changes and informally through the interpretations of the document itself. Informal adaptation develops through judicial interpretation and through the actions of legislators, governors, and electorates as they all apply the meaning or intent of the explicit documentary language to the particular problems of the day. The latter process is held implicit in written law; the former calls for more constitutional authority, governing documentary revision by a) adding of amendments or b) the work of a specially called constitutional convention.

REVISION BY AMENDMENT

Adding amendments involves two major steps—submission and ratification. All states with the exception of New Hampshire authorize their legislatures to submit amendments, and all states with the exception of Delaware provide for the electorate to approve or reject such amendments (see Table 7). The type of majorities required, the details of procedures, and the extent of other "hurdles" vary greatly from state to state.[24]

By insisting on favorable action by two successive legislative sessions, fourteen states clearly indicate their wish to slow down the process of submitting amendments. In the states in which but one session is needed only eight—Arizona, Arkansas, Minnesota, Missouri, North Dakota, Oklahoma, Oregon, and South Dakota—are satisfied to leave the legislative initiation up to a simple majority vote; the remainder require either a two-thirds or a three-fifths vote for passage.

For popular ratification of amendments, most constitutions provide for adoption by two types of majorities: a majority of all voters participating in the general election or merely a majority of those voting on the amendment. The former plan, used in Minnesota, Mississippi, New Jersey, Oklahoma, Tennessee, and Wyoming, may constitute a genuine obstacle to ratification since voter interest and participation in the choice of candidates usually exceeds the interest or understanding of the often technical and complex provisions of an amendment.

---

[24] For discussions regarding three states, see William C. Havard, "Notes on a Theory of State Constitutional Change: The Florida Experience," *Journal of Politics*, February, 1959; J. A. Millimet, "The Proposals to Amend the Constitution with Respect to the Judicial Dept. and the Power of Taxation," *New Hampshire Bar Journal*, April, 1964 (Symposium on the 1964 New Hampshire Constitutional Convention); and G. Theodore Mitau, "Constitutional Change by Amendment: Recommendations of the Minnesota Constitutional Commission in Ten Years' Perspective," *Minnesota Law Review*, January, 1960.

TABLE 7. CONSTITUTIONAL AMENDMENT PROCEDURE:

State or other jurisdiction	Legislative vote required for proposal(a)	Approval by two sessions	Ratification by electorate	Limitations on the number of amendments submitted at one election
Alabama	$\frac{3}{5}$	No	MA	None
Alaska	$\frac{2}{3}$	No	MA	None
Arizona	Maj.	No	MA	None
Arkansas	Maj.	No	MA	(b)
California	$\frac{2}{3}$	No	MA	None
Colorado	$\frac{2}{3}$	No	MA	None(c)
Connecticut	(d)	Yes	MA	None
Delaware	$\frac{2}{3}$	Yes	None	None
Florida	$\frac{3}{5}$	No	MA	None
Georgia	$\frac{2}{3}$	No	MA(e)	None
Hawaii	(f)	(f)	MA(g)	None
Idaho	$\frac{2}{3}$	No	MA	None
Illinois	$\frac{2}{3}$	No	(h)	None(i)
Indiana	Maj.(j)	Yes	MA	None
Iowa	Maj.	Yes	MA	None
Kansas	$\frac{2}{3}$	No	MA	3
Kentucky	$\frac{3}{5}$	No	MA	2
Louisiana	$\frac{2}{3}$	No	MA	None
Maine	$\frac{2}{3}$	No	MA	None
Maryland	$\frac{3}{5}$	No	MA	None
Massachusetts	(k)	Yes	MA	None
Michigan	$\frac{2}{3}$	No	MA	None
Minnesota	Maj.	No	ME	None
Mississippi	$\frac{2}{3}$	No	ME	None
Missouri	Maj.	No	MA	None
Montana	$\frac{2}{3}$	No	MA	3

MA—Majority vote on amendment.
ME—Majority vote in election.
(a) In all states not otherwise noted, the figure shown in this column refers to percentage of elected members in each house required for approval of proposed constitutional amendments.
(b) General Assembly limited to 3; no limit on number of initiative proposals.
(c) Legislature may not propose amendments to more than six articles at the same session.
(d) Majority of House of Representatives; next Assembly, $\frac{2}{3}$ each house.
(e) Amendments of a local nature must receive a majority vote only in subdivision affected.
(f) Approval at two successive sessions required if votes in each house are majority but less than $\frac{2}{3}$.
(g) Amendment altering the ratification provision or the representation from any senatorial district requires a majority of votes on the question in a majority of the counties.
(h) Majority voting in election or $\frac{2}{3}$ voting on amendment.
(i) Legislature may not propose amendments to more than three articles at the same session.
(j) No new amendments may be proposed while an amendment is awaiting its second legislative action or action of the electors.
(k) Majority members elected sitting in joint session.
(l) Votes cast in favor of amendment must be at least 35% of total vote at election.
(m) No provision for proposal of amendments by legislature. Constitution amended only by constitutional convention.

A relatively easy amendment formula does not, of course, necessarily assure a high rate of adoption of proposals submitted as shown in Table 1. In only three states (Minnesota, Missouri, and South Dakota) of the eight which follow the "simple legislative majority" and the "one session" provision, is a 50 per cent adoption rate attained. On the other hand, amendments can be

BY THE LEGISLATURE

State or other jurisdiction	Legislative vote required for proposal(a)	Approval by two sessions	Ratification by electorate	Limitations on the number of amendments submitted at one election
Nebraska	⅗	No	MA(l)	None
Nevada	Maj.	Yes	MA	None
New Hampshire	(m)			
New Jersey	(n)	(n)	ME	None
New Mexico	Maj.(o)	No	MA(o)	None
New York	Maj.	Yes	MA	None
North Carolina	⅗	No	MA	None
North Dakota	Maj.	No	MA	None
Ohio	⅗	No	MA	None
Oklahoma	Maj.	No	ME(p)	None
Oregon	Maj.	No	MA	None
Pennsylvania	Maj.	Yes	MA	None
Puerto Rico	⅔(q)	No	MA	3
Rhode Island	Maj.	Yes	(r)	None
South Carolina	⅔	Yes(s)	MA	None
South Dakota	Maj.	No	MA	None
Tennessee	(t)	Yes	ME(u)	None
Texas	⅔	No	MA	None
Utah	⅔	No	MA	None
Vermont	(v)	Yes	MA	None
Virginia	Maj.	Yes	MA	None
Washington	⅔	No	MA	None
West Virginia	⅔	No	MA	None
Wisconsin	Maj.	Yes	MA	None
Wyoming	⅔	No	ME	None

(n) Three-fifths of all members of each house; or majority of all members of each house for two successive sessions.
(o) Amendments dealing with certain sections on elective franchise and education must be proposed by ¾ vote of the legislature and ratified by ¾ vote of the electorate and ⅔ vote in each county.
(p) The legislature, by ⅔ vote, may require a special election on amendments. If the amendment is voted upon at a special election, ratification is by a majority vote on the amendment. The legislature may amend certain sections of the constitution relating to the Corporation Commission by simple majority vote, without popular ratification.
(q) If proposed amendment approved by a ⅔ vote in the legislature, it is submitted to voters at a special referendum; if approved by a ¾ vote in the legislature, the referendum is held at next general election.
(r) Three-fifths of voters on amendment.
(s) Final approval in legislature by majority vote after popular ratification.
(t) Majority members elected, first passage; ⅔ members elected, second passage.
(u) Majority of all citizens voting for Governor.
(v) Two-thirds vote Senate, majority vote House, first passage; majority both houses, second passage. Since 1910, amendments may be submitted only at 10-year intervals.

SOURCE: *Book of the States, 1964–1965*, p. 13.

adopted with considerable frequency even in states with difficult provisions. For example, only six of the thirty-one states requiring either a two-thirds legislative vote for submission or passage at two successive sessions fall below the 50 per cent figure.

There are some alternative methods of bringing amendments before the electorate. New Hampshire requires and Hawaii merely enables constitutional conventions to perform the task of submitting amendments. Fourteen states authorize the electorate to initiate the amendments through petition and then have it submitted directly for a referendum vote.[25] Most typically in these states, the number of signatories for the petition is based on a percentage— eight, ten, or fifteen—of voters having cast ballots for governor at the preceding election; for the referendum to be successful, an affirmative simple majority vote usually suffices.

REVISION BY CONSTITUTIONAL CONVENTION

This is the more difficult process of formal change—full of political, legal, and procedural obstacles despite the fact that all but eleven states have provisions in their constitutions for just such conventions. Here again are involved two distinct and important steps: the legislative decision to submit to the voters the issue of calling a convention and the electoral decision of authorizing it through an affirmative vote and then acting on the proposals or revisions that such a convention may draft for consideration. Since only the constitutions of Alaska, Hawaii, Iowa, Maryland, Michigan, Missouri, New Hampshire, New York, and Oklahoma demand that the issue be submitted periodically for popular decision, legislatures for various reasons may wish to avoid the issue of submission altogether. Even if it passes the legislature successfully (usually requiring a two-thirds or three-fifths majority vote), the electorate may reject such a proposed convention at the referendum stage (eleven states stipulate approval by a majority of those casting ballots at the general election), or it may finally turn down the laboriously worked-up revisions after considerable expense has been incurred and after the elapse of much valuable time—perhaps four to six years from when the issue of submission was originally presented (see Table 8). It is not surprising then that (Alaska and Hawaii excepted) during the last ninety-five years major conventions were held only in Michigan and Missouri. Limited conventions, that is, assemblies which, by the explicit terms of their calling, might address their deliberations to only a few enumerated subjects and which could thus find broader legislative and electoral support, were convened in New Hampshire, New Jersey, New York, Rhode Island, Tennessee, and Virginia.

TO AMEND OR TO REVISE—THAT IS THE QUESTION

The volume of constitutional amendments proposed is enormous and the number actually adopted is certainly impressive. Based on a recent study, a total of 1,584 propositions were submitted between 1946 and 1956 of which 1,172 were adopted, encompassing 1,589 different subject matter changes.

---

[25] For a recent discussion of the use of initiative, referendum, and recall in the states, see Daniel S. McHargue, *Direct Government in Michigan* (Lansing, 1961).

TABLE 8. CONSTITUTIONAL CONVENTIONS

| State or other jurisdiction | Procedure for calling constitutional convention | | | Popular ratification of convention proposals |
	Vote required in legislature(a)	Approval by two sessions	Referendum vote	
Alabama	Maj.	No	ME	(b)
Alaska	Maj.(c)	No	MP	Y
Arizona	Maj.	No	MP	MP
Arkansas	Maj.(d)	No	—	MP
California	⅔	No	MP	ME
Colorado	⅔	No	MP	ME
Connecticut	Maj.(d)	No	—	X
Delaware	⅔	Yes	MP	X
Florida	⅔	No	MP	X
Georgia	⅔	No	—	MP(e)
Hawaii	(c)	No	MP	MP(f)
Idaho	⅔	No	MP	MP
Illinois	⅔	No	ME	ME
Indiana	(g)	—	—	—
Iowa	(h)	—	MP	X
Kansas	⅔	No	MP	X
Kentucky	Maj.	Yes	MP(i)	X
Louisiana	Maj.(d)	No	MP	X
Maine	⅔	No	—	X
Maryland	(j)	No	ME	MP
Massachusetts	Maj.(d)	No	MP	X
Michigan	Maj.(k)	No	MP	MP
Minnesota	⅔	No	ME	(l)
Mississippi	Maj.	No	—	X
Missouri	(m)	No	MP	MP
Montana	⅔	No	MP	ME
Nebraska	⅗	No	MP(n)	MP
Nevada	⅔	No	MP	X
New Hampshire	(o)	No	MP	(p)
New Jersey	(g)	—	—	—
New Mexico	⅔	No	MP	MP
New York	Maj.(q)	No	MP	MP
North Carolina	⅔	No	ME	X
North Dakota	(g)	—	—	—
Ohio	⅔	No	MP	MP
Oklahoma	(r)	No	MP	MP
Oregon	Maj.	No	MP	X
Pennsylvania	Maj.(d)	No	—	Y
Puerto Rico	⅔	No	MP	MP
Rhode Island	Maj.(d)	No	MP	MP
South Carolina	⅔	No	ME	X
South Dakota	⅔	No	ME	X
Tennessee	Maj.(s)	No	MP	MP
Texas	Maj.(d)	No	MP	MP
Utah	⅔	No	ME	ME
Vermont	(g)	—	—	—
Virginia	Maj.	No	MP	X
Washington	⅔	No	ME	ME

TABLE 8 (*continued*)

State or other jurisdiction	Procedure for calling constitutional convention			Popular ratification of convention proposals
	Vote required in legislature(a)	Approval by two sessions	Referendum vote	
West Virginia _____ Maj.		No	ME	ME
Wisconsin _____ Maj.		No	MP	X
Wyoming _____ ⅔		No	ME	Y

ME—Majority voting in election.
MP—Majority voting on the proposition.
X—There appears to be no constitutional or general statutory provision for the submission of convention proposals to the electorate in these states, but in practice the legislature may provide by statute for popular ratification of convention proposals in specific instances.
Y—Popular ratification required but no provision for size of vote.
(a) The figure shown in this column refers to the percentage of elected members in each house required to initiate the procedure for calling a constitutional convention.
(b) In 1955 the Alabama Supreme Court, in an advisory opinion, indicated that a constitutional convention could not adopt a constitution without submitting it to popular ratification.
(c) Question must be submitted to the electorate every 10 years.
(d) In the following states—Arkansas, Connecticut, Louisiana, Massachusetts, Pennsylvania, Rhode Island and Texas—the constitution does not provide for the calling of a constitutional convention but legislative authority to call such a convention has been established in practice by statute, opinions of Attorneys General, and court decisions.
(e) Amendments of a local nature must receive a majority vote only in subdivision affected.
(f) Majority must be 35% of total vote cast at election; at a special election, the majority must be 35% of the number of registered voters.
(g) In the following states—Indiana, New Jersey, North Dakota and Vermont—the constitution does not provide for the calling of a constitutional convention and there appears to be no established procedure in this regard.
(h) Proposal automatically put on ballot every 10 years since 1870.
(i) Must equal ¼ of qualified voters at last general election.
(j) Question must be submitted to the electorate every 20 years beginning 1970.
(k) Question must be submitted to the electorate every 16 years beginning with the general election in 1978.
(l) ⅗ voting on question.
(m) Question must be submitted to the electorate every 20 years.
(n) Must be 35% of total vote cast at election.
(o) Question must be submitted to the electorate every seven years.
(p) ⅔ voting on question.
(q) Question must be submitted to the electorate every 20 years beginning 1957.
(r) Question must be submitted to the electorate every 20 years since 1907.
(s) Convention may not be held oftener than once in six years.
SOURCE: *Book of the States, 1964–1965*, p. 15.

Involved in most of these amendment changes were provisions dealing with such areas as taxation, finance, education, veterans, highways, the executive, and the judiciary.[26]

Those who favor constitutional change by amendment rather than by revision stress the relative speed with which amendments can be added, the more than even chance of success at the polls, the willingness of legislatures to submit proposals to the electorate, the inexpensiveness, and the limited risk of the method.

[26] W. Brooke Graves, "Use of Amending Procedure Since World War II," in Graves, p. 103; for an interesting appraisal of rejected amendments in Michigan, see Sidney Glazer, *Rejected Amendments to the Michigan Constitution 1910–1961* (Lansing, 1961).

While acknowledging the great contributions made by the amendment process to facilitate adaptation to badly needed governmental changes, most political scientists still view the constitutional convention "to be the most efficacious method of conducting thoroughgoing constitutional reform." Harrassed legislators, it is contended, cannot give the care and the attention to proposed amendments so necessary for excellence in wording and clarity in meaning. Piecemeal amendments make difficult an orderly arrangement of related subject matter and may thus invite inconsistencies between constitutional provisions with subsequent uncertainties entailing an excessive reliance on judicial reconciliation. While necessarily short and precise, amendments for that very reason do not lend themselves as well to offering basic and, therefore, often controversial institutional changes. A constitutional convention with careful preparation, with wide representation and adequate professional and consultative staffs, offers a better forum in which to debate and to compromise basic policies and in which to work out their application to all of the relevant sections of the constitution simultaneously.

CONSTITUTIONAL CONVENTIONS—POLITICAL OBSTACLES AND OPPORTUNITIES

Political scientists may be asked to serve at constitutional conventions, but as a rule they do not call them. Legislatures which generally do have to call them are reluctant to submit the initial question to the voters for complex and even selfish reasons.

A constitutional convention once assembled represents the democratically representative will of the electorate which may wish to mold a constitution that may rearrange certain political balances. Thus, it may seek to strengthen the governorship at the expense of the legislature; it may establish new bases of representation; it may provide more effective sanctions to force reapportionment; it may remove the principle of dedicating taxes, impose new taxes, reallocate tax burdens, or alter the distribution formula for certain types of revenues between county, city, and state. In brief, it may seriously alter the status quo. Legislative apprehension, if not successful in blocking the submission of the issue, may be reinforced in the course of the referendum campaign. For example, interest groups opposed to altering the basic charter or its provisions may stress the great expense involved in the operation of a convention or the danger that might befall the state should radical reformers with their untried and socially dangerous ideas obtain a majority of delegates in the proposed assembly. Taxpayer groups may express their fears of higher taxes; local government officials, of more centralization; state officials, of more departmental consolidations; business groups, of more power in the hands of organized labor; farmers, of loss of legislative representation in the face of urban pressures. Rural and conservative interests almost prevented the calling of the recent constitutional convention in Michigan. Only four —all in the metropolitan Detroit area—of the state's eighty-three counties gave the convention proposal sufficient support to overcome the negative outstate vote. Voters in Pennsylvania in November, 1963 defeated a proposal to call a constitutional convention despite widespread legislative and bi-partisan citizen support for constitutional revision.

Something of the political strength offered by a combination of these forces and factors can be seen from the fact that even when a convention finally did materialize, in all but two (Missouri—1945 and Michigan—1963) of the thirteen conventions held in eight states since 1938 specific limitations were imposed in the enabling act. In like manner, entire articles were excluded from consideration by the convention. The price for New Jersey's 1947 convention was the debarring of senatorial reapportionment.

On the other hand, there was nothing in the unlimited conventions held in Alaska, Hawaii, or Michigan either in terms of membership or in terms of achievements that would sustain the serious charge of radicalism. The constitutions that the conventions in Alaska and Hawaii submitted—that the people accepted and that Congress approved—were shorter, more flexible, better integrated but deviated in no major respect from long established democratic principles. The executive was strengthened and so was the judiciary, but separation of powers was retained as the axiom of American state government as was bicameralism. The new Michigan constitution is essentially a conservative document. It retained the bicameral legislature, separation of powers, the four-cent limitation on the sales tax, the prohibition on the levying of a graduated income tax, and traditional forms of local government. Democratic party delegates to the convention felt that the document was so conservative that all but five of them voted against it on final passage. Despite Democratic party opposition the constitution won the necessary approval in the statewide ratification vote of April 1, 1963. Little, if anything, was entirely new or experimental in either of these three constitutions.

CONSTITUTIONAL CONVENTIONS

THE PRELIMINARIES

After the legislature submits the question "Shall a constitutional convention be called," and the necessary majority of the electorate vote affirmatively (in nine states, including Georgia and Maine, there is no requirement for such a referendum), generally it is the duty of the legislature at an ensuing general election to proceed by law with the arrangements for the selection of candidates.[27] In 1951 the Maryland legislature did not see its duty in this light and chose to override the popular expression and kill the convention before it was born.

In the majority of the states, the number of delegates is constitutionally determined, but the site of the convention, the nature of the ballot, the time of

[27] Albert L. Sturm, *Methods of State Constitutional Reform* (Ann Arbor, 1954), p. 92.

election, the method of nomination, and the compensation for delegates is left to the legislature.

While procedural steps take their course, those concerned with the success of the convention must plan carefully. Conventions have to deliberate on weighty problems. Research must be prepared professionally, consultants employed, comparative data gathered: New York's legislature in 1956 established a fifteen-member Temporary State Commission on the Constitutional Convention under the chairmanship of Nelson Rockefeller preparatory to the referendum in the following year; the Alaskan Statehood Commission asked the Public Administration Service of Chicago to "provide the necessary research and provide reports for use by the Convention delegates" some months before the convention ever assembled; the Hawaiian Statehood Commission started work on the constitution for that state at least two years before the delegates were even elected; and the W. K. Kellogg Foundation provided the necessary funds in Michigan to support preparatory studies by the eighteen-member Constitutional Convention Preparatory Commission when the legislature failed to appropriate the money.

Above all, a politically favorable climate has to be created, prior, during, and after the convention lest much effort and expense be in vain. Gubernatorial leadership and widespread cooperation between responsible segments of the major parties, of bar and bench, and of the civic-minded in all sections of the population is nearly indispensable if the inherent obstacles to constitutional revision are to be met and overcome. Activities by reform groups such as the League of Women Voters, volunteer efforts by scholars and students, and informational programs and discussions in the press and on radio and television must provide the educational background to help overcome voter apathy and unfounded hostilities.

Closely linked to the political climate and to the likelihood of voter acceptance of the revised or new constitution is, of course, the quality of statesmanship possessed by the potential delegates and their representativeness of the state's population and interests.

THE CONVENTION AT WORK

The internal organization of a state constitutional convention resembles that of a lower house of a typical legislature. Presiding officers (chairman or president and vice-chairman) have to be elected, rules of procedure adopted, committees designated, a secretariat appointed, consultants selected, and agendas prepared. Limited only by the United States Constitution and the provisions of the enabling act, these conventions as plenary "spokesmen" for the electorate must then proceed to draft, debate, and recommend a new constitution or a revision of the old.

As in all other assemblies of this type, the human factor figures prominently. While there may not be a Benjamin Franklin for each state, each convention that does succeed can proudly boast of parliamentarily skillful and politically sensitive leaders without whom victory would have been less certain. "To be close to a constitutional convention that approaches the greatness of which such a body is capable," a participant of the Alaska convention confided, "is to have something akin to a religious experience. In such a body members may attain heights of statesmanship seldom equaled in their political or private lives." [28] The delegates to the recent Michigan convention have been characterized as "outstanding and competent." A profile analysis by the University of Michigan's Institute of Public Administration found that the education and the incomes of the delegates were well above average. "Lawyers were the largest single occupational group and a great majority of the delegates had had considerable previous political experience either in their own parties or in civic organizations. Their competence and experience were far above those of the average legislator and the convention was treated with respect." [29]

RECOMMENDATIONS FOR CHANGE ONLY—THE CONSTITUTIONAL COMMISSION

Practical-minded politicians have come up with still one more device when the pressure for constitutional reforms is heavy, the legislature unwilling, and the public either unconcerned or uninformed—the constitutional study commission. Although this device is not new, New Jersey having established its first commisson over one hundred years ago, its attractiveness has increased to the point where since 1950 fourteen or more states have utilized it in some form. The typical constitutional commission, created by statute, provides for a membership of less than thirty, includes legislators and gubernatorial appointees, and is given authority to study the constitution and to report on the changes deemed necessary. These may then take the form of suggestions for amendments or serve as preparatory drafts for a more thorough consideration by a constitutional convention.

Some of these commissions are strictly legislative in character (California, 1947; Maine, 1961; Massachusetts, 1962; New York, 1958; Oregon, 1953; West Virginia, 1957); some were established by executive order only (Florida, 1958; Kansas, 1957; Kentucky, 1949; Michigan, 1942; Washington, 1934); and some by special agencies (Kentucky, 1952, by the Committee on Functions and Resources of State Government; Louisiana, 1946, by the Louisiana State Law Institute; Oklahoma, 1947 and Texas, 1957, by their Legislative Councils; Connecticut, 1949, by the Commission on State Government).[30]

---

[28] John E. Bebout and Emil J. Sady, "Staging a State Constitutional Convention," in Graves, p. 85.

[29] James K. Pollock, "Opportunity in Michigan," *National Civic Review*, March, 1963, p. 140. For further studies of the Michigan convention, see Dr. Pollock's *Making Michigan's New Constitution 1961–1962* (Ann Arbor, 1963) and "Making a Constitution," *National Civic Review*, January, 1964, pp. 14–26.

[30] Bennett M. Rich, "Revision by Constitutional Commission," in Graves, p. 91.

By themselves these commissions cannot directly make any constitutional reforms. But if the entire membership is carefully selected, if they are dedicated and serious and their investigations thorough, they could help to prepare the ground and focus attention on possible solutions. Yet even scholars friendly to these commissions will hasten to point out that they can in no way serve as convention substitutes and that "on balance over a period of several decades the record of the constitutional commission has been undistinguished." [31]

SOME UNRESOLVED ISSUES OF CONSTITUTIONAL REFORM—THE "MODEL CONSTITUTION"

The constitutions of Alaska, Hawaii, and Michigan represent without doubt some of the best contemporary professional thought as to what a good constitution should contain. They reflect the ideas contained in the various *Model State Constitutions* sponsored by the National Municipal League first published in 1921 and revised five times since. The last revision appeared in 1963, and yet there are a number of provocative provisions in the *Model* that have not so far found much acceptance or favor. These may be unsound, impractical, or as yet too advanced. One of them is given here as basis for discussion and thought as an unresolved issue of constitutional reform.

This is the recommendation for a unicameral legislature. Delaware, Georgia, and Pennsylvania had a unicameral legislature during the colonial period, and Vermont "entered the Union with a one-house legislature which it maintained until 1836:" However, with the exception of Nebraska (1937) none of the states despite numerous proposals have been willing to make this change. In the light of the recent Supreme Court decisions eliminating "area" as a criterion for apportionment, it seems quite plausible that renewed attention will be given by the states to the usefulness of the unicameral legislature.

WHAT THEN IS A "GOOD" CONSTITUTION?

There will be some disagreement on the proposition that no one single constitution can meet democratically and effectively the needs of the fifty different states. And yet it is possible to set out a few central criteria that might apply to nearly all of them.[32]

First, a constitution should be brief and to the point. Unnecessary detail obstructs the vision and prevents adaptability to inevitable institutional changes. A constitution should not be a legislative code. By dealing with fundamentals only it establishes the framework within which legislators and executives can then implement the policies periodically reviewed by the voters at election time.

Second, a constitution should make possible the fusion of political power

[31] *Ibid*, p. 97.
[32] See David Fellman, "What Should a State Constitution Contain?" in Graves, pp. 137–138.

with political responsibility so that those who have power can be held account-able and that those who are held accountable may then in turn have the power commensurate with their responsibilities. In practical terms this means that the three branches must not only be distinct but should be permitted to make their own internal administrative decisions and rulings.

Third, a constitution which is to enable a democratic state and local government of the second half of the twentieth century to respond to the needs of the public—to protect the rights of individuals, and to render the services demanded in an efficient and humane manner—must be amenable to orderly and periodic change. To meet the nearly inevitable population in-crease and metropolitan growth, enforceable provisions for reapportionment constitute elemental justice. To permit local governmental consolidation and charter revision represents an enlightened understanding of the modern meaning of home rule and self-government. Above all, the type of numerical majority required for the amendment or revision of the state constitution, while necessarily extraordinary to distinguish it from the mere passage of statutes, must not be too unrealistically high or cumbersome. When the required majority is unusually high, experience has shown that recourse to somewhat unconstitutional processes is likely to be taken.

CASE PROBLEMS FOR CLASS DISCUSSION

1. You are the clerk of a state legislative committee which has before it a bill calling for a constitutional convention. The chairman of your committee has asked you to summarize briefly the testimony offered by proponents and opponents to the bill. You have just completed your report. Which major organizations appeared before the committee and what was the central thrust of their remarks?
2. You have been elected a member of a state constitutional convention and ac-cepted appointment on the committee which will scrutinize proposals for changes in the executive article. What would be some of the key recommendations with which your group will have to wrestle, and which social, economic, and political interests are expected to offer testimony favoring or opposing these various recommendations?
3. You are the executive secretary of your state's municipal home rule association which has decided to lobby for an amendment which would strengthen constitu-tional home-rule provisions. It is now August; the legislative elections are sched-uled for November, and the legislature will convene in January. How would you plan your strategy for the upcoming session?
4. Assume that your state includes an economically-depressed mining area. Mining companies have promised major capital investment (and employment) in the area if a constitutional amendment were to be adopted which would guarantee them no increase in taxation for a period of fifteen years. As editor of your paper, you would like to take a public position on this important issue. To acquire an adequate background what information would you need and which sources would you have to consult?

SELECTED BIBLIOGRAPHY

Advisory Commission on Intergovernmental Relations, *State Constitutional and Statu-tory Restrictions on Local Government Debt* (Washington, 1961).

Advisory Commission on Intergovernmental Relations, *State Constitutional and Statu-tory Restrictions on Local Taxing Power* (Washington, 1962).

Advisory Commission on Intergovernmental Relations, *State Constitutional and Statutory Restrictions upon the Structural, Functional, and Personnel Powers of Local Government* (Washington, 1962).

Tip H. Allen, Jr. and Coleman B. Ransone, Jr., *Constitutional Revision in Theory and Practice* (University, Ala., 1962).

Wendell M. Bedichek, *The Texas Constitutional Amendments of 1962* (Austin, 1962).

Rosalind L. Branning, *Pennsylvania Constitutional Development* (Pittsburgh, 1960).

A Comparative Analysis of the Michigan Constitution, 2 vols. (Lansing, 1961).

A Comparison of the Organization and Procedures of Six State Constitutional Conventions (Detroit, 1961).

Constitutional Earmarking of State Tax Revenues (Detroit, 1961).

Constitutional Revision in Kansas: The Executive and the Legislative (Lawrence, 1960).

Constitutional Revision in Kansas: The Issues (Lawrence, 1960).

A Digest of the Proposed Constitution (East Lansing, 1962).

Robert B. Dishman, *State Constitutions: The Shape of the Document* (New York, 1960).

Rob Downey *et al., Convention Report* (East Lansing, 1963).

Martin L. Faust, "Constitutional Convention in Missouri," *Business and Government Review*, March–April, 1962, pp. 15–24.

James T. Fleming, *Kentucky's Constitutional Development* (Frankfurt, 1960).

Morris M. Goldings, "The Use of the Popular Initiative Petition for a Constitutional Convention Act," *Massachusetts Law Quarterly*, December, 1962, pp. 367–377.

A. James Heins, *Constitutional Restrictions Against State Debt* (Madison, 1963).

Bernard L. Hyink, "The California Legislature Looks at the State Constitution," *Western Political Quarterly*, March, 1962, pp. 157–169.

Charlotte Irvine and Edward M. Kresky, *How to Study a State Constitution* (New York, 1962).

Paul G. Kauper, *The State Constitution: Its Nature and Purpose* (Detroit, 1961).

Alfred H. Kelly, *The Meaning of American Constitutional Government* (Lansing, 1961).

Robert S. Ketchum, *The 1958 Constitutional Revision Campaign in Michigan* (Ann Arbor, 1960).

Bruce B. Mason and Heinz R. Hink, *Revision of the Arizona Constitution: A Commentary* (Tempe, 1961).

The Proposed Constitution: A Comparison with the Present Constitution (Lansing, 1962).

George Romney, "Michigan's New Constitution," *State Government*, Winter, 1964, pp. 2–7.

Frank G. Schlosser, *Dry Revolution: Diary of a Constitutional Convention* (Newton, N. J., 1960).

John R. Schmidhauser, *Iowa's Campaign for a Constitutional Convention in 1960* (New York, 1963).

Dick Smith, "Constitutional Revision in Texas, 1876–1961," *Public Affairs Comment*, September, 1961, pp. 1–4.

"State Constitutional Limitations on the Power of Eminent Domain," *Harvard Law Review*, February, 1964, pp. 717–729.

Carolyn Stieber, *Focus on Con Con* (East Lansing, 1961).

Albert L. Sturm, *Constitution-making in Michigan 1961–1962* (Ann Arbor, 1963).

Albert L. Sturm, *Major Constitutional Issues in West Virginia* (Morgantown, 1961).

Albert L. Sturm, "Making a Constitution," *National Civic Review*, January, 1964, pp. 14–26.

The Texas Constitutional Amendments of 1960 (Austin, 1960).

John P. Wheeler, Jr. (ed.), *The Constitutional Convention: A Manual on its Planning, Organization, and Operation* (New York, 1961).

John P. Wheeler, Jr., *Salient Issues of Constitutional Revision* (New York, 1961).

John M. Winters, *State Constitutional Limitations on Solutions of Metropolitan Area Problems* (Ann Arbor, 1961).

Dean Zenor, *State Constitutional Conventions: The Legislature's Role Preparing for a Convention* (Iowa City, 1960),

▶ Chapter III

THE STATE
LEGISLATURE

Who are the legislators, whom do they represent, how do they operate, and why do some bills pass and others fail?

Who manages the legislatures and who advises them?

IN a representative democracy the major task of policy-making is given to the legislature. Here hundreds, even thousands, of measures are introduced in every session that require decision and disposition. These measures affect the citizen in terms of the following: the organizational structure of state and local governments under which he lives; the services that may be rendered him in the areas of health, education, and welfare; the protection that may be afforded him in the control of crime, in the regulation of gambling, liquor, and narcotics; and certainly not least, in terms of the types and rates of taxation that may be necessary to help finance all of these multitudinous activities.

These thousands of legislative proposals may be buried in committee, amended beyond recognition by either friend or foe, debated on the floor, killed on the floor, filibustered to death, or recommended for passage. As of December 31, 1963 for the biennium then closing, a total of over 37,000 enactments were passed in the fifty states and these only in the course of regular sessions.

Senators and representatives elected in their respective constituencies may speak and vote on behalf of farmers, workers, and businessmen, may speak and vote on behalf of city or country, may speak and vote for their own consciences, may speak and vote as Americans, and may speak and vote as members of chambers which are organized, in the majority of states, into two distinct groupings—one labeled Democratic, the other, Republican. The precise meaning of these party designations is not unambiguous. For example, can there be much legislative responsibility when legislators are elected in campaigns where, as a rule, no explicit effort is made to relate candidates to party platforms or positions? Do Republican or Democratic electors in exchange for their votes expect or have the right to expect Republican or Democratic legislators to support their respective parties and leaderships in the House and Senate? Some students of government will argue that there can be no legislative responsibility without such discipline and interrelationship. A more detailed consideration of these important issues must be deferred for the next chapter.

The doctrine of separation of powers was never designed to smooth the path of legislators and executives. Under the state constitutions both branches are directly accountable to the electorate, both interpret its wishes, and neither can function without the other's cooperation. But "cooperation" is a

48

slippery concept subject to diverging interpretations by strong-willed governors imbued with the need for gubernatorial leadership and by strong-minded legislators eager to assert their independence and prerogative.

Governors not only execute the laws but are eager to influence the making of them; legislators not only pass the laws but are also concerned with their administrative impact. For the legislature to play a more efficient role in this necessary and ongoing struggle for power, there is needed a more adequate staff for research, study and analysis, an improved internal organization through fewer committees, more realistic rules, and a greatly strengthened apparatus for the legislative post audit of state expenditures. An increased avoidance of strictly local issues and a reduced concern for administrative detail may be the price the legislature will have to pay in order to gain the time necessary for more penetrating deliberations of basic policy. To debate and act (with statesmanship and the highest concern for the general good) on these fundamental and increasingly complex questions, the legislature of the 1960's will more than ever need dedicated public servants of the highest personal integrity.

INTERNAL LEGISLATIVE ORGANIZATION AND OPERATION

THE PERSISTENCE OF BICAMERALISM

Despite the unicameralism of the eighteenth-century Georgia, Pennsylvania and Vermont legislatures, the 1934 adoption of the one-house principle in Nebraska, and the urgings of the National Municipal League *Model Constitution,* the states' preference for bicameralism persists and in the main unabatedly.

There are a number of reasons for this other than mere tradition and precedent.

Those that argue in support of the *status quo* may stress the safety factor. Two chambers are better than one in scrutinizing dangerous legislation, in checking popular passions to which one of the houses may have fallen victim. John Adams' warning may be cited: "A single assembly is liable to all the vices, follies and frailties of an individual; subject to fits of humor, starts of passion, flights of enthusiasms, partialities or prejudices, consequently productive of hasty results and absurd judgments." Second, it is contended, the 1964 Supreme Court decision in *Reynolds* v. *Sims* to the contrary notwithstanding, that two houses permit "area" (such as counties or towns) as the basis for apportioning seats in one house, with "population" as the basis for the other chamber as in the "federal plan." Third, bicameralism offers greater protection against special interest groups and their possibly insidious designs.

Proponents of unicameralism rely heavily on the example of Nebraska. They see in it adequate evidence of greater efficiency and lower costs. It is possible to avoid duplicate committees, memberships, and staffs for two houses, and the requirements for two distinct legislative gauntlets before bills become law. Moreover, it is suggested that nothing has happened in Nebraska to prove the charge that popular radicalism could seize power more easily or that injurious lobbies were more effective there in their efforts than in bicameral systems.

The debate continues but the delegates of Hawaii and Alaska chose to put their faith in the traditional bicameral structure.

STATE HOUSE OF REPRESENTATIVES AND SENATE— SIZE, TERMS, AND SALARIES

The "lower" or larger chamber is called the "House of Representatives"; typically it has a membership between ninety-nine and one hundred and fifty representatives who are elected for two-year terms and work through standing committees varying in number from eleven to thirty. California, New Hampshire, New York, and Wisconsin prefer to call their lower house "Assembly," and in Virginia and West Virginia, it is still the "House of Delegates." Four-year terms are now the rule in four states—Alabama, Louisiana, Maryland, and Mississippi. All of the states call their upper chambers "Senate," and all but thirteen give their senators four-year terms. The typical Senate has between thirty-five and fifty members and works through eleven to twenty standing committees (see Table 1).

There are considerable differences between states in the level and basis of pay received by their legislators. (The term "legislator" properly applies to members of both House and Senate). The biennial salary range includes New York with a maximum of $20,000 followed by Massachusetts with $15,600; a majority of the states, however, are found in the $2,000 to $5,000 category. New Hampshire with its enormous House of 400 members and its Senate of twenty-four members pays a mere $200. A daily amount between five and fifty dollars is set by nineteen states, eighteen of which limit the number of days from thirty-six in Alabama to one hundred and twenty in Kansas, North Carolina, and Oregon. All but one state make provision for travel allowances, and all but eleven states permit additional mileage appropriations while the legislators are at the Capitol (see Table 2).

LEGISLATIVE DISTRICTS

Approximately half of the representatives and nine-tenths of the senators are elected in single-member districts or constituencies; the others come from multimember districts.[1] Generally speaking, a majority party receives a distinct advantage under the multimember district scheme. Voters may be persuaded to cast their two or three votes for candidates of the locally dominant party while the minority party may be too discouraged to offer

[1] See Maurice Klain, "A New Look at the Constituencies: The Need for a Recount and a Reappraisal," *American Political Science Review*, December, 1955, pp. 1105–1119.

e or other jurisdiction	House committees appointed by Speaker	Senate committees appointed by	No. of standing committees at 1962 and 1963 regular sessions			Range in size of committees †			Hearings open to public †
			House	Senate	Joint	House	Senate	Joint	
bama	*	President	19	30	0	7–15	3–21	-----	Dis.
ska	(a)	(a)	9	9(b)	0	7–11	5–7	-----	Dis.
ona	*	President	21	21	0	9–15	7–14	-----	Dis.
ansas	*	President	26	25	1	5–20	4–12	12	Dis.
fornia	*	Comm. on Rules	26	21	4	3–20	5–13	6–14	Yes
rado	*	Resolution	17	20	1	4–19	5–15	6	Dis.
necticut	*(c)	Pres. pro tem(c)	0	0	28	-----	-----	26–36	Yes
aware	*	Pres. pro tem	26	22	1	5	5	-----	Dis.
ida	*	President	51	45	0	7–25	7–15	-----	Yes(d)
rgia	*	President	24	18	0	5–51	5–23	-----	Dis.
vaii	*	President	21(e)	18(f)	0	3–14	5–10	-----	Dis.
ao	*	President	15	14	0	7–13	5–11	-----	Dis.
ois	*	Comm. on Comms.	26	25	0	6–40	3–33	-----	Yes
ana	*	Pres. pro tem	28	29	0	7–16	5–11	-----	Dis.
a	*	President	42	30	0	5–52	3–31	-----	Dis.
sas	*	Comm. on Comms.	45	31	1	3–23	5–13	12	Dis.
tucky	(g)	Comm. on Comms.	45	37	1	3–46	3–23	9	Dis.
siana	*	President	17	18	0	9–20	3–17	-----	Dis.
ne	*	President	6	3	26	4–16	4–12	7–10	Yes
yland	*	President	15	16	3	6–31	3–15	6–10	Yes
sachusetts	*	President	6	4	31	3–16	3–10	15–19	Yes
higan	*	Comm. on Comms.	48	21(h)	0	5–15	6–10	-----	Dis.
nesota	*	Comm. on Comms.	36	23	0	4–29	7–27	-----	Yes
issippi	*	President	50	46	5	5–33	3–26	5–13	Dis.
ouri	*	Pres. pro tem	45	28	2	5–44	5–15	15	Dis.
tana	*	Comm. on Comms.	18	23	0	5–17	3–11	-----	Dis.
raska	(i)	Comm. on Comms.	(i)	14	(i)	(i)	1–8	(i)	Yes
ada	*	President	22	19	0	5–9	3–5	-----	Yes
Hampshire	*	President	24	18	1	5–22	3–7	8	Yes
Jersey	*	President	16	16	4	7–8	5–22	12	Dis.
Mexico	*(j)	Comm. on Comms.	16(k)	7(l)	0	7–14	7–11	-----	Dis.
York	*	Pres. pro tem	36	28	0	5–20	6–25	-----	Dis.
h Carolina	*	President	46	34	4	11–62	7–26	-----	Yes
h Dakota	*	Comm. on Comms.	14	11	0	22	10–19	-----	Dis.
	*	Pres. pro tem	21	13	0	7–25	7–9	-----	Yes
homa	*	(m)	39	34	0	3–31	3–20	-----	Dis.
on	*	President	20	20	1	9	5–8	14	Yes
sylvania	*	Pres. pro tem	30	21	0	10–19	9–23	-----	Dis.
le Island	*	Named in rules	15	17	1	8–17	5–10	9	Dis.
h Carolina	*	Elected(n)	8	25	5	5–27	5–18	6–15	Dis.
h Dakota	*	President	23	16	0	3–15	3–9	-----	Dis.
essee	*	Speaker	17	17	0	17–30	9–17	-----	Dis.
s	*	President	43	24	1	5–21	5–21	6	Yes
	*	President	16	14	1	7–18	4–12	30	Yes
ont	*	Special comm.	18	18	3(o)	10–25	5–18	6–56	Yes
nia	*	Elected	34	21	3	NA	NA	NA	Dis.(p)
ington	*	President	21	20	0	11–41	10–36	-----	Dis.
Virginia	*	President	24	28	4	10–25	5–18	5	Dis.

TABLE 1 (*continued*)

State or other jurisdiction	House committees appointed by Speaker	Senate committees appointed by	No. of standing committees at 1962 and 1963 regular sessions			Range in size of committees †			Hearin open public
			House	Senate	Joint	House	Senate	Joint	
Wisconsin_____*		Comm. on Comms.(q)	23	11	5	3–11	3–5	5–14	Yes
Wyoming_____*		President	18	16	1	7–9	2–5	_____	Dis.
Puerto Rico_____*		President	17	17	6	7–23	5–17	7–16	Dis.

† Abbreviations: Dis.—Discretionary; NA—Information not available.
 (a) Nominated by Committee on Committees and elected by House and Senate respectively.
 (b) Ten during 1962 session; 9 during 1963 session.
 (c) Minority party members are nominated by the minority party leader of each house.
 (d) Senate committees sometimes meet in executive session.
 (e) Twenty-five during 1962 session; 21 during 1963 session.
 (f) Twelve during 1962 session; 18 during 1963 session.
 (g) Committee on Committees.
 (h) Twenty during 1962 session; 21 during 1963 session.
 (i) Unicameral legislature.
 (j) Standing Committee on Committees advises him.
 (k) Only 12 consider legislation; 4 are procedural.
 (l) Also the Committee on Committees.
 (m) Senate elects Senate standing committees. Appointments to temporary and special committees, in Oklahoma, are made by the Senate presiding officer.
 (n) Special committees are appointed.
 (o) Corresponding committees of each house usually meet jointly.
 (p) Final vote by a House committee must be in open session.
 (q) Confirmation by Senate.
SOURCE: *Book of the States, 1964–1965*, p. 51.

spirited opposition and may even fail to enter a full slate of candidates. Illinois, on the other hand, which employs a multimember district arrangement actually encourages the minority party to contest all seats. Under the cumulative voting system operative there, a voter may split his votes. He is permitted to "give all three of his votes to one candidate, give a vote and a half each to two, give a single vote to each of three, or give two to one and one to another." [2]

LEGISLATIVE LEADERS AND OFFICIALS

To those who can command a majority in the House goes the key position of influence and power—the speakership. As presiding officer, the speaker can set the general tone of the assembly. He can preserve the decorum and order which may entail clearing the galleries, lobbies, or corridors. In nearly all of the states he refers bills to committees and generally signs all acts, addresses, resolutions, writs, and warrants. Subpoenas for persons and records issued by committees may also require his signature.

As parliamentarian he recognizes (or fails to recognize) those who wish to obtain the floor. He must state the motions before they can be put to a vote.

[2] Malcolm E. Jewell, *The State Legislature* (New York, 1962), p. 35; see also George S. Blair, *Cumulative Voting: An Effective Electoral Device in Illinois Politics* (Urbana, 1960).

He must decide questions of parliamentary procedure (with the aid of his parliamentarian) and he must announce the results when a vote is taken.

As head of his legislative party or majority group (Nebraska and Minnesota do not have party-designated legislatures and nearly all of the Southern chambers have only Democrats), he must work closely with the majority leader and his fellow members of the powerful rules committee on the major decisions that affect party programs and interests. When the governor in office belongs to the same party, the speaker, majority leader, and floor leaders (party whips) may have to meet frequently with the chief executive and other major committee chairman to confer on the priority of legislative measures and on ways of best overcoming opposition forces.

The speaker has important administrative duties affecting the efficient operation of the legislature. Legislative employees, clerical and professional, authorized and paid by the rules of the House usually work under his or the chief clerk's supervision. These are usually appointments of political patronage (except in Wisconsin), not covered by civil service protection and may include clerks, messengers, doorkeeper, sergeants-at-arms, janitors, parking marshalls, elevator operators, and chaplains.

The one great power, perhaps the greatest power—long ago taken from the speaker of the national House of Representatives—is that of appointing committees. Speakers of all state legislatures except those of Alaska, Kentucky, and Nebraska still possess this power, although in some states the House must formally ratify his appointments (see Table 1). To be sure, this is not a power entirely unshared with others. Before a session is even formally organized certain critical negotiations are carried on among the leaders of the majority group with the aim of designating individuals for the key positions. These negotiations may be very delicate and may involve reciprocal commitments as well as policy. The more closely the parties are matched in numbers, the greater the demand for prudence and tact. Sometimes there may be other types of pressure. In 1961, Republicans in the Illinois legislature found that their majority proved insufficient to elect a speaker. The fact that six Republicans held jobs through the generosity of the Chicago Democratic machine may have had something to do with their failure to stay with their party during the critical organizational vote. A Democratic speaker was elected. Sometimes a speaker-designate may have to weigh an appointment for the majority leadership and committee chairmanship because of his state's sectional or religious politics. At the beginning of the 1961 New York legislative session Speaker of the Assembly Carlino, a Catholic Republican from a metropolitan downstate area, with his party having a majority of only eight votes, was under pressure to appoint a Protestant from an upstate county to the majority leadership post.

In thirty-nine states the presiding officer of the Senate is the lieutenant governor. Where no such office exists (as in Alaska, Arizona, Florida, Maine, Maryland, New Hampshire, New Jersey, Oregon, Utah, West Virginia, and Wyoming), one of the members of the chamber is elected president by

TABLE 2. SALARIES AND COMPENSATION

	SALARY AND DAILY PAY PLANS						
	Regular session			Special session			
	Daily pay plan		Salary plan				
State or other jurisdiction	Amount per day	Limit on no. of days of pay	Amount of salary calculated for biennium	Amount of pay per day	Limit on no. of days of pay	Basic salary is fixed by	Date basi salar estab lishe
Alabama	$10	36 L(a)	—	$10	36 L	Const.	194
Alaska	—	—	$ 5,000(b)	—	—	Stat.	196
Arizona	—	—	3,600(b,d)	—	—	Const.	195
Arkansas	20	60 C	2,400(e,f)	6	—	Const.	195
California	—	—	12,000(b)	—	—	Const.	195
Colorado	—	—	6,400(b,h)	h	—	Stat.	196
Connecticut	—	—	2,000	—	—	Stat.	195
Delaware	—	—	6,000(b)	—	—	Const.	195
Florida	—	—	2,400	—	—	Const.	195
Georgia	10	(b,j)	—	10	70 C(k)	Const.	194
Hawaii	—	—	4,000(b,l)	(l)	—	Const. & Stat.	195
Idaho	10	60 C	—	10	20 C	Const.	194
Illinois	—	—	12,000	—	—	Stat.	195
Indiana	—	—	3,600	—	—	Stat.	195
Iowa	30	—	—	30	—	Stat.	195
Kansas	10	120 C(b,m)	—	10	30 C	Stat.	196
Kentucky	25	60 L(n)	—	25	—	Stat.	195
Louisiana	50	90 C(b,o)	—	50	30 C	Stat.	195
Maine	—	—	1,600	10	—	Stat.	195
Maryland	—	—	3,600(b)	—	—	Const.	194
Massachusetts	—	—	15,600(b)	(q)	—	Stat.	196
Michigan	—	—	14,000(b)	—	—	Stat.	196
Minnesota	—	—	4,800	25	—	Stat.	195
Mississippi	—	—	3,000	22.50	—	Stat.	195
Missouri	—	—	9,600	—	—	Stat.	196
Montana	20	60 C	—	20	60 C	Stat.	195
Nebraska	—	—	4,800	—	—	Const. & Stat.	196
Nevada	25	60 C	—	25	20 C	Stat.	195
New Hampshire	—	—	200	3	15 L	Const.	188
New Jersey	—	—	10,000(b)	—	—	Const. & Stat.	194
New Mexico	20	60 C	—	20	30 C	Const. & Stat.	194
New York	—	—	20,000(b)	—	—	Const. & Stat.	194
North Carolina	15	120 C	—	15	25 C	Const.	19

ADDITIONAL COMPENSATION FOR LEGISLATORS

Travel allowance		Additional expense allowances during session
Amount per mile	Number of trips during session	Additional expense allowances during session
10c	One round trip	$20 per day(a)
15c	One round trip(c)	$35 per day; $300 postage-stationery allowance; presiding officers receive an extra annual allowance of $500
10c	-------------------	$12 per day subsistence for legislators from outside city limits of capital(d)
5c	One round trip	---------
5c(g)	One round trip	$19 per day(f)
(i)	One round trip	None during session(g)
10c	Each day	$500 expense allowance
15c	Unlimited mileage	$25 stationery and supplies
10c	Round trip per week	$25 per day
10c	Four round trips	$40 per day
20c	One round trip	$32.50 per day for members from Oahu; $45 for legislators from neighbor islands
10c	One round trip	Additional $15 a day for committee members
10c	Round trip per week	$50 for postage and stationery
7c	Round trip per week	---------
7c	One round trip	---------
7c	Six actual round trips during regular and three actual round trips during special or budget session	$15 per day; not to exceed $1,350 during regular session nor $450 during special or budget session; $50 per month between sessions
15c	One round trip	$25 a day; $50 in lieu of stationery
10c	Eight round trips and four round trips during budget session	$250 per month while legislature not in regular session
5c	Round trip per week	Small allowance for postage, telephone, etc.
20c(p)	One round trip	$2,400 per biennium
8c(p)	Each day(r)	$1,200 per biennium; weekly expense allowance according to distance from capital(q)
10c	Two round trips per month	$2,500 per biennium; plus allowance for postage, telephone and telegraph
15c	One round trip	In 1963, $18 per day except that legislators who did not have to leave their homes to attend session received $12 per day
10c	One round trip(s)	$100 per month between sessions
10c	Twice per month	$10 per day
8c	One round trip	---------
8c	One round trip	$100 postage allowance
10c	Daily commuting(t)	$15 per day(t); $60 for postage, etc.
(u)	Daily round trip(u)	---------
—	State railroad pass	---------
10c	One round trip	Stationery, postage, telephone and telegraph allowance
(i)	Round trip per week	$2,500 expense allowance at 1963 annual sessions
8c	One round trip per week	$12 per day subsistence

TABLE 2 (continued)

State or other jurisdiction	SALARY AND DAILY PAY PLANS					
	Regular session			Special session		
	Daily pay plan		Salary plan			
	Amount per day	Limit on no. of days of pay	Amount of salary calculated for biennium	Amount of pay per day	Limit on no. of days of pay	Basic salary is fixed by
North Dakota	5	60 L	—	5	—	Const.
Ohio	—	—	10,000	—	—	Stat.
Oklahoma	15	75 L(v)	3,900(v)	15	75 L(v)	Const.
Oregon	20(w)	120 C	6,000	20	120 C	Const.
Pennsylvania	—	—	12,000(b)	—	—	Stat.
Rhode Island	5	60 L(b)	—	—	—	Const.
South Carolina	—	—	3,600(b)	45	40 L	Stat. & Const.
South Dakota	—	—	3,000(b)	10	—	Stat.
Tennessee	10	75 C	—	10	20 C	Stat.
Texas	—	—	9,600(x)	—	—	Const.
Utah	—	—	1,000	—	—	Const. & Stat.
Vermont	(y)	—	—	—	—	Stat.
Virginia	—	—	1,080	30	30 C	Stat.
Washington	—	—	2,400	25	—	Stat.
West Virginia	—	—	3,000(b)	—	—	Const.
Wisconsin	15	110 L	10,800	15	20 L	Stat.
Wyoming	12	40 C	—	12	—	Stat. Act
Puerto Rico	—	—	5,400(b)	—	—	Stat.

Abbreviations: L—Legislative days; C—Calendar days.

(a) In practice the legislature meets for 18 weeks. Legislators receive $210 a week in combined daily salary and expense allowance, a total of $3,780 for each regular biennial session.
(b) Annual sessions.
(c) Plus excess baggage allowance.
(d) Plus $20 per day salary (limited to $1,800 in a year) for special sessions and interim committee meetings; $12 per day subsistence for days required to attend interim commitee meetings, plus 10c a mile or first class public carrier.
(e) Payable at rate of $100 each month. Speaker of the House receives $2,700.
(f) Legislators receive $100 a month for each of the 24 months in the biennium, plus a per diem of $20 a day for each of the 60 calendar days of the biennial legislative session.
(g) 12½c a mile for interim committee meetings and $25 a day for maximum of 60 days for interim committee meetings.
(h) Legislators receive $100 a month during biennium plus $4,000, paid at rate of $25 a day during regular and special sessions up to a total of 160 days each biennium with remainder paid as a lump sum. Legislators also receive $20 per day, not to exceed $600 in any calendar year, while not in session, for attendance at legislative meetings, plus actual and necessary traveling expenses.
(i) Actual and necessary expenses.
(j) Not to exceed 40 days in even years; 45 days in odd years.
(k) 70-day limit on special sessions called by Governor except for impeachment proceedings; 30-day limit on sessions convened by legislature except for impeachment proceedings.
(l) $2,500 per general session; $1,500 per budget session; $750 for each special session.
(m) 120 C-days biennial total; 90 C-day regular session; 30 C-day budget session. Legislators are paid additional allowance of $50 per calendar month, except for January, February and March in odd years, and January during even years to defray expenses incurred between sessions.

ADDITIONAL COMPENSATION FOR LEGISLATORS

Travel allowance		
Amount per mile	Number of trips during session	Additional expense allowances during session
10c	One round trip	$20 per day
10c	Round trip per week	Postage and stationery
10c	One round trip per week	Postage, stationery, telephone and telegraph allowance and shipping legislative supplies
10c	-------------------	-------
10c	Round trip per week	$6,000(b)
8c	-------------------	-------
9c	Round trip per week	$15 per day for maximum of 40 days per annual session
5c	One round trip	-------
16c	One round trip	$5 per day
10c	One round trip	Per diem of $12 for first 120 days of regular session and for 30 days of each special session; postage, stationery, supplies, telephone and secretarial assistance
10c	One round trip per week, if incurred	$5 per day
20c	One round trip	
7c	One round trip	$720 for regular session; $360 for special sessions
10c	One round trip	$25 per day
10c	One round trip	-------
(z)	Rate-distance ratio(z)	(aa)
8c	One round trip	$20 per day
15c	Round trip per week (ab)	$10 per day(ac); $200 for telephone; $100 for postage; $100 for stationery

Legislators are paid for Sundays and holidays during session, consequently compensation period usually is 72 to 74 days.
90 days biennial total; 60-day regular session, 30-day budget session.
In terms of fixed amounts for each legislator.
Determined at each session in Massachusetts.
Within 40-mile radius, 8c a mile daily to amount to not less than $7 a week; outside 40-mile radius, $60 per week living expenses plus 8c a mile for one round trip per week.
Plus one extra round trip each 7 days at 6c a mile.
10c a mile for daily commuting or $15 per day if living in capital.
25c per mile for first 25 miles, 20c for next 20 miles, 8c for next 25 miles, 6c for the next 25 miles, 5c over 95 miles.
Figure shown is approximate for biennium in which no special session is held. In 1961–62 biennium, combined per diem and salary totaled $3,908.32. Legislators receive $15 for first 75 legislative days, including intervening nonlegislative days, for regular or special session; otherwise $100 a month.
Expenses plus salary.
Members receive an annual salary of $4,800.
Members receive $85 for each week or portion thereof during regular session.
10c a mile for one round trip; thereafter, 7c a mile for first 2,000 miles per month, 6c a mile for each additional mile once a week during the session.
Interim expense allowance paid for each full calendar month when legislature not in session, as follows: for district of one county or less—Assemblyman, $25 per month; Senator, $40 per month. For each additional county or part of county in district—Assemblyman, $15 per month; Senator, $20 per month.
Minimum $10.
$15 per day within 25–50 kilometers radius; $25 per day beyond.

ᴀᴄᴇ: *Book of the States, 1964–1965*, pp. 46–47.

majority vote.[3] In states having a lieutenant governor, he is, of course, elected on a statewide basis which may mean that he could be of a different political party than the Senate majority. This possibility has caused some states to take away from this office the power of appointing committees. See Table 1 for the variety of methods used in appointing committees.

Though shorn of this important power as well as certain other administrative duties possessed by the speaker of the House, the lieutenant governor still retains his position as the ceremonial and parliamentary head of the Senate. In this capacity he is also ordinarily given the duty of signing legislative acts, memorials, addresses, resolutions, writs, warrants, and subpoenas and of referring all bills to a standing committee. The appointing of the other Senate employees and officials is usually left in the hands of the committee on rules or some other special committee. Much of the Senate's actual political power is thus held not by the lieutenant governor but by the president *pro tem* (an elective officer of the Senate) or in his place by the chairman of the rules committee.

LEGISLATIVE COMMITTEES—SEATS OF POLITICAL POWER

High in the power structure of any legislature stand the committees and their chairmen. This is the place where most bills are made and unmade, where legislative careers are born and broken. Appointment to a major committee may yield influence on legislative substance and opportunities for public attention and acclaim.

Little wonder then, that a doctrine like "every man a king" or "every legislator a chairman" has an appealing quality to an assembly wishing to spread or distribute these legislative prizes to as large a group of deserving fellow party members as possible. Incidentally, it also facilitates the placating of a disappointed candidate for speaker or majority leader or the "indenturing" of a well-known opponent of a particularly important administration measure.

Actually the need for such committees inheres in the very nature of the legislative process. House and Senate by their size alone make it impossible to give to bills—many of them full of technical details—the attention and scrutiny they deserve. Legislators—lawyers, businessmen, farmers, or school teachers—are essentially generalists as all successful politicians must be. They know and can work with people and in addition to their own occupations or fields of specialization may have a very wide understanding of many facets of everyday life. However, the minutiae of taxation, conservation, transportation, or education should be considered by those legislators who have some special competence. Actually most subject-matter committees tend to reflect considerable background experience in their membership—a fact which less charitable critics may liken to a built-in lobby.

[3] *Book of the States, 1964–1965,* p. 142.

The Senate banking committee in Alabama, for example, a few years ago had a majority of bankers. The alcoholic beverage control committee in the Maryland House recently consisted mostly of tavern-keepers, beer distributors, and lawyers representing liquor interests. Florida committees dealing with citrus products and forestry have been made up almost entirely of citrus-growers and representatives of the forestry interests. In a recent session of the Kentucky legislature all members of the House who were veterans were put on the veterans' committee, all insurance agents were on the insurance committee, and most of those on the agricultural committees were farmers.[4]

There is also the sheer volume of bills introduced in sessions still rigidly limited as to length in the majority of states. Committees are a means of breaking down the legislative work load, of screening the irrelevant from the relevant, and of consolidating related proposals into integrated measures.

Hearings have to be held, studies prepared, and investigations conducted. Much of this activity, to be sure, is entirely within the discretion of the committee and not infrequently the chairman's prerogative. Hearings can be avoided or, if held, conducted to maximize the influence of the proponents, or so scheduled as to make attendance of the opponents of the measure difficult, or outright impossible. Studies that are prepared by either the committees (as a rule infinitely less well-staffed than those of Congress) or by outside experts may reflect a bias favorable or unfavorable. These are some of the tools of power for leadership or partisanship depending on one's frame of reference.

NUMBER, SIZE, AND WORK LOAD OF COMMITTEES

The number of standing committees of the lower chambers ranged in number at the beginning of 1963 from a high of fifty-one in Florida to six in Maine and Massachusetts. It might be expected that the more populous states would be found near the upper limit of the range. As shown by Table 1, this was generally not true.

Explanations for committee proliferation as indicated earlier must, therefore, be sought more in terms of the complexities of politics underlying legislative organization than in mere population statistics. Although there are some exceptions, it is generally true that states preferring a large number of committees in their lower chambers tend to have an equally large number of committees for their Senates as well.

If the number of committees becomes excessively large, the legislature pays a price in duplication of effort, wasted manpower, overcrowded hearing schedules, and in poor committee and session attendance. Among its sixty-one standing House committees during the 1957–1958 session, the Missouri legislature had in its roster separate committees for Agriculture, Dairying,

---

[4] Jewell, p. 99. For further discussions of legislative committees, see Henry W. Lewis, *Law and Administration: Legislative Committees in North Carolina* (Chapel Hill, 1952); Loren P. Beth and William C. Havard, "Committee Stacking and Political Power in Florida," *Journal of Politics*, February, 1961, pp. 57–83; and Dean E. Mann, "The Legislative Committee in Arizona," *Western Political Quarterly*, December, 1961, pp. 925–941.

Seeds and Grain, and Rural Electrification; separate committees on Criminal Jurisprudence, Criminal Justice and Cost, and Judiciary; separate committees for Education, Universities and School of Mines, State Teachers Colleges, and Public Schools. Based on studies of actual legislative needs, it has been suggested that state legislatures could, by proper arrangement of subject matter, operate with a dozen standing committees. Missouri under such a pattern would have to be satisfied with one committee for each: agriculture, judiciary, and education.

Despite such newer areas of emphasis as turnpikes, metropolitan annexation, juvenile delinquency, or pollution control (and the desire to create separate committees for each of these areas), there has been a fortunate tendency as shown in the following table to actually reduce committees.

| | House | | Senate | |
Number of standing committees	1946	1963	1946	1963
10 or under	0	5	0	5
11–20	2	15	8	21
21–30	9	16	15	18
31–40	15	4	13	4
41–50	12	8	9	2
51–60	7	1	2	0
61–70	2	0	1	0

SOURCE: *Book of the States, 1964–1965*, p. 40.

A few states make use of joint committees with membership drawn from both House and Senate, thereby eliminating some of the duplication due to bicameralism in the hearing, study, and consideration of bills. Valuable legislative time is thus conserved and more intensive attention given to each measure. Presently, all of Connecticut's twenty-eight committees are joint; Maine and Massachusetts mostly work through joint committees and twenty-two other states do have one or more joint committees with their other standing committees.

The average membership of committees in most of the states ranges somewhere between five to twenty-five in the House and five to fifteen in the Senate. Some very large House committees are noted in North Carolina–62, Iowa–52, Georgia–51, Kentucky–46, and Missouri–44. Since referral to committees (and thus work loads) varies greatly within a legislature, most states have avoided fixing a uniform size.

How these work loads may differ from committee to committee was brought out in a recent study of the Missouri legislature. It was found that over 50 per cent of the load in the House was carried by only four committees: Judiciary, Government Organization, Fees and Salaries, and Appropriations. In the Senate the busiest committees tended to be: Judiciary, Education, Public Health and Welfare, Municipal Corporations, and Roads and Highways.

An earlier study of the New York Senate revealed that of all bills referred, the Judiciary and the Finance committees together received 26.6 per cent of the assignments. For that same 1945 session, approximately six of the Assembly's thirty-six committees were given an average of 315 bills each while another six averaged only sixteen bills each.[5]

Legislative committees also indicate diverse policies with respect to "controversial" bills. Analysis of the Illinois practice revealed that bills are not buried or pigeonholed in committees, that "chairmen do not kill bills," but that hearings are held and that of over 3,000 referrals in the 1955 session only 103 or 3.3 per cent received "Do Not Pass" recommendations.[6] Missouri, revealing a very dissimilar pattern, found Senate committees may refuse to report on "from one-third to half or more of the bills referred to them," whereas House committees stamp approximately one-third of all measures "Do Not Pass" (which constitutes a formal report), rather than killing the measure outright.[7]

A study of committee action in Alabama for the period 1907–1943 showed that of all measures referred to them Senate committees would, on an average, report 5.8 per cent of the bills unfavorably and pigeonhole 15.8 per cent. Percentages for the House were 13.2 and 15.6, respectively.[8]

That Missouri and Alabama rather than Illinois come closer to representing a pattern typical for most state legislatures is underscored by the widespread concern for devices to remove bills from committee consideration.

Fourteen states as of 1963 stipulate that committees must within stated periods report *all* bills referred to them. Explicit constitutional provisions in Hawaii, Kentucky, and Missouri permit recall of such bills either by special motion or through discharge petitions. The discharge petition has the advantage of a selected recall and thus does not inundate the chamber with all of the committee's bills. Legislative leaders seeking to avoid an embarrassing or controversial chamber action and opposed to the petition can cause the defeat of such motions with some ease. In the Missouri study covering four successive sessions, its use was found to be quite rare, "no more than once or twice a session." [9]

COMMITTEE CHAIRMEN

The congressional pattern of awarding committee chairmanships to the majority party members with the highest seniority in terms of service is not uniformly followed in state legislatures. Not only has the seniority rule been

---

[5] Belle Zeller (ed.), *American State Legislatures: Report of the Committee on American Legislatures, American Political Science Association* (New York, 1954), p. 99.

[6] Gilbert Y. Steiner and Samuel K. Gove, *Legislative Politics in Illinois* (Urbana, 1960), p. 63.

[7] Robert F. Karsch, *The Standing Committees of the Missouri General Assembly* (Columbia, 1959), pp. 27–28.

[8] Hallie Farmer, *The Legislative Process in Alabama* (University, Ala., 1949), p. 156.

[9] Karsch, p. 29.

ignored by some legislatures but previous legislative experience itself has been minimized as well in view of the high turnover among legislators. There just are not enough deserving and competent "old-timers" to fill the vacant positions.

In 1950, for example, 76 per cent of the Senate committee chairmen in Alabama, 50 per cent in Maryland, 50 per cent in Kentucky, and 43 per cent in Georgia had but a single term of previous legislative experience. By way of contrast in nine other states not even one of their committees was chaired by a "sophomore."

Previous legislative experience seems to have been heaviest in the following six states where 50 per cent or more of the Senate chairmen had served upwards of five previous terms: California, 90 per cent; Minnesota, 80 per cent; Iowa, New York, and Wyoming, 70 per cent; and Kansas, 55 per cent.

House committee chairmen generally do not have the extent of seniority of their Senate colleagues. In very large chambers such as Vermont with 246 members and New Hampshire with 399 members, the percentages of no previous experience are 50 per cent and 44 per cent, respectively. Other Houses with large numbers of chairmen having a single term of previous experience include Alabama, 100 per cent; Kentucky, 83 per cent; Montana, 43 per cent; and Nevada and Tennessee with 43 per cent each.[10]

It could certainly be maintained that those who are in such responsible legislative positions as that of chairman should have the widest possible experience with the complexities of legislation. Understanding technical subject matter, legislative skill, and a profound perception of the political implications of proposed legislation is not something that can be quickly absorbed. It simply takes time to learn the ropes of writing laws.

But seniority can also deny the legislature a fresh point of view, enthusiasm, the uplifting idealism of the relatively unentangled, lobby-resistant young public servant, and last, the rich professional background or experience possible in a successful citizen only lately turned politician. As in so many other phases of government it is difficult to set down any hard and fast rule even here. How much stability is necessary for effective government and how much is too much? The more populous states, states with more extensive governmental machinery, and states where political party organizations tend to be stronger and better organized have preferred stability and chosen the majority of their committee chairmen from the ranks of older statesmen.

LEGISLATORS

Who are these busy legislators? They may be hurrying about the Capitol, listening to constituents, sitting in committee rooms, participating in a floor debate, addressing a P.T.A. meeting, drawing up a bill, studying in the law

[10] Zeller, pp. 68–69.

library, conferring with lobbyists, writing letters to the home newspaper, attending a party caucus, or worrying about the next campaign, the next vote, the next appointment, or the next batch of mail. Since most of them have a business, farm, or other occupation aside from lawmaking, which is but a part-time job, and since most of them are family men as well, they also have the usual concerns of other mortals for bills that must be paid, for children and wives who may be neglected, and for a future which at times may seem clouded and precarious.

QUALIFICATIONS

In the majority of the states any person who is by law qualified to vote in terms of his age, residence, and citizenship is also qualified to be a candidate for the legislature.

There are, however, some notable exceptions. Clergymen are ineligible in Tennessee and Maryland. In fifteen states "collectors or holders of public moneys," that is, tax collectors and treasurers, must by constitutional directive give "public accounting" before they can qualify; in other states age becomes an issue. For House membership, age twenty-four is specified in Delaware, Kentucky, and Missouri; twenty-five in Arizona, Colorado, Hawaii, South Dakota, and Utah. For the Senate, twenty-two states stipulate the age of twenty-five; seven, the age of thirty; Montana insists on twenty-four; Texas, on twenty-six; and Delaware, on twenty-seven.

OCCUPATIONS AND BACKGROUND

While nearly everyone may attempt to become a legislator, a survey of the nearly eight thousand members serving fifty state legislatures will readily disclose a group with marked common characteristics.

First, in every legislature the occupations most prominently represented are those of law, business, and farming.

Second, as distinct groups, women, skilled laborers, and Negroes are significantly underrepresented.

Third, legislative turnover is heavy. A 1950 study showed "over half of the state legislators are new at each session, the lower chamber having a greater percentage of new members than the Senate." [11]

Fourth, the majority of legislators are likely to be in the forty to sixty age category.

Some of these characteristics are interrelated and pertain to the very nature of the legislature. To afford legislative service and to live up to its

[11] *Ibid.*, p. 65. For more recent studies of the backgrounds of legislators, see Heinz Eulau, William Buchanan, LeRoy Ferguson, and John C. Wahlke, "The Political Socialization of American State Legislators," *Midwest Journal of Political Science*, May, 1959, pp. 188–206 and Duncan MacRae, Jr. and Edith K. MacRae, "Legislators' Social Status and their Votes," *The American Journal of Sociology*, May, 1961, pp. 599–603.

demands requires money, time, mobility, and personal dispensability from business, law office, shop, or farm. While legislators do not have to be wealthy persons—and the majority are not—their personal affairs have to be so ordered as to enable them to spend three, four, and five months at a time away from their homes and occupations at daily legislative pay and allowances which are minimal at best (see Table 2). This factor alone makes legislative service impossible for persons in a large number of occupations. Lawyers, on the other hand, are particularly attracted to a legislative career for a variety of reasons. Much in their own professional curriculum in the areas of taxation, banking, judicial procedures, labor law, negotiable instruments, trusts, and social legislation prepares them and serves as valuable background for the actual process of lawmaking. Work for their clients' interests has led to contacts in courthouse, city hall, and state Capitol. Legislative prominence itself has become a valuable and respectable method of attracting new legal business.

To those in the legal profession who are interested in building a political career, the legislature has often been a useful steppingstone. Of the governors in office in 1964, twenty-two had at one time or another served in a state legislature. In addition to these elective posts, lawyers have found their legislative experience and associations most helpful in obtaining important judicial and administrative posts.

INSTRUCTING THE NEW LEGISLATOR

Whatever the reasons for rapid turnover among legislators (personal, political, or the result of disappointments due to the subordinate position of a freshman lawmaker), in the majority of the states each session opens with an impressive number of inexperienced legislators. In thirty-six states this fact has been considered sufficiently significant to develop some form of orientation program for new legislators. Sponsorship, content, and objectives differ. The most widely-used pattern involves general presentations by legislative leaders with special topics assigned to legislative clerks, experts from the legislative councils, bill-drafting officials, and administrative officers. In some instances the governor as well as leading members of the bar and bench along with specialists from university faculties of law and public administration may be invited to address these conferences on particular phases of the legislative and executive process. A recent sampling of the topics discussed by these pre-legislative conferences is found in the following table. Some of these conferences are held prior to the actual beginning of the session; others are convened in the opening days of a new session.

During the last few years an attempt has been made in a number of states to broaden the scope of these pre-legislative conferences and to go beyond the technical and procedural questions to a discussion of policy issues. These sessions before the session can thus teach the new legislator not only the techniques of passing laws but give him the opportunity to listen and

Topics	State
Organizations, rules and procedures of the legislature	California, Florida, Georgia, Maryland, New Mexico, Oklahoma, South Dakota, Texas, Utah, Wyoming
Bill drafting	Florida, Texas, Wyoming
How a bill becomes a law	Florida, Missouri, New Mexico, Texas, Wyoming
Budgets and financing	Georgia, Maryland, Missouri
Legislative services and service agencies	California, Georgia, New Mexico, Oklahoma, South Dakota, Texas
Relations with the press	California, Oklahoma, South Dakota, Wyoming

SOURCE: Adapted from James B. Kessler, *Pre-Legislative Conferences: An Appraisal* (Bloomington, 1960), p. 10.

discuss with experts issues confronting the legislature in taxation, public education, highway construction, urban development, or in any of the other complex areas of legislative action on which he may be expected to cast an informed vote and in which he may claim no special knowledge.

LEGISLATIVE SESSIONS AND RULES

HOW LONG A SESSION?

Biennial sessions convening regularly in January of the odd-numbered years and limited in length to between sixty and 120 days still constitute the characteristic pattern for the majority of the states although some states exceed this range. In nineteen states annual sessions are held; eight of these states have "split" sessions; and in seven of these eight states, the even-numbered year is the "budget" session (see Table 3). Annual and unlimited sessions are presently possible in seven states only: Alaska, Massachusetts, Michigan, New Jersey, New York, Pennsylvania, and South Carolina.

Originally these constitutional restrictions were imposed to guard against legislative irresponsibility resulting in excessive legislation, in "riotous" living at public expense, or to prevent an unnecessarily prolonged session from interference with the harvest. As the volume and needs of legislation increased and as the complexity of legislation demanded more extensive hearings and deliberations, the pressure for removal of these restrictions gradually led the public to accept changes in the direction of longer or of annual sessions.

Reluctance to change is great. There are still fourteen states with biennial sessions of sixty days or less. Pressure for more adequate and thorough attention to bills introduced in ever-increasing quantities has forced these and many other states to resort to various alleviating alternatives. Special sessions may be called to complete work on measures left in suspense

TABLE 3. LEGISLATIVE SESSIONS

State or other jurisdiction	Years in which sessions are held	Sessions convene	
		Month	Day
Alabama	Odd	May	1st Tues.(a)
Alaska	Annual	Jan.	4th Mon.
Arizona	Annual	Jan.	2nd. Mon.
Arkansas	Odd	Jan.	2nd. Mon.
California	Annual(e)	Jan.	Odd-Mon. after Jan. 1
		Feb.	Even-1st Mon.
Colorado	Annual(e)	Jan.	Wed. after 1st Tues.
Connecticut	Odd	Jan.	Wed. after 1st Mon.
Delaware	Annual(e)	Jan.	Odd-1st Tues.
		Feb.	Even-1st Tues.
Florida	Odd	Apr.	Tues. after 1st Mon.
Georgia	Annual	Jan.	Odd-2nd Mon.
		Jan.	Even-2nd Mon.
Hawaii	Annual(e)	Feb.	Odd-3rd Wed.
		Feb.	Even-3rd Wed.
Idaho	Odd	Jan.	Mon. after Jan. 1
Illinois	Odd	Jan.	Wed. after 1st Mon.
Indiana	Odd	Jan.	Thurs. after 1st Mon.
Iowa	Odd	Jan.	2nd Mon.
Kansas	Annual(e)	Jan.	Odd-2nd Tues.
		Jan.	Even-2nd Tues.
Kentucky	Even	Jan.	Tues. after 1st Mon.
Louisiana	Annual(e)	May	Even-2nd Mon.
		May	Odd-2nd Mon.
Maine	Odd	Jan.	1st Wed.
Maryland	Annual(e)	Jan.	Odd-1st Wed.
		Feb.	Even-1st Wed.
Massachusetts	Annual	Jan.	1st Wed.
Michigan	Annual	Jan.	2nd Wed.
Minnesota	Odd	Jan.	Tues. after 1st Mon.
Mississippi	Even	Jan.	Tues. after 1st Mon.
Missouri	Odd	Jan.	Wed. after Jan. 1
Montana	Odd	Jan.	1st Mon.
Nebraska	Odd	Jan.	1st Tues.
Nevada	Odd	Jan.	3rd Mon.
New Hampshire	Odd	Jan.	1st Wed.
New Jersey	Annual	Jan.	2nd Tues.
New Mexico	Odd	Jan.	2nd Tues.
New York	Annual	Jan.	Wed. after 1st Mon.
North Carolina	Odd	Feb.	Wed. after 1st Mon.
North Dakota	Odd	Jan.	Tues. after 1st Mon.
Ohio	Odd	Jan.	1st Mon.
Oklahoma	Odd	Jan.	Tues. after 1st Mon.
Oregon	Odd	Jan.	2nd Mon.
Pennsylvania	Annual(e)	Jan.	1st Tues.
Rhode Island	Annual	Jan.	1st Tues.
South Carolina	Annual	Jan.	2nd Tues.
South Dakota	Annual	Jan.	Odd-Tues. after 3rd Mon.
		Jan.	Even-Tues. after 1st Mon.
Tennessee	Odd	Jan.	1st Mon.
Texas	Odd	Jan.	2nd Tues.
Utah	Odd	Jan.	2nd Mon.
Vermont	Odd	Jan.	Wed. after 1st Mon.

Limitations on length of sessions		Special sessions	
Regular	Special	Legislature may call	Legislature may determine subject
36 L	36 L	No	⅔ vote those present
None	30 C	Yes	Yes(b)
63 C(c)	20 C(c)	Petition ⅔ members	Yes
60 C	15 C(d)	No	(d)
120 C(f)	None	No	No
30 C			
160 C(c)	None	No	No
150 C(g)	None	Yes	Yes
90 L	30(c)	No	Yes
30 L			
60 C(h)	20 C(i)	(i)	Yes(i)
45 C(j)	(k)	Petition ⅗ members(l)	Yes(m)
40 C			
60 C(n)	30 C(n)	(o)	(o)
30 C(n)			
60 C(c)	20 C	No	No
None(p)	None	No	No
61 C	40 C	No	Yes
None	None	No	Yes(q)
90 L(c)	30 L(c)	No	Yes
30 C			
60 L	None	No	No
60 C	30 C	Petition ⅔ elected members each house	No(r)
30 C			
None	None	No	Yes
90 C	30 C	No	Yes
30 C			
None	None	Yes	Yes
None	None	No	No
120 L	None	No	Yes
None	None	No	No
195 C(g)	60 C	No	No
60 C	60 C	No	No
None	None	Petition ⅔ members	No
60 C(c)	20 C(c)	No	No
July 1(c)	15 L(c)	Yes	Yes
None	None	(s)	Yes
60 C	30 C(t)	Yes(t)	Yes(t)
None	None	No	No
120 C(c)	25 C(c)	No	Yes
60 L	None	No	Yes
None	None	No	No
None	None	No(u)	No
None	None	No	Yes
None	None	No	No
60 L(c)	None	No	No
None	40 L(c)	No	Yes
45 L	None	No	Yes
30 L			
75 C(c)	20 C(c)	No	No
140 C	30 C	No	No
60 C	30 C	No	No
None	None	No	Yes

TABLE 3 (continued)

State or other jurisdiction	Years in which sessions are held	Sessions convene	
		Month	Day
Virginia_____	Even	Jan.	2nd Wed.
Washington_____	Odd	Jan.	2nd Mon.
West Virginia_____	Annual(e)	Jan.	Odd-2nd Wed.
		Jan.	Even-2nd Wed.
Wisconsin_____	Odd	Jan.	2nd Wed.
Wyoming_____	Odd	Jan.	2nd Tues.
Puerto Rico_____	Annual	Jan.	2nd Mon.

Abbreviations: L—Legislative days; C—Calendar days.

(a) Legislature meets quadrennially on second Tuesday in January after election for purpose of organizing.
(b) Unless Governor calls and limits.
(c) Indirect restriction on session length. Legislators' pay, per diem, or daily allowance ceases but session may continue. In Colorado the 160-day limitation applies to the legislative biennium. In New Hampshire travel allowance ceases after July 1 or 90 legislative days, whichever occurs first.
(d) Governor may convene General Assembly for specified purpose. After specific business is transacted, a ⅔ vote of members of both houses may extend sessions up to 15 days.
(e) Budget sessions held in even-numbered years, except in Louisiana.
(f) Exclusive of Saturdays and Sundays.
(g) Approximate length of session. Connecticut session must adjourn by first Wednesday after first Monday in June, Missouri's by July 15, and Puerto Rico's by April 30.
(h) Length of session may be extended by 30 days, but not beyond Sept. 1, by ⅔ vote of both houses.
(i) Twenty per cent of the membership may petition the Secretary of State to poll the legislature; upon affirmative vote of ⅗ of both houses an extra session, no more than 30 days in length, may be called. Extra sessions called by the Governor are limited to 20 days.
(j) Convenes for no longer than 12 days to organize. Recesses and then reconvenes 2nd Monday in February for not more than 33 calendar days. Budget presently considered in odd-year session only.
(k) Seventy-day session limit except for impeachment proceedings if Governor calls session; 30-day limit except for impeachment proceedings if Governor calls session at petition of legislature.

during the regular session although here, too, some legislatures are hemmed in by specific limits.

To add a complicating but tactically often critical factor, special sessions in a majority of states may not be called by the legislature on its own motion but require gubernatorial initiative. Moreover, in only sixteen of the thirty-one states with biennial sessions is the legislature in the position to determine the subjects to be considered in such an extended session.

Another device for easing some of the effects of an all too brief session has been the interim commissions or committees. These groups composed of House and Senate members meet between sessions, conduct hearings and studies, and may prepare bills or reports for the upcoming session. They usually work closely with a legislative council or legislative research committee, the major fact-gathering agency for nearly all of the state legislatures. There is, of course, no assurance that the regular session and its committees may not ignore the efforts of these interim committees and start their

Limitations on length of sessions		Special sessions	
Regular	Special	Legislature may call	Legislature may determine subject
60 C(c,v)	30 C(c,v)	Petition ⅔ members	Yes
60 C	None	No	Yes
60 C(w)	None	Petition ⅔ members	No
30 C(w)			
None	None	No	No
40 C	None	No	Yes
111 C(g,x)	20 C	No	No

(l) Thirty-day limit except for impeachment proceedings.
(m) If legislature convenes itself.
(n) Governor may extend any session for not more than 30 days. Sundays and holidays shall be excluded in computing the number of days of any session.
(o) Legislature may convene in special session on 45th day after adjournment to act on bills submitted to the Governor less than ten days before adjournment if Governor notifies the legislature he plans to return them with objections.
(p) By custom legislature adjourns by July 1, since all bills passed after that day are not effective until July 1 of following year.
(q) Iowa constitution requires the Governor to inform both houses of the General Assembly the purpose for which a special session has been convened.
(r) Unless legislature petitions for special session. However, no special session may be called during the 30 days before or the 30 days after the regular fiscal sessions in the odd years without the consent of ¾ of the elected members of each house of the legislature.
(s) Petition by majority of members of each house to Governor, who then "shall" call special session.
(t) Limitation does not apply if impeachment trial is pending or in process. Legislature may call 30-day "extraordinary" session if Governor refuses to call session when requested by ⅔ of legislature.
(u) Governor may convene Senate alone in special session.
(v) May be extended up to 30 days by ⅔ vote of each house, but without pay.
(w) Must be extended by Governor until general appropriation passed; may be extended by ⅔ vote of legislature.
(x) Session may be extended by adoption of joint resolution.
SOURCE: *Book of the States, 1964–1965*, pp. 44–45.

legislative activities *de novo*. Poor attendance at interim committee meetings, inadequate research facilities, and a membership that may not reflect the actual power configurations of the regular session have so far prevented these committees from becoming a very satisfactory answer to the problems created by the short session.

The search for other methods continues. Thirteen states have been experimenting with a pre-session filing process. This would permit legislators to introduce bills prior to the opening of a session. Some other states in the annual session category are considering an adaptation of the congressional practice which makes possible a carry-over of unfinished calendars from one session to another within the span of one legislative term. Hawaii has adopted a procedure under which legislators may introduce their bills in an abbreviated form, on one page or so, which will be printed and processed further only if the committee considers it of sufficient merit.

And still the demands for longer and annual sessions remain unabated largely because the alternatives have not come to grips with fundamentals. Business cycle fluctuations can affect tax and relief needs in a way that makes biennial budgetary anticipations difficult and unrealistic. Federal programs in welfare and highway development are often dependent upon state implementation and cooperation which goes beyond a governor's administrative authority. The increase in the states' financial burdens from an added legislative payroll could result in more judicious and less-hurried policy decisions of wider benefit to the entire community.

LEGISLATIVE RULES

On initial inspection the rules of a legislature seem inordinately complex and bewildering. Actually they are designed to permit the efficient and democratic operations of the assembly, allowing the majority to carry out its "mandate" without denying to the minority the opportunity to criticize, to question, to delay, to dissent, and to lay its case before the public.

Nearly every set of legislative rules includes the following: powers of the presiding officer; list of standing committees; method of committee appointment; order of legislative business; rules for debate and placing of motions; method of voting and roll call; procedures for a House or Senate sitting as a committee of the whole; form of bills and the process of their introduction and printing; rules governing the various readings of bills; privileges possessed by members; types and character of calendars and journals; size of the quorum; and number and duties of legislative employees. Then there are also separate rules governing the legislature when sitting in joint session.

COURSE OF A BILL

A few of these rules need further comment. The order of legislative business represents the formal sequence of events transpiring in a chamber during the course of a legislative day. A typical Senate order of business will likely include most of these items:

1. Call to order by the presiding officer.
2. Chaplain offers invocation.
3. Reading of official communications including executive messages.
4. The previous day's journal is customarily accepted without formal reading; corrections may be suggested by any member.
5. Introduction, "first reading," and referral of Senate bills. Reading is by title only.
6. First reading of House bills.
7. Reports from standing and special committees.
8. Second reading of Senate bills.
9. Second reading of House bills.
10. Receiving of motions and resolutions.
11. Third reading of Senate bills.
12. Third reading of House bills.
13. Calendar of the day. This is the stage when the chamber will transform itself by a motion into a committee of the whole to discuss, debate, and amend the bills that have had a second reading. Someone other than the

speaker or lieutenant governor will customarily take the chair. Procedure is more informal and permits all members to scrutinize the proposed legislation. Bills must usually be in printed form and have lain on the legislator's desk for forty-eight hours.

14. General orders of the day. This stage includes all bills to be taken up in order in which they are numbered unless moved ahead on a Special Order which requires generally a two-thirds vote and a two-day notice.

15. Announcements and miscellaneous business.

Most states provide that bills must be printed on introduction, that they be read on three different days, and that they must be considered in the committee of the whole before they can come up for final passage on third reading.

Although two-thirds of the states require at least one reading in full, and eight states insist on three readings at length, such requirements can simply not be met in view of the hundreds of measures to be considered. When challenged, courts have been unwilling to strike down laws passed without meeting the letter of these stipulations (even if of constitutional origin). They rest their reasoning on the theory that this would constitute an infringement of separation of powers or that legislative journal entries stating that the bill had been properly read and passed is sufficient and has to be presumed correct.

Of all the various hurdles over which a bill has to pass before becoming law, five may be singled out for special attention. A bill's substance or main idea may spring from the mind of a legislator, lobbyist, constituent, or administrator or from a legislative committee or legislative council. Whatever its source, a bill that is to pass must first of all be properly drafted and introduced in time. Legislatures operating under fixed calendar limits in order to minimize a last-minute rush often stipulate that no bills may be introduced following a certain day of the session unless the sponsors can obtain an extraordinary majority or gubernatorial consent to lift such restrictions. Second, in view of the great reliance a legislature places on its committees and their work, a bill's course will be significantly smoothed and the chance of its passage greatly enhanced if in addition to merely reporting the measure and placing it on General Order for second reading, it is accompanied by a positive report ("that it do pass"), or that it pass under suspension of rules (if urgent). A re-referral of a bill to another committee constitutes in the majority of legislatures an unmistakable burial ritual, except when, under the rules of the chamber, a re-referral to the appropriations committee is made obligatory for measures involving the expenditure of funds.

THE DISCUSSION STAGE FOLLOWING

The discussion stage following the second reading when the chamber resolves itself into the committee of the whole points up the third hurdle. Now the entire membership is given an opportunity to question, amend, pass, or refer the bill back to the parent committee.

If the bill has successfully survived action in two chambers, any minor

TABLE 4. LEGISLATIVE PROCEDURE-

State or other jurisdiction	Days after which bill becomes law (before adjournment) unless vetoed†	Fate of bill after adjournment		Item veto on appropriations bills	Votes required in House and Senate to pass bills or items over veto(a)	Constitution pro. Governor from ve	
		Days after which bill is law unless vetoed†	Days after which bill dies unless signed†			Initiated measures	Refe meas
Alabama	6	—	10	*	Majority elected	(b)	(l
Alaska	15	20	—	*	Three-fourths elected	*	—
Arizona	5	10	—	*	Two-thirds elected(c)	*	*
Arkansas	5	20(d)	—	*	Majority elected	*	*
California	10	—	30	*	Two-thirds elected	*	*
Colorado	10(d)	30(d)	—	*	Two-thirds elected	*	*
Connecticut	5(e)	15(d)	—	*	Majority present	(b)	(l
Delaware	10	—	30(d)	*	Three-fifths elected	(b)	(l
Florida	5	20(d)	—	*	Two-thirds present	(b)	(l
Georgia(f)	5	30	—	*	Two-thirds elected	(g)	—
Hawaii	10(e)	45(e,h)	(e,h)	*	Two-thirds elected	(b)	(l
Idaho	5	10	—	*	Two-thirds present	—	—
Illinois	10	10	—	*	Two-thirds elected	(b)	(l
Indiana	3	5(d,i)	—	—	Majority elected	(b)	(l
Iowa	3	(j)	(i)	—	Two-thirds elected	—	—
Kansas	3	—	(k, l)	*	Two-thirds elected	(b)	(l
Kentucky	10	10	—	*	Majority elected	—	—
Louisiana	10(d,m)	20(n)	—	*	Two-thirds elected	(b)	(l
Maine	5	(o)	—	—	Two-thirds present	(p)	*
Maryland(ad)	6	—	6(q)	*	Three-fifths elected	(g)	—
Massachusetts	5(e)	—	(r)	*	Two-thirds present	*	*
Michigan	10(s)	—	5	*	Two-thirds elected(t)	*	*
Minnesota	3	—	3	*	Two-thirds elected	(b)	(l
Mississippi	5	(o)	—	*	Two-thirds elected	(b)	(l
Missouri	(u)	—	45	*	Two-thirds elected	*	*

† Sundays excepted.

(a) Bill returned to house of origin with objections, except in Georgia, where Governor need not state objections in Kansas, where all bills are returned to House.
(b) No provision for initiative or referendum in state.
(c) Three-fourths in case of an emergency measure.
(d) Sundays not excepted.
(e) Sundays and legal holidays excepted.
(f) Constitution withholds right to veto constitutional amendments.
(g) No provision for initiative in state.
(h) If bill is presented to Governor less than 10 days before adjournment and he indicates he will return it with o tions, legislature can convene on 45th day after adjournment to consider the objections. If, however, legisl. fails to convene, bill does not become law.
(i) Bill becomes law if not filed with objections with Secretary of State within 5 days after adjournment in Ind and 15 days after adjournment in Wyoming.
(j) Bills forwarded to the Governor during the last 3 days of the General Assembly session must be deposited b Governor with the Secretary of State within 30 days after the adjournment of the General Assembly. The Gov must give his approval if approved or his objections if disapproved.
(k) Bills unsigned at the time of adjournment do not become laws.
(l) In practice, the legislature closes consideration of bills 3 days before adjournment sine die. However, some may be "presented" to Governor during last 3 days of session. In 1963, the interpretation was followed tha Governor had 3 days to sign or veto bills after they were presented irrespective of whether the legislature ha journed sine die or not.
(m) Governor has 10 days in Louisiana and 6 days in Wisconsin from time bill was presented to him in which to app or disapprove.
(n) Becomes effective in 20 days, if not vetoed. Sundays not excepted, unless a later date is set in the act.

or other jurisdiction	Days after which bill becomes law (before adjournment) unless vetoed†	Fate of bill after adjournment		Item veto on appropriations bills	Votes required in House and Senate to pass bills or items over veto(a)	Constitution prohibits Governor from vetoing	
		Days after which bill is law unless vetoed†	Days after which bill dies unless signed†			Initiated measures	Referred measures
ana	5	—	15(d,v)	*	Two-thirds present	*	*
aska	5	5	—	*(w)	Three-fifths elected	*	*
da	5	10	—	—	Two-thirds elected	*	*
Hampshire	5	—	(r)	—	Two-thirds present	(b)	(b)
Jersey	10(x)	45	—	*	Two-thirds elected	(b)	(b)
Mexico	3	—	20(v)	*	Two-thirds present	(g)	—
York	10	—	30(d)	*	Two-thirds elected	(g)	—
h Carolina	(y)	(y)	(y)	(y)	--------------------	(b)	(b)
h Dakota	3	15(d)	—	*	Two-thirds elected	*	*
	10	10	—	*	Three-fifths elected	*	—
homa	5	—	15	*	Two-thirds elected(c)	*	*
on(ad)	5	20	—	*(z)	Two-thirds present	—	*
sylvania	10(d)	30(d)	—	*	Two-thirds elected	(b)	(b)
de Island	6	10(d)	—	—	Three-fifths present	(b)	(b)
h Carolina	3	(o)	—	*	Two-thirds present	(b)	(b)
h Dakota	3	10(d)	—	*	Two-thirds present	*	*
essee	5	10	—	*(aa)	Majority elected	(g)	—
s	10	20	—	*	Two-thirds present	(b)	(b)
	5	10	—	*	Two-thirds elected	*	*
ont	5	—	(k)	—	Two-thirds present	(b)	(b)
nia	5	—	10(d)	*	Two-thirds present(ab)	(b)	(b)
hington(ad)	5	10	—	*	Two-thirds elected	*	*
Virginia	5(ac)	5(d)	—	—	Majority elected	(b)	(b)
onsin	6(m)	—	6(m)	*	Two-thirds present	(b)	(b)
ming	3	15(d,i)	—	*	Two-thirds elected	(b)	(b)

Bill passed in one session becomes law if not returned within 3 days after reconvening in Maine and Mississippi and within 2 days after reconvening in South Carolina.
Constitution provides that Governor may veto initiated measures and if legislature sustains veto, measure is referred to vote of people at next general election.
Within 6 days after presentation to the Governor, regardless of how long after adjournment.
Within 5 days of receipt by Governor. In Massachusetts, in practice General Court not prorogued until Governor has acted on all bills.
After January 1, 1964, under new constitution, will be 14 days, Sundays not excepted.
After January 1, 1964, will be two-thirds elected and serving.
If Governor does not return bill in 15 days, a joint resolution is necessary for bill to become law.
Governor must file bills with Secretary of State.
Governor may not veto items in budget submitted by himself after it has passed legislature with three-fifths vote.
If house of origin is in temporary adjournment on tenth day, Sundays excepted, after presentation to Governor, bill becomes law on day house of origin reconvenes unless returned by Governor on that day. Governor may return bills vetoed, suggesting amendments, and bills may be passed in amended form, but must be approved by Governor in amended form within 10 days after presentation to him.
No veto; bill becomes law 30 days after adjournment of session unless otherwise expressly directed.
Also may veto items in new bills declaring an emergency.
Governor may reduce or eliminate items but must give written notice of item veto either 3 days before adjournment or 1 day after bill is presented for signature.
Including majority elected.
Budget (appropriation) bill not submitted to Governor after passage.
Constitution provides that any bill vetoed after adjournment be returned to the legislature when it next convenes for a vote on overriding the veto. In Maryland the requirement is not applicable if a new General Assembly has taken office since the passage of the vetoed bill.

CE: *Book of the States, 1964-1965*, pp. 58-59.

or major variation between its Senate and House versions necessitates a conference committee referral. This presents a fourth hurdle of no small proportion. Should this committee fail to iron out the differences, should additional and/or controversial clauses be inserted, should the conference committee "managers" appointed by the speaker of the House and the Senate presiding officer fail to agree and remain deadlocked, an almost inevitable result is the measure's heroic or ignominious failure. Pressures of calendar and business would in most cases preclude any promising resuscitation efforts.

Fifth, and lastly, the governor may kill the bill through the use of his veto, provided, of course, this action is sustained in the legislature. All of the states but North Carolina give to their chief executive a general legislative veto exercisable generally within three to five days of receiving the bill, and all but nine give him an item veto on appropriation measures (see Table 4).

In the majority of the states a bill can only be passed over his veto by a two-thirds vote (present or elected) in both chambers. See Table 4 which indicates the different methods used by legislatures to pass a bill over a gubernatorial veto.

These five hurdles represent checkpoints in a legislative process that is designed to afford diverse segments of the political community an effective opportunity to register objections and to mold policy. Considerations of either speed or efficiency should not blur the primary objective of seeing that those who may be affected by a law have the right and the duty to voice their positions and where necessary to force through debate and lobbying a bill's modification, defeat, or passage.

Underlying a legislature's responsible performance in terms of rules and procedure are a number of fundamental assumptions. No one interest group, be it labor, business, veterans, lawyers, church groups, or the League of Women Voters, can be presumed to embody the sum total of the state's virtue, wisdom, or knowledge. This is true despite the almost ever-present tendency to loudly and proudly identify the good of one group with the good of the entire state. Inherent in the legislative process is the further assumption that legislative truth or the long-range interests of the community will best emerge through conflict, compromise, and consensus. That means that in all probability no one interest group can get all that it wants nor will all get more than that which is possible or practically attainable.[12]

The difficulty most frequently encountered in legislative rules is not that there are an insufficient number of rules but that the rules are overly rigid, excessively detailed, occasionally totally outdated, and not infrequently de-

[12] For discussions of representation by state legislators, see Heinz Eulau, John C. Wahlke, William Buchanan, LeRoy C. Ferguson, "The Role of the Representative: Some Empirical Observations on the Theory of Edmund Burke," *American Political Science Review*, September, 1959, pp. 742–756 and Wilder W. Crane, Jr., "Do Representatives Represent?" *Journal of Politics*, May, 1960, pp. 295–299.

TABLE 5. PROPOSALS PASSED 1962–63 LEGISLATIVE SESSIONS

Percentage	State
Under 10%	Hawaii
11–20%	Massachusetts, Minnesota, New Jersey, New York, Washington
21–30%	Alaska, Arizona, Kentucky, Michigan, Missouri, Ohio, Pennsylvania, West Virginia, Wisconsin
31–40%	Alabama, Connecticut, Delaware, Iowa, Louisiana, New Mexico, Oklahoma, Texas, Utah
41–50%	Arkansas, California, Colorado, Florida, Indiana, Maine, Maryland, Mississippi, Montana, Oregon, Rhode Island, Tennessee, Wyoming
51–60%	Georgia, Illinois, Kansas, New Hampshire, North Dakota, South Carolina, South Dakota, Vermont
61–70%	Idaho, Nebraska, Nevada, North Carolina, Virginia
Over 70%	None

SOURCE: Adapted from *Book of the States, 1964–1965*, pp. 60–61.

signed to permit a few individual legislators placed in critical posts to preclude responsible exercise of the majority will.

Along a more humorous vein, even the most elaborate hurdles and rules cannot prevent a practical joker from upsetting his colleagues. During the 1961 session, for example, both houses of the Alaska legislature unsuspectingly accepted a conference report on a bill dealing with notaries public to which one of their colleagues had attached a rider cancelling the legislative pay for the session. Fortunately for all, it was caught in time. Both houses promptly rescinded their actions, and the culprit could proudly claim that his experiment proved "some members did not know what they were voting for." [13]

Majority will and minority interests can be best accommodated when committee hearings are scheduled and properly publicized; when electrical voting devices are used to facilitate taking roll call votes without an excessive burden on valuable legislative time; when committee meetings are opened to the public and the press and executive sessions reduced to a minimum; and when legislative journals and committee records and minutes show not only the final votes but reflect *in toto* the discussions, testimony, and all other relevant background information. Connecticut, Maine, Nebraska, and Pennsylvania are the only four states which keep verbatim records of all House and Senate proceedings, and only fifteen other states have anywhere near complete records of the House and Senate committee proceedings available.

Such records are of tremendous significance if the press and through it

---

[13] *The New York Times*, April 1, 1961, p. 7.

the public are to follow and understand the course of legislative affairs. Even more important, without such records legislators can avoid or circumvent their public accountability, making campaign promises which remain unfulfilled when the roll is called. Without committee records and detailed journals a bill's true friend or foe cannot easily be identified, its history of failure or success cannot be accurately traced, nor can legislative intent guide its proper interpretation by law enforcement officials and the courts.

ADVICE FOR ALL LEGISLATORS

LEGISLATIVE REFERENCE AND LEGAL SERVICES

A number of states provide their individual legislators with legal assistance through a legislative council so that bills may be expressed in proper technical form and language. Spot as well as major research may be done by the legislative reference or library service agencies now operating in eighteen states. In practice these services, though much in demand by legislators who are often overwhelmed by the sheer volume of highly intricate legislation, rarely prove adequate due to insufficient appropriations for professional and clerical staff.

Table 6 and 7 not only indicate something about the insufficiency of both reference and legal services, but also reveal that states which provide one set of services do not necessarily provide the other, and that there is little direct relationship between work load and size of staff. An even more detailed analysis would point up a wide variety among the states as to titles, ratings, and salaries of personnel and to the designation of the agency.

What all of this adds up to is the inevitable necessity for most legislators to rely on their own resources, on committee staffs, on services rendered by lobbies, and on constituents, or on such help as their more expert fellow legislators are willing to offer them.

Dependence on specialists within the legislature itself appears to be an important fact of legislative life. A few years ago, by way of illustration, the New York State legislature placed its faith largely in the competence of one bill-drafting expert when it enacted the New York City administrative code comprising 3,500 pages, weighing twenty-one pounds, repealing no less that 35,000 obsolete or inapplicable provisions and covering a period of nearly three hundred years.[14] A survey of 471 state legislators in California, New Jersey, Ohio, and Tennessee showed that "specialization was widely regarded as accepted and acceptable practice; 91 per cent named one or more members they considered specialists in some substantive field, and 83 per cent named fields in which they themselves were or were becoming expert." [15] Fields of specialization most frequently mentioned were law, finance, education, con-

[14] *Ibid.*, April 5, 1961, p. 23.
[15] William Buchanan, Heinz Eulau, LeRoy C. Ferguson, and John C. Wahlke, "The Legisla tor as Specialist," *Western Political Quarterly,* September, 1960, pp. 639–640.

TABLE 6. LEGISLATIVE REFERENCE AND LIBRARY SERVICES—
BILLS INTRODUCED AND NUMBER OF LEGISLATORS

State	Number of professional employees	Number of clerical employees	Number of bills introduced	Number of legislators
California	3	2	5,479	120
Connecticut	1		3,971	315
Delaware	1	2	780	52
Hawaii	9	4	3,454	76
Illinois	5	5	2,699	235
Maine	2	1	2,276	184
Massachusetts	3		8,081	280
Michigan	4	6	1,981	144
Nevada	4		866	64
New Hampshire	1		772	424
New Jersey	4	6	1,823	81
New York	4	3	16,372	208
Ohio	1	1	1,607	172
Oklahoma	1	1	1,096	165
Pennsylvania	8	5	3,737	260
Texas	3	1	1,486	181
Vermont *	2			276
Wisconsin	9	5	2,066	133

* Figure for number of bills introduced not available.

SOURCE: Adapted from The Council of State Governments, *Legislative Reference Bureaus and Library Services* (Chicago, August, 1960), pp. 6–8. Heads of staff agencies counted as professional personnel.

servation, local government, and industrial relations. Statistically significant differences were also noted between the four states in terms of the relative emphasis placed on the various specialties. A definite relationship was disclosed between the predominance of certain socio-economic problems of

TABLE 7. LEGISLATIVE LEGAL SERVICES—BILLS INTRODUCED
AND NUMBER OF LEGISLATORS

State	Number of professional employees	Number of clerical employees	Number of bills introduced	Number of legislators
California	29	28	5,479	120
Colorado	2	2	992	100
Connecticut	5	3	3,971	315
Florida	3	9	3,792	133
Hawaii	2	1	3,454	76
Kansas	3	4	981	165
Minnesota	4	4	3,571	198
Nebraska	1	1	739	43
Nevada	8	5	866	64
New York	4	3	16,372	172
North Carolina	2	1	1,880	170
Oregon	7	4	1,474	90
South Carolina	3	1	2,189	170
Virginia	2	2	1,078	140
Washington	5	5	1,444	148
Wisconsin	4	2	2,066	133

SOURCE: Adapted from The Council of State Governments, *Legal Services for State Legislatures* (Chicago, August, 1960), pp. 39–43. Heads of staff counted as professional personnel.

the state and the need for experts in those fields. In California it was conservation (water problems); in Tennessee, agriculture; in New Jersey, finance and education; and in Ohio, finance, education, and law.

LEGISLATIVE COUNCILS

To assist with research or to help solve basic substantive problems in such areas as taxation, education, and highway expansion, legislatures in forty-two states have established by statute a permanent council or joint committee composed of senators, representatives, and certain ex-officio members. These legislative councils or legislative research committees, involving groups of twelve to twenty-five legislators or, as in Nebraska, Oklahoma, Pennsylvania, or South Dakota, the entire legislative membership, have stressed either a fact-finding or recommending role. Kansas has developed the programming pattern in which the council through its various subcommittees not only supervises and directs a department of research but submits its recommendations in the form of bills which will be referred to the regular standing committees of the House and Senate. In Illinois, on the other hand, the legislative council does not initiate legislative recommendations but "conscientiously regards as one of its major functions [that of] insulating the research staff from policy influence. . . ." [16] Factual, analytical, and practical studies were to be conducted with major stress on objectivity and professional detachment. Whereas the Kansas council is considered a little legislature, the Illinois council is limited to simply furnishing impartial information. In both Kansas and Illinois despite the differences in role, the councils have been highly regarded and considered very influential.

Which pattern a legislature will prefer involves more than questions of organizational detail and design. Where political party competition is keen and the alignments are closely matched (as in Illinois), it will be more difficult to surrender to a super-legislature the prerogative of initiating policy than where a legislature is relatively free from intense party combat and the political waters are generally much calmer (as in Kansas). Nor can the role of the governor be ignored. A strong chief executive will likely consider it to be his function to suggest legislative policies through special messages and personal leadership. In a politically charged setting of this character a legislative council would quickly be embroiled in partisan warfare were it to go beyond study and fact-gathering.

What must never be neglected in reflecting upon a discussion of the structure, composition, and work of a legislature is that political considerations and alignments give direction and meaning to the legislative process. Rules, procedures, and working arrangements are merely channels through which the political processes operate. They are not to be perceived as ends in

[16] Cited by William J. Siffin, *The Legislative Council in the American States* (Bloomington, 1959), p. 137; see also William H. Cape and John Paul Bay, *An Analysis of the Kansas Legislative Council and its Research Department* (Lawrence, 1963).

themselves. Those who have the power to make the politically significant decisions usually have the necessary skill and experience to mold the process for the effective achievement of their objectives.

CASE PROBLEMS FOR CLASS DISCUSSION

1. Assume that you plan to run for the state House of Representatives. Politically, you are a "moderate" Republican. Your urban district is relatively equally divided between high, medium, and low income areas. Party organization is practically non-existent. What type of campaign organization would you establish? What issue or issues would you stress? How much money would you need?
2. You have been asked to identify three or four of the key senators who are the most important "decision-makers" in the state Senate. What would be your research design?
3. The rules committee of your legislature has before it a proposal to permit the televising of legislative sessions. You are the public relations director of the local station and wish to testify in favor of the measure. What sources would you consult in preparation for your appearance? What would be the nature of your argument? What are the objections that you may have to rebut?
4. You would like to make civics instruction more meaningful to your students. As a social studies teacher in a senior high school within walking distance of the state Capitol, you have decided to assign a group of students to follow a workmen's compensation law from its introduction through its (assumed) enactment. How would you organize this project? How many students would be required? What are some of the limitations that would characterize the findings?

SELECTED BIBLIOGRAPHY

"American State Legislatures in Mid-Twentieth Century," *State Government*, Autumn, 1961, pp. 245–252.

Council of State Governments, *Our State Legislatures*, rev. ed. (Chicago, 1960).

DAVID R. DERGE, "The Lawyer in the Indiana General Assembly," *Midwest Journal of Political Science*, February, 1962, pp. 19–53.

ERNEST A. ENGELBERT, "Legislative Reorganization in California," *State Government*, Winter, 1963, pp. 58–64.

CHARLES B. HAGAN, "The Bicameral Principle in State Legislatures," *Journal of Public Law*, 1962, pp. 310–327.

ROBERT J. HUCKSHORN, EDWARD S. MIDDLEMIST, and C. A. BOTTOLFSEN, *The Idaho Legislature* (Moscow, 1960).

MALCOLM E. JEWELL, "State Legislatures in Southern Politics," *Journal of Politics*, February, 1964, pp. 177–196.

JAMES B. KESSLER, *Pre-Legislative Conferences: An Appraisal* (Bloomington, 1960).

PAUL MASON, "Procedure in State Legislatures: The Nature of Rules," *State Government*, Spring, 1963, pp. 101–107.

ARTHUR A. OHNIMUS, *The Legislature of California 1959* (Sacramento, 1959).

KENNETH D. PATTERSON, "Legislative Budget Review: An Economist's Viewpoint," *Public Administration Review*, March, 1964, pp. 7–13.

ROBERT R. ROBBINS (ed.), *State Government and Public Responsibility 1962: The Role of the General Court in Massachusetts* (Medford, 1962).

EDWARD V. SCHTEN, "Administration and Legislative Research," *Public Administration Review*, June, 1963, pp. 81–86.

CECIL H. UNDERWOOD, *The Legislative Process in West Virginia* (Morgantown, 1953).

HARVEY WALKER, "The Legislature Today," *National Civic Review*, November, 1960, pp. 530–536.

HARVEY WALKER, "The Role of the Legislature in Government," *State Government*, Spring, 1960, pp. 96–102.

✔ Chapter IV

LEGISLATIVE
POLITICS AND
APPORTIONMENT

Is there much party discipline in state legislatures? Should there be? What about the Independents?

How sound is the federally-imposed standard—one man, one vote?

PARTIES AND LEGISLATURES—SOME MAJOR ISSUES

ALL but two of the fifty states—Nebraska and Minnesota constituting the exceptions—have party labels attached to their legislators. How significant are these parties in determining the outcome of legislative battles? Can the party organizations discipline their membership? Are legislative party loyalties undermined by urban-rural splits, i.e., do the city legislators tend to vote together regardless of party when confronted with issues that might separate their interests from those of their rural colleagues? Do strongly competitive state party systems denote equally competitive legislative politics? Are there telling regional differences between the performances of parties? Do legislative parties have significant cohesion when confronted with critical roll calls or do members place the interests of home constituency, section, economic blocs, or ethnic or religious allegiances above those of party policy? What are the standards and ingredients of a responsible party organization within the framework of a state legislature?

Questions such as these have concerned political scientists and politicians for many years. Certain basic philosophical considerations are interrelated as to the "ought." Whom *ought* the legislator represent when there is a conflict between different sets of pressures: between the diverse conceptions of the community's well-being and between a legislator's perception of the demands of his conscience; between the possibly conflicting expectations of those who had helped campaign for and win his present office and between the demands of legislative compromise?

There are very few if any broad generalizations regarding the operations or effectiveness of parties that can validly be applied to all of the state legislatures. If these performance factors were to be quantified, they could be plotted on a continuum with one end symbolizing the most competitive and highly organized and the other symbolizing the weakest and least competitive party system.

Using the roughest possible approximation, one might assert that one-third of the states have a fairly strong and competitive system, another third a

80

very weak one and the final third a moderately disciplined legislative party pattern.

LEGISLATURES WITH FAIRLY STRONG COMPETITIVE AND COHESIVE PARTIES

States belonging most definitely in this category would be New York, Connecticut, Rhode Island, Massachusetts, Ohio, and Michigan.

New York: The legislature of the state possesses a party discipline far superior to that found either in the United States Congress or in all but a few state Capitols. Almost all major issues are determined by party-line votes; when dissenting votes are cast by party members, they are ordinarily cast by permission of the party leaders. Consequently, the process of legislation consists of a process of negotiation among the legislative leaders of the two houses and the governor.[1]

Connecticut, Rhode Island and Massachusetts: Party cohesion has been found to be very high in all of these three New England states; including issues involving substantive policies in such areas as labor, education, welfare and health.

The following quotation by the author of a classic study of New England politics characterizes his findings for the above three states:

As in Massachusetts and Connecticut, the public policy battles in the Rhode Island legislature are fought out between the parties. Interest groups make their special pleas as to any legislative body, but in Rhode Island even more than in Massachusetts the pleaders turn to the party leaders for help. Here too the subsurface political maneuvering on major issues is hidden behind closed doors, but it is apparent that those behind the doors virtually always include those high up in the party hierarchy. The governor, the state chairman of both parties, and the formal legislative leaders control the legislature. Conflicts may arise, and members of the General Assembly may at times upset the plans of the leadership, but in the vast majority of the cases the final word rests with the leaders.[2]

Ohio: A study of party voting in the 1935, 1949, 1955 and 1957 sessions of the Ohio legislature permitted the following observations:

[P]arty opposition votes are fairly common; the number ranges from 33 per cent in the 1935 House to 60 per cent in the 1949 Senate . . . the average indices of cohesion are usually high, sometimes very high . . . indicating that party conflict is frequent in the Ohio legislature. . . . Urban-rural factionalism is unimportant in the Ohio General Assembly. . . .[3]

Michigan: In 1925–1926 there was not a single Democrat in either Senate or House. Michigan belonged to the solid phalanx of Midwestern Republicanism. Depression politics, the rise of the United Auto Workers to

[1] Ralph A. Straetz and Frank J. Munger, *New York Politics* (New York, 1960), p. 61.

[2] Duane Lockard, *New England State Politics* (Princeton, 1959), p. 212.

[3] Thomas A. Flinn, "The Outline of Ohio Politics," *Western Political Quarterly*, September, 1960, pp. 719–721.

political power, and G. Mennen Williams' six gubernatorial victories changed the political complexion of that state so radically that Democrats became major contenders for office.

Here is a 1960 appraisal of Michigan legislative politics:

> In Michigan . . . both parties are relatively free of internal rivalries and meet one another head-on . . . both Republican and Democratic Senators tend to vote as a bloc on partisan issues . . . Michigan's Democratic party is supported by organized labor and "liberal" elements whereas, the Republican party is backed, primarily, by the business and farm communities.[4]

There are certainly states other than these that could be classified as having competitive and cohesive legislative party politics. Prominent among these are Delaware, Indiana, New Jersey, and West Virginia. A 1954 study relying on questionnaires sent to "two or more competent persons in each state, including political scientists" and other specialists of state politics, listed a total of seventeen states in this category.[5]

If legislative politics is viewed from the perspective of how many years one party or the other had a working control of the legislature, a somewhat different scheme of classification appears to emerge. New York, for example, was cited as an illustration of a state characterized by intense party competition yet its House and Senate during the last fifty years have been under Democratic control only once although Democrats captured the governorship more than 50 per cent of the time.[6] Thus, if alternating control among the two major parties is used as a decisive criterion, New York's legislature would have to be classified as one in which the Republican party was dominant to a degree similar to that in the legislatures of Iowa, Kansas, Maine, and North Dakota.

In an excellent recent study of state legislative politics, the author classifies as two-party states those in which neither "had a dominant legislative control, and [in which] party control of [the] legislature approximate[s] control of [the] governorship." [7] Table 1 shows the nine states that fit into this category.

STATES WITH NON-COMPETITIVE AND RELATIVELY WEAK LEGISLATIVE PARTY POLITICS

Included in this category are the one-party Democratic systems of eleven Southern states, and the overwhelmingly Democratically-controlled legislatures of Kentucky and Oklahoma. Today the Republican equivalent is found

4 John H. Fenton, "Northern Politics," an unpublished paper prepared for delivery at the annual meeting of the American Political Science Association, New York City, September, 8–10, 1960, pp. 9–10.

5 Belle Zeller (ed.), *American State Legislatures: Report of the Committee on American Legislatures, American Political Science Association* (New York, 1954), p. 192.

6 *The New York Times*, June 18, 1964, p. 34.

7 Malcolm E. Jewell, *The State Legislature: Politics and Practice* (New York, 1962), p. 11. For a recent study of legislative partisanship in California, see William Buchanan, *Legislative Partisanship: The Deviant Case of California* (Berkeley, 1963).

TABLE 1. CLASSIFICATION OF STATE LEGISLATURES ACCORD-
ING TO DEGREE OF TWO-PARTY COMPETITION, 1947–1962

State	Years of party control							
	Senate			House			Governorship	
	D	R	Tie	D	R	Tie	D	R

1. Limited Two-Party States: Same party controlled both houses throughout most of the period and the governorship at least half of the time.

State	D	R	Tie	D	R	Tie	D	R
South Dakota	2	14	—	0	16	—	2	14
Wisconsin	0	16	—	2	14	—	4	12
Missouri	14	2	—	12	4	—	16	0
Illinois	4	12	—	0	16	—	6	10
Indiana	2	14	—	4	12	—	6	10
New Mexico	16	0	—	14	2	—	8	8
Wyoming	0	16	—	2	12	2	8	8
New Jersey	0	16	—	4	12	—	8	8

2. Limited Two-Party States: Same party controlled both houses throughout most of the period but usually not the governorship.

State	D	R	Tie	D	R	Tie	D	R
Michigan	0	16	—	0	14	2	14	2
Ohio	4	12	—	4	12	—	12	4

3. Limited Two-Party States: Two houses controlled by different parties
during most of the period.

State	D	R	Tie	D	R	Tie	D	R
Nevada	16	0	—	0	16	—	8	8
Rhode Island	4	6	6	16	0	—	14	2
Connecticut	10	6	—	2	14	—	10	6
Massachusetts	4	10	2	12	4	—	8	8

Two-Party States: Neither party had dominant legislative control, and
party control of legislature approximated control of governorship.

State	D	R	Tie	D	R	Tie	D	R
Pennsylvania	0	14	2	6	10	—	8	8
Idaho	6	10	—	2	14	—	6	10
California	4	10	2	4	12	—	4	12
Oregon	4	10	2	6	10	—	2	14
Montana	6	10	—	8	8	—	4	12
Washington	8	6	2	12	4	—	8	8
Utah	8	8	—	6	8	2	2	14
Colorado	6	10	—	8	8	—	12	4
Delaware	10	6	—	8	8	—	6	10

SOURCE: Malcolm E. Jewell, *The State Legislature: Politics and Practice* (New
York, 1962), p. 11.

only in Maine, New Hampshire, and possibly Vermont. Some years ago this
list could have included the Dakotas as well.

A word of caution is needed to place these dominant one-party patterns
in perspective. While there is little that minority parties can do very positively
when their numbers are so small as to be nearly negligible, it cannot be
assumed that there is no grouping at all or that there is total absence of
internal legislative conflict. Even a dominant party's leadership may discover
that they cannot have *carte blanche*. Instead of parties there may be caucuses
and factions that take on a character not too dissimilar from parties. These
groupings may focus along "liberal" versus "conservative" or "urban" versus
"rural" lines. They may wish to be identified either as the "governor's" caucus
or as the "legislative" caucus. Their base of power may be economic, sectional,
or personal—they may be known as the "labor bloc," the "farm bloc," or the

"business interests." Some may favor or oppose certain structural changes in the executive departments or rally around such issues as reapportionment or constitutional reform.

To complicate the picture a little further, there are a number of states with considerable party competition for statewide and federal office in which, however, legislative party alignments are not very pronounced and in which party discipline as measured by coefficients of cohesion is very low.

For example, in Colorado in 1965, seven votes separate Democrats from Republicans in the Senate while nineteen votes separate them in the House. Party competition for federal and gubernatorial office is keen. Mr. Nixon carried the state in the presidential election of 1960 and so did the incumbent Republican United States Senator. Four seats in Congress are divided evenly between the two parties. The governor elected for a four-year term in 1958 was a Democrat; the governor elected in 1964 is a Republican. Yet the state's legislative politics were described in the following terms:

> [In the legislature] . . . functional and geographic interests are often more decisive than party affiliation. In 1961, for instance, the question of reapportionment of the legislature . . . [was] discussed. A rural Democrat was appointed as chairman of the legislative committee to make a study of the problem. In turn, he appointed a rural Republican as chairman of a subcommittee to make the actual study, and most of the members of the subcommittee [were] rural representatives, regardless of their party affiliation. On issues involving moral or ethical considerations, the representatives of small towns and rural areas tend to align themselves on one side of such questions, while representatives of urban centers and strongly Roman Catholic districts will be found on the other side—in each case without regard to party affiliation in the main. . . . In the legislature, the club spirit that prevails is more significant than party affiliation, and this spirit tends to over-ride party lines and to reinforce bipartisan and nonpartisan influences and brings in its wake a tendency toward conflict between the legislature and the governor, regardless of the party affiliations involved on either side.[8]

Illinois politics offers an even clearer illustration that a state may have intense inter-party conflict without a well-disciplined and cohesive legislative party system. A roll call analysis of the 1949 and 1951 General Assembly indicates that the actual instances where 80 per cent or more of the members of one party voted together against 80 per cent of the other party amounted to only 3.95 per cent of 2,324 roll calls in the 1949 session, and that a large number of substantively important legislative issues were decided without any very noticeable or statistically significant reference to party alignments.[9] Party considerations were not without influence in the Assembly, but they were not the primary forces motivating its major legislative decisions. What counts more in Illinois is leadership—gubernatorial and lobbyist. However,

[8] Curtis Martin, "The Colorado Pre-Primary Convention System and Party Cohesion," an unpublished paper prepared for delivery at the annual meeting of the Midwest Conference of Political Scientists, Columbia, Mo., May 12, 1961, pp. 12–13.

[9] William J. Keefe, "Party Government and Lawmaking in Illinois General Assembly," *Northwestern University Law Review*, March–April, 1952, p. 68.

thc deepest imprint is left by the cleavage between the politics of Chicago (Cook County) and the politics of downstate Illinois.

NEBRASKA AND MINNESOTA—LEGISLATURES WITHOUT PARTY DESIGNATION

Strongly backed by the late George W. Norris and by Depression-conscious appeals for efficiency and economy, a constitutional amendment providing for a unicameral legislature was overwhelmingly ratified by the people of Nebraska in 1934. The politics of this chamber, whose members are elected without party labels, have been characterized as follows:

> The party affiliation of each member is usually known. . . . For some years, the Republicans have had an overwhelming majority in [the] legislature, but that apparently has no effect upon the organization or procedure. At least twice, the man elected speaker was known to be a Democrat, and during the last session of the legislature, several of the most powerful committee chairmanships, including the one on budget and finance, went to Democrats. I could not say that a spirit of partisanship has never appeared in the legislature, but I can say that there has been amazingly little partisanship.[10]

Minnesota has the distinction of having the only non-party designated bicameral legislature in the United States. Its party status had been discarded in 1913 "as the result of a parliamentary struggle between the 'drys' and the 'wets' in which the opponents of prohibition working with liquor interests exploited sentiments within the legislature that were strongly critical of party machine and boss control." [11] Since then its 135 representatives and 67 senators have structured themselves in two caucuses, one designated "conservative" and the other "liberal." To consider these two groups non-partisan, however, would be far from accurate.

> Four-fifths or more of the Liberals in the legislature openly identify themselves with the DFL; many of them have served as county or district committeemen. . . . [The Democratic-Farmer-Labor Party] gives the weight of party endorsement to approved candidates for the legislature, prints their names on its sample ballots, and sends its leaders into their districts to speak on their behalf.[12]

The relationship between the conservative caucus in House and Senate and the state Republican party is not quite that close. Although only about 40 per cent of the House and 28 per cent of the Senate actively participate in Republican politics, many of the key leaders in these caucuses have held significant positions in that party's leadership at one time or another. Failure of the conservative caucus to be more closely associated with the party is predominantly due to the relatively large number of rural legislators who look with some suspicion and often criticism at the more liberal, city-based Republican leadership.

[10] Zeller, p. 212.
[11] G. Theodore Mitau, *Politics in Minnesota* (Minneapolis, 1960), p. 57.
[12] *Ibid.*, pp. 66–67.

THE CASE FOR LEGISLATIVE PARTY COHESION AND DISCIPLINE

Around the turn of the century it was customary for reformers to blame most of the ill-functioning of American government, particularly widespread legislative corruption, on self-seeking political bosses and machines. California's 1913 and 1916 primary laws with their peculiar cross-filing feature represented something of a high-water mark in the Progressive movement's campaign "to return to the people" the task of picking candidates unhampered by party labels in primaries open to all. The practice of cross-filing, which was ended in 1959, was one of the major factors in weakening the role of the two major parties in that state's legislature. Weakened parties did not, however, produce the millennium. On the contrary, "with parties playing less than the usual role in state politics, pressure groups have tended to operate directly in primary and general election campaigns and have crossed party lines in their lobbying activities." [13] Out of such conditions evolved the "secret boss of California—not a party boss, but a master lobbyist" who held no office but who "could push laws through the legislature or stop them cold." His powers were enormous. He could name an attorney general, a police commissioner, a mayor of San Francisco and "make or break governors." [14]

Those who favor a more cohesive and disciplined legislative party see the California experience as merely a crasser manifestation of what has happened and what will tend to happen in all states in which election laws militate against the development of a viable two-party system.

First and foremost, it is contended, a more cohesive party system would be in a superior position to protect the legislators against the pressure of special interests. Second, political parties by the nature of their composition and structure are especially well suited to bring about the widely-based coalition of locality, section, and socio-economic grouping without which no legislature can view the public interest in its broadest perspective. At the same time it would be utterly unrealistic to insist that decisions in such fields as taxation, welfare, labor, housing, and economic development could or should be taken independently or in isolation from partisan positions on the congressional level. A majority of Republicans and Democrats do, after all, vote and think differently on these matters. Why not let these differences be argued and resolved on state legislative levels as well? Third, campaigns would lose some of their "beauty contest" quality and would become more issue-centered if legislators were pledged to the support of party programs and platforms and if their accountability to the voters were made more explicit.

New meaning would be given to election promises of those seeking the governorship if executive leadership were to be buttressed by legislative majorities not only nominally of the same party but also sympathetic as to program.

[13] Winston W. Crouch, Dean E. McHenry, John C. Bollens, and Stanley Scott, *California Government and Politics*, 2nd ed. (Englewood Cliffs, 1960), p. 64.
[14] Lester Velie, "The Secret Boss of California," *Colliers*, August 13, 1949, p. 12.

Fourth, all legislatures are necessarily run by the few. But the power of the few and their anonymity is often assured and greatly enhanced in caucus, committee, and clique when their decisions can be taken outside of the framework of political parties. Party members must operate in the proverbial goldfish bowl. This too contributes to greater public responsibility.

THE CASE FOR THE "INDEPENDENTS"

Those opposed to greater party discipline believe that absence of party control cannot be equated with the irresponsible machinations of wirepullers and self-seekers. On the contrary, it is the absence of party control, permitting maximization of the individual legislator's sense of freedom and his direct accountability to the particular needs of his and only his constituency, which assures legislative responsibility. Parties at best should be used for strictly parliamentary purposes of organizing the chamber and of regularizing its procedures. When parties become disciplining caucuses, they may serve to advance the interest of bosses and machines and thus drive a wedge between the legislator and the people whom he represents.

These are more than mere academic contentions. Legislators who advance this case usually find themselves opposed to gubernatorial innovations in centralized administrative designs as well as to broadly-gauged experimentation with the newer forms of social legislation. They are frankly critical of ever-expanding governmental services and rising costs which these innovations tend to imply or make necessary. They genuinely suspect that the real forces underneath this drive for party discipline are collectivistically-inclined labor interests whose tentacles are reaching deeper into Democratic party organizations. They may reflect in their own thinking rural hostility to much of what the city and its politics represent and specifically fear what the urban masses may view as equitable in reapportionment and a more generous share of the state's tax dollar. Not infrequently legislators of this persuasion can count favorably on a significant segment of the press and on campaign support from certain farm and business organizations to whom the move towards more disciplined parties represents a threat real or alleged.

Summing up, aside from rhetoric and preference, there is increasing evidence that the trend towards tighter party control of legislatures is becoming more pronounced. This is due to a number of factors. With industrialization and urban growth following World War II, Republican party activity has increased in certain Southern and border states, and the Democratic party has made noticeable gains in many of the one time solidly Republican Midwestern states. This has been particularly true of Illinois, Michigan, Minnesota, Ohio, and Wisconsin and to a lesser extent in the Dakotas, Indiana, and Iowa.

Campaigning has become more expensive and extensive which has forced legislators to look to broader bases of electoral support. Increases in governmental services have increased the stakes in governmental policy-making. Urban-rural conflicts have been somewhat blunted and become more complex by suburban developments and by needs for transportation, water, air pollution control, and other public services with regional implications. Some recent studies of legislatures have pointed up that

> conflicts which superficially may be described as setting urban areas against rural areas are more satisfactorily explained in terms of conflict among social, economic and cultural interests which have incidentally been associated with urban and rural areas, at least in the past. Present trends . . . find these interests rearranging themselves in such a way that within the foreseeable future the ability to describe conflict in terms of urban-rural differences, even superficially, will disappear.[15]

Similar findings are reported in studies of the Illinois and Missouri legislatures.

GOOD LOBBYING AND BAD LOBBYING

Lobbies are as old as legislatures. The right to plead a cause, to petition a legislature, to organize with others in order to strengthen the presentation of a point of view, proposal, or bill is constitutionally safeguarded in state and nation. This may involve buttonholing legislators, publishing pamphlets, inserting advertisements, entertaining legislators socially, presenting research, working in alliance with other groups, or contesting the efforts of others. It includes appearances before the committees of the legislature (or administrative and regulatory agencies) by interested "volunteer" citizens who are members of the organization as well as by agents or lawyers who, as employees, will do this on a full or part-time basis.

It may involve an organized effort to support or oppose candidates and after the election is over to urge constituents to write or contact their legislators in support of or in opposition to certain legislative measures.

Lobbyists can represent powerfully entrenched groups reflecting the homogeneity of certain interests in labor, business, or agriculture that have long been active on national and state levels, or they may speak for less powerful economic and social groups formed only recently in response to particular legislative issues. In brief, lobbyists and lobbies whether big or small represent an organized effort to influence legislators and legislation on behalf of causes deemed important to those for whom they speak.

It is the method of influence or technique of lobbying which more than

---

[15] Robert S. Friedman, "The Urban-Rural Conflict Revisited," *Western Political Quarterly,* June, 1961, p. 485; see also David R. Derge, "Metropolitan and Outstate Alignments in Illinois and Missouri Legislative Delegations," *American Political Science Review,* December, 1958, pp. 1051–1065; Thomas R. Dye, "A Comparison of Constituency Influences in the Upper and Lower Chambers of a State Legislature," *Western Political Quarterly,* June, 1961, pp. 473–495; and John P. White and Norman C. Thomas, "Urban and Rural Representation and State Legislative Apportionment," *Western Political Quarterly,* December, 1964, pp. 724–741.

any other factor has concerned legislators in Washington as well as at the state Capitol. At issue is the practical differentiation of the legitimate from the illegitimate, the good from the bad lobbying, and then to effect controls over the corrupting influences of an irresponsible lobbyist or of an even more irresponsible principal. The federal approach, parts of which are followed by those states having any type of lobby control is centered on the identification of the lobbyist through registration and disclosure provisions which would indicate the name of the lobbyist, his employer, the purpose for which lobbying was carried on, the moneys received and disbursed in connection with furthering these purposes and the sources and recipients of the disbursements. A failure to file these reports periodically and truthfully results in fines and disbarment from further lobbying.

The essential weakness of this approach is its concentration on the paid lobbyist only, its reliance on public disclosure as the major sanction, its inadequate report forms which neglect to reveal the complete scope of lobby influence, and its restrictive application to only those groups whose primary and avowed purpose is the influence of legislation. It also fails to bring within effective control those lobby pressure tactics that are aimed not directly at the legislator while at the Capitol but at him indirectly at the grass roots level from where his support must ultimately come.

Following the federal model most of the states also exempt from coverage certain categories of individuals: citizens who merely testify in support of or in opposition to a legislative measure pending before a committee, public officials in their official capacity, and representatives of the news media.

Some of the states have not even gone that far with their regulations of lobbies. In Colorado, Florida, Iowa, Minnesota, and Washington, the requirement for registration rests not on statute but merely on the internal rule of the chamber before which the lobbyist may wish to practice. Among the states experimenting with stronger provisions are California, Illinois, New York, and Wisconsin.

California has prohibitions against a legislative advocate who places the legislator under personal obligation, deceives him, creates a fictitious appearance of public favor or disfavor for a measure, or represents an ability to control votes of legislators. Perhaps the strongest feature of the law is its enforcement machinery. Committees of each chamber can "grant, revoke and suspend certificates of registration" and are also given the power through investigation and hearings to go behind the registration reports of lobbyists in order to ascertain the objectives and interests of those supporting the lobbyist financially.

Wisconsin and Illinois require not only the registration of the agent but of the principal as well. Prohibited also by the Wisconsin statute as well as in twenty-five other states are contingent fee employment contracts "where the compensation is paid conditionally on successfully opposing or favoring legislation."

DIRECT LEGISLATION—INITIATIVE, REFERENDUM, AND RECALL

The Progressive movement of the early twentieth century was disdainful and distrustful of legislatures and legislators. They considered them purchasable, greedy, and dominated by political bosses and ruthless machines which sought to exploit the public and the country for the benefit of the monopolists, railroads, and industrial empires. With legislative channels blocked and public officials deaf to the demands of the voters, the ills of democracy could only be cured by more democracy—by letting the people legislate directly rather than indirectly.

Despite the early momentum and enthusiasm behind these "tools of populism" only twenty states, nearly all in the West, have constitutionally incorporated initiative and referendum provisions and all but one of them, Alaska, did so between 1898 and 1918. Besides this group, New Mexico and Maryland also accepted the referendum but not the initiative.

Initiatives may be direct or indirect—both are in use. The former involves a group of citizens actually drawing up a law themselves. After a certain number of signatures on a direct initiative petition have been obtained, usually between 5 and 10 per cent of the votes cast during a previous election for governor or some other office, this proposed law will then be placed on the ballot and thus submitted to the electorate at the next general election for its approval or rejection. The indirect initiative operates a little differently. Under this form the legislature, having been presented with the petition, is given an opportunity to enact the proposed law. Then, if it fails to avail itself of this opportunity and refuses to pass the measure, the measure must be placed on the ballot and if approved by the electorate will then become law without the legislature.

There are two general types of referenda: one is optional and the other legislative. An optional referendum interposes a thirty- to ninety-day period before the law is allowed to have effect. During this interval voters can circulate petitions and if they obtain a sufficient number of signatures, the measure will then be placed before the electorate for its decision. Unless approved by a majority of the voters, such a measure cannot become law. Constitutionally exempt from such referenda may be laws considered essential to the public peace or those of an emergency nature.

Legislative referenda leave it to the discretion of the legislature to submit bills to the electorate for its judgment. Some states also have what is called a mandatory referendum. This means that the legislature must submit the bill to the voters and obtain their approval before it can become a law. The most common form is the constitutional amendment since only ratification by the electorate can give it legal effect.

What has been the extent and effect of I. and R.? Has it been used excessively, and has it led to radical and irresponsible legislation? It has been charged that under I. and R. minority interests have been able to impose their will on a reluctant legislature or on an apathetic and uninformed electorate and that legislatures ducked their responsibilities and referred controversial measures to the electorate instead of assuming their proper duties as prescribed by a representative democracy.

These are just a few of the questions and charges raised by I. and R.'s friends and foes. From California where in forty years a total of 348 constitutional amendments and 102 legislative proposals was submitted to the electorate comes this observation: "Broadly speaking, the voters have shown remarkable judgment and discrimination in their use." [16] A thorough and comparative study of I. and R. in California, Colorado, Michigan, Oregon, and Washington arrived at a similar judgment. It was found that I. and R. did not destroy legislative responsibility and the number of measures submitted to the electorate constituted a very small portion of legislative business.

Another and more recent survey of the Washington experience with popular lawmaking concluded that "the people have been generally selective in what they have approved and that a proposition has about a fifty-fifty chance of acceptance." [17]

In Colorado by way of contrast where a total of 170 I. and R. proposals was submitted to the electorate between 1912 and 1960, only 32 per cent were accepted.[18] Of the sixteen initiatives attempted in Massachusetts since 1919, the electorate approved but six.[19] Partially explaining the very small number of proposals in Massachusetts is the requirement which removes as a subject of direct legislation such matters as religion, the judiciary, or local affairs.

I. and R. has brought success and failure to various causes, some liberal, some conservative. California, for example, had its "Ham and Eggs" pension plans and the famous Townsend proposals of "$60 at 60," all of which were defeated. Initiatives supported by the single tax movement met a similar fate in 1916, 1918, and 1920.[20] Labor lost an eight-hour day proposal in 1914, and the "full crew" law for railroads in 1948. Other rejected proposals were those dealing with antivivisection, compulsory vaccination, and the reading of the Bible in the public schools.

Voter approval of I. and R. proposals included such important matters as the establishment of a state civil service system, reforms in judicial trial procedures, abolition of the poll tax, school reorganization legislation, a voter registration system, the executive budget, and the defeat of a "right-to-work" law.

The "stick in the closet" possibilities of I. and R. were particularly well illustrated only recently when voters of Washington (1956) and Oregon (1952) used it in successfully overcoming and modifying legislative resistance to reapportionment.

[16] Joseph P. Harris, *California Politics* (Stanford, 1955), p. 54.
[17] Daniel M. Ogden, Jr. and Hugh A. Bone, *Washington Politics* (New York, 1960), p. 67.
[18] Curtis Martin, *Colorado Politics*, 2nd ed. (Denver, 1962), p. 75.
[19] Earl Latham and George Goodwin, Jr., *Massachusetts Politics* (Medford, 1960), p. 68.
[20] Harris, pp. 51–55 and Crouch *et al.*, p. 87.

Yet on the whole, I. and R. is generally on the decline and certainly so if compared with its heavy pre-World War I use. There are a number of reasons for this phenomenon. Signature requirements for petitions and expenses are burdensome. In California a petition requires approximately 330,000 names; in Washington, about 100,000; and in Colorado, 44,000. Additional campaign expenditures for such items as radio and TV time, literature, advertisements, speakers, rents, secretarial costs, transportation, etc., may run upward of a hundred thousand dollars. Legal and political obstacles in the form of challenged petitions, or subsequent actions by a legislature seeking to "amend" the initiated law or to ignore the demands of the electorate all together are risks which must weigh heavily in any group's decision to embark on such a campaign. Nor is there any certainty that voters even after such an expensive effort would not be confused or "over-burdened" by the nature of the issue itself. An experience in Michigan pointed this up sharply in 1952. After an intensive and well-organized campaign by the U.A.W. on behalf of an initiative that would have reapportioned both houses of the legislature on population, "only 56 per cent of the *registered* U.A.W. members in a sample had even so much as heard of the proposal, and only 23 per cent could show that they knew something about it which could serve as a basis for an intelligent vote." [21]

If I. and R. was shown to have its limited application, the other device of direct democracy, recall, has had even less use and greater problems.

The concept of "recalling public officials" made its first statewide appearance in Oregon in 1908 and was then followed by California in 1911 and by nine other states in subsequent years. Judges are specifically exempted in three states, and Kansas restricted the recall to appointed officers only.

Following presentation of petitions which must bear charges and carry from 10 to 25 per cent of the voters' signatures for most state offices, the individual in question may vacate the office "voluntarily." But should he fail to do so, a formal recall election will be held to determine his continuance in office.

Recalls have been invoked only twice on a statewide basis. In Oregon it involved two public utilities commissioners; and in North Dakota, a governor and two state officials. Although a few local officials have been threatened with it (the number of signatures required is higher for local than for state offices), only three mayors have actually been recalled, one each in Los Angeles, Seattle, and Detroit.

Since the recall is even more complex than I. and R. in procedure, this may help to explain why resort to it has not been as intense. Unwillingness to invoke it could also be due, at least partially, to the voters' faith in the effectiveness of checks and balances inherent in state and local governmental arrangements or to the relatively satisfactory quality of the public servant. Not unrelated to the lack of enthusiasm for the recall and even for the I. and R., are such modern developments as improvements in public administration,

[21] Charles R. Adrian, *State and Local Governments: A Study in the Political Process* (New York, 1960), p. 154.

election law reforms, and the increased sense of public responsibility by political parties and organizations.

REAPPORTIONMENT—OBSTACLES AND POLITICAL CONSEQUENCES

State legislatures have come a long way from the days of the seventeenth century when there was a reluctance to be represented and when, for example, Virginia in 1670 "levied a fine of 10,000 pounds of tobacco for any county failing to send two burgesses to the assembly." [22] For the next two hundred years in a largely rural and frontier America, there was little disagreement with the view that representation should be equal, based on population or based proportionately on a properly qualified electorate.

As the population increased, legislatures simply enlarged their membership by adding new districts. But then towards the end of the nineteenth century cities grew faster than other areas of the state with rural-urban antagonisms intensifying as their social and economic interests collided. It became obvious that the legislature could not go on indefinitely increasing its size and that some rearrangement of districts would have to be accomplished. Some areas would have to lose seats so that others could be more fairly represented. The battles for reapportionment, joined at the beginning of the twentieth century, have become more significant with every generation, reaching something of a crescendo during the last thirty years when the urban share of the national population increased from about one-half to about two-thirds. In the course of the past decade alone the metropolitan areas gained more than thirty million more people, an increase of close to 30 per cent. Yet at the beginning of the 1950's the country's ten largest cities had less than half of their proportionate share of legislative representation. A vote for state senator in Los Angeles had approximately 500 times less power than that of a rural California vote. Nor was New England's record better. Providence, Rhode Island, with almost one-third of the state's population only had five senators out of a total of forty-four. In Connecticut, four towns each with a population of 100,000 composing nearly one-third of the population received eight seats or 2.9 per cent of the voting power in the state House, and in the lower chamber of Vermont, towns with about 40 per cent of the state's population had approximately 6 per cent of the representatives. [23] Rural interests in Kansas were able to keep the four most populous counties with a total of 810,000 persons comprising 40 per cent of the state's population down to a total of four senators. This represented a mere 10 per cent of the forty-member Kansas Senate. In Vermont, the disparity in the House of Representatives "between the largest and smallest district . . . ran as great as 676

[22] Gordon E. Baker, *State Constitutions: Reapportionment* (New York, 1960), p. 3. Other general works on legislative reapportionment include the following: Paul T. David and Ralph Eisenberg, *Devaluation of the Urban and Suburban Vote: A Statistical Investigation of Long-Term Trends in State Legislative Representation* (Charlottesville, 1961) and Malcolm E. Jewell (ed.), *The Politics of Reapportionment* (New York, 1962).

[23] Lockard, pp. 178, 273, and 36.

to 1"; [24] in Tennessee, there was one district with 3,900 population, another with 75,000.[25] And in Connecticut's House, Hartford with a population of 116,000 had two representatives—the same number given to the town of Colebrook, population 547.[26] In New York, Yates County had one assemblyman for its population of 17,461 while in Bronx County one assemblyman represented a population of 115,000.[27]

A 1964 study of the extent of malapportionment revealed that (1) in twenty-two states a majority of the Senate was elected by less than one-third of the state's population, and (2) that one-third of the people or less elected a majority of the House of Representatives in fifteen of the fifty states (see Table 2 and Figure 1).

Prior to the reapportionment of Illinois in 1955, the first since 1901, Chicago and Cook County with a population of 4.5 million had only nineteen senators, whereas the rest of the state with a population of only 4.2 million held the remaining thirty-one Senate seats. Chicago with 40 per cent of the state's population had only about one-third of the House membership. Redistricting under this act considerably improved the Illinois picture, though the requirement that "area" was to be given "prime consideration" made it necessary for Cook County to accept a constitutionally frozen minority status in the Senate, a maximum of twenty-four seats (18 for Chicago and 6 for suburban Cook County) in a Senate of fifty-eight members.[28] No reapportionment is required of the Senate; however, if the Illinois lower House fails to redistrict itself, a commission appointed by the governor may redistrict the Senate (within the area restrictions) as well as the House. This is what happened in January of 1964, and as a consequence all 177 Illinois House members had to run at-large.

PATTERNS OF APPORTIONMENT

A variety of formulas are used by the fifty states to govern legislative apportionment. Table 3, which utilizes basic categories identified by Malcolm E. Jewell, indicates that six different methods are used for apportionment in the states.[29]

[24] The New York Times, March 15, 1961, p. 39. On Kansas reapportionment, see Thomas Page, Legislative Apportionment in Kansas (Lawrence, 1952) and James W. Drury and James E. Titus, Legislative Apportionment in Kansas: 1960 (Lawrence, 1960).

[25] Saturday Evening Post, April 22, 1961, p. 10.

[26] The New York Times, November 22, 1960, p. 29.

[27] Ibid., May 2, 1961, p. 28. On reapportionment in New York, see three articles by Ruth C. Silva: "Apportionment of the New York State Legislature," American Political Science Review, December, 1961, pp. 870–881; "Legislative Representation—With Special Reference to New York," Law and Contemporary Problems, Summer, 1962, pp. 408–433; and "Population Base for Apportionment of the New York Legislature," Fordham Law Review, October, 1963, pp. 1–50.

[28] Gilbert Y. Steiner and Samuel K. Gove, Legislative Politics in Illinois (Urbana, 1960), p. 85.

[29] Malcolm E. Jewell, "Constitutional Provisions for State Legislative Apportionment," Western Political Quarterly, June, 1955, pp. 272–279; see also William J. D. Boyd, Patterns of Apportionment (New York, 1962).

TABLE 2. STATE LEGISLATIVE DISTRICTS

WASHINGTON, June 16—The table below shows the extent to which the 50 state legislatures now depart from the standard of population equality in their districts. The population figures are for the most-populous and least-populous district in each House. The other columns show the smallest percentage of each state's population that can elect a majority in each house. The lower the percentage, the less representative of population is the apportionment; for example, the 10.7 per cent figure for the California Senate means that percentage of the population could theoretically elect control of the Senate. The source of the table is the National Municipal League.

State	Senate Largest	Senate Smallest	Pct.	House Largest	House Smallest	Pct.
Alabama	634,864	31,715	27.6	50,718	10,726	37.9
Alaska	88,021	4,603	41.9	7,174	2,945	47.3
Arizona	331,755	3,868	12.8	30,438	5,754	46.0
Arkansas	80,993	35,983	43.8	31,686	4,927	33.3
California	6,038,771	14,294	10.7	306,191	72,105	44.7
Colorado	73,340	19,983	33.0	35,123	20,302	45.1
Connecticut	175,940	21,627	32.0	81,089	191	12.0
Delaware	64,820	4,177	22.4	58,228	1,643	18.5
Florida	467,525	17,711	15.2	66,788	2,868	26.9
Georgia	95,032	52,572	48.3	185,442	1,876	22.2
Hawaii	63,620	8,518	18.1	23,779	5,030	38.4
Idaho	93,460	915	16.6	15,576	915	32.7
Illinois	565,300	53,500	28.7	160,200	34,433	39.9
Indiana	73,329	28,135	40.5	35,651	16,503	47.6
Iowa	88,771	27,703	38.9	31,078	13,916	44.8
Kansas	61,920	47,114	47.8	47,800	2,241	19.4
Kentucky	120,700	62,048	46.6	40,480	20,166	44.8
Louisiana	248,427	31,174	33.0	57,622	6,909	33.1
Maine	45,687	16,146	46.9	13,102	2,394	39.7
Maryland	492,428	15,481	14.2	37,879	6,541	42.3
Massachusetts	199,107	86,355	44.6	49,478	3,559	45.3
Michigan	363,187	79,950	41.3	101,120	48,395	46.4
Minnesota	99,446	26,458	40.1	99,446	8,343	34.5
Mississippi	187,045	20,987	37.2	26,361	3,576	41.2
Missouri	160,288	96,477	47.8	53,015	3,936	20.3
Montana	79,016	894	16.1	12,537	894	40.8
Nebraska	36,393	21,703	43.9	(Unicameral Legis.)		
Nevada	127,016	568	8.0	12,525	568	29.1
New Hampshire	41,457	15,829	45.3	1,779	8	43.9
New Jersey	923,545	48,555	19.0	143,913	48,555	46.5
New Mexico	262,199	1,874	14.0	16,198	1,874	42.0
New York	650,112	168,398	41.8	314,721	15,044	34.7
North Carolina	148,418	65,722	47.6	82,059	4,520	27.1
North Dakota	42,041	4,698	31.9	8,408	2,665	40.2
Ohio	439,000	203,163	44.8	148,700	10,274	29.4
Oklahoma	61,866	24,393	44.5	62,789	11,706	32.5
Oregon	69,634	29,917	47.8	39,660	18,955	48.1
Pennsylvania	352,629	130,498	43.4	81,534	4,485	42.7
Rhode Island	47,080	486	18.1	18,977	486	46.5
South Carolina	216,382	8,629	23.3	29,490	8,629	46.0
South Dakota	43,288	10,039	38.4	16,688	3,531	38.6
Tennessee	133,248	83,031	44.5	50,105	22,275	39.7
Texas	1,243,158	147,454	30.3	105,725	33,987	38.7
Utah	64,760	9,408	21.3	32,380	1,164	33.3
Vermont	16,014	2,927	47.0	35,531	24	11.9
Virginia	163,401	61,730	41.1	95,064	21,825	40.5
Washington	145,180	20,023	33.9	57,648	12,399	35.3
West Virginia	73,590	37,042	46.7	27,233	11,584	40.6
Wisconsin	137,134	100,615	48.4	52,368	22,268	45.4
Wyoming	30,074	3,062	24.1	7,929	3,062	46.5

SOURCE: *The New York Times*, June 17, 1964, p. 29.

FIGURE 1

MAKE-UP OF STATE LEGISLATURES AS SUPREME COURT RULES THAT DISTRICTS MUST BE SUBSTANTIALLY EQUAL IN POPULATION

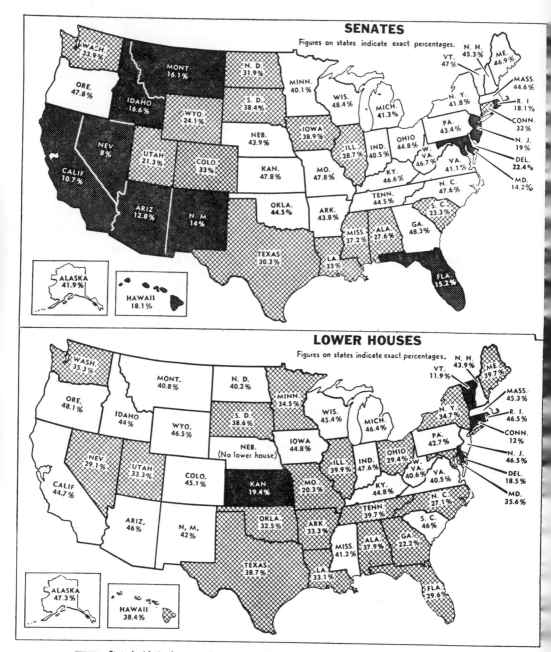

SENATES

Figures on states indicate exact percentages.

WASH. 33.9%
ORE. 47.8%
MONT. 16.1%
IDAHO 16.6%
NEV 8%
CALIF 10.7%
UTAH 21.3%
ARIZ 12.8%
WYO 24.1%
COLO 33%
N. M. 14%
N. D. 31.9%
S. D. 38.4%
NEB. 43.9%
KAN. 47.8%
OKLA. 44.5%
TEXAS 30.3%
MINN. 40.1%
IOWA 38.9%
MO. 47.8%
ARK. 43.8%
LA. 33%
WIS. 48.4%
ILL. 28.7%
IND. 40.5%
KY. 46.6%
TENN. 44.5%
MISS. 37.2%
ALA. 27.6%
GA. 48.3%
FLA. 15.2%
MICH. 41.3%
OHIO 44.8%
W. VA. 46.7%
VA. 41.1%
N. C. 47.6%
S. C. 23.3%
N. H. 45.3%
VT. 47%
ME. 46.9%
MASS. 44.6%
N. Y. 41.8%
R. I 18.1%
PA. 43.4%
CONN. 32%
N. J. 19%
DEL. 22.4%
MD. 14.2%
ALASKA 41.9%
HAWAII 18.1%

LOWER HOUSES

Figures on states indicate exact percentages.

WASH. 35.3%
ORE. 48.1%
IDAHO 44%
MONT. 40.8%
N. D. 40.2%
MINN. 34.5%
S. D. 38.6%
WIS. 45.4%
NEV 29.1%
CALIF 44.7%
UTAH 33.3%
WYO. 46.5%
COLO. 45.1%
NEB. (No lower house)
IOWA 44.8%
KAN. 19.4%
MO. 20.3%
ARIZ. 46%
N. M. 42%
OKLA. 32.5%
ARK. 33.3%
TEXAS 38.7%
LA. 33.1%
MISS. 41.2%
ALA. 37.9%
GA. 22.2%
FLA. 29.6%
ILL. 39.9%
IND. 47.6%
KY. 44.8%
TENN. 39.7%
S. C. 46%
MICH. 46.4%
OHIO 29.4%
W. VA. 40.6%
VA. 40.5%
N. C. 27.1%
N. H. 43.9%
VT. 11.9%
ME. 39.7%
MASS. 45.3%
N. Y. 34.7%
R. I. 46.5%
PA. 42.7%
CONN. 12%
N. J. 46.5%
DEL. 18.5%
MD. 35.6%
ALASKA 47.3%
HAWAII 38.4%

State legislative houses with greatest population imbalance in election districts. (Less than 20 per cent of the state's population can elect a majority of the chamber.)

State legislative houses with next greatest population imbalance in election districts. (20 to 40 per cent of the state's population can elect a majority of the chamber.)

State legislative houses with least population imbalance in election districts. (More than 40 per cent of the state's population is required to elect a majority of the chamber.)

SOURCE: *The New York Times*, June 21, 1964, p. E3.

TABLE 3. STATE LEGISLATIVE APPORTIONMENT BASES

Basis	Senates	Houses	Total
Population	17	16	33
Population, but with weighted ratios	1	5	6
Combination of population and area (including one unicameral)	21	27	48
Equal apportionment for each unit	8	1	9
Fixed constitutional apportionment	2	0	2
Apportionment by taxation	1	0	1
Total	50	49	99

SOURCE: Compiled from information in *Book of the States, 1964–1965*, pp. 62–66. For earlier compilations of state legislative apportionment bases, see Gordon E. Baker, *State Constitutions: Reapportionment* (New York, 1960), p. 5 and Malcolm E. Jewell, "Constitutional Provisions for State Legislative Apportionment," *Western Political Quarterly*, June, 1955, p. 272.

(1) One-third of all legislative bodies use "population" as the standard of apportionment although definitions of "population" vary from state to state. Indiana, for example, counts only male inhabitants over 21, Massachusetts and Tennessee use the concept of "legal or qualified" voters, and California and North Carolina base their apportionment on "citizens" only. In the deep South, rural "Black Belt" counties receive disproportionate representation by including their largely disenfranchised Negroes in computing their "population" for determining their legislative representation. Arizona reapportions its lower House every four years on the basis of each county's actual vote in the previous gubernatorial election.

That neither fair nor periodic reapportionment is realistically assured in states where the constitution establishes population as the basis, is now well known. In fact, a 1960 study found that "resistance to reapportionment among lawmakers is often the strongest in those states where the constitutions contain a population standard, since the legislatures are usually controlled by the areas of declining population." [30]

(2) A population standard with "weighted ratios" is now used in one Senate (Oregon) and five lower Houses (Alaska, Hawaii, New Hampshire, Oregon, and Tennessee). The purpose of such ratios is to assure more favorable voting power to the rural or less populated areas.

(3) A formula which utilizes both population and area as the basis for apportionment of legislative bodies is employed in almost one-half of the states. Here again there are different patterns; some states will rate area as more important than population, while in others the emphasis is reversed. Another widely-adopted arrangement will allot at least one representative to each county or district in the upper House (Connecticut, Vermont, and Wyoming) or in the lower House (Arkansas, Florida, Idaho, Iowa, Kansas,

[30] Baker, p. 7.

Louisiana, Maine, Mississippi, Missouri, Montana, New Jersey, New Mexico, New York, North Carolina, North Dakota, Ohio, Pennsylvania, South Carolina, Utah, and Wyoming). Still another variation, used as the basis in the upper Houses of Florida, Iowa, and Texas, prohibits the apportionment of more than one senator to each county. Several states employ both variations of the population and area basis. For example, California provides that no county, or city and county, may have more than one senator, while guaranteeing that no more than three thinly-populated counties may be combined into any district. A new variation of the population-area standard that has recently been adopted as the basis for apportionment of the Senate in Michigan (1963) and the unicameral legislature of Nebraska (1962) calls for a formula which combines population to the extent of 80 per cent with area held down to a mere 20 per cent.

(4) Equal apportionment to each county is guaranteed in the Senates of Arizona, Delaware, Idaho, Montana, Nevada, New Jersey, New Mexico, and South Carolina and to towns in the lower House of Vermont.

(5) There are now only two legislative bodies in the nation in which the districts are specified in the state constitutions. In Arkansas and Hawaii, Senate districts may be reapportioned only by constitutional amendment.

(6) The Senate of New Hampshire is the only legislative body in the nation apportioned on the basis of direct taxes paid by each district. Reapportioned in 1961, the new Senate districts give the urban areas of the state fairly equitable representation.

A 1962 study of the Advisory Commission on Intergovernmental Relations indicates that there has been a trend toward so-called "federal plans"—where the Senate is partially area-based and the lower House population-based—for apportioning bicameral state legislatures. The study found that "the original constitutional provisions of thirty-six states contained apportionment provisions based completely or substantially on population," while in 1962 only twenty-four constitutions contained such provisions. In addition, three original state constitutions based both houses on political subdivisions. Today no constitutions contain such a provision for both houses. The federal plan, a concept not found in any original state constitutions, appeared in the constitutions of twelve states in 1962.[31] Since then, voters in Colorado (1963) have approved federal plans, while constitutional amendments for such plans were defeated by the action of urban areas in both Iowa (1963) and North Carolina (1964).

There is obviously more involved in the laying out of "compact and contiguous" legislative districts (so generously ordered in many state constitutions) than mere arithmetic and geography. "No taxation without representation," a once stirring battle cry, may be ignored for awhile (except in New Hampshire), but it cannot easily be forgotten since the distribution of

---

[31] Advisory Commission on Intergovernmental Relations, *Apportionment of State Legislatures* (Washington, 1962), p. 14. For a discussion of the federal plan of apportionment, see Robert B. McKay, *Reapportionment and the Federal Analogy* (New York, 1962).

political powers within the state is directly affected by the numerical leverage that can be marshalled on the floor of a legislature. One of the critical concerns in all representative assemblies has always been and probably will always be—who speaks for whom and for what. Reapportioning districts nearly always result in the strengthening of one set of interests at the expense of another and most fatally of all, in forcing some legislators into political oblivion so that others may have their day in the sun.

First, then, there is the human factor resisting change, "the desire of each legislator to be in a 'safe' district" reinforced by the law of mutual preservation, "the willingness of members to cooperate with each other in protecting incumbents against political challengers." [32] This was stated most succinctly by a Washington state legislator some years ago: "I saw to it that there was no redistricting of the state . . . and I'm going to see to the same thing again this year. Self-preservation is the first law of nature." [33]

Second, there is the frankly anti-urban bias—the fear of the cities. Few illustrations could be more unadorned than this 1947 statement by a one-time president of the National Association of Real Estate Boards:

> Today the greatest threat to democratic institutions, to the republican form of government, and ultimately to freedom itself, lies in our big cities. They are populated for the most part with the mass-man, devoid of intelligence, devoid of civic responsibility. He talks only about rights and has no conceptions of responsibilities. He will vote for anyone who offers something for nothing, whether it be subway fares at half-price or public housing at one-third price . . . our one hope of survival as a free country is that rural and semi-rural areas still dominate most of the state legislatures through their representatives and still dominate the House of Representatives at Washington. Our best hope for the future is to keep it that way.[34]

Third, there are certain identifiable interest groups—social, economic, or ideological—that are opposed to any move upsetting the legislative status quo. Farm and business organizations may jointly fear that reapportionment will yield more power to the leaders of organized labor. Rural Protestants and urban minorities may be apprehensive about the influence of the Roman Catholic church and its hierarchy upon Catholic voters concentrated in the metropolitan centers.

Conservatively-inclined voters in cities, towns, and villages may see extension of expensive social programs, in welfare, health, education or unemployment benefits through reapportionment; Republican politicians strong in small towns and on farms may be reluctant to weaken their electoral and organizational bases by further strengthening the hold exercised by

---

[32] Steiner and Gove, pp. 86–87.

[33] Gordon E. Baker, *The Politics of Reapportionment in Washington State* (New York, 1960), p. 2.

[34] Quoted from *Madison (Wisconsin) Capitol Times*, August 26, 1947 by August Norman Renner, in "Legislative Apportionment in Wisconsin," an unpublished M.S. thesis, University of Wisconsin, 1948, p. 18.

Democrats on urban politics; and rural Democrats may view with much trepidation any rebirth of Republicanism in industrial and middle-class Southern urban constituencies.

REAPPORTIONMENT BY INITIATIVE

Legislative reluctance for self-reapportionment has sufficiently aroused citizens of some states to the point of resorting to the initiative as a method of obtaining more equitable representation. In recent years such initiatives (constitutional or legislative) led to reapportionment action in Michigan (1952), Oregon (1952), and Washington (1956).

In 1960 a California petition to correct the severe apportionment discrimination assuring continued Senate domination by northern counties over the southern area where 60 per cent of California's population is located was defeated. Other than the likelihood of defeat, there are a number of additional difficulties that need to be mentioned, to assess the usefulness of the process.

First, the legislative or the constitutional initiative can only be used in twenty states.[35] Second, the necessary percentage of required signatures for the petition is often difficult and expensive to obtain; bipartisan cooperation, as demonstrated in Oregon, may often be the "crucial" and even the indispensable factor in success.[36] Third, the passage of an initiative does not automatically assure legislative compliance.

This last point was dramatically illustrated in the state of Washington where the 1957 legislature defied the will of the 1956 electorate as expressed in the acceptance of the petition and substituted a bill of its own significantly different in its terms—rendering the results of the "initiative largely ineffective." An appeal to the state supreme court, brought by the League of Women Voters, the force behind the successful initiative, was turned down in a split decision. The power of amending an initiative (given to the legislature under the terms of an earlier amendment), the court ruled, included the authority to "change the law completely, within the realm of the subject matter contained in the act." [37]

Even where the initiative is successful, rural forces are able to demonstrate considerable ability in exacting a fairly high price for its passage. This was true in Michigan (1952) and in Illinois where in 1954 the legislature submitted and the electorate ratified a redistricting proposal in the form of an amendment.

In both states the supporters of reapportionment had to accept as a

---

[35] Constitutional and statutory—Arizona, Arkansas, California, Colorado, Idaho, Massachusetts, Michigan, Missouri, Nebraska, Nevada, North Dakota, Ohio, Oklahoma, and Oregon; statutory only—Alaska, Maine, Montana, South Dakota, Utah, and Washington.

[36] Gordon E. Baker, "Reapportionment by Initiative in Oregon," *Western Political Quarterly*, June, 1960, p. 519.

[37] Baker, *The Politics of Reapportionment in Washington State*, p. 28.

necessary compromise the federal plan. Under it, Senate districts based primarily on area and secondarily on population were more or less made constitutionally permanent while the lower House districts were to be apportioned on basis of population only and reapportioned regularly following each federal census. As a result of these changes, the urban and more populous centers undoubtedly improved their position. But at the same time the insistence on area meant that in Michigan the Senate districts varied in population as much as five to one [38] and that in Illinois one Senate district downstate included 53,989 people and another district in Chicago included a population of 383,803.[39] The initiative process was also used in Arkansas (1956) to freeze the Senate districts permanently into the constitution.

REAPPORTIONMENT—SOME EXTRA-LEGISLATIVE PATTERNS

The facts of political life being what they are, some states have endeavored to develop reapportioning machinery that could affect the desired changes even in the face of a relatively unwilling legislature. Two basic approaches have developed. First, there are those states which give the legislature an opportunity to discharge their proper and periodic reapportionment responsibilities. Should these assemblies then fail to live up to their duties, the job is taken out of their hands and located somewhere else. Included in this group are California, Illinois, North Dakota, South Dakota, Texas, Oregon, and Maine. In the first five states, redistricting is to be accomplished by an executive commission; in Oregon, by the secretary of state; and in Maine, by the supreme judicial court. These reapportioning measures are subject, of course, to certain limitations set out in the constitutions, which affect particularly the upper houses.

The exact composition of the executive commissions varies, but the officers most frequently mentioned are the lieutenant governor, the attorney general, the secretary of state, and the superintendent of public instruction.

Second, there is the other group of states in which the reapportioning responsibilities are either in their entirety or in part removed from the legislature altogether. This group includes Alaska, Arizona, Arkansas, Delaware, Hawaii, Maryland, Michigan, Missouri and Ohio.

> In *Alaska, Hawaii* and *Maryland,* the governor is given the power to reapportion the House following each federal census. Alaska provides for a bi-partisan advisory board with regional representation. Both Alaska and Hawaii provide for judicial review of reapportionment.

> In *Delaware* and *Ohio,* reapportionment of both houses and in *Arkansas,* reapportionment of the lower House is in the hands of an executive board.

[38] Robert H. Pealy, *The Voter and the Michigan Constitution* (Ann Arbor, 1960), p. 44. For other discussions of Michigan reapportionment, see Herbert Garfinkel and Leonard J. Fein, *Fair Representation: A Citizen's Guide to Legislative Apportionment in Michigan* (East Lansing, 1960) and Karl A. Lamb, William J. Pierce, and John P. White, *Apportionment and Representative Institutions: The Michigan Experience* (Washington, 1963).
[39] Steiner and Gove, p. 115.

The Delaware commission includes the governor, the majority and minority leaders of the Senate, the president of the University of Delaware, and the president of the Farmers' Bank of the State of Delaware; the Ohio board includes the governor, the auditor and the secretary of state; and the Arkansas board includes the governor, the secretary of state and the attorney general.

In *Missouri*, the Senate is to be reapportioned by a bi-partisan ten-member board appointed by the governor from lists submitted to him by the two major political parties. The House redistricting is to be initiated by the secretary of state who apportions the seats among the counties and then the county boards will have the responsibility of apportioning the totals within their counties.

In *Michigan*, both houses are to be reapportioned by a Commission on Legislative Apportionment, composed of four members selected by each political party and four by area.

In *Arizona*, automatic reapportionment is to be carried out biennially for the House based on the last gubernatorial vote cast. The secretary of state then certifies the total number of representatives to be elected from each county and the County Boards of Supervisors do the redistricting.

Patterns such as these that place the responsibility for the actual reapportioning of districts in administrative rather than legislative hands have helped improve the situation in the states involved. This is even true for states in which the administrative procedures are used only as alternative methods in case of legislative inactivity. The matter of drawing districts that are compact, contiguous, equal in population and that constitute (in the words of the Alaskan constitution) "relatively integrated socio-economic areas" is greatly aided by these devices and by the judicial review feature. There is, in other words, the problem of avoiding the gerrymandering of districts.

The practice of drawing odd-shaped legislative districts in order to maximize one party's representation, attributed to the machinations of Governor Gerry of Massachusetts, was neither originated by him nor can it be considered something unique to his state. Few, if any, legislative maps are free of these strangely-shaped districts. Legislative majorities, regardless of party, have long considered this one of the spoils of victory.

No reapportionment machinery can be entirely effective as long as counties and towns are given representation unrelated to equality in population. Many constitutional provisions express this barrier by prohibiting any part of one county from forming part of another in the creation of a legislative or assembly district. This restriction, of course, makes population equality of districts impossible. In states where the reapportionment machinery has been strengthened with respect to the lower House, the more rural and less populous sections appear to have been successful in blocking any major move to relinquish the area or local government factors in the Senate.

There are at least two major sets of recommendations for additional reform. Neither has so far been received with any significant sign of enthusiasm by the political practitioners.

One of these, suggested by the State Constitutional Studies Project of

The National Municipal League (1963) would replace bicameralism with a unicameral chamber based on single-member districts. The power of legislative reapportionment would be given to the governor, with judicial review possible.[40] The other recommendation submitted in a report of the Committee on State Legislatures of the American Political Science Association (1954) would retain bicameralism only if "not inconsistent with the principle of equal population constituencies. . . ." It envisages a Senate that "might be elected from multi-member districts laid out with regard to important economic regions with or without proportional representation for each district."[41]

REAPPORTIONMENT—THE ROLE OF THE COURTS

Supplementing human and political obstacles to reapportionment have been some inherent in the process itself. A constitution might declare that "the legislature shall fix the number of assemblymen after each decennial United States census" or that the legislature "shall have the power" to reapportion, or that both houses "shall be apportioned equally throughout the different sections of the state" but, and this was often the very crux of the problem, there was little that could be done until 1962 if the statesmen for whatever reason wished to ignore such a mandate.

Before 1962 Alabama had had no reapportionment since 1901, Delaware since 1897, Indiana since 1921, Louisiana since 1921, Mississippi since 1916, North Dakota since 1931, Tennessee since 1901, and Wyoming since 1931. In Iowa, the House had not been redistricted since 1927 and the Senate since 1911. New Hampshire had not reapportioned its Senate since 1915 and Vermont's House as well as Senate had not been changed since the adoption of the state constitution in 1793. When a taxpayer initiated a suit prior to 1962 to compel reluctant legislatures to reapportion, the courts were generally unwilling to assume jurisdiction or to demand that the legislature apportion seats fairly on the theory noted earlier that the separation of powers doctrine makes these issues essentially "political" and thus unjusticiable. Until the latter half of the 1950's, federal courts followed the reasoning and decision laid down by the United States Supreme Court in *Colegrove* v. *Green* (1946).[42] This case grew out of an attempt to invoke federal assistance to force the Illinois legislature to rectify vast inequalities in congressional districting resulting in gross discrimination against the voters of Chicago. A four to three majority of the court speaking through Mr. Justice Felix Frankfurter refused to intervene on the theory that "Courts ought not to enter this political thicket. The remedy for unfairness in districting is to secure state legislatures that will apportion properly, or to invoke the ample powers of Congress." (Art. I, Section 4).[43]

[40] National Municipal League, *Model State Constitution,* 6th ed. (New York, 1963), pp. 4–5.
[41] Zeller, p. 46.
[42] 328 U. S. 549 (1946). For a discussion of court decisions prior to *Baker* v. *Carr,* see James E. Larson, *Reapportionment and the Courts* (Birmingham, 1962).
[43] 328 U. S. 549, at 556.

But the pressures favorable for federal judicial intervention on behalf of reapportionment persisted as legislatures continued to ignore constitutional mandates and as population shifts and growth further accentuated the disparities in districts.

A 1956 federal court in Hawaii (*Dyer* v. *Kazuhisa Abe*) [44] successfully upheld the contention of some Oahu voters that the failure of the territorial legislature to reapportion for over fifty years in direct violation of mandatory language in the Organic Act constituted in effect a clear denial of due process of law warranting judicial attention and action. From its opinion, two major premises succinctly emerged. First, a state has a perfect right to assure representation to geographic areas which may entail something less than an equal voice for each voter, but "where the fundamental law provides for equal rights of suffrage, each citizen should have the right of judicial redress if the law is violated." [45] Second, in an era when courts are busy assuring equal rights to all "it is ludicrous to preclude judicial relief when a mainspring of representative government is impaired. Legislators have no immunity from the Constitution. The legislatures of our land should be made as responsible to the Constitution of the United States as are citizens who elect legislators." [46] The court ordered at-large elections for the territorial legislature, but they never did take place. Instead, Congress amended the Organic Act to redraw the district lines, to shift responsibility for reapportionment from the legislature to the governor, and to provide for judicial review of the governor's action.

Two years later a group of Minnesota voters were able to have a federal district court assume jurisdiction in a case (*Magraw* v. *Donovan*) [47] challenging forty-five years of legislative inaction on reapportionment. In this instance the court not only acknowledged the inequalities that had developed since 1913 and the present inadequacy of the last reapportioning act, but also offered the legislature one more face-saving device. "It is not to be presumed," the court said in addressing itself to the upcoming session, "that the legislature will refuse to take such action as is necessary to comply with its duty under the state constitution," but it then retained jurisdiction just in case the conscience of the legislature were to prove silent.[48] At the 1959 session of the legislature, a reapportionment bill was passed which gave the urban areas of Minnesota greater representation, and the suit was then dismissed by the court.

State courts, like federal courts, had generally been unwilling prior to 1962 to assume jurisdiction in cases involving legislative malapportionment. One exception occurred in 1960 when the supreme court of New Jersey assumed jurisdiction in a suit (*Asbury Park Press* v. *Wooley*) [49] challenging

---

[44] 138 F. Supp. 220 (1956).
[45] *Ibid.*, at 236.
[46] *Ibid.*, at 236.
[47] 163 F. Supp. 184 (1958).
[48] *Ibid.*, at 188.
[49] 161 A. 2nd 705 (1960).

the apportionment of the New Jersey legislature. Although the court did not grant relief to the petitioners, it did retain jurisdiction until 1961 when the legislature reapportioned itself.

Another attempt to invoke the "due process of law" and "equal protection" clauses of the 14th Amendment on the behalf of legislative apportionment was brought before the United States Supreme Court in 1961 by a group of Tennessee voters in *Baker* v. *Carr*.[50] Although required by the Tennessee constitution to reapportion following each federal census, a rural bloc controlling two-thirds of the seats in each house had been successfully preventing such action since 1901. Explicitly overruling its previous decision in *Colegrove* v. *Green*, the Court on March 26, 1962, by a vote of six to two held "(a) that the court possessed jurisdiction of the subject matter; (b) that a justiciable cause of action is stated upon which appellants would be entitled to appropriate relief; and (c) because appellees raise the issue before this Court, that the appellants have standing to challenge the Tennessee apportionment statutes." [51] In making its decision on the merits of the case, and remanding the case to the district court, the Supreme Court provided no special guidelines for the lower courts to follow. Mr. Justice Brennan, speaking for the Court, said that it would be "improper now to consider what remedy would be most appropriate if appellants prevail at the trial." [52] Instead, the majority opinion centered on the question of whether legislative reapportionment was a "political question," as had been established in *Colegrove* v. *Green*. Addressing himself to this issue, Mr. Justice Brennan said:

> The question here is the consistency of state action with the Federal Constitution. We have no question decided, or to be decided, by a political branch of government coequal with this Court. Nor do we risk embarrassment of our government abroad, or grave disturbance at home if we take issue with Tennessee as to the constitutionality of her action here challenged. Nor need the appellants, in order to succeed in this action, ask the Court to enter upon policy determinations for which judicially manageable standards are lacking. Judicial standards under the Equal Protection Clause are well developed and familiar, and it has been open to courts since the enactment of the Fourteenth Amendment to determine, if on the particular facts they must, that a discrimination reflects *no* policy, but simply arbitrary and capricious action.[53]

Mr. Justice Frankfurter, who had authored the majority opinion in *Colegrove* v. *Green*, dissented:

> [T]here is not under our Constitution a judicial remedy for every political mischief, for every undesirable exercise of legislative power. The framers carefully and with deliberate forethought refused so to enthrone the judiciary. In this situation, as in others of like nature, appeal for relief does not belong here. Appeal must be to an informed, civically militant electorate. In a democratic society like ours, relief must come through an aroused popular conscience that sears the conscience of the people's representatives.[54]

[50] 369 U. S. 186 (1962).
[51] *Ibid.*, at 197–198.
[52] *Ibid.*, at 198.
[53] *Ibid.*, at 226.
[54] *Ibid.*, at 270.

The majority opinion in *Baker* v. *Carr* settled the question of whether courts could assume jurisdiction in suits challenging legislative apportionment; it did not assert that apportionment of both legislative bodies must be based solely on population. Nor did it delineate the point at which a legislative apportionment is in violation of the "equal protection" clause of the 14th Amendment. It also failed to answer the question of whether state constitutional provisions which prevent equal representation of urban areas are incompatible with the "equal protection" clause.

In the two years following the *Baker* v. *Carr* decision, judicial, legislative, or referendum actions on the issue of legislative apportionment have taken place in at least forty-three states leaving only seven states—Alaska, Arizona, Arkansas, Hawaii, Montana, South Carolina, and South Dakota—without any significant action on reapportionment.[55]

Although the Supreme Court threw out the Georgia county unit system in *Gray* v. *Sanders* (1963)[56] a number of highly important questions continued to remain unanswered as to what type of apportionment would satisfy the Court's standard. Did the equal protection of law clause of the 14th Amendment rule out altogether the use of *area* as a constitutionally acceptable basis of apportionment? Must both houses of the legislature be based on population? May states retain the "federal plan" under which each county is assigned one representative irrespective of size or population?

Most of these questions were answered by the Court on June 15, 1964, in a group of opinions which decided issues of apportionment raised in six different states—in Alabama, Colorado, Delaware, Maryland, New York, and Virginia. In striking down all the various state contentions, Mr. Chief Justice Warren, speaking for a six to three majority, held in his history-making decision that the equality clause of the 14th Amendment did in law demand that all states apportion both houses of their legislatures into districts "substantially equal" in population.

A few of the most relevant passages from the *Reynolds* v. *Sims*[57] group will illustrate the enormous impact that this decision is bound to have on legislative apportionments in all states:

    A. Legislators represent people, not trees or acres. Legislators are elected by voters, not farms or cities or economic interests.[58]
    B. Once the geographical unit for which a representative is to be chosen is designated, all who participate in the election are to have an equal vote—

---

[55] *Congressional Quarterly Weekly Report*, December 27, 1963, pp. 2258–2264 and *National Civic Review*, May, 1964, pp. 259–262. For discussions of apportionment after the *Baker* v. *Carr* decision, see Robert G. Dixon, Jr., "Legislative Apportionment and the Federal Constitution," *Law and Contemporary Problems*, Summer, 1962, pp. 329–389; Paul T. David and Ralph Eisenberg, *State Legislative Redistricting: Major Issues in the Wake of Judicial Decision* (Chicago, 1962); and Charles A. Barnett, "Reapportionment and the Courts," *State Government*, Summer, 1962, pp. 138–143.

[56] 373 U. S. 368 (1963).

[57] 377 U. S. 533 (1964).

[58] *Ibid.*, at 562.

whatever their race, whatever their sex, whatever their occupation, whatever their income, and wherever their home may be in that geographical unit.[59]

C. Diluting the weight of votes because of place of residence impairs basic constitutional rights under the 14th Amendment just as much as individual discriminations based upon such factors as race. . . .

D. A nation once primarily rural in character becomes predominantly urban. Representation schemes once fair and equitable become archaic and outdated. But the basic principle of representative government remains, and must remain, unchanged—the weight of a citizen's vote cannot be made to depend on where he lives.[60]

'Nag, Nag! That's all you and the
Supreme Court ever do!'

SOURCE: Paul Conrad in the *Los Angeles Times;* reprinted in *The Minneapolis Tribune,* July 28, 1964.

[59] *Gray* v. *Sanders,* 373 U. S. 368, at 379 cited in *Reynolds* v. *Sims.*
[60] 377 U. S. 533, at 566, 567.

Alabama's effort to justify its pattern of representation under which each of the state's sixty-seven counties was allotted one senatorial seat by analogy to the United States Senate where each state is given two votes was declared "inapposite and irrelevant."

> Political subdivisions of states—counties, cities or whatever—never were and never have been considered as sovereign entities. Rather, they have been traditionally regarded as subordinate governmental instrumentalities created by the state to assist in the carrying out of state government functions.[61]

The essential function of bicameralism, according to the Chief Justice, "is to insure mature and deliberate consideration of, and to prevent precipitate action on, proposed legislative measures." This thoroughly worthwhile objective may be attained by having one chamber composed of single-member districts and the other of multi-member districts, or "one house could be arranged so as to balance off minor inequities in the representation of certain areas in the other house." What is fundamental, however, is that "both are apportioned substantially on a population basis." [62]

Justices Tom C. Clark, John Marshall Harlan, and Potter Stewart were the three dissenters.

Mr. Justice Harlan who dissented in all of the eight cases saw nothing in the 14th Amendment and its history to substantiate and warrant the approach taken by the Chief Justice. He rejected the notion that the Supreme Court had any right to supervise the composition of state legislatures or that there was anything in the Constitution which prevented states from selecting criteria for districting other than that of population.

> [I]t is . . . obvious . . . that people are not ciphers and that legislators can represent their electors only by speaking for their interests—economic, social, political—many of which do reflect the place where the electors live.[63]

Mr. Justice Stewart, who filed a separate dissent in the New York and Colorado cases, objected to the "arbitrary application of the 'one man, one vote' principle." He complained that

> What the Court has done is to convert a particular political philosophy into a constitutional rule, binding upon each of the 50 states . . . without regard and without respect for the many individualized and differentiated characteristics of each state . . . stemming from [its] distinct history, distinct geography, distinct distribution of population and distinct political heritage. . . . [It] forever denies to every state any opportunity . . . to accommodate within a system of representative government the interests and aspirations of diverse groups of people, without subjecting any group or class to absolute domination by a geographically concentrated or highly organized majority.[64]

While it is true that the Court did not in its ruling lay down any precise mathematical formula for deciding what constitutes a properly apportioned

[61] *Ibid.*, at 575.
[62] *Ibid.*, at 576, 577.
[63] *Ibid.*, at 623–624.
[64] 377 U. S. 713 (1964), at 748–749.

legislature, it is widely assumed that it will consider violative of the equal protection clause any legislature in which a majority can be elected by less than 40 per cent of the population. If this estimate should be accurate, no less than four-fifths of all the fifty states will be confronted with the necessity of reapportionment within the very near future.[65] For although no deadline was given, the Chief Justice did consider speedy implementation of sufficient importance to warn the states that "it would be the unusual case in which a court would be justified in not taking appropriate action to insure that no further elections are conducted under the invalid plan." [66]

As expected, legislative resentment to this landmark decision is running deep. Among the various congressional proposals to bar implementation of the court's standard for equal apportionment is that of the Senate Minority Leader, Senator Everett M. Dirksen of Illinois, granting the states a two-year delay for compliance. Even stronger proposals urge a constitutional amendment explicitly authorizing states to incorporate the area factor in either their House or Senate. The 1964 Republican party platform included a plank which would enable "states having bicameral legislatures to apportion one house on the basis of their choosing including factors other than population."

Whether a constitutional amendment embodying proposals such as these will ever receive favorable action by the required number of states is difficult to predict (as of January 1, 1965, only 16 of the necessary 34 state legislatures agreed to petition the Congress for such a constitutional amendment).[67]

There can be little doubt, however, that the demands for reapportionment which grew out of the various Supreme Court decisions already constitute a most serious challenge to many of the state party systems. Whether or not state legislatures operate with "disciplined" or "undisciplined" caucuses, whether or not interparty relationships are competitive, or whether or not party voting cohesion is significant—the essence of political parties is to build broad electoral coalitions of support which tend to minimize the divisive and maximize the consensus. To the degree to which urban areas will now be pitted against rural areas, and suburb against core city, the task of parties becomes more onerous. Reapportionment affects the selection of legislative candidates, the formation of issues, the source of votes, the composition of committees and the general make-up of the legislature. Present positions of legislative leadership and privilege are threatened as the formerly underrepresented areas gain in power, and as newer interests assert their influence. Most battles for reapportionment sharpen what most parties wish to avoid—an

[65] Anthony Lewis, "Districts Ruling Shocks Capital," *The New York Times*, June 17, 1964, p. 29. On measuring legislative malapportionment, see Alan L. Clem, "Measuring Legislative Malapportionment: In Search of a Better Yardstick," *Midwest Journal of Political Science*, May, 1963, pp. 125–144 and Glendon Schubert and Charles Press, "Measuring Malapportionment," *American Political Science Review*, June, 1964, pp. 302–327.

[66] 377 U. S. 533, at 585.

[67] *The New York Times*, December 28, 1964, p. 24; a year end, state-by-state survey of the apportionment situation in each of the states can be found in this issue.

internecine warfare which turns brother against brother at the expense of party harmony and effectiveness. Fortunately for the preservation of a viable major party system, in most of the states neither the Democrats nor the Republicans can ever be too certain of the legislative prospects of a particular reapportionment proposal or of the electoral consequences of a particular reapportionment scheme. Complexity in the state lawmaking process, high population mobility, and the presence of a considerable number of unknown variables all combine to make apparent the need for reasonably sound compromises. While these might weaken one of the parties in one part of the state, they will not be so radical as to obliterate that party politically in all parts of the state.

CASE PROBLEMS FOR CLASS DISCUSSION

1. If you wish to determine the extent of party discipline in your legislature, which issues would you elect as significantly indicative of party alignment? How would you find the index of party cohesion? What qualifications or limitations would you have to add to your statistical findings?
2. As a member of your legislative research committee, you have the responsibility of drawing up a lobby registration law. Would your definition of "lobbyist" include: departmental spokesmen seeking legislative appropriations and support, representatives of church social action committees pleading for higher ethical standards in government, local school board officials asking for an increase in state aids? Would your proposal hold lobbyists personally liable for misrepresentations before legislative committees?
3. Assume that the electors of your state will have to cast their ballots on a referendum outlawing the sale of liquor by any establishment within a five-mile radius of all state highways. As an expert on state politics you have been retained by an important public relations firm which includes among its accounts the leading liquor distributors in the state. You are now in the process of preparing a memorandum which is to be presented to an upcoming "strategy" meeting. What are some of the central decisions that would have to be made very early in the campaign to defeat the referendum? What would be your suggestions with respect to the organization of the campaign? What should be the approach to the various business, social, and political interest groups in the state?
4. You have been requested to draw up a reapportionment plan for your state legislature in which a majority of the electorate can elect a majority of the members in both House and Senate. Would this require the creation of multiple-member districts? Would some of the single-member districts have to exceed variations of more than 15 per cent from the statewide standard? Would district lines have to cut across counties, municipalities, or across certain geographic entities?

SELECTED BIBLIOGRAPHY

RAYMOND V. ANDERSON, "The Operation of the Initiative, Referendum and Recall in North Dakota," unpublished Ph.D. dissertation, University of Minnesota, 1962.

ALFRED BANDZA, "An Analysis of the Electoral Response to the Initiative and Referendum in North Dakota, 1918–1960," unpublished M.A. thesis, University of North Dakota, 1963.

TWILEY W. BARKER, JR., "A Long, Long Ballot," National Civic Review, April, 1964, pp. 170–175.

WILLIAM V. CHAPPELL, JR., "Florida's Hot Struggle," National Civic Review, April, 1964, pp. 188–193.

RICHARD S. CHILDS (ed.), Compendium on Legislative Apportionment (New York, 1962).

"Conflicts of Interest of State Legislators," *Harvard Law Review*, April, 1963, pp. 1209–1232.

WILDER W. CRANE, JR., "A Test of Effectiveness of Interest Group Pressures on Legislators," *Southwestern Social Science Quarterly*, December, 1960, pp. 335–340.

WALTER D. DEVRIES, "The Michigan Lobbyist: A Study in the Bases and Perceptions of Effectiveness," unpublished Ph.D. dissertation, Michigan State University, 1960.

ROBERT G. DIXON, JR., "Representation Goals," *National Civic Review*, November, 1963, pp. 543–547.

RALPH EISENBERG, "Power of Rural Vote," *National Civic Review*, October, 1962, pp. 489–492, 530.

WAYNE L. FRANCIS, "Influence and Interaction in a State Legislative Body," *American Political Science Review*, December, 1962, pp. 953–960.

ROBERT S. FRIEDMAN, "Reapportionment Myth," *National Civil Review*, April, 1960, pp. 184–188.

JOHN F. GALLAGHER, "Apportionment in California Counties," *State Government*, Winter, 1964, pp. 36–41.

SLADE GORTON, "New Methods Urged," *National Civic Review*, April, 1964, pp. 176–181.

HOWARD D. HAMILTON, "Consensus or Tyranny?" *National Civic Review*, May, 1964, pp. 244–248, 263.

ROYCE HANSON, "Fight for Fair Play," *National Civic Review*, February, 1961, pp. 70–75.

WILLIAM C. HAVARD and LOREN P. BETH, *The Politics of Mis-Representation* (Baton Rouge, 1962).

FREDERICK C. IRION, *Reapportionment and Districting in New Mexico* (Albuquerque, 1963).

JAMES E. LARSON, *Reapportionment and the Courts* (University, Alabama, 1962).

FRANK P. MAGGIO, "Lobbying—Multi-State Statutory Survey—Requirements and Procedures for Lobbying Activities," *Notre Dame Lawyer*, December, 1962, pp. 79–88.

R. P. MALONEY, "Easy Does It!" *National Civic Review*, May, 1964, pp. 239–243.

NORMAN MELLER, "Legislative Behavior Research," *Western Political Quarterly*, March, 1960, pp. 131–153.

SAMUEL C. PATTERSON, "The Role of the Deviant in the State Legislative System: The Wisconsin Assembly," *Western Political Quarterly*, June, 1961, pp. 460–472.

SAMUEL C. PATTERSON and ROBERT S. WALKER, "The Role of the Lobbyist: The Case of Oklahoma," *Journal of Politics*, February, 1963, pp. 72–92.

NOEL PERRIN, "In Defense of Country Votes," *The Yale Review*, Autumn, 1962, pp. 16–24.

ROBERT J. PITCHELL, "Reapportionment as a Control of Voting in California," *Western Political Quarterly*, March, 1961, pp. 214–235.

JOSEPH C. PRAY and GEORGE J. MAUER, *The New Perspective of Legislative Apportionment in Oklahoma* (Norman, 1962).

JOHN S. RADABAUGH, "Tendencies of California Direct Legislation," *Southwestern Social Science Quarterly*, June, 1961, pp. 66–78.

ERNEST C. REOCK, JR., "Measuring Compactness as a Requirement of Legislative Apportionment," *Midwest Journal of Political Science*, February, 1961, pp. 70–74.

WILLIAM R. ROSS, *House of Delegates Apportionment in West Virginia* (Morgantown, 1961).

RUTH C. SILVA, "Making Votes Count," *National Civic Review*, October, 1963, pp. 489–492.

RUTH C. SILVA and WILLIAM J. D. BOYD (comps.), *Selected Bibliography on Legislative Apportionment and Districting* (New York, 1963).

WILLIAM A. STEIGER, "Form or Substance?" *National Civic Review*, April, 1964, pp. 182–187.

GUS TYLER, "Court Versus Legislature," *Law and Contemporary Problems*, Summer, 1962, pp. 390–407.

JOHN C. WAHLKE, WILLIAM BUCHANAN, HEINZ EULAU, and LEROY C. FERGUSON, "American State Legislators' Role Orientations Toward Pressure Groups," *Journal of Politics*, May, 1960, pp. 203–227.

JOHN C. WAHLKE, HEINZ EULAU, WILLIAM BUCHANAN, and LEROY C. FERGUSON, *The Legislative System: Explorations in Legislative Behavior* (New York, 1962).

JOHN P. WHEELER and JOHN E. BEBOUT, "After Reapportionment," *National Civic Review*, May, 1962, pp. 246–250, 262.

⮤ Chapter V

THE EXECUTIVE

What do governors do and how do they try to lead their legislatures, their administrators, their party, and the public?

Are there too many elected state executive officers—should the ballot be shortened and some of these positions made appointive?

For many years the road from the state executive mansion to the White House seemed the most direct when compared to the steppingstone qualities of other state or national offices.

To men with imagination, competence, leadership, perseverance, and a keen sense and love for political power, there is much in a governorship that lends itself to building a public image that might just turn a gubernatorial into a presidential dream. Men like Woodrow Wilson and Franklin D. Roosevelt made it on their first attempt; others like Charles Evans Hughes, James M. Cox, Alfred E. Smith, Alfred Landon, Thomas E. Dewey, and Adlai E. Stevenson had to be content with a mere nomination (or two). Theodore Roosevelt and Calvin Coolidge did have the experience of a governorship behind them, but reached the presidency initially through succession from the vice-presidency.

This favored approach from the governorship to the presidency may now appear somewhat overshadowed by the prominence of such senators as Kennedy, Johnson, Kefauver, Humphrey, Nixon, and Goldwater. These men found the Senate chamber to be a forum peculiarly suitable for attracting public attention to the most crucial issues of domestic and foreign policy. Moreover, in this arena senators rather than governors were making the ultimate decisions.

But neither President Johnson nor the other senators could ever completely ignore the governors from the populous states of the East and West; and these states will continue to offer ambitious and able governors whose talents the nation will wish to utilize for its highest elective office simply because a governorship if for no other reason is an excellent training ground for executive leadership.

Constitutional and political realities in most of the states have by design sought to minimize strong gubernatorial leadership and maximize legislative independence and power. Executive powers are divided between the governor and the major elective officers of the state—attorney general, secretary of state, treasurer, auditor, and others. In place of departments headed by one person, there are a multitude of boards or commissions with membership drawn from more than one party and with terms overlapping and rarely coextensive with that of the governor. Power corrupts, it is asserted, but does the absence of power denote either administrative efficiency or justice? If not leadership, can a governor exercise sufficient administrative supervision to assure the speedy and fair carrying-out of existing laws in an executive branch where diffusion of power is accompanied by clouded channels of communication and accountability?

The people can judge. Let them elect these major offices of state; it will increase their political interest and involvement; it will make certain that ambitious governors will not build machines geared to their personal aggrandizement and insensitive to popular scrutiny and criticism. If two heads are better than one, why not apply this to the business of state and make sure that decisions affecting thousands will be given careful consideration and will protect the minority interests? As a result of this thinking, ballots have grown longer, voters have become more confused, administrative efficiency has been sacrificed and governmental costs have increased correspondingly.

To be discussed in the following pages will be some of the powers that governors have and can use in their multiple roles as chief executives, as party leaders, as administrators, and as innovators of legislation. What will also become apparent are some of the stubborn problems and obstacles encountered as strong governors wrestle with equally strong or even stronger legislatures about the how and why of their most cherished legislative programs and objectives.

GOVERNORS NOW IN OFFICE—A PROFILE

The "typical" state governor today is a lawyer, married, the father of two or three children, a Methodist, between forty and fifty years of age, a veteran of World War II, and a native of his state. As to his political affiliation, he is either a Democrat or a Republican—the last significant third party having merged with the Democrats in 1944, the Democratic-Farmer-Labor Party of Minnesota.[1]

When the polls closed in the 1964 election, which had included contests for twenty-five governorships (see Figure 1), the voters had returned to office twelve incumbents—nine Democrats: Faubus (Arkansas), Kerner (Illinois), Hughes (Iowa), Morrison (Nebraska), King (New Hampshire), Campbell (New Mexico), Guy (North Dakota), Connally (Texas), and Hoff (Vermont); and three Republicans: Romney (Michigan), Babcock (Montana), and Chafee (Rhode Island).

Seventeen of the twenty-five contests resulted in victory for the Democrats bringing that party's 1965 national total to thirty-three, one less than before the election. Although the Democrats had won from the Republicans the governorships of Arizona (Sam Goddard defeated Richard Kleindienst)

[1] For a profile study of the governors of the 1950's, see Samuel R. Solomon, "Governors: 1950–1960," *National Civic Review*, September, 1960, pp. 410–416.

and of Utah (Calvin L. Rampton defeated Mitchell Melich), Democrats lost to the Republicans the governorships of Massachusetts, Washington, and Wisconsin.

Thirteen of the victorious candidates that comprised the "class of 1964" were not incumbents. Of this group five held no elective office before their election as governor; six came directly from legislative service; none from law enforcement positions; and three held an elective statewide office such as auditor, attorney general, or lieutenant governor. The newly-elected governor of Massachusetts, John Anthony Volpe, a construction company executive and one-time federal roads administrator in the Eisenhower Administration, had served as governor between 1960 and 1962 when he was narrowly defeated by Endicott Peabody. Florida's new governor, Haydon Burns, had served as mayor of Jacksonville for five terms—the longest tenure in that city's history.

FIGURE 1

DEMOCRATIC GOVERNORSHIPS   REPUBLICAN GOVERNORSHIPS

* INDICATES PARTY SWITCH IN 1964

GOVERNORS FOR 1965

SOURCE: *Congressional Quarterly Weekly Report*, November 6, 1964, p. 2637.

In terms of their previous office experience the "class of 1964" conforms quite closely to the normal pattern. In a study of all governors elected between 1870 and 1950, "promotion" from a statewide elective office to the governor-

TABLE 1. GOVERNORS–1965: YEARS OF EXPERIENCE IN PUBLIC OFFICE PRIOR TO ELECTION

State	Governor	Post prior to election	Local gov't.	State gov't. Ex-Adm.	Leg.	Jud.	Nat'l. gov't. Adm.	Leg.	Jud.	Total
na	Wallace(D)	Attorney		2	6	6				14
	Egan(D)	Terr. Sen.			14			2		16
a	Goddard(D)	Dem. State Chmn.								0
as	Faubus(D)	Editor	8	4						12
nia	Brown(D)	Atty. Gen.	8	8						16
do	Love(R)	Attorney								0
ticut	Dempsey(D)	Lt. Gov.	15	6	6					27
re	Terry(D)	Chief Justice			4	26				30
	Burns(D)	Mayor	10							10
a	Sanders(D)	State Sen.			8					8
	Burns(D)	Businessman						3		3
	Smylie(R)	Atty. Gen.		8						8
	Kerner(D)	County Judge	7				7			14
a	Branigin(D)	Bus. & Law								0
	Hughes(D)	Commerce Comr.		4						4
	Avery(R)	Farmer				4		10		14
ky	Breathitt(D)	Pub. Serv. Comr.		4	6					10
na	Davis(D)	Pub. Serv. Comr.	4	2						6
	Reed(R)	State Sen.				7				7
nd	Tawes(D)	St. Compt.		16						16
husetts	Volpe(R)	Businessman		2			1			3
an	Romney(R)	Businessman								0
ota	Rolvaag(D)	Lt. Gov.		8						8
ippi	Johnson(D)	Lt. Gov.		4						4
ri	Hearnes(D)	Sec. of State		4				10		14
a	Babcock(R)	Lt. Gov.		1	8					9
xa	Morrison(D)	Attorney	8							8
	Sawyer(D)	County Atty.	9							9
ampshire	King(D)	State Rep.			6					6
rsey	Hughes(D)	Attorney	4			6	6			16
exico	Campbell(D)	House Speaker			8					8
rk	Rockefeller(R)	Businessman					11			11
Carolina	Moore(D)	Lawyer				8				8
Dakota	Guy(D)	State Rep.			2					2
	Rhodes(R)	State Auditor	12	10						22
na	Bellmon(R)	Farmer			2					2
	Hatfield(R)	Sec. of State		2	6					8
vania	Scranton(R)	Congressman					1	2		3
island	Chafee(R)	State Rep.			6					6
Carolina	Russell(D)	Attorney					5			5
Dakota	Boe(R)	Lt. Gov.		2	8					10
ee	Clement(D)	Attorney		5						5
	Connally(D)	Sec. of Navy					2			2
	Rampton(D)	Attorney								0
t	Hoff(D)	State Rep.			2					2
	Harrison(D)	Atty. Gen.		4	10					14
gton	Evans(R)	Engineer			8					8
rginia	Smith(D)	Businessman		2						2
in	Knowles(R)	Lt. Gov.		6	14					20
g	Hansen(R)	Banker								0

ship was found to be the "most clearly defined" path.[2] For a summary of the previous experience of governors in office in January, 1965, see Tables 1 and 2.

Tables 3, 4, and 5 reveal something about the political background against which the "classes of 1960, 1962, and 1964" were elected and give eloquent testimony of the ticket-splitting habits of American voters. For example, in 1960 five Democrats were elected to governorships in states that

TABLE 2. GOVERNORS–1965: SUMMARY OF EXPERIENCE
IN PUBLIC OFFICE PRIOR TO ELECTION

Type of experience	Number of governors
Local Government	11
State Legislative	21
State Executive-Administrative	21
State Judicial	4
National Legislative	4
National Administrative	7
National Judicial	0

TABLE 3. TICKET-SPLITTING IN 1960

State	Governor	Legislature		Presidential choice
		House	Senate	
Arizona	R	D	D	R
Florida	D	D	D	R
Illinois	D	R	R	D
Indiana	D	R	D	R
Massachusetts	R	D	D	D
Michigan	D	R	R	D
Minnesota	R	Lib.	Cons.	D
Mississippi	D	D	D	Other
Montana	R	R	D	R
New Mexico	R	D	D	R
North Dakota	D	R	R	R
Utah	R	D	D	R
Washington	D	D	D	R
Wisconsin	D	R	R	R

gave their presidential ballots to Mr. Nixon while two Republicans won in states that went for Mr. Kennedy. Politically "loneliest" Democrats were Governors Guy of North Dakota and Nelson of Wisconsin whose states went for Nixon and whose legislatures were also under Republican control.

On the other hand, a Republican who experienced political claustrophobia was Governor Volpe of Massachusetts. Not only because of Kennedy's win or because the legislature was solidly under Democratic management, but every statewide elective office—lieutenant governor, secretary of the common-

[2] Joseph A. Schlesinger, *How They Became Governor: A Study of Comparative State Politics, 1870–1950* (East Lansing, 1957), p. 16.

TABLE 4. TICKET-SPLITTING IN 1962

| State | Governor | Legislature | |
		House	Senate
Arizona	R	D	D
Connecticut	D	R	R
Iowa	D	R	R
Minnesota	D	Cons.	Cons.
Nebraska *	D		
Nevada	D	D	R
New Hampshire	D	R	R
North Dakota	D	R	R
Oklahoma	R	D	D
Oregon	R	D	D
Pennsylvania	R	D	R
Rhode Island	R	D	D
Vermont	D	R	R
Wisconsin	D	R	R

* Technically, the Nebraska one-house legislature is considered nonpartisan.

TABLE 5. TICKET-SPLITTING IN 1964

| State | Governor | Legislature | | Presidential choice |
		House	Senate	
Arizona	D	D	D	R
Kansas	R	R	R	D
Massachusetts	R	D	D	D
Michigan	R	D	D	D
Montana	R	D	D	D
New Hampshire	D	R	R	D
North Dakota	D	D	R	D
Rhode Island	R	D	D	D
South Dakota	R	R	R	D
Vermont	D	R	R	D
Washington	R	D	D	D
Wisconsin	R	D	R	D

wealth, attorney general, treasurer, and auditor—all were filled by Democrats.

As a result of the 1962 elections six Democrats occupied governorships in states where both houses of the legislature were controlled by the Republicans. Five of these six—Hughes of Iowa, Morrison of Nebraska, Guy of North Dakota, Hoff of Vermont, and Reynolds of Wisconsin—had to run their states with the assistance of elective officers from the Republican party.

Following Lyndon Johnson's landslide victory in 1964, (in which the GOP lost over five hundred legislative seats in the forty-three states where such elections were held) the "loneliest" Republicans must be Governors Volpe of Massachusetts, Romney of Michigan, Babcock of Montana, Chafee of Rhode Island, and Evans of Washington—all are confronted by legislatures in which the Democrats control both House and Senate (see Table 5). Only two Democrats find themselves in similar solitude—Governors King of New

Hampshire and Hoff of Vermont, both of whom are incumbents reelected with majorities of 66.8% and 64.8% respectively.

Although Johnson carried Michigan by over one million votes, Governor Romney won reelection with 56.3% and while Senator Pastore and the President won handily in Rhode Island, the incumbent Republican Governor John H. Chafee was returned by the voters with 61.3%. Similar splits occurred in Massachusetts, Washington, and Wisconsin, where voters favored a Democratic president and a Republican governor.

Thus ticket-splitting is deeply entrenched in American politics. Some of the implications of these voting patterns for legislative policy, state administration and party organization should become apparent throughout this chapter.

GOVERNORS—THEIR QUALIFICATIONS, TERMS, AND SALARIES

In the majority of the states thirty is the minimum age for gubernatorial eligibility. Oklahoma specifies thirty-one; Hawaii, thirty-five; four states, twenty-five (Arizona, California, Minnesota, and Nevada); and the rest omit any constitutional age requirement implying that being a qualified voter denotes the right age for becoming governor. South Carolina declares ineligible any person "who denies the existence of a Supreme Being."

Among the residence requirements, eight states provide for a two-year period, fifteen states for a five-year period, and five for a seven-year period. All in all, the variations run from a one-year minimum in Minnesota to a ten-year maximum in Missouri. In thirty-seven states governors now have a four-year term of office; however, in twenty-two of them, there is a two-year limitation or a prohibition against a governor succeeding himself. Two-year terms are found in the remaining states but even these short terms are further restricted in South Dakota and New Mexico where they are constitutionally held to a maximum of two consecutive terms. That an absence of formal restrictions may occasionally invite record tenures is illustrated by Michigan where Governor Williams won six terms (1948–1960) and by Arkansas where Governor Faubus was elected to his sixth consecutive term in 1964.

Salaries for most governors fall into the $15,000–$25,000 range. New York pays $50,000; California, $44,100; Massachusetts, New Jersey, and Pennsylvania, $35,000; and Illinois, $30,000. This figure does not include additional allowances for travel and maintenance of an executive mansion. Some of the states in the lower salary ranges have become increasingly conscious of the inadequacy of their pay scales for the responsibilities commensurate with the office. Utah recently raised its governor's pay from $13,000 to $15,000; Idaho from $12,500 to $15,000; Indiana from $15,000 to $25,000; Wyoming from $15,000 to $20,000. When Washington raised the salary of its governor from $15,000 to $22,500, Governor Rosellini (D) vetoed the measure, but the legislature overrode his objections. "The position itself is worth $22,500," one of the GOP legislators was quoted as saying, "even if the man is not." [3]

WHAT GOVERNORS DO—AN OVERVIEW

Governor Rockefeller issued an executive order providing for a Code of Fair Campaign practices applicable to the executive branch of New York State government. Governor Otto Kerner spoke at a women's luncheon on recent legislative developments in Illinois. Governor John A. Love of Colorado, with legislative approval, transferred control of the Natural Resources Department to his office. Pennsylvania's Governor William W. Scranton urged the calling of a convention to revise the state's constitution. Governor George Romney proposed that the Michigan legislature enact his program of tax reform—a state (non-progressive) income tax, exemption of groceries and prescription drugs from the 4 per cent sales tax, and real estate tax relief. Mississippi's Governor Paul Johnson called a special session of the legislature to enact laws aimed at circumventing federal court orders to desegregate some Mississippi schools. Governor Mark O. Hatfield called a special session of the Oregon legislature to deal with an estimated $55 million budget deficit. In Florida, the legislature received a proposal from Governor Farris Bryant that the state cigarette tax be increased from 5 to 8 cents a pack to provide added income for cities. Iowa's Governor Harold Hughes created a commission on state and local government "to develop and strengthen cooperative relationships between state and local governments and between the various jurisdictions of local government." [4] Governor Karl Rolvaag of Minnesota ordered a 5 per cent cutback in state expenditures when he learned that the legislature had overestimated tax revenues for the current biennium. Governor Robert E. Smylie of Idaho recommended a change in the state's minimum wage law to make it conform with the level of the federal minimum wage law. Vermont's governor Philip H. Hoff called for modernization of the governmental organization in his state.

Governors address legislatures. They issue pardons and call emergency meetings with mayors to discuss flood damages. They may have to activate the state guard to suppress riots.[5] They urge party members to go to their precinct caucuses and county conventions. They fly to Washington in search of federal assistance for state drought victims. They instruct department heads to cut down their budgetary requests. They may appeal to the public to write to their

---

[3] *The New York Times*, May 14, 1961, p. 51.

[4] *National Civic Review*, May, 1964, p. 251.

[5] For a discussion of one governor's use of the national guard, see G. Theodore Mitau, "The Governor and the Strike," in Richard T. Frost (ed.), *Cases in State and Local Government* (Englewood Cliffs, 1961), pp. 207–218.

state representatives to support their programs on mental health or penal reform. These, then, are some of the activities and concerns of America's state governors as they assume their various roles as legislative leaders, chief executives, party heads, and spokesmen for the states.

GOVERNORS AS LEGISLATIVE LEADERS

Like a strong president, a strong governor is not satisfied with merely carrying out the laws passed by the legislature or with performing routinely the other duties given him by the constitution or devolving upon him in his capacity as chief executive. If he wishes to lead, what are the tools that he can use?

After the swearing-in ceremony is completed, the legislature assembles to hear the governor's inaugural message. If he is the incumbent or if his predecessor belonged to the same party, much of the comment will reflect favorably upon the accomplishments of the past. Aside from such standard rituals of politics, these messages outline the fiscal conditions of the state, the budgetary requirements for the future, and the governor's specific legislative recommendations. Usually special sections are devoted to such topics as administrative reorganization, law enforcement, improvement in the state's economic or industrial climate as well as such other legislative or constitutional issues to which the governor may wish to call the attention of the lawmakers.[6] Obviously these messages are important not only as inventories of the past but as a preview of things to come. They frequently do much to disclose the general tone of the new administration and the particular role that the new chief executive envisages for himself vis-à-vis the legislature and legislation.

The messages of 1963 were not devoid of their share of gubernatorial vision for progress through executive leadership. There were major requests for authority to reorganize the executive branch of government in Arizona, Georgia, Hawaii, Massachusetts, Missouri, Nevada, Oklahoma, Pennsylvania, Texas, Utah, Vermont, and Wisconsin. Constitutional amendments to permit four-year terms for the office of governor were suggested in Iowa, Massachusetts, New Mexico, and Wisconsin and to pair the offices of governor and lieutenant governor were recommended in Colorado, Hawaii, Massachusetts, and Wisconsin. Many legislatures were urged to reapportion, and the New Mexico governor requested annual sessions in place of the present biennial sessions. Reorganization of court systems was demanded in Delaware, New Hampshire, and Tennessee. Stronger provisions against corrupt and unethical practices in government were included in the messages of the governors of at least four states. Attention was called to questions of constitutional revision and for "continuity of government in event of disaster" by the governors of fourteen states. "Education received far more attention in the messages than

---

[6] See "Trends of State Government . . . as Indicated by the Governors' Messages," in each Spring issue of *State Government.*

any other public service." [7] Recommendations for highway building figured prominently in the message of the Montana governor. Greater highway safety through such devices as expanded patrols, maximum speed limits, tightened licensing systems, and mandatory chemical tests for drunken drivers was requested by the governors of thirteen states. Fifteen governors asked for greater concern and increased funds to improve mental health programs and institutions.

Tax relief for the aging, or special commissions on the problem of aging, were proposed by at least three governors. Suggestions for economic growth and industrial development included such programs as the establishment of a commission on economic expansion in Michigan, a department of state development in Nebraska, and an office of economic development in Texas. Numerous proposals were made to improve unemployment compensation and to raise the level of benefit payments and state minimum wage rates. Eleven governors expressed their state's concern for the proper control and development of water, parks, and other natural resources. The problems of juvenile delinquency were given special attention by two governors.

To pay for the increasing costs of governmental and social services, some governors were forced to suggest not merely higher but additional or new sources of revenue.[8] Different forms of income taxes were recommended by the governors of Idaho, Iowa, Massachusetts, New Mexico, Oregon, and Wisconsin, and income tax withholding was urged in California and Iowa. Additional excise taxes were recommended in Arizona, Connecticut, Idaho, Indiana, Nebraska, Oregon, Pennsylvania, Tennessee, Utah, and Wisconsin. Other than in Colorado where Governor Love suggested a 15 per cent cut in income tax obligations and a relatively minor income tax adjustment in North Carolina, nearly every other gubernatorial message was replete with recommendations for the unpopular, for digging deeper into the taxpayers' pockets, lest the "public sector" be starved.

Necessarily, this enumeration of subjects can only represent a very small proportion of the hundreds of executive proposals addressed to the 1963 legislatures. Suggestions to the 1965 legislatures reflected a similar diversity of proposals.

Also, of course, while governors may propose legislation, it is the legislature that can and does dispose of it. Just how much will actually become law depends on the interplay of such factors as the governor's statewide popularity, his personal relationship with key legislative leaders, his party's legislative strength, the degree of its discipline, his use or threatened use of the veto, his willingness to use pressures of patronage and the extent to which this is available, and his ability to mobilize and handle effectively the media of public opinion in support of his program. True, it also helps if the

[7] "Trends of State Government in 1963 as Indicated by the Governors' Messages," *State Government*, Spring, 1963, p. 82.

[8] See Leon Rothenberg, "State Budgets—1963," *State Government*, Spring, 1963, pp. 84–93.

gubernatorial program has significant elements in it that make it attractive to legislators in terms of its own merit.

Some items in this long list need to be examined further. The frequent division between legislature and executive is usually the greatest obstacle to a governor who seeks to give legislative leadership. Since 1931 governors in all but fourteen states have found themselves confronted with legislatures under opposition party control.[9] This tendency of the electorate to vote one party into the governorship and the other into a legislative majority greatly aggravates all of the divisiveness inherent in the separation of powers doctrine. It contributes, however, in no small measure to the frustration of program-centered party politics which some people may view as highly desirable.

Whether this ticket-splitting is caused by a built-in unwillingness of voters to give "all power" to one party, or whether reapportionment failure has put the Democrats with their urban strengths into a relatively more unfavorable position in legislatures generally, the fact is that Democratic governors more often than Republicans have been faced with hostile legislatures.

The presidential sweep of 1964 clearly reversed the picture. Following that election, eight or nearly one-half of all GOP governors found themselves confronted by legislatures in which both houses were controlled by Democrats. Included in this list were such important states as Massachusetts, Michigan, and New York. By contrast only two Democrats, Governors King of New Hampshire and Hoff of Vermont, grappled with legislatures led by Republicans.

But whether Democrat or Republican, during the period 1931–1952 in nearly half of the states in which there was any degree of party competition at all, there existed for about a third of the time open warfare between the party of the governor and the majority party of the legislature.[10]

Now governors in nearly half of such states will find one or the other house under control of the opposite party. Were party discipline genuinely severe, which as noted earlier is certainly not the case, the governors' lament would no doubt re-echo throughout the land.

The veto feared in the eighteenth century because of its "royal" associations, and at that time avoided in nearly all state constitutions, constitutes another source of gubernatorial power vis-à-vis the legislature. Forty-nine states (North Carolina is the exception) give their governors a general veto but only forty-one permit him to veto items in appropriation bills (in actuality, it is rarely used), and three states authorize their governors not only to reject items but to reduce them. Also some of the states have strong veto provisions and others have weak ones. What makes one veto provision effective and the other not depends on such variables as the number of days that a governor may be permitted to hold a bill before vetoing it, the type of legislative

[9] Malcolm E. Jewell, *The State Legislature: Politics and Practice* (New York, 1962), p. 15.
[10] V. O. Key, Jr., *American State Politics: An Introduction* (New York, 1956), p. 55.

majority required to override it, and the opportunity afforded a governor for holding a measure and pocket-vetoing it after the legislature has adjourned. Generally, how effective has the veto power been? Careful analysis has shown that,

First, the gubernatorial veto has been strengthened over the years by more states giving their governors both pocket and item vetoes and by lengthening the time given them to consider measures after formal presentation;

Second, the number of bills passed over a governor's veto has decreased continuously to the point where it represents a fraction of one per cent. For example, in the course of nearly one-half century only thirty-eight vetoes were overridden in Alabama, twenty-eight in California, thirteen in Michigan, and one in Pennsylvania.[11] Thus the veto or its threatened use, although in essence more of a negative than a positive device, represents very much of a weapon in the arsenal of gubernatorial leadership.

Does a governor's power of appointment when based largely on the principles of patronage—rewards for party loyalty and effort—help in obtaining favorable legislative action for his program? At first glance there appears to be a considerable opportunity for a governor to place his political friends or, more important here, a legislator's friend into public office. Most states permit the governors to appoint judges or to fill judicial vacancies pending an election. Beyond this, the power of appointment extends to positions on numerous state administrative bureaus, boards, agencies, commissions, councils, and committees as well as notaries public and the state guard. For upper-echelon appointments, senatorial confirmation is usually required and given without much obstruction. Yet legislatures reinforced by popular fears that a governor might become "too ambitious" or too powerful have built significant obstacles to the effective exercise of patronage.[12] These have taken various forms. Statutes may specify that boards shall have bipartisan representation, that public officials may not be removed except for cause, that applicants for certain positions must have certain qualifications, and that boards and not the governor are to appoint the functional directors or department heads. This last qualification is used widely in administrative agencies concerned with education, health, welfare, taxation, and highways.

Civil service reform movements also have sought to clip the governors' patronage powers. Protection of employees against political reprisals and a job tenure resistant to the shifting political winds have long been part of their sacred writ. Still the careful use of patronage has always had its defenders and

[11] Frank W. Prescott, "The Executive Veto in American States," *Western Political Quarterly*, March, 1950, p. 104.

[12] For a recent case study of the use of patronage by the governor of one state, see Daniel P. Moynihan and James Q. Wilson, "Patronage in New York State, 1955–1959," *American Political Science Review*, June, 1964, pp. 286–301. See also Frank J. Sorauf, "State Patronage in a Rural County," *American Political Science Review*, December, 1956, pp. 1046–56; James Q. Wilson, "The Economy of Patronage," *The Journal of Political Economy*, August, 1961, pp. 369–380; and Frank J. Sorauf, "Patronage and Party," *Midwest Journal of Political Science*, May, 1959, pp. 115–126.

even "reformers" are beginning to wonder whether the emphasis upon the politically antiseptic civil servant may not have gone too far. A second sober look might reveal that with ever-shrinking patronage governors are deprived of an important source of eager, devoted, and at the same time thoroughly competent party men who have labored hard to build the political foundation for their program in precinct and caucus.

Beyond veto and patronage there are still many less formal sets of influences inherent in his office that a governor who is at all adept at politics can bring to bear upon a reluctant legislature. As head of the administration there are important discretionary powers which only he or his appointees may exercise in filling in the numerous details that a legislature must necessarily leave to executive discretion. Laws can only constitute the framework of social policy. Administrators must work out the implementing rules, the specific provisions which by their very specificity will affect the citizen in his day-to-day relationships to the law. Legislators running errands for their constituents will soon discover that a friendly governor can be of immense value. Governors may need legislative support, but legislators also will appreciate a mutually beneficial relationship, a *quid pro quo,* in which a call from the governor's office might accelerate action on a tardy relief payment, insure a prisoner's transfer to another institution, arrange for the review of a highway department's financial award, or result in background information immensely useful in a forthcoming tax committee meeting.

Incomparably more persuasive than the veto or some of the other leadership devices is the ability of a governor to marshal the forces of public opinion, to enthuse his audiences, to dramatize his program and to convince the public to become a "people's lobby." Issues are then reduced to their simplest expression. It is the governor, symbol of all the people, versus the legislature, subservient to local pressures, petty considerations, and selfish interests and this is how the following governors phrased it: G. Mennen Williams of Michigan, Franklin D. Roosevelt and Al Smith of New York, Earl Warren of California, Robert LaFollette of Wisconsin, Luther Youngdahl and Harold Stassen of Minnesota, and Huey Long of Louisiana, Republicans, Democrats, and Progressives—strong governors all.

And the legislators fought back. They assailed the governors for not understanding their constituents, for not appreciating the problems of the farmer, the businessman, the private utility; for wanting power and expanding the bureaucracy; for using the state and the office to build themselves a platform for national office. They castigated them for running for the presidency and caring little for the taxpayers of the state. But when the votes were counted after the battle had run its course, these governors won not all that they had asked for but enough to write into law substantial segments of the program they had championed so vigorously. They had traveled thousands of miles, given hundred of speeches, shaken hands from morning till night, pleaded their cause, worked their deals, threatened the opposition, promised victory, and driven themselves relentlessly as if possessed.

GOVERNORS AS CHIEF EXECUTIVES

Myth and reality are the key words in this discussion. Somehow Americans think of a governor as a chief executive in fact as well as in theory. They think of him as the one upon whose shoulders rests the enforcement of all the laws that affect them and as the one to whom to address all the protests that arise from the faulty, overzealous, or inefficient administration of the laws. In reality all of the governors except those of Alaska (see Figure 2), Hawaii, Michigan, and New Jersey (see Figure 3) are much to their annoyance and regret far from being able to exert direction of their executive establishments.[13] They must share their powers with at least four different types of agencies or persons. (For a typical chart of one state's executive branch, see Figure 4.)

(1) Nearly all states have in addition to the governor a number of elective officers specifically provided for in the constitution. Customarily this includes the lieutenant governor, secretary of state, attorney general, treasurer, and auditor. Some of these individuals may actually be members of the party opposing the governor and look impatiently to the day when they might themselves be able to ascend to the governorship.

(2) Departments established by statute may be headed by officials whose terms of office may not be coextensive with that of the governor. This means that an incoming governor may find a tax commissioner or a labor commissioner appointed by his predecessor who had initiated or supported policies that the new governor campaigned against.

(3) Multi-headed agencies created by statute or by the constitution include memberships with overlapping terms. A governor will have some appointments but may find himself opposed by the remaining majority.

(4) Lastly, in each state there are some offices, commissions, or boards, the personnel of which are designated by the legislature. Although these agencies or individuals may have functions of an executive character, they owe no accountability to the governor. For example, in South Carolina the legislature elects the public utility commissioner; in Maine, the secretary of state, auditor, treasurer, attorney general and commissioner of agriculture; and in New Hampshire, the secretary of state and treasurer.

Other than sharing executive power with officials not responsible to them and being held politically liable for their actions, governors have found the sheer diffusion and size of the administrative apparatus to represent an even more difficult obstacle to their leadership. As state governments increased their activities in response to demands for special services and economic regulation growing out of the needs of industrialization, urbanization, and depressions, new offices were established, lines of accountability became blurred, and jurisdictions overlapped. It is difficult or nearly impossible for governors to personally supervise and direct effectively an administrative establishment

[13] For two points of view on the issue of the "strong governorship," see Sherrill D. Luke, "The Need for Strength," *National Civic Review*, March, 1964, pp. 126–130 and Samuel K. Gove, "Why Strong Governors?" *National Civic Review*, March, 1964, pp. 131–136.

FIGURE 2

ALASKA STATE GOVERNMENT

ORGANIZATION OF THE EXECUTIVE BRANCH

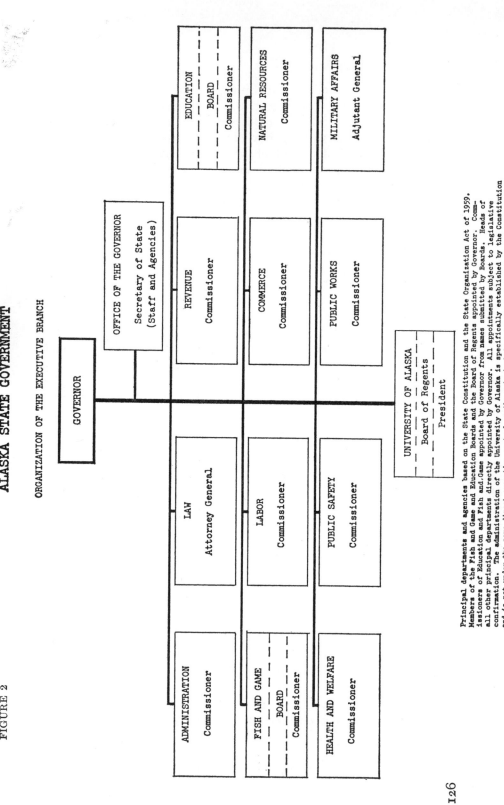

Principal departments and agencies based on the State Constitution and the State Organization Act of 1959.
Members of the Fish and Game and Education Boards and the Board of Regents appointed by Governor. Commissioners of Education and Fish and Game appointed by Governor from names submitted by Boards. Heads of
all other principal departments directly appointed by Governor. All appointments subject to legislative
confirmation. The administration of the University of Alaska is specifically established by the Constitution
and is not under the same direct executive control as the principal departments included here.

Prepared by the Alaska Legislative Council, June, 1959

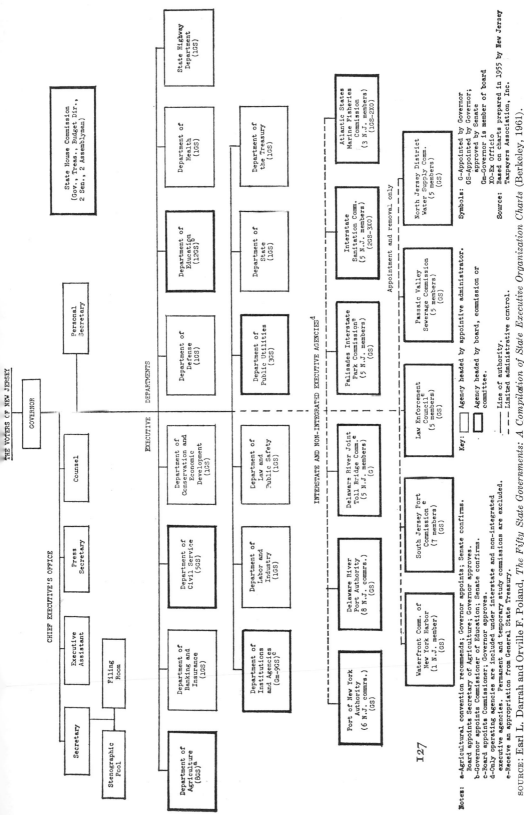

Notes: a—Agricultural convention recommends; Governor appoints; Senate confirms.
Board appoints Secretary of Agriculture; Governor approves.
b—Governor appoints Commissioner of Education; Senate confirms.
c—Board appoints Commissioner; Governor approves.
d—Only operating agencies are included under interstate and non-integrated executive agencies. Permanent and temporary study commissions are excluded.
e—Receive an appropriation from General State Treasury.

SOURCE: Earl L. Darrah and Orville F. Poland, *The Fifty State Governments: A Compilation of State Executive Organization Charts* (Berkeley, 1961).

| | ATTORNEY GENERAL | | SECRETARY OF STATE | | GOVERNO |

Functional Area	Administration	Agriculture	Commerce	Conservation	Educatio
ELECTIVE OFFICIALS	Attorney General Secretary of State State Auditor State Treasurer		Railroad and Warehouse Comm. Secretary of State		
ADMINIS- TRATIVE DEPTS.	Dept. of Administration Dept. of the Public Examiner	Dept. of Agriculture, Dairy and Food	Dept. of Aeronautics Dept. of Business Development Commissioner of Iron Range Resources and Rehabilitation Div. of Banking Div. of Insurance Div. of Securities	Dept. of Conservation Surveyor General of Logs and Lumber	
ADMINIS- TRATIVE BOARDS	Archives Comm. Bd. of Investment Civil Service Bd. Municipal Comm. State Employees' Retirement Assn. Veterans' Service Bldg. Comm.	Livestock Sanitary Bd. Soil Conservation Comm.	Compensation Insurance Bd. Athletic Comm.	Game Wardens' Retirement Assn. Water Resources Bd.	State Bd. of Education State College Teachers' Retirement Assn.
POLICY BOARDS, COMMIS- SIONS & COM- MITTEES	Executive Council Publication Bd. Canvassing Bd. Comm. on Uniform State Laws Voting Machine Comm. Employees' Insurance Bd. Employees' Merit Award Bd.	Bd. of Grain Appeals Poultry Improvement Bd.	Great Lakes Comm. Great Lakes St. Lawrence Tidewater Comm. Tri-State Waters Comm. Upper Mississippi and St. Croix Improvement Comm. Iron Range Resources and Rehabilitation Comm.	Geographic Bd. Land Exchange Comm. Land Use Comm. So. Dakota– Minn. Boundary Water Comm. State Mapping Advisory Bd.	School Loan Committee
EXAMINING & LICENSING BOARDS		Veterinary Examining Bd.	Accountancy Abstractors Architects, Engineers and Land Surveyors Barber Electricity Hairdressing and Beauty Culture Watchmaking		
INDEPEND- ENT OR SEMI-STATE AGENCIES		State Agricultural Society State Horticultural Society			State Art Soc State Histori Society University of Minnesota

SOURCE: Earl L. Darrah and Orville F. Poland, *The Fifty State Governments: A Compilation of State Executive Organiz*

STATE AUDITOR   STATE TREASURER

'Health	Highways	Labor	Public Safety	Taxation	Welfare
			Attorney General	Secretary of State State Treasurer	
	Dept. of Highways	Dept. of Employment Security Div. of Conciliation	Civil Defense Agency Bur. of Criminal Apprehension Liquor Control Commissioner ¦ Dept. of Military Affairs	Dept. of Taxation	Dept. of Corrections Dept. of Public Welfare Dept. of Veterans' Affairs
e Bd. of lth er Pollution trol Comm.	Highway Patrolmen's Retirement Assn.	Industrial Comm.	Armory Building Comm.	Bd. of Tax Appeals	Governor's Human Rights Comm. Soldiers' Home Bd. Fair Employment Practices Comm.
	Historic Sites and Markers Comm.			Equalization Aid Review Committee	Bd. of Pardons
c Sciences opody opractic tal lical sing ometry opathy rmacy chologists			Society for the Prevention of Cruelty		

comprising, to mention a few illustrations, 177 units with 676 individual positions as in Massachusetts, or 106 departments and independent committees or agencies as in New York, or 363 boards or commissions as in California, or 117 separate officials, departments, or commissions as in Montana, or 135 units as in Texas. Despite these examples and others that could be shown, state governorships have already been significantly strengthened during the last generation. Ballots have become shorter (as in New Jersey and Michigan) and gubernatorial terms longer. Through wider use of the executive budget, governors have been able to offer legislatures an integrated fiscal program in support of the substantive programs they wished to see enacted into law. Collating departmental requests gave to the chief executive important controls over departments and their functions.[14] More and more states have moved in the direction of creating departments of administration whose heads are directly responsible to the governor and who assist him in the preparation of budgets and the tasks of overall administrative supervision. Purchasing and personnel management have become more centralized and the single-headed and consolidated agency has increasingly taken the place of separate and multiheaded boards, commissions, and committees.[15]

Most of these developments in administrative reorganization were based on certain canons strongly advocated by the Council of State Governments. Here are a few of these principles:

A. Consolidate all administrative agencies into a small number of departments (usually ten to twenty) organized by function. Functional consolidation will eliminate costly overlapping and duplication, settle questions of uncertain authority and responsibility, and encourage intelligent, thorough performance of related functions.

B. Establish clear lines of authority running from the governor at the top of the hierarchy through the entire organization. The governor's authority over the organization can be implemented in several ways:

    1. Shorten the ballot by eliminating most elective administrative officials;

    2. Give the governor powers of appointment and removal over all department heads;

    3. Round out the governor's usually vague "supreme executive power" with other specific authorities that go to make up the complete chief executive, such as the authority to require reports and to investigate any administrative activity.

C. Establish appropriate staff agencies responsible to the governor:

    1. An adequate personal office staff;

    2. A functioning cabinet, composed of department heads clearly responsible to the governor;

    3. A central budget office, with authority to prepare an executive budget;

    4. A central accounting office, with authority to prescribe an accounting system, allot appropriated funds, pre-audit expenditures;

[14] For a case study of the operation of an executive budget system in one state, see Thomas Flinn, "Governor Freeman and the Minnesota Budget," in Edwin A. Bock (ed.), *State and Local Government: A Case Book* (Birmingham, 1963).

[15] See Joe E. Nusbaum, "State Depts. of Administration: Their Role and Trends of Development," *State Government*, Spring, 1962, pp. 124–129.

    5. A central personnel office, which will link a technically sound merit system to the governor's office for purpose of over-all coordination;

    6. A central purchasing office;

    7. A planning agency to carry on research, evaluate programs in terms of general coordination, and advise the governor with respect to future needs.

  D. So far as possible, eliminate the use of boards and commissions for administrative work. Plural-headed agencies tend toward lethargy, indecision, and an undesirable diffusion of responsibility. . . .[16]

Massive reorganization programs submitted within the last few years by Governor Rockefeller in New York, Governor Hatfield of Oregon, and Governor Brown in California were built around these principles in the hope of bringing greater economy, greater efficiency, and greater responsibility into state administration. The California proposals were closely fashioned after the federal pattern of administrative reorganization in that they would allow the governor not only to submit his proposals for consolidation but actually proceed with their implementation unless the legislature were to veto them by affirmative resolution within a specified period of time.[17]

Not everyone approves of this type of administrative centralization. Some see in it an unwarranted expansion of bureaucracy under new names and new designs for essentially old purposes—the gaining of personal power. Diffusion of power may well invite inefficiency or even confusion, but is this not true also for the system of separation of powers itself? Madison strongly favored this system, because, "Ambition must be made to counteract ambition."

State legislatures as a rule have not been overly sympathetic to gubernatorial pressures for administrative reorganization. The diverse and separate bureaus and agencies have many friends both among the legislators and among interest groups throughout the state. They are not eager to see established programs and personnel jeopardized by consolidations and changes in emphasis.

Administrators are fearful that the combining of related functions may well endanger their positions, and empires may feed legislative committees inside information on the disastrous effects of the impending arrangements.

---

[16] The Council of State Governments, *Reorganizing State Government: A Report on Administrative Management in the States and a Review of Recent Trends in Reorganization* (Chicago, 1950), pp. 3–4.

[17] See James R. Bell and Earl L. Darrah, *State Executive Reorganization* (Berkeley, 1961) and James R. Bell, "State Government Reorganization in California," *State Government,* Spring, 1962, pp. 130–135; in this connection, note also Stephen B. Sweeny and James C. Charlesworth (eds.), *Achieving Excellence in the Public Service, a Symposium* (Philadelphia, 1963); Bennett M. Rich, "Administrative Reorganization in New Jersey," *Public Administration Review,* Autumn, 1952, pp. 251–257; Ferrel Heady and Robert H. Pealy, "The Michigan Dept. of Administration; A Case Study in the Politics of Administration," *Public Administration Review,* Spring, 1956, pp. 83–89; and Karl A. Bosworth, "The Politics of Management Improvement in the States," *American Political Science Review,* March, 1953, pp. 84–99.

Where party divisions are numerically close between legislature and governor, or within the legislature itself, any effective reorganization effort is dependent on bipartisan cooperation. This again may not be easy to secure since success readily grants campaigning benefits to the governor. He would then be in the position to point with pride to a record of achievements that made possible new savings and better business methods.

GOVERNORS AS PARTY LEADERS

While the president is regarded as national head of his party, a governor is usually but not always considered to be the leader of his state party organization. This somewhat weaker position of the state chief executive is due less to theory than to political realities. Few would doubt, for instance, that Senator Byrd of Virginia is the head of his state's Democratic party or that a senior senator generally does not have claims of party leadership difficult to contest by a governor only recently elected or only eligible for a relatively short and fixed tenure.

But in the majority of states and under normal circumstances it is the governor who is head of the party; it is the governor who picks the party chairman; it is the governor who is to be consulted in questions of party platform, campaign tactics, nominations for party office, slate for public office, and party finances.

But here also generalizations must be avoided. To some governors the building of party organizational strength is a major objective of policy leadership. To others it is not. In most of the Southern states governors seek to build personal followings within the framework of the Democratic party.[18] Sometimes a governor may with charm and skill seek to soft pedal his party affiliation, stress selected issues and administrative competence, and seek to attract dissidents from across the political aisle. Warren of California, Youngdahl of Minnesota, Rockefeller of New York, and Lausche of Ohio have tended to follow this pattern. Among recent governors who have worked hard to build party organization and to strengthen party programs centered in their state's politics are Brown of California, Bowles of Connecticut, Williams of Michigan,[19] Freeman of Minnesota, Hatfield of Oregon, Scranton of Pennsylvania, and Nelson of Wisconsin, all of them proudly partisan. These men worked aggressively and tirelessly along with their state chairmen at special workshops and rallies to activate organizations from precinct and township caucus level to the convention level. Before primary and general elections they campaigned actively on behalf of legislators and candidates for state office who promised to support the party's program. Much of the post-World War II

---

[18] See Robert B. Highsaw, "The Southern Governor—Challenge to the Strong Executive Scheme?" *Public Administration Review*, Winter, 1959, pp. 7–11 and Coleman B. Ransone, Jr., "Political Leadership in the Governor's Office," *Journal of Politics*, February, 1964, pp. 197–220.

[19] See G. Mennen Williams, *A Governor's Notes* (Ann Arbor, 1961).

resurgence of Democratic party strength was owed to the efforts of such governors.

A word about the role of governors at the quadrennial presidential nominating conventions. Although American gubernatorial politics has a quality and dimension of its own, it certainly does not operate independently from the mainstream of presidential politics.

Governors have not merely been nominated for president and become president, but they have also played important roles in influencing the selection of the final candidate. No doubt the most outstanding recent illustration was Governor Thomas E. Dewey's domination of the 1952 Republican convention which nominated General Eisenhower. One of the tactical highlights was the now famous telegram of the twenty-two Republican governors in which they urged the convention to rally behind Eisenhower as the candidate most likely to succeed. Significant data about some of the activities of governors at these conventions has come to attention only recently as a result of a thorough-going analysis of presidential nominating politics.[20]

First, governors have participated as delegates in ever-increasing numbers. In 1964, however, a number of Southern governors were conspicuously absent from Atlantic City. Among Republican governors who failed to attend the San Francisco convention were Chafee of Rhode Island and Anderson of Kansas (who had been rejected as a delegate on the issue of the Goldwater candidacy).

Second, as shown in Table 6, since the turn of the century eight incumbent governors as compared to two senators received their party's presidential nomination.

Something of an additional clue about the convention influence of governors can be gathered by noting that of the state governors who attended the Republican and Democratic conventions of 1952 and 1956, 80 per cent chaired their state delegations.

> A delegation chairman occupies a strategic position. He is frequently approached by emissaries of all kinds on the assumption which may or may not be correct, that he is in a position to negotiate for his delegation. . . . In delegations that are cohesive and disciplined the chairman's powers, during the short period while the convention is in session, may approach those of the traditional boss.[21]

At the 1960 Republican convention, West Virginia's Governor Cecil Underwood was temporary chairman of the convention, Arizona's Governor Fannin nominated Senator Goldwater for president; Idaho's Governor Robert Smylie introduced the permanent chairman; Montana's Governor J. Hugo Aronson was selected to pay a special tribute to President Eisenhower; and

---

[20] See Paul T. David, "The Role of Governors at the National Party Conventions," *State Government,* Spring, 1960, pp. 103–110.

[21] Paul T. David, Ralph M. Goldman, and Richard C. Bain, *The Politics of National Party Conventions* (Washington, 1960), pp. 357–358.

TABLE 6. GOVERNMENTAL POSITIONS HELD BY PRESIDENTIAL
NOMINEES WHEN FIRST NOMINATED, 1896–1960

Governmental position [a]	Democratic 1896–1960	Republican 1896–1960	Both parties 1896–1960
No governmental position [b]	2	1	3
State executive other than governor	—	—	—
House of Representatives	—	—	—
Senate	1	1	2
Governor	5	3	8
Federal appointive office [c]	—	2	2
General, Regular Army	—	1	1
Federal and state judiciary	1	1	2
Vice president	—	1	1
Number of cases	9	10	19

[a] Governmental position held at the time of first nomination if a nominee.
[b] Military service has been disregarded in determining governmental experience except in the case of the generals of the regular army.
[c] In the executive branch, other than military.

SOURCE: Adapted from Table 7.10 in Paul T. David, Ralph M. Goldman, and Richard C. Bain, *The Politics of National Party Conventions* (Washington; 1960), p. 148.

New York's Governor Nelson Rockefeller, himself one of the key contenders for nomination, played a major role in the writing of the platform and in the building of the coalition that made possible Mr. Nixon's speedy selection as the GOP standard-bearer.

Governors played a prominent role in the "Kennedy convention" also. Governor Collins of Florida was convention chairman; Governor Freeman of Minnesota gave the nominating speech for Senator Kennedy; Governor Brown of California helped to contain the Stevenson drive; Governor Hodges of North Carolina assisted in "calming" the South; and former Governor Bowles of Connecticut was chairman of the platform committee. Governor Ribicoff of Connecticut was one of the major Kennedy convention floor leaders; Governor Williams kept reins taut on strong liberal labor forces that had felt themselves betrayed or sold out by the Kennedy-Johnson deal and were considering protest demonstrations. Moreover, until Senator Johnson's selection as vice-presidential candidate became final, a number of governors, mostly from the Midwest, were given serious attention as possible running mates by the Kennedy managers.

In the 1964 Republican convention the governors again played a significant, although perhaps a somewhat less prominent role. What challenge there was to Senator Goldwater's overwhelming control of his party's presidential convention was provided by three governors—William Scranton of Pennsylvania, Nelson Rockefeller of New York, and George Romney of Michigan. Among convention leaders raising criticisms concerning the tenor of the Republican platform and strategy were Governors Mark Hatfield of Oregon and John Love of Colorado and former Governor Elmer Andersen of

Minnesota. Governors also were conspicuous at the Democratic convention of 1964 when President Johnson invited Governors Pat Brown of California and John Connally of Texas to be his co-nominators, when Governor Carl Sanders of Georgia was asked to serve as co-chairman of the Rules Committee, and when former Governor David Lawrence of Pennsylvania was called upon to chair the Credentials Committee.

It was true, however, that in both conventions of 1964 the Congress rather than the state legislatures served as a more prominent power base for convention leadership and party nomination. In the GOP convention, for example, great influence was wielded by Senator Carl Curtis of Nebraska (Senator Goldwater's floor manager), Senator Everett Dirksen of Illinois (who nominated Senator Goldwater), Representative Melvin Laird of Wisconsin (Chairman of the Resolutions Committee), Senator Thruston Morton (Convention Chairman), and former Senator William Knowland (chairman of the crucial California delegation). On the Democratic side the names of Senators Hubert Humphrey and Eugene McCarthy of Minnesota, Thomas Dodd of Connecticut, Edmund Muskie of Maine, and Mike Mansfield of Montana dominated the pre-convention speculation for the greatly-enhanced and pivotal position of vice-president.

MISCELLANEOUS POWERS AND DUTIES OF GOVERNORS

CALLING SPECIAL SESSIONS OF THE LEGISLATURE

In the majority of states, governors are given the power of convening the legislature although only a few constitutions permit him to designate the particular agenda for the course of that session. Thus governors with proposals for immediate legislative action may find that once in session a legislature can with impunity attend to measures they, rather than he, would like to see acted on and passed. This makes the threats or use of special sessions politically a risky affair. There is nothing quite like an unproductive session to arouse the public against politics and the politicians for wasting the taxpayers' hard earned money. Still this may be the only way left for a governor to dramatize his own legislative frustrations. When the Republican-controlled legislature of Ohio, for example, cut $38 million of the governor's biennial requests at the end of the 1961 session, Michael V. DiSalle, a Democrat, proceeded to item veto more than half of the entire state budget with the result that a special session became inevitable. Then, by way of building up support for the post-Labor Day special session, Governor DiSalle embarked on a "campaign" tour against the record of the legislature, stressing its failure to provide the finances that he considered the necessary minimum for the state's mental health and welfare programs. His political risk was even more pronounced since the legislature had already overridden eight of his twenty-three vetoes during the regular session. In Ohio the battlelines were drawn with significant portents for not only the next session but for the 1962 elections as well. One of the major factors contributing to the defeat of DiSalle in 1962 was his fiscal differences with the legislature.

Of course, there are all kinds of special sessions. In approximately three-fifths of the states they are nearly a regular occurrence in any given biennium. Over half of them are quite brief, rarely exceeding one week and mostly a result of excessively rigid calendar limitations under which the regular session has to operate. It is either "covering the clock" and pretending that there is still time left, or calling a special session and finishing up properly. Genuine deadlocks over basic policy—taxation, budgets, reapportionment—occur in perhaps a dozen states. These deadlocks do not necessarily have to be an outgrowth of gubernatorial initiative on behalf of programs he may favor. A relatively lengthy special session recently ended in Minnesota, for instance, with the adoption of a strenuously fought income tax withholding scheme which did not at all represent a gubernatorial proposal but was forced on the chief executive and the conservative and disinclined Senate by the aggressive, liberal (DFL) House majority.

PARDONS AND REPRIEVES

With the exception of Idaho, South Carolina, and Virginia, all states give the power of pardoning or reprieving criminals—one of the traditional royal prerogatives—to the state's chief executive or jointly to him and a board or council or jointly to him and the state Senate. To give a few examples, in Maine, Massachusetts, and New Hampshire, the Governor's Council functions also as the pardon board. In Nebraska the board is composed of the governor, secretary of state, and attorney general. In Minnesota, it is the governor, attorney general, and chief justice of the state supreme court. Georgia provides for a three-man board appointed by the governor with the consent of the Senate. And in Rhode Island the governor must obtain the "advice and consent" of the Senate for the exercise of pardons. Pardons may be conditional or absolute depending on the state's constitutional or statutory provisions.

In forty-seven states there are now full-time or part-time pardon boards. Law generally governs the composition of the boards, the nature of the hearings that are to be required, and the procedures that must be followed in the processing of petitions. The three members of such a "typical" statutory board are appointed by the governor for staggered terms of six years and must be confirmed by the Senate. A full-time chairman heads the board, and the membership may include professionally-trained persons in such fields as law, sociology, probation, and law enforcement. Rhode Island includes a psychiatrist while ministers serve on pardon boards in Alabama, Arizona, Indiana, Kansas, Minnesota, Pennsylvania, and Washington.

Briefly, this is how these boards operate. A person after conviction and incarceration in a state penal institution files for application for a pardon with the secretary or chairman of the board. In addition to certain personal data of identification, this application must contain such information as his claims to innocence or to the nature of errors allegedly committed in trials or sentencing. The board may then investigate on its own motion the circumstances of the trial, the opinions of the judge and the prosecuting attorney, the records of prison conduct, previous parole experience, if any, and any other pertinent data. Commutation of sentences may also be granted if the board is convinced that the convict could realistically be considered rehabilitated or that the maximum benefit of confinement has been reached or that continued confinement would constitute a serious threat to the prisoner's health.

Now and then a governor may be faced with immense pressure to pardon a notorious criminal or to commute a death sentence to life imprisonment. Caryl Chessman's twelve-year legal battle against California's gas chamber will long be remembered. He was sentenced for his conviction as the infamous red light bandit for committing seventeen felonies and was reprieved eight times. His final petitions were again based on alleged errors in the trial court procedures as well as on a plea of having suffered an unusual punishment as a result of having had to face eight execution dates already. The events of this fantastic case climaxed in February of 1960. Protests against his execution came from all over the world. Giovanni Leone, President of the Italian Chamber of Deputies, asked President Eisenhower to intervene.

> Protests came from all strata of society. Millions signed petitions in Brazil, thousands in Switzerland. The Queen of Belgium pleaded for his life, as did Dr. Albert Schweitzer, Aldous Huxley, and Pablo Casals. So did the Vatican through its newspaper *L'Osservatore Romana.*[22]

His case had been before the United States Supreme Court fifteen times. Governor Brown although personally and publicly opposed to capital punishment deemed himself unable to extend clemency under provisions of the California constitution which, in Chessman's case, called for a majority vote by the Supreme Court affirming gubernatorial action. This the court refused to do three times in three months. Finally on February 19, ten hours before the execution was to take place, Governor Brown did grant Chessman one more sixty-day reprieve. The governor did more. He called for a special session of the California legislature for the specific purpose of abolishing capital punishment entirely. "Conscientious people may differ," wrote Governor Brown in his message, "but the ultimate issue here is clear. Can law and order be maintained as well or better if capital punishment is abolished?" [23] After questioning witnesses for sixteen hours, the Senate's fifteen-member judiciary committee voted eight to seven to kill the abolition bill. A sixteenth attempt to have the United States Supreme Court stay the execution failed and Chessman died on May 2, 1960. Near the end the governor was again put under enormous pressure. Special delegations and pickets circling his office at

[22] *The New York Times*, May 3, 1960, p. 22.
[23] Lawrence E. Davies, "Brown Asks Death Penalty Ban at Special Legislative Session," *The New York Times*, March 3, 1960, p. 18.

Sacramento urged further gubernatorial intervention, telegrams pleading for clemency came in by the hundreds, and on the day of execution a Los Angeles psychiatrist called Brown "The Hangman of California."

Governor Brown's opposition to capital punishment reflects a very large segment of thinking among state chief executives as reflected in a recent poll. Of all the governors queried, thirty-five responded and seventeen of them were personally opposed to capital punishment; eight were in favor, five of these from the South; and the remaining ten were either unwilling to express an opinion or were noncommittal.[24]

Abolition bills were introduced in 1961 in eighteen states. Only in Delaware, however, were the proponents successful. Nineteen sixty-three legislative sessions abolished the death penalty for persons under 17 in Georgia, for the offense of treason in Michigan (which had been the only offense punishable by death), and submitted to the voters in Oregon the question of eliminating the death penalty for first degree murder.[25]

GOVERNORS AS LEADERS OF THE TROOPS AND PRESERVERS OF THE PEACE

MARTIAL LAW AND THE MILITIA

Most state constitutions provide that the governor may call out the state militia to execute the laws, suppress riots, and repel invasions. To be sure, the military efforts now rest primarily with the federal government in the form of the nation's military forces, regular and reserve, and with national guard divisions. Although state-based and subject to gubernatorial direction in emergencies, the guard has been increasingly integrated into the national establishment.

Profound hostility to martial law was the prevailing mood of the framers of constitutions in colonial America. There also have been deep controversies as to just when a governor may call out the state militia, declare martial law, and have the judicial branch of government acknowledge his actions as binding and his judgment as conclusive as to the necessity or justification of his actions.

Some courts have argued that there is no such thing as martial law at all. Some have insisted that if the necessity should demand it, martial law can be invoked even in the absence of constitutional authority as a power inherent in the sovereignty of the state, a power necessary for the very survival of government itself, the law of self-defense. Only a few have held that the invoking of martial law replaces the functioning of all civil government. A majority of the courts have viewed the governor and his troops as merely assisting the regular police power and the civil law enforcement machinery of the state. Behind this diversity in approach among courts and between governors and courts lie some strong traditions: the supremacy of the civilian

[24] *New York Herald Tribune,* April 24, 1960, pp. 1, 24.
[25] *Book of the States, 1964–1965,* p. 92.

arm of government over the military, the protection of civil and property rights by the judiciary, and the continued availability even in times of tumult and turbulence of the privilege of the writ of *habeas corpus* as long as the courts are still functioning.

Governors have called out the troops for various purposes—some serious and some less so. Small detachments have been activated in connection with emergencies arising from civil commotion or natural disasters when local officials were unable to cope with them. A number of the more serious instances in Colorado, Idaho, and Pennsylvania arose out of bitter and bloody management-labor disputes in the coal mining industry. Strikes and lockouts during one of the worst Depression years alone involved 8,216 guardsmen in twenty-eight states. Generally speaking, the courts have upheld the use of the guard in labor-management conflicts only where violence and the threat of violence constituted a very real and major part of the factual situation.

Where, in their judgment, these ingredients were lacking, courts have shown no hesitancy to enjoin gubernatorial declarations of martial law as an unwarranted executive discretion. The latest conflict between courts, in this instance a federal district court and a governor, occurred in Minnesota in 1959 when Governor Orville Freeman called out the guard, declared martial law, and closed a plant in connection with riots and violence growing out of a nationwide strike by the United Packing House Workers of America against the meat packing house of Wilson & Company at Albert Lea. In the opinion of the court "the use of martial law under the conditions prevailing in Albert Lea would in effect constitute, 'a surrender to mob rule. . . and that the hazard, inconvenience, and expense involved in suppressing the violence [cannot] justify the state in refusing to enforce the law or in depriving the owner of his property or his right to enjoy it.' " [26]

As the court perceived the situation, the governor had the responsibility to use the guard not only to keep the peace, but if necessary to keep the plant open and permit "scabs" to enter. This the governor refused to do. "I closed the plant . . . and I would do it again," contended Freeman, "I don't know if any of you people have ordered troops to use bayonets. I have. I have used them and it wasn't nice. I don't want to use bayonets on the people of Minnesota. . . . Thank God, no one was killed. I felt I made a right decision. . . ." [27] However, reluctantly the governor obeyed the terms of the injunction, and the plant was reopened.

THE GOVERNOR'S ROLE IN CIVIL DEFENSE

Nuclear war poses possibilities of devastation of gigantic proportions. Twenty-six states have already approved the so-called "continuity in government" amendments first suggested jointly by the Office of Civil Defense and the Council of State Governments.

[26] Mitau, in Frost, p. 213.
[27] *Ibid.*, p. 218.

These amendments provide for:

A. Continuity of leadership and authority in executive, legislative, and judicial branches of state and local government through proper lines of succession in public office.
B. Reducing the chances of the unlawful assumption of authority in state and local government.
C. Assurance that government can function legally and effectively in an emergency.
D. Preservation of civil government while minimizing the need for martial law in meeting emergency situations.[28]

It is only natural that governors or their successors in their roles as state chief executive officers will have to perform many of the critical functions in the civil defense establishments. The Model State Civil Defense Act suggested by the federal Office of Civil and Defense Mobilization has served as a legislative guide to the states most of which have as a consequence either adopted identical or very similar provisions.

Within the executive branch is to be established a department of civil defense headed by a director, appointed by the governor with the advice and consent of the Senate. The governor is given general direction and control of this agency "and in the event of disaster beyond local control, may assume direct operational control over all or any part of the civil defense functions" within the state. He is authorized to make the necessary rules, prepare comprehensive civil defense programs, coordinate these plans and programs with those of the federal government, local governments, or other states, conduct surveys of the state's industrial resources pertaining to civil defense, and "to plan for the most efficient emergency use thereof." He shall have the power to declare the existence of a state of civil defense emergency if he (or the legislature by concurrent resolution) "finds that an attack upon the United States has occurred or is anticipated in the immediate future. . . ." He shall have the power to "sell, lend, lease, give, transfer or deliver materials or perform services for civil defense purposes on such terms and conditions as [he] shall prescribe and without regard to the limitations of any existing law, and to account to the (State Treasurer) for any funds received for such property." Under his direction the population can be compelled to evacuate any stricken or threatened area. He may remove public officials for "willful failure to obey an order, rule or regulation adopted pursuant to this Act," and by appointment fill any such resulting vacancy. All law enforcement officers of the state must "execute and enforce such orders, rules and regulations as may be made by the Governor under authority of this Act." [29]

Legislators who voted for these sweeping provisions and electors who approved the continuity in government amendments may well have uttered a silent prayer that none of these far-reaching proposals would ever be put to the ultimate test.

[28] Leo A. Hoegh, "Planning for Survival," *National Civic Review,* September, 1960, pp. 423–424.
[29] Office of Civil and Defense Mobilization, Executive Office of the President, *Comparison of State Civil Defense Legislation* (Washington, 1960), pp. 1–22.

STATEWIDE ELECTIVE EXECUTIVE OFFICERS— HOW MANY IS TOO MANY?

In nearly all of the states, in addition to the governor, constitutions provide for the election of such officers as lieutenant governor, secretary of state, treasurer, auditor, and attorney general. Exceptions to the rule of the "long ballot" are New Jersey which elects the governor only and lets him appoint the rest of the major state officials, Alaska which elects a secretary of state (but no lieutenant governor), and Hawaii which elects a lieutenant governor who also performs the duties of a secretary of state. New Yorkers cast one ballot for governor and lieutenant governor and only for one other executive official, the attorney general.

Political scientists have long questioned the wisdom of asking people to vote for officials whose duties are mostly non-policy making and whose discretion is relatively minimal. But the power of tradition is strong and the antagonism to an over-centralized executive branch even stronger. Yet whenever and wherever administrative reorganization is studied, the demand for reducing the number of elective officials persists, although differing with intensity for the different offices. Of all executive officials, it is the secretary of state on whose appointment rather than election there is generally the widest consensus.

Some of the reasons for eliminating or for retaining all or some of these positions as elective offices will emerge from an analysis of the functions commonly assigned to them.

THE LIEUTENANT GOVERNOR

When Lieutenant Governor Robert B. Crosby of Nebraska wrote an article entitled "Why I Want to Get Rid of My Job," [30] he had the "temerity" to express sentiments that may have been the unexpressed sentiments of more than one occupant of this position. This honorable office, still on the ballot in thirty-nine states, goes back in origin to the Massachusetts charter of 1691 and, with the exception of New Jersey and New Hampshire, was included at one time or another in the structure of all state governments. The office has generally had two basic functions. Lieutenant governors were to be in direct line of succession to the governor and were to be the presiding officers of the Senate. Not unlike the vice-presidency, the resulting amalgam has as a rule not been able to attract the ablest politicians. If, perchance, the occupant of this "spare tire" office had the competence and imagination to make a meaningful contribution to public life, the circumscribed duties of the job often left him frustrated and unhappy.

There have been some efforts to build up this office by assigning to a lieutenant governor certain statutory responsibilities or membership on certain commissions or boards. To cite a few illustrations, in Colorado he is a

[30] *State Government*, July, 1947, pp. 193–194.

member of the Parole Board; in Michigan and Kansas, a member of the Commission on Intergovernmental Cooperation; in Delaware, Missouri, Nebraska, and Pennsylvania, a member of the Pardon Board; in North Carolina, a member of the State Board of Education; in California and Texas, a member of the legislative redistricting board (which apportions the state if the legislature fails to do so); in California, a member of the toll bridge authority and an ex-officio member of the Board of Regents of the University of California; and in Massachusetts, a member of the Governor's Council. Lieutenant governors also serve as members of legislative councils in approximately one-third of the states. In Hawaii, Michigan, Nebraska, and Washington, his additional powers and duties can be legislatively defined.

Summing up the record of all of these gestures, the plain truth of the matter is that the lieutenant governor has not become the assistant governor and in most instances not even an assistant to the governor; this despite the fact that state government and governors are increasingly vexed by the need to coordinate the sprawling executive establishment and by the need for administrative supervision. What is done along these lines of management control is done by executive assistants or administrative directors appointed by the governor and responsible to him. They compose his executive office, but the lieutenant governor is not included.

There are some explanations for ignoring lieutenant governors. In the decade 1950–1960, there were thirteen administrations in which governors and lieutenant governors belonged to different political parties. Presently there are twelve states in this category: Colorado, Idaho, Indiana, Iowa, Michigan, Nebraska, Nevada, North Dakota, Oklahoma, Rhode Island, Vermont, and Wisconsin. Obviously a setting of this kind makes it practically impossible to tie the lieutenant governor into the administrative "team." [31]

Even belonging to the same party does not and cannot guarantee that a lieutenant governor with ambitions of his own will self-effacingly stay in the background and submerge his political individuality for the greater glory of the governor and the success of the administration. While not a particularly good steppingstone to the top job itself, the lieutenant governorship does rank third as the immediately preceding office from whence candidates reached the governorship between 1870 and 1950.[32]

A lieutenant governor does have his legislative responsibilities. With the exception of Massachusetts and Hawaii, all of the constitutions that provide for a lieutenant governor make him also the presiding officer of the Senate. Therefore, it is imperative that, during the course of such a session, his entire attention be given to duties connected with that position. In most instances this involves not only essential parliamentary tasks but the referral of bills and, in a few instances, the appointment of committees.

Without doubt the greatest concrete service that the office renders presently arises, of course, when a vacancy suddenly occurs in the governor-

[31] See I. Ridgway Davis, "Divided Leadership," *National Civic Review*, July, 1961, pp. 356–361.
[32] Schlesinger, p. 11.

ship. It thus adds an element of stability to government in that it helps to clarify the line of successorship. Unfortunately, however, the constitutions of too many states still do not define the meaning of "vacancy." Does a vacancy result from a governor's sudden death, from his temporary absence from the state, or from an incapacitating but not fatal illness? Since these are by no means academic questions, a number of courts have had to untangle or interpret constitutional language often after unsettling and perplexing developments grew out of competing claims by rivals for the office. In doing so, two judicial approaches crystallized. Some courts held that in filling the "vacancy" the successor becomes the "bona fide" governor, others that he merely becomes acting-governor and that the assumption of power can be of a temporary character only.

No such doubt could exist in states that have as clear a constitutional directive as that of Hawaii:

> Section 4. When the office of governor is vacant, the lieutenant governor shall become governor. In the event of absence of the governor from the state, or his inability to exercise and discharge the powers and duties of his office, such powers and duties shall devolve upon the lieutenant governor during such absence or disability.

Hazards and volume of modern travel, not to mention the catastrophic conditions that may grow out of a sudden military assault on this country, have recently led a number of states to re-examine their succession provisions. Clear lines of succession going beyond the assumption of power by a lieutenant governor have now been incorporated into the basic charters of Arizona, California, Michigan, Minnesota, Oregon, and Texas.

Most of the changes provide not only for a number of specified officials who would be in direct line of succession such as the president *pro tempore* of the Senate, the speaker of the Assembly, the secretary of state, the attorney general, the treasurer, and the comptroller as, for example, in California, but authorize the legislature to provide by law for further successions should the need ever arise.

Aside then from their constitutional role as governors-potential and from their role as the Senate's presiding officer, whatever influence a lieutenant governor may have will have to depend largely on his personal relationships with governmental and political leaders in general and with the governor in particular.

Few lieutenant governors served their senior partners with greater candor and devotion than did Herbert H. Lehman of New York under Franklin D. Roosevelt. Roosevelt in turn assigned to Lehman important political missions which called for legislative leadership in the Senate, for conciliatory efforts in the settling of bitter inter-party squabbles. In 1930 when Lehman indicated some interest in returning to private life, Roosevelt pleaded with him to join him for another term; he needed his "good right arm" to complete the unfinished program.[33]

[33] Bernard Bellush, *Franklin D. Roosevelt as Governor of New York* (New York, 1955), p. 151.

THE ATTORNEY GENERAL

Next to the governorship itself, probably no other state executive office
has the power potential of an attorney general. The office of the "King's
council" is now constitutionally anchored in all states except in Indiana,
Oregon, Tennessee, and Wyoming where it is established by statute alone.
Attorneys general are elected by the voters in forty-one states, by the state
supreme court in Tennessee, by the legislature in Maine, and are appointed by
their governors with the advice and consent of the Senate (or the Governor's
Council) in Alaska, Hawaii, New Hampshire, New Jersey, Pennsylvania, and
Wyoming. In about three-fourths of the states they are given four-year terms;
in Kentucky and Alabama, they may not succeed themselves; in five states the
attorney general's term may not be coextensive with that of the governor, and
in Pennsylvania he may be removed by the governor at will. Fifteen states
have a constitutionally fixed minimum age qualification ranging from twenty-
five to thirty-one, and four states specify as an additional qualification
experience gained from having spent a certain number of years in legal
practice.

The powers and duties of an attorney general, as those of any other state
executive official, are derived from the constitution, state statutes, and the
common law. He is the state's chief legal officer, which means that he
represents the state in suits with the federal government, with other states,
and with private parties who claim interests adverse to the state. He is the governor's chief legal advisor and other state executive officials seek his advice
and legal service.

The legislature may ask for his views on proposed measures in order to
ascertain their constitutional compatibility. In the majority of the states the
legal business and personnel of administrative departments, agencies, commissions, and boards are subject to varying degrees of supervision by the office of the attorney general. In some states such as in Alabama, California,
Illinois, Indiana, Michigan, and Ohio, the attorney general is given the power
to "approve any counsel hired" by such agencies. Other states including New
Jersey insist that departmental counsels are in effect assistants to the attorney
general and that their work is carried on under the immediate supervision of
the central office.

Other than functioning as counsel to the governor, the executive officers,
administrative agencies, and the legislature, the attorneys general may also
act as legal advisors to county attorneys and city attorneys.

What makes the position of most attorneys general such a powerful one
is his quasi-judicial duty of rendering formal or written opinions in response
to a request from any one of these sources. These opinions when formally
handed down have the power of law pending their challenge in court. They
may involve the interpretation of constitutional language, statutes, city
ordinances, or administrative rulings.

With regard to an attorney general's role in local law enforcement, there are considerable differences. Approximately one-third of the states now endow his office with supervisory powers over local officials, including the right to supersede or dismiss local prosecutors. Somewhat fewer states give him no such powers at all, and in the remaining states there are no formal constitutional or statutory provisions related to this subject.

In the absence of such authority, courts have been quite reluctant to grant centralizing powers to the attorney general on the basis of the common law alone.

Aside from the question of supervising local law enforcement personnel, thirty-eight states allow the attorney general to initiate criminal proceedings on his own motion and nearly all states assign to him the responsibility of handling the state's criminal business in the appellate courts of the state. California, Kansas, North Carolina, Rhode Island, South Carolina, and South Dakota give him statutory authority over certain units of the state police, and some other states, including Minnesota, give him supervisory control over state bureaus of criminal apprehension. California's constitution has perhaps gone farther in facilitating a highly integrated and centralized attorney general's office than any other state.

> Subject to the powers and duties of the Governor vested in him by Article V of the Constitution, the Attorney General shall be the chief law officer of the state and it shall be his duty to see that the laws of the State of California are uniformly and adequately enforced in every county of the State. He shall have direct supervision over every district attorney and sheriff and over such other law enforcement officers as may be designated by law, in all matters pertaining to the duties of their respective offices, and may require any of said officers to make to him such written reports concerning the investigation, detection, prosecution, and punishment of crime in their respective jurisdictions as may seem advisable. . . .

Is such centralization desirable? The arguments for giving the attorney general supervisory responsibilities over the legal staffs of administrative departments and agencies rest on considerations of economy, efficiency, and safety. Centralized staffs, it is contended, would assure better handling of uneven workloads and would permit the accumulation of valuable experience by the full-time professional employees who are working for the state. This experience would be lost if attorneys were employed by the individual department or agency on a contract or part-time basis.

Moreover, the public interest would likely be in safer hands since a highly centralized staff could resist more effectively the pressures of politics and special interests that tend to converge on a particular administrative department. Centralized control over law enforcement personnel and especially granting to the attorney general power to supersede reluctant or incompetent local district attorneys in criminal prosecutions is often justified as the singularly best method of attaining more uniformly high standards of law enforcement throughout the entire state.

Critics of centralization see in it a genuine threat to local government, local responsibility, and local identity. Some stress the need for distinguishing between police work and investigative work and the danger of combining both in one office, a practice they deem dangerous to civil liberties. Inasmuch as such centralization will tend to result in the need for large and professionally-trained staffs, and since the prevailing pattern is not to apply the civil service system to assistant attorneys general, tremendous political patronage would be placed in the hands of such a department of law enforcement. The attorney general as the head of this department would emerge as much too powerful an official.

Closely related to this controversy is another one. Should the office of attorney general be appointive or elective? As noted earlier, the two newest constitutions, those of Hawaii and Alaska, have given the governor the power of appointing the state's chief attorney; the two legislatures have treated his office structurally like any of the other departments of state.

Curiously enough, the admittedly powerful nature of the office has served equally as a rallying point for proponents and opponents of its elective status. Those favoring the traditional pattern see in it an opportunity for greater political independence held highly important for its quasi-judicial functions; those favoring the process of appointment see in it far greater opportunity for political independence since an integrated executive branch under a strong governor would be in a much better position to keep particular activities of government free from the persuasive entanglements of narrow economic or sectional interests. Further, outright hostility between a governor and an attorney general is second only in significance to executive-legislative "warfare" as a potential for paralyzing the activities of state government. Executive orders, departmental contracts, bond issues, investment policies—these are but a few of the multitudinous activities of an administration that call for legal scrutiny and appraisal and sometimes for even formal opinions which involve discretion and which could thus very easily constitute a battleground between a governor and "his" attorney general. Should these two officials come from different political parties or only from different factions within a major party, very real obstruction could be interposed to gubernatorial programs regardless of how strong a popular mandate there may have been in support of them.

"Fine," the traditionalists would say. "Let there be this friction." They would argue that no greater benefit could come to the public than a careful check of any and all of an administration's activities particularly as they affect wider and wider areas of private interests and lives. An attorney general only if elected by the voters can find the political strength to fight a gubernatorial machine aggressively and with hope for success as he exposes corruption, inefficiency, and the betrayal of the public's trust. Governors whose administrations live up to the law have nothing to fear; they could thus only welcome the exposures of errors and the opportunities for reform than inhere in them.

STATE TREASURERS AND COMPTROLLERS

Of all state executives these two officials are the individuals most directly concerned with the state's fiscal transactions, with money in all of its various aspects—warrants, bonds, investments, and cash. Treasurers have as their primary duties the actual custody of state funds whereas the primary responsibility of comptrollers (in some states they are auditors and given slightly different duties) is that of post-auditing state funds. Post-auditing is the process of assuring fiscal accountability and of making sure that state expenditures and investments have been made in accordance with constitutional and statutory directives.

Statewide election of treasurers is still the major method of filling the office; forty states follow this procedure. Treasurers are appointed by the governor in Alaska, Hawaii, Michigan, New Jersey, and Virginia, by the legislature in Maine, Maryland, New Hampshire, and Tennessee, and by the Commissioner of Taxation and Finance in New York.

Four-year terms are now the law in one-half of the states, two-year terms in eighteen states, and in seven states (Alaska, Hawaii, Maryland, Michigan, New Jersey, New York, and Virginia) the treasurers serve "at the pleasure of the appointing authority." Sixteen states also impose a limitation of from one to three terms on the eligibility of treasurers to succeed themselves, singling out this office along with that of the governorship as functioning best, that is, most safely, considering its fiduciary character, when operating under the principle of rotation.

There is considerable variation in the nature of the duties assigned to the state treasurer. As custodian of state funds he may also be given such functions as that of collecting taxes; acting as paymaster to state departments, to the legislature, and to the judiciary; and administering the investment of the state's diverse trust funds. In this latter capacity a majority of the states provide for investment boards, councils, or commissions which must be consulted on matters of policy and to which the treasurer (usually a member of the board himself) is expected to give periodic reports concerning the status of the funds under his control. A few of the states leave the selection of banks in which the state may deposit its funds entirely to the discretion of their state treasurers, but the majority either designate such depositories by statute or consider this a policy matter weighty enough to be decided by the state investment boards as a group.

Nearly all states require their treasurers to serve in ex-officio capacity on a wide variety of boards and commissions, many of them only tangentially related to their central duties. A 1957 survey found Florida's treasurer to have been the most burdened in this respect; he was required to serve on a total of nineteen boards and commissions.

Much of a treasurer's day-to-day office routine is taken up with the payment of departmental or agency requisitions for funds to be paid to those furnishing the state with goods or services. As a general rule each one of these requests for funds must be accompanied by a certificate or voucher showing proper legislative authority for such items. A number of states will stipulate a pre-audit by the auditor's office as further proof that the encumbrance is in line with matching appropriations made by the legislature before a treasurer's warrant can be drawn on a state depository (bank) or before a cash settlement at the treasurer's office itself can be legally executed.

It would be incorrect to assume on the basis of what has been said so far, that the treasurer, as a rule, is the state's chief receipts and disbursements officer. In any one state it is not at all unusual to have taxes collected by the commissioner of taxation, beer taxes by the liquor control commission, motor vehicle taxes by the secretary of state's office, and aviation license fees by the commissioner of aviation. Authority to make independent disbursements may be shared by various agencies or departments such as purchasing, printing, finance, state employees' retirement bureau, or buildings and grounds. This very diffusion and resulting confusion has caused a certain amount of agitation for the establishment of an integrated department of revenue or finance under an administrator not elected but appointed directly by the governor.

The "Founding Fathers" of Alaska and Hawaii consonant with their concept of a strong governorship have entirely eliminated the elective position of treasurer. Alaska placed in its department of revenue the enforcement of tax laws as well as collection, custody, investment, and management of all state moneys. Hawaii created a department of treasury and regulation with functions mostly centering around the regulation of banks, insurance companies, and other financial institutions and licensing boards, leaving money matters divided between the department of taxation and the department of accounting and general services.

Governor Brown's comprehensive reorganization proposals for California planned to retain the constitutionally elective office of treasurer, assign to him the state's major investment responsibilities but centralize all revenue and general service agency functions in one single department of revenue. This proposal to establish a revenue and general service agency has failed to receive legislative approval.

Reorganization proposals in Kansas, Minnesota, and Washington, on the other hand, have envisaged a department of revenue and a shortened ballot, omitting altogether the position of treasurer. None of these proposals has yet been enacted.

Departmental status similar to that of the treasurer is now also urged in these plans for the state executive post-auditing position. Here again the practice of Alaska and Hawaii will be closely watched, for neither the constitution nor statute provides for either an auditor or a comptroller.

Presently, approximately one-half of the states have an official known as a comptroller, and the remainder designate an official with similar duties as state auditor, post-auditor, supervisor of public funds, or director of departments of budget, finance, or accounts. Positions of state auditor are more likely to be elective, those of comptrollers are more likely to be appointive. Four-year terms are most common but there are also a number of states with two-year terms, a few with longer and some with indefinite terms. Although verification of current and trust fund accounts and periodic reports on the status of these to governors and legislatures are generally basic responsibilities, there appears to be an enormous variation of additional statutory functions given to comptrollers and auditors. A listing of these more or less important duties (though extraneous to the office) would have to include purchasing, motor transport, pre-audits, collections, disbursements, etc. What this indicates, quite obviously, is a failure in a number of states to define clearly the nature of the post-audit role, for no one can doubt that a thorough analysis and verification of numerous state accounts should keep any one official sufficiently occupied without having to assume collateral responsibilities. Moreover, like their fellow treasurers, comptrollers and auditors are given ex-officio membership in a very large number of boards, commissions, and committees.

In all of this compounding of functions, auditors, not infrequently, are also asked to perform pre-audits for the departmental and agency vouchers. A sound case can be made for drawing a basic distinction between the character of pre-audits which essentially represent executive functions and that of post-audits which most fundamentally represent an assurance to the legislature that expenditures and investments have been made in accordance with law. Some of the reorganization proposals now under consideration have argued for creating a post-audit office fashioned after that of the United States Comptroller's, the occupant of which would be elected by and be responsible to the legislature. He would be a watchdog for the legislature.

Where comptrollers or auditors are now constitutionally established offices, political realities appear to have militated against their removal from the ballot through constitutional revision or amendment. Even Governor Rockefeller's massive reorganization program which sought to reduce to forty-one New York's one hundred and six separate executive agencies pointedly did not suggest the elimination of the comptroller's office held at the time of its submission by the state's only Democratic executive official. California's program equally avoided the issue and restricted itself to certain internal shifts of workloads but retained all of the comptroller's fiscal functions including accounting and auditing. When the 1957 Illinois legislature proceeded to reorganize the state's fiscal controls following revelations of "irregularities in the office of the Auditor of Public Accounts," a number of basic changes were authorized including the creation of a legislative audit commission. But the constitutional office of auditor was not among the changes finally adopted.

SECRETARIES OF STATE

In surveying the nature and duties of this office, it is difficult to escape the conclusion that many legislatures may have adopted the attitude "when in doubt let the secretary of state do it." Actually, the multiplicity of functions that have accrued to this office was neither accidental nor designed to demean its occupants. The office of the secretary of state is one of the oldest, perhaps the oldest next to that of the governor. Some of its roots go back to fifteenth-century Britain. In different form it was one of the key executive offices during the colonial era. It existed in each of the original thirteen states. The Northwest Ordinance of 1787, providing for United States territorial government, mentioned it specifically as a companion office to that of governor.

Originally a gubernatorially appointive office, it became a statewide elective office under the impact of Jacksonianism. Secretaries of state are presently elected in thirty-nine states; appointed by the governor in Delaware, Maryland, New Jersey, New York, Pennsylvania, Texas, and Virginia; and elected by the legislature in three—Maine, New Hampshire, and Tennessee. Hawaii, the one state which does not have a secretary of state, consolidated the office with that of lieutenant governor. Four-year terms are now the pattern for the majority of the states; most of the rest still cling to the more traditional two-year term.

Duties most indigenous to the office of secretary of state are two: Custodial-documentary and election law administration. (1) Filed for safekeeping and public record with the secretary of state may be such documents as state constitutions, amendments, legislative acts, committee reports, mortgages, and land surveys. In most of the states the secretary of state functions as the keeper of the official seal, and as the state's chief certification officer.

In this custodial-documentary role, he may also be given the responsibility to act as filing officer for incorporations of businesses, banks, insurance companies, and other associations.

(2) A significant part of a secretary of state's work in nearly all of the states is performed in connection with the operation of state and national elections. Omitting much detail and inter-state differences, a "typical" secretary of state's office has important statutory responsibilities:

A. Accepting filing statements of candidates for statewide offices both in primary and general elections;
B. Supervising the preparation and printing of ballots;
C. Certifying election results and officially notifying those elected;
D. Instructing and supervising county auditors in their respective roles as registration and certification officers for county-wide election operations;
E. Organizing and convening canvassing boards for the determination of official election results;
F. Directing the compilation and publication of state election laws;
G. Issuing state legislative manuals containing certain basic historical, governmental, and political data.

Also, secretaries of state, either alone or in conjunction with the governor, will certify the state's presidential choice and when United States constitutional amendments are submitted to the electorate, the outcome of such a vote.

These are only the more traditional and widely representative activities. Among many other duties in Colorado, for example, the secretary of state appoints notaries public; in California, Georgia, and Illinois, he is also state archivist; in Ohio, he publishes the opinions of the attorney general; in Oklahoma, he records "applicants in the healing arts"; in Rhode Island and Wisconsin, he registers lobbyists; and in Georgia, he is the "keeper of buildings and grounds."

And secretaries of state, just as all the other state executive officers, must serve also on numerous state councils, boards, and commissions officio and ex-officio. Wyoming with its list of fourteen such board memberships must certainly keep its secretary busy.

Heavy duties, workloads, and board memberships notwithstanding, much of the reorganization literature finds little reason for providing such an elective office and urges transfer of its functions to regularly constituted administrative departments wherever possible. Its essentially "ministerial" character, it is urged, leaves little discretion of a policy-making nature, and little on which voters can acquaint themselves for a sufficient understanding to cast an informed ballot. While Alaska does have an elective officer known as secretary of state, he is also, in effect, the lieutenant governor of the state and must appear jointly with the governor on the same ballot. Hawaii, as indicated earlier, has consolidated the offices reversely, giving to its lieutenant governor many of the duties of a secretary of state as well.

Defenders of the status quo who wish to keep as elective such positions as secretary of state, treasurer, auditor, and comptroller, refer the reformers to the lessons of reality. As they read election returns, in nearly one-half of the states voters seem to favor individuals in such positions with frequent re-elections. Long tenure in these offices is taken as an expression of confidence that the public expressed in these officials with little regard for their political party affiliations.

If as a result of such voter decisions, there should be party divisions between governors and certain of the other members of the state executive officials, this might well be taken as the public's desire to have certain individuals serve as their state's watchdogs over finances and records.

THE GOVERNOR'S PERSONAL STAFF AND THE EXECUTIVE OFFICE

Given the complexity of modern American state government, a governor's managerial effectiveness can rarely transcend the sufficiency and competency of his personal staff. His staff must handle the hundreds of letters, messages, telephone calls, and visitors, and the enormous number of requests for favor and friendship that pour into a typical governor's office each day. In addition, it must help to protect the governor's time from unwarranted intrusion and ruthless exploitation; yet at the same time, a governor must be kept readily accessible to department heads, legislators, and political party leaders for consultation, discussion, and decision on policy matters. Ideally, for a governor to have time to think, to plan, to act, and to react, he must have a staff that is ample, devoted, able, politically skilled, and above all tactful and sensitive.

A governor's personal staff will obviously vary from state to state depending on such factors as scope of governmental operations, willingness of the legislature to provide funds for staff positions, and size and population of the state. More than that, the precise character of a governor's staff will also depend on the type of governor and his concept of office. A strong governor with imagination and perseverance who feels keenly about the merit and need of his program will wish to surround himself with equally inspired or inspirable individuals. A governor's previous career and background also will have much influence on the make-up of the "inner" cabinet, whether he likes "egg-heads," or businessmen, or professional politicians, and whether he likes the independently minded or the sycophantly inclined.

Money-conscious legislatures have at times been too willing to "starve" gubernatorial staffs, to keep them small and ineffective. When confronted with such inadequate appropriations, governors occasionally find it necessary to add personally financed or volunteer workers to their statutory allotments in order to support their legislative recommendations with more comprehensive research and with special briefs.

A minimal staff organization beyond strictly clerical employees will make provision for a personal secretary, press secretary, appointment secretary, and administrative assistants for legislation, research, and legal problems. Some of these functions in smaller staffs are, of course, performed by doubling up.

How G. Mennen Williams of Michigan, a governor with very long tenure in office, staffed his "inner cabinet" emerges from the following characterization of some of the key personalities and their duties:

> *Press Secretary:* "a white haired reporter-editor of long experience . . . served since Williams' first day in office . . . has a sense of humor which is a safety valve in times of tension and trouble . . . knows intimately the press, wire, television and newspaper business from wide experience in many cities. He understands thoroughly every operation of state government."

> *Administrative Assistant for Legislation:* ". . . youngest member of the staff at 34, is the son of an Alabama Methodist Minister. . . . His headache is from morning until night, smoothing over legislative rows, rounding up votes, threshing out arguments, attending the caucuses which boil up with the frequency of summer storms, passing out small assists and other favors."

> *Personal Secretary:* ". . . a sparkling, pretty and highly intelligent woman, has been Williams' personal secretary since the day he opened his first campaign office. The daughter of a New Jersey Irish coal miner . . . moved out to Detroit in 1940, and went to work in the Detroit offices of the Air Forces

as secretary to the Commanding General, and finally became director of personnel. Her responsibilities in the Governor's office range across the activities of Government, as well as handling the speaking schedules, all correspondence and personal business of the Governor."

Legal Advisor: ". . . son of a retired Presbyterian minister . . . a graduate of Yale (B.A.) and a Juris Doctor from the University of Michigan Law School. He is razor-sharp in legal matters, restless in manner, blunt in speech, deeply wedded to principle which he sees in inflexible terms, combative in argument. . . ."

"Another Assistant": ". . . an 'old pro,' with a delightfully iconoclastic wit . . . recruited from the staff of the *Detroit Free Press* . . . privately paid by the Governor, has his own office in quarters removed from the Capitol. It is quiet, filled with books and reference works. . . . He is the department of the 'long look,' the idea man who helps prepare Williams' speeches."

Head of the Department of Administration: "[This department] oversees all spending and budgeting, serves as the Governor's eyes, ears, cash register, and right arm . . . son of a Scotch baker, who lived in Brockton, Massachusetts, and one of the brightest scholastic lights in all of the Williams' entourage. . . ."

Executive Secretary: "a quiet, shyly introspective, drivingly efficient young man . . . a University of Michigan graduate in economics and political science . . . first became slightly acquainted with Williams at political meetings . . . in the 1948 campaign. In 1950, he accepted an invitation to direct and coordinate all campaigns and did the job so efficiently that he has drawn the same assignment in each fall campaign since . . . a dedicated political liberal . . . a troubleshooter in state offices. . . ." [34]

Concern for improving administrative channels of communication among California's widely diffused and numerous governmental departments and bureaus led former Governor Earl Warren to establish a special staff position, the coordinator for state agencies. This departmental staff secretary was given major responsibilities for coordinating executive policies, for following up policy directives, and for acting as the governor's personal troubleshooter whenever bureaucratic intransigence prevented speedy action for crisis situations.[35]

In most of the states that have a department of administration, this agency is usually located structurally outside the governor's personal staff but works in closest association with it. In many states the head of this important department has political power second only to the governor and the attorney general. This is the official who assists the governor in preparing the budget and in supervising state administrative practices and rules and who often has the major responsibility in such additional areas as purchasing, administrative research and planning, state personnel systems, public property management, and administrative supervision over state buildings and con-

[34] Frank McNaughton, *Mennen Williams of Michigan: Fighter for Progress* (New York, 1960), pp. 167–171. Copyright © by Frank McNaughton 1960; reprinted by permission of Oceana Publications, Inc.

[35] See James R. Bell, "A Coordinator for State Agencies," *Public Administration Review,* Spring, 1958, pp. 98–101.

structions. Through him a governor can more effectively perform the essential responsibilities of public management—the planning, supervising, controlling, and evaluating of governmental activities and services.

In the final analysis, the American governorship is a highly political office. Those of its occupants who are able to practice the art and science of politics with competence and imagination are able to overcome the constitutional and statutory limitations of the office with notable success. Those who lack these requisites often find themselves beset by frustrations and helplessness. They are the mere executors of a law defined by the legislature, circumscribed by the constitution, and weakened through administrative diffusion and apathy.

STATE PERSONNEL SYSTEMS AND MANAGEMENT

No discussion of state executives can be complete without a word about the civil service—the system of personnel management under which the majority of the nearly two million state government workers are presently organized and under which are performed the ongoing day-to-day activities of state government.

Actually there is no such a thing as *the* civil service. While at least thirty-two states now cover state employees generally, the remaining eighteen states extend civil service coverage only to employees in agencies receiving federal grants-in-aid.[36] Moreover, "general coverage" does not imply that governmental employees of counties are automatically included in the state personnel system either as to the terms of their employment or as to the protections afforded them. While recognizing important organizational differences between state civil service laws, it is still possible to stress a few structural and administrative elements that are common or typical to the systems of a majority of the states.

The central objective of a civil service system generally is to staff government through competitive and standardized procedures with personnel that is competent, reliable, and freed from partisan political pressures or involvement. To attain these ends laws have been enacted and rules promulgated which govern the announcement, recruitment, examination, evaluation, certification, assignment and promotion of employees into positions which have been classified as to their particular skill requirements, duties, and salary levels.

Not subject to the customary testing and recruitment procedures are the employees of the unclassified systems which include certain types of professional personnel—physicians, engineers, academic employees of the universities, the immediate personal staffs of governors, the higher executive officers, and department heads.

Whereas most state laws place the administration of the civil service in the hands of a civil service department or commission, they reserve for a

[36] *Book of the States, 1964–1965,* pp. 178–181.

separate, bipartisan or "nonpartisan" board the more controversial matters of rule-making and of handing down decisions of a quasi-judicial nature. Such a board, usually composed of three members, appointed by the governor for six-year terms (overlapping), and representative of both parties, may also have the responsibility for conducting hearings and for deciding appeals arising out of disciplinary actions that have been taken against employees of the classified system.

Among the many administrative problems continually confronting state personnel systems, one of the most crucial is that of the degree of cooperation that is legally possible or that can be developed between the central civil service department (or commission) on the one hand and the operating or line department on the other. Executives from the operating departments—highway, welfare, or education—conscious of the imperatives of getting a particular job done or mission accomplished, may, for example, charge the men from the civil service with a lack of sympathy or understanding of the particular personnel requirements of their department when the rules of the service call for policies, clearances, consultations, and checks that tend to cramp their style. The possibilities for friction and misunderstanding are rich indeed. A central civil service department may under the law have the responsibility for recruiting and testing, for certifying eligibles, for maintaining the registers (lists of applicants with passing grades), and for the uniform and consistent application standards of performance, rating, promotion, demotion, dismissal, and pay. Yet the actual selection of employees, their evaluation, promotion, demotion, or dismissal must of course be left to the operating departments. Unless, therefore, the civil service department and the line department coordinate their policies with respect to recruitment, job classification, and personnel standards, confusion abounds, duplication of efforts heightens costs, and the overall efficiency and responsibility of the public service is greatly impaired.[37]

Even without such internal administrative problems, the tasks of civil service personnel management are complex enough. The public image of the service has not enhanced its attractiveness to the competitively minded or the ambitious. Salary levels (especially among the middle levels) have lagged behind those prevalent in the private sector of the economy and of the professions; possibilities for advancement have been slowed by veterans' preference and by the rigidities in standards for promotions; legitimate concerns for job security have been allowed to contribute to overly cumbersome procedures in the dismissal of the incompetent; and the letter and intent of civil service law has too often been avoided by recourse to the devices of extended probationary or temporary appointments.

[37] For a more detailed discussion and illustration of these personnel management problems, see Oakley Gordon, Reed Richardson, and J. D. Williams, *Personnel Management in Utah State Government* (Salt Lake City, 1962); consult also such standard texts as O. Glenn Stahl, *Public Personnel Administration*, 5th ed. (New York, 1962) and Norman J. Powell, *Personnel Administration in Government* (Englewood Cliffs, N. J., 1956).

Difficulties such as these persuaded leaders in the profession of public personnel management to suggest a variety of reforms which aim at strengthening the service; only a few can be mentioned here:

Recruitment. Increased budgets for recruitment to attract qualified college and professional school graduates; better advertising of public service opportunities and benefits; improved and more imaginative communications with professional associations; upward revision of job requirements; summer internships in state government for students interested in a career in state government; establishment of trainee positions to which graduates with a general college education would wish to apply.[38]

Testing and Selection of Candidates. Greater use of "unassembled" examinations (non-standardized tests which place more reliance on experience and education) and of performance tests; elimination of the "rule of one, or two, or three" (ranked order of eligibles) which would allow department employment officers more discretion in the selection of qualified applicants whose names appeared further down on the list of eligibles.

Promotion, Placement, and Transfers. Permit the promotion of employees without examination when their jobs have been upgraded, when work assignments were changed, or when the employee showed unusual enterprise and talent; greater care in departmental management to assure "the most efficient combination of human resources, space, equipment and supplies"; liberalization of transfer policies to help employees avoid "dead end jobs or jobs for which they are poorly suited."

Employee Training and Development Programs. Extend state financial assistance to employees for the payment of tuition for courses professionally helpful and of value to their service; expand use of management development institutes and in-service training opportunities; improve career planning and orientation programs; wider adoption of incentives for improved performance and expanded use of monetary and non-monetary recognition awards.[39]

Many questions concerning the scope of the civil service have remained unanswered. Where, for example, should the line be drawn between policy-making officials who should not be covered by the provisions of the civil service and career officials who can and should serve regardless of which party won the election and captured the key administrative and executive positions? In the name of standardization and uniformity, how much power and discretion should be allowed the central civil service staff agency over the personnel policies of the line departments? In recruiting for supervisory officials, should the pre-government, practical on-the-job experience of an applicant be stressed or should greater emphasis be laid on educational

[38] See Ray Ferris, "Internship for Leadership in North Carolina," *State Government*, Winter, 1964, pp. 42–46 and Franklin K. DeWald, "A Ten-Year Personnel Plan For State Government," *State Government*, Winter, 1964, pp. 47–50.

[39] David T. Stanley, assisted by William C. Kroeger, Jr., W. Richard Lomax, Murray B. Nesbitt, Frederick J. Roberts, Lucille Rosenbluth, Doris E. Silberstein, and Katherine W. Strauss, "The Professional Personnel Crisis of the City of New York," *Professional Personnel for the City of New York* (Washington, 1963); the material cited here was taken from the *Brookings Institution Research Report No. 13,* which presented the highlights of their recommendations, p. 6.

qualifications and general administrative qualities which might prepare the applicant for a variety of duties or positions once he successfully completed a departmental in-service training program?

Obviously, there is no simple way of raising the efficiency or attractiveness of the civil service. As in so many other areas of governmental reform, the necessary consensus in and outside of government grows slowly and unevenly. For the building of such a consensus the supportive leadership of governors and departmental executives is, however, quite indispensable. More than others in government, these men must know that the most imaginatively conceived plans and programs require for their implementation clear lines of direction and communication. Demanded above all is the loyalty, effectiveness, and cooperation of the thousands of governmental workers—unskilled, skilled, and professional, who must serve the public by typing letters, processing forms, nursing the sick, guarding the prisons, paving the roads, teaching the young, and staffing the laboratories.

CASE PROBLEMS FOR CLASS DISCUSSION

1. As an executive secretary to the governor you have been handed a letter alleging corruption in the state highway department. The governor has made it your responsibility to check into the charges and to ascertain the facts. How would you proceed?
2. You have been asked to address a group of British journalists visiting this country comparing the American presidency with the American governorship. What would be the main points you would want to stress in your speech?
3. The civil administration committee of your state legislature has before it a proposed constitutional amendment which would abolish the attorney general as an elective office and give to the governor the power to fill the office by appointment (with senatorial confirmation). The incumbent attorney general has urged you, the assistant attorney general, to testify in opposition to this proposal. What would you emphasize in your presentation? What kinds of evidence would you be able to introduce? What type of approach, if any, would you make towards the various blocs in your state legislature and towards interest groups throughout the state?
4. A seven-month smoldering civil rights dispute in a small town in your state finally erupted in mass violence. Local police officials and the county sheriff called on the governor for immediate assistance. Assume that your state does not have a state police force. The governor is out of town and instructs you, his administrative assistant, over the phone to convene an emergency staff session in his office pending his return. He tells you to invite all the necessary departmental personnel and to come up with a solution. Whom would you call in? What information would need to be assembled? What decisions would have to be made? What recommendations for action would you submit to the governor?

SELECTED BIBLIOGRAPHY

Byran R. Abernethy, *Some Persisting Questions Concerning the Constitutional State Executive* (Lawrence, 1960).

Clark D. Ahlberg and Daniel P. Moynihan, "Changing Governors—and Policies," *Public Administration Review*, Fall, 1960, pp. 195–204.

CURTIS O. BAKER, *A Guide to the Work of Executive Agencies in Michigan* (Ann Arbor, 1960).

DAVID CARLEY, "Legal and Extra-Legal Powers of Wisconsin Governors in Legislative Relations—Part I," *Wisconsin Law Review*, January, 1962, pp. 3–64.

DAVID CARLEY, "Legal and Extra-Legal Powers of Wisconsin Governors in Legislative Relations—Part II," *Wisconsin Law Review*, March, 1962, pp. 280–341.

EARL L. DARRAH and ORVILLE F. POLAND, *The Fifty State Governments: A Compilation of State Executive Organization Charts* (Berkeley, 1961).

PAUL FANNIN, ERNEST W. McFARLAND, LEONARD E. GOODALL, and JOHN P. WHITE, *The Office of Governor in Arizona* (Tempe, 1963).

CHARLES GIBBONS, "Transition of Government in Massachusetts," *State Government*, Spring, 1961, pp. 100–101.

KLAUS HERMANN, "The Politics of Administrative Reorganization in Minnesota State Government, 1949–1959," unpublished Ph.D. dissertation, University of Minnesota, 1960.

LUTHER H. HODGES, *Businessman in the Statehouse: Six Years as Governor of North Carolina* (Chapel Hill, 1962).

DANIEL KLEPAK, "Organizing for Effective Centralized Services," *State Government*, Summer, 1962, pp. 176–181.

FRANK LOMBARDI, "State Planning in Hawaii," *State Government*, Autumn, 1961, pp. 226–232.

JOHN P. MALLAN and GEORGE BLACKWOOD, "The Tax That Beat a Governor: The Ordeal of Massachusetts," in Alan F. Westin (ed.), *The Uses of Power* (New York, 1961), pp. 285–322.

LLOYD D. MUSOLF, "Independent Hearing Officers: The California Experiment," *Western Political Quarterly*, March, 1961, pp. 195–213.

THOMAS PAGE, *State Personnel Reorganization in Illinois* (Urbana, 1961).

MALCOLM B. PARSONS, "The Suspension and Removal of Florida Public Officers by the Governor, 1945–1960," *University of Florida Law Review*, Fall–Winter, 1962, pp. 400–409.

ROBERT E. RIGGS, *The Movement for Administrative Reorganization in Arizona* (Tucson, 1961).

ROBERT E. RIGGS, "The Politics of State Administrative Reorganization in Arizona," *Arizona Review of Business and Public Administration*, February, 1961, pp. 1–4.

EDWARD V. SCHTEN, "Forward in Kentucky," *National Civic Review*, June, 1960, pp. 302–307.

REED M. SMITH, *State Government in Transition: Reforms of the Leader Administration 1955–1959* (Philadelphia, 1963).

WILLIAM E. STEVENSON, "The Place of Purchasing in State Government," *State Government*, Winter, 1962, pp. 40–44.

KENNETH O. WARNER, "Planning for Transition," *State Government*, Spring, 1961, pp. 102–103.

RICHARD A. WATSON, *Law Enforcement in Missouri: Office of Attorney General* (Columbia, 1962).

FRANK B. WOODFORD, *Alex J. Groesbeck: Portrait of a Public Man* (Detroit, 1962).

JOSEPH F. ZIMMERMAN, "The Executive Veto in Massachusetts," *Social Science*, June, 1962, pp. 162–168.

Chapter VI

LAW ENFORCEMENT

How adequate are state and local police forces in the face of steeply-rising crime rates?

Are law enforcement agencies unfairly handicapped, and the public at large endangered as a result of recent Supreme Court decisions strengthening the rights of the accused?

ONE of the most tragic aspects of American life has been the pathetic increase in crimes, individual and organized. Since 1940, crimes have outrun population growth by a rate of four to one; since 1958, the increase in crime has been almost 6 times greater than the population growth. The more than 2,600,000 serious offenses in 1964 involved a murder every 60 minutes, a rape every 26 minutes, and an aggravated assault every 3 minutes. Arrests of juveniles increased 17 per cent over 1963. Juvenile arrests in cities, where the volume is highest, rose 17 per cent. In suburban and rural areas the increases were 21 per cent and 22 per cent respectively. The suburban crime rate (including juvenile and adult) showed the sharpest increase—17 per cent.[1]

Hearings before the McClellan and Kefauver committees have revealed the cancerous quality and frightening magnitude of organized crime in gambling, business and labor racketeering, vice, narcotics, and extortion.

Crimes are not mere private wrongs; they are public wrongs. They constitute violations of a public law and impair rights and duties that belong to the community as a whole. Not only are individuals likely to be injured, but the public is also injured by the contravention of its formal laws, and government as protector of individuals and of the public peace must, therefore, bring the offender to justice. But in the United States there are at least two major "publics," speaking through two major systems of prosecutors and courts, federal and state. Inevitably law enforcement and crime prevention become complex, often indefinite, sometimes plainly ineffective.

This may be the price of federalism. Although there is considerable cooperation between the federal, state, and local law enforcement personnel, there is in this country no single national police force. The F.B.I. is an investigative agency operating only in a jurisdiction defined by the enumerated, implied, concurrent, and resultant powers of the federal government. Federal law officers including the Federal Bureau of Investigation are held responsible specifically for the enforcement of approximately six hundred

---

[1] Federal Bureau of Investigation, U. S. Department of Justice, *Uniform Crime Reports for the United States, 1964* (Washington, 1965), pp. 1, 3, 16, 24.

statutes affecting the integrity of the federal government, the safeguarding of the postal system, the channels of interstate commerce, and the protection of government reservations. Therefore, most of the actual police efforts in fighting crime are left to the law enforcement agencies of state and local governments.

A NOTE ON THE EXTENT OF CRIME

An up-to-date and comprehensive picture of crimes committed throughout the United States can be obtained from an annual survey, the *Uniform Crime Reports,* a publication issued by the F.B.I., comprising police data furnished on a cooperative basis by over 7,000 state and local law enforcement agencies.

Its reliability, while considerable, is, of course, affected by reporting deficiencies, diverse definitions of crime, lack of formal verification procedures, and differences in legal practices and standards among the states. Breakdowns by regions, size of cities, category of crimes, age groups and other social groupings invite comparisons, facilitate the detection of trends, and serve public and police officials with important background information for managerial decisions. As in all these types of comparative data, care must be taken not to oversimplify numerical indices. Two cities equal in population with equally competent and conscientious law enforcement personnel may vary radically in such factors as population stability, employment rates, income levels, educational facilities, age distribution, and community attitude towards crime. Obviously in the battle against crime, the interaction of police, prosecutors, and courts cannot occur in a vacuum but reflects very directly the dominant social tensions and values that characterize the particular community.

With all of these limitations in mind, it is difficult to avoid a deep sense of frustration at the tragic persistency of the steeply rising rate of crime and the enormity of waste and loss entailed in life and property.

Each year the crime rate continues to rise at a greater rate than the population growth. The end is not yet in sight (see Figure 1). Reporting only on those cases which had actually reached formal court proceedings, the number of cases in 1961 reached a high of 801,000 cases involving 691,000 children ten to seventeen years old.[2]

According to the Bureau of the Census, total United States population grew 1.5 per cent in 1964. In the same year, the national crime rate was 1,361 offenses per 100,000 population. This was an 11 per cent rise over 1963. Juvenile delinquency offers an even worse picture. Nationally, juveniles (persons under 18) comprise 48 per cent of all police arrests for serious offenses.[3] Up to 4 million young people will have an encounter with a court

---

[2] See Donald M. Pilcher, Leonard W. Stern, and I. Richard Perlman, "Juvenile Delinquency," *Health, Education, and Welfare Indicators,* June, 1963, pp. v-xviii.

[3] *Uniform Crime Reports, 1964,* pp. 3, 24.

FIGURE 1

CRIME AND POPULATION
1958-1964
PERCENT CHANGE OVER 1958

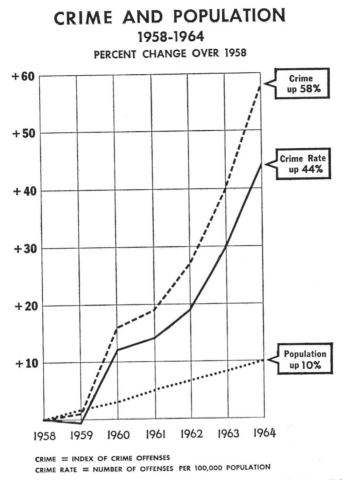

CRIME = INDEX OF CRIME OFFENSES
CRIME RATE = NUMBER OF OFFENSES PER 100,000 POPULATION

SOURCE: Federal Bureau of Investigation, U. S. Department of Justice, *Uniform Crime Reports for the United States, 1964* (Washington, 1965), p. 4.

within the next decade, according to a recent estimate by the Secretary of Health, Education and Welfare.[4]

Organized crime in the form of interstate and international syndicates constitutes another complex, baffling, and ominous object of law enforcement activity. The late Senator Kefauver and his Senate Crime Investigating Committee noted that "infiltration of legitimate business by known hoodlums has progressed to an alarming extent. . . ."[5] Working with and through corrupt politicians, ruthless and vicious criminals in various parts of the country were shown to have achieved considerable influence in paralyzing the

[4] *The New York Times*, May 12, 1961, p. 14.
[5] Estes Kefauver, *Crime in America* (Garden City, 1951), p. 16.

machinery of the law. Here is a sampling of chapter headings in *Crime in America*, the popularized version of the Senator's formal report:

Chicago—The Heritage of Al Capone
Miami—Polluted Playground
Tampa—The Strange Domain of a Sheriff Called Melon Head
Kansas City—The Law of the Jungle
The Cleveland Area—Middletown of Crime
Detroit—Where Underworld and Business World Merge
Louisiana—Fantasia in Law Enforcement

One of the most forceful statements about this peculiar problem was made by former Senator Kenneth Keating (R-N.Y.) in an address to the Cornell Law School:

These syndicates are not controlled by the weak and depraved men who are responsible for the bulk of our petty crimes. They are in the hands of a new criminal type—suave, impeccable figures, masterminds, who hide behind a screen of respectability, who utilize every modern tool in their operation, who carry out their schemes with the efficiency and planning of a modern industrial enterprise. The Frank Costellos and Joe Adonis' of today are a different breed from the Baby Face Nelsons and Dillingers of past decades. The new criminal of this type comes equipped with the best legal adviser, highly trained accountants, the best connections, and influence which sometimes reaches into high levels of government. These men are cunning, resourceful, and powerful.[6]

POLICE FORCES—STATE POLICE, SHERIFFS, AND CITY POLICE

Of the approximately 350,000 persons directly engaged in law enforcement work in the United States including uniformed, administrative, clerical, and custodial personnel, nearly 95 per cent are employed by state and local governmental agencies. The combined total of federal law enforcement personnel, the F.B.I., Immigration and Naturalization Service, Bureau of Narcotics, and the Secret Service does not exceed 21,000. Clearly then, the major responsibility for crime prevention and criminal apprehension rests squarely on the shoulders of state and local governments.

STATE POLICE

Developments leading to an establishment of a state police system have been sporadic and spasmodic. Although nearly all states now have some type of police force or establishment, not more than a third have permitted their police forces to mature into comprehensive law enforcement agencies with

---

[6] *Congressional Record*, May 5, 1960, p. A3882. On the question of organized crime, see also Earl Johnson, Jr., "Organized Crime: Challenge to the American Legal System," *The Journal of Criminal Law, Criminology, and Police Science*, December, 1962, pp. 399–425; March, 1963, pp. 1–29; and June, 1963, pp. 127–145.

statewide and general criminal jurisdiction. Only four states, California, Michigan, New York, and Pennsylvania, have uniformed forces in excess of 1,000 men, and the total strength for all state police does not exceed 14,000.

There is no one single pattern of state police organization. Some states have consolidated the highway patrol with the state police; in others they exist side by side. Some have varying degrees of separate and distinct law enforcement agencies to handle liquor control, gambling, criminal identification, and crime detection. New York, Pennsylvania, and West Virginia have built the most systematically integrated and centralized forces with broad enforcement powers.

Personnel in these organizations is carefully recruited, intensively trained, highly disciplined, and equipped much like the highway patrols in many other states with two-way radios, communication networks, and patrol vehicles.

Historically, state police systems developed in response to a variety of needs and situations. The oldest unit, the Texas Rangers, was founded in 1835 largely to augment military forces and to do border patrol work. Much later more general police duties were added. Most of the state police establishments evolving in the early twentieth century grew out of less martial settings: the need to fight vice, to enforce gambling and liquor regulations, to maintain law and order in strife-torn shops and mines, or to maintain highway safety and assure the orderly movement of traffic. Inadequate local law enforcement personnel or frankly uncooperative officials were in most instances among the major contributory factors in overcoming the public's traditional and deeply-held reluctance to entrust police duties to the state. Communities resented and feared state intervention or meddling in local affairs. Labor engaged in union-building recognition efforts viewed state police forces with much apprehension for their potential as a strike-busting device. Rival political camps saw no reason to provide a governor and his friends with a "private" army that could easily turn into a job-rewarding political machine. Sheriff and police chief associations viewed a strong centralized state police as constituting a very real threat to their prerogatives and powers. Legislators reflecting these and other attitudes and pressures found it not too difficult to circumscribe these state police forces with elaborate statutory limitations as to jurisdiction and size.

But as the crime rate shot up, as criminals resorted to speedier methods of escape, as they crossed county and city lines, and as organized crime syndicates adopted more sophisticated techniques of dodging the law, demands became more insistent that the state police be strengthened or at the very least, that more efficient patterns of intrastate cooperation be evolved between state and local law enforcement agencies. In this way a state could, and many of them do, for example, serve as a clearinghouse for criminal intelligence, as well as provide the investigative and scientific laboratory facilities that can greatly enhance the effectiveness of a sheriff, a rural constable, or a city police department.

THE SHERIFF—HIS OFFICE AND ITS POWERS

The office of sheriff has been one of great honor and great power in England for at least a thousand years. In pre-Norman times the sheriff functioned as keeper of the king's peace, as royal revenue collector, and as the one local official who combined most of the judicial, ministerial, and law enforcement powers of the entire shire or county.

But as governmental institutions became more specialized over the centuries, as courts evolved, and as administrative control over the state was lodged more frequently in a formal bureaucracy attached to the court itself, sheriffs were left mostly with law enforcement as their major responsibility. In America from the colonial beginnings to the present, sheriffs have functioned primarily as law officers of the county. Some of the Southern and Southwestern states used sheriffs also in connection with tax collecting.

Currently there are some 3,000 sheriffs in the United States of which approximately one-half are elected by the citizens of the county for four-year terms; Massachusetts provides for six-year terms; Indiana, for four-year terms; New Jersey and New York for three-year terms; and the remainder of the states for two-year terms. Ten states impose a limit on the number of terms a sheriff may serve. Seven sheriffs receive their commission by appointment—five in Rhode Island (governor), one in New York City (civil service), and one in Denver (mayor).

To many TV enthusiasts, the office of sheriff calls to mind a hard-riding, tough-fisted, fast-shooting, and incorruptible fighter for law and order who personally leads the *posse comitatus* in hot pursuit of cattle thieves and murderers. In many a Western frontier community this was undoubtedly true. But times have changed. Most of the present-day sheriffs are much less heroically employed. They are busy with administrative and civil duties, serving legal writs, posting court orders, maintaining records, transporting criminals, and operating the county jail.

Statutes define their duties and their fees. Out of these fees they must pay the deputies as well as the administrative and custodial expenses of office and jail. Most sheriffs make a modest living, but a few have become quite wealthy. Income and attractiveness of the office vary enormously and so do personal standards, qualifications, and influence.

Depending on the size of the county, its population and work load, a modern sheriff's office will be built around four major divisions: records, jail, patrol, and civil.

Studies of the operations of sheriffs conducted in California, Connecticut, Indiana, Kentucky, Missouri, Montana, New Jersey, North Carolina, and Texas have yielded a rather unfavorable picture as to their effectiveness. All too often sheriffs were found to have been ill-trained, insufficiently aggressive in law enforcement, underpaid, preoccupied with their private business interests, politically overinvolved, and inadequately equipped to fight modern criminals. One authority concluded on the basis of these findings that "in the vast majority of American counties the sheriff system has already collapsed. . . . In a day of highly developed police techniques, elected police administrators are an anachronism . . . the long descending curve marking the decline of the Shrievalty's [sheriff's] prestige promises to remain unbroken." [7] Other critics attribute much of the increasing rural crime rate despite declining rural populations to the basic inadequacy or incompetency of the present sheriff system.

Among the reforms which would retain the system but improve it are the following: legislatures authorizing counties to put the sheriff on a salary and in return allow the county to receive all or a share of all the collected fees; statutory standardization and uniformity of fees; professional training programs for sheriffs and deputies in modern methods of crime prevention, detection, and apprehension; civil service selection and appointment procedures for deputies, administrative staff personnel, and even for sheriffs themselves; and legislation integrating sheriffs and their staffs into a state-wide pattern of cooperative law enforcement. These reforms have been attempted in some states and suggested in others.

Little need be added about the role of another old English law official and servant of the court, the constable. Although nearly one-half of the state's constitutions still make some kind of reference to his office, and Alabama devotes over one hundred valuable words merely to describing certain conditions under which he may be removed, there is hardly any doubt about the fading quality of the office. "In state after state the evidence accumulates that the constable has outlived his usefulness, and the time has come when he can be abolished without any concern about the effect such action would have upon the administration of justice." [8] Where still in office, part-time constables as township and village law officers are now mostly concerned with traffic violations and with serving court papers.

Their terms of office are either two or four years; they are elected by the qualified voters of the township, district or precinct, or they may be appointed by the county commissioners. Compensation is customarily based on the fee system. As police officers, most of the constables have neither the physical conditioning, education, experience, nor training that would qualify them to be considered as a regular arm of the state's law enforcement machinery.

CITY POLICE SYSTEMS

In 1960, 70 per cent of the population of the United States, 125 million people, lived in urban areas, defined by the census bureau as population centers of 2,500 or more. Analysis of crime rates will show not only that crime is more rampant in urban than in rural areas but that, generally, the larger the community, the higher the rate.

[7] Bruce Smith, *Police Systems in the United States*, 2nd rev. ed. (New York, 1960), p. 79; see also Samuel G. Chapman and T. Eric St. Johnston, *The Police Heritage in England and America* (East Lansing, 1963).

[8] Smith, p. 84.

For example, in 1964 in rural areas there were 549.2 crimes committed per 100,000 population; in urban areas, 948.9; and in the 212 standard metropolitan areas (which include 126.5 million people), 1,699.1.[9]

This progression is true notwithstanding the fact that the larger cities have not stood by idly, that they do have more policemen, more and better equipment, more formalized recruitment and training programs, and even slightly higher salaries. New York has 27,100 police employees; Chicago, 11,700; Philadelphia, 6,500; and Los Angeles, 6,300.[10] Figure 2 clearly illustrates the average number of police employees per 1,000 inhabitants in cities of varying population size.

FIGURE 2

POLICE EMPLOYEE DATA

AVERAGE NUMBER OF POLICE DEPARTMENT EMPLOYEES, AND RANGE IN NUMBER OF EMPLOYEES, PER 1,000 INHABITANTS

BY POPULATION GROUPS, DECEMBER 31, 1964

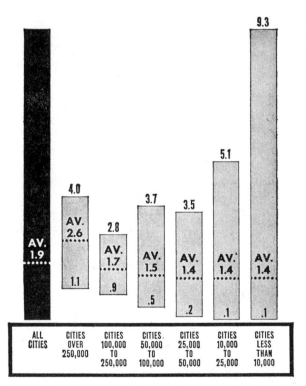

SOURCE: Federal Bureau of Investigation, U. S. Department of Justice, *Uniform Crime Reports for the United States, 1964* (Washington, 1965), p. 37.

[9] *Uniform Crime Reports, 1964*, p. 49.
[10] *Ibid.*, pp. 150–156.

Aside from the question of numbers, all major city police departments do have some similarities as to use of personnel, organization of functions, and administrative structure (for a typical department, see Figure 3). Patrolmen form the numerical backbone of all departments. Some of them may be motorized or mounted. Their duties may involve making arrests, walking the beat, rendering reports, testifying in courts, controlling traffic, guarding property, and assisting the general public. Most of them are uniformed, some are not. When motorized, one or two-man patrols may cruise on regular schedules through specially hazardous areas, or respond to emergency calls.

Specialized patrol personnel may include policewomen, juvenile delinquency officers, and jail attendants. Many departments employ civilian personnel for administrative work and for work in connection with radio dispatching, communications, parking-meter attending, chemical testing, toxicology, photographing, fingerprinting, and vehicle maintenance. Criminal investigating duties are usually performed by detectives, the plainclothesmen. Their responsibilities center on following up leads, rounding up suspects, interrogating them, questioning witnesses, and on all the other steps involved in arresting criminals, obtaining testimony, securing the evidence, and bringing them to justice.

The hierarchical command structure of a department will usually include a police chief or superintendent, his deputy, assistant chiefs or inspectors, captains in charge of certain divisions such as the uniformed patrol division or the division of detectives, and lieutenants and sergeants and specialized squads such as homicide, auto theft, forgery, morals, and juvenile protection.

A 1960 survey of one hundred and twenty-five cities and towns (5,000 population and over) in Texas throws some light on the status and problems of modern policemen.

> Although auto patrols are used increasingly, foot patrolmen are still relied on heavily for inspection and other patrol duties.
>
> Only about a third of the cities had a formalized civil service system for their policemen; most of the systems were found in the larger cities.
>
> Average beginning salaries for patrolmen ranged from a monthly high of $370 in Houston (938,000) to a low of $175 in Lampass (5,061).
>
> Average monthly salaries for police chiefs ranged from a maximum of $1,126 (Dallas—680,000) to a minimum of $260 (Hillsboro—7,402).
>
> Approximately 70 per cent of the cities require a high school education or its equivalent for prospective police officers; about 65 per cent specify a medical examination; entrance age specifications range from a minimum of 21 to a maximum of 35 years; intelligence tests are made mandatory in only about two-fifths of the communities.
>
> The predominant pattern of selecting police chiefs is by appointment by city mayors or managers.
>
> More than three-fourths of the cities have their own training programs for recruits; some systems insist on a brief pre-duty training period. Nearly all cities permit their personnel to attend brief in-service training courses in such areas as delinquency, narcotics, traffic control, etc.

FIGURE 3

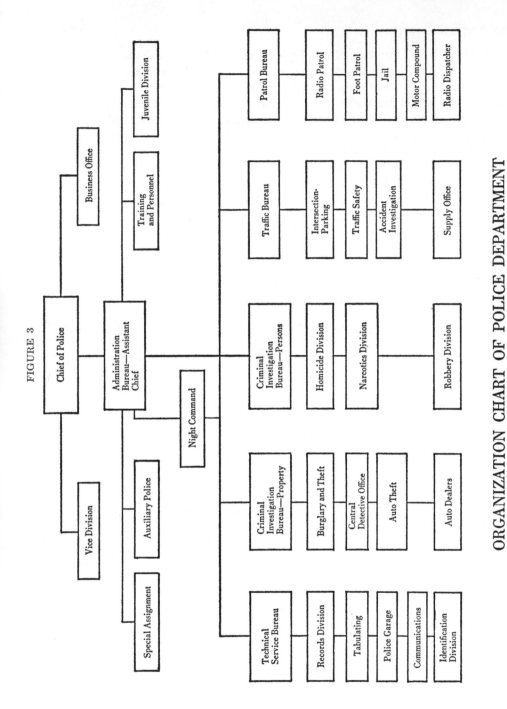

ORGANIZATION CHART OF POLICE DEPARTMENT
CITY OF HOUSTON

The average work week for policemen in cities over 10,000 population was 48.15 hours; the average for all cities was 52.2 hours. Outside, part-time employment or activities in private business are permitted but departmental approval is required in most cities.

A little over 70 per cent of the cities provide uniforms (mostly two per year) but less than one-third grant clothing allowances to their plainclothesmen. Less than one-half of the communities only provide their policemen with such basic equipment as ammunition, night sticks, sidearms, Sam Browne belts, holsters, riot guns, badges, etc.[11]

Salaries and working conditions for many of America's 186,000 policemen are improving, especially in the larger cities. New York now has a $135.00 weekly minimum for its patrolmen. Beginning minimum salaries of $5,000 or more are no longer a rarity in cities of over 100,000 population, and more cities than ever are permitting overtime pay. Improvements also are noted in provisions governing tenure, retirement, pension rights, health insurance programs, and standards of promotion.

Yet progress is slow and poor salaries, long hours, and low morale still characterize many a police system, particularly those of the medium and smaller cities.

There are some more basic weaknesses. Modern police work becomes increasingly complex and bewildering. Will the metropolitan systems be able to attract and hold the type of personnel that has the educational, emotional, and intellectual qualifications to deal effectively with the increases in juvenile crime and with minority problems accentuated by relocations in housing growing out of urban renewal and highway building programs or by the Negroes' sharpened insistence for equal citizenship and justice? Demands on a modern police force far exceed the requirements of being able to shoot straight, be morally straight, walk straight, and think straight. More than ever departments will be forced to seek men skilled in handling human and intercultural relations, men who can handle social maladjustments with firmness and candor. More and more departments aim their recruiting efforts at recent college graduates. Personnel already recruited continue to need more training. Statewide in-service training programs established by legislatures are now in force in California, Illinois, Maine, Minnesota, and New York. New York considers its six-month basic course containing eighty hours of instruction in seventeen subjects a prerequisite for policemen who wish to attain permanent civil service status. Between 1950 and 1960, 2,423 Bachelor of Arts degrees and 93 Masters degrees were granted in Law Enforcement and Criminalistics by a dozen different state colleges and universities. Additional institutions of higher learning are offering special certification programs or Associate of Arts degrees in police science and administration.[12] A typical curriculum will include such courses as police supervision and leadership,

---

[11] *Municipal Police Administration in Texas: A Survey* (Austin, 1960), pp. 18, 24–25, 29, 32–36, 40–41, 50.

[12] *Municipal Year Book, 1961*, p. 394.

criminal investigation, criminal law and procedure, social aspects of police administration, police organization and administration, juvenile laws, crime and delinquency, probation and parole administration, introduction to criminology, laboratory technique, evidence and court procedure, traffic engineering and control, and personal property and sales.[13]

But even the best-paid force, the best-trained force, and the best-equipped force cannot function effectively without public cooperation and public understanding of the mission it is asked to perform. What New York policemen may be up against was revealed in an angry blast by the city's police commissioner, Michael J. Murphy, who saw "a trend toward mob violence against police and apathy from onlookers who watch cops beaten with unconcern. . . . In one week policemen in New York were severely attacked by criminals and mobs on 32 occasions. There were 1,787 such cases in the past year." [14]

Cities eager to rid themselves of corrupted police systems (in which "crooked cops" fix traffic tickets, collude with the underworld, and flaunt the law) may wish to take a leaf out of Chicago's recent history as to how reforms can be successfully carried out. About five years ago Chicago was rocked by one of the worst police scandals in its history, and there have been some bad ones. Officers on duty were found selling narcotics from squad cars, policemen were taking part in burglaries, and the city was known as an inviting haven for crime. Mayor Daley handed the cleanup job to one of the nation's outstanding authorities on police administration, Orlando W. Wilson, Dean of the School of Criminology at the University of California. Responsible only to a five-member, nonpartisan citizens' police committee, Dr. Wilson quickly established inspectional services within the force (including a division of internal investigations), tightened up the overall administration of the 10,000 man department, modernized record-keeping, and greatly speeded patrol service for emergency calls. Chicago's department is now rated well along the way to becoming one of the most effective and best organized among big cities.

One of the most hopeful developments in the uneasy race relation picture of the South has been the increasing awareness among influential citizens (church groups, chambers of commerce, leaders of bench and bar) that a breakdown of law and order must under all circumstances be avoided and that this could be best accomplished by well-trained police forces that are "color blind." Highly successful along this line have been the efforts of Atlanta's police department and those of the "human relations" seminar for police officers at Little Switzerland, North Carolina, organized under the leadership of the Southern Police Institute of Louisville, Kentucky.[15]

COUNTYWIDE POLICE SYSTEMS

Surburban growth, particularly since World War II, has multiplied the number of small and often inadequately staffed police departments. A 1952 study noted forty independent police departments within a radius of fifteen

[13] *Congressional Record,* August 15, 1961, p. A6403.
[14] *The Minneapolis Star,* August 11, 1961, p. 286.
[15] *The Wall Street Journal,* August 18, 1961, p. 1.

miles from the center of Boston and three hundred and fifty such departments within a radius of fifty miles from Chicago. Nearly all booming metropolitan areas characterized by heavy population shifts from core city to the suburbs find themselves with a large number of governmental units, each with its own police force. A few counties which encompass such metropolitan areas did overcome powerful political pressures—local pride and status considerations of their officialdom, all strongly resisting consolidation attempts—and successfully brought about patterns of countywide police systems. Four such examples are Fulton County (Atlanta, Georgia), Nassau County (New York, New York), San Francisco County (San Francisco, California) and Dade County (Miami, Florida).

Los Angeles County is experimenting with a pattern short of actual consolidation but, in the judgment of some observers, in the direction of it. Under constitutional authority and state law, the Los Angeles county sheriff is empowered to render law enforcement assistance to the various municipalities of Los Angeles County, an area comprising 3,417 square miles and including a population of 1,500,000. On an annual budget of $22,000,000 the sheriff's office employs 3,800 people, and provides a "package" service to twenty-two contract cities and to other unincorporated areas within the county at a cost of $78,000 per year for one patrol unit, fully equipped along with other supplementary headquarters' services.[16]

COMPLAINT BOARDS AND POLICE DEPARTMENTS—
THE PHILADELPHIA PATTERN

Tensions between ethnic minorities and police departments are not restricted to the South. Charges of police brutality figured prominently in the racial and social strife which exploded with such terrifying force in New York and Rochester in 1964 and Los Angeles in 1965. In the overcrowded urban ghettoes of these Northern cities, Negroes and Puerto Ricans have bitterly resented treatment by the police they considered abusive, harrassing, and glaringly discriminatory. Responsible leaders in these and other racially tense communities have been searching for measures which would help to change the image of the police from that of an enemy to that of an even-handed protector of the public peace, who fairly balances restraint with severity and law enforcement with the preservation of civil rights.

Among the various plans suggested, considerable attention had been given to the establishment of civilian complaint boards. Aggrieved citizens, it was thought, might tend to be less constrained to present their allegation of police brutalities to a civilian group than to the regular departmental authorities.

Philadelphia adopted this approach in 1958 when Mayor Richardson

---

[16] See Howard H. Earle, *Contract Law Enforcement Services by the Los Angeles County Sheriff's Department* (Los Angeles, 1960), Chapter 4. For a discussion of metropolitan police districts, see Max A. Pock, "Are Metropolitan Police Districts Legally Feasible?" *Journal of Public Law*, XII, 1963, pp. 313–336.

Dilworth established the city's civilian Police Advisory Board through executive action. The eight-member board is authorized to hear "grievances of citizens who have a complaint against any member of the Philadelphia Police Department, based upon a charge of brutality, racial or religious discrimination, or violation of state or federal constitutional rights." Board membership includes prominent leaders in labor, business, civil rights, the churches, and the legal profession; a Negro minister functions as executive secretary.

Under the rules of the board, a complainant may appear before the board in person or may be represented by counsel (either of his own choosing or, upon request, by a board-appointed attorney). A written complaint setting out the allegations must include the name of the police officer and must be filed within a specified period with the executive secretary of the board. If informal settlement proves impossible, a copy of the complaint is then passed on to the police department with a request for investigation. After the board receives the results from the department (and there is authority for the board to conduct its own investigations), a hearing date is set and the parties are notified to appear. Police personnel are invariably assisted by counsel furnished by the Fraternal Order of Police. The rules of evidence are formal and governed by the law of the commonwealth; witnesses may be cross-examined (the board does not possess the power of subpoena); board decisions are reached by majority vote.

The board may recommend to the mayor that the police officer be dismissed from the department, that he be suspended from active duty without pay (for not more than 30 days), that he be reprimanded, or that he be exonerated.[17]

Philadelphia's Police Advisory Board operates out of a two-room business office. Its annual budget is a mere $12,000, its staff and publicity insufficient, its effectiveness limited, yet the community reaction to the program as such appears to have been generally positive. Even the police, despite its basic and frank opposition to review procedures of this type, cooperated willingly with the board and its activities. Spokesmen for the police in Philadelphia and throughout the nation have never hidden their concern that the discipline of the force may be undermined and law enforcement weakened when civilians without the appropriate professional training and experience are charged with judging police activities. Police administrators prefer intra-departmental review procedures in which qualified and responsible upper-echelon officers are given adequate power to evaluate and dispose of citizen complaints in a setting that is kept as free from outside interference and political considerations as possible.[18]

[17] *Annual Report, Police Advisory Board, City of Philadelphia* (Philadelphia, 1963), p. 4.

[18] An excellent description of the Philadelphia Police Advisory Board is found in "Who Shall Judge a Policeman?" *The New York Times Magazine*, August 2, 1964; for a comparison of departmental and civilian police review boards, see Harold Beral and Marcus Sisk, "The Administration of Complaints by Civilians Against the Police," *Harvard Law Review*, January, 1964, pp. 499–519; a brief summary of the F.B.I. Report to the President on the 1964 summer riots in nine cities can be found in *The New York Times*, September 24, 1964.

STRENGTHENING POLICE EFFORTS: FEDERAL–STATE
COOPERATIVE PATTERNS

Even the most exuberant defenders of local police control and administration cannot easily ignore the very real contributions made by the F.B.I.
during the last twenty-five years toward the raising of local standards and
techniques of law enforcement.

This federal assistance has taken various forms. Over 4,300 graduates of
the F.B.I.'s National Police Academy are now actively engaged in law-enforce-
ment activities. Among these graduates nearly a third presently head up local
police systems.

On file and available from the F.B.I. are over 167 million fingerprints.
Local agencies may call on F.B.I. laboratory assistance, and federal experts
may be invited to testify in local trials. During the fiscal year 1963 alone there
were numerous requests for assistance involving 247,894 scientific examinations of 196,057 specimens of evidence. Hundreds of regional police schools
and law enforcement conferences have been held by officials of the F.B.I. to
acquaint police officers with the latest methods in fighting crime. In 1963
105,209 local law enforcement officers attended 3,801 such police training
schools.[19]

The Federal Fugitive Felon Act passed about fifteen years ago permits
state and local law enforcement officers to call on federal assistance in
locating and returning those who fled in order to avoid prosecution or the
giving of testimony. While it is not designed to supplant ordinary extradition
procedures under which the governor of the state of refuge may be requested
to return a fugitive to the state claiming jurisdiction for the crime, the federal
act does seek to deny to criminals the possible sanctuary of interstate movements.

More than that is involved. Organized crime has long lost its purely local
character. In their vicious activities criminal syndicates "spill over into neighboring jurisdictions"; criminality does not end at the state's border whereas
the state's law machinery does.

To pick up where the states under federalism are forced to leave off,
Robert Kennedy as attorney general felt it necessary in 1961 to recommend to
Congress a six-point program for fighting organized crime throughout its
manifold interstate operations. He urged:

    A. Laws which would prohibit the interstate use of telephone and telegraph
       communications for betting and gambling purposes.
    B. Laws which would prohibit interstate travel in support of racketeering.
    C. Laws which would provide immunity for certain witnesses in labor-
       management investigations.
    D. Laws which would prohibit the shipment in interstate commerce of betting
       paraphernalia such as numbers slips, lottery tickets, or facsimiles or plates
       from which they can be reproduced.

[19] Department of Justice, FBI Annual Report: Fiscal Year 1963 (Washington, 1963), pp.
   31–32.

E. Laws which would prohibit the intimidation of witnesses in administrative investigations such as questioning by the F.B.I. or other similar agencies.

F. An amendment to the Federal Fugitive Felon Act which would extend the range of present crimes (murder, kidnaping, burglary, robbery, mayhem, rape, assault with a dangerous weapon, arson, and extradition) to make it applicable to all state offenses punishable by death or imprisonment for a term exceeding one year.[20]

Objections to these proposals come largely from two sources, those who fear further accumulation of power in the federal government and those who view apprehensively the breadth of the Fugitive Felon provisions under which the Department of Justice might be placed in the position of being compelled to "enforce" laws essentially archaic or obnoxious to a large segment of the American public.

The 87th Congress enacted into law all of the Attorney General's proposals but two—the ones providing immunity for witnesses in labor-management investigations and prohibiting intimidation of witnesses. And in 1965 President Johnson appointed a nineteen member National Crime Commission to study and report on various aspects of the administration of criminal justice, law enforcement procedures, programs for the rehabilitation of criminals, and on the broader implications of the relationship of poverty to crime.

PUBLIC PROSECUTORS AND SOME ASPECTS OF PRE-TRIAL PROCEDURES

Routine procedure when a crime has been committed is for the police to investigate the circumstances of the crime, to locate and arrest a probable suspect, to question him, to secure if possible a confession, to obtain statements from witnesses and to present the person to be charged with the crime to a magistrate for a preliminary hearing. Unless the charges are clearly unsubstantiated or readily rebutted by the defendant, the magistrate may then order him held for trial or order him released on bail pending the trial, assuming, of course, that the crime is bailable and that bail can be arranged.

The decision to proceed with a case and to prosecute is generally that of the county or district attorney. The titles of these officials vary. In Ohio they are called prosecuting attorneys; in New Hampshire, county solicitors; in Virginia, commonwealth attorneys; and in Alabama, circuit solicitors. They are elective officials in all but three states.

Most widely representative are two- or four-year terms of office; terms are fixed constitutionally at six years in Kentucky and at eight in Tennessee. Four states stipulate a minimum age of twenty-four or twenty-five, and a few states including Georgia, Kentucky, Louisiana and New Jersey insist on a minimum period of previous legal experience, usually three years, as a necessary qualification for the office. In Delaware and Rhode Island they are appointed by the

---

[20] See *Congressional Quarterly Weekly Report*, April 14, 1961, p. 630.

attorney general; and in Connecticut, by the judges of the courts. While most states do not have a blanket prohibition against private practice by county attorneys, eight states do have such rules. Tennessee and Oklahoma prohibit all their prosecutors from engaging in private practice but the remaining six states have rules applicable only to selected counties, most of them the larger metropolitan ones. Salaries are highest, not unexpectedly, in the populous metropolitan counties (usually $3,000 less than the salary paid the chief county executive). Nearly one-third of the states in 1959 offered their prosecuting attorneys annual minimum salaries of less than $2,500. No doubt many of these attorneys were retained on a part-time basis by mostly smaller, rural counties. Partially unreflected in these lower salaries is the relic of the past, the fee system, which in a number of the states, particularly Arkansas, Florida, Georgia, Kentucky, and Oklahoma, may then be combined with a basic salary from regular public tax funds. Where county attorneys are compensated by fees, they usually serve on a part-time basis.[21]

A decision to prosecute necessarily involves a number of discretionary aspects. Prosecutors before proceeding in the courts will weigh the probability of success, the substantiality of the evidence, the reliability and availability of witnesses, and the sufficiency of the investigative work carried out by the police. It is not at all unusual for some jurisdictions to have rarely more than 50 per cent of the cases go beyond the preliminary hearing stage.

In about one-half of the states where grand juries are still functioning, prosecutors will then present to them a request for indictment, setting forth the facts of the crime and the relationship of the accused to it. After outlining the case, prosecutor or grand jury may wish to call witnesses and question them.

Grand juries possess great common law power in forcing attendance, requiring testimony, and citing uncooperative witnesses for contempt. They may also grant immunity to witnesses who contend that their testimony might be self-incriminating. Proceedings are kept secret, and no one may be forced to reveal their contents. Neither the accused nor his counsel may participate in these proceedings. At the end of the proceedings grand juries may, by majority or two-thirds vote, either refuse to indict or indict, and if the latter, they formally charge the accused with having committed crime. Trial in a criminal court then ordinarily follows as a matter of course.

The role played by the prosecutor is often pivotal throughout these proceedings before the grand jury and the twelve to twenty-three citizen-members that compose it. Ordinarily he initiates the process by seeking the indictment. He selects the witnesses to be heard; he presents the evidence; he "instructs" the grand jury in the complexities of the law; and he determines who shall be summoned and the order in which those summoned shall appear. A grand jury's dependence on the prosecutor, the dominant role that he can

21 Duane R. Nedrud, "The Career Prosecutor," *The Journal of Criminal Law, Criminology and Police Science,* September–October, 1960, pp. 343–355.

assume in its proceedings, and the one-sidedness of the deliberations have certainly not gone unchallenged. These factors when combined with criticisms as to the expense of the grand jury, as to its failure to meet with sufficient frequency particularly in rural areas, causing unwarranted delays, and as to its tendency to duplicate the preliminary hearing before a magistrate have contributed much to the search for and adoption of alternatives.

In the twenty-eight states that do permit such alternatives, formal charge through "information" in place of indictment by grand jury has been resorted to in 95 per cent of the cases.[22] Filed by the prosecuting attorney, it sets forth the necessary essentials of the charge unrestricted by the legalisms of the common law and permits the earliest possible arraignment of the accused on the assumption that sufficient cause exists to proceed with the actual trial.

Supporters of the grand jury, however, remain unpersuaded. Stressed in their rebuttal is the fact that prosecutors do not have the power of subpoena, that they cannot grant immunity to witnesses and that in their judgment a politically ambitious prosecutor or the compulsively possessed grand "inquisitor" type could be more effectively contained by a corporate body like a jury than by an individual magistrate.

Even in old England the grand jury at times found it possible to stand courageously against the despotism of the Crown and for the rights of the accused.

A second alternative to the grand jury is the one-man jury, or judge-jury for which authority exists in about a dozen states, which is employed to a moderate extent in three states, and which has been most frequently used in Michigan, and there often in connection with a number of juicy political scandals.[23] Under Michigan law, for example, prosecutors or any other persons may file a charge with a judge to the effect that a crime has been committed and that probable cause exists to accuse a particular individual with having committed it.

In the course of a thirty-year period ending in 1948, Michigan's one-man jury conducted about 300 investigations and received testimony from about 15,000 witnesses.[24]

There are certain obvious advantages that one-man juries possess over the "information" process. Unlike prosecutors, judges can, of course, compel testimony and subpoena persons and documents. Such advantages can be abused and were in at least one instance, when a Michigan judge in investigating alleged gambling and corruption adopted procedures reminiscent of the Court of Star Chamber of 1641. A pinball machine operator was called before the judge. He was afforded no counsel, given neither the chance to prepare his case, nor the opportunity to cross-examine witnesses testifying

---

[22] Ernst W. Puttkammer, *Administration of Criminal Law* (Chicago, 1953), p. 149.

[23] Robert G. Scigliano, "Grand Jury, the Information, and the Judicial Inquiry," *Oregon Law Review*, June, 1959, p. 306; see also his *The Michigan One-Man Grand Jury* (East Lansing, 1957).

[24] Scigliano, "Grand Jury, the Information, and the Judicial Inquiry," p. 307.

against him. The public was excluded, and then suddenly the judge decided that the pinball machine operator was lying, that he should be held in contempt. Promptly he charged, convicted, and sentenced him to sixty days in jail. A writ of *habeas corpus* filed by his attorney was turned down by the state supreme court. Fortunately for this defendant and others, the United States Supreme Court reversed the decision finding gross violations of rights under the due process of law clause of the Fourteenth Amendment. Mr. Justice Black speaking for the court wrote in part:

> [N]o court in this country has ever before held, so far as we can find, that an accused can be tried, convicted, and sent to jail, when everybody else is denied entrance to the court, except the judge and his attachés. And without exception all courts have held that an accused is at the very least entitled to have his friends, relatives, and counsel present, no matter with what offense he may be charged.[25]

An important limiting change in Michigan's one-man jury growing out of this decision and subsequent state legislation has taken from a judge, acting in such capacity, the power to try contempts against himself or to punish the witness in his own court. These are matters that must now be turned over to another judge thus separating and delineating the grand jury's functions from the traditional judicial functions. This is but another way of making certain that under the Bill of Rights one may not be at once judge, jury, and prosecutor.

False arrest or imprisonment on false charges must be an enormously traumatic experience for the innocent as he finds himself in abject dependence upon the jailer's tender mercies. A society that treasures such possibly unpopular concepts as the presumption of innocence and which abhors police brutality and the third degree no matter how heinous the crime and how despicable the criminal must be as constantly vigilant about the rights of the accused as about the protection of the public lest law enforcement become enforcement without law.

That these nobler precepts of the criminal law have not been followed with regularity in frontier communities or in communities caught in a dehumanizing turmoil of racial tensions or mass violence is a well-known matter of historical record that needs little amplification.

Suspects belonging to certain groups were found to be more vulnerable to legal short cuts than others. Somehow police officers, sheriffs, and prosecutors with "blood in their eyes" harried by a hate-charged community found it easier to ignore the more stringent demands of the rule of law when their potential victims belonged to such ethnic minority groups as Chinese, Negro, or Mexican, or when they were union organizers or strike leaders, or civil rights workers, or when they came from the ranks of the dispossessed, the vagrants, the drunks, or the friendless.

By failing to obtain bail (an assurance that the accused will be present in court as required), over a million and a half indigent defendants every year

25 *In re Oliver* 333 U. S. 257 (1948), at 271–272.

are forced to languish in jails as they await trial. While state constitutions and laws do give to judges the power to release the accused under bail, the decision of whether or not bail will in fact be furnished is left to commercial bondsmen and not to the government. Although bail may be modest for lesser crimes, a recent study in New York City revealed that 28 per cent of the defendants were unable to post $500 bail and that 45 per cent could not secure a bond when their bail was set at $2,000.[26] What makes the entire bail granting process so inequitable and grossly unfair is the ease with which professional criminals and members of the syndicates can secure bail bonds while the little fellow or first-time offender is unable to avail himself of these constitutional guarantees. Commentators on criminal procedures have long assailed the widespread corruption which pollutes the bail bond business and the system which gives to the bondsman "the keys to the jail." Too many of these bondsmen were inadequately supervised; courts have failed to order the collection of forfeited bonds; venal lawyers and bondsmen have split fees and manipulated bond rates at the expense of bewildered and helpless defendants.[27]

Pre-trial incarceration necessarily places profound psychological and economic burdens on the accused and his family. Time spent in awaiting trial may be considerable. (New York City in 1962 reported an average twenty-eight day period for its 58,458 adult prisoners and thirty-two days for its 12,955 adolescent prisoners.)[28]

Studies by the Manhattan Bail Project have shown that aside from the burdens of awaiting trial, jail prisoners when compared to those on bail seem to experience considerable disadvantages with respect to their chances of jury acquittal. Individuals who are jailed are less able to assist in the preparation of their defense, less effective in court, and less likely to shake a jailbird appearance despite their legally presumed innocence. What the New York study also showed was that the overwhelming majority of prisoners awaiting trial could be safely released both for their own benefit and for the very substantial savings of public expenditures.

> Between October 16, 1961, and April 8, 1964, the Manhattan Bail Project interviewed approximately 10,000 defendants . . . and recommended almost 4,000 of these for release on their own recognizance. Of these, 2,600 defendants have been released on their own recognizance and only 23, less than one per cent, have "jumped." [29]

[26] Robert F. Kennedy, "The Department of Justice and the Indigent Accused," *Journal of the American Judicature Society*, January, 1964, p. 184. In this connection, see also Charles Ares and Herbert Sturz, "Bail and the Indigent Accused," *Crime and Delinquency*, January, 1962, pp. 12–20 and Gertrude Samuels, "Bail: Justice for Far From All," *The New York Times Magazine*, August 19, 1962, pp. 13, 74–75.

[27] Murray Teigh Bloom, "Must It Be Bail or Jail?," *The Kiwanis Magazine*, April, 1964, pp. 33–35.

[28] Ronald Goldfarb, "The Great Bail Scandal," *The New Republic*, June 6, 1964, p. 15.

[29] *Ibid.*, p. 16.

Similar findings are reported from California. In March of 1963, Attorney General Kennedy who strongly favored this approach instructed the United States District Attorneys to release defendants awaiting trial on their own recognizance "when no substantial risk is involved."

FEDERAL ASSISTANCE AND CHECKS

Standards in law enforcement have fortunately been improving progressively over the years. While leaders of state and local bar and bench as well as other civic-minded reform groups may rightfully claim a share in the developments toward a more responsible enforcement of the laws, an ever larger share must be reserved for another source. To the federal government must go a great deal of credit, more specifically to the Department of Justice and to the United States Supreme Court. The former made its contributions through its training of police personnel in which stress is laid on the more scientific approach to criminal work, the latter by insisting on procedural fairness. Repeatedly the Supreme Court threw out convictions in which the defendant did not have counsel, in which confessions or testimony were obtained under duress, and in which the officers of the court and jurors blatantly ignored the most rudimentary facets of due process of law.

Parenthetically, among some of the weird practices specifically struck down by the United States Supreme Court was an Ohio law which tied the fee that a justice of the peace might collect for his labors to his conviction of the defendant.

And still much remains to be done. Too many suspects are taken into custody and held for questioning by the police on the mere ground of suspicion—on the optimistic assumption that their testimony might yet yield something of value.

Easy arrests may well be the earmark of "lazy" police, of a police unwilling or incapable of doing the hard and patient investigative work required by our law. In the words of Mr. Justice Douglas, "under our system the arrest is warranted not by what the police discover afterwards but by what they knew at the time." [30] Based on the F.B.I.'s *Uniform Crime Reports, 1964,* a total of 102,106 persons were arrested on the grounds of suspicion. [31]

Closely related to issues inherent in arrests for suspicion are arrests for vagrancy, although one involves by itself no violation of statute by the defendant whereas the other may. Vagrancy charges reaching a total of 132,955 (1964) are used increasingly by some cities against transients in search of employment, residence, or welfare payment and by some as a catchall weapon to rid the community of those deemed undesirable. [32] There are records of persons arrested for vagrancy and kept in jail for days without benefit of

[30] William O. Douglas, "Vagrancy and Arrest on Suspicion," *Minority of One,* May, 1960.
[31] *Uniform Crime Reports, 1964,* p. 107.
[32] *Ibid.,* p. 107.

counsel or formal presentation of charge. A community's concern for fair procedures is perhaps most difficult to arouse for those least appealing, least powerful, and those often most in need of succor.

One of the traditionally most perplexing problems in American federalism is the extent to which the safeguards of the Bill of Rights can be made applicable to criminal proceedings in state courts.

At the turn of the century, minimal indeed were the standards used by the United States Supreme Court in testing these state proceedings against the requirements of due process of law as contained in the Fourteenth Amendment. All that was federally demanded then was that state courts had adequate jurisdiction to try the case in question, and that the parties in the case had been given a proper hearing.[33]

Left in the hands of state legislatures, state courts, and state law enforcement officials (unless governed by state constitutions) were such matters as the use or non-use of juries, the nature of evidence admitted in a court, the protection against self-incrimination, the rules controlling searches and seizures, the right to counsel, the meaning of coerced confessions, and the elements constituting a fair trial.

Not all members of the United States Supreme Court shared the majority view that these procedural matters were to be kept beyond the reach of the federal amendments. In *Hurtado* v. *California* (1884) Mr. Justice Harlan (a grandfather of the present Justice Harlan), dissenting, took the position that the due process of law clause of the Fourteenth Amendment should impose upon the states "the same restrictions in respect of proceedings involving life, liberty, and property which had been imposed upon the general government." [34] This attempt to channel through the due process clause of the Fourteenth Amendment all of the commands of the first ten amendments and thus require state criminal procedures to match federal standards had been rejected by the majority of the Supreme Court until very recently.

What subsequent decisions did establish gradually over the years was that the Fourteenth Amendment absorbed a few of the more basic assurances of the first ten amendments. Their assurances of liberty and procedural safety were deemed so fundamental to a fair trial that a majority of the Supreme Court felt compelled to strike down their denial or violation by the states.

For example, the Court insisted that confessions could not be secured by duress, terror, or torture or by unintermittent questioning of prisoners "extending over a period of thirty-six hours." In crimes punishable by death the defendant had to be given the opportunity of having assistance of counsel. But in non-capital cases such assistance needed only to be provided "in circumstances where an accused could not have an adequate and fair defense without a lawyer." [35]

Federal courts have for some years operated under the rule that the

---

[33] C. Herman Pritchett, *The American Constitution* (New York, 1959), p. 534.
[34] 110 U. S. 516 (1884).
[35] Rocco J. Tresolino, *American Constitutional Law* (New York, 1959), p. 551.

"police must with reasonable promptness show legal cause for detaining arrested persons," on the theory that this procedural requirement "checks resort to those reprehensible practices known as the third degree which, though universally rejected as indefensible, still find their way into use." [36] Also ruled inadmissible in the *Mallory* case are confessions obtained by the police while the defendant is illegally detained.[37]

When a Negro was kept incommunicado for a period of a week, questioned unintermittently by the police, and not arraigned before a magistrate, Mr. Justice Frankfurter in a 1957 case (*Fikes* v. *Alabama*), writing the majority opinion for a divided court, argued that the combination of the circumstances in the case constituted procedural violations by state authorities clearly within the orbit of "due process of law" prohibitions.[38]

Four years later, Justice Frankfurter speaking once again for the court, overturned a murder conviction (*Culombe* v. *Connecticut*) on the ground that prolonged detention had in effect made the questioning of the defendant "an effective instrument for extorting an unwilling admission of guilt." [39]

THE INDIGENT DEFENDANT AND THE RIGHT TO COUNSEL

The problem of obtaining justice for the indigent defendant is likely to be even more crucial to those concerned with improving the administration of law than the issues posed by arrest for suspicion or vagrancy. Though it may seem strange, the "principle that every person accused of a serious crime should as a matter of legal right have counsel to represent him" is of relatively recent origin and can certainly lay no claim on the sanction of English precedents, since it was entirely alien to the common law.

One of the requirements of the Sixth Amendment granting to the defendant the right to counsel in other than capital cases has been held applicable to the states only since 1963.

Federal and state statutes making available paid legal assistance to the indigent defendant have been urged for adoption for at least a generation. Committees of the American Bar Association, of the Judicial Conference of the United States, of the Conference of Chief Justices, as well as prominent individual jurists, law professors, and individual members of the bar have recommended such reforms as indispensable to elemental justice.

Testimony in 1961 before the subcommittee on constitutional rights of the Senate Committee of the Judiciary indicated that forty-nine states had some statutes which provided for the assignment of counsel to defendants in criminal cases.

---

[36] *NcNabb* v. *United States*, 318 U. S. 332 (1943).

[37] *Mallory* v. *United States*, 354 U. S. 449 (1957).

[38] *Fikes* v. *Alabama*, 352 U. S. 191 (1957).

[39] *Culombe* v. *Connecticut*, 367 U. S. 568 (1961). For a discussion of coerced confessions, see H. Frank Way, Jr., "The Supreme Court and State Coerced Confessions," *Journal of Public Law*, XII, 1963, pp. 53–67.

A. Counsel can be assigned for *capital cases only* in Alabama, Florida, Maine, Massachusetts, Mississippi, Pennsylvania, South Carolina, and Texas.
B. In only eighteen other states are there provisions for *mandatory assignment* of defense counsel.
C. In twenty-two states the assignment of counsel is "discretionary with the court or only at the request of the defendant."
D. Right to counsel may be waived. "In a number of jurisdictions if [defendant] does not demand his right at the trial, he will be presumed to have waived it."
E. In other than capital cases, only twenty-three states provide compensation for counsel. At best no more than two states (California and Wisconsin) have statutory authority under which necessary trial expenses, other than counsel, may be incurred and paid.[40]

Not until 1963 did the United States Supreme Court extend to all crimes tried in state courts the defense counsel guarantees of the Sixth Amendment by holding these to be incorporated in the due process of law clause of the Fourteenth Amendment. A unanimous court overruling a 1942 case (*Betts* v. *Brady* which had held that state courts were required to appoint defense counsel only in capital crimes or under "special circumstances") [41] now insisted in *Gideon* v. *Wainwright* that states must provide indigent defendants with counsel in all "serious criminal cases" or cases involving the likelihood of a substantial prison sentence.[42]

Mr. Justice Black speaking for the court wrote

[R]eason and reflection require us to recognize that in our adversary system of criminal justice, any person haled into court, who is too poor to hire a lawyer cannot be assured a fair trial unless counsel is provided him. This seems to us to be an obvious truth.[43]

What gave the court the opportunity to overturn the *Betts* case was a misspelled handwritten note from Clarence Earl Gideon, a former skid row resident from Panama City, convicted of having burglarized a pool hall.[44] At

[40] Senate Judiciary Committee, *Legal Counsel for Indigent Defendants in Federal Courts*, study by the Subcommittee on Constitutional Rights, 87th Cong., 1st Sess. (Washington, 1963), p. 8. See also Senate Judiciary Committee, *Criminal Justice Act of 1963* (*Public Defender*), Hearings, May 13, 20, and 27, 1963, 88th Cong., 1st Sess. (Washington, 1963); Arthur J. Goldberg, "Equality and Governmental Action," *New York University Law Review*, April, 1964, pp. 205–227; Junius L. Allison, "Poverty and the Administration of Justice in the Criminal Courts," *The Journal of Criminal Law, Criminology and Police Science*, June, 1964, pp. 241–245; Joint Committee on Continuing Legal Education of the American Law Institute and the American Bar Association, *The Problem of the Indigent Accused* (Philadelphia, 1961); Yale Kamisar, "The Right to Counsel and the Fourteenth Amendment: A Dialogue on 'the Most Pervasive Right' of an Accused," *University of Chicago Law Review*, Autumn, 1962, pp. 1–77; and Attorney General's Committee on Poverty and the Administration of Criminal Justice, *Poverty and the Administration of Federal Criminal Justice* (Washington, 1963).
[41] 316 U. S. 455 (1942).
[42] 372 U. S. 335 (1963).
[43] *Ibid.*, at 344.
[44] See Anthony Lewis, *Gideon's Trumpet* (New York, 1964).

the occasion of his trial his request for counsel was denied on the ground that Florida law authorized the appointment of counsel for indigent defendants only for capital offenses. Gideon's petition for a writ of *certiorari* which originated in a Florida prison cell and ended up before the United States Supreme Court was bound to have a massive impact. This was especially true since the Court had decided in an earlier but related case that relief afforded an improperly convicted defendant was retrospective in its effect. On the basis that their new trials would be either impossible or impractical, Florida quickly decided to release nearly a thousand prisoners. As a result of *Gideon* and of *White* v. *State of Maryland* (another case decided in 1963 which stipulated that counsel for an indigent defendant in criminal proceedings had to be present at as early a stage as that of the preliminary examination),[45] new public defender laws were enacted and old ones were strengthened within a few months in Colorado, Florida, Kansas, Maine, Michigan, Minnesota, Nevada, North Carolina, Oklahoma, and Pennsylvania. Additional bills seeking to implement these new standards of criminal procedure are pending in nearly all of the legislatures.

A defendant's right to counsel while in police custody continues to receive strong support from the Warren Court. For example, held violative of the Fourteenth Amendment in *Escobeda* v. *Illinois* was the failure to permit a defendant arrested on suspicion of murder to consult with his counsel during his interrogation by the police, in the course of which incriminating evidence was obtained.[46]

Under the terms of such bills indigent defendants will be aided by a public defender, by legal aid societies, by local defender systems or by a combination of arrangements with funds coming from both state and local tax sources. How much financial support these governments will be able to furnish the defense for investigative and expert services, however, is far from clear.

SEARCH AND SEIZURE

The Fourth Amendment, extolling "a man's house to be his castle" by securing him privacy against unreasonable searches and seizures, has for many years offered dramatic examples in the divergence of federal and state standards of criminal procedure. Whereas courts in nearly one-half of the states will admit evidence illegally obtained, federal courts are not permitted to do this. On the contrary, following the *Weeks* case, federal courts have repeatedly insisted that evidence without a search warrant is evidence seized

[45] 373 U. S. 59 (1963). The decision of the Court in the *Gideon* case has been further modified by decisions in two recent cases: *Escobeda* v. *Illinois*, 378 U. S. 478 (1964) and *United States ex rel Durocher* v. *LaVallee*, 330 F. 2d 303 (1964).
[46] 378 U. S. 478.

in violation of the Fourth Amendment and thus inadmissible.[47] An effort to extend this federal exclusionary rule via the Fourteenth Amendment to states not excluding such evidence was denied as late as 1949 in *Wolf* v. *Colorado* by the Court over the most strenuous objections of Justices Murphy, Rutledge, and Douglas.[48]

Yet only twelve years later, again in 1961, a divided court in *Mapp* v. *Ohio* [49] went beyond *Wolf* v. *Colorado* and held that the rule of exclusion as part and parcel of the Fourth Amendment was absorbed by the Fourteenth Amendment and thus became binding upon the states. Mr. Justice Clark's majority opinion in effect denied the validity of a dual standard for "search and seizure" by holding that a) "the exclusionary rule is an essential part of both the Fourth and the Fourteenth Amendments," [50] b) "the State, by admitting evidence unlawfully seized, serves to encourage disobedience to the Federal Constitution which it is bound to uphold," [51] and that c) "the ignoble shortcut to conviction left open to the State tends to destroy the entire system of constitutional restraints on which the liberties of the people rest." [52]

Mr. Justice Harlan entered a vigorous dissent on behalf of the right of states to define their own standards of law enforcement regardless of the inherent desirability or undesirability of the exclusionary rule. "The preservation of a proper balance between state and federal responsibility in the administration of criminal justice," he maintained, "demands patience on the part of those who might like to see things move faster among the states in this respect." [53] He did not conceive it to be within the province of the Supreme Court to sit in judgment of state variations in trial procedures nor did he believe "that the Fourteenth Amendment empowers . . . [the] Court to mold state remedies effectuating the right to freedom from 'arbitrary intrusion by the police' to suit its own notions of how things should be done." [54]

EAVESDROPPING AND WIRETAPPING

Interrelated with the search and seizure issue is the even more baffling and heatedly debated constitutional status of wiretapping and eavesdropping when carried out by federal or state officials. Of all the procedural problems of law enforcement affecting constitutional rights there is no other more complex, more replete with stinging dissents, or more beset with conflicting

[47] *Weeks* v. *United States*, 232 U. S. 383 (1914). For a discussion of the Fourth Amendment, see Richard M. Leagre, "The Fourth Amendment and the Law of Arrest," *The Journal of Criminal Law, Criminology and Police Science*, December, 1963, pp. 393–420; see also Frank D. Day, "Criminal Law Enforcement and a Free Society," *ibid.*, September, 1963, pp. 360–365.
[48] 338 U. S. 25 (1949).
[49] 367 U. S. 643 (1961).
[50] *Ibid.*, at 657.
[51] *Ibid.*, at 657.
[52] *Ibid.*, at 660.
[53] *Ibid.*, at 680.
[54] *Ibid.*, at 682.

testimony by prosecuting attorneys, police officials, legislators and defense counsels.

All that can be done here is to point up briefly in outline form the configuration of the law and the dilemma that inheres in it and in its enforcement.

First, ambiguity and diversity will have to be the key words in describing federal and state laws affecting wiretapping and eavesdropping. Section 605 of the Federal Communications Act of 1934 declares it to be a crime for any person unless authorized by the sender to intercept communications by wire or radio and to divulge or publish their content. Yet former Attorneys General Jackson and Biddle publicly stated that "tapping and use of the information did not violate the statute absent a divulgence" and there is uncontradicted evidence to the fact that the F.B.I. does engage in some wiretapping in connection with certain types of crimes.[55] J. Edgar Hoover in testifying before the House Appropriations Subcommittee on February 5, 1959, acknowledged that "[taps] are utilized only in cases involving the internal security of the nation or where a human life may be imperiled." [56]

Second, over thirty states entirely outlaw wiretapping although some states merely prohibit the physical interference with communications such as the injuring or cutting of wires. In Louisiana, Maryland, Massachusetts, Nevada, New York, and Oregon, statutes permit wiretapping by law enforcement officers, but in some of these prior judicial permission must be secured. Six states, Illinois, Maryland, Nevada, Oregon, Pennsylvania, and Rhode Island, not merely prohibit wiretapping but make it unlawful to introduce in courts evidence so obtained.[57]

Third, while the Supreme Court had relatively little difficulty in upholding Section 605 and in precluding in federal courts the introduction of wiretapped evidence obtained by federal officers (*Nardone* v. *United States*),[58] the question of reconciling differences between state and federal

---

[55] Senate Judiciary Committee, *Wiretapping, Eavesdropping and the Bill of Rights*, Subcommittee on Constitutional Rights, Hearings, December 15–16, 1959, Pt. 5, 86th Cong., 1st Sess. (Washington, 1960), pp. 1714–1715. For a discussion of wiretapping laws in the states, see Senate Judiciary Committee, *State Statutes on Wiretapping*, compiled by the Subcommittee on Constitutional Rights, 87th Cong., 1st Sess. (Washington, 1961). For recent hearings, see Senate Judiciary Committee, *Wiretapping—The Attorney General's Program*, Hearings, March 29, April 4–6, May 10, 17, and 24, 1962, 87th Cong., 1st Sess. (Washington, 1963).

[56] Quoted in Thomas C. Hennings, Jr., "The Wiretapping-Eavesdropping Problem: A Legislator's View," *Minnesota Law Review*, April, 1960, p. 832. In the same issue, see also Edward S. Silver, "The Wiretapping-Eavesdropping Problem: A Prosecutor's View," pp. 835–854; Edward Bennett Williams, "The Wiretapping-Eavesdropping Problem: A Defense Counsel's View," pp. 855–871; Harold K. Lipset, "The Wiretapping-Eavesdropping Problem: A Private Investigator's View," pp. 873–889; and Yale Kamisar, "The Wiretapping-Eavesdropping Problem: A Professor's View," pp. 891–940.

[57] *Wiretapping, Eavesdropping, and the Bill of Rights*, Pt. 5, pp. 1527–1528; see also *State Statutes on Wiretapping*, p. iii.

[58] 302 U. S. 379 (1937).

law proved once again to be the more complex problem. Thus while the Court was able to rule in *Schwartz* v. *Texas* [59] that wiretapping evidence procured by state officers even in violation of Section 605 was admissible in a state court, five years later in the *Bernanti* case [60] Chief Justice Warren concluded that wiretapped evidence could not be admitted in a federal court even when obtained by state officers operating under the authority of state law. The Court rejected the argument of the prosecutor that there was nothing in the wording of Section 605 to prevent a state from authorizing wiretapping "in the exercise of its legitimate police function." Chief Justice Warren contended that the act of 1934 was "a comprehensive scheme for the regulation of interstate communication," that "it applies both to intrastate and to interstate communications," and that as a matter of public policy, Congress "did not mean to allow state legislation which would contradict that section and that policy." [61]

No one can really be too surprised at the resulting confusion about the status of the wiretapping law. "There is no uniformity among states and there is conflict between the laws of the several states and the federal law," notes a well-known commentary on wiretapping. "Picture the dilemma of the New York City police officer. The New York Constitution and the statutes of New York authorize him to wiretap if he first obtains a warrant from a judge. . . . Yet the Supreme Court of the United States . . . has told him that the supreme law of the land is the United States congressional prohibition against wiretapping, embodied in the Federal Communications Act, and that the New York constitutional and statutory authorization of police wiretapping is invalid." [62] To compound the dilemma even more, two New York state judges gave public notice of their intention to rely on the *Benanti* ruling and issue no further permits to tap wires notwithstanding the enabling provisions of their state. [63]

Actually despite the glaring conflict between federal and New York state law, there has not as yet been a single prosecution of a state officer for violating the federal wiretapping prohibitions. [64]

Fourth, what is the actual extent of wiretapping? Since private individuals as well as public officers tap wires, and since in many instances the results of wiretapping may under law not be revealed nor its practice admitted, no authoritative answer can be given this question.

A further complication and cause for caution is the matter of definition. Actually eavesdropping rather than wiretapping is the more generic term. The former denotes the practice of employing electronic or mechanical apparatus in overhearing the conversation of two or more persons without such persons'

---

[59] 344 U. S. 199 (1952).

[60] *Benanti* v. *United States*, 355 U. S. 96 (1957).

[61] *Ibid.*, at 104–106.

[62] Samuel Dash, Richard F. Schwartz, and Robert E. Knowlton, *The Eavesdroppers* (New Brunswick, 1959), p. 4.

[63] Hennings, p. 826.

[64] *Wiretapping, Eavesdropping and the Bill of Rights*, Pt. 5, p. 1716.

permission or knowledge whereas the latter, wiretapping, in its strictest sense, refers to the interception of telephonic, telegraphic, or radio communication only. Some writers, however, also include "bugging" in their discussion of wiretapping and eavesdropping issues. "Bugging" ordinarily refers to eavesdropping accomplished through the use of microphones or transmitters placed strategically for the purpose of intercepting and recording private conversations of the parties under surveillance.

Eavesdropping when accomplished "by means of an unauthorized physical penetration into the premises occupied by the petitioner" was held to constitute a violation of Fourth Amendment safeguards by the Supreme Court in a 1961 case (*Silverman* v. *United States*).[65] In this instance a "spike mike" was attached to the heating ducts of the person's house, turning the duct into a "gigantic microphone, running through the entire house" occupied by the petitioner. The admissibility or inadmissibility of "other frightening paraphernalia which the vaunted marvels of an electronic age may visit upon human society" is left legally very much in limbo by the court's own frank admission in the *Silverman* case. The court referred to such devices as the parabolic microphone which can pick up conversation three hundred yards away and a sonic wave device as yet experimental that could overhear "everything said in a room without entering it or going near it."

With these qualifications in mind, a few of the following findings and observations by a leading national authority may be indicative of the scope of the eavesdropping problem:

> In February of 1955, the news broke in New York about a central wiretap station set up by private detectives and able to monitor over 100,000 lines in the mid-Manhattan area. . . . Taps by Maryland police in bookmaking cases led the Baltimore *Sun* to attack the "wide open, indiscriminate use of wire tapping" in that state. In Las Vegas, Nevada, hidden microphones were installed by a private investigator at the direction of a newspaper editor who wanted to secure proof that prominent gamblers and State officials were in connivance, and in the wake of this exposure, it was proved that Nevada's leading brothels made a practice of wiring their rooms to collect useful facts about clients. . . . In California, eavesdropping practices by police and private detectives included microphone installations which were kept for months on end in the bedrooms of suspects. . . .[66]

In New Jersey where wiretapping is prohibited, a report of the Joint Legislative Committee to Study Wiretapping and the Unauthorized Recording of Speech found this:

> [P]rivate individuals and private detectives participate in eavesdropping activities, not only by wiretapping, but by placing hidden microphones and transmitters. . . . [E]avesdropping is sometimes employed in matrimonial cases, and sometimes at the request of an employer to check on the activities

---

[65] 365 U. S. 505 (1961).

[66] Alan F. Westin, "Wiretapping: The Quiet Revolution," *Commentary*, April, 1960, pp. 333–334.

of employees. The State Police, County Prosecutors and Municipal Police also employ eavesdropping methods in the detection of crime.[67]

And in New York, where wiretapping is legal (but subject to a judicial warrant), a poll of that state's district attorneys revealed a total of 2,392 taps for a period of five years, 1950–1955.[68]

THE CASE FOR AND AGAINST WIRETAPPING

Bitter controversy has raged around the practice of wiretapping ever since its prominent use by the police in battling bootleggers during the prohibition era. Is wiretapping really the indispensably necessary law enforcement tool as claimed by those who view the battle against the dirty business of crime as tragically handicapped and the odds unjustifiably uneven? Or must wiretapping be classed among the despicable weapons of police terror reminiscent of a police state, an instrument adopted by individuals who care little for civil liberties and even less for the subtler ethical dimensions of the means and ends relationship—individuals possessed in their fight against crime? But then perhaps it is not primarily a matter of either tapping or not tapping, but a question of surrounding the operations with restrictions and safeguards which would permit its careful use by professionally competent investigators in cases involving major crimes only.

Speaking in favor of wiretapping, this is the opinion of a police chief of Los Angeles:

> It is often a dirty business—a very dirty business—because of the warped nature of the criminals with whom the police must often deal. But history has shown and is continuing to show that it is a necessary business. . . . The men of the police service are aware of this responsibility, and in choosing their profession voluntarily assume it. They can discharge that responsibility only to the extent that society supports them. If society chooses, for reason of its own, to handicap itself so severely that it cannot or will not deal effectively with the criminal army, it is doubtful that free society as we now enjoy it will continue . . .[69]

Some of the critics are not unaware of the risks involved in denying to the police the power to tap wires or eavesdrop, but deem of higher value a noble concept of the common law that was enunciated so eloquently by Pitt in 1765, "That the poorest man may, in his cottage, bid defiance to all the force of the Crown."[70] Others granting the usefulness of these devices and the greater security it could afford the public are still unwilling to pay a price they view as exorbitant for a liberty-loving people.

[67] *Report of the New Jersey Joint Legislative Committee to Study Wiretapping and the Unauthorized Recording of Speech* (Trenton, 1958), p. 25.

[68] Dash, Schwartz, and Knowlton, p. 42.

[69] W. H. Parker, "Surveillance by Wiretapping or Dictograph: Threat or Protection? A Police Chief's Opinion," *California Law Review*, December, 1954, pp. 727–728.

[70] Quoted in *Wiretapping, Eavesdropping, and the Bill of Rights*, Pt. 5, p. 1956.

If wiretapping is an aid to the police in frustrating foreign agents, so is rifling the mails, so is unrestricted search of private homes, so is summary arrest on suspicion—the ominous knock on the door by night that came to be the symbol of the Gestapo's terror. A great deal could be learned about crime by putting recording devices in confessionals and in physicians' consulting rooms, by compelling wives to testify against their husbands, by encouraging children to report the dangerous thoughts uttered by their parents. The trouble with these techniques, whatever their utility in safeguarding national security, is that a nation which countenances them ceases to be free.[71]

As in so many other areas of sharp controversy, accommodations do emerge which endeavor to reconcile the apparently unreconcilable. Some states—Maryland, Massachusetts, Nevada, New York, and Oregon—now permit wiretapping only "if [law enforcement officers] can present evidence before a State judge showing reasonable cause to believe that a crime . . . is about to be committed, and that telephone interceptions are essential to the processing of the case." [72]

A noted authority on the subject has stressed a number of national reforms which would aim at even more effective controls. Among the proposals he advocates were the following:

First, if eavesdropping is necessary, let this be done not by the police but let it be "lodged entirely in the hands of the District Attorneys . . ."; second, since the enforcement of wiretapping statutes is not "self-executing"—what is needed is an alert community which would keep "recalcitrant police officials" under surveillance, if necessary, through special legislative committees or grand jury investigations. "The key to success is constant supervision and enforcement—by police superiors, district attorneys, bar associations, newspaper reporters, governors, civil liberties organizations, and other opinion-forming elites." Third, helpful also would be statutes which would recognize "an actionable right of privacy" so that the affronted party could recover damages from the wiretapper (Pennsylvania permits suits for treble damages); fourth, by no means least in significance, Congress should "drop its Hamlet-like indecisiveness and enact a tightly guarded court-order system to control F.B.I. wire tapping." [73]

Congress has already wrestled with the eavesdropping problem for years. There are at least three major bills that have been before the Subcommittee on Constitutional Rights which has held a number of public hearings on this subject since 1958.

Limited to certain types of cases and subject to court order, at least two of these bills would permit wiretapping by state as well as by federal officials and would permit also the disclosure of findings and their use as trial evidence. When queried on their views by the committee, of forty-five state attorneys general replying, somewhat surprisingly only fourteen endorsed

[71] Alan Barth, *The Loyalty of Free Men* (New York, 1951), p. 174.
[72] Westin, p. 335.
[73] *Ibid.*, p. 338.

wiretapping by law enforcement officers without major qualifications.[74] Resolution of this controversy does not promise to be either speedy or simple.

CASE PROBLEMS FOR CLASS DISCUSSION

1. Your city has under consideration the establishment of a civilian review board to hear charges of alleged police brutality which grew out of a series of civil rights demonstrations. You are the administrative assistant to the mayor and it is your responsibility to prepare a draft proposal for eventual submission to the city council. How would you proceed?
2. Assume that you are the executive secretary of a private foundation which has decided to sponsor a conference on "capital punishment." How would you structure this conference as to participants, topics, bibliographies, and publications?
3. You have been asked to design a research project which would reveal public attitudes about the effectiveness of law enforcement in your community. Assuming that you are acquainted with the essentials of survey research methods and procedures, what types of questions would you wish to include in your questionnaire?
4. As an assistant to the commissioner of police in your city, it is now your responsibility to prepare a manual for use by the force which describes in nontechnical language the various constitutional and legislative restrictions on search and seizure and on wiretapping. What kind of an outline would you suggest?

SELECTED BIBLIOGRAPHY

"Bail: An Ancient Practice Reexamined," *Yale Law Journal*, May, 1961, pp. 966–977.

EMANUEL CELLER, "Federal Legislative Proposals to Supply Paid Counsel to Indigent Persons Accused of Crime," *Minnesota Law Review*, April, 1961, pp. 697–714.

SAMUEL G. CHAPMAN and T. ERIC ST. JOHNSTON, *The Police Heritage in England and America: A Developmental Survey* (East Lansing, 1962).

ELLIOTT E. CHEATHAM, "A Lawyer When Needed: Legal Services for the Middle Classes," *Columbia Law Review*, June, 1963, pp. 973–986.

ELLERY E. CUFF, "Public Defender System: The Los Angeles Story," *Minnesota Law Review*, April, 1961, pp. 715–735.

WILLIAM M. FERGUSON, "Legal Search and Seizure," *State Government*, Summer, 1963, pp. 152–156.

WARREN FREEDMAN, "News Media Coverage of Criminal Cases and the Right to a Fair Trial," *Nebraska Law Review*, April, 1961, p. 391.

ABRAHAM S. GOLDSTEIN and EDITH W.

FINE, "The Indigent Accused, the Psychiatrist, and the Insanity Defense," *University of Pennsylvania Law Review*, June, 1962, pp. 1061–1093.

VICTOR E. GRIMM, "Wiretapping: The Federal Law," *Journal of Criminal Law, Criminology and Police Science*, November–December, 1960, pp. 441–448.

BRUCE J. HAVIGHURST and PETER MACDOUGALL, "The Representation of Indigent Criminal Defendants in the Federal District Courts," *Harvard Law Review*, January, 1963, pp. 579–618.

ROY E. HOLLADAY, "The Police Administrator—A Politician?" *Journal of Criminal Law, Criminology and Police Science*, December, 1962, pp. 526–529.

FRED E. INBAU, "Public Safety v. Individual Civil Liberties: The Prosecutor's Stand," *Alabama Lawyer*, October, 1961, pp. 414–421.

LESTER D. JANOFF and PHILIP I. AARON, "The Law of Search and Seizure—Federal Standards of Reasonableness," *Brooklyn Law Review*, April, 1962, pp. 302–323.

YALE KAMISAR, "Public Safety v. Individual Liberties: Some 'Facts' and 'Theories',"

[74] Senate Judiciary Committee, *Wiretapping and Eavesdropping Legislation*, Subcommittee on Constitutional Rights. Hearings, May 9–12, 1961, pp. 539–575.

Journal of Criminal Law, Criminology and Police Science, June, 1962, pp. 171–193.

JOHN KAPLAN, "Search and Seizure: A No-Man's Land in the Criminal Law," *California Law Review,* August, 1961, pp. 474–503.

ABE KRASH, "The Right to a Lawyer: The Implications of *Gideon* v. *Wainwright,*" *Notre Dame Lawyer,* February, 1964, pp. 150–160.

ELIOT H. LUMBARD, "Local and State Action Against Organized Crime," *Annals of the American Academy of Political and Social Science,* May, 1963, pp. 82–92.

HERBERT J. MILLER, JR., "A Federal Viewpoint on Combating Organized Crime," *Annals of the American Academy of Political and Social Science,* May, 1963, pp. 93–103.

GORDON E. MISNER, "Recent Developments in Metropolitan Law Enforcement," *Journal of Criminal Law, Criminology and Police Science,* January–February, 1960, pp. 497–508, and July–August, 1960, pp. 265–272.

JAMES H. NEWHOUSE, "Interference with the Right to Free Movement: Stopping and Search of Vehicles," *California Law Review,* December, 1963, pp. 907–922.

MONRAD G. PAULSEN, "Civil Liberties and the Proposals to Curb Organized Crime," *Notre Dame Lawyer,* Symposium, 1963, pp. 699–711.

MORRIS PLOSCOWE, "New Approaches to the Control of Organized Crime," *Annals of the American Academy of Political and Social Science,* May, 1963, pp. 74–81.

HERMAN J. POLLOCK, "Equal Justice in Practice," *Minnesota Law Review,* April, 1961, pp. 737–752.

"Search and Seizure in the Supreme Court: Shadows on the Fourth Amendment," *University of Chicago Law Review,* Summer, 1961, pp. 664–706.

THORSTEN SELLIN, "Organized Crime: A Business Enterprise," *Annals of the American Academy of Political and Social Science,* May, 1963, pp. 12–19.

HELEN B. SHAFFER, "Public Defenders," *Editorial Research Reports,* February 27, 1963, pp. 151–166.

ALAN H. SWANSON, "Wiretrapping: The State Law," *Journal of Criminal Law, Criminology and Police Science,* January–February, 1961, pp. 534–544.

CHARLES D. TARLTON, "The Mentally Ill in Criminal Cases: The Constitutional Issue," *Western Political Quarterly,* September, 1960, pp. 525–540.

O. W. WILSON, "Police Authority in a Free Society," *Journal of Criminal Law, Criminology and Police Science,* June, 1963, pp. 175–177.

PAUL E. WILSON, *Basic Rules of Arrest, Search and Seizure* (Lawrence, Kansas, 1961).

Should judges be elected or appointed?
If elected, should they run on a partisan
or nonpartisan ballot?

Should the rights of defendants and all
state criminal procedures be based on one
national standard?

THE STATE JUDICIARY

ORGANIZATION AND JURISDICTION

Most simply stated the state judiciary consists of at least three, sometimes four, major levels of court organizations. At the bottom of the hierarchy are found the minor courts, or the courts of limited jurisdiction. Their names and functions vary: police courts, family courts, county courts, probate courts, small claims courts, magistrate courts, juvenile courts, justice of the peace courts, etc. These specialized courts hear and settle controversies of a limited nature (in civil matters, generally up to $300), have the power to impose small fines (usually up to $100) or short jail terms (usually up to ninety days), and perform their judicial functions in a setting of informality both of record and procedure. The multiplicity of courts on this level lowest in the hierarchy but closest to the public is not only impressive, but is still characterized in too many states by overlapping jurisdictions, duplicated efforts, antiquated rules, wasteful employment of judicial manpower, and lack of administrative supervision. A 1948 survey of such courts in Detroit noted for example a total of 145 separate tribunals including 104 township justices, eighteen city justices, and six probate and juvenile courts.[1] In Ohio, there are at least 330 separate and distinct courts of limited jurisdiction.[2] New York City until recently could "boast" of over a dozen such separate local courts— none of which constituted a division or branch of a central citywide court and many having exclusive jurisdictions and procedures.[3]

Although many states are replacing rural justices of the peace with county or district courts, those still in existence continue to come under heavy criticism for the abuses that grow out of the fee system, the "informality of the proceedings," judicial incompetence, and many other reasons. And still, the justice of the peace

[1] Maxine B. Virtue, *Survey of Metropolitan Courts: Detroit Area* (Ann Arbor, 1950), p. 6.
[2] Ohio Legislative Research Commission, *The Ohio Court System: Its Organization and Capacity* (Columbus, 1961).
[3] Jewell Cass Phillips, *Municipal Government and Administration in America* (New York, 1960), p. 341.

tries misdemeanor cases in some 32 states. . . . He appears most active in the mountain and western states of Arizona, New Mexico, Wyoming, South Dakota, Idaho, Montana, Oregon, and Washington, and in the southern states of Mississippi and Alabama.[4]

County courts usually handle probate cases, traffic violations, minor civil controversies, misdemeanors, and juvenile offenses. Increases in work load and population as well as demands for professional specialization have led many states to establish separate probate and juvenile courts or to make significant shifts in case loads. In Colorado, for example, mental and juvenile cases now constitute a large share of the county courts' judicial business.

Municipal courts derive their authority from either special acts, statewide general laws, or charter provisions. Much of their time is taken by traffic cases. Of over a million complaints brought before the New Jersey municipal courts between 1954–1955, 93 per cent were in that category.[5] The rest of the cases dealt with the enforcement of city ordinances, settlement of petit causes, or misdemeanors. At issue within the limited jurisdiction of such courts are such matters or charges as disorderly conduct, child abandonment or desertion, vacating of an alley, zoning violations, garnishment of wages, or the interpretation of building codes and ordinances governing the rights and duties of tenants, landlords, retail establishments, or licensees.

Courts of general criminal and civil jurisdiction represent the second major tier in most of the state court hierarchies. Approximately one-third of the states call them circuit courts, in another third they are known as superior courts, and in the remaining third as district courts (see Table 1). As trial courts they form the core of the state judiciary for the important criminal work (felonies) and for the settlement of civil controversies involving monetary amounts substantial enough to exceed the lower court jurisdictions. In some states these courts serve as appellate tribunals for cases initiated in the lower and local courts, but in the majority of states both criminal and civil cases start *de novo* with these higher courts of record where the legal rules and procedures are formal and where the judges are learned in the law and members of the bar.

At the top of the state judiciary stand the courts of last resort. These courts are called Courts of Appeal in Kentucky, Maryland, and New York, Supreme Judicial Courts in Maine and Massachusetts, Supreme Courts of Error in Connecticut, Supreme Courts of Appeal in Virginia and West Virginia, and Supreme Courts in the remaining states (see Table 2). They are courts of from three to nine members. They hear and decide mostly appellate cases. They have the power of judicial review and have original jurisdiction of a restricted nature only. These are the courts of highest prestige and competence.

In order to relieve the courts of last resort from their heavy appeal work,

---

[4] Kenneth E. Vanlandingham, "The Decline of the Justice of the Peace," *The University of Kansas Law Review*, March, 1964, p. 390.

[5] Phillips, p. 342.

TABLE 1. CLASSIFICATION OF COURTS

| State or other jurisdiction | Appellate Courts | | Major Trial Courts | | |
	Court of Last Resort	Intermediate Appellate Court	Chancery Court	Circuit Court	District Court
Alabama	6	6	—	6	—
Alaska	10	—	—	—	—
Arizona	6	—	—	—	—
Arkansas	8	—	6	4	—
California	12	12	—	—	—
Colorado	10	—	—	—	6
Connecticut	8	—	—	—	—
Delaware	12	—	12	—	—
Florida	6	6	—	6	—
Georgia	6	6	—	—	—
Hawaii	7	—	—	6	—
Idaho	6	—	—	—	4
Illinois	10	10	—	6	—
Indiana	6	4	—	6	—
Iowa	8	—	—	—	6
Kansas	6	—	—	—	4
Kentucky	8	—	—	6	—
Louisiana	14	12	—	—	6(m)
Maine	7	—	—	—	—
Maryland	15	—	—	15	—
Massachusetts	Life	—	—	—	Life(r)
Michigan	7	—	—	6	—
Minnesota	6	—	—	—	6
Mississippi	8	—	4	4	—
Missouri	12	12	—	6	—
Montana	6	—	—	—	4
Nebraska	6	—	—	—	6
Nevada	6	—	—	—	4
New Hampshire	To age 70	—	—	—	—
New Jersey	7 with reappointment for life	7 with reappointment for life	—	—	—
New Mexico	8	—	—	—	6
New York	14	5(z)	—	—	—
North Carolina	8	—	—	—	—
North Dakota	10	—	—	—	6
Ohio	6	6	—	—	—
Oklahoma	6	—	—	—	4
Oregon	6	—	—	6	—
Pennsylvania	21	10	—	—	—
Puerto Rico	To age 70	—	—	—	—
Rhode Island	Life	—	—	—	—
South Carolina	10	—	—	4	—

		Terms in years				
		Courts of Limited Jurisdiction				
Major Trial Courts					Justice, Magistrate or	
Superior Court	Other Trial Courts	Probate Court	County Court	Municipal Court	trate or Police Court	Other Courts
—	—	6	—	—	4	—
6	—	—	—	—	(a)	—
4	—	—	—	—	4(b)	—
—	—	—	2	2–4	2	2(c)
6	—	—	—	6	6	—
—	—	—	4	—	2	—
8	—	4	—	—	—	4(c), 4(d) 6(e)
12	—	—	—	12	4	12(c), 12(f)
—	4–6(g)	4	4	2–4	4	4(e,h)
4–8	—	4	—	1–4	4	6(e)
—	—	—	—	2(i)	—	—
—	—	2	—	2	2	—
—	—	(j)	(j)	(j)	(j)	—
4	4(k)	4	—	4	4	4(e)
—	—	—	—	4	2	4(l)
—	—	2	2	2	2	—
—	—	—	4	—	4	—
—	—	—	—	4–6(n)	4	6–8(e)
7	—	4	—	—	—	7(i)
—	15(o)	4	—	8–10(p)	2	4(q)
Life	—	Life	—	Life	—	Life(s)
6	6(t)	6	—	6	4	6(c)
—	—	4	—	4	2	—
—	—	—	4	—	4	(u)
—	4(c)	4	—	—	4	4(v)
—	—	—	—	2	2	—
—	—	—	4	4	2	6(w)
—	—	—	—	4	2	—
To age 70	—	To age 70	—	To age 70	—	To age 70(i)
7 with reappointment for life	5(x)	—	—	3	—	5(e,y)
—	—	2	—	—	2	2(h)
—	6(w), 14(aa)	6	—	—	4	—
8	—	—	2–4	2	2–6	2(e)
—	—	—	2	—	2–4	—
—	6(c)	6	4	6	4	6(e)
4	—	—	2	—	2	4(c), 6(e)
—	—	—	6	—	6	6(l)
—	10(c)	10	10	—	6	—
12	—	—	—	—	4	8(i)
Life	—	—	—	—	—	3(i),(f)
—	—	4	4	—	(ab)	—

TABLE 1 (*continued*)

| State or other jurisdiction | Terms in years | | | | |
| | Appellate Courts | | Major Trial Courts | | |
	Court of Last Resort	Intermediate Appellate Court	Chancery Court	Circuit Court	District Court
South Dakota	6	—	—	4	—
Tennessee	8	8	8	8	—
Texas	6	6	—	—	4
Utah	10	—	—	—	6
Vermont	2	—	—	—	—
Virginia	12	—	8	8	—
Washington	6	—	—	—	—
West Virginia	12	—	—	8	—
Wisconsin	10	—	—	6	—
Wyoming	8	—	—	—	6

(a) At pleasure of Presiding Judge of Superior Court.
(b) For justices of the peace. Terms of city and town magistrates provided by charter or ordinance.
(c) Courts of common pleas. In Missouri, now presided over by circuit judges.
(d) Circuit Court.
(e) Juvenile courts; in Florida, New Jersey and Virginia, juvenile and domestic relations courts.
(f) Family courts. In Rhode Island, judges serve during "good behavior."
(g) Courts of record.
(h) Small claims courts.
(i) District courts.
(j) Effective January 1, 1964, part of circuit court system.
(k) Criminal courts.
(l) Statutory courts; superior, district, civil, small claims.
(m) Judges in New Orleans serve 12 years.
(n) Judges in Baton Rouge serve four years.
(o) Supreme Bench of Baltimore.
(p) People's Courts of Baltimore City and Montgomery County; Municipal Court of Baltimore City.
(q) People's Court of Baltimore County.
(r) Includes Boston Juvenile Court.

fourteen states, among them California, Illinois, New Jersey, New York, Ohio, Pennsylvania, and Texas, have interposed between trial courts of general jurisdiction and supreme courts an intermediate appellate court, empowered by statute to serve as a tribunal of final determination for a wide variety of cases.

JUDICIAL TERMS, TENURE, AND SELECTION

One of the sadder aspects of American justice is that at the points of contact between the largest number of people and the judiciary stand the local or minor courts, all too often physically least attractive, undignified in their lack of decorum, most informal in their procedures, and presided over by judges untrained in the law who grind out sentences mechanically. Even the most conscientious are frequently worn down by the sheer pressure of work or feel unchallenged by the relative monotony characteristic of a traffic calendar or magistrate's night term.

| Major Trial Courts | | Courts of Limited Jurisdiction | | | | |
Superior Court	Other Trial Courts	Probate Court	County Court	Municipal Court	Justice, Magistrate or Police Court	Other Courts
—	—	—	2	4	2–4(ac)	—
—	8(k)	—	(ad)	—	6	8(ae)
—	—	—	4	—	4	—
—	—	—	—	6	4	6(e)
—	2(x)	2	—	2	2	—
—	8(af)	—	4	4	4	4–6(e)
4	—	—	—	—	4	—
—	—	—	6	(ag)	(ag)	6–8(ah)
—	—	—	6	—	2	—
—	—	—	—	—	2	—

Terms in years

(s) Land Court of Massachusetts.
(t) Recorder's Court of Detroit.
(u) City courts.
(v) St. Louis Court of Criminal Corrections.
(w) Workmen's Comp. courts; Court of Ind. Relations.
(x) County courts.
(y) County district courts.
(z) Justices are designated for five-year terms while retaining status as elected Supreme Court Justices.
(aa) Supreme Court, to age 70; judges may be certified thereafter for two-year terms, up to age 76.
(ab) Terms not uniform; fixed by General Assembly.
(ac) Township justices and police magistrates, two years; county justices of the peace, four years
(ad) Six years for county chairmen; terms of county judges fixed by private acts.
(ae) Courts of general sessions.
(af) Corporation, hustings, law and equity courts, law and chancery courts.
(ag) Municipal and police courts variable.
(ah) Common pleas, domestic relations, criminal, intermediate and juvenile courts.

SOURCE: *Book of the States, 1964–1965*, p. 125.

Fortunately, the pattern rapidly becoming the stipulated norm for the more important county and municipal judges now is a legal education, and in place of the old fee system, a fixed salary paid out of public funds.

Typical also for these local courts is a two- or four-year term of office, popular election rather than appointment, and with the exception of many Southern and New England states, a nominally nonpartisan rather than a partisan ballot.

For major trial and appellate courts the prevailing length of term is either four or six years while for the courts of last resort, the supreme courts, the common patterns are six, eight, ten, twelve years or even life (or age 70) terms (see Table 1). Annual compensation for most of these judges falls between $15,000 and $25,000.

When the federal Constitution was written, it was decided that the theory of judicial separateness and independence would be served more effectively if the president were to appoint the members of the federal bench for life terms. Some of the state constitutions gave similar power to governors, but the impact of Jacksonian populism was too strong. Democracy was identified with rotation in office, with short terms and with long ballots, and with a judiciary close to the people. However, the panacea of curing the ills of democracy with more democracy proved to be chimerical, and instead of being close to the people, too many judges were found closer to venal bosses, to favor-seeking political machines, and to selfish economic interests. During the reform era of the early twentieth century judicial terms were lengthened, and even the gubernatorial appointment of major court judges rather than their election was considered occasionally essential to progressive government.

Presently statutes and constitutions provide for four methods of selecting major trial court and appellate court judges (see Table 3).

(1) In eleven states the governor appoints major court judges: Alaska (initially), California (initially), Delaware, Hawaii, Iowa (initially), Maine, Massachusetts, Missouri (initially), Nebraska (initially), New Hampshire, and New Jersey. Appellate court judges only are appointed in California and Kansas. In Rhode Island only trial court judges and justices of the peace are so selected.

(2) In eighteen states judges are elected at partisan elections: Alabama, Arkansas, Colorado, Florida, Georgia, Illinois, Indiana, Kansas (except supreme court judges), Kentucky, Louisiana, Mississippi, New Mexico, New York, North Carolina, Oklahoma, Pennsylvania, Texas, and West Virginia.

(3) Seventeen states elect their major court judges initially at nonpartisan elections: Arizona, California (trial courts only), Idaho, Maryland, Michigan, Minnesota, Montana, Nevada, North Dakota, Ohio, Oregon, South Dakota, Tennessee, Utah, Washington, Wisconsin, and Wyoming.

(4) Major court judges in five states are elected by the legislature: Connecticut, Rhode Island (supreme court only), South Carolina, Vermont, and Virginia.

Surveying these diverse methods of judicial selection at least three observations may be made. First, for whatever reasons, historical or political, the American state electorate has not been able to arrive at a clear consensus regarding its preference for an elective or appointive judiciary; second, there do appear to be significant regional differences—the Midwestern states heavily leaning in the direction of nonpartisan elections, whereas the Southern states seem to prefer the partisan pattern; third, gubernatorial appointment is favored by the two youngest states, Alaska and Hawaii, and retained by some of the oldest states, Massachusetts, Maine, and New Hampshire.

THE SELECTION OF JUDGES—APPOINTMENT OR PARTISAN ELECTION

Whether judges should be appointed or elected has been argued for years by members of the American Bar Association, judges, judicial reformers, legislators, governors, and political scientists. The case for gubernatorial appointment of the major court judges rests frequently on two central premises: (1) a claim of insulating the judges from personal political involve-

TABLE 2. STATE COURTS OF LAST RESORT

State or jurisdiction	Name of court †	Number of justices	At large	By dist.	Method of selection ‡	Term ‡
ıa..........	S.C.	7	*	—	Popular election	6 yrs.
....	S.C.	3	*(a)	—	Nominated by Judicial Council; appointed by Governor	Remainder of term as Justice
....	S.C.	5	*	—	Selected by Court	Unspecified
as........	S.C.	7	*	—	Popular election	8 yrs.
ıia........	S.C.	7	*(a)	—	Appointed by Governor	Remainder of term as Justice
lo........	S.C.	7	*	—	Appointed by Court-rotation	1 yr.
ticut........	S.C.E.	5	*(b)	—	Nominated by Gov. Apptd. by Gen. Assembly	8 yrs.
re........	S.C.	3	*(c)	—	Appointed by Governor. Confirmed by Senate	12 yrs.
....	S.C.	7	*	—	Appointed by Court-rotation	2 yrs.
....	S.C.	7	*	—	Appointed by Court	Remainder of term as Justice
....	S.C.	5	*(c)	—	Appointed by Governor with consent of Senate	7 years
....	S.C.	5	*	—	Justice with shortest time to serve	Remainder of term as Justice
....	S.C.	7	—	*	Appointed by Court-rotation	3 yrs.
....	S.C.	5	*	—	Appointed by Court-rotation	6 mos.
....	S.C.	9	*(a)	—	Selected by Court	Remainder of term as Justice
....	S.C.	7	*(a)	—	Seniority of service	Remainder of term as Justice
ky.......	C.A.	7(d)	—	*	Seniority of service-rotation	18 mos.
ıa	S.C.	7	—	*	Seniority of service	Remainder of term as Justice
....	S.J.C.	6	*(c)	—	Appointed by Governor	7 yrs.
ıd.......	C.A.	7	—	*(a)	Selected by Governor from Judges	Remainder of term as Judge
ıusetts...	S.J.C.	7	*(c)	—	Appointed by Governor	Life
ın........	S.C.	7	*	—	Appointed by Court	Pleasure of Court
ota........	S.C.	7	*	—	Popular election	6 yrs.
ppi........	S.C.	9	—	*	Seniority of service	Remainder of term as Justice
i........	S.C.	7(d)	*(a)	—	Appointed by Court-rotation	4 yrs.
a........	S.C.	5	*	—	Popular election	6 yrs.
ka........	S.C.	7	—	*(a,e)	Popular election	6 yrs.
....	S.C.	3	*	—	Seniority of service-rotation	2 yrs.
mpshire..	S.C.	5	*(c)	—	Appointed by Governor and Council	To age 70
sey......	S.C.	7	*(c)	—	Appointed by Governor with consent of Senate	7 yrs. with reappointment for life
exico.....	S.C.	5	*	—	Justice with shortest term to serve	Remainder of term as Justice
rk........	C.A.	7	*	—	Popular election	14 yrs.
arolina...	S.C.	7	*	—	Popular election	8 yrs.
akota....	S.C.	5	*	—	Justice with shortest term to serve	2 yrs.
....	S.C.	7	*	—	Popular election	6 yrs.
ıa.......	S.C.(f)	9	*(g)	*(g)	Appointed by Court	2 yrs.
....	S.C.	7	*	—	Majority vote of members of Supreme Court	6 yrs.
vania....	S.C.	7	*	—	Justice with shortest time to serve	Remainder of term as Justice
₹ico......	S.C.	9	*(c)	—	Appointed by Governor with consent of Senate	To age 70
sland....	S.C.	5	*(h)	—	Elected by Legislature	Life
arolina...	S.C.	5	*(h)	—	Elected by General Assembly	10 yrs.
akota....	S.C.	5	—	*	Appointed by Court-rotation	1 yr.
ce.......	S.C.	5	*(i)	—	Appointed by Court	Pleasure of Court
....	S.C.(f)	9	*	—	Popular election	6 yrs.
....	S.C.	5	*	—	Justice with shortest time to serve	Remainder of term as Justice

TABLE 2 (continued)

State or other jurisdiction	Name of court †	Number of justices	At large	By dist.	Method of selection ‡	Chief Justice Term ‡
Vermont_____S.C.		5	*(h)	—	Elected by General Assembly	2 yrs.
Virginia_____S.C.A.		7	*(h)	—	Seniority of service	Remainder of term as
Washington_____S.C.		9	*	—	Appointed by Court-rotation	2 yrs.
West Virginia____S.C.A.		5	*	—	Appointed by Court-rotation	1 yr.
Wisconsin_____S.C.		7	*	—	Seniority of service	Remainder of term as
Wyoming_____S.C.		4	*	—	Justice with shortest time to serve	Remainder of term as

† Explanation of symbols:
S.C.   Supreme Court.
S.C.E. Supreme Court of Errors.
C.A.   Court of Appeals.
S.J.C. Supreme Judicial Court.
S.C.A. Supreme Court of Appeals.
‡ Method of selection and term as Chief Justice rather than term as Justice on the Court.
(a) Justices originally appointed by Governor, elected subsequently.
(b) Justices are nominated by Governor, appointed by General Assembly.
(c) Justices are appointed by Governor, with consent of Senate; in Maine, Massachusetts, New Hampshire w: sent of Council.
(d) In addition, there are 4 commissioners assisting the Court in Kentucky and 6 in Missouri.
(e) Chief Justice is chosen at large.
(f) There is a separate 3-judge Court of Criminal Appeals which is the court of last resort in criminal cases.
(g) Nominated by district, elected at large.
(h) Justices are elected by legislature.
(i) Justices are chosen at large (each voter may vote for 5) but not more than two may reside in any one of t! geographical regions of the state.

SOURCE: *Book of the States, 1964–1965*, p. 132.

ments, and (2) a claim of removing from the general public an electoral choice they cannot intelligently make since the evaluating of judicial competence is a professional and not a layman's task.

(1) If an attorney wishing to become a judge must seek office via the party ballot, and if he wishes to do this successfully, he is forced to become a politician or a politician's friend. This, the critics of the elective method contend, may seriously compromise his future judicial independence. Moreover, an election requires money and organization, neither of which can be obtained without a "sense of indebtedness" that could lead to subsequent pressures and favor-seeking. Some highly qualified attorneys who would make exceptionally able members of the bench may find this political involvement repugnant and unworthy of their professional talents. However noble the techniques of campaigning—a dinner in honor of the candidate, a volunteer committee of prominent party attorneys (even with some sprinkling of opposition party names), or endorsements from nonpartisan groups—the partisan nature of the office cannot easily avoid some future partisan liability.

(2) How can a voter distinguish a "good" judicial candidate from one "not so good"—by his platform, his promises, his character, by the source of his law degree, by his academic record, or by the severity of his sentences, in case he is the incumbent? Let the governor make this choice. He has the knowledge and the staff to screen the candidates and to evaluate their accom-

TABLE 3. FINAL SELECTION OF JUDGES OF ALL STATE COURTS

na_____	All elected on partisan ballot except that some juvenile court judges are appointed. Of these appointments, some are by Governor, some by legislature and some by county commissions.
_____	Supreme Court Justices and superior court judges appointed by Governor from nominations by Judicial Council. Approved or rejected at first general election held more than three years after appointment, on non-partisan ballot. Re-elected on non-partisan ballot—Supreme Court Justices every 10 years, superior court judges every 6 years. Magistrate judges appointed by and serve at pleasure of Presiding Judge of Superior Court.
a_____	Supreme and superior court judges elected on non-partisan ballot; justices of the peace elected on partisan ballot; city and town magistrates selected as provided by charter or ordinance.
as_____	All elected on partisan ballot.
nia_____	Supreme Court and district courts of appeals judges appointed by Governor with approval of Commn. on Judicial Appointments. Run for re-election on record. All judges elected on non-partisan ballot.
do_____	All elected on partisan ballot except that municipal judges and police magistrates are appointed by the municipality's governing body unless a home rule charter provides otherwise.
ticut_____	All selected by legislature from nominations submitted by Governor except that probate judges are elected on partisan ballot.
re_____	All appointed by Governor with consent of the Senate.
_____	All elected on partisan ballot.
a_____	All elected on partisan ballot except county and some city court judges are appointed by the Governor with the consent of the Senate.
_____	Supreme Court Justices and circuit court judges appointed by the Governor with consent of the Senate. District magistrates appointed by Chief Justice of the state.
_____	Supreme Court and district court judges are elected on non-partisan ballot; probate judges on partisan ballot; justices of the peace appointed by board of county commissioners and probate judge with approval of senior district judge.
_____	All elected on partisan ballot; run on record for re-election. Magistrates, appointed by circuit judges, serve at pleasure of judges.
a_____	All elected on partisan ballot except that judge of municipal court is appointed by Governor.
_____	Judges of Supreme and district courts appointed initially by Governor from lists submitted by non-partisan nominating commission. Run on record for retention in office. Municipal and superior court judges elected on non-partisan ticket and justices of the peace on partisan ticket.
a_____	Supreme Court Judges appointed by Governor from list submitted by nominating commission. Run on record for re-election. All other judges elected on partisan ballot.
ky_____	All elected on partisan ballot.
na_____	All elected on partisan ballot.
_____	All appointed by Governor with consent of Executive Council except that probate judges are elected on partisan ballot.
nd_____	Judges of Court of Appeals, Circuit Courts and Supreme Bench of Baltimore appointed by Governor, elected on non-partisan ballot after at least one year's service. Trial magistrates appointed by Governor. People's Court judges in Baltimore City appointed initially; present incumbents run on record for re-election. Those subsequently appointed run for election. People's Court judges in Baltimore County appointed initially by Governor with consent of Senate, thereafter appointed by Governor. People's Court judges of Montgomery County appointed by County Council. Judges of Municipal Court of Baltimore City elected on non-partisan ballot.
husetts_____	All appointed by Governor with consent of the Council.
an_____	All elected on non-partisan ballot.
sota_____	All elected on non-partisan ballot.
sippi_____	All elected on partisan ballot.
ri_____	Judges of Supreme Court, appellate courts, circuit and probate courts in St. Louis and Jackson County and St. Louis Court of Criminal Corrections appointed initially by Governor from nominations submitted by special commissions. Run on record for re-election. All other judges elected on partisan ballot.

TABLE 3 (*continued*)

Montana_____	All elected on non-partisan ballot except that some judges of police courts are appointed councils or commissioners.
Nebraska_____	Judges of Supreme and District Courts and some juvenile court and municipal judges ap by Governor from lists submitted by non-partisan nominating commissions. Run on re retention in office. Workmen's Compensation Court and Court of Industrial Relations ap by Governor. Other judges elected.
Nevada_____	All elected on non-partisan ballot.
New Hampshire____	All appointed by Governor with confirmation of the Council.
New Jersey_____	All appointed by Governor with consent of Senate except that surrogates are elected, gistrates of municipal courts serving one municipality only are appointed by governing
New Mexico_____	All elected on partisan ballot.
New York_____	All elected on partisan ballot except that Governor appoints judges of Court of Claims ar nates members of appellate division of Supreme Court, and Mayor of New York appoint of some local courts.
North Carolina_____	All elected on partisan ballot except that a few county court judges are appointed by Gov county commissioners, some magistrates are appointed by Governor or General Assembly venile court judges are appointed by county commissioners or city boards.
North Dakota_____	All elected on non-partisan ballot.
Ohio_____	All elected on non-partisan ballot.
Oklahoma_____	All elected on partisan ballot except judge of Tulsa County Juvenile Court who is appoint a list submitted by a committee of lawyers and laymen.
Oregon_____	All elected on non-partisan ballot.
Pennsylvania_____	All elected on partisan ballot.
Puerto Rico_____	All appointed by the Governor with consent of the Senate.
Rhode Island_____	Supreme Court Justices elected by legislature. Superior, family and district court jud justices of the peace appointed by Governor, with consent of Senate (except for justice peace); probate judges appointed by city or town councils.
South Carolina_____	Supreme Court and circuit court judges elected by legislature. City judges, magistrates ar county judges appointed by Governor. Probate judges and some county judges elected o san ballot.
South Dakota_____	All elected on non-partisan ballot, except county justices of the peace, who are appointed senior circuit judge of the judicial circuit in which the county is located.
Tennessee_____	All elected on non-partisan ballot.
Texas_____	All elected on partisan ballot.
Utah_____	All elected on non-partisan ballot except that juvenile court judges are appointed by Go with consent of Department of Welfare and town justices appointed by town trustees.
Vermont_____	Supreme Court and county court presiding judges elected by legislature. Municipal jud pointed by Governor. Assistant judges of county courts and probate judges elected on p ballot.
Virginia_____	Supreme Court of Appeals and all major trial court judges elected by legislature. Practic judges of courts of limited jurisdiction appointed by judges of major trial courts. Some, hc are elected by popular vote, some by the legislature, and some by city councils.
Washington_____	All elected on non-partisan ballot.
West Virginia_____	All elected on partisan ballot.
Wisconsin_____	All elected on non-partisan ballot.
Wyoming_____	Supreme Court justices and district court judges elected on a non-partisan basis and other on a partisan basis.

SOURCE: *Book of the States, 1964–1965*, p. 126.

plishments and should he fail to do this well, the responsibility for an inferior appointment would clearly be his. No incumbent state executive cherishes the thought of a judicial scandal at the next general election.

The case for retaining the party ballot for selecting the judiciary, of course, has its supporters also.

Parties have in the past and will continue in the future to select able judges, men in whose integrity the public can place its faith. Were this not so, democracy would have failed long ago. If the electorate is held competent to decide intelligently and choose professional politicians to run their legislatures and their executive branches, why can they not select equally well the judiciary, the professionals of the bench?

Furthermore, there is nothing wrong with reflecting party opinion, suggests one supporter of the case for the judicial party ballot:

> The judgments of the courts reflect not only the established body of substantive law but also reflect in their opinions the changed economic conditions and social mores of our times. Therefore, it is to be hoped that a judge's political affiliation, which cannot help but have a substantial impact on his decisions, should be representative of the party which elects him. Any system which makes more remote the influence of the free electorate on those who hold high office should be discarded.[6]

THE MISSOURI PLAN

Missouri's method of selecting members of the supreme court and other major courts in Jackson County and St. Louis represents an attempt to combine a nonpartisan system of election with that of the gubernatorial appointment. Briefly, its essential features are these:

A. Judicial nominations for the appellate divisions are made by a special nonpartisan commission composed of seven members—the chief justice of the supreme court (chairman), three laymen appointed by the governor, and three attorneys selected by the bar association.

B. This commission submits a list of three names for each judicial vacancy from which the governor must then select one to fill the office.

C. At the next general election, after the judge has served at least one year, his name is placed on a nonpartisan ballot without any other name in opposition.
   "Shall Judge _____
   (Here the name of the judge shall be inserted)
   of the _____
   (Here the title of the court shall be inserted)
   Court be retained in office.   Yes   No
                                      (Scratch one)"

D. A full, regular term following an affirmative vote is twelve years for the appellate courts and six years for the major trial courts.

[6] William J. Keefe, "Judges and Politics: The Pennsylvania Plan of Judge Selection," *University of Pittsburgh Law Review*, May, 1959, p. 628. See also Claude J. Davis, *Judicial Section in West Virginia* (Morgantown, 1959).

Iowa, Kansas, and Nebraska have adopted a similar system. In Kansas, its operation is limited to the membership of the supreme court only, but in Iowa, it applies to the district courts as well, and in Nebraska, to some municipal and juvenile courts.

California also has a form of appointment-election system for selecting its judiciary, but the governor must first select the candidate and then submit his name to a qualifications commission for approval before he is entitled to a full term (twelve years for the supreme court and district court of appeals; six years for the superior court). This qualifications commission which includes the chief justice, a presiding justice of the district court of appeals, and the attorney general, has to date turned down only one gubernatorial nomination.

California's ballot:

> Shall John T. Johanson   Yes_____
> be elected to the office for the   No_____
> term expiring January 1, 1970.

Rejection of the nomination either by the commission or by the majority of the voters will make it necessary for the governor to submit another name and repeat the process again.

In Alaska judicial nominations to the governor are made by a seven-member judicial council composed of three attorneys appointed by the bar association, three non-attorney members appointed by the governor (but subject to confirmation by a majority vote of the legislature), and the chief justice (ex officio and chairman). Once appointed, the name of the supreme court justice must then be placed on a nonpartisan ballot and voted on at the next general election following the completion of the judge's third year in office. Unless rejected by the electorate, a supreme court justice will then be given his full ten-year term and a superior court judge his full six-year term of office.

Alaska, California, Iowa, Kansas, Missouri, and Nebraska have thus sought to strengthen their judiciaries by assuring their judges long tenure, by giving the bar association a significant role in the nomination process, and by devising a nonpartisan ballot with a built-in advantage to the incumbent. Judicial reformers who praise the Missouri Plan which these states have adopted tend to stress that the pattern

A. Removes judges from politics and politicians and thus contributes to attracting more qualified candidates to the bench.
B. Prevents the bench from being staffed with judges who are politically indebted by restricting the governor's choice to the three nominees of the nonpartisan commission.
C. Saves the electorate from having to vote on competing judicial candidates of whom they know little and whose backgrounds and professional qualifications they cannot properly evaluate.

Critics of the Missouri Plan meanwhile contend that:

A. Judges are policy-makers whose decisions affect important areas of public life which means that their nomination, even if it should be desirable, cannot, in fact, be removed from political considerations.
B. They are unwilling to place such great powers over the recruitment and selection of judges in the representatives of a conservative bench and bar who would tend to dominate the nominating commissions.
C. They see nothing wrong in the more democratic and traditional patterns where judges regardless of whether they reached the bench by gubernatorial appointment or by direct election have shown themselves generally responsible and judicially competent.

Research findings to date have not yet been able to demonstrate that the Missouri Plan is superior to older methods of securing the services of more highly qualified judges. So far, little is known about the hidden political interplay between governors, bar association representatives, judges, and laymen in the composition and work of the nominating commissions.[7] What is quite clear, however, is that no bar association can be considered politically antiseptic. Political considerations may operate with more subtlety and refinement than they do in a party caucus or convention, but there is little doubt about the party inclination or ideological position of leading members of the bar. Most of them tend to reflect the views of economic interest groups whose attitudes about political candidates and governmental policies—especially those affecting property, labor, civil rights, and taxation—can hardly be considered vacuous.

Until fairly recently very little scholarly research had been devoted to analyzing the relationships between the political party identification of the judiciary and the process of judicial decision-making.[8] Does the fact that a judge may have been identified as a Republican or Democrat, or that he may

[7] A careful study of the Missouri Plan's operation is presently being conducted under a grant from the Social Science Research Council by Professors Ronald G. Downing, Frederick C. Spiegel, and Richard A. Watson (all of the University of Missouri); special attention is focused on the roles and actions of the various participants in the nominating commissions and how their actions affect the recruitment of judges; see the paper "Judicial Selection Under the Missouri Plan," delivered by the group of authors at the annual meeting of the Midwest Conference of Political Scientists, Madison, Wisconsin, May 2, 1964. See also John E. Crow, "Subterranean Politics: A Judge is Chosen," Journal of Public Law, XII, 1963, pp. 275–289.

[8] Among some of the major studies in the field of judicial decision-making, the following should be mentioned: Glendon Schubert, Quantitative Analysis of Judicial Behavior (Glencoe, 1959); C. Herman Pritchett, The Roosevelt Court: A Study in Judicial Politics and Values, 1937–1947 (New York, 1948); Pritchett, Civil Liberties and the Vinson Court (Chicago, 1954); S. Sidney Ulmer, "The Analysis of Behavior Patterns in the United States Supreme Court," Journal of Politics, November, 1960, pp. 629–653; Schubert, "The Study of Judicial Decision-Making as an Aspect of Political Behavior," American Political Science Review, December, 1958, pp. 1007–1025; Schubert, "The 1960 Term of the Supreme Court: A Psychological Analysis," American Political Science Review, March, 1962, pp. 90–107; Schubert, "Judicial Attitudes and Voting Behavior: the 1961 Term of the United States Supreme Court," Law and Contemporary Problems, Winter, 1963, pp. 100–142; and Eloise C. Snyder, "Political Power and the Ability to Win Supreme Court Decisions," Social Forces, October, 1960, pp. 36–40

have been active politically, have any significant and legitimate bearing upon his approach to cases involving public issues which basically divide the parties? Does his new role on the bench remove from him all of his former partisan predilections of ideology or program? These are extremely difficult questions.

Most judges regardless of their present or past political attachments will assert their judicial independence and stress the irrelevancy, if not the impropriety, of the query. Judicial nonpartisanship is a deeply embedded value in this country's legal and political ethos. Its wide acceptance in public opinion is underscored by the large number of states which elect their judges on a nonpartisan ballot.

Further complicating any determination of the role of party in the decision-making process is the fact that party labels as such offer little assurance of clearly delineated ideological affinities or positions. There are liberal and conservative Republicans and liberal and conservative Democrats, and as far as judicial decision-making is concerned, such denotations as "liberal" and "conservative" may in fact describe much more accurately a judge's political value framework than his former "party membership" ever could. (Chief Justice Warren, a Republican from California, and Associate Justice Tom Clark, a Democrat from Texas, are two excellent cases in point.) Still, if it is proper to assume that a majority of Northern Democrats are more liberally inclined than a majority of Republicans, is it also possible to assume that Democratic judges would tend to be more liberal in their decisions than their Republican colleagues? A recent study of the relationship between political party and judicial decision-making among 313 state and federal supreme court justices serving on multimember courts attempts to suggest that this may actually be the case.

The author of this study selected certain types of cases which raised questions that he considered ideologically significant in that they dealt with issues that touched on the very basic role and function of government in society.

Among a group of fifteen such issues, he found that "Democratic judges sitting on the same supreme court with Republican judges were more prone to favor

    A. the defense in criminal cases;
    B. the administrative agency in business regulation cases;
    C. the claimant in unemployment cases;
    D. the finding of a constitutional violation in criminal-constitutional cases;
    E. the government in tax cases;
    F. the tenant in landlord-tenant cases;
    G. the consumer in sales-of-goods cases;
    H. the injured party in motor vehicle accident cases;
    I. the employee in employee injury cases." [9]

[9] Stuart S. Nagel, "Political Party Affiliation and Judges' Decisions," American Political Science Review, December, 1961, p. 845; see also his "Unequal Party Representation on the State Supreme Courts," Journal of the American Judicature Society, August, 1961,

While such findings may raise more questions than they answer (such as the appropriateness of the cases and the scheme of classification), they do lend support to those who maintain that the overrepresentation of Republicans on state supreme courts (67 per cent to 33 per cent in the North, in 1955, when the area was nearly evenly divided in congressional vote) constitutes a politically built-in conservative bias against the governmental policies and attitudes reflected among Democrats.

A PROFILE OF TRIAL PROCEDURES

A political society that treasures its individualism, its emphasis on the equality of all before the law, and its doctrine of the presumption of innocence of those accused of a crime will likely need to have trial procedures that are somewhat complex and cumbersome. Life is complex and so are the factual situations which form the heart and substance of the many human conflict situations that seek court litigation and settlement. Trial procedures in state courts have grown out of precedents of common law and equity originally transplanted to this country from England.

These precedents were then modified or adapted by American courts and legislatures to meet this country's indigenous legal climate and needs. Court practices continue to differ notably from state to state and often from court to court within a state. And yet there are major procedural stages common to nearly all jurisdictions.

In a civil suit,

A. Plaintiff through his attorney files a declaration, complaint or petition with a clerk of court setting out the nature of the case. In equity proceedings he may file a bill.

B. Defendant through his attorney will answer such a declaration with a demurrer or denial of allegation.

C. Judge will rule on the adequacy or sufficiency of the response—if not sustained or given judgment in his favor defendant must then prepare for trial, unless an out of court settlement can be reached by agreement between the parties.

D. Trial may or may not involve a jury. In equity proceedings juries are generally not called, although there are some situations in which a limited factual question may be submitted to them subject to the court's discretion.

E. When juries are used most of them will include twelve persons but there are significant variations. In forty states provisions exist which permit courts of limited jurisdiction to use smaller juries. Only sixteen states will permit such smaller juries for civil trials in courts of general jurisdiction.

pp. 62–65. In another article, Professor Nagel concluded that federal and state supreme court judges "who are white Anglo-Saxon Protestants (or at least Anglo-Saxon Protestants) tend to be found on the conservative side of split decisions on their respective courts more so than do non-Anglo-Saxon non-Protestants (or at least non-Anglo-Saxon Catholics)." "Ethnic Affiliations and Judicial Propensities," *Journal of Politics*, February, 1962, pp. 109–110.

F. The swearing-in of jurors may involve some time since each side to the controversy is given a number of challenges which entitles it to object to the inclusion of this or that person for such causes as bias, personal connection with the case, incompetence, etc. A certain number of challenges can be peremptory which means that no basis for obligation need be given.

G. Witnesses are called, sworn, examined, and cross-examined by counsel for plaintiff and defendant. Evidence is introduced. Counsel has the right to enter objections to statements or evidence which then forces the judge to rule on the question of sustaining or of overruling such objections. Such rulings based on the judge's interpretation of the applicable law may then subsequently be used as basis for appeal by the losing party.

H. After the presentation of the case and after each side has attempted to tear down or cast a shadow of doubt on the veracity of witnesses and evidence adduced by the other party, the judge may order the jury to bring in a verdict—a directed verdict, if he decides the issues to have been resolved preponderantly in favor of the plaintiff's case, or he may let the case go to jury determination.

I. After summation of the arguments—but in some states before—the judge will have to instruct the jury in the applicable law and outline to the jury the framework within which they must assess the conflicting factual content of the trial.

J. The jury's verdict or judgment may be in favor of the plaintiff, in favor of the defendant, or may set forth the damages that are to be paid to the winning party. If it cannot arrive at a verdict—and this does not require unanimity in most civil cases—a new trial will have to be ordered.

K. Upon arriving at the verdict, the losing party may move for a new trial. The petition for such a trial may be based on an allegedly erroneous ruling of the judge on motions (such as an initial motion to dismiss the case) or on objections, or on alleged failure to provide the jury with the proper instructions in the law.

L. Not all judgments can be taken to an appellate court as a matter of right. If the case does so qualify in the opinion of the reviewing court, it will be the briefs and the records of the court that customarily form the basis of a second hearing (process in appellate courts does not involve a trial *de novo*). Appellate courts may affirm, reverse, or remand for a retrial the judgments of a lower court. If affirmed, the winning party may have an execution of judgment which ordinarily means that money must be paid, or property given by the defendant.

Criminal procedure varies from civil procedure in at least four major respects:

A. Following the issuance of a warrant for the arrest of the accused, his arraignment before a magistrate, the conclusion of preliminary hearings (and the possible release of the defendant on bail), it becomes the responsibility of the state's district attorney or county prosecutor to charge the defendant with having committed the particular crime. The formal legal charge is obtained either through an indictment by a grand jury or through a writ of information (in about half of the states) which the prosecuting attorney presents to the trial court.

B. Upon the plea of "not guilty," the trial begins with the selection of a petit jury of twelve unless a jury trial is waived (which is not very frequent and is impossible in some states). The number of peremptory challenges permitted the defense is usually greater in criminal proceedings than it is in civil suits. Depending on the nature of the crime, some of the states allow the use of smaller juries.

C. Throughout the trial, counsel will attempt to conduct his defense tactics in such a way as to maximize doubt in the minds of the jury that the defendant could or actually did commit the crime while the prosecutor must establish the defendant's guilt "beyond a reasonable doubt."

D. After the jury arrives at its verdict, and following possible pleas for leniency, the judge will pronounce sentence and then order the defendant turned over to the sheriff. Under the indeterminate sentence statutes, judges will be required to determine the maximum sentence only, thus leaving the state administrative agencies—parole or prison boards—possible discretion to release the defendant conditionally (prior to having served the maximum length of his sentence) on basis of his penal record or on other grounds which to them indicate that the optimum rehabilitative effort has been achieved and that society would be better served by the defendant's release from incarceration.

THE DILEMMA OF PUNISHMENT

Even the most cursory glance at state criminal statutes and sentencing practices reveals enormous differences. Median terms served by all persons sent to prison for all offenses in Vermont is a period of ten months, but in Illinois it is thirty-eight months. For manslaughter the range of median time served is from 17 months in Tennessee to 54 months in New York. And so it goes for nearly all offenses.

What then is the essence of punishment? Fundamentally, is it to punish the criminal for the crime that he has committed, society's institutionalized lesson in place of personal revenge? Is it to deter others from following a similar anti-social conduct, frightening them with the consequences of such action? Is it to protect society and remove the offender or isolate him so that he will not be in a position to repeat a similar crime? Does rehabilitation rather than punishment constitute society's major answer to a deviant's behavior? Should the heaviest emphasis be laid not so much on punishment as on the re-education of the offender while in confinement so that his sense of values might be reoriented and his personality be reintegrated to permit a constructive rather than destructive pattern of expression? Theories of punishment may stress one or the other or a combination of these views. Raising these questions is no mere academic exercise. Much of the penal apparatus and entire probation programs derive their justification from assumptions concerning the nature of crime and the punishment that the state should exact.

Actually most states greatly emphasize "punishment" in their practices rather than rehabilitation, a fact which, in the judgment of some penal experts, may have much to do with this country's high level of recidivism. Programs of rehabilitation are expensive, and many are still experimental. It is widely agreed that rehabilitation programs, whatever their detail, will necessarily have to give much more attention to the psychiatric aspects of crimes and criminals.

It might be added parenthetically that the traditional sanity tests for criminal responsibility are currently undergoing a most vigorous debate. Under the old McNaughton rule, announced by an English court in 1843 in connection with a case arising out of an attack on Sir Robert Peel, the defense of insanity could be called into effect only if the defendant were shown not "to know the nature and quality" of his act, i.e., if he were unable to tell right from wrong. Many psychiatrists have long contended that psychiatric deviants other than imbeciles and idiots may well know the difference between right and wrong but that such a deviant's sickness may prevent him from applying his knowledge to effectively control his conduct.

The McNaughton rule, accepted in nearly all states and slightly modified in nineteen with the so-called "irrepressible impulse" test, attempts to draw a clear line of demarcation between sanity and insanity—a concept untenable to many psychiatrists. A 1954 District of Columbia Court of Appeals case accepted a different psychiatric test for criminal responsibility. Under the Durham rule, psychiatric testimony was held admissible as a defense which would persuade a jury that the act was the "product of mental disease or defect" even though the defendant may otherwise have known the difference between right and wrong. Critics of the Durham rule appear to be concerned that its adoption would "contribute to a growing cult of irresponsibility" and that it would unduly enhance the influence of psychiatrists in the administration of justice.[10]

Something about the gap between theory and practice in the application of newer medical insights in rehabilitational work alone can be seen in the startling fact that presently thirty-eight states do not even have one single full-time psychiatrist on their penal staffs.

The indefinite sentence practice is used now in approximately one-half of the states. California law has gone furthest in placing sentences exclusively in the hands of administrative boards. Underlying this trend towards the indefinite sentence system is the search for greater professionalization in tailoring punishment and rehabilitation to the needs of the criminal and of society, to achieve a flexibility and discretion in sentencing that judges with traditional legal training and courts with crowded calendars are not as likely to provide.

Some states permit the incarcerated criminal to initiate a petition for probation as early as six months after beginning his sentence. Among the many factors that a parole board takes into consideration when acting upon such a petition are the following:

A. The nature and gravity of the inmate's offense against society;
B. The deviant history of the person seeking parole or the absence of any misconduct in his past life;
C. The inmate's total personality as the same reflects the presence or absence of potential and capacity for serious harm to society;

[10] *The New York Times*, March 9, 1961, p. 19. For a favorable discussion of the Durham rule, see Winfred Overholser, "Some Psychiatric Aspects of Criminal Responsibility," *State Government*, Spring, 1961, pp. 124–129.

D. The likelihood that on release the offender will return, or will not return, to a life of criminal conduct and the probable injury society will suffer should the prisoner become a recidivist;

E. What efforts have been made, or not made, by the prisoner since imprisonment by way of improvements in habits of social conduct—education or skills—to demonstrate an honest desire to live in harmony with society and its laws;

F. How effective or ineffective the efforts of the inmate seem to have been and will probably be when released in aiding him or her toward living a life free of crime.[11]

JUVENILE COURTS AND JUVENILE DELINQUENTS

While the law of the old equity courts of England did afford some humanizing elements, youthful offenders found the common law by contrast stern and inflexible. Children over seven years of age were considered responsible for their criminal conduct and treated by adult standards particularly when the charge involved the more serious crimes. Beginning with the juvenile probation system of Massachusetts (1869) and the juvenile court code of Illinois (1899), all of the states gradually adopted some form of juvenile court and code which removed from the family and granted to the state certain controls over the delinquent child.

Actually there is no single pattern for juvenile courts. Specialized and separate juvenile courts generally developed only in the larger urban and metropolitan areas. Some of the smaller states like Connecticut and Rhode Island developed a single statewide juvenile court. Other states favored a system whereby the juvenile court was attached to a domestic relations court, family court, or probate court (rural areas) or where the juvenile court operated as a special term or session of the regular court of limited or local jurisdiction.[12]

Regardless of whether or not the juvenile courts were organized as separate courts, their practices and procedures with respect to trial and sentencing were at least in theory to operate under a similar set of special premises.

A. During the pre-sentence phase of the judicial process optimum use was to be made of professional diagnostic services and counsel.

B. The court hearing was to be characterized by a sympathetic and informal proceeding.

C. The stigma of a criminal record was to be avoided since it might seriously handicap the youth in his later life.

D. Juveniles were not to be detained or incarcerated on a non-segregated basis in jails or penal institutions housing adult offenders.

Youth in the Toils,[13] a book published in 1938, effectively presented a record of failures in attempts to correct delinquent behavior with traditional

---

[11] American Correctional Association, *Proceedings of the Eighty-Eighth Annual Congress of Correction* (New York, 1958), p. 226.

[12] Paul W. Tappen, *Crime, Justice and Correction* (New York, 1960), p. 390.

[13] Leonard V. Harrison and Pryor M. Grant, *Youth in the Toils* (New York, 1938).

patterns of punishment. Stressed also was the likelihood of hardening the youthful offender into a probable recidivist through brutalizing reform school experiences. A Youth Correction Act drafted by a committee of the American Law Institute in 1940 sought to provide constructive alternatives in rehabilitation to some of the dramatic failures in correction highlighted in *Youth in the Toils* and reflected for years, though more prosaically, in penal surveys and statistics.

Presently adopted in modified form by at least seven states—California, Illinois, Kentucky, Massachusetts, Minnesota, Texas, and Wisconsin (and the federal government)—these acts address themselves primarily to the problems of rehabilitating young criminals in the sixteen to twenty-one year age groups.[14] Central to the philosophy of the Youth Correction Act is the concept of the indeterminate sentence under which the court, instead of prescribing a particular sentence, orders the young offender turned over to the control of an administrative agency, a youth commission or board, which is given the responsibility after proper diagnosis to order the most promising rehabilitative effort for the particular offender. To accomplish its mission, most of the states have given these agencies the power (though rarely sufficient funds) to establish diagnostic centers, special youth camps, separate probational staffs, and vocational training programs.

Despite the sincere effort of its supporters and despite some notable progress towards a more humane and scientific approach to the juvenile delinquent and his problems, the high expectations of the juvenile court and the rehabilitation movements have fallen far short of their objectives. Here are a few, and only a few, of the many obstacles:

A. Annually between 50,000 and 100,000 children are still confined in jails and police stations.[15]

B. Less than 50 per cent of this country's 3,000 counties have any juvenile probation services at all; only one-tenth of such personnel have any specialized training. One-half of the cities with 10,000 or more population do not have specially trained juvenile officers.[16]

C. Most of the juvenile institutions or reformatories are still characterized by crowded facilities, inadequate staffs, an atmosphere of fear and a considerable extent of corporal and degrading punishment.[17]

D. Punishment rather than rehabilitation remains a dominant theme in too many juvenile court proceedings reinforced by the "retributive drive that sustains much of society's attacks upon the offender, regardless of age." [18]

E. "Confidentiality" of juvenile proceedings is widely violated. ". . . [P]olice records of juvenile arrests are generally kept on the same blotters as

[14] Tappen, p. 460.

[15] Frederick B. Sussman, *Law of Juvenile Delinquency*, rev. 2nd ed. (New York, 1959), p. 41. A study in 1964 of Georgia jails revealed that there were 195 inmates younger than 17, *The New York Times*, October 28, 1964.

[16] Orman W. Ketcham, "The Unfulfilled Promise of the Juvenile Court," *Crime and Delinquency*, April, 1961, quoted in *Congressional Record*, June 6, 1961, p. 8969.

[17] *Ibid.*, June 6, 1961, p. 8970.

[18] Paul W. Tappen, *Juvenile Delinquency* (New York, 1949), p. 428.

those of adults without any special confidentiality. Finger-printing and to a lesser extent, photographing of arrested juveniles are likewise common practice. . . ." [19]

F. Judges are overworked. A Philadelphia juvenile judge reports of having to dispose of 20,000 cases per year.[20]

G. Probation personnel are overworked. Many metropolitan centers report that their probation workers on an average must be assigned twice the case load prescribed by the standards of the profession.

As late as 1962 there were

sixteen states in which it was "legally possible to execute children as young as 7;"

three states where children of 8 could be sentenced to death;

three others where the minimum age was 10;

and nineteen other states in which the age of youngsters subject to the death penalty ranged from 12 to 18.[21]

As juvenile crime rates continue to rise, public understanding is blurred by a mixture of criticism from "coddling youth" and failing to shock these young people or their parents into an appreciation of the seriousness of their criminal conduct to criticisms growing out of frustrations with the "unfulfilled promises" of juvenile reform programs. Voices also question the wisdom of conducting juvenile court hearings and procedures in a legal climate in which the youth finds himself unprotected by long established constitutional safeguards which are automatically invoked for the protection of the ordinary criminals.[22] To many persons most baffling and worrisome is the increase in youth gang warfare, no doubt accentuated in the larger cities by major population shifts which often disrupted socio-economic and ethnic living patterns. Rare are the days when the metropolitan press of New York, Philadelphia, Chicago, Los Angeles, and many other cities do not reveal some acts of violence, of theft, or vandalism, or of "rumbling" involving more or less organized groups of juveniles bent on a thrill, on revenge, or on social protest, real or imagined. Precise causes are most difficult to define. Nor are all gangs criminal in nature. But of the more than 100 separate fighting gangs operating in each of these four cities and involving thousands of youngsters (an

[19] Ketcham, in *Congressional Record,* June 6, 1961, p. 8969.

[20] Senate Judiciary Committee, *Juvenile Delinquency,* Subcommittee to Investigate Juvenile Delinquency, Senate Report No. 1593, June 15, 1960, 86th Cong., 2nd Sess. (Washington, 1960), pp. 20–21.

[21] *The New York Times,* January 7, 1962, p. 81; a tabulation, by states, of criminal offenses on which capital punishment is imposed (prepared by the American Law Division of the Library of Congress) can be found in the *Congressional Record,* March 1, 1962, pp. 3019–3023; on the notion that capital punishment serves as a deterrent to murder, see William O. Reichert, "Capital Punishment Reconsidered," *Kentucky Law Journal,* 1958–1959.

[22] See Lewis Diana, "The Rights of Juvenile Delinquents: An Appraisal of Juvenile Court Procedures," *The Journal of Criminal Law, Criminology and Police Science,* January–February, 1957, pp. 561–569.

estimated 3,000 girls and 8,000 boys in New York City alone), enough is known to present a depressing picture of alcoholism, drug addiction, sexual promiscuity, muggings, robbery, and other crimes as well as patterns of inter-gang warfare characterized by numerous instances of intensive personal violence. Gang arsenals include guns, knives, clubs, bottle openers, straight-edge razors, and other assorted "weapons."

A Senate Judiciary subcommittee on juvenile delinquency conducting hearings in these and other cities found much concern about the extent of

SOURCE: Herb Ticklen in *The Dallas News*, reprinted in *The New York Times*, August 10, 1958.

juvenile crime and diverse efforts to stem its tide.[23] Some cities, counties, and state governments have developed certain types of preventive programs including youth councils, gang specialists, guidance clinics for juveniles, club houses, etc.; others have concentrated their efforts on developing work camps or boys' villages. Nearly all hearings reported serious difficulties in coordinating volunteer and public agency programs and in obtaining the necessary funds to provide the already existing activities and institutions with professionally competent staffs. On the basis of its findings, the Senate committee urged Congress to come to the assistance of the states by providing

23 See Senate Judiciary Committee, *Juvenile Delinquency*, Senate Report No. 1593.

$10,000,000 grants for a period of five years for projects aimed at developing preventive methods and control programs for juvenile delinquents. President Kennedy's original proposals to Congress were of a more comprehensive nature and envisaged the establishment of an urban service corps for youths who have shown signs of getting into serious trouble. They would be given employment in connection with conservation, forest, and park projects.[24]

SOME OTHER TRENDS IN COURT REFORM

"The Popular Causes of Dissatisfaction of the Administration of Justice," a speech delivered in 1906 by Roscoe Pound, later Dean of Harvard Law School, is often designated as a significant point of departure for nearly all of the major recommendations for judicial reform which have been proposed in the following half century. Pound expressed his concern about the multiplicity of courts, and the waste of judicial manpower. He urged that judges be taken out of partisan politics and that certain procedural reforms be introduced that would tend to eliminate unwarranted trial obstructions and excessive court costs. Bar associations ought to be strengthened and interest in jury service revitalized. These and some other of his recommendations were subsequently stressed or enlarged by the more formal recommendations and studies of the American Bar Association, the Institute of Judicial Administration, the National Conference of Chief Justices, the National Conference of State Trial Justices, the National Conference of Court Administrative Officers, the Council of State Governments, and by many of the other committees, public as well as private, that concerned themselves with improving the administration of justice.[25]

Although political and legal traditions vary in each state, and although factors such as population, size, and the extent of urbanism must inevitably require local adaptations of the "reform" pattern, there are nonetheless a few salient aspects of these recommendations that have found widespread acceptance. Emerging rather distinctly is an integrated court system—at the bottom one local court with limited jurisdiction operating through various divisions, above it one general trial court with unlimited jurisdiction, and at the top one supreme court as the court of last resort. This means a reduction in specialized courts and the gradual elimination of overlapping and concurrent jurisdictions by courts operating on the same level of the judicial hierarchy. Chief justices are given greater administrative control over the entire system. Administrative officers serving under their direction conduct studies of calendar status and work load which may eventually lead to the reassignment of judges or to proposals for additional judges in districts with a chronic backlog of cases. Judicial councils composed of prominent members of the bar and bench are to assist the supreme court in recommending procedural changes

[24] *The New York Times*, May 25, 1961, p. 29.
[25] See *The Ohio Court System*, pp. 54–61; and Colorado Legislative Council, *Judicial Administration in Colorado* (Denver, 1960), pp. 53–77.

and in the promulgation of rules. States where in recent years significant judicial reforms have already been enacted into law or have remained under active consideration include California, Colorado, Florida, Idaho, Illinois, Iowa, Maine, Minnesota, Nebraska, New Mexico, New York, North Carolina, Ohio, Oregon, Rhode Island, Utah, Washington, Wisconsin, and Wyoming.

Here is only a small sample of some of the latest reform proposals and actions:

> *Nebraska* voters in 1962, approved a plan for nominating judges to the major courts patterned after the Missouri Plan.[26]

> *North Carolina*—An amendment was adopted in 1962 which among other provisions (1) abolishes the justice of peace courts, (2) vests administrative responsibility over the courts in a central office, (3) gives to the supreme court greater rule-making power (subject to legislative amendment and review), and (4) gives to the chief justice of the supreme court the right to make judicial assignments and transfer district judges from one district to another for temporary or specialized duties.[27]

> *Colorado*—A constitutional amendment was adopted by the voters in 1962 (1) abolishing the justice of peace courts, (2) increasing the membership of the state supreme court from seven to nine, (3) enlarging the jurisdiction of the district courts, (4) upgrading the county courts, and (5) providing the state with a three instead of four-level court system.[28]

> *Illinois* voters in 1962 approved a new judiciary article to the constitution which provides for a three-tiered system headed by a seven-member supreme court. The new article eliminates a maze of courts at the trial level by creating a single circuit court for each judicial circuit. Judges under the new article will be elected initially on a partisan ballot. After their first term is completed, they will stand for re-election on their records without opposition. The supreme court is given general administrative power over all courts in the system.[29]

> *Iowa*—A judicial reform amendment to the constitution was adopted by the state's voters in June, 1962, providing for appointment by the governor of district and supreme court judges from a list of candidates provided by nominating commissions. The district and supreme court judges so appointed must be approved by popular vote after one year in office. Again within one year of the expiration of their first term they must be voted upon as to whether they shall continue in office.[30]

Judicial reform must be a continuous process. Court calendar studies of personal injury cases by the Institute of Judicial Administration have yielded shocking statistics of calendar congestions and delayed justice. A recent

---

[26] See *National Civic Review*, October, 1961, p. 486 and January, 1963, pp. 25–26.

[27] *Ibid.*, September, 1961, p. 427; December, 1962, pp. 613–614; November, 1963, pp. 552–553; and June, 1964, p. 316.

[28] *Ibid.*, April, 1962, pp. 212–213 and February, 1963, p. 90.

[29] *Ibid.*, February, 1963, pp. 87–89.

[30] *Ibid.*, September, 1962, pp. 462–463 and December, 1963, p. 601. For a study of judicial reform in another state, see Sidney Schulman, *Toward Judicial Reform in Pennsylvania: A Study in Court Reorganization* (Philadelphia, 1962). For a discussion of the court system in Georgia, see Robert H. Hall, "Improving the Administration of Justice," *Journal of Public Law*, XII, 1963, pp. 376–382.

survey found 18.7 months to be the average time needed for major state courts to bring a personal injury case to the jury trial stage "after the parties were 'at issue.'" In heavily-populated metropolitan areas—counties with populations over 750,000—the average delay was as high as 29.2 months.

Among counties with 500,000 or more population having an average delay of more than 49 months were the following:

Superior Court, Cook County (Chicago), Ill. (5,129,725)	68 months
Court of Common Pleas, Allegheny County (Pittsburgh), Pa. (1,628, 587)	67 months
Supreme Court, Nassau County (Mineola), N. Y. (1,300,171)	60 months
Supreme Court, Queens County (New York), N. Y. (1,809,578)	49 months
Court of Common Pleas, Philadelphia County (Philadelphia), Pa. (2,002,512)	49 months
Supreme Court, Suffolk County (Riverhead), N. Y. (666,748)	49 months [31]

As in all studies of this nature, considerable caution is necessary in the evaluation of such findings. In some states and courts the parties are not considered at issue until the pleadings are completed, whereas in others the point is reached upon filing of the pleadings.[32] Differences such as these cannot help but affect the meaningfulness of figures reporting court delays.

Also, it must be emphasized that in placing a civil case on calendar an attorney (or the party that he represents) does not necessarily wish to see the case actually go to trial. What is attempted by this act may often be merely a tactical move—a threat—in a complex set of rituals which have as their true aims a settlement reached out of court rather than in court. Personal injury case disposition in New York City shows that of an annual total of approximately 50,000 cases only about 14 per cent reach trial of which less than one-third proceed to a verdict.

Nevertheless, however realistic these qualifications may be, they cannot detract from the central need to meet the challenge of crowded civil calendars. It is no mere cliché to assert that justice delayed is justice denied. With the passage of time, facts become blurred, witnesses die or move away or will be unable to recall necessary details, legal costs increase and many other inequities are likely to occur.

Bar, bench, and law school have long been aware of the problem and a number of reforms have been suggested or already put into operation. Bronx County City Court under its rotating calendar plan calls a very large number of cases daily and readily grants delays unless both parties are prepared to go to trial immediately. So-called "blockbuster sections" have been added to the Appellate Division of the Supreme Court for Manhattan and the Bronx to work on the disposition of very old cases that have long acted as a roadblock to calendar clearings. These sections are given to special judges with power to set calendar and to conduct the necessary hearings to bring the cases quickly

[31] Institute of Judicial Administration, *State Trial Courts of General Jurisdiction Calendar Status Study—1963: Personal Injury Cases* (New York, 1963), pp. ii–iii.
[32] *The New York Times*, February 9, 1961, p. 30.

to court or to settlement.[33] Colorado courts have made considerable progress in eliminating crowded and clogged calendars by an elaborate attack on many fronts. Among others, use was made of visiting and temporary judges. The court year was lengthened. Calendars were more carefully planned and consolidated, and the number of law clerks was increased.[34]

Another subject of judicial reform concerns the problem of removing judges unfit to continue their service because of unethical, unjudicial, or incompetent conduct—nearly always a most delicate, difficult, and cumbersome process. In most states it requires either a formal impeachment proceeding or a *legislative address* whereby an extraordinary majority in both houses of the legislature votes the removal of a judge (without a trial). Arizona, California, Colorado, Kansas, Nevada, North Dakota, Oregon, and Wisconsin provide for the *recall* of judges, a clumsy and little-used device.

Steps to facilitate the removal of unfit judges have recently been incorporated into the law of a number of states. In Hawaii and Alaska, the governor may appoint a special three-member commission for the purpose of inquiring into the alleged disability of a member of the supreme court and, upon positive findings, may order his retirement. Members of the lower courts of Alaska and New Jersey may be removed by direct action of their respective state's court of last resort.

New York gives the power of removal to a *Court on the Judiciary*, a special group composed of one judge from each of the four appellate court divisions, the senior associate justice of the court of appeals and the chief justice of the court of appeals. The move may be initiated in various ways—by the governor, by the chief judge of the court of appeals, by the presiding justice of any intermediate court of appeals, or by the executive committee of the state bar association.

In California, the state's supreme court, as a result of a 1960 constitutional amendment, may order the removal of a judge "for cause" upon the recommendation of a nine-member state Commission on Judicial Qualifications. Five members of this group are named by the supreme court, two by the state bar association, and two by the governor. During the first two years of its operations, the commission received 163 complaints:

> Of the 163 complaints, 46 merited further investigation. In ten cases the judges involved resigned or retired because of the commission's inquiry. In three of these cases, drinking was the problem. In three it was absenteeism. In three other cases it was emotional disturbance: one judge made improper comments to jurors, went out of his way to embarrass witnesses, had fits of rage at counsel; another was admitted by his psychiatrist to be "very disturbed" and emotionally unsuited to making judicial decisions.[35]

[33] Russell Porter, "Court Procedure Revised to Speed Accident Cases," *The New York Times,* September 17, 1961, pp. 1, 51.

[34] William E. Doyle, "Battle of the Backlog in the Colorado Supreme Court," *Journal of the American Judicature Society,* June, 1961, pp. 19–23.

[35] Murray Teigh Bloom, "Unseating Unfit Judges," *National Civic Review,* February, 1963, p. 119.

Judicial reforms, like many of the other efforts to improve governmental institutions, involve more than a search for a better rearranging or restructuring of offices, procedures, or policies. All such reforms involve extending political advantages to some groups and not to others, but in the realm of the judiciary, the issues are often more subtle and the benefits more hidden. This is not to suggest anything sinister or necessarily undesirable. What is suggested is that the "good" and "bad" of judicial reform require standards of assessment as critical and sophisticated as those used for all the other more political branches and agencies of government.

CASE PROBLEMS FOR CLASS DISCUSSION

1. You have been asked to give a speech in support of the Missouri Plan at a state bar convention. What evidence would you be able to cite in support of your position? What are some of the objections to the plan that you would have to meet? What steps would you propose that might lead to the adoption of the plan in your state?

2. The governor in your state is about to appoint a judge to a recently vacated district bench. Assume that the judge will have two years before he comes up for election on a partisan ballot, that you are an observer studying the judicial selection process of your state, and that you have been asked to sit in at the crucial meeting at which the governor is to make his decision. Also present are the chairman of the governor's party, the president of the state bar association, and the dean of the state university law school. What would likely be some of the considerations expressed at this conference?

3. Your state legislature is exploring the possibility of establishing a youth conservation commission for the treatment and rehabilitation of juvenile delinquents. Assume that you are a member of your legislative research committee and that you have been asked to prepare a background study. Which state laws would you use as "models"? What type of administrative structure would you suggest for your state? Which interest groups in the community would you consult?

4. You have been asked to write a campaign speech for an incumbent candidate to the state supreme court. Assume that the members of this court are elected on a nonpartisan ballot and also that crowded calendars have become an issue of controversy throughout the state. Which themes would you stress in the speech and which would you wish to avoid? Would you work in any proposals for calendar reforms?

SELECTED BIBLIOGRAPHY

M. GLENN ABERNATHY, "The South Carolina State Court System," *University of South Carolina Governmental Review*, May, 1963, pp. 1–6.

ELBERT M. BYRD, JR., *The Judicial Process in Maryland* (College Park, 1962).

JOHN H. CRABB, "The Court of Appeal of England and the Supreme Court of North Dakota: A Psychological Comparison," *North Dakota Law Review*, October, 1962, pp. 554–562.

I. RIDGWAY DAVIS, "Connecticut's New Circuit Court," *State Government*, Winter, 1964, pp. 51–59.

JOHN R. DETHMERS, "Delay in State Appellate Courts of Last Resort," *The Annals of the American Academy of Political and Social Science*, March, 1960, pp. 153–163.

JAMES P. ECONOMOS, "Justice Court Improvement and Traffic Courts," *State Government*, Spring, 1962, pp. 118–123.

THOMAS A. EWERS, "A Study of the Background of the Successful and Unsuccessful Candidates for the Iowa Supreme Court," unpublished M.A. thesis, State University of Iowa, 1960.

EDWARD FERGUSON III, "Some Comments on the Applicability of Bloc Analysis to

State Appellate Courts," paper presented to the Midwest Conference of Political Scientists, Columbia, Mo., May 11–13, 1963.

HERBERT JACOB, "The Effect of Institutional Differences in the Recruitment Process: The Case of State Judges," *Journal of Public Law*, 1964, pp. 104–119.

CALVIN R. LEDBETTER, "The Arkansas Supreme Court: 1958–1959," unpublished Ph.D. dissertation, Northwestern University, 1961.

STUART S. NAGEL, "Judicial Backgrounds and Criminal Cases," *Journal of Criminal Law, Criminology and Police Science*, September, 1962, pp. 333–339.

STUART S. NAGEL, "Testing Relations Between Judicial Characteristics and Judicial Decision-Making," *Western Political Quarterly*, September, 1962, pp. 425–437.

"Pennsylvania's Minor Courts: An Assessment," *Horizons*, in *Pennsylvanian*, May, 1963, pp. 19, 22.

WILLIAM M. TRUMBULL, "The State Court Systems," *The Annals of the American Academy of Political and Social Science*, March, 1960, pp. 134–143.

S. SIDNEY ULMER, "The Political Party Variable in the Michigan Supreme Court," *Journal of Public Law*, 1962, pp. 352–362.

KENNETH N. VINES and HERBERT JACOB, *Studies in Judicial Politics* (New Orleans, 1962).

MAXINE B. VIRTUE, "The Two Faces of Janus: Delay in Metropolitan Trial Courts," *The Annals of the American Academy of Political and Social Science*, March, 1960, pp. 125–133.

RUTH Y. WETMORE, *The Justice of the Peace in Kansas* (Lawrence, 1960).

✔ *Chapter VIII*

POLITICAL

PARTIES

IN THE STATES

How reliable are generalizations about the nature of political alignments and bases of support in American state politics?

What is the power structure in the various state party systems?

WHEN mention is made of America's two major parties, one basic fact, both legal and political, cannot be ignored: each national party is composed of fifty separate state parties. Yet for many years textbooks treated the indigenous quality of American state politics in a somewhat cavalier fashion.

There are many reasons for such treatment. Little research had in fact been done on the detailed aspects of state politics (and generalizations are always so much more appealing). National politics were much more dramatic and seemed so much more significant in an era characterized by an enormous increase of power in Washington and by the simultaneously shrinking state sovereignty. The need to keep big government responsible and to give direction to big government seemed to point toward the existence of much more disciplined and active parties—to a truly national party system.

But even the most enthusiastic exponents of unified national parties could not avoid coming to grips with the realities of state politics. After all, United States senators and representatives are nominated and elected largely as the result of state party activity. True, there is the quadrennial national convention, but here again the national convention delegates are state party officials who in the final analysis must give account of their stewardship to the state organization and to the state party electorate. The national committee, although presided over by a national chairman, is composed of national committeemen and committeewomen who are state party officials and who are little more than ambassadors sent by the state organization to the national group. Even presidents must win state electoral votes on a state party ticket. Much of the money and most of the campaign effort spent on behalf of the national ticket is actually borne by state party organizations and state volunteers and not by the national party officers.

This chapter is designed to provide a better understanding of the operation of the state party systems, their structure, their constitutions, their programs, their officers, their socio-economic bases of support and most of all, their peculiar differences. The regional and state differences that emerge are the result of history, tradition, socio-economic factors, election law, campaign calendar, rural-urban conflicts, governmental structure, and metropolitanism. Many of these same factors help to explain, moreover, why in some states interparty competition is quite keen, while in others it is only moderately so, and why in a few it is relatively nonexistent at least as far as a general election is concerned.

There has been much talk about reforming political parties. Should parties become more disciplined, more program-centered, or would this lead to monolithic politics devoid of the flexibility demanded by a pluralistic culture and the existence of powerful economic interest groups with strong loyalties and stronger pocketbooks? Should state parties become links in a unitary national system or in a federated national system, or should they develop their candidates' platforms and programs independently of national currents with attention consciously focused on state issues and state needs?

State parties, just as the national parties, have long been accused of being merely loosely knit coalitions of social and economic interests held together by nothing but their collective appetites for office and patronage. Among some of the methods by which the various state parties have become more programmatic or principle-conscious in their orientation and approach in recent years are those of pre-primary endorsements, party research, annual conventions, and monthly contributions by the membership to the party's sustaining fund.

Critics of such party reforms, particularly of such techniques as the pre-primary endorsement, emphasize that an inordinate concentration of power would most likely be gathered in the hands of a new party oligarchy. New bosses and new machines would take the place of the older bosses and machines, and the "independently-minded" rank and file voter and candidate would find himself once again out-organized and out-maneuvered by the professionals.

THE PROBLEM OF CLASSIFICATION

The fact that the American party system is a composite or confederation of fifty fairly distinct state systems is far more than mere rhetoric. It is this fact which becomes crucial when a president seeks national legislative support to implement the campaign promises of his party's platform, when the public demands more effective presidential leadership, or when the economic interests of the nation call for a higher loyalty than that of region or state.

Superficially, there is much that these fifty Republican and Democratic state parties have in common. With some occasional exceptions, they nearly always support the national ticket. They nominate and seek to elect candidates to congressional and state offices. They conduct campaigns, organize the electorate, formulate platforms and resolutions, and assist in the distribution of patronage.

To be sure in performing all these varying roles, parties vary considerably from state to state in their competence, their enthusiasm, and their effectiveness. Just how responsibly they will carry out their functions of providing the voter with meaningful alternatives in personnel and policy and how much power they can marshal to give direction to government in the executive and legislative branches will to no small extent depend on the degree of competition between the parties within each state.

Using interparty competition as the criterion for classifying state parties, at least three major patterns emerge with some degree of clarity: (1) the one-party system, (2) the modified one-party system, and (3) the two-party competitive system.[1]

THE ONE-PARTY SYSTEM

In the South the systems of Alabama, Arkansas, Florida, Georgia, Louisiana, Mississippi, South Carolina, Texas, and Virginia fit fairly well into the one-party category. This is true despite the fact that Alabama, Louisiana, Mississippi, and South Carolina bolted the Democratic national ticket in 1948 and again in 1964 and that Mississippi did not pledge its eight electors nor Alabama six of its eleven electors to the Kennedy ticket in 1960. None of these states, except Louisiana, had ever "gone Republican" in presidential, congressional, or state elections before 1964 when they became the only states aside from Arizona, which Senator Goldwater carried against the Johnson landslide. Although Republicans registered gains in a number of state legislatures as a result of the 1964 election (Georgia–11, Louisiana–2, South Carolina–1, and Tennessee–6), these gains were offset by losses suffered in North Carolina–8, Texas–7, and West Virginia–9.

Then there are the one-party states of the South which despite their party monopoly on the state level have strayed in national elections. Texas voted for Hoover in 1928, for Eisenhower in 1952 and again in 1956. Virginia and Florida followed the same pattern and continued it in 1960 by voting for Nixon despite Lyndon Johnson's place on the Democratic ticket. In May of 1961, Texas elected its first Republican senator since 1877, John G. Tower, a strong conservative. Before this happened, Texas and Florida had one Republican congressman each and Virginia two. In the 1962 congressional elections, Florida and Texas each elected an additional Republican to the House of Representatives. In the 89th Congress (1965), Southern congressional delegations included eighteen Republicans, seven from states that had not sent a Republican congressman to Washington since Reconstruction (Alabama–5, Georgia–1, and Mississippi–1).

Outside the South, Vermont has come closest to a one-party system. Only once since 1856 have the citizens of this state voted Democratic in a national election. In 1962, Philip H. Hoff was narrowly elected the first Democratic governor in 109 years and then reelected in 1964 by 64.8 per cent of the vote.

[1] For a discussion of classificatory patterns for state party systems, see Austin Ranney and Willmoore Kendall, "The American Party Systems," *American Political Science Review,* June, 1954, pp. 477–485.

Over 70 per cent of the membership of the Vermont House of Representatives in 1962 as well as in 1964 was Republican.

In denoting certain states as one-party, nothing could be further from the truth than to assume that in such states there is a general lack of intraparty competition for power. Detailed studies of factional struggles in one-party states in the South and in New England led one authority to discern the following variations:

A. Machine-led; one faction predominant
  1. Clear, continuous leadership
  2. Control over nominations and advancement in the hands of organization leaders
  3. Considerable influence over legislative policy in the hands of the organization
      a. Dominated by one or two powerful interests (such as those based on a natural resource or an important farm crop), or
      b. A more confusing array of economic powers controlling decision-making
B. Bifactional party structure
  1. Two contesting factions with relatively continuous and identifiable leaderships
  2. In varying degree some question of policy transferred to primary contests
  3. Moderate to minor legislative policy identification of factions
C. Multifactional party structure
  1. Party organizations as holding companies—virtual non-participants in policy-making
  2. Factions and their leaderships ever shifting and non-continuous and without clear identification
  3. Personality conflicts dominate in primaries
  4. Policy formation—a lottery in which the "haves" use the disorganization of politics to achieve their conservative ends [2]

For more than thirty years the Byrd machine has controlled Virginia politics "with a tightly knit, well-defined group of leaders that maintains an existence from election to election." [3] Presided over by Senator Harry Flood Byrd, a state senator at 28, one-time state governor (1926–1930) and a leading conservative Democrat in the United States Senate since 1933, the machine recruits candidates, carries them through the primary, and then gives policy direction to governors, congressmen, and members of the Virginia legislature whom they have helped to elect.

Strongly supported by the business and financial community of Virginia, the organization successfully resisted most of the demands for expanded social welfare programs and racial integration and defeated anti-organization forces composed of New Deal liberals and members of organized labor in election after election.

There are a number of reasons why the Byrd machine triumphed and why

[2] Duane Lockard, *New England State Politics* (Princeton, 1959), pp. 325–326. Reprinted with permission of Princeton University Press.

[3] V. O. Key, Jr., *Southern Politics in State and Nation* (New York, 1950) p. 27.

it was able to reward its friends and punish its enemies. It had the financial resources for campaigning. It had centralized control over the nomination process, and it kept the electorate small. It appointed the key officials in the county courthouses or assured their elections. It had the power of opening up channels to higher offices and positions of prestige to those who accepted its discipline. Avoiding the extremes of rabid racism and blatant corruption, the machine was enormously successful in demonstrating to a sufficient number of Virginians that stable government should be conservative and "gentle-

'I Can't Understand It . . . It Used to Run So Well'

SOURCE: James Berryman. Courtesy of *The Washington Star*.
Reprinted in *The New York Times*, February 8, 1959.

manly" and that no one was better qualified to help them select the proper officials than the distinguished Senior Senator from Berryville, Virginia, and his associates.

There is still much life left in the old oligarchy. Once again in July of 1961 the headlines proclaimed that the Byrd machine swept Virginia when Albertis S. Harrison and his ticket defeated A. E. S. Stephens, a state lieutenant governor, who had broken with the machine at a primary at which less than one-third of the registered and qualified voters felt it necessary to participate.[4]

For some years now the classical illustration of a bifactional one-party

4 *The New York Times*, July 12, 1961, p. 14 and July 13, 1961, p. 61.

system has been that of Louisiana, a state where politics has all too often been conducted along lines neither "gentlemanly" nor responsible. Louisiana's political struggles were dominated by deep religious, cultural, and racial cleavages, by conflicts between urban New Orleans and the upstate rural counties and by the clash of interests between the plantations of the lowlands and the farmers of the hills. With enormous poverty and a barely literate white electorate, spokesmen for utilities, railroads, sugar, oil, and commerce frequently considered it necessary for the preservation of the status quo to establish electoral alliances with wild and woolly populist idols extolling white supremacy and fundamentalist evangelism and damning the sinfulness of urban life.

The "Robin Hood politics" of Huey Long, Louisiana's kingfish, brought undeniable economic benefits to the forces of agrarian discontent. Roads, schools, hospitals, and bridges were built, and the loyalties fashioned in those days formed the electoral foundations upon which Long and anti-Long factions campaigned for nearly a generation, each claiming to be the authentic heir to Huey Long. These factions carefully structured their tickets from the governorship to local and legislative offices by balancing Protestants with Catholics, the French with the non-French, the cities with the rural areas.[5] Winners disbursed patronage or disciplined the disaffected. Louisiana though certainly lacking in the fundamentals of a genuinely competitive two-party system, developed something vaguely akin to it—an identifiable, continuous, personality-centered bifactional system.

Among the Northern one-party states, North Dakota's Republican hegemony during the nineteen twenties and thirties provided a typical illustration of bifactionalism. Working within the Republican party were two major groups, the Republican Organizing Committee representing the eastern part of the state and its more conservative farm and urban interests and the Non-Partisan Leagues, spokesmen for the agrarian discontent of the western and southern counties of North Dakota.

Many Non-Partisan Leaguers after 1956 found it more advantageous to move into the Democratic party. One of these people, Quentin N. Burdick, son of the N.P.L. Congressman Usher Burdick, was elected congressman-at-large on the Democratic ticket in 1958 and United States senator in 1960. Two years later, a sixteen-year Republican hold on the governorship was broken by the election of William L. Guy, a Democrat. He was reelected in 1962 and in 1964.

Multi-factional politics characterize the one-party system that is least well structured. Power here is widely diffused; winning coalitions may center around economic or regional loyalties, around local concerns and friendships, or more often around strong candidates with an intense personal following.

Other than their segregationist ideas, there was little consensus or party program that was held in common by such former Southern politicians as

5 Key, p. 170.

Theodore Bilbo of Mississippi, Herman Talmadge of Georgia, or "Cotton Ed" Smith of South Carolina. Their support was personal, their policy inclinations populist though rarely radical. Going along with those aspects of the New Deal that brought financial assistance to their states for highways, agriculture, and welfare, they never ceased to oppose the power of organized labor and the demands for more effective federal civil rights legislation.

As spokesmen for the people from the hills against the people from the delta, or as defenders of the Old South against the industrialism of the New South, they may have been railing with evangelic fervor against the sins of the cities or the evils of the corporation. Yet the legislation that finally emerged while they were in the governor's chair, rhetoric notwithstanding, was rarely anti-business and never very liberal.

Thus, whether North or South, the politics of one-party states reflects the power configurations within the dominant party. Whether a particular party system tends to be multi-factional, bifactional, or single-factional, its particular characteristics will significantly affect the manner in which nominations are made and campaigns conducted, in which legislatures organize and governors lead. Throughout the one-party system there is a wide variety of political style and tone.

The Southern One-Party System in Transition

No one can predict with much certainty the particular consequences for Southern politics likely to emerge from the enormous social and economic changes that have occurred there during the last two decades. Something of the rate of progress made in the Deep South since 1940 can be gleaned from the experiences of Alabama, Georgia, Louisiana, Mississippi, and South Carolina. Income per person has multiplied nearly five times. Almost twice as many persons work in factories. Bank assets have increased five times and manufacturing output seven times. So many thousands of small farmers and sharecroppers have left the land and moved to the cities that the area is now nearly 50 per cent urban compared to 30 per cent in 1940. Negroes have moved into Northern cities to the extent that the five states have only 26 per cent of all the Negro population in the United States—in 1940 they had 37 per cent. Adult illiteracy has decreased, the overall level of education has been raised, and the number of university and professional school graduates has doubled. Substantial amounts of Northern capital have been invested in textiles, aircraft industries, chemicals, and electrical machinery. Cotton production has decreased about 50 per cent, and cash returns from livestock have doubled. Atomic energy installations and missile production centers have given the Old South new population centers and new sources of income.

What all of this means politically is difficult to assess. There can be little doubt, however, that the rapid rate of urbanization and industrialization cannot help but upset traditional political patterns and practices. Among the factors greatly accentuating these social and economic disruptions is, of course, the drive by various civil rights groups to register and bring to the polls the nation's largest reservoir of relatively untapped voters—the Southern Negro.

Negro Registration and Voting

Although the Negro and other minority groups suffer from disenfranchisement in the North as well as the South, it is in the South where enfranchisement of the Negro will have the greatest effect on future voting patterns. Viewing the South as a whole (that is, all of the eleven former Confederate states), out of a total of over five million Negroes of voting age, only about 40 per cent were registered to vote as of March, 1964. In the Deep South, the percentages of Negro registration were even lower: Alabama 21.6%, Georgia 39.1%, Louisiana 31.6%, Mississippi 6.7%, and South Carolina 34.2%.[6]

Still more disturbing was the extent of Negro disenfranchisement found by the United States Civil Rights Commission in a 1959 study of 158 counties comprising the so-called "black belt" that extends westward from Virginia into Louisiana.[7] In each of these old counties, most of them still heavily rural and cotton-growing, the Negro represented a majority of the population, yet very few, if any, Negroes were found on the voting register. Sixteen of these counties did not have a single Negro registrant. Fifty-one counties had a Negro registration of 3 per cent or less of those of voting age; forty-one counties, 10 per cent or less; 39 counties, between 10 and 30 per cent; and only eleven counties had a Negro registration of more than 30 per cent. Two years later the commission reported that thirteen of the sixteen counties which had no Negro registrants in 1959 still had none.[8]

When the Civil Rights Commission analyzed more closely the socio-economic levels of the Negro in seventeen of such non-voting counties (selected at random), they found in a majority of such counties to no one's great surprise much unemployment, low cash incomes, poor housing conditions, segregation of all public facilities, minimal education, insufficient skills, decreasing populations, and one-crop cotton economies.

Reasons for the Negro's failure to register and vote are complex and mutually reinforcing. They include "fear of economic or physical reprisals, official discrimination, blatant or subtle, and lack of education and motivation." [9]

[6] For recent statistics on Negro voter registration in the South, see *Congressional Quarterly Weekly Report*, August 14, 1964, pp. 1755–1756 and Pat Watters, "Negro Registration in the South: The Significance for November," *The New Republic*, April 4, 1964, pp. 15–17.

[7] *1959 Report of the United States Commission on Civil Rights* (Washington, 1959), pp. 40–54.

[8] *1961 Report of the United States Commission on Civil Rights, I, Voting* (Washington, 1961), p. 143.

[9] *Ibid.*, p. 196; see also Charles V. Hamilton, "Minority Politics in Black Belt Alabama," *Eagleton Institute Cases in Practical Politics* (New York, 1960).

There are available—some as a result of recent legislative action—certain legal tests for the would-be voter which in the hands of registrars bent on keeping Negroes from the polls can be administered in such a manner as to leave little doubt as to the outcome. Among the requirements that an applicant may have to meet to the satisfaction of the registrars are the following:

A. A literacy test
B. An adequate explanation of selected sections of the state or national constitutions
C. Established proof of good character
D. A specified number of registered voters who must vouch for the identity of the applicant

If racial discrimination is the avowed intent of these tests, any minor discrepancy in information or technical error on the forms could then, of course, be judged "fatal" to the applicant. Unavailable or inaccessible registrars can, of course, further complicate the process.

Of the numerous incidents of discriminatory tactics and practices noted in the *1961 Report of the Civil Rights Commission*, a few will suffice as examples:

Franklin County, North Carolina. All of the complainants [10] were required to read designated passages from the United States, or the North Carolina constitutions. Five alleged denials were for reading deficiencies: "missed words, mispronounced words," and "just didn't read well enough." . . . On six occasions Negro applicants alleged that they were rejected because they did not answer questions to the registrar's satisfaction, among them: "What does 'create' mean?" "Who was the Creator?" . . . "Are all people born alike?" "Was I born like Queen Elizabeth?" "When God made you and Eisenhower, did He make both of you the same?" [10]

The commission pointed out that such questions were not authorized by the laws of North Carolina.

Jackson Parish, La. A young Negro veteran was in the . . . registrar's office. It was his first effort to register to vote. He completed his application card . . . and handed it to the registrar. She examined the card and exclaimed: "No, no, no; I see one mistake." She returned the card to him to examine. He checked it, then double checked it. He could not see anything wrong. He told the registrar he saw no mistake, and returned the card to her. "Oh, yes," she said, "but there is one. . . . you underlined 'Mr.' when you should have circled it." (His application was denied.)

Subsequently, when the registrar was given an opportunity to contradict the testimony she added that he had two additional mistakes. "He had misspelled the words 'October' and 'Democratic.'" She also "testified that she rejected registration of applicants for any misspelling at all." [11]

A major registration drive in 1959 involving about 1,500 Negro citizens in Fayette County, Tennessee, brought into open relief some of the more extreme forms of economic reprisals applied by merchants in the area. These were the

[10] *Ibid.*, p. 33.
[11] *Ibid.*, pp. 54–55.

practices listed by the Department of Justice in its application for an injunction:

Termination of sharecropping and tenancy relationships

Termination of employment

Refusal to sell on credit to Negroes who had previously obtained it

Refusal to sell other goods and necessaries and services (even for cash)

Refusal to make loans to qualified Negro borrowers, many of whom had formerly been granted loans

Cancellations of (refusal to renew) various types of insurance

Refusal to supply goods to merchants and others suspected of selling to Negroes

Circulation of lists of Negro registration leaders, and the "inducing, encouraging, and assisting of merchants, landowners, and others to penalize economically" such persons

Inducing wholesale suppliers not to deal with Negro merchants suspected of being sympathetic to Negro registration [12]

Similar tactics of reprisals and intimidation with varying degrees of severity and effectiveness were reported from other Southern counties, especially those in the black belt. The organizational impetus behind these efforts to keep the Negro from exercising his franchise was found not infrequently to come from local residents active in the White Citizens' Councils.

Progress in Negro Enfranchisement

The Thirteenth and Fourteenth Amendments notwithstanding, only thirty years ago less than one hundred thousand Negroes were permitted to cast a general election ballot in Alabama, Arkansas, Florida, Georgia, Louisiana, Mississippi, North Carolina, South Carolina, Tennessee, Texas, and Virginia.[13] As mentioned before, these states presently are able to point to a Negro registration figure of almost 2,000,000 which represents nearly 40 per cent of all that area's non-white population of voting age.[14] Of the various factors and forces contributing to progress in this direction, those most decisive have been without doubt the general and basic socio-economic changes which are transforming the South itself. Parallelling and occasionally highlighting these developments were certain critically significant court cases and instances of federal intervention through statute, litigation, and investigation.

The Grandfather Clause was a state provision under which voters were to be exempted from taking literacy or understanding tests if they could trace

---

[12] *Ibid.,* p. 163.

[13] U.S. Department of Justice, *Protection of the Rights of Individuals* (Washington, 1952), p. 4.

[14] *The New York Times,* February 17, 1964, p. 22 and May 12, 1964, p. 28.

their lineage back to those who were able to vote prior to the adoption of the Fifteenth Amendment. This clearly paved the way for the white voter. The Supreme Court in *Guinn* v. *United States* (1915) [15] saw through the disguise and declared the Grandfather Clause unconstitutional being in clear contravention of the very purpose of the Fifteenth Amendment.

Next came the White Primary. State and local party organizations adopted constitutions and rules which barred participation by all but white voters. Since the results of primary elections in one-party states have the force of deciding the contests, general elections being mere formalities, an exclusionary rule of this type could scarcely fail to keep political power and effective choices in the hands of the white electorate. When, however, the Texas legislature attempted to make the White Primary binding on the Democratic party as a matter of law, the United States Supreme Court in *Nixon* v. *Herndon* (1927) [16] struck down the law as constituting state action in defiance of the "equal protection of the laws" clause of the Fourteenth Amendment.

But the White Primary was not dead yet. A few years later when the Democratic party of Texas through its state convention issued the ruling that only white citizens could hold membership in the party and vote in the party's primary, the United States Supreme Court in *Grovey* v. *Townsend* (1935) [17] sustained the arrangement on the basis that this was no longer the action of the State of Texas but the action of a private and voluntary political association that could not as such be reached by the commands of the Fourteenth Amendment.

Before the White Primary was legally ended in 1944, the primary itself was brought within the protective orbit of the federal Constitution.

While the courts under the provisions of Article II, Sections 2 and 4, of the United States Constitution have for years granted Congress the power to protect by appropriate statutes the integrity of congressional elections against fraud and corruption, primary elections, unknown devices to the Founding Fathers of 1787, were judged in a Michigan primary election dispute as late as 1921 (*Newberry* v. *United States*) [18] as constituting a distinct and separate type of election beyond the reach of congressional control. In 1941 the United States Supreme Court was presented with a Louisiana case (*United States* v. *Classic*) [19] in which certain election commissioners were found to have "willfully altered and falsely counted and certified the ballots of voters cast in the primary election."

Acknowledging the critical state of primary elections in a one-party state, the Court now held that "where the state law has made the primary an integral part of the procedure of choice, or where in fact the primary effec-

[15] 238 U. S. 347 (1915).
[16] 273 U. S. 536 (1927).
[17] 295 U. S. 45 (1935).
[18] 256 U. S. 232 (1921).
[19] 313 U. S. 299 (1941).

tively controls the choice, the right of the elector to have his ballot counted at the primary is likewise included in the right protected by Article I, Section 2." [20]

All that now remained to give the White Primary its legal obituary was to apply to the federally-protected primary the standards of the Fourteenth Amendment. This was accomplished in *Smith* v. *Allwright* (1944), when the Supreme Court after overturning in effect *Grovey* v. *Townsend,* declared "when primaries become a part of the machinery for choosing officials, state and national, as they have here, the same tests to determine the character of discrimination or abridgement should be applied to the primary as are applied to the general election." [21]

More significant and direct federal intervention on behalf of Negro voting became possible only after passage of the Civil Rights Acts of 1957 and 1960. Statutory language assuring all citizens the right to vote had actually been on the books since 1870 as implementing provisions of the Fifteenth Amendment:

> All citizens of the United States who are otherwise qualified by law to vote at any election by the people in any State, Territory, district, county, city, parish, township, school district, municipality, or other territorial subdivision, shall be entitled and allowed to vote at all such elections, without distinction of race, color, or previous condition of servitude; any constitution, law, custom, use or regulation of any State or Territory, or by or under its authority, to the contrary notwithstanding.[22]

The law was there but the enforcement was largely missing.[23] This was changed in 1957. Among the major provisions of the Civil Rights Act then added were the following:

A. The federal government was given authority "[T]o bring civil actions for injunctive relief where discrimination denied or threatened the right to vote."

B. The Attorney General was given "power to institute civil suits when the rights declared in that section were in jeopardy."

C. The sections of the federal code concerned with the prevention of "intimidation, threats, and coercion for the purpose of interfering with the right to vote in federal elections" were strengthened.

D. Contempt proceedings were authorized in the event of disobedience of court orders.

E. The Civil Rights division of the Department of Justice was enlarged.

F. The Federal Civil Rights Commission was established with power:
   1. to investigate formal allegations of voting rights violations,

---

[20] *Ibid.,* at 318.

[21] 321 U. S. 649 (1944), at 664.

[22] *United States Code Annotated,* Title 42, Sec. 1971(a) (St. Paul, 1963).

[23] Sections 19 and 20 of the U. S. Criminal Code were involved in the *Classic* case and provided penalties against persons injuring, oppressing, threatening, or intimidating any citizen "in the free exercise or enjoyment of any right or privilege secured to him by the Constitution" or the laws of the United States. Sec. 20 prohibits any action under "color of law" interfering with the rights of citizenship.

2. to study and collect information concerning legal developments which constitute a denial of equal protection of the laws under the Constitution,
3. to appraise the laws and policies of the federal government with respect to equal protection of the laws under the Constitution,
4. to prepare and submit reports to the president and the Congress.

The Civil Rights Act of 1960 further strengthened the power of the federal government in at least three major respects: First, it entitled the Attorney General to have access to voting records, and it required the preservation of such public documents by the local registrars for a minimum of twenty-two months. Second, in such cases where an uncooperative registrar resigns his office or is relieved of his office, the Attorney General is empowered to institute suit against the state itself. Third, where discrimination is found by the court upon petition by the Attorney General to be so widespread as to constitute a "pattern or practice," the Attorney General may ask the court or a party designated by the court, to act as a federal election referee. Any person who considers himself deprived of his voting privileges because of race or color may then apply to such a referee for an order declaring him to be a qualified voter provided, of course, that he meets all the other standard requirements for voting. Where state law specifies a literacy test, this would also have to be administered by the referee. If the state attorney general and the other interested parties, who are to receive copies of the referee's determination, enter no exception to the findings within a specified period of time, voters having received their certificates of qualification from the referee can be turned down by local registrars only under penalty of contempt of court.

In their 1961 report, the United States Civil Rights Commission found that "substantial numbers of Negro citizens are, or recently have been, denied the right to vote on grounds of race or color in about 100 counties in eight Southern states: Alabama, Florida, Georgia, Louisiana, Mississippi, North Carolina, South Carolina, and Tennessee." [24] These 100 counties, where only 8.3 per cent of the eligible Negroes were registered to vote in 1962, became the target of Justice Department suits against alleged discrimination or intimidation by individuals which hamper the Negro's constitutional right to vote. As of September 30, 1963, suits had been filed in 29 of the 100 counties. In addition, the Justice Department had filed suits in eleven other counties in the Southern states. [25] The constitutionality of the Civil Rights Commission itself was sustained by the United States Supreme Court in *United States* v. *Raines* (1960). [26] As a result of federal action consummating in *United States* v. *McElveen* (1960), [27] 1,377 Negroes previously registered but removed from the rolls in Washington Parish, Louisiana, largely due to an alliance of

[24] *1961 Report of the United States Commission on Civil Rights*, I, Voting, p. 135.
[25] *1963 Report of the United States Commission on Civil Rights: Civil Rights '63* (Washington, 1963), p. 15.
[26] 362 U. S. 17 (1960).
[27] 180 F. Supp. 10 (1960). For further litigation in this case see *United States* v. *Thomas,* 362 U. S. 58 (1960).

members of the White Citizens' Councils and local registrars, were restored to the voting lists. No significant registration gains have been made in Washington Parish since the Court action. An attempt to "fence Negro citizens out of Tuskegee," Alabama, by means of "an irregular, 28-sided gerrymander" was unanimously struck down by the Supreme Court as a violation of the Fourteenth Amendment in *Gomillion v. Lightfoot* (1960).[28]

Much of the momentum for registering Negroes has come, as might be expected, from the ranks of the Negro community itself, more particularly from such organizations as the National Association for the Advancement of Colored People (N.A.A.C.P.), the Southern Christian Leadership Conference, the Congress of Racial Equality, and Student Non-Violent Coordinating Committee.

Inspired by such leaders as Rev. Martin Luther King, Jr., deeply conscious of the changes in the New Dixie, and enormously impressed by the rapid strides towards political identity now characterizing the new nations of Africa, America's Negro youth are committed to an assertion of first-class citizenship.

The focal point in reaching this goal is the voter registration drive now carried on, not infrequently at considerable personal risk, by Negro and white college students, housewives, ministers, teachers and other segments of the community in the urban and rural areas of Alabama, Georgia, Louisiana, Mississippi, and North Carolina.

The drive for increased Negro voter registration has also spurred Negroes into becoming candidates for political office in the South. Georgia voters in Atlanta in 1962 elected their first Negro state senator, Leroy R. Johnson, a lawyer. His opponent was also a Negro. In Macon County, Alabama, four Negroes were nominated for countywide office in the May, 1964, Democratic primary. Negro voters now outnumber white voters in Macon County as a result of federal court actions. Four Negroes in Mississippi entered the Senate and three the House Democratic primary races in June, 1964, but received only a scattering of votes. At the same time as Negroes have become active in seeking political office in the South, a United States Supreme Court decision has removed an artificial barrier from the path of potential Negro office-seekers. In *Anderson v. Martin* (1964) [29] the court ruled that a Louisiana statute requiring that the race of every candidate be designated on the ballot violated the equal protection clause of the Fourteenth Amendment.

The Fifteenth Amendment right to vote was further reinforced by the Civil Rights Act of 1964. The Voting Rights Title of the act requires election officials to apply uniform standards in registering voters and prohibits them from disqualifying persons for immaterial errors or omissions on applications for voting in federal elections. In voting rights suits, a "rebuttable presumption" is created that a person who has completed a sixth grade education in a

28 364 U. S. 339 (1960).
29 375 U. S. 399 (1964).

predominantly English language school is sufficiently literate to vote. When literacy tests are used, they must be given in writing unless an agreement between the attorney general and state or local authorities provides otherwise. The Voting Rights Title of the law also authorizes the attorney general or any defendant to request a three-judge court to hear suits involving discrimination against voting rights. Another title of the act directs the Bureau of the Census to compile statistics of registration and voting by race, color, and national origin in areas of the country recommended by the Commission on Civil Rights.[30]

The Voting Rights Act of 1965 (P. L. 89–110), signed by President Johnson on August 6, 1965, on the very spot where Lincoln signed the Emancipation Proclamation, represents the latest and probably most significant federal measure designed to remove major barriers remaining to Negro voting in the South. Among its principal provisions with respect to the enfranchisement of Negroes are the following:

A. Literacy or competence tests used to determine voter registration are automatically suspended in any state or county in which less than 50% of the voting-age population voted in the presidential election of 1964 or were registered on November 1, 1964.
B. The Attorney General and the Bureau of the Census are empowered to determine which counties or states are covered by the law.
C. Federal examiners may be sent by the Attorney General either on his own motion or on receipt of complaints to any county covered by the law for the purpose of making investigations and registering qualified voters.
D. Federal authorities are to commence legal action to have the poll tax declared unconstitutional where used as a basis for eligibility for voting in state and local elections. (The Federal poll tax has already been outlawed by the 24th Amendment to the Constitution).

The effect of this act is to take voter registration out of the hands of local registrars whose recalcitrance precludes otherwise qualified persons from registering. Where the law is operative all voting tests are suspended and the only prerequisites to registration are proper age, residence, and absence of criminal record.

[30] For the full text of the act, see the *Congressional Record*, May 26, 1964, pp. 11537–46. An excellent discussion of recent political changes in the South is found in this series of articles: Leslie W. Dunbar, The Changing Mind of the South: The Exposed Nerve"; William H. Nicholls, "The South as a Developing Area"; Lawrence L. Durisch, "Southern Regional Planning and Development"; Robert H. Connery and Richard H. Leach, "Southern Metropolis: Challenge to Government"; Donald R. Matthews and James W. Prothro, "Southern Images of Political Parties: An Analysis of White and Negro Attitudes"; Alfred Clubok, John DeGrove and Charles Farris, "The Manipulated Negro Vote: Preconditions and Consequences"; Samuel DuBois Cook, "Political Movements and Organizations"; George W. Spicer, "The Federal Judiciary and Political Changes in the South"; Malcolm E. Jewell, "State Legislatures in Southern Politics"; Coleman B. Ransome, "Political Leadership in the Governor's Office"; O. Douglas Weeks, "The South in National Politics"; in *Journal of Politics* (25th Anniversary Issue: The American South: 1950–1970), February, 1964.

Republican Efforts in the South—Towards a Two-Party System?

This is how an account of the 1960 presidential campaign portrayed the reception given the Republican nominee in one of the Southern states:

> The Atlantans waved their banners, shouted, screamed, crowded thicker and thicker until the procession slowed to an ooze, and then at Atlanta's famous Five Points, where Peachtree turns left to Edgewood to descend to Hurt Park, they burst out of control to overwhelm him completely. From then on down to Hurt Park there was no order to the procession as the white-helmeted police, the middle-aged ladies, the sober young men, all trotted after him as if he were magic. . . . At Hurt Park there were two or three acres of people, crowding over the limestone parapet above, sitting on the ledges of the swimming pool, yodeling and yipping rebel yells, yearning to listen to him, waiting to be taken. It was, Dick Nixon was later to remark, the most impressive demonstration he had seen in fourteen years of campaigning . . .[31]

Ten weeks later Mr. Nixon did not carry Georgia (he received 37.4 per cent of the vote); the enthusiasm of campaign crowds can seldom be considered a very reliable barometer of a party's true strength. Yet the fact remains that since 1948 the electorate of such former Confederate states as Florida, Louisiana, Texas, and Virginia split their tickets in support of the Republican presidential nominees.[32] Additionally, as noted before, three of these states now also have two Republicans in their congressional delegations, and Texas, following the special election of 1961, elected a Republican senator to take the seat vacated by Lyndon B. Johnson.

Republicans in Florida were encouraged by reports in 1962 from Sarasota County along the Gulf where G.O.P. registration for the first time in 100 years exceeded those of the Democrats and by registration figures in the counties around Orlando where Edward J. Gurney was elected in 1962, the second Republican congressman joining William C. Cramer.[33] In March, 1963, the Florida G.O.P. captured twelve of forty vacant legislative seats in a special election to fill vacancies created by the state's new reapportionment law.[34] In Louisville, Kentucky, Republicans won, in 1961, forty-two out of forty-four city and county offices including the mayorality despite a two to one Democratic registration advantage.[35] In the 1962 congressional elections, Senator Thruston B. Morton carried Louisville by 22,000 votes in his successful contest against Wilson W. Wyatt, helping to carry M. G. Snyder, the G.O.P. House candidate in the Third District, to a 2,000-vote victory over the Democratic incumbent.[36] The 1963 Kentucky G.O.P. gubernatorial candidate, Louis

[31] Theodore H. White, *The Making of the President* (New York, 1961), pp. 268–269.

[32] Donald S. Strong, "The Presidential Election in the South, 1952," *Journal of Politics*, August, 1955, pp. 343–389 and Bernard Cosman, "Presidential Republicanism in the South, 1960," *Journal of Politics*, May, 1962, pp. 303–322.

[33] *The New York Times*, October 8, 1961, p. 49 and November 7, 1962, p. 44.

[34] *Ibid.*, March 28, 1963, p. 4.

[35] *Ibid.*, November 12, 1961, p. 67.

[36] *Ibid.*, November 7, 1962, p. 33.

B. Nunn, won a 4,000-vote margin in Louisville but was unable to poll enough votes outstate to win the election.[37]

What is still most inconclusive and tenuous is whether these figures add up to anything more than that in some of the Southern states Republicans have at times captured a local office, national office, or even their state's presidential electors.

The significance, for example, of the Texas senatorial election, the G.O.P.'s most dramatic recent success, is far from clear. Republican conservative John Tower defeated the interim incumbent, William A. Blakely, a conservative Democrat, by 10,000 out of 887,000 votes in a contest where Lyndon Johnson, liberal Democrats, organized labor, and many Negroes refused to support Blakely. It was a special election (no party labels shown) where the total electorate was only a third of that which had cast ballots for the presidency just six months before.[38] Johnson, when running for reelection in 1960, defeated Tower by 379,972 votes. In the 1962 gubernatorial election, former Secretary of the Navy John B. Connally defeated the G. O. P. candidate, Jack Cox, by polling 54.2 per cent of the vote. Ed Foreman became the second G.O.P. congressman from Texas when he ousted the Democratic incumbent in the Sixteenth District of West Texas.

Despite President Eisenhower's tremendous personal popularity and his carrying Texas, Virginia, and Florida twice and despite the organizational efforts of his party to add G.O.P. congressmen from Dixie, the party's total popular vote for Congress in twelve Southern states increased from 19.0 per cent in 1952 to only 24.1 per cent in 1960.[39] In 1962, the G.O.P. polled 42.4 per cent of the congressional vote in the districts which the party contested, while winning five additional seats in the South. Although garnering only 39.4 per cent of the congressional vote in 1964, the G.O.P. was able to elect four additional congressmen from the South while incurring a net loss nationally of thirty-eight seats.

Even more disturbing to those who wish to see the Republican party make major advances in Southern politics has been the obvious problem of translating these occasional victories on the national level into concrete gains in county and state houses.[40] This has been particularly true for the managers of the newer industries and the young businessmen in the urban chambers of commerce, of whom many would find G.O.P. affiliations much more congenial. To date there have been no significant breaches in the Democratic party's monopoly hold on state executives, state legislatures, or state judiciaries. It is still the Democratic party primary restricted generally to all but registered Democrats that furnishes the arena in which contests for these offices are fought out.

[37] Ibid., November 7, 1963, p. 30.
[38] The Wall Street Journal, May 31, 1961, p. 12.
[39] The 1960 Elections: A Summary Report with Supporting Tables (Washington, 1961), p. 29.
[40] Donald S. Strong, Urban Republicanism in the South (University, Ala., 1960).

If a state Republican party were established prematurely, it might well rob the Republicans of any effect or voice that they can exercise to greater advantage by continuing to vote for state and local contests within the Democratic primary.

There is now in the South much political frustration, considerable diversity in social and political thought, and a wide variety of conflicting counsels concerning the direction that Southern politics should take in the future. Conservative Southern Democrats detest what they consider to be the domination of their party's national councils and conventions by "socialistically oriented labor bosses, by N.A.A.C.P. spokesmen, and by professional liberals." Yet twenty-two congressional standing committee chairmanships and the power that they and the seniority system have afforded weigh heavily on practical-minded politicians. Many of the most vociferous defenders of states' rights have found it so far impossible to turn their backs on such material manifestations of the new federalism as grants-in-aid to hospitals, roads, welfare, agriculture, and housing.

Right-wing extremists like the White Citizens' Councils and the Ku Klux Klan warn their fellow Southerners never to forget that "integration of the races and destruction of White America is one of Communistic Russia's objectives." [41] Senator William J. Fulbright, chairman of the Senate Foreign Relations Committee has been a major target of such groups, not so much for his positions on the race issue (he is a moderate and even a signer of the Southern Manifesto against integration), but for his alleged softness on the Communist issue in defending the sale of jets to Tito's Yugoslavia, and in urging a more flexible approach to the problems of Laos, South Vietnam, Cuba, Berlin, and more recently Santo Domingo.

The lot of liberal Democrats is not a happy one either. In spite of rapid urban growth, Southern legislators have kept their cities more underrepresented than their Northern colleagues. Georgia (before it was forced to reapportion) represented the most glaring illustration. Fulton County (Atlanta), with a population in excess of 500,000, had a delegation of three state representatives, the same number as Charlton, Echols, and Lanier counties near the Florida line which have a total population of less than 10,000. Most anti-urban was, of course, Georgia's unique county unit system of nomination. Under this arrangement the eight most populous counties were each given six unit votes, the next thirty most populous four unit votes, and the 121 least populous two unit votes. In this manner the 121 least populous counties were assured of 59 per cent of the total unit votes cast. For nomination, candidates needed only to obtain a majority of the unit votes; a popular majority was not necessary. Likened to the presidential electoral college in its operation, the county unit system greatly accentuated the political power of rural and

---

[41] Marian D. Irish, "Political Thought and Political Behavior in the South," *Western Political Quarterly,* June, 1960, p. 413.

[42] *The Wall Street Journal,* November 24, 1961, p. 1; *The Washington Post,* September 16, 1965, pp. 1, 7.

small-town conservatism. Due to the notable failure of organized labor to make significant progress in unionizing Southern workers with social views still heavily rural, liberal Democratic politicians even within the cities have not yet been able to build the type of political machines that proved so successful in the Northern and Eastern industrial centers.

If there is a single force that is likely to have profound effect on the direction that Southern politics might take in the years ahead, it will probably be the Negro.

Should the present rate of their registration continue, as it is likely to do following the enactment of the Civil Rights Act of 1965, approximately 2 million Negro voters could be added to the voting lists during the next two years. Increasingly conscious of political power, urged to register and vote, will these newly enfranchised Negro masses then forgive or forget the Democrats?

That the Negro community does not represent a homogeneous political orientation is a well-known fact. Yet considering present needs and realities, demands for civil rights, for better housing, more jobs, and social security will presumably force many of the Negroes to keep their political focus centered for some time to come on federal action in addition to that which may be rendered by state and local governments. Whether the platform promises and Washington achievements of the Northern, more liberal Democratic party will prove sufficiently strong to make the Southern Negro forget the past and remain Democratic on state and local levels as well, will depend to a large extent on how well these promises are kept and the nature of the G.O.P. alternatives. Which alternative to offer the Negro electorate constitutes a major dilemma for Southern Republicanism. A conservative Republicanism favoring states' rights and a restricted role for the federal government, a position quite appealing to large numbers of Southern voters, urban as well as rural, and especially appealing to the newer business and industrial segments of the South might further cement Negro affinities for the Democrats. A more liberal Republicanism might prove popular with Negro voters but fail to attract sufficient supporters from the basically conservative states' rights faction of the white Southern electorate and thus retard G.O.P. power on the state level.

Should, on the other hand, the former alternative materialize as it appears to have through the capture of the G.O.P. machinery by conservative Republicans, and the Negro decide to find his political expression and future within the Democratic party, then it will probably be the moderates or liberals and not the conservatives among the Democratic party's candidates who would gain significant allies.

It was this kind of support from Negroes and white moderates that proved decisive on November 3, 1964, when Charles L. Weltner from Georgia's 5th Congressional District (Atlanta), the only Democratic congressman from the Deep South who had voted for the Civil Rights Act of 1964, received 54.5 per cent of the vote against an avowed segregationist.

Numerically the Negro electorate in the South is not yet of sufficient strength to decide the outcome of many contests. But the day is not far off when few if any Southern candidates whether local, state, or national, Democratic or Republican, will be able to afford the risk of ignoring the wishes of this still largely untapped reservoir of voting power (see Figure 1).

THE MODIFIED ONE-PARTY SYSTEM

A study of American political parties based on election returns for the office of president, United States senator, and governor over the period of 1914 to 1952 suggested the modified one-party system classification for the following twelve states: Iowa, Kansas, Kentucky, Maine, New Hampshire,

FIGURE 1

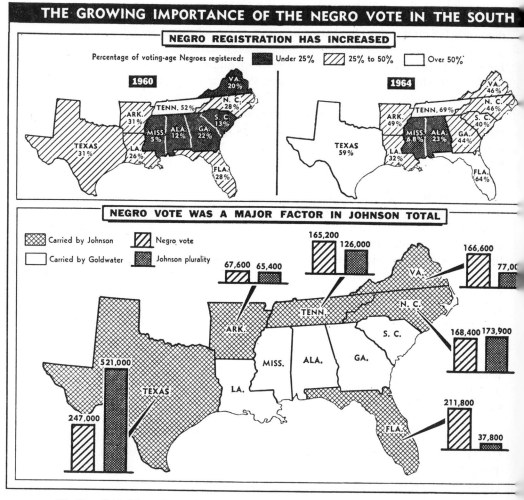

SOURCE: *The New York Times,* November 22, 1964, p. E5.

TABLE 1. THE MODIFIED ONE-PARTY SYSTEM

State	1 Total Republican wins (1914–1952)	2 Total Democratic wins (1914–1952)	3 Per cent of second party wins (1914–1952)	4 Per cent of second party wins (1954–1962)	5 No. of seats of second party in state House			
					1950	%	1965	%
	34	10	22.7	27.2	29	26.8	101	81.4
as	36	7	16.2	16.7	30	24.0	39	31.2
ucky	8	27	22.8	60.0	25	25.0	37	37.0
e	40	3	7.0	40.0	26	17.2	70	52.3
Hampshire	37	6	14.0	15.4	145	36.3	176	44.7
Carolina	1	33	3.0	0.0	13	10.8	14	11.7
Dakota	36	8	18.1	27.3	2	1.8	64	58.2
oma	6	27	18.1	33.3	23	19.5	21	21.7
n	26	7	23.5	50.0	11	18.3	28	46.6
sylvania	28	7	20.5	62.5	91	43.7	119	52.0
Dakota	34	9	21.0	18.2	11	14.7	30	40.0
essee	4	40	9.0	25.0	19	19.0	25	25.5

CE: Adapted from Table II in Austin Ranney and Willmoore Kendall, "The American Party Systems," *American Political Science Review*, June, 1954, p. 483.

North Carolina, North Dakota, Oklahoma, Oregon, Pennsylvania, South Dakota, and Tennessee. In each of these states, the second party, either Democratic or Republican, "while winning less than 25 per cent of all elections, [had] won over 30 per cent of the vote in over 70 per cent of all elections and [had] won over 40 per cent of the vote in over 30 per cent of all elections." [43] Thus while not strong enough to win many elections, second parties in these states did offer at times sufficiently substantial opposition to merit voter attention as a functioning and possible alternative to the dominant party.

As shown in Table 1 modified one-party systems are found in almost all regions of the United States.

Republicans have the advantage of being the dominant party in eight of the twelve states. Interparty competition appears to be increasing in all but three or four states. Based on column (4) Democrats have made their most notable gains in Maine, Oregon, and Pennsylvania; Republicans, in Kentucky and Oklahoma.

Iowa's Republican party suffered its most disastrous defeat in 1964. In addition to winning the state for Johnson, the Democrats picked up five seats in Congress, twenty-three seats in the state Senate, and seventy-two seats in the state House.

Democrats, although they were the political underdogs in two-thirds of the modified one-party states, were able to point to more substantial advances. Presidential victories were scored only in Pennsylvania where Kennedy carried the state by 116,326 out of over five million votes cast. Between 1952 and 1965 Democrats in Maine won three gubernatorial and one senatorial elec-

[43] Ranney and Kendall, p. 484.

tion; Democrats in Oregon won one gubernatorial and four senatorial elections; and Democrats in Pennsylvania won two gubernatorial and two senatorial elections. Moreover, Democrats not only increased their party's strength in the legislatures of all three of these states but they made important gains also in the state Houses of North and South Dakota as well.

Since there are no simple explanations in American politics, none should be looked for to account for this increasingly competitive stance of the Democrats. As so often in state and national politics, there were strong personalities that played a major role in the resurgence. In Maine, it was Governor Edmund S. Muskie, now a United States senator, a moderate liberal, an able administrator, and a successful legislative leader. The two key figures in Oregon were the late Senator Richard L. Neuberger, a nationally famous liberal journalist and effective speaker, and Congresswoman Edith Green, a hard-working, widely respected legislator and an excellent campaigner and party organizer. Pennsylvania Democrats long torn by intraparty fratricide between the western part of the state and the "Philadelphia machine" achieved their renaissance largely through the activities of three mayors and one congressman. The western leader was David Lawrence, the former mayor of Pittsburgh, and governor between 1958 and 1962. He is also one of the most influential "elder statesmen" of the Democratic party. From Philadelphia came two "reformers," Mayor Joseph S. Clark, now senator, who in 1951 was elected as that city's first Democratic chief executive in sixty-seven years, and the mayor until 1963, Richardson Dilworth. The late William J. Green, Jr., northeastern Philadelphia's seven-term congressman, provided the organizational support—or as his critics pointed out, the "boss-controlled" machine vote fed by patronage and favoritism.

At best these are only partial explanations. Of aid and benefit to the Democratic candidates' cause were such substantial campaign factors as organized labor's concentrated registration drives, extensive unemployment, real or threatened, and a drop in farm income in the Dakotas.

Nor can the effect of the Kennedy candidacy be ignored. Special enthusiasm for Kennedy among labor, Negro, Catholic, and Jewish voters helped to boost Philadelphia's Democratic vote from 57.0 per cent in 1956 to 68.1 per cent in 1960.

THE TWO-PARTY COMPETITIVE SYSTEM

The line of demarcation between the modified one-party and the competitive two-party system is neither a sharp nor a constant one. For example, Pennsylvania and Oregon, classified by the Ranney-Kendall study as belonging to the modified one-party system may now have moved from that category into the two-party system (see Table 2).

The authors placed into this category twenty-six states in which the second party won between 1914 and 1952 one-fourth or more of all presidential, senatorial, and gubernatorial elections (see Table 3). In nearly two-

TABLE 2. MAJORITY PARTY VOTES IN PENNSYLVANIA AND OREGON

	Pennsylvania		Oregon	
	Democrat	Republican	Democrat	Republican
Presidential Election (1960)	51.2%	48.8%	52.6%	47.4%
(1964)				
Gubernatorial election (1958)	51.0%	49.0%	44.7%	55.3%
(1962)	44.4%	55.6%	43.4%	56.6%
Senatorial election (1958)	48.6%	51.4%	No Election	
(1960)	No Election		54.6%	45.4%
(1962)	51.2%	48.8%	54.2%	45.8%
(1964)	49.4%	50.6%	No Election	
Party membership in state legislature (1963–1964)				
House	101	109	31	29
Senate	23	27	21	9
(1965)				
House	119	90	28	32
Senate	23	27	19	11

SOURCE: Adapted from Richard M. Scammon (ed.), *America Votes, A Handbook of Contemporary American Election Statistics* (Pittsburgh, 1962), pp. 338–340, 346–349, and 354–355.

TABLE 3. THE TWO-PARTY SYSTEM

	1	2	3	4	5			
			Per cent of second party wins	Per cent of second party wins	No. of seats of second party in state House			
	Total Republican wins (1914–1952)	Total Democratic wins (1914–1952)	(1914–1952)	(1954–1962)	1950	%	1965	%
	12	32	27.2	60.0	7	12.1	35	43.8
ia	22	11	35.3	33.3	35	43.8	48	60.0
n	22	21	48.8	40.0	41	67.2	42	68.9
icut	31	15	32.6	75.0	92	33.8	110	37.3
e	22	11	33.3	42.9	17	48.6	30	85.7
	26	18	40.9	20.0	24	40.7	37	46.8
	21	14	40.0	50.0	81	52.9	118	66.7
	21	13	38.2	42.9	60	60.0	79	79.0
d	11	23	32.3	50.0	36	29.3	25	17.6
usetts	24	19	44.2	54.5	122	50.9	172	71.7
n	30	13	30.2	80.0	39	39.0	72	72.0
ta	28	15 *	34.8	80.0	42 †	32.1	56	41.5
i	13	22	37.1	0.0	60	38.9	39	24.4
a	9	24	27.2	55.5	35	38.9	38	40.4
a	30	14 *	31.8	27.3	- - -	- - -	- - -	- - -
	11	25	30.5	22.2	18	41.9	12	32.4
sey	24	13	35.1	62.5	16	26.6	28	46.6
xico	14	29	32.5	30.0	19	38.8	18	23.4
rk	17	23	42.5	75.0	87	58.0	62	41.3
	23	22	48.8	50.0	16	11.5	62	45.3
sland	17	26	39.5	30.0	35	35.0	23	23.0
	13	21	38.2	14.3	19	31.7	30	43.5
ton	15	19	44.1	28.6	32	32.3	40	41.2
rginia	12	21	36.3	33.3	16	17.0	9	9.0
in	31	13 *	29.3	54.5	25	25.0	52	52.0
g	15	20	42.8	66.7	28	50.0	27	44.2

party victories added to second party totals.
al" Members of state House—Minnesota does not have party designation.
Adapted from Table I in Austin Ranney and Willmoore Kendall, "The American Party Systems," *American Political Science Review*, June, 1954, p. 482.

thirds of these states, all of them north of the Mason-Dixon Line, the advantage lay with the Republican party. But here too politics since 1952 has become much more competitive. In more than one-half of the twenty-six states the second party has made notable gains, gains which often were accompanied by additional seats won for the respective party delegations in the state House.

Most of the significant augmentations in Republican votes occurred in Maryland and New York and in the Western mountain states of Arizona, Montana, and Wyoming.

Among Republicans, other than President Eisenhower himself, who contributed most to lifting the G.O.P. from its second-party status in these states since 1952, the most prominent were Governor Nelson Rockefeller of New York, former Governor Cecil Underwood of West Virginia, former Governor Theodore McKeldin of Maryland, former Governor J. Hugo Aronson of Montana, Senator Milward L. Simpson of Wyoming, and former Senator Barry Goldwater of Arizona. In political philosophy these Republican leaders, who were so successful in bucking traditional Democratic strength in their states, represented every shade of the ideological spectrum from the near left to the right. It is often difficult to tell the difference between Rockefeller and his Democratic predecessor with regard to legislative programs and administrative leadership in public housing, civil rights, social security, income tax withholding, education, governmental reorganization, and public planning. No such potential criticism of "me-tooism" has ever been leveled at the spokesman for the other end of the ideological continuum, Arizona's Barry Goldwater. Believing in states' rights and advocating a greatly reduced role for the federal government in the areas of taxation, grants-in-aid, and management-labor relations, the Republicanism of Senator Goldwater and Governor Paul Fannin proved highly attractive to Arizona's ranchers and businessmen, as well as to the thousands of newcomers pouring into the state every year in search of health and sunshine to retire or to begin a new life. Between 1950 and 1960, both Tucson and Phoenix more than quadrupled their populations.

Democrats scored some of their most notable advances in moving away from second-party status in Connecticut, Illinois, Michigan, Minnesota, New Jersey, and Wisconsin. In Connecticut, major credit would have to go to senator and former Governor Abraham Ribicoff, former governor and Congressman Chester Bowles, and to the party's State Chairman John Bailey, now Democratic National Chairman. New Jersey's former Governor Robert B. Meyner proved to be a highly able administrator in the nation's constitutionally strongest governorship, and Michigan's G. Mennen Williams achieved the nation's record for gubernatorial tenure by winning six successive terms in addition to building one of the most program-conscious parties in the United States. A very similar type of programmatic, as well as liberal, party was developed in Minnesota by former Senator Hubert H. Humphrey, former Governor Orville L. Freeman, and Senator Eugene J. McCarthy; and in

Wisconsin, by Senator William Proxmire, Senator Gaylord Nelson and former Governor John W. Reynolds.

Undoubtedly, Illinois' most famous Democrats were the late Governor Adlai Stevenson and the present Senator Paul Douglas. During the last few years, however, when it came to making key decisions affecting the party's state and local issues and nominations, in place of these two national figures, the actual power was wielded frequently by Chicago's Mayor Richard Daley, Governor Otto Kerner, Chicago's Congressman William L. Dawson, and the downstate legislative leader and former speaker of the House, Paul Powell.

Why should Democrats have experienced such electoral prosperity in Midwestern states where they had been traditionally weak and the Republicans strong? Reasons most often given are the personal charm of some of the candidates, administrative leadership of their state governors, effective and large-scale campaign and party organizational work, increased political efforts by organized labor and by the Farmers' Union, and in Illinois, occasional moments of truce in the intraparty battles between the Democrats of Cook County and the Democrats from downstate.

ETHNIC, RELIGIOUS, ECONOMIC, AND RACIAL FACTORS IN STATE POLITICS

A person's voting behavior or party preference is a necessarily complex phenomenon.[44] Each person stands at the center of pressures and influences—family, social, religious, or economic—all of which may demand loyalties or affirmations to certain candidates, issues, or parties but all of which can rarely be obeyed simultaneously. Few of them, if any, will combine neatly to point in one and the same direction. While it, therefore, continues to be difficult to predict with certainty what a particular individual may finally do with his ballot under the impact of such forces, the political behavior of groups as such does tend to follow general trends and patterns which are certainly no longer shrouded in mystery.

[44] On some basic studies in this area, see Paul H. Appleby, "The Influence of the Citizen," in Frank Munger and Douglas Price (eds.), *Readings in Political Parties and Pressure Groups* (New York, 1964), pp. 408–420; Phillips Cutright and Peter H. Rossi, "Grass Roots Politicians and the Vote," *American Sociological Review*, April, 1958, pp. 171–179; John Foster, "Campaigning for the Ethnic Vote," in Munger and Price, pp. 385–391; Robert T. Golembiewski, "The Group Basis of Politics: Notes on Analysis and Development," *American Political Science Review*, December, 1960, pp. 962–971; Edward G. Janosik, *Report on Political Activity of Philadelphia Businessmen* (Philadelphia, 1958); V. O. Key, Jr. and Frank Munger, "Social Determinism and Electoral Decision: The Case of Indiana," in Munger and Price, pp. 366–384; Earl Latham, "The Group Basis of Politics: Notes for a Theory," *American Political Science Review*, June, 1952, pp. 376–397; David Riesman, "The Political Man: Two Views," in Munger and Price, pp. 1–9; E. E. Schattschneider, "The Scope and Basis of the Pressure System," *ibid.*, pp. 130–147; David B. Truman, "Group Politics and Representative Democracy," *ibid.*, pp. 118–130; David B. Truman, "The Group Concept," *ibid.*, pp. 57–71; and James Q. Wilson, "Two Negro Politicians: An Interpretation," *Midwest Journal of Political Science*, November, 1960, pp. 346–369.

Sufficient research has already been conducted into the political habits of major voting groups to identify some of their gravitational patterns. Take, for example, New England. Religio-ethnic groupings in state politics there have had an opportunity to crystallize more succinctly over a longer period than in some of the other regions of the country.

The Irish, French-Canadian, Italian, and Polish groups—the most numerous minorities in the region—have been largely Democratic since the 1920's. Certain other ethnic groups—the Germans and the Swedes, for example—have chosen to be Republicans in the main, but relatively few of them came to New England. . . . Why these ethnic groups have either come to or stayed with the Democratic party is apparently a question both of tradition and of pocketbook voting. Since the Whigs, the Know Nothings and the Republicans, who derived from the remnants of these earlier parties, were largely anti-Catholic and anti-immigrant, it was natural that the Irish as the first comers turned to the Democratic party. The Democrats made a special appeal to the Irish in these early days, and it paid off handsomely.[45]

TABLE 4. IRISH AND ITALIAN NAMES IN THE MASSACHUSETTS HOUSE OF REPRE-SENTATIVES, 1900 AND 1955

| | 1900 | | | | 1955 | | | |
| | Republicans | | Democrats | | Republicans | | Democrats | |
	No.	Per cent	No.	Per cent	No.	Per cent	No.	Per cent
Total representation	165	100.0	71	100.0	113	100.0	127	100.0
Irish names	2	1.2	33	46.5	5	4.4	59	46.5
Italian names	0	0.0	0	0.0	5	4.4	22	17.3
Other	163	98.8	38	53.5	103	81.2	46	36.2

SOURCE: Duane Lockard, *New England State Politics*, (Princeton, 1959), p. 134.

Nor has this pattern changed very much during the last half century as the following study of names in the Massachusetts legislature suggests (see Table 4).

Within the Democratic party councils Irish political power grew. Eventually so did that of other, later arriving ethnic minorities, most of whom were Catholic and came from eastern Europe. Their power became particularly effective as cities grew and became industrialized. This influx of Democratic strength was by no means unique or restricted to New England but became a fairly typical phenomenon for most of the urban centers of the eastern United States which proceeded to absorb these new masses of workers and immigrants. The event that cemented many members of the ethnic or religious minorities to the Democrats and especially to the New Deal was, of course, the shattering experience of the Depression years. Beset by mass unemployment, poverty, immobility, and a profound sense of helplessness, many thousands from these low-income groups along with organized labor attached them-

[45] Lockard, pp. 311–312. Reprinted with permission of Princeton University Press.

TABLE 5. DEMOCRATIC PRESIDENTIAL PERCENTAGES IN TEN MAJOR CITIES

	1936	*1940*	*1944*	*1948*	*1952*	*1956*	*1960*	*1964*†
Baltimore	68.3	64.0	59.2	53.3	51.7	44.2	63.9	76.0
Boston	69.9	63.3	62.3	69.2	59.6	53.8	74.7	86.4
Chicago	66.9	58.5	61.4	58.6	54.4	49.0	63.6	63.2‡
Cleveland	76.5	69.9	67.9	61.8	59.9	54.6	70.9	82.8
Detroit	68.9	63.0	65.0	59.6	60.5	61.8	71.0	80.0
Milwaukee	82.1	64.1	61.7	59.4	51.5	47.3	61.8	70.0
New York	75.4	61.2	61.6	51.1*	55.4	51.0	62.8	73.2
Philadelphia	62.1	60.0	58.9	49.2*	58.4	57.1	68.1	73.7
Pittsburgh	70.7	61.6	60.8	60.1	56.1	52.3	67.0	74.7
St. Louis	67.0	58.1	60.4	64.3	02.0	61.0	66.6	77.7

* The Progressive party of Henry Wallace polled 13.5% in New York City and 2.4% in Philadelphia.
‡ Percentage figures for 1964 are based on unofficial returns.
† Cook County returns.
SOURCE: Adapted from *The Political Almanac*, 1952, compiled by George Gallup and the American Institute of Public Opinion Staff (New York, 1952) and Richard M. Scammon (ed.), *America Votes, A Handbook of Contemporary American Election Statistics*, Vol. IV (Pittsburgh, 1962).

selves throughout the 1930's to Roosevelt's leadership and aggressively supported most of the various public works, labor, social welfare, and fiscal measures collectively identified as the New Deal. The political loyalties forged during these memorable years proved strong enough to keep nearly all of these major industrial cities solidly in the Democratic column for nearly a generation (see Table 5).

In New York City, as in probably no other city, ethnic, religious (see Table 6), social, and economic factors combined with such force as to make quite dismal the prospects for Republican victories on either national, state, or local levels except for an unusual combination of circumstances.

For example, between 1920 and 1962, Democrats in New York City won nine out of eleven presidential elections and more than 85 per cent of the city's congressional delegation. Only once did they elect less than two-thirds of the city's state senators and only twice less than three-fourths of the city's state assemblymen. In city government after La Guardia's three terms as mayor (1933–1945) on an anti-Tammany Republican-Fusion ticket, Democrats were

TABLE 6. RELIGIOUS GROUPINGS IN NEW YORK CITY *

	Protestant	*Roman Catholic*	*Jewish*	*Other*
Bronx	12.4%	50.2%	35.2%	2.2%
Kings	19.5%	44.4%	33.9%	2.2%
Manhattan	36.5%	43.6%	17.7%	2.2%
Queens	20.4%	57.7%	19.7%	2.2%
Richmond	24.2%	68.5%	5.1%	2.2%
City average	22.6%	48.6%	26.6%	2.2%

* By "identification," not church membership.
SOURCE: Ralph A. Straetz and Frank J. Munger, *New York Politics*, (New York, 1960) p. 37.

able to keep the Republican vote for mayor uniformly under the 35 per cent level. In 1965, Democrats held in addition to the offices of mayor and comptroller twenty-eight out of thirty-five seats in the city council. The religious distribution of these offices in 1960 before the increase in council size was as follows: Mayor—Catholic; Comptroller—Catholic; 5 borough presidents— four Catholics, one Protestant; and City Council—12 Catholics, 11 Jews, and 2 Protestants.

While the other nine cities (Table 5) might not be able to match the intensity of New York's devotion to the Democrats below the office of president, they continue to provide substantial majorities to Democrats on senatorial, congressional, and statewide tickets.

Negro voters represent another minority group which has enormously strengthened the political hold that the Democrats have on the larger metropolitan centers (see Table 7).

TABLE 7. PERCENTAGE OF NEGRO VOTERS WHO VOTED FOR
DEMOCRATIC PRESIDENTIAL NOMINEE *

	1948	1952	1956
Chicago	70.4%	74.7%	62.6%
Cincinnati	75.0%	81.2%	72.2%
Cleveland	71.3%	78.8%	62.7%
Detroit	83.9%	89.9%	84.4%
Kansas City	77.3%	81.8%	70.0%
New York City (Manhattan)	71.8%	83.2%	68.9%
Pittsburgh	77.6%	82.0%	76.9%
St. Louis	68.4%	79.6%	74.8%

* Based on data for sample areas.

SOURCE: Oscar Glantz, "The Negro Voter in Northern Industrial Cities,"
The Western Political Quarterly, December, 1960, p. 1008.

Right up to the Depression, the Northern Negroes' political affinities were strongly Republican. Roosevelt in 1932 "received only 23 per cent of the Negro vote in Chicago and 29 per cent in Cincinnati." Negro workers "last to be hired and first to be fired" were hit even harder by the Depression than their fellow white workers. Racial discrimination, lack of skill, or insufficient educational background accentuated their problems. They found much to attract them in the programs of the New Deal and Fair Deal and in the sympathetic attitudes on civil rights displayed by both Roosevelt and Truman. In 1948, after a campaign in which Truman vigorously advocated a greater federal role in the civil rights fields (voting, housing, and employment), it was the Negro vote that provided the critical margins of victory in Ohio and Illinois.

Next to regaining about 60 per cent of the Catholic voters who had defected to Eisenhower in 1952 and 1956, Kennedy made some of the most impressive net gains in Negro precincts (see Table 8).

TABLE 8. SPOT CHECKS OF PREDOMINANTLY NEGRO PRECINCTS
AND WARDS IN 1956 AND 1960 PRESIDENTIAL ELECTIONS

	Stevenson	Eisenhower	Kennedy	Nixon
Cleveland (8 precincts)	1,231	993	1,992	506
East St. Louis, Ill. (4 precincts)	2,342	761	2,734	534
Pittsburgh (2 wards)	13,940	8,922	14,892	5,272
Buffalo, N. Y. (4 wards)	12,119	14,850	21,712	7,329
New York, Manhattan (3 A.D.'s)	66,527	32,356	71,445	20,367
Brooklyn (1 A.D.)	13,754	8,973	22,777	5,808
Richmond, Va. (3 precincts)	588	1,287	1,286	762
Houston, Texas (23 precincts)	11,592	6,006	22,156	3,393
Tampa, Fla. (3 precincts)	1,011	995	1,980	558
Louisville, Ky. (5 wards)	23,067	26,183	28,613	23,405
Nashville, Tenn. (3 wards)	2,861	3,258	5,710	2,529

SOURCE: *The New York Times*, November 27, 1960, p. 51.

Contributing to these shifts may have been three primary factors: (1) Depressed economic conditions which although generally relatively mild, proved quite severe as far as their impact on Negroes were concerned; (2) Kennedy's campaign emphasis on civil rights and his prompt message of encouragement to Mrs. King when her husband, the Rev. Martin Luther King, Jr. was arrested; (3) Heavy Northern Negro migrations during the 1950's. There are now five Northern cities which have Negro populations greater than any Southern city.

When the 1964 election returns came in they once again illustrated the tenaciousness with which certain voting blocs retain their attachments to the Democratic party and its presidential nominees (see Tables 9 and 10).

Election results in the presidential primaries of Indiana and Wisconsin in

TABLE 9. THE ETHNIC GROUPS: AGAIN HEAVILY DEMOCRATIC

Democratic percentage of vote		Democratic percentage of vote	
1960 Kennedy	1964 Johnson	1960 Kennedy	1964 Johnson
Italian precincts—		Irish precincts—	
Massachusetts 85% 89%		Massachusetts 81% 88%	
Illinois 75% 75%		Illinois 80% 69%	
Ohio 83% 78%			
New York State 67% 68%			

Democratic percentage of vote		Democratic percentage of vote	
1960 Kennedy	1964 Johnson	1960 Kennedy	1964 Johnson
Slavic precincts—		Jewish precincts—	
Wisconsin 78% 80%		New York State 84% 90%	
Michigan 89% 88%		California 81% 89%	
Illinois 74% 72%		Colorado 70% 80%	
Ohio 88% 86%		Florida 78% 89%	

TABLE 10. THE NEGRO VOTE: HEAVY GAIN FOR
DEMOCRATS

	Democratic percentage of vote	
	1960	1964
	Kennedy	Johnson
Southern Negro precincts	55%	88%
Georgia	42%	99%
Florida	70%	88%
Northern Negro precincts	71%	89%
Illinois	76%	97%
Michigan	85%	98%
Ohio	71%	98%
New York State	74%	96%

SOURCE: Compiled by NBC-AP in *U. S. News & World Report*,
November 16, 1964, pp. 40–41.

the spring of 1964 when Governor George Wallace of Alabama challenged
regulars supporting President Johnson seemed to reveal a "white backlash" in
areas which voted traditionally Democratic or Liberal. That most of the
Democratic fears were ungrounded and that such voter reaction to the civil
rights demonstrations and freedom rides did not actually materialize becomes
apparent from Table 11.

Prediction of future voting behavior patterns of ethnic, religious, economic, and racial groups will always be complicated. Upward economic
mobility of an immigrant minority or ethnic group, for example, often is
accompanied by the shedding or weakening of past loyalties to liberal welfare
programs and candidates. Here is a great opportunity for the Republican

TABLE 11. EFFECT OF "BACKLASH": WHAT A SURVEY SHOWS

Reports from three areas where Alabama's segregationist Governor George Wallace got
a larger vote than expected in 1964 presidential-primary elections—

	Wallace (presidential primary)	Goldwater (November 3 election)
Maryland		
16 counties carried by Governor Wallace	64.4%	42.3%
9 precincts, 27th ward, Baltimore	50.0%	42.7%
2 precincts, 1st ward, Baltimore	56.9%	27.3%
2 precincts, 2nd ward, Baltimore	58.7%	25.3%
Lake County, Ind.		
(industrial area around Gary)		
Entire county	51.5%	35.2%
Precinct 94, Gary (white neighborhood		
where there has been talk of bringing in		
Negro pupils to integrate schools)	76.7%	50.9%
Milwaukee, Wis.		
Ward 14—predominantly Polish	32.0%	18.1%
Ward 12—predominantly Polish	32.3%	16.4%

SOURCE: Compiled by the *Baltimore Sun*, *Hammond (Ind.) Times*, and *Milwaukee
Journal* in *U. S. News & World Report*, November 16, 1964, p. 40.

party to gather in disenchanted Democrats. In this connection Republicans might well study the remarkable victory of Edward W. Brooke, a Negro who was elected attorney general of Massachusetts in 1962 (the only Republican to win a statewide office at that time) and reelected in 1964 with a two-to-one majority while President Johnson carried the state by 76.4 per cent and Senator Edward Kennedy by 74.4 per cent.

Also, the social and economic advancement of the Negroes, for example, may now constitute a serious threat in status to low-income whites (many of them of recent immigrant background) who are fearful of Negro competition for jobs and housing. There has been a certain reluctance on the part of some smaller labor unions to accept Negroes as apprentices in their specific trades. Such reluctance on the part of a predominantly Democratic sector of the community may deflect votes to the Republican party.

Uncertainty throughout the political system will be accentuated by a number of other factors also. Traditional voting patterns among Democrats and Republicans are breaking up in the South as well as in New England. There is a surge of political moderation that has shifted the Democrats towards the ideological center, causing serious divisions within their party and within the Republican party; there is the struggle between certain Republican governors and the party's congressional contingent for national leadership; and there is the problem of a serious party realignment in the South.

What the 1964 election continued to make abundantly clear is that interest groups—ethnic, racial, religious, social, and economic—can effectively demonstrate an impressive voting solidarity when they believe their particular interests are threatened. At the same time the election underscored the remarkable quality of American federalism which makes it possible for strong state party organizations with locally attractive leaders and candidates to resist successfully a national political tide of major magnitude.

INTENSE PARTY COMPETITION—
POLITICAL PROFILES OF NEW YORK AND CALIFORNIA

Eighty-three electoral college votes or 31 per cent of the 270 necessary to elect a president come from these two politically-competitive states.

NEW YORK

In brief, here is how the major public offices are divided:

U. S. Senator	Jacob K. Javits	Republican	(1962–58.8%)
U. S. Senator	Kenneth R. Keating	Republican	(1958–51.2%)
U. S. Senator	Robert F. Kennedy	Democrat-Liberal	(1964–54.5%)
Governor	Nelson Rockefeller	Republican	(1962–54.7%)
Lieutenant Governor	Malcolm Wilson	Republican	(4-year term)
Attorney General	Louis J. Lefkowitz	Republican	
Comptroller	Arthur Levitt	Democrat	

	1963	1965
U. S. House of Representatives		
Republicans	21	14
Democrats	20	27
State legislature		
Senate: Republicans	33	24
Democrats	25	34
House: Republicans	85	62
Democrats	65	88

The heaviest concentration of Democratic party strength in New York is located in New York City, more particularly in Manhattan, the Bronx, and Brooklyn. Richmond County is heavily Republican and Queens County is a toss-up. When Rockefeller swept the state in 1962, winning with a plurality of over 500,000 votes carrying all but five of the sixty-two counties, his Democratic opponent Robert M. Morgenthau was able to win in the Bronx by 60.4 per cent, in Manhattan by 55.3 per cent, and in Brooklyn (Kings County) by 58.7 per cent. Albany County, the fourth county bucking the trend, voting 51.1 per cent for Morgenthau, represents one of the few upstate areas that has remained consistently Democratic for at least forty years. Erie County (Buffalo), the fifth county supporting Morgenthau (54.9 per cent), had been voting consistently Republican until it supported President Kennedy in 1960.

There are other indices of New York City's overwhelmingly Democratic leanings (see Table 12). Of New York state's twenty Democratic congressmen, sixteen were from constituencies located in New York City. Of the sixty-five Democrats in the state Assembly, New York City alone elected fifty-five which gave the Democrats 85 per cent of the city's total Assembly delegation in Albany. The mayor was a Democrat, the City Council was Democratic

TABLE 12. NEW YORK DEMOCRATIC CONGRESSMEN AND ASSEMBLYMEN

	1963		1965
Congressmen from New York State		41	
Congressmen from New York City		19	
Democrats/Liberals	16		16
Congressmen from Suburban and Upstate Counties		22	
Democrats/Liberals	4		11
Assemblymen in State Legislature		150	
Assemblymen in State Legislature from New York City		65	
Democrats/Liberals	55		57
Assemblymen in State Legislature from Suburbs and Upstate Counties		85	
Democrats/Liberals	10		27
Democrats in New York City's Congressional Delegation	84.2%		84.2%
Democrats in New York City's Assembly Delegation	84.6%		87.7%
Democrats in Upstate New York and Suburban Congressional Delegation	18.2%		50.0%
Democrats in Upstate New York and Suburban Assembly Delegation	11.8%		31.8%

twenty-eight to seven, and the powerful Board of Estimate did not have a single Republican member.

New York City without its suburbs casts approximately 40 per cent of the total vote for statewide offices. For Republican candidates to carry the state against this heavy vote means that they must attempt to hold down Democratic majorities in the city to less than 65 per cent of the combined totals.

In accomplishing this, Republicans have generally found that their greatest support comes from the suburbs of New York City (see Table 13) as well

TABLE 13. PERCENTAGES OF MAJOR PARTY VOTE

| | | New York City counties | | | vs. | | Suburban counties | | |
	Bronx	Kings (Brook-lyn)	New York (Man-hattan)	Queens	Rich-mond	Nassau	Rock-land	Suffolk	West-chester
1952 Presidential Eisenhower (R) Stevenson (D)	38.1	40.5	40.2	57.6	66.4	70.1	64.7	74.7	67.7
1954 Gubernatorial Harriman (D) Ives (R)	72.3	70.2	67.6	53.7	48.6	36.1	40.7	30.9	35.3
1956 Senatorial Javits (R) Wagner (D)	36.8	39.7	40.7	51.9	60.2	62.7	60.3	67.0	63.2
1956 Presidential Eisenhower (R) Stevenson (D)	42.8	45.2	44.3	59.9	76.6	69.1	71.0	77.6	72.2
1958 Gubernatorial Rockefeller (R) Harriman (D)	37.7	39.4	41.9	51.7	61.8	63.0	60.6	66.1	69.0
1958 Senatorial Keating (R) Hogan (D)	32.2	33.3	36.9	45.0	52.4	60.9	56.8	64.4	63.5
1960 Presidential Kennedy (D) Nixon (R)	68.1	66.4	65.6	54.8	43.4	44.8	45.1	40.6	43.3
1962 Gubernatorial Rockefeller (R) Morganthau (D)	39.6	41.3	44.7	54.2	61.2	65.7	64.1	66.0	66.9
1962 Senatorial Javits (R) Donovan (D)	48.4	50.5	52.1	58.9	57.5	70.2	66.0	66.1	68.8
1964 Presidential Johnson (D) Goldwater (R)	74.8	74.8	80.7	66.7	54.1	60.4	63.8	55.3	61.5
1964 Senatorial Kennedy (D) Keating (R)	68.1	65.0	63.5	56.0	51.2	47.4	49.3	49.1	46.4

SOURCE: Compiled from data in Richard M. Scammon (ed.), *America Votes, A Handbook of Contemporary American Election Statistics*, Vols. I–IV (Pittsburgh, 1962) and *The New York Times*, November 5, 1964.

as from the cities and rural areas of upstate New York. To cite just one illustration, in 1958 there were only seven counties out of the fifty-seven in upstate New York in which Rockefeller was not able to win at least 65 per cent or more of all the votes cast outside the city limits. Such upstate cities as Rochester and Syracuse have a long record of Republican victories. Rockefeller carried these as well as six other of the nine biggest cities upstate. Only Albany and Buffalo held out for Morgenthau.

The 1965 special election in New York state has altered to some degree the preceding figures. However, the election results do not substantially affect the underlying facts of New York state politics.

New York Party Leaders—Republicans and Democrats

New York City's political composition has made its impact felt not only on the Democrats but also on the choice of Republican candidates who successfully sought statewide office. Generally speaking, New York's Republican governors and senators have come mostly from the more moderate or liberal wing of their party. Governor Thomas E. Dewey (1946–1954) in fact gave much the same support as Governor Rockefeller (1958–   ) does to legislative programs encouraging public housing, public health, rent control, and fair employment practices—measures more often identified with the Democratic party. In the United States Congress, New York's Republican (until 1965, Keating and Javits) senatorial delegation could be counted among the most determined opponents of the conservative coalition. In 1963 on such issues as foreign aid, debt limitation, mass transportation, college aid, and manpower retraining, Senator Jacob K. Javits (1956–   ), for example, voted against the congressional coalition of Southern conservative Democrats and Northern conservative Republicans on 63 per cent of the roll calls. His Republican colleague, Senator Kenneth B. Keating (1958–1964) had an opposition of 70 per cent. As might be expected, New York's G.O.P. delegation in the United States House of Representatives follows a more conservative line, most of them coming from upstate districts. Two members of the delegation had an 80 per cent record of supporting the conservative coalition, Carleton King and J. Ernest Wharton, who both represented upstate districts. Manhattan's only Republican, Representative John Lindsay (Seventeenth District), by way of contrast opposed the coalition in 80 per cent of the roll call votes.[46]

In state politics, Republicans of a more conservative brand have long had at least two influential spokesmen. Leonard Hall was national chairman of the Republican party before resigning his office to seek the gubernatorial nomination against Rockefeller in 1958 and Walter J. Mahoney, a state senator from Buffalo, New York, led a conservative opposition of rural upstate Republicans against welfare and taxation measures proposed by Dewey and

[46] *Congressional Quarterly Weekly Report*, April 17, 1964, pp. 744–746.

Rockefeller, from his vantage point as president pro tempore of the Senate at Albany.

Democrats too have had their problems with factionalism, most of it arising out of the politics of New York City. At issue for the past few years has been the widening cleavage between Tammany Hall, Manhattan's regulars or "machine" Democrats led by Carmine De Sapio from Greenwich Village, and the so-called "reform" Democrats, led by former Governor (1934–1946) and United States Senator (1949–1952) Herbert Lehman, Mrs. Franklin D. Roosevelt, and David Dubinsky, Liberal Party leader.

Although backed by De Sapio for the mayoralty of the city in 1953 and again in 1956 for his unsuccessful bid for the United States senatorship against Jacob Javits, Mayor Robert Wagner, hard-pressed by a reform coalition, broke with the Tammany leader during his 1961 campaign for reelection after a bitter exchange of epithets and after charging the county leader with "bossism" and a variety of unethical practices. Arrayed against the Mayor in the September primary and supporting his opponent State Comptroller Arthur Levitt were in addition to De Sapio such Democratic organization leaders as Congressman Charles A. Buckley of the Bronx, Joseph T. Sharkey of Brooklyn, majority leader and vice chairman of the City Council, and Herbert A. Koehler of Queens and the five county organizations including approximately 20,000 elected party officials. Despite dissensions in his own party and the eruption of a number of major scandals in an administration often characterized by indecisiveness and unimaginativeness, Mayor Wagner emerged from the primary with a majority of 150,000 votes and won the general election by over 400,000 votes against two opponents, State Attorney General Louis J. Lefkowitz, the Republican candidate, and City Controller Lawrence E. Gerosa heading up an independent ticket. At stake had been not merely the mayoralty of the city, but the leadership of New York's state Democratic party. In this context, Wagner was supported, in addition to the reform leadership, by such old "pros" as former Postmaster General James A. Farley, Paul O'Dwyer, brother of former Mayor William O'Dwyer, Louis A. Harris, a polling expert, and Alex Rose, vice chairman of the Liberal party. The White House also had given Mayor Wagner its blessing.

The mayor's prestige was greatly enhanced in June, 1964, when reform candidates, with his backing, defeated fourteen-term Congressman Charles A. Buckley, Chairman of the House Public Works Committee and head of the Bronx County Democratic organization, and Congressman James C. Healey, one of Buckley's top lieutenants, in the Democratic primary. President Johnson had supported Buckley with a letter of endorsement and Attorney General Robert F. Kennedy had made a campaign appearance for him. In addition, Carmine De Sapio, Tammany Hall leader until 1961, lost his second bid to regain the district leadership of Greenwich Village.[47]

On the other hand, a new and significant challenge to Mayor Wagner's

[47] *The New York Times,* June 3, 1964, p. 1.

party leadership developed in the spring of 1964, when Robert F. Kennedy officially decided to seek the party's convention nomination for the race against the G.O.P. incumbent, Senator Kenneth Keating. Wagner swallowed his objections and backed Kennedy, who then went on to defeat Keating, receiving 54.5 per cent of the vote. Wagner's coolness to the Kennedy candidacy revealed the Mayor's early awareness of the impending struggle for power within the Democratic party of New York. The enormous difficulties that the Democrats encountered in organizing the two houses of the state legislature at Albany, after taking control from the Republicans for the first time in a generation, gave further vivid testimony to the depth of their factional divisions.

Along with the mayor, other key state and national Democratic candidates have sometimes found the necessary winning margins through the endorsement and support given them by New York City's Liberal party. Here are four of the most famous instances:

PRESIDENT—1944

Franklin D. Roosevelt		*Thomas E. Dewey*	
Democratic party	2,478,598	Republican party	2,987,647
Am. Liberal party	329,325		
Am. Labor party	496,405		

UNITED STATES SENATE—1949

Herbert H. Lehman		*John Foster Dulles*	
Democratic party	2,155,763	Republican party	2,384,381
Liberal party	426,675		

GOVERNOR—1954

W. Averell Harriman		*Irving M. Ives*	
Democratic party	2,296,645	Republican party	2,549,613
Liberal party	264,093		

PRESIDENT—1960

John F. Kennedy		*Richard M. Nixon*	
Democratic party	3,423,909	Republican party	3,446,419
Liberal party	406,176		

In 1961 when Wagner defeated Lefkowitz by 401,730 votes, the American Liberal party contributed 211,175 votes to his election.

New York City's American Liberal party, one of the few remaining minor parties in American politics, developed as a protest against the American Labor party (1936–1956) after that group's infiltration in the late nineteen thirties by Communists and Communist sympathizers. Among the anti-Communist leaders of the American Liberal party (1944–   ) were such well-known labor supporters of Franklin D. Roosevelt as the late Sidney Hillman of the Amalgamated Clothing Workers and such liberal intellectuals as George S. Counts and Reinhold Niebuhr. Dedicated to the socio-economic policies of the New Deal, of the Fair Deal, and of the New Frontier, New York's Liberal party has long been critical of Tammany bossism and of Democratic machine politics for their alleged lack of social consciousness. It has consistently favored governmental reforms for the city and in local and judicial elections has not been adverse to breaking with the Democrats in order to support liberal Republicans or party independents on a fusion basis. The most recent illustration was its endorsement and support of Representative John V. Lindsay (R., 17th District, Manhattan) for mayor of New York City.

CALIFORNIA

Between 1950 and 1960, California increased its population by 48.5 per cent, or by 5.1 million. This vast influx of people brought to California new job-seekers and new jobs, more school children and new schools, welfare recipients and new taxpayers, hundreds of thousands of automobiles and more smog and congestion—all constituting enormous problems and opportunities for the various levels of state and local government but also yielding to this new most powerful state of the Union eight additional highly treasured congressional districts.

U.S. Senator	Thomas H. Kuchel	Republican	(1962—56.5%)
U.S. Senator	George Murphy	Republican	(1964—51.3%)
Governor	Edmund G. Brown	Democrat	(1962—52.6%)
Lieutenant Governor	Glenn M. Anderson	Democrat	(4-year term)
Secretary of State	Frank M. Jordan	Republican	
Attorney General	Stanley Mosk	Democrat	
Treasurer	Bert A. Betts	Democrat	
Controller	Alan Cranston	Democrat	

U.S. House of Representatives		1963	1965
Democrats		23	23
Republicans		15	15
State legislature			
Senate:	Democrats	27	27
	Republicans	13	13
House:	Democrats	52	48
	Republicans	28	32

Although the preceding indicates considerable Democratic majorities in the House of Representatives and the state legislature, the actual voting strength of the two parties is much more evenly balanced. It just happened that the Democrats scored unusual election successes in 1958, a feat to which a telling contribution was made by deep Republican intraparty cleavages and the exceptionally bitter personal rivalry between Governor Knight and Senator Knowland.

Until the end of the nineteen fifties, as clearly shown in Table 14, Republicans in California outvoted Democrats in the overwhelming majority of contests for state and national office. Between 1946 and 1958 Republicans

TABLE 14. RECENT CALIFORNIA ELECTIONS

Vote for President

Year	Republican Vote *	Per cent	Democratic Vote	Per cent	Minority party Per cent
1948	1,895	47.1	1,913	47.6	5.3
1952	2,897	56.3	2,197	42.7	less than 1
1956	3,027	55.4	2,420	44.3	" " "
1960	3,260	50.1	3,224	49.6	" " "
1964	2,879	40.8	4,172	59.2	" " "

Vote for Governor

Year	Republican	Vote	Per cent †	Democratic	Vote	Per cent †
1946	Earl Warren	2,345	100.0	No Candidate	—	—
1950	Earl Warren	2,462	64.9	James Roosevelt	1,334	35.1
1954	Goodwin J. Knight	2,291	56.8	Richard P. Graves	1,739	43.2
1958	William F. Knowland	2,111	40.2	Edmund G. Brown	3,140	59.8
1962	Richard M. Nixon	2,740	47.4	Edmund G. Brown	3,037	52.6

Vote for Senator

Year	Republican	Vote	Per cent	Democratic	Vote	Per cent
1946	William F. Knowland	1,428	55.0	Will Rogers	1,167	45.0
1950	Richard M. Nixon	2,183	59.2	Helen G. Douglas	1,503	40.8
1952	William F. Knowland	3,982	100.0	No Candidate	—	—
1954	Thomas H. Kuchel	2,091	53.9	Samuel W. Yorty	1,788	46.1
1956	Thomas H. Kuchel	2,893	54.2	Richard Richards	2,446	45.8
1958	Goodwin J. Knight	2,204	43.0	Clair Engle	2,928	57.0
1962	Thomas H. Kuchel	3,180	56.5	Richard Richards	2,453	43.5
1964	George Murphy	3,629	51.5	Pierre Salinger	3,412	48.5

Vote for United States Congressmen

Year	No. of Republicans	No. of Democrats
1952	19	11
1954	19	11
1956	16	14
1958	14	16
1960	14	16
1962	14	24
1964	15	23

Party composition of the state legislature

Year	State Senate R	State Senate D	State Assembly R	State Assembly D
1946	27	13	48	32
1948	25	15	46	34
1950	27	13	47	33
1952	29	11	54	26
1954	24	16	48	32
1956	20	20	42	38
1958	12	28	32	47 (1 vacancy)
1960	10	30	33	47
1962	13	27	28	52
1964	13	27	32	48

* Rounded in thousands.
† Percentage of the major party vote.

SOURCE: Adapted from Richard M. Scammon (ed.), *America Votes*, A *Handbook of Contemporary American Election Statistics*, Vols. I–IV (Pittsburgh, 1962) and unofficial 1964 election returns.

won all the gubernatorial as well as the senatorial elections, the congressmen representing the state in Washington during these twelve years were at two sessions nearly two-to-one Republican, and Republicans controlled the Senate and Assembly in every session of the state legislature except in the Senate in 1956.

Still, throughout this era of Republican predominance, it was the Democratic totals in terms of individual party registrations that continuously exceeded Republican totals by impressive and evidently misleading margins.[48]

VOTER REGISTRATION BY PARTY
(Per cent)

Year	Republican	Democratic
1944	37.4	58.4
1948	37.6	57.2
1952	40.9	55.2
1954	41.0	55.5
1958	39.6	57.4
1960	39.2	57.5
1962	39.8	56.9
1964	38.9	57.9

How could Democrats outregister Republicans so heavily and yet lose elections so consistently? A group of scholars well versed in the vagaries of California politics suggests that:

A. Many of the "Democrats" are such in name only, having long since abandoned voting for the party of their youth, family connection, section of origin, or Depression loyalty.
B. Republicans are more apt to vote on election day than are Democrats.
C. The Democratic party has been short on attractive candidates.
D. Republicans have made skillful use of their greater monetary resources and newspaper support.
E. State legislative and congressional districts in the 1940's and 1950's were gerrymandered to give Republican candidates the advantage.[49]

Another factor contributing to Republican successes in the past had been the operation of California's unique system of permitting candidate cross-filing in party primaries, a device which prior to its repeal in 1959 had tended to greatly benefit the incumbent at the expense of the challenger. Originally enacted in 1913 under prodding by Governor Hiram Johnson (running mate of Theodore Roosevelt on the Bull Moose ticket of 1912) for the purpose of assisting fellow Progressives in their efforts to capture Republican primary votes as well, this arrangement made it possible for candidates to file for office in more than one party. If victorious in two such party primaries, these

[48] Eugene C. Lee, *California Votes, 1928–1960 (with 1962 Supplement): A Review and Analysis of Registration and Voting* (Berkeley, 1963), p. 29.
[49] Winston W. Crouch, *et al.*, *California Government and Politics*, 2nd ed. (Englewood Cliffs, 1960), p. 57.

candidates could show on the general election ballot that they were the official nominees of both parties. A highwater point for this system was reached in the 1940 primaries when 55 per cent of the state's congressional candidates were so nominated and in the 1944 primaries when 90 per cent of the state Senate and 80 per cent of the state Assembly districts gave to their winners such two-party endorsements.[50] That candidates even for the top offices can under certain circumstances secure such a broad bipartisan level of approval was demonstrated by Earl Warren in 1946 when both Democrats and Republicans nominated him for the governorship, by Hiram Johnson whom both parties nominated for United States senator in 1934 and again in 1940, and by William Knowland who had received similar support in his 1952 senatorial bid. Something of the extent to which cross-filing had made the primary more important and the general election less so emerges from the record of a twelve-year period, 1940 to 1952 in which 84 per cent of the members of the state Senate and 72 per cent of the members of the state Assembly found themselves without opposition in the final contest.[51]

Cross-filing was born in an era of outspoken hostility to political parties and partisanship. Reformers had identified good government as being government without politics. Subsequent weakening of the parties, promises and predictions notwithstanding brought neither efficiency nor responsibility as pressure groups took the place of parties and as lobbyists became the new bosses. The task of rebuilding the parties in a setting where election laws were expressly designed to frustrate them proved to be painfully slow and uneven.

Somewhat parallelling the official but ineffective shell of their parties, Republicans and Democrats began to organize and work through unofficial but increasingly powerful groups such as the Republican Assembly (1934) and the California Democratic Council (1953). These organizations rather than the formal party structures proceeded to formulate the issues, collect the funds, carry out the research, encourage the faithful, conduct the campaigns, and engage in all the complicated but indispensable operations that center around the recruitment, endorsement, and support of candidates for public office.

In the light of these developments and others that grew out of California's unique rate of immigration and economic growth during the post-war years, the patterns of Republican and Democratic voting strengths within the state could not be expected to be as relatively stable or distinct as those prevailing in the older parts of the country where party loyalties are stronger and voting traditions are more deeply rooted.

Nearly all generalizations about California's contemporary politics are risky at best. It is true generally, but only generally, that Republicans have been more successful in the southern cities and counties of the state while Democrats have done better in the upper two-thirds of the state, north of Bakersfield and north of the East-West line formed by the boundaries of three

[50] *Ibid.*, pp. 43–45.
[51] Joseph P. Harris, *California Politics,* rev. ed. (Stanford, 1961), p. 42.

counties—San Bernadino, Kern, and San Luis Obispo. In the metropolitan areas of southern California, Republicans tend to find their major support in San Diego, Santa Ana, Santa Barbara and in such suburbs of Los Angeles as Long Beach, Santa Monica, Glendale, Pasadena, Alhambra and Whittier.

Heavy majorities in these and other suburban-urban communities enabled the Republicans to overcome the strong Democratic voting tendencies in industrial and working-class precincts in the city of Los Angeles and in the south coastal, southeastern, and eastern (Norwalk) sections of Los Angeles County. Of the elections shown on Table 15, the county of Los Angeles produced Republican majorities with regularity until 1958. Two years later, Los Angeles County again went Democratic, although this time by a greatly-reduced margin. Kennedy took the county from Nixon, a former congressman from Whittier, by a mere 21,000 votes. In 1962, Brown (D) won 52.5 per cent of the county's vote in the gubernatorial race, while Kuchel (R) received 52.8 per cent in the senatorial contest.

In northern California, Democrats obtain their majorities in San Francisco, Oakland, Berkeley, and Sacramento, and in the Oakland-Alameda industrial area. Considerable Democratic strength is found also in the Central Valley, a region formed by the Sacramento and San Joaquin rivers comprising the state's major agricultural lands, as well as along the western slopes of the Sierra-Nevada where some of the mining, timber, cattle, and sheep-grazing counties developed a Democratic tradition.

After the 1960 ballots were counted, Democrats took inventory and discovered that things could have been a lot worse. Although Kennedy finally lost the state by 36,000 votes and although the Democratic percentage of the two-party vote declined from the record level of 1958 (see Table 16), nearly all of the incumbents were reelected. Also left unaffected was the numerical

TABLE 15. SUBURBS OF LOS ANGELES REPUBLICAN PERCENTAGES OF MAJOR PARTY VOTE, 1952–1964

Assembly district	Pres. 1952	Gov. 1954	Sen. 1954	Pres. 1956	Sen. 1956	Gov. 1958	Sen. 1958	Pres. 1960	Pres. 1964	Sen. 1964	Assembly 1964
k	42	58.1	56.5	51.6	55.7	52.9	40.8	45.0	49.2	51.0	62.5	43.1
e	43	72.4	72.5	70.4	72.1	70.1	59.9	60.1	67.9	63.4	71.8	66.9
each	44	56.5	58.8	55.0	57.1	54.8	43.8	48.2	53.1	47.3	60.3	45.2
a	47	70.6	65.5	69.6	70.9	68.8	59.5	58.7	65.9	52.6	60.9	69.4
r	50	62.9	61.8	58.6	60.7	57.6	45.1	46.1	54.6	60.0	71.2	48.5
ra	53	67.5	54.9	64.4	66.3	64.2	53.1	54.6	60.1	52.3	51.0	9.4
Ionica	60	69.1	68.6	67.9	68.0	66.6	59.9	61.4	61.3	48.4	58.1	59.4

STATEWIDE ASSEMBLY VOTE, 1964

R   3,107,670   46.7
D   3,550,398   53.3

Adapted from Richard M. Scammon (ed.), *America Votes, A Handbook of Contemporary American Election Statistics*, Vols. I–IV (Pittsburgh, 1962) and unofficial 1964 election returns.

TABLE 16. DEMOCRATIC PERCENTAGE OF TWO-PARTY VOTE FOR MAJOR OFFICES

Year	President	Governor	U. S. Senate	House of Representatives *	Assembly *
1948	52.6 †			40.6	40.2
1950		35.1	40.8	45.8	43.0
1952	43.1		‡	46.0	32.4
1954		43.2	46.1**	51.5	49.0
1956	44.4		45.8	52.4	53.4
1958		59.8	57.1	60.6	58.9
1960	49.7			53.9	54.0
1962		52.6	43.5	51.8	53.9
1964	59.2		48.5	52.5	53.3

* These figures are based on the total of Democratic plus Republican candidates' votes. In the earlier years, when a large proportion of legislators took their seats without a contest, the congressional and assembly totals are not as meaningful, since they include many voters who ratified the election of successful cross-filers (mostly Republican incumbents).
† Truman plus Wallace.
‡ Knowland won by cross-filing.
** Special senatorial election.
SOURCE: Totten J. Anderson and Eugene C. Lee, "The 1962 Election in California," *Western Political Quarterly*, June, 1963, p. 397; 1964 figures added.

advantage the Democrats had scored in the makeup of the state's congressional delegation and the majorities with which they controlled the legislature.

California Political Leaders—Republicans and Democrats

Taking a fair view of the arena of American national politics during the 1950's, it is doubtful whether any single state could quite match the records attained by the three Republicans from California—Richard M. Nixon, Earl Warren, and William Knowland. Strong and controversial men, they reflected three major ideological positions in the spectrum of California Republicanism: Knowland on the right, as spokesman of conservatism, Warren on the left, as spokesman of liberalism, and Nixon in the center as spokesman of the moderates.

For various reasons—historical, sectional, seniority, and others—positions of policy leadership in the Senate's Republican caucus have generally gone to conservatives. This tradition continued when William Knowland inherited Taft's mantle of leadership in 1953. Appointed to fill the unexpired term of the immensely popular Hiram Johnson, Knowland was first elected to the Senate in 1946 and then reelected in 1952 with the largest majority in the history of California politics. As the Senate's youngest majority leader (1953–1954) and minority leader (1955–1956), he not only battled his Democratic opponents across the aisle, but he also proceeded to attack major foreign and domestic policies of a fellow Republican in the White House. Eisenhower supporters in the Senate soon discovered that in their fight against Joseph

McCarthy and the Bricker amendment, Senator Knowland could not be found in their corner. His uncritical endorsement of Chiang Kai-shek and the vehemence with which he objected to any reexamination of America's China policy earned him among his detractors the title of "Senator from Formosa." As leader of the California Goldwater forces in the 1964 presidential primary, he made a very significant contribution to the Senator's crucial victory over Rockefeller.

Knowland's decision in 1958 to exchange his Senate seat for the gubernatorial chair in Sacramento, a position he may have viewed as a springboard for the presidential nomination two years hence, embarked him on a collision course with another Republican with similar presidential ambitions, Goodwin J. Knight, the incumbent governor who liked his job and wanted another term. Knight, who had been lieutenant governor since 1946, succeeded to the governorship in 1953 when Warren was appointed by President Eisenhower to be the Chief Justice of the United States Supreme Court. Though originally far from qualifying as a political liberal, Knight, upon becoming governor, carefully cultivated the leaders of organized labor, the independent voters, and Democrats in his efforts to keep intact Warren's winning coalition. His efforts and considerable personal charm proved extremely successful. In 1954 he won the governorship by more than half a million votes.

Republicans in California will not readily forget the *Götterdämmerung* of 1958. Knowland who was United States senator and minority leader but wanted to become governor received the gubernatorial nomination and lost the election. Knight who was governor but was forced to seek the senatorship lost also. Democrats who exploited the Republican fracas, won the governorship, and the senatorship, and control of both houses of the state legislature.[52] The Warren era which began so auspiciously in 1943 had come to an end. A Warren protégé still left in a major office is Thomas H. Kuchel whom the governor appointed to the United States Senate in 1952 after Nixon resigned his seat to become Vice-President. Since then Kuchel, an Eisenhower Republican, a former state senator (1940–1946) and state controller, and now Senate Republican whip, received approximately 54 per cent of the total vote in each of his two elections, a special election in 1954 and an election for a full term in 1956. In his bid for reelection in 1962, he increased his percentage of the two-party vote to 56.4 per cent.

Another tremendously popular Republican, Earl Warren, spent most of his adult life in the public service of his state. Among the various offices that he held before becoming governor in 1943 was that of city attorney (Oakland), district attorney (Alameda County), and state attorney general. As governor, Warren strongly advocated measures in support of social welfare, health, and education. He also initiated significant penal and administrative reforms.

In a state where party lines had crumbled or where party affiliations had

[52] Totten J. Anderson, "The 1958 Election in California," *Western Political Quarterly,* March, 1959, pp. 276–300.

lost much of their former meaning, Warren was able to build a following that cut across a very wide range of socio-economic interests. His moderate politics appealed alike to many Democrats, Republicans, and Independents. It helped to make possible the huge majorities with which he regularly won reelection. In 1950, for example, when he waged his third campaign for the governorship, Warren defeated Democrat James Roosevelt by more than one million votes.

Richard M. Nixon's meteoric rise to fame and power needs no detailed recounting. When the Republican Assembly in 1946 picked the young Navy veteran to represent the Twelfth District (eastern Los Angeles County), they never dreamed that after two terms in Congress, he would be elected to the United States Senate in 1950 with a majority of over 600,000 votes, that two years later he would be vice-president of the United States and that in 1960 he would come within one-tenth of one per cent of winning the popular vote for the presidency. Warren and Knight, whose relationships with Nixon were far from friendly, attempted to avoid political turbulence and controversy. Nixon on the other hand sought it and thrived on it with remarkable results. His opponents, Jerry Voorhis, a liberal and five-term incumbent congressman, and then Helen Gahagan Douglas, a former congresswoman and liberal Democratic senatorial nominee, were charged with softness towards Communism and Communists in Nixon's campaigns which were hard-hitting and single-minded. These campaigns earned him the hostility not only of the politically vanquished but also of those liberals throughout the country to whom the campaigns became symbols of how not to exploit the anti-Communist issue. In Washington, Nixon's moderately conservative voting record was quickly overshadowed by the persistent and skillful manner with which he, as a member of the House Un-American Activities Committee, uncovered the perplexing details that connected Alger Hiss to a Communist espionage ring operating in the nation's capital. Hiss was a former law clerk to Justice Oliver Wendell Holmes, an official of the State Department, a member of the Roosevelt delegation at Yalta, secretary general of the San Francisco conference which established the United Nations, and president of the Carnegie Foundation for International Peace. In a national climate where confidence in the internal security machinery was shaken, the Hiss case was instrumental in making Nixon senator and later vice-president.[53]

The clearly dominant figure among California Democrats during the 1950's was that of Governor Edmund (Pat) Brown. During most of the decade

[53] With reference to the 1950 senatorial election, Earl Mazo, in his friendly and penetrating profile of Nixon, wrote that the "articulate young Congressman" was viewed by party professionals as a " 'real comer' because of the skill in which he 'got Alger Hiss'." When former Senator Knowland presented Nixon's name to the 1960 presidential nominating convention he termed Nixon"—the man whose 'bulldog determination' enabled 'the government to hunt out and unravel the Alger Hiss case' . . ."; Earl Mazo, *Richard Nixon, A Political and Personal Portrait* (New York, 1959, 1960), pp. 79, 90.

Brown, as Attorney General, was the lone Democrat among the state's executive officers. He was elected to that post in 1950 after serving as district attorney in San Francisco for seven years (1943–1950). For Brown, whose cautiousness and political moderation were well-known, 1958 proved to be the most propitious year in which to seek and win the governorship. His one million vote victory over Knowland established him as the most likely leader to bring order and future successes to California's squabbling Democrats. But party unity was hard to come by, particularly in the nation's second most powerful state at the beginning of a bitter struggle for the presidential nomination. In order to keep the party from being torn apart and to strengthen his own hand at the impending national convention in Los Angeles, Governor Brown decided to run as California's "favorite son" candidate in the presidential primary. This holding operation, however, in no way diminished the enthusiasm and efforts of the followers of Stevenson, Kennedy, Symington, and Johnson to garner converts among the delegates so pledged. Although he had been personally leaning towards Kennedy, Brown's role at the convention was not a happy one. While he was able to persuade the delegates to elect his candidate, Stanley Mosk (state attorney general) as national committeeman in place of the incumbent Paul Ziffren, who was a powerful leader of the liberally-orientated and Stevenson-inclined California Democratic Council and a critic of the governor, the governor's own position at the head of his large and strategically valuable delegation became increasingly unenviable and vulnerable. Caught in the middle, Brown was pressured by the insistent demands from the Kennedy managers to release his delegation promptly and by the equally insistent demands from the managers of a potential anti-Kennedy coalition (Stevenson sentiment was quite strong in California) that he keep control of his delegation in order to prevent a Kennedy bandwagon movement from forming even before the actual balloting began. The governor's image meanwhile, as portrayed by the press, television, and radio, was one of vacillation, indecision, or helplessness. Since Los Angeles and following Kennedy's narrow defeat in California, which the governor attributed largely to religious factors rather than to party disunity or lack of effort,[54] Brown's popularity has again been on the upswing. In no small measure this is due to his legislative leadership on behalf of increased outlays for school construction and welfare payments for the aged, blind, and needy, as well as to his urging of a major overhauling and streamlining of the state's complex and sprawling administrative establishments. Also helpful was the adoption by the voters of his gigantic one and three quarter billion dollar river development program which will bring sorely needed water five hundred miles from northern to southern California.

The next major challenge to Governor Brown, and in a larger sense to all of California's Democrats, came in 1962 when much was at stake. Former

[54] Eugene C. Lee and William Buchanan, "The 1960 Election in California," *Western Political Quarterly*, March, 1961, pp. 309–326.

Vice-President Nixon, the G.O.P. candidate for governor, and Senator Thomas Kuchel, the incumbent in a state which rarely votes against incumbents, constituted a formidable team, and Democrats were well aware of it. Their awareness of the imperative of party unity was reflected in Kennedy's personal and emphatic endorsement of Brown and in the intensity of effort with which the Ziffren-Mosk factions were urged towards an early and effective rapproachement.

That Republicans, too, would have their problems in achieving party unity become quite apparent. First, former Governor Knight proclaimed his interest in contesting Nixon for the gubernatorial nomination. Then both Nixon and Kuchel came under vigorous criticism by the extreme right for being too liberal and too far to the left. Hundreds of organizations like or similar to the Christian Anti-Communism Crusade and the John Birch Society claimed thousands of zealous supporters in many of the cities of southern California. Nixon, however, was able to defeat the candidate of the conservatives, Assembly minority leader Joseph C. Shell, by over 625,000 votes. In an election campaign, which was highlighted by charges of extremism, Brown was reelected by a margin of over 295,000 votes.[55]

A lack of unity was once again revealed in the Democratic party during the 1964 primary campaign to fill the seat of Senator Clair Engle. State Controller Alan Cranston entered the campaign early and received the endorsement of the California Democratic Council, Governor Brown, and the AFL-CIO. On the last day for filing, the press secretary to President Kennedy and to President Johnson, Pierre Salinger, flew in from Washington and filed for the seat. Salinger during the campaign received support from the powerful assembly speaker, Jesse Unruh, Attorney General Mosk, and Mrs. Clair Engle. In what has been interpreted as a rebuff for Governor Brown, the Democratic voters selected Salinger by a margin of approximately 140,000 out of a total of over 2,000,000 votes.[56] Following the death of Senator Engle in late July, Governor Brown appointed Salinger to fill the remainder of the term. Neither the fact of his "incumbency" nor Lyndon Johnson's nearly two-to-one victory over Goldwater proved strong enough to help Salinger keep his seat. George Murphy, for years a leader in the Motion Picture Alliance for the Preservation of American Ideals and a conservative Republican, was able to defeat Salinger, winning 51.5% of a total vote of over 7 million. Murphy, who ran strongly in populous Los Angeles county, apparently benefitted considerably from the backlash produced by Salinger's vocal opposition to the highly controversial Proposition 14. This repealer of the Rumford law, California's Fair Housing Act, received almost a two-thirds majority.

[55] Totten J. Anderson and Eugene C. Lee, "The 1962 Election in California," *Western Political Quarterly*, June, 1963, pp. 396–420; and Totten J. Anderson, "Extremism in California Politics: The Brown-Knowland and Brown-Nixon Campaigns Compared," *Western Political Quarterly*, June, 1963, pp. 371–372.

[56] *The New York Times,* June 4, 1964, p. 29.

SOME GENERALIZATIONS ABOUT REPUBLICANS AND DEMOCRATS
AT THE LEVEL OF STATE POLITICS

A number of characteristics of contemporary American state politics should already emerge with reasonable clarity from what has so far been presented about state party systems, about the uniqueness of Southern politics, and about the strengths and weaknesses of the major parties in the political configurations of New York and California.

First, American politics as a rule appear to have become more competitive. It can no longer be considered a novelty for a Republican south of the Mason-Dixon Line to be elected congressman or even senator; or for a Republican presidential ticket to emerge victorious in Florida, Louisiana, Tennessee, Texas and Virginia. In states where a modified one-party system prevailed, the second or weaker party has improved its position notably to the point of offering much more effective opposition and of increasing its percentage of winning candidates.

Second, rapid industrialization and urbanization has tended to benefit Democrats although failure to reapportion legislative districts has prevented them, in most of the states, from gaining a proportionate share of House and Senate seats. While it was shown to be true that most of the larger cities voted generally for Democrats—Kennedy, for example, carried 26 out of 40 cities in the United States having 300,000 or more population—it was also noted especially in upstate New York and in southern California that some fairly large cities have remained Republican. Moreover, in these and other Northern states Democratic voting strength in the center of the cities was often counterbalanced by suburban areas in which Republican candidates showed up very well. To be sure, there are all kinds of suburbias so that here too oversimplifications must be avoided.

Following the 1960 election, Republican researchers discovered that it was in the suburban areas, especially those with heavy concentrations of Catholic voters, where Kennedy was able to draw back into the Democratic fold significant numbers of Eisenhower supporters (see Table 17).

Third, outside of the South the great majority of non-metropolitan or rural counties favored the Republicans. But here again generalizations have to be qualified by the fact that a number of such counties in California were found to have persistently voted for Democrats in state and national elections.

Fourth, the practice of electors splitting their tickets and of "voting for the man rather than the party" is "as American as apple pie." Thousands of voters in New York and California apparently saw nothing wrong in voting for the presidential candidate of one party and for the state legislative, House, or Senate candidates of the other party. In the 1960 and 1962 elections, North Dakota Republicans retained their customary control of the House, but a Democrat captured the governorship. Massachusetts voted overwhelmingly

TABLE 17. SUBURBAN AREAS AND THE PRESIDENTIAL VOTE,
1956 AND 1960

Suburban area	Change in Republican from 1956	Change in Democratic from 1956
New York	−95,447	+163,210
Chicago	+ 6,986	+142,745
Los Angeles	+62,061	+192,075
Philadelphia	+15,008	+104,568
Baltimore	− 5,504	+ 58,114
Pittsburgh	−21,140	+ 76,429
Newark	−36,046	+ 49,553

SOURCE: Republican National Committee, *The 1960 Elections: A Summary Report With Supporting Tables* (Washington, 1961).

for its favorite son for president in 1960, but elected a Republican governor. Kennedy, in 1960, carried Minnesota, the Liberals (D.F.L.) retained their majority in the state House, but a Republican became governor. Other states in which voters split their presidential and gubernatorial tickets were Nebraska, New Mexico, Washington, and Wisconsin.

Table 18 provides a convenient summary of the extent to which divided party control between governor, state House, or state Senate prevails presently throughout the states.

Why do people insist on split-ticket voting? Many explanations have been given. Some voters frankly contend that they suspect politics and the politi-

TABLE 18. TWENTY-TWO STATES WITH DIVIDED PARTY CONTROL, 1965

State	Governor	State Senate	State House
Colorado	R*	R	D
Connecticut	D*	D	R
Illinois	D	R	D
Maine	R*	D	D
Massachusetts	R	D	D
Michigan	R	D	D
Minnesota	D*	C(R)	C(R)
Montana	R	D	D
Nevada	D*	†	D
New Hampshire	D	R	R
New Jersey	D*	R	R
New York	R*	D	D
North Dakota	D	R	D
Ohio	R*	†	R
Oklahoma	R*	D	D
Oregon	R*	D	R
Pennsylvania	R*	R	D
Rhode Island	R	D	D
Vermont	D	R	R
Washington	R	D	D
Wisconsin	R	R	D
Wyoming	R*	R	D

* Denotes state in which there was no gubernatorial election in 1964.
† Denotes Senate evenly divided D and R.

cian and that they refuse to vote for the candidates of one party only since this would tend to concentrate too much power in the hands of the few. Power corrupts. Also was it not the very purpose of those who designed our system of separation of powers to assure and maximize liberty by having executives confront legislators and legislators, executives? To govern safely is not necessarily to govern efficiently.

Others suggest that it is the candidate-centeredness of American politics which is at the bottom of it all. Voters, believing that there are no real or significant differences anyway between the parties as such, might as well choose the man rather than decide their vote on the basis of party platforms which are written more likely to confuse or to appease than to serve as "contracts" to which the electors might hold those candidates who by their label at least ought to be guided by its provisions.

If it were agreed that divided party government represents an undesirable obstacle to the building of a responsible and program-centered party system in the states, much of the blame must be placed on constitutions and statutes which have so spaced the elections of governors that their terms of office do not coincide with quadrennial presidential contests. What such an election calendar has in effect accomplished is to isolate state from national issues and to deny to a party winning state presidential majorities the opportunity to implement on the state levels policies for which it campaigned so successfully or which its presidential candidate symbolized so successfully.

CASE PROBLEMS FOR CLASS DISCUSSION

1. As a member of your political party's state platform committee you have been listening to all the various interest groups and their representatives for the inclusion of certain policy recommendations into the state party platform. You are now ready to fashion the different planks. What should be written about legislative reapportionment, urban renewal, taxation, school aids, administrative reorganization?
2. At the state convention a session of the rules committee is in the process of composing a set of rules that will govern the operation of the convention about to convene. You are chairman of the committee and it is your responsibility to make sure that the convention will operate smoothly and efficiently. What will you suggest to the committee with respect to such subjects as reducing county voting power proportionately to actual delegate strength on the floor, adoption or rejection of the unit rule, use of the secret ballot on nominations?
3. The county convention of your party, meeting in April of the election year, is torn by a fiery discussion concerning the desirability of endorsing candidates for governor and attorney general prior to the September open primary. You are representing a candidate for governor who does not have much support among the members now attending the convention but who does have support among the so-called independent voters. It is now your turn to take the floor and to persuade the convention to hold off on their gubernatorial endorsement. What would be your major arguments? What are some of the arguments for immediate endorsement that you would have to refute?
4. You are asked to provide "answers" for the following questions which were raised about the 1964 presidential election outcome in your state. How much of a role

was played by the so-called "white backlash"? Were domestic issues generally more or less important than foreign policy? Compared with the 1960 election, what happened in the suburbs? To find solutions to these problems what would have to be your research design?

SELECTED BIBLIOGRAPHY

ROBERT R. ALFORD, "Role of Social Class in American Voting Behavior," *Western Political Quarterly*, March, 1963, pp. 180–194.

BRUCE R. ANDREWS, "Religious and Ethnic Influences on Voting Behavior: A Study of the Syracuse Electorate from 1918 to 1957," unpublished Ph.D. dissertation, Syracuse University, 1961.

JOSE ARMILLA, "Leader-Follower Frame of Reference in Political Behavior," unpublished Ph.D. dissertation, University of Michigan, 1961.

ANDREW R. BAGGALEY, "Religious Influence on Wisconsin Voting, 1928–1960," *American Political Science Review*, March, 1962, pp. 66–70.

DONALD G. BALMER, "The 1962 Elections in Oregon," *Western Political Quarterly*, June, 1963, pp. 453–459.

EDWARD BANFIELD, *Political Influence* (Glencoe, 1960).

E. J. BAUR, "Opinion Change in a Public Controversy," *Public Opinion Quarterly*, Summer, 1962, pp. 212–226.

CHARLES BEALL, "The 1962 Election in Wyoming," *Western Political Quarterly*, June, 1963, pp. 477–482.

ROBERT W. BECKER, FRIDA L. FOOTE, MATHIAS LUBEGA, and STEPHEN B. MONSMA, "Correlates of Legislative Voting: Michigan House of Representatives 1954–1961," *Midwest Journal of Political Science*, November, 1962, pp. 384–396.

JOSEPH L. BERND, *Grass Roots Politics in Georgia* (Atlanta, 1960).

DONALD C. BLAISDELL, "The Riverside Democrats," in Paul Tillett (ed.), *Cases on Party Organization* (New York, 1963), pp. 64–92.

HUGH BONE, "The 1960 Election in Washington," *Western Political Quarterly*, March, 1961, pp. 373–382.

HUGH BONE, "The 1962 Election in Washington," *Western Political Quarterly*, June, 1963, pp. 467–476.

BELMONT BRICE, JR., "Absentee Voting and the Character of the Electorate," *BGR Observer*, June, 1961, pp. 1–4.

FRANCIS M. CARNEY, "The Decentralized Politics of Los Angeles," *The Annals of the American Academy of Political and Social Science*," May, 1964, pp. 107–121.

JACQUELYNE MARY JOHNSON CLARKE, "Goals and Techniques in Three Negro Civil-Rights Organizations in Alabama," unpublished Ph.D. dissertation, The Ohio State University, 1960.

ALAN L. CLEM, "Analysis of the 1958 Campaign in Nebraska's Third Congressional District," unpublished Ph.D. dissertation, American University, 1960.

ALAN L. CLEM, "The 1962 Election in South Dakota," *Public Affairs*, February, 1963, pp. 1–6.

ALAN L. CLEM, *Spirit Mound Township in the 1960 Election* (Vermillion, S. D., 1961).

ELMER E. CORNWELL, JR., "Bosses, Machines, and Ethnic Groups," *The Annals of the American Academy of Political and Social Science*, May, 1964, pp. 27–39.

ELMER E. CORNWELL, JR., "Party Absorption of Ethnic Groups: The Case of Providence, Rhode Island," *Social Forces*, March, 1960, pp. 205–210.

EDMOND COSTANTINI, "Intraparty Attitude Conflict: Democratic Party Leadership in California," *Western Political Quarterly*, December, 1963, pp. 956–972.

EDWARD F. COX, "The Measurement of Party Strength," *Western Political Quarterly*, December, 1960, pp. 1022–1042.

WILDER CRANE, JR., "A Caveat on Roll-Call Studies of Party Voting," *Midwest Journal of Political Science*, August, 1960, pp. 237–249.

PHILLIPS CUTRIGHT, "Activities of Precinct Committeemen in Partisan and Non-Partisan Communities," *Western Political Quarterly*, March, 1964, pp. 93–108.

PHILLIPS CUTRIGHT, "Measuring the Impact of Local Party Activity on the General Election Vote," *Public Opinion Quarterly*, Fall, 1963, pp. 372–386.

PHILLIPS CUTRIGHT, "Nonpartisan Electoral Systems in American Cities," *Comparative Studies in Society and History*, January, 1963, pp. 212–226.

PHILLIPS CUTRIGHT, "Urbanization and Competitive Party Politics," *Journal of Politics*, August, 1963, pp. 552–564.

BENJAMIN DEMOTT, "Party Apolitics," *American Scholar*, Autumn, 1962, pp. 595–602.

JOHN M. DIGMAN and DANIEL W. TUTTLE, "An Interpretation of an Election by Means of Obverse Factor Analysis," *Journal of Social Psychology*, April, 1961, pp. 183–194.

RICHARD W. DODGE and EUGENE S. UYEKI, "Political Affiliation and Imagery Across Two Related Generations," *Midwest Journal of Political Science*, August, 1962, pp. 266–276.

DON W. DRIGGS, "The 1960 Election in Nevada," *Western Political Quarterly*, March, 1961, pp. 347–349.

THOMAS R. DYE, "Certain Political Correlates of Social and Economic Differentiation Among Suburban Communities," unpublished Ph.D. dissertation, University of Pennsylvania, 1961.

THOMAS R. DYE, "Popular Images of Decision-Making in Suburban Communities," *Sociology and Social Research*, October, 1962, pp. 75–83.

STEVEN EBBIN, "Personality and Politics: A Qualitative Analysis of the Basic Factors of Political Success," unpublished Ph.D. dissertation, Syracuse University, 1960.

ROLAND H. EBEL, *The Political Professionals: Summary of a Study of the Permanent Staff of Political Parties in the United States* (East Lansing, Mich., 1960).

FRANKLIN O. FELT, "A Study of a Nonpartisan Political Organization: The Arlingtonians for a Better County (ABC)," unpublished Ph.D. dissertation, Michigan State University, 1961.

G. JAMES FLEMING, *An All-Negro Ticket in Baltimore* (New York, 1961).

THOMAS A. FLINN, "Continuity and Change in Ohio Politics," *Journal of Politics*, August, 1962, pp. 521–544.

THOMAS A. FLINN, "How Mr. Nixon Took Ohio: A Short Reply to Senator Kennedy's Question," *Western Political Quarterly*, June, 1962, pp. 274–279.

THOMAS A. FLINN, "Party Responsibility in the States: Some Causal Factors," *American Political Science Review*, March, 1964, pp. 60–71.

PAMELA S. FORD, *Political Activities and the Public Service: A Continuing Problem* (Berkeley, 1963).

ROY E. FOSSETT, "The Impact of the New Deal on Georgia Politics, 1933–1941," unpublished Ph.D. dissertation, University of Florida, 1960.

LOUIS L. FRIEDLAND, "Organized Labor and the City Boss," *The Annals of the American Academy of Political and Social Science*, May, 1964, pp. 40–51.

ROBERT S. FRIEDMAN, "The Urban-Rural Conflict Revisited," *Western Political Quarterly*, June, 1961, pp. 481–495.

RICHARD T. FROST, "Stability and Change in Local Party Politics," *Public Opinion Quarterly*, Summer, 1961, pp. 221–235.

CHARLES GARRETT, *The LaGuardia Years: Machine and Reform Politics in New York City* (New Brunswick, 1961).

CHARLES E. GILBERT, "National Political Alignments and the Politics of Large Cities," *Political Science Quarterly*, March, 1964, pp. 25–51.

CHARLES E. GILBERT, "Some Aspects of Nonpartisan Elections in Large Cities," *Midwest Journal of Political Science*, November, 1962, pp. 345–362.

CHARLES E. GILBERT and CHRISTOPHER CLAGUE, "Electoral Competition and Electoral Systems in Large Cities," *Journal of Politics*, May, 1962, pp. 323–349.

MARILYN GITTELL, "Metropolitan Mayor: Dead End," *Public Administration Review*, March, 1963, pp. 20–24.

OSCAR GLANTZ, "The Negro Voter in Northern Industrial Cities," *Western Political Quarterly*, December, 1960, pp. 999–1010.

DAVID GOLD and JOHN R. SCHMIDHAUSER, "Urbanization and Party Competition: The Case of Iowa," *Midwest Journal of Political Science*, February, 1960, pp. 62–75.

IRWIN GOLDBERG, "Democracy in Detroit," unpublished Ph.D. dissertation, University of Michigan, 1961.

ROBERT A. GOLDWIN (ed.), *Political Parties, U.S.A.* (Chicago, 1964).

ROBERT T. GOLEMBIEWSKI, "A Taxonomic Approach to State Political Party Strength," *Western Political Quarterly*, September, 1958, pp. 494–513.

FRED I. GREENSTEIN, "The Changing Pattern of Urban Party Politics," *The Annals of the American Academy of Political and Social Science*, May, 1964, pp. 1–13.

SCOTT GREER, "Catholic Voters and the Democratic Party," *Public Opinion Quarterly*, Winter, 1961, pp. 611–625.

MORTON GRODZINS, "American Political Parties and the American System," *Western Political Quarterly*, December, 1960, pp. 974–998.

STEWART L. GROW, "The 1962 Election in Utah," *Western Political Quarterly*, June, 1963, pp. 460–466.

ANDREW HACKER, "Pressure Politics in

Pennsylvania," in Alan F. Westin (ed.), *The Uses of Power* (New York, 1961), pp. 323–376.

CHARLES B. HAGAN and CARL D. McMURRAY, "Rural Midwestern Voting Trends," *Illinois Business Review*, September, 1960, pp. 6–8.

A. CLARKE HAGENSICK, "Influences of Partisanship and Incumbency on a Nonpartisan Election System," *Western Political Quarterly*, March, 1964, pp. 117–124.

SAMUEL HALPERIN, *A University in the Web of Politics* (New York, 1960).

MARVIN A. HARDER and THOMAS UNGS, "Notes Toward a Functional Analysis of Local Party Organization," paper presented to the Midwest Conference of Political Scientists, University of Chicago, May 2–4, 1963.

LOUISE HARNED, "Authoritarian Attitudes and Party Activity," *Public Opinion Quarterly*, Fall, 1961, pp. 393–399.

WILLIAM C. HAVARD, "From Bossism to Cosmopolitanism: Changes in the Relationship of Urban Leadership to State Politics," *The Annals of the American Academy of Political and Social Science*, May, 1964, pp. 84–94.

JANE HENDRA, "The 1960 Democratic Campaign in Wisconsin," unpublished M.S. thesis, University of Wisconsin, 1961.

ROBERT E. HENNINGS, "California Democratic Politics in the Period of Republican Ascendancy," *Pacific Historical Review*, August, 1962, pp. 267–280.

ROBERT S. HIRSCHFIELD, BERT E. SWANSON, and BLANCHE D. BLANK, "A Profile of Political Activists in Manhattan," *Western Political Quarterly*, September, 1962, pp. 489–506.

HARRY HOLLOWAY, "The Negro and the Vote: The Case of Texas," *Journal of Politics*, August, 1961, pp. 526–556.

HARRY HOLLOWAY, "The Texas Negro as a Voter," *Phylon*, Summer, 1963, pp. 135–145.

JOHN E. HORTON, "The Angry Voter, A Study in Political Alienation," unpublished Ph.D. dissertation, Cornell University, 1960.

FREDERICK C. IRION, "The 1960 Election in New Mexico," *Western Political Quarterly*, March, 1961, pp. 350–354.

FREDERICK C. IRION, "The 1962 Election in New Mexico," *Western Political Quarterly*, June, 1963, pp. 448–452.

ERWIN A. JAFFE and STANLEY A. PEARL, "The 1962 Election in Nevada," *Western Political Quarterly*, June, 1963, pp. 443–447.

MALCOLM E. JEWELL, "Party and Primary Competition in Kentucky State Legislative Races," *Kentucky Law Journal*, Summer, 1960, pp. 517–535.

BENTON JOHNSON, "Ascetic Protestantism and Political Preference," *Public Opinion Quarterly*, Spring, 1962, pp. 35–46.

FRANK H. JONAS, "The 1960 Election in Utah," *Western Political Quarterly*, March, 1961, pp. 365–372.

CONRAD JOYNER, "The 1962 Election in Arizona," *Western Political Quarterly*, June, 1963, pp. 390–395.

DANIEL KATZ and SAMUEL J. ELDERSVELD, "Impact of Local Party Activity Upon the Electorate," *Public Opinion Quarterly*, Spring, 1961, pp. 1–24.

WALTER C. KAUFMAN and SCOTT GREER, "Voting in a Metropolitan Community: An Application of Social Area Analysis," *Social Forces*, March, 1960, pp. 192–204.

V. O. KEY, JR., *American State Politics: An Introduction* (New York, 1956).

EUGENE C. LEE, *The Politics of Nonpartisanship: A Study of California City Elections* (Berkeley, 1960).

MARTIN L. LEVIN, "Social Climates and Political Socialization," *Public Opinion Quarterly*, Winter, 1961, pp. 596–606.

MURRAY B. LEVIN, *The Alienated Voter: Politics in Boston* (New York, 1960).

MURRAY B. LEVIN, *The Compleat Politician: Political Strategy in Massachusetts* (Indianapolis, 1962).

MURRAY B. LEVIN and MURRAY EDEN, "Political Strategy for the Alienated Voter," *Public Opinion Quarterly*, Spring, 1962, pp. 47–63.

WILLIAM O. LEWIS, "The 1962 Election in Idaho," *Western Political Quarterly*, June, 1963, pp. 432–438.

CHARLES S. LIEBMAN, "Some Political Effects of the Functional Differentiation of Suburbs," unpublished Ph.D. dissertation, University of Illinois, 1960.

JOHN H. LINDQUIST, "Businessmen in Politics: An Analysis of Political Participation in Syracuse, New York, 1880–1959," unpublished Ph.D. dissertation, Syracuse University, 1961.

EDGAR LITT, "Ethnic Status and Political Perspectives," *Midwest Journal of Political Science*, August, 1961, pp. 276–283.

EDGAR LITT, "Jewish Ethno-Religious Involvement and Political Liberalism," *Social Forces*, May, 1961, pp. 328–332.

EDGAR LITT, "Status, Ethnicity, and Patterns of Jewish Voting Behavior in Baltimore," *Jewish Social Studies*, July, 1960, pp. 159–164.

N. I. Lustig, "Relationships Between Demographic Characteristics and Pro-Integration Vote of White Precincts in a Metropolitan Southern County," *Social Forces*, March, 1962, pp. 205–208.

Herbert McClosky, Paul J. Hoffmann, and Rosemary O'Hara, "Issue Conflict and Consensus Among Party Leaders and Followers," *American Political Science Review*, June, 1960, pp. 406–427.

John B. McConaughy and John H. Gauntlett, "The Influence of the Social Factor Upon the Voting Behavior of South Carolina Urban Negroes," *PROD*, May, 1960, pp. 15–17.

John B. McConaughy and John H. Gauntlett, "The Influence of the S Factor Upon the Voting Behavior of South Carolina Urban Negroes," *Western Political Quarterly*, December, 1963, pp. 973–984.

John B. McConaughy and John H. Gauntlett, "A Survey of Urban Negro Voting Behavior in South Carolina," *South Carolina Law Quarterly*, Spring, 1962, pp. 365–380.

W. H. McCree, Jr., "Negro Renaissance in Michigan Politics," *Negro History Bulletin*, October, 1962, pp. 7–9.

Edward L. McDill and Jeanne C. Ridley, "Status, Anomia, Political Alienation, and Political Participation," *American Journal of Sociology*, September, 1962, pp. 205–213.

Joseph E. McGrath and Marion F. McGrath, "Effects of Partisanship on Perceptions of Political Figures," *Public Opinion Quarterly*, Summer, 1962, pp. 236–248.

Duncan MacRae, Jr., and J. A. Meldrum, "Critical Elections in Illinois: 1888–1958," *American Political Science Review*, September, 1960, pp. 669–683.

James W. Markham and G. H. Stempel, "Press Treatment of the 1958 State Elections in Pennsylvania," *Western Political Quarterly*, December, 1961, pp. 912–924.

Boyd A. Martin, "The 1960 Election in Idaho," *Western Political Quarterly*, March, 1961, pp. 339–342.

Curtis Martin, "The 1960 Election in Colorado," *Western Political Quarterly*, March, 1961, pp. 327–330.

Curtis Martin, "The 1962 Election in Colorado," *Western Political Quarterly*, June, 1963, pp. 421–425.

Dwaine Marvick (ed.), *Political Decision-Makers* (New York, 1961).

Roger H. Marz, "Voting Shifts in a Suburban Community: A Study of Migrants from Detroit, 1952–1956," unpublished

Ph.D. dissertation, Michigan State University, 1960.

Norman Meller, "Major Issues in Hawaiian Politics," *Western Political Quarterly*, September, 1960, pp. 18–20.

G. Theodore Mitau, *Politics in Minnesota* (Minneapolis, 1960).

Joan W. Moore, "Social Deprivation and Advantage as Sources of Political Values," *Western Political Quarterly*, June, 1962, pp. 217–226.

R. Joseph Monsen, Jr. and Mark W. Cannon, *The Makers of Public Policy: American Power Groups and Their Ideologies* (New York, 1965).

Daniel P. Moynihan, " 'Bosses' and 'Reforms': A Profile of New York Democrats," *Commentary*, June, 1961, pp. 461–470.

Raymond J. Murphy and Richard T. Morris, "Occupational Situs, Subjective Class Identification, and Political Affiliation," *American Sociological Review*, June, 1961, pp. 383–392.

Virgil Miller Newton, *Crusade for Democracy* (Ames, Iowa, 1961).

Mary Peret Nichols, "The Politics of Virtue, or, The New Tammany," *Dissent*, Summer, 1961, pp. 366–370.

Charles R. Nixon, "The Coming Electorate: 1965–1970," *Western Political Quarterly*, September, 1960, pp. 620–635.

Lloyd B. Omdahl, *The Insurgents* (Brainerd, Minn., 1961).

Malcolm B. Parsons, "Quasi-Partisan Conflict in a One-Party Legislative System: The Florida Senate 1947–1961," *American Political Science Review*, September, 1962, pp. 605–614.

Samuel C. Patterson, "Characteristics of Party Leaders," *Western Political Quarterly*, June, 1963, pp. 332–352.

Samuel C. Patterson, "Dimensions of Voting Behavior in a One-Party State Legislature," *Public Opinion Quarterly*, Summer, 1962, pp. 185–200.

Samuel C. Patterson, "Legislative Leadership and Political Ideology," *Public Opinion Quarterly*, Fall, 1963, pp. 399–410.

Samuel C. Patterson and Robert S. Walker, "The Political Attitudes of Oklahoma Newspaper Editors: The Prohibition Issue," *Southwestern Social Science Quarterly*, December, 1961, pp. 460–472.

Lois M. Pelekoudas (ed.), *Illinois Political Parties* (Urbana, 1960).

Pertti Pesonen, "Close and Safe Elections in Massachusetts," *Midwest Journal of Political Science*, February, 1963, pp. 54–70.

THOMAS PETTIGREW and ERNEST Q. CAMP-
BELL, "Faubus and Segregation: Analysis
of Arkansas Behavior," *Public Opinion
Quarterly*, Fall, 1960, pp. 436–447.

HUGH D. PRICE and BRUCE B. MASON,
Florida Voters' Guide (Gainesville, 1960).

JAMES A. RIEDEL, "Boss and Faction," *The
Annals of the American Academy of
Political and Social Science*, May, 1964,
pp. 14–26.

ROBERT E. RIGGS, "The District Five Primary—A Case Study in Practical Politics," *Arizona Review of Business and
Public Administration*, March, 1963, pp.
1–14.

GEORGE ROBERTS, "The Democratic Party
of Indiana, 1952–1958," unpublished
Ph.D. dissertation, Indiana University,
1962.

JAMES A. ROBINSON and WILLIAM H.
STANDING, "Some Correlates of Voter Participation: The Case of Indiana," *Journal of Politics*, February, 1960, pp. 96–
111.

LEONARD C. ROWE, *Preprimary Endorsements in California Politics* (Berkeley,
1961).

KENNARD W. RUMAGE, "Some Spatial Characteristics of the Republican and Democratic Presidential Vote in Iowa, 1900–
1956," *Iowa Business Digest*, February,
1960, pp. 17–21.

ROBERT H. SALISBURY, "St. Louis Politics:
Relationships Among Interests, Parties,
and Governmental Structure," *Western
Political Quarterly*, June, 1960, pp. 498–
507.

ROBERT H. SALISBURY and GORDON BLACK,
"Class and Party in Partisan and Nonpartisan Elections: The Case of Des
Moines," *American Political Science Review*, September, 1963, pp. 584–592.

JACK SAWYER and DUNCAN MACRAE, JR.,
"Game Theory and Cumulative Voting in
Illinois: 1902–1954," *American Political
Science Review*, December, 1962, pp. 936–
946.

ROBERT LEE SAWYER, JR., *The Democratic
State Central Committee in Michigan,
1949–1959: The Rise of the New Politics
and the New Political Leadership* (Ann
Arbor, 1960).

JOSEPH A. SCHLESINGER, "Stability in The
Vote for Governor, 1900–1958," *Public
Opinion Quarterly*, Spring, 1960, pp. 85–
91.

JOSEPH A. SCHLESINGER, "The Structure of
Competition for Office in the American
States," *Behavioral Science*, July, 1960,
pp. 197–210.

JOSEPH A. SCHLESINGER, "A Two-Dimen-
sional Scheme for Classifying the States
According to Degree of Interparty Competition," *American Political Science Review*, December, 1955, pp. 1120–1128.

LESTER G. SELIGMAN, "Political Recruitment
and Party Structure: a Case Study,"
American Political Science Review,
March, 1961, pp. 77–86.

RICHARD B. SHERMAN, "The Status Revolution and Massachusetts Progressive Leadership," *Political Science Quarterly*,
March, 1963, pp. 59–65.

HERMAN E. SLOTNICK, "The 1960 Election
in Alaska," *Western Political Quarterly*,
March, 1961, pp. 300–304.

HERMAN E. SLOTNICK, "The 1962 Election
in Alaska," *Western Political Quarterly*,
June, 1963, pp. 386–389.

JOEL SMITH, HERMAN TURK, and HOWARD
P. MYERS, "Understanding Local Political
Behavior: The Role of The Older Citizen,"
Law and Contemporary Problems, Spring,
1962, pp. 280–298.

FRANK J. SORAUF, "*Party and Representation, Legislative Politics in Pennsylvania*
(New York, 1963).

ROBERT H. STOUDENMIRE, "Political Party
Organization in South Carolina," *Univer-
sity of South Carolina Governmental
Review*, November, 1961, pp. 1–4.

WILLIAM L. STRAUSS, "The 1960 Election
in Arizona," *Western Political Quarterly*,
March, 1961, pp. 305–308.

JOHN M. SWARTHOUT, "The 1960 Election
in Oregon," *Western Political Quarterly*,
March, 1961, pp. 355–364.

HENRY J. TOMASEK, "North Dakota's Ad-
vent as a Two Party System," *North Dakota Quarterly*, Summer, 1960, pp. 57–61.

HERMAN H. TRACHSEL, "The 1960 Election
in Wyoming," *Western Political Quarterly*, March, 1961, pp. 383–385.

DANIEL W. TUTTLE, JR., et al. (comps.),
"The 1960 Elections in Hawaii," *Western
Political Quarterly*, March, 1961, pp. 331–
338.

DANIEL W. TUTTLE, JR., et al. (comps.),
"The 1962 Election in Hawaii," *Western
Political Quarterly*, June, 1963, pp. 426–
431.

DANIEL W. TUTTLE, JR., et al. (comps.),
*The Hawaii Democratic and Republican
Party Platforms, 1952–1962* (Honolulu,
1962).

"Group Voting in the 1961 Los Angeles
Mayoral Election," *BGR Observer*, November, 1961, pp. 1–4.

JAMES W. VANDER ZANDEN, "Voting on Segregationist Referenda," *Public Opinion Quarterly*, Spring, 1961, pp. 92–105.

JOHN A. VIEG, "A New Design for California Politics," *Western Political Quarterly*, September, 1960, pp. 692–701.

DAVID B. WALKER, *Politics and Ethnocentrism: The Case of the Franco-Americans* (Brunswick, Me., 1961).

DAVID WALLACE, "The Sociology of Stability and Change in One Suburb's Voting," unpublished Ph.D. dissertation, Columbia University, 1962.

RICHARD A. WATSON, *The Politics of Urban Change* (Kansas City, Mo., 1963).

O. DOUGLAS WEEKS, *Texas in the 1960 Presidential Election* (Austin, 1961).

E. A. WILKENING and RALPH K. HUITT, "Political Participation Among Farmers as Related to Socio-Economic Status and Perception of the Political Process," *Rural Sociology*, December, 1961, pp. 395–408.

JAMES Q. WILSON, *Negro Politics: The Search for Leadership* (Glencoe, 1960).

RAYMOND E. WOLFINGER, "The Influence of Precinct Work on Voting Behavior," *Public Opinion Quarterly*, Fall, 1963, pp. 387–398.

Are party organizations kept accountable
to the rank and file membership—who
speaks for whom?

How easy should it be for people to vote
or to back the candidates of their choice
with financial contributions, unpublicized
and unreported?

STATE POLITICAL PARTIES—THEIR LEGAL SETTING AND ORGANIZATION

In state constitutions there is very little substance dealing with party organizations. Legal provisions regarding political parties that do exist are statutory in origin and are mostly concerned with the relationship of parties to the nomination and election process. Most state laws avoiding ideological criteria for party membership, or requirements for political programs, platforms, or organizational detail tend to define political parties in terms of a minimum percentage of electors who wish to file a petition to constitute themselves as a political party organization in the state or its subdivision in order to nominate and support candidates for public office.

To assure party stability and to make it more difficult for new parties to get on the ballot or for factional groupings within the major parties to become independent parties, laws have been passed to protect the names of the existing parties. For example, no new party may use the name of an existing party as part of its own name. Delays are also written into the laws so that petitions can be adequately scrutinized for legal sufficiency and particularly for violations of residence requirements by petition signatories. Some states additionally specify a fixed geographic distribution of petitioners that calls for a minimum quota of registrants from all or from a majority of the state's counties or election districts.

Some form of parties existed throughout our history but the modern system clearly developed from social, political, and economic consequences that characterized the post-Jacksonian era and even more significantly the post-Civil War era. The extension of the suffrage, mass immigration, and urbanization made necessary institutional arrangements to organize the electorate, nominate candidates, conduct campaigns, and provide the voters with policy alternatives. Of all these various functions that they were to perform, parties, even on the state level, were soon to discover that the last one—that of giving the electorate a set of policy alternatives—was chimerical.

If party discipline is defined as holding an elective official on a policy-making level to the support of a set of resolutions or principles which were enacted into a platform by his party at its convention and on whose ticket he

276

had then offered his candidacy to the electorate at the polls—if such is party discipline, precious little exists now or has ever existed in American politics. Presidents, governors, legislators, mayors, and councilmen ignored platforms and yet won smashing endorsements at the polls from an electorate which viewed platforms or formal party pronouncements with disdain.

Among the factors contributing to this lack of party discipline a few stand out: the doctrine and operation of separation of powers which pits executives against legislators; staggered terms for state senators, precluding a party from maximizing its strength at a given moment of popularity; voter concern with and stress on local issues rather than statewide issues; the system of single-member constitutencies which requires building winning coalitions composed of widely divergent interests; and the system of primary elections which emphasizes persons and personalities rather than issues. Most state parties operate in a political climate which extolls independence over party discipline and prefers interest group and personal politics to party politics.

Consequent then with this legal and political setting, parties developed structures which are primarily those of electoral associations. Some general observations are valid for a majority of state party organizations although no two of the fifty are structured identically, and no two assign to their various officers, committees and conventions the same type of functions or powers.

PARTY CONVENTIONS AND COMMITTEES

Most of the work that the parties do is carried out by two parallel hierarchies of committees and conventions.

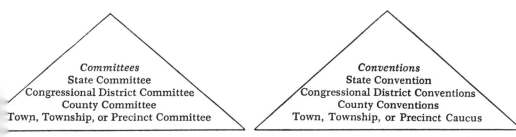

State laws usually name these committees and conventions and define their membership but leave much of the internal organizational and procedural details to the governing bodies of the parties and their constitutions and rules. Courts as a rule have been most reluctant to settle intraparty disputes or factional controversies of these unincorporated voluntary associations. However, there are a number of cases in which they were forced to make final judicial determination of questions involving the exclusion of otherwise qualified voters, the recognition of new parties, or the administration of funds, property, or aspects of state law governing nominations, voting, and ballots.

Under law, the state convention is the highest governing tribunal of the party. Standing at the apex of the pyramid of caucuses and conventions and meeting at least once every two years, it has the final word on what is to go into the party platform, constitution, and rules and how these are to be applied. It nominates and elects state party officers; it may nominate or endorse candidates for statewide public office, approve or reject nominations for county or districtwide office, designate the national committeeman and woman, and in a presidential year, select the delegates who are to be sent to the national nominating convention. Presidential electors whose names will appear on the November ballot are also chosen then.

Generally, the rank and file party voters who compose the precinct or town (the lowest election district) elect the membership of the county convention. They do this by voting at a regular public election or by sitting as a caucus. The county convention in turn elects the membership of the congressional district convention which then elects the membership of the state convention.

Each of these caucuses or county conventions performs on its respective level organizational and electoral duties that correspond roughly to those of the state convention but that vary greatly in importance and in scope with the nature of its jurisdiction. For example, conventions may be held also in judicial districts (to endorse or nominate judges), in senatorial districts (to endorse or nominate senators), or in legislative districts (to endorse or nominate legislators).

Each county convention also elects the party officers for the committees that are to operate and carry out party and campaign work while the larger group is not in session—the precinct committeemen, the county committeemen, the district committeemen, and the state committeemen. At the state level some parties now employ a paid, professional staff and an executive secretary who functions under the direction of the state chairman or of a state executive committee and whose major responsibility consists of assisting party volunteers with the ever-increasing scope of work connected with party publications, research, correspondence, and voter registration drives as well as with the many details involved in day-to-day office management.

The precinct captain or committeeman no longer has the power that he once had. Before there were civil service rules, restrictive immigration laws, public employment agencies, and state welfare programs, the precinct captain played a pivotal role in building loyalties to the party organization, candidate, boss, or machine, by rendering personal services to the needy, the indigent, and the newcomer. What has not changed is that today, party victories, like those in the past, still depend on the effectiveness with which local workers distribute the literature, canvass the neighborhood, collect the funds, reassure the faithful, and register the potential voters.

With this general picture in mind, what then are some of the variations in party organizations now operative in the several states? In California, for example, the state convention has very little to do beyond approving the party's platform after the primary and electing the presidential electors in presidential years. Convention membership does not emerge from below through election, but consists of the party members (or their delegates) who were nominated or elected to public state or national office. Illinois also does not leave much to the state convention except permitting it to adopt the platform, to nominate the presidential electors and the trustees for the University of Illinois, and to select "the delegates- and alternates-at-large (the *district* delegates and alternates are elected in the primary) to the national nominating convention. . . ."[1]

By way of contrast, New York's practice of not nominating statewide candidates through the direct primary—not even the governor—has left great powers in the hands of the state convention. Delegates to this important assembly are formally elected at the primaries but in fact are "selected by the county chairman, placed on the ballot, and ratified automatically by the handful of voters who typically participate. . . ."[2] Therefore, those in search of a gubernatorial or senatorial nomination must begin to cultivate county chairmen long before the convention is called to order. Indiana and Connecticut are two states in which the conventions still nominate candidates for statewide office in this manner although there are also a number of Southern states including Alabama, Arkansas, Georgia, South Carolina, and Virginia in which the Republican party uses the convention method when it cannot qualify under the primary laws due to lack of party registration.

Some of the state parties have placed major responsibility for supervising or directing the execution of convention determined policies in the hands of state central or state executive committees. But here again there are important variations among the states as to powers, composition, and size of these committees. California's state central committee has about eight hundred delegates who meet once every two years to do little more than elect the state party officers and the executive committee. Its membership includes the party nominees for office, the 58 county chairmen, five additional members who are appointed by each incumbent nominee, and three additional members who are appointed by each non-incumbent nominee.

In 1964 followers of Barry Goldwater helped to capture control of the G.O.P. central committee by becoming G.O.P. candidates in districts which were often uncontested by the party. Such nominees then exercised the privilege of appointing members of the central committee who reflected a more conservative point of view.

In New York party officers are also elected by the state central committee, a group composed of two delegates elected at the primary from each election district, and while smaller than the California committee, it again is too large "to permit deliberation over party policy."[3] State central committeemen in Illinois are elected at the April primaries in the even-numbered years and are

---

[1] Austin Ranney, *Illinois Politics* (New York, 1960), p. 13.

[2] Frank J. Munger and Ralph A. Straetz, *New York Politics* (New York, 1960), p. 58.

[3] *Ibid.*, p. 64.

given voting power equal to that of the total cast for their party in the congressional district primary. The committee elects its chairman but has "no legal power of discipline or command over any other party organization . . ." and "almost never does . . . itself act as the decision-making body." [4]

In the South where party organization is generally more informal and less structured, state central committeemen are elected either at the party primaries or at state conventions. Election law in Alabama, Florida, and Louisiana, for example, has given them considerable power over the affairs of the party. In practice, however, such power is more often exercised by the chairman personally than by the entire committee.

Pennsylvania represents a group of states including such Midwestern states as Minnesota and Michigan and such Far Western states as Washington and Colorado in which the state central committee is "active in raising funds, advising candidates on campaign tactics, disbursing money for election expenses, arranging meetings and rallies, and printing and distributing campaign literature." [5] Committees in Pennsylvania and Minnesota may even make recommendations or "endorse" candidates prior to the primary. The 113 members of the Pennsylvania committee are elected for two-year terms in the spring primaries in even-numbered years and include one man and one woman from each of the state senatorial districts.

A somewhat typical state central committee will include approximately 150–250 members. Since this large a group is difficult to convene quickly and too large to engage in effective policy discussion, many states have developed an alternative group, a state executive committee, composed of state party executives, i.e., only the state chairman, vice chairman, secretary, treasurer, national committeeman and woman, and congressional district chairmen, etc. Some states like Texas, for example, do not have a central committee at all. There it is the state executive committee elected at state conventions "that determines how party funds will be spent and recommends the seating of delegates at the state convention." [6] Small wonder then that this committee and its chairman represent one of the major prizes in the often bitter conflicts which agitate the conservative and liberal wings of the Democratic party of Texas.

From what has been said so far it might possibly appear that state parties generally have central bodies with decisive powers of discipline over county committees or over the committees or conventions of other subdivisions of the state or party organization. Nothing could be further from depicting the reality of American politics. Nearly all state party organizations are still very much beset by traditions of localism and decentralization both of which tend to accentuate the concerns and interests of "the folks back home" over those of the state as a whole. Town, city, or county chairmen and the town, city, or

[4] Ranney, p. 12.
[5] Edward F. Cooke and G. Edward Janosik, *Guide to Pennsylvania Politics* (New York, 1957), p. 24.
[6] Wilbourn E. Benton, *Texas: Its Government and Politics* (Englewood Cliffs, 1961), p. 117.

county committees that they more or less control still form the factional centers of power that state chairmen and state leaders must seek to combine and weave into a coalition if they or their candidates are to emerge successfully at the state party convention or at the statewide general election. How much of a price will have to be paid to satisfy the local leadership or the interests for which they speak depends largely on the political skill and on the political power possessed by those who build the coalition.

Outstanding among the many factors that make this task of exercising central state party leadership such a difficult one are at least two: the operation of the direct primary and the strength of interest group politics.

NOMINATIONS AND THE DIRECT PRIMARY

In this section a few fundamentals concerning the manner in which candidates are picked for local, state, and national office will be discussed. The following outline briefly annotated with reference to current provisions endeavors to present a profile of major nominating patterns (see also Table 1):

A. The direct primary is used in all fifty states except Delaware and Indiana.
B. Connecticut, Iowa, Maryland, Michigan, New Mexico, New York, South Dakota, Texas, Utah, and Virginia employ the convention method for many offices.
C. In some Southern states such as Alabama, Georgia, and South Carolina, election law has left to the political parties the decision of whether they wish to nominate by primaries or by conventions.[7]
D. Many states permit an individual to be filed by petition when he is unable to secure nomination either by convention or party primary.
E. Some state election laws permit their political parties to combine the convention system of nominating with the operation of the direct primary. In Colorado, for example, pre-primary party conventions generally select the candidates whose names will appear in the primary,[8] while in Connecticut, primary elections will be held only "if convention action is contested by a candidate receiving at least 20 per cent of the convention vote."[9] By way of contrast, according to the election laws of Iowa and South Dakota, a convention may be held if a candidate fails to receive at least 35 per cent of the votes cast at the primary.
F. Alaska, Michigan, Minnesota, Montana, Utah, Washington, and Wisconsin employ an "open" primary in which voters do not need to identify their party membership in order to be able to cast their ballot in either party column.[10] Washington's "blanket primary" goes even further by permitting the voter to roam also between party columns in his choice of candidates, a practice reserved in all other states to voting in general elections only.[11] "Nonpartisan primaries," i.e., direct primaries for offices which do not

[7] V. O. Key, Jr., *Southern Politics in State and Nation* (New York, 1950), p. 439.
[8] Curtis Martin, *Colorado Politics*, 2nd ed. (Denver, 1962), pp. 9–10.
[9] *Book of the States, 1964–1965*, p. 20.
[10] *Ibid.*, p. 20.
[11] Daniel M. Ogden, Jr. and Hugh A. Bone, *Washington Politics* (New York, 1960), pp. 3–4.

TABLE 1. PRIMARY ELECTIONS

| | Dates of 1964 primaries for state officers elected by statewide vote (a) | | General provisions | | |
| | | | Voters receive ballots of | | Nomination of candidates elected by statewide vote* |
State	Primary 1964	Runoff primary (b) 1964	All parties participating	One party	
Alabama	May 5	May 26(c)	—	X	C,P(b,d)
Alaska	Aug. 4	None	X(e)	—	P
Arizona	Sept. 8	None	—	X	P
Arkansas	July 28(f)	Aug. 11	—	X	P(b)
California	June 2	None	—	X	P
Colorado	Sept. 8	None	—	X	P(g)
Connecticut	(h)	None	—	X	X(h)
Delaware	None	None	—	—	C
Florida	May 5	May 26	—	X	P(b)
Georgia	(i)	(i)	—	X	C,P(b,d)
Hawaii	Oct. 3	None	—	X	P
Idaho	Aug. 4	None	—	X	P
Illinois	April 14	None	—	X	P
Indiana	None	None	—	—	C
Iowa	June 1	None	—	X	X(j)
Kansas	Aug. 4	None	—	X	P
Kentucky	May 26	None	—	X	P
	(1965) May 25				
Louisiana	Dec. 7, 1963	Jan. 11	—	X	P(b)
Maine	June 15	None	—	X	P
Maryland	May 19	None	—	X	CP
Massachusetts	Sept. 15	None	—	X	P
Michigan	Aug. 4	None	X	—	CP
Minnesota	Sept. 8	None	X	—	P
Mississippi	June 2	June 27	—	X	P(b)
Missouri	Aug. 4	None	—	X	P
Montana	June 2	None	X	—	P

* Abbreviations: P—direct primary; C—convention; CP—some candidates in direct primary, some in convention; C, P—convention or direct primary; X—combination of direct primary and convention; CX—some candidates in convention, some combination of direct primary and convention.
(a) States which hold primaries for statewide offices in 1965 are indicated by the figure 1965 in parentheses preceding the date.
(b) Run-off primary if necessary.
(c) An act passed in a 1961 special session provides that on the first Tuesday in May, 1962, and every 2 years thereafter until the state is divided into congressional districts a candidate for election may be named by the voters of each of the 9 congressional districts. In those districts where no candidate receives a majority of the votes cast there shall be a runoff primary election on the second Tuesday following the first primary. On the fourth Tuesday following the first primary the voters from the state at large shall nominate 8 candidates for election to the U.S. Congress.
(d) Usually Democratic party nominates in primary and Republican party in convention.
(e) Party-column ballot; voter restricted to marking on one column only.

have party designation are resorted to in many states to nominate candidates for local and judicial posts. Minnesota and Nebraska even hold such primaries to select candidates for their state legislature. All other states use "closed" primaries which are restricted to those voters who have registered their party preference.

G. In order to avoid primary nominations in which candidates win by a mere plurality of the votes cast, a "runoff" or second primary may be required

FOR STATE OFFICERS

| | Dates of 1964 primaries for state officers elected by statewide vote (a) | | General provisions | | |
| | | | Voters receive ballots of | | Nomination of candidates elected |
State	Primary 1964	Runoff primary (b) 1964	All parties participating	One party	by statewide vote *
Nebraska	May 14	None	—	X	P
Nevada	Sept. 1	None	—	X	P
New Hampshire	Sept. 8	None	—	X	P
New Jersey	April 21	None	—	X	P
New Mexico	May 5	None	—	X	X(k)
New York	(l)	None	—	X	CP
North Carolina	June 30	June 27	—	X	P(b)
North Dakota	June 30	None	—	X	P
Ohio	May 5	None	—	X	P
	(1965) May 4	None	—	X	P
Oklahoma	May 5	May 26	—	X	P(b)
Oregon	May 15	None	—	X	P
Pennsylvania	April 28	None	—	X	P
	(1965) May 18	None	—	X	P
Rhode Island	Sept. 15	None	—	X	P
South Carolina	June 9	(m)	—	X	C,P(b,d)
South Dakota	June 2	None	—	X	CX(j)
Tennessee	Aug. 13	None	—	X	P
	(1965) Aug. 10				
Texas	May 2	June 6	—	X	CP(b)
Utah	Aug. 11	None	X	—	X
Vermont	Sept. 8	None	—	X	P
Virginia	(1965) July 13	None	—	X	CP(b)
Washington	Sept. 15	None	X(n)	—	P
West Virginia	May 12	None	—	X	P
Wisconsin	Sept. 8	None	X	—	P
Wyoming	Aug. 18	None	—	X	P

(f) It is provided that the general primary shall be held the second Tuesday in August. However, a preliminary or "preferential" primary is also provided for, to be held two weeks earlier. If a candidate receives a majority of the votes cast for a given office in the preliminary primary, the general primary is not used for that office.

(g) Pre-primary endorsing conventions are usually held.

(h) A post-convention primary can be held during June or July if convention action is contested by a candidate receiving at least 20 per cent of convention vote.

(i) Primary election to be held the second Wednesday in September in 1964 and every year in which a regular general election is held.

(j) If for any office no candidate receives 35 per cent of votes cast at the primary, a convention is held to select a candidate.

(k) Candidates may be put on the primary ballot by petition if not chosen by convention.

(l) Date to be set.

(m) First runoff held two weeks after primary; second runoff held two weeks after that if necessary.

(n) May vote in the primary of more than one party.

SOURCE: *Book of the States, 1964–1965*, p. 20.

in such instances in Alabama, Arkansas, Florida, Georgia, Louisiana, Mississippi, North Carolina, Oklahoma, South Carolina, Texas, and Virginia.

H. Preceding the quadrennial presidential nominating conventions, fifteen states and the District of Columbia provided by law for a presidential preferential primary which is administered separately and distinct from the direct primary (see Table 2).

TABLE 2. STATE PRESIDENTIAL PRIMARIES

State	Type
New Hampshire	Non-binding preference poll; election of delegates who may be pledged to a candidate.
Wisconsin	Election of delegates who may be pledged to a candidate. No write-in votes.
Illinois	Non-binding preference poll. Election of unpledged district delegates; at-large delegates chosen by party committees.
New Jersey	Non-binding preference poll; election of delegates who may be pledged to candidate.
Massachusetts	Non-binding, write-in preference poll; election of delegates who may be pledged to candidate.
Pennsylvania	Preference poll; election of district delegates who may state willingness to be bound by preference poll; at-large delegates chosen by party committees.
Indiana	Preference poll which is binding on delegates (chosen by state convention) for one ballot.
Ohio	Election of delegates who must be pledged to first and second choice candidates.
Nebraska	Non-binding preference poll; election of unpledged district delegates; at-large delegates chosen by party committees.
West Virginia	Non-binding preference poll; election of unpledged delegates. Write-in votes do not count.
Oregon	Binding preference poll; election of delegates who may state preference for candidate on ballot.
Maryland	Binding preference poll; delegates chosen by convention.
Florida	Election of slate of delegates which may be pledged to candidate.
California	Election of slate of delegates either pledged to a presidential candidate or unpledged.
South Dakota	Election of slate of delegates which may be pledged to candidate.

Alabama and New York elect unpledged convention delegates in spring primaries.

SOURCE: From the *New York Herald Tribune*, January 12, 1964 in *National Civic Review*, March, 1964, p. 148.

Under the impact of the Progressive movement, most of the states adopted the direct primary sometime during the first two decades of the twentieth century. Wisconsin, under Robert La Follette's leadership, enacted the first mandatory statewide primary law in 1903.

Reformers like La Follette viewed the direct primary as much superior to the conventions and as one of the most decisive weapons in the battle to liberate the nomination process from the stranglehold of party bosses and machines. It was thought that primaries would return to the rank and file voters what was properly theirs, the right to select the candidate. This would improve the quality of candidates and put an end to the irresponsible wire-pulling and machinations through which party oligarchs controlled raucous conventions and caucuses which had come to resemble more often the atmosphere of a beer garden than that of a deliberative assembly.

Did the voters, so re-enfranchised, actually assert their right to nominate and did the quality of candidates improve in fact? While there is nothing in the research done so far to justify a pronouncement that primary-nominated candidates are clearly superior to those formerly or currently nominated by conventions, the answer to the question of voter participation, on the other hand, is quite simple. Returns from primary elections outside of the South show that rarely more than a fourth to a third of the eligible electorate participate in the direct primary. Blame for this poor showing by the voters is laid to lack of interest, absence of competition, or unwillingness of voters (in the closed primary states) to identify with one or the other party. Those who look to a more centralized party system as a major avenue to more responsible state government can point to findings which substantiate the distinctly decentralizing quality of the primary. One of the most thorough studies of the effect of primaries on central party organizations concluded that:

> Statewide party hierarchies seem to disintegrate under the impact of the influences given free play by the primary. They cannot thrive under repeatedly successful assaults upon their proposals by those who, on the basis of some special or parochial appeal, can manage to win nominations through the primary. Only under rather exceptional sets of circumstances—of party homogeneity, of monopolization of sources of campaign funds, of common desire for victory—can formal party leadership maintain much control over the nominating process. The more common tendency seems to be that competing centers of power—competing informal hierarchies based on localities, regions, groups, personal followings—develop their electoral support in the direct primary.[12]

In some open primary states like California, Michigan, Minnesota, and Wisconsin, party reformers have increasingly resorted to pre-primary endorsements to tie candidates to programs or issues and to concentrate party organization support behind these convention or committee screened individuals. While supporters of the pre-primary endorsements contend that their practice would rid primaries of the popularity or beauty contest quality, critics of such endorsements insist that this represents but another circumvention of the very purpose for which primaries were designed and that this would only return to the bosses and to their "palace guards" the enormous powers over nominations that they once possessed when the convention system was at its prime.

THE POLITICS OF INTEREST GROUPS

American politics on national, state, and local levels have long been characterized by the interaction of relatively weak parties with relatively strong interest groups. In this widely-accepted arrangement the political

12 V. O. Key, Jr., *American State Politics: An Introduction* (New York, 1956), p. 167.

parties working within a functional "division of labor" were to concern themselves mostly with the election of candidates and with the writing of platforms whereas interest groups were to be nonpartisan and to operate primarily as lobbies or pressure groups advocating particular issues or causes. Power relationships in this marriage of convenience as in any marriage consummated under similar circumstances cannot be delineated quite that simply. Major interest groups do not function as parties but the programs and causes they support with money, publicity, lobbyists, and pressure are rarely if ever nonpartisan in their implications. Also, while these groups do not ordinarily select candidates, candidates can and often are made to feel their approval or disapproval with telling consequences at the polls.

No one would be particularly surprised if Republican candidates for statewide office campaigning on a platform of economy in government and opposing further expansions of the "welfare state" should find favorable reception with the local or state Employers' Association, state Chambers of Commerce, state Manufacturers' Association, state Grange, state Farm Bureau Federation, and state taxpayers' associations.

Equally normal would be the support given to a statewide Democratic officeseeker advocating public welfare programs for the state by such groups as C.O.P.E. (AFL-CIO Committee for Political Education), the Farmers' Union, or the United Mine Workers.

These listings of groups can obviously not purport to offer anything approaching an inventory of political inclinations or power. Newspapers, television, and radio may play crucial roles in particular elections with effects that are far from nonpartisan. There are interest groups, however, that are so specialized in their composition and so concerned about the damage they might incur through partisan identification or attachments as to clearly preclude their classification. Among these will be found church councils, Leagues of Women Voters, educational associations, and state Parent-Teacher Associations.

MONEY AND STATE ANTI-CORRUPT PRACTICES ACTS

Campaigns are necessarily expensive. Parties and candidates collect large funds from wealthy contributors and at the special appreciation and testimonial dinners from some of the not so wealthy. Democrats have their Jefferson-Jackson Day dinners; Republicans their Lincoln Day dinners. To replenish their nearly always empty treasuries and to reach also the smaller contributors, parties sponsor Fun Fests, Bean Feeds, Neighbor-to-Neighbor drives and sustaining fund systems which call for regular monthly donations. The American Heritage Foundation through its widely publicized national campaigns repeatedly urges all citizens to contribute "a dollar to the Party of their choice." Despite these and other efforts to have more people contribute to the campaign funds of parties and candidates, the best available studies and estimates indicate that only 10 per cent of the public contributed any money to campaigns and that only 1 per cent of the population continues to provide approximately 90 per cent of the money spent in all elections. This great financial dependence on the few has long been deplored by many practical politicians and the civic-minded as undesirable not only for its failure to involve more people in democratic political processes but for its dangers as well. Which state is free from illustrations where in one election or another unscrupulous individuals or interests did not use or attempt to use their large campaign contributions as weapons to place candidates or officeholders under undue pressure or obligation?

To protect the integrity of the ballot, to insure that public office shall not go to the highest bidder, to keep crime and gambling syndicates from buying candidates, to let the public know who contributes what and how much— these were among the major objectives to which federal and state anti-corrupt practices laws were addressed during the last eighty years. The beginning was relatively easy. Ballot stuffing, bribery, and intimidation caused no great legal problems in definition or in enforcement. Requiring proper identification or labeling of campaign literature also was not too difficult, but when it came to fixing dollar limits on contributions or disbursements, defining legitimate expenditures, determining the nature of required reports to be filed by candidates, parties and committees, or assuring the effective enforcement of these laws, Congress and state legislatures soon found themselves confronted with basic problems of policy and of political reality that are still essentially unresolved.

Presently, candidates for federal office and their financial campaign activities are, of course, subject to the provisions of several statutes—among them the Corrupt Practices Act of 1925, the Hatch Political Activities Act of 1939, and the Taft-Hartley Act of 1947.

Briefly, these laws:

A. Set limits on maximum expenditures by candidates for House and Senate, $5,000 and $25,000, respectively;
B. Prohibit direct campaign contributions by labor unions, national banks, and corporations;
C. Make it a crime to solicit federal employees or state employees connected with activities financed "in whole or in part" by loans or grants from the United States government;
D. Place a maximum of $5,000 on individual contributions;
E. Require the candidates to file periodic reports with the Secretary of the Senate or the Clerk of the House;
F. Limit political committees functioning in two or more states or as subsidiaries of a national committee to collecting or expending not more than $3,000,000 during any calendar year.[13]

Testimony before congressional committees has shown most of these provisions to be unrealistic, unenforceable, and unobeyed. The prescribed

[13] G. Theodore Mitau, "Selected Aspects of Centralized and Decentralized Control over Campaign Finance: A Commentary on S. 636," *University of Chicago Law Review,* Summer, 1956, pp. 623–624.

expenditure maxima are ridiculously low in terms of what is needed to finance a modern campaign. Based on a recent survey of campaign costs in one Midwestern state with a population of less than four million, it costs approximately

$3,500 for a one-half hour statewide TV program
$5,500 for one full page ad in three metropolitan papers
$25,000 for one statewide mailing to voters
$420 for one minute prime time TV rates (one station)
$800 for one newspaper advertisement, ⅓ page with pictures

Estimates generally place total expenditures for a typical senatorial campaign, with a contest in primary and general election, at more than $100,-000.[14]

There are other basic weaknesses in the federal laws. Most of the provisions, for example, are not applicable at all to nominations or primary elections which constitute the critical election in nearly one-third of the states. Yet approximately one-half of all congressional committee chairmen, in House and Senate, are elected in states and districts in which they encounter in the general election almost no opposition whatsoever.

Not all expenditures moreover need to be reported nor are contributions accounted for which involve services or efforts of a character not readily translatable into cash or "something of value." Inevitably, "much voluntary work is involuntary, when it is done under pressure from an employer or a union. . . ."[15] Nor have the explicit prohibitions against corporate or union donations been found to constitute a major legal obstacle to financial and other contributions that these powerful interests wish to make. Individual board members of a corporation may wish to make a cash contribution to the candidate, to his committee, or to his party. Some office facilities and services may be volunteered. Labor groups establish "educational" campaign committees placing newspaper advertisements and posters, or publishing literature favorable to the candidate or his cause. Complimentary editorials may appear in house organs or trade journals. Public endorsements may be voted at organizational meetings or conventions. Membership lists and volunteer workers may be put at the candidate's disposal. There are literally hundreds of ways in which groups and individuals may come to the aid of the candidate without violating at least the letter of these federal election laws or the formal rules of their own organizations. Among the most serious weaknesses of federal (and state) laws other than their inherent vagueness and the widespread reluctance to enforce them has been their tendency to encourage volunteer committees to proliferate and to decentralize to a point where candidates and parties are no longer in the position to exercise effective

[14] League of Women Voters of Minnesota, *Money in Elections: A Study of Corrupt Practices* (Minneapolis, 1960), p. 2.

[15] Herbert E. Alexander, *Money, Politics, and Public Reporting* (Princeton, 1960), p. 26; see also his *Financing the 1960 Election* (Princeton, 1962) and *Responsibility in Party Finance* (Princeton, 1963).

control over their activities which were allegedly undertaken on their behalf and in support of their cause. Too frequently now funds are collected, literature is composed and distributed, and statements or promises made—all without the candidate's knowledge or approval.

Another serious problem has been the relative ease with which wealthy contributors have been able to exceed the nominal limits on individual contributions. This was accomplished by splitting gifts between national, state, and local committees, or by using the names of family members or friends as dodges or dummies. Congressional proposals to close the loopholes in the anti-corrupt practices laws and to assure these statutes more effective enforcement have been numerous. Senate and House committees have urged that state primaries be subjected to federal supervision, that the expenditure ceiling be lifted or removed entirely, that the candidate be given more control over the financial affairs of his own campaign, and that report provisions be tightened and standardized. While something of a consensus may have been reached that without many of these reforms much cynical disobedience and widespread evasion of the law will persist, the consensus has obviously not been sufficiently strong to overcome the resolute opposition of powerful states' rights interests.

Most of the forty-seven state anti-corrupt practices laws (Delaware, Nevada, and Rhode Island are the exceptions) aim at objectives similar to those of the federal laws. They impose limits on expenditures and contributions; they seek to provide the public with some information as to the source and objectives of expenditures, and they prohibit certain types of campaign activities. Yet they vary greatly in their approach and provisions (see Table 3).

A. Four states—Idaho, Mississippi, Vermont, and Washington—place a limit on expenditures in primaries only. Eighteen states have separate limits for primaries and general elections.

B. Thirty-two states require statements of campaign receipts to be filed by either candidates or their committees, whereas thirty-five states demand such reports for campaign disbursements as well.

C. Some states specify dollar limits for the major offices. For governor the limits range from $2,000 in Idaho to $50,000 in Alabama and New Jersey. Some states use a percentage of the office's annual salary. For the office of governor, Iowa and South Dakota, for example, fix a 50 per cent maximum of the annual gubernatorial salary; Kansas, Montana, New Mexico, and Oregon specify 10 per cent. A third group of states including Connecticut, Maryland, Michigan, Missouri, and Virginia base their maxima on a figure determined at least in part by multiplying a given number of cents or dollars per vote by the number of votes cast at the last gubernatorial election for the gubernatorial candidates. Nineteen states—Alaska, California, Colorado, Delaware, Florida, Georgia, Hawaii, Illinois, Louisiana, Maine, Massachusetts, Nebraska, Nevada, North Carolina, Pennsylvania, South Carolina, Texas, Utah, and Washington—impose no maximum limitation whatever on expenditures by the candidate.

D. Thirty-four states prohibit corporations from making contributions and four states—Indiana, New Hampshire, Pennsylvania, and Texas—impose similar restrictions on labor unions.

TABLE 3. LIMITATIONS ON CAMPAIGN

| State or other jurisdiction | Applies to | | Filing of statements required | | | |
	Elections*	Candidates†	Campaign receipts by parties	Campaign receipts by candidates	Campaign disbursements by parties	Campaign disbursements by candidate
Alabama	P,G	Statewide, Sen., Rep.	No	Yes	No	Yes
Alaska	P,G	Statewide, Sen., Rep.	No	No	No	No
Arizona	P,G	Statewide, Sen. (b), Rep. (b),	Yes	Yes	Yes	Yes
Arkansas	–P,G	Statewide, Sen., Rep.	No	No	No	Yes
California	P,G	Statewide, Sen., Rep.	Yes	Yes	Yes	Yes
Colorado	P,G(e)	Statewide, Sen., Rep.	Yes	Yes	Yes	Yes
Connecticut	P,G	Statewide, Sen., Rep.	Yes	Yes	Yes	Yes
Delaware	(g)	(g)	No	No	No	No
Florida	P,G	Statewide, Sen., Rep.	Yes	Yes	Yes	Yes
Georgia	P,G	Statewide, Sen., Rep.	No	No	No	No
Guam	P,G	Statewide	Yes	Yes	Yes	Yes
Hawaii	P,G	Statewide, Sen., Rep.	No	No	Yes(h)	Yes
Idaho	P	Statewide, Sen. , Rep.	No	No	No	Yes
Illinois	(g)	(g)	No	No	No	No
Indiana	P,G	Statewide, Sen., Rep.	Yes	Yes	Yes	Yes
Iowa	P,G	Statewide Sen., Rep.	Yes	Yes	Yes	Yes

ired times for statements	Contributions by corporations prohibited	Contributions by unions prohibited	Contributions from other sources prohibited or limited ‡	Restrictions on character of expenditures	Total expenditures by candidate limited	Amount spent in behalf of candidate limited
in 15 days after a ary and within 30 after a general election	Yes	No	No	Yes	Yes(a)	No
	--	--	No	No	No	No
pts and expenditures election	Yes	No	No	No	Yes(c)	--
pt practice pledge e, candidate expenses election	--	--	No	No	Yes(d)	No
election	No	No	Campaign contributions solicited or received from a licensee by an elective state officer issuing licenses	Yes	No	No
n 10 days after a ry and within 30 after a general or l election	No	No	No	No	No	No
election	Yes	No	Contributions by person under an assumed name	Yes	Yes	No(f)
	No	No	No	No	No	No
e and after election	Yes	No	Limit of $1,000 contribution from any one person; contributions prohibited from holders of horse or dog racing permits and licenses for sale of intoxicating beverages, operators of public utilities franchised or regulated by the state, or partners, officers, or directors of unincorporated or incorporated holders of such permits, licenses or franchises	Yes	No	No
n 20 days after elec-	Yes	No	No	No	No	No
15 days after elec-	No	No	No	--	--	--
20 days	No	No	No	Yes	No	No
20 days after elec-	No	No	No	Yes	Yes(b)	No
	(i)	No	No	No	No	No
30 days after elec-	Yes	Yes	No	Yes	Yes	Yes
dates: within 30 fter election; parties: 30 days after gen- ection	Yes	No(j)	Funds donated by a nonresident person, firm, or corporation may not be used by any person or political organization for the purpose of conducting a campaign for political office	No	Yes	No

TABLE 3 (*continued*)

State or other jurisdiction	Applies to		Filing of statements required			
	Elections *	Candidates †	Campaign receipts by parties	Campaign receipts by candidates	Campaign disbursements by parties	Campaign disbursement candidat
Kansas	P,G	Statewide	Yes	Yes	Yes	Y
Kentucky	P,G	Statewide, Sen., Rep.	No	Yes	No	Y
Louisiana	P.G	Statewide, Sen.,Rep.	No	No	No	I
Maine	P,G	Statewide	Yes	Yes	Yes	Y
Maryland	P,G	Statewide, Sen., Rep.	Yes	Yes	Yes	Y
Massachusetts	P,G	Statewide, Sen., Rep.	Yes	Yes	Yes	Y
Michigan	P,G	Statewide, Sen., Rep.	Yes	Yes	Yes	Y
Minnesota	P,G	Statewide, Sen., Rep.	Yes	Yes	Yes	Y
Mississippi	P	Statewide, Sen., Rep.	No(b)	Yes(b)	No(b)	Y
Missouri	P.G	Statewide, Sen., Rep.	Yes	No	Yes	Y
Montana	P,G	Statewide, Sen., Rep.	Yes	Yes	Yes	Y
Nebraska	P,G	Statewide, Sen., Rep.	Yes	No	Yes	Y
Nevada	(g)	(g)	No	No	No	I

...ired times for ...g statements	Contributions by corporations prohibited	Contributions by unions prohibited	Contributions from other sources prohibited or limited ‡	Restrictions on character of expenditures	Total expenditures by candidate limited	Amount spent in behalf of candidate limited
r election	Yes	No	No	Yes	Yes	No
ays before and 30 days r election	Yes	No	Persons with whom candidate must deal in his official capacity	Yes	Yes	Yes
e	Yes	No	All state and city classified employees; members of state and city civil service commissions; registrars of voters and employees; certain classified police and firemen; all municipal officers and employees operating under commission form of government	No	No	No
iminary report not less 10 nor more than 15 before election; final rt within 30 days after ion	No	No	No	Yes	No	No
in 20 days after elec-	Yes	No	Limit of $2,500 contribution by any one source not a candidate	Yes	Yes(k)	Yes
in 14 days after pri-; second Tuesday preg general election and in 14 days after general ion	Yes	No	By public officers or employees	Yes	No	No
election but before fication to office	Yes	No	No	Yes	Yes	Yes
s before and within 10 following primary; 8 before and 10 days fol-g general election	Yes	No	No	Yes	Yes	Yes
ribution statements 1st and 15th each h of campaign	No	No	No	No	Yes	Yes
in 30 days after elec-	Yes	No	No	No	Yes	No
idates, within 10 days election; parties, with-days after election	Yes	No	No	No	Yes(l)	No
election	Yes	Only if union is a corpotion	No	Yes	No	No
--------------------	No	No	No	No	No	No

TABLE 3 (*continued*)

| State or other jurisdiction | Applies to | | Filing of statements required | | | |
	Elections *	Candidates †	Campaign receipts by parties	Campaign receipts by candidates	Campaign disbursements by parties	Campaign disbursements by candidates
New Hampshire	P,G	Statewide, Sen., Rep.	Yes	Yes	Yes	Yes
New Jersey	P,G	Statewide, Sen., Rep.	Yes	Yes	Yes	Yes
New Mexico	P,G	Statewide, Sen., Rep.	Yes	Yes	Yes	Yes
New York	P,G	Statewide, Sen., Rep.	Yes	Yes	Yes	Yes
North Carolina	(g)	(g)	Yes	Yes	Yes (in general elections)	Yes
North Dakota	P,G	Statewide, Sen., Rep.	No	No	No	Yes
Ohio	P,G	Statewide, Rep.	Yes	Yes	Yes	Yes
Oklahoma	P,G	Statewide, Sen., Rep.	Yes	No	Yes	Yes
Oregon	P,G	Statewide, Sen., Rep.	Yes	Yes	Yes	Yes
Pennsylvania	P,G	Statewide, Sen., Rep.	Yes	Yes	Yes	Yes
Puerto Rico	(g)	(g)	No	No	Yes(t)	No
Rhode Island	(g)	(g)	No corrupt practices act (t)			--
South Carolina	P,G	Statewide, Sen., Rep.	No	No	No	Yes
South Dakota	P,G	Statewide, Sen., Rep.	Yes	Yes	Yes	Yes
Tennessee	P,G	Statewide, Sen., Rep.	No	No	Yes	Yes
Texas	P,G	Statewide, Sen., Rep.	No	Yes	No	Yes

ed times for statements	Contributions by corporations prohibited	Contributions by unions prohibited	Contributions from other sources prohibited or limited †	Restrictions on character of expenditures	Total expenditures by candidate limited	Amount spent in behalf of candidate limited
tement Wednesday s) before; 2nd, second (10 days) after elec-n)	Yes	Yes	Any partnership as such or any partner acting in behalf of such partnership; any person employed in the classified service of the state; a personal contribution in excess of $5,000 except by candidate himself; or a contribution if made anonymously, or in guise of a loan, or concealed, or without knowledge of candidate or his agents or political committee	Yes	Yes(a)	Yes
or Saturday before days after election	Yes(i)	No	No	Yes	Yes	No
dates, within 10 days lections; parties, 30 days after election	No	No	No money of political party may be spent on behalf of primary candidate	No	Yes(o)	No
and after elections	Yes	No	Contributions by owners of polling places barred	No	Yes	Yes
and after elections	Yes	No	No	No	No	No
s after elections	Yes	No	A contribution made or received under other than the donor's own name	Yes	Yes(p)	Yes
0 P.M. 45th day after n	Yes	No	No	Yes	Yes	No
dates within 15 days ny election; party ign committees with-ays after any general n	Yes	No	No	No	Yes	Yes
s after election	(q)	No	----------------------	Yes	Yes(l,r)	No
30 days after each y and general elec-	Yes	Yes	No	Yes	No	No
first 10 days of each	No	No	Individual contributions are restricted up to the amount of $300 in an election year, and $200 in other years	(s)	No	No
elections	No	No	No	Yes	No	No
30 days after elec-	Yes	No	No	Yes	Yes(u)	Yes
ate's statement 5 to s before convention ion; manager's with-ays after	Yes	No	No	No	Yes	Yes
and after elections	Yes	Yes	No	Yes	No	Yes

TABLE 3   (continued)

| State or other jurisdiction | Applies to | | Filing of statements required | | | |
	Elections *	Candidates†	Campaign receipts by parties	Campaign receipts by candidates	Campaign disbursements by parties	Camp. disbu ment. candi.
Utah	P,G	Statewide, Sen., Rep.	Yes	Yes	Yes	Y
Vermont	P	Statewide, Sen., Rep.	No	No	No	Y
Virginia	P,G	Statewide, Sen., Rep.	---	---	---	Y
Washington	P	Statewide, (v) Sen., Rep.	No	Yes	No	Y
West Virginia	P,G	Statewide, Sen., Rep.	Yes	Yes	Yes	Y
Wisconsin	P,G	Statewide, Sen., Rep.	Yes	Yes	Yes	Y
Wyoming	P,G	Statewide, Sen., Rep.	Yes	Yes	Yes	Y

* P—primary election; G—general election.
† The abbreviations Sen. and Rep. in this column stand for United States Senator and United States Represei
‡ This column only shows prohibitions and restrictions on sources and limitations on amounts of contributions.
  not include procedural limitations such as prohibitions on making gifts directly to candidates shortly before ele
(a) Newspaper and radio advertising exempt.
(b) Only in primary election.
(c) Expenditures limited at primary election, exclusive of money expended for stationery, postage, printing a
    vertisements in newspapers, motion pictures, radio and television broadcasts, outdoor advertising sig
    necessary personal, traveling or subsistence expenses.
(d) Travel and hotel expenses of candidate exempted.
(e) Also applies to special elections to fill vacancies in U.S. Congress.
(f) If spent by independent political committee.
(g) No limitation.
(h) By agent or committee acting for or on behalf of any candidate.
(i) Illinois: by insurance corporations only; New Jersey: by public utilities, banks and insurance corporat
(j) State statute prohibits contribution only if union is a corporation.
(k) Postage, telegrams, telephoning, stationery, printing, advertising, radio and television programs, publish
    pressage, travel and board exempted.
(l) Expenditures of relatives and associates deemed to be those of candidate himself.

Enacting anti-corrupt practices statutes is one thing; enforcing them is quite another. In most of the public efforts to help keep elections honest reliance was placed on three major forms of sanctions: (1) public disclosure of the source and expenditures of campaign finances; (2) specified criminal penalties for failure to obey the anti-corrupt practices laws; and (3) disqualification of the candidate; this would preclude a candidate from appearing on the ballot, or if already elected, it would bar him from serving in an office which he may have reached through fraudulent or corrupt campaign practices.

red times for statements	Contributions by corporations prohibited	Contributions by unions prohibited	Contributions from other sources prohibited or limited ‡	Restrictions on character of expenditures	Total expenditures by candidate limited	Amount spent in behalf of candidate limited
at. after 1st disburse-; 2nd Sat. each calen-onth thereafter; Sat. ding any primary or on	Yes	No	No	Yes	No	No
n 10 days after pri-	No	No	No	No	Yes	Yes
n 30 days after elec-caucus, convention or ry election	- - -	- - -	No	Yes	Yes	- - - - -
primary only	No	No	No	No	No	No
and after elections	Yes	No	No	Yes	Yes	Yes
P.M. on Tues. preced-imary or election; Sat. ing primary or elec-	Yes	No	Contributions by cooperative associations	Yes	Yes	No
n 20 days after elec-	Yes	No	No	Yes	Yes(w)	Yes

andidates for State Senator or Representative to the General Court who have expended a sum in excess of $200 re required to file second statement only (not later than second Friday after primary or election).
andidate's contribution to the state committee, his filing fee, personal travel and subsistence expenses, or services f his regular employees in discharging duties of a public office, are exempt.
xclusive of sums expended for necessary personal, traveling or subsistence expenses. No limit for candidate for tate Representative in primary election.
xpenses for personal travel and printing in state publicity pamphlet exempted.
ertain corporations only.
rimary election: 15 per cent of 1 year's compensation or salary of office for which candidate; General election: 0 per cent of 1 year's compensation or salary for which candidate. Not restricted to less than $250.
ct No. 110, 1957, created an electoral fund against which each principal political party in the commonwealth an draw up to $75,000 annually, or up to $150,000 in election years. The act enumerates the character of the xpenditures which can be paid from the fund.
nly restrictions are those imposed by federal statutes.
rinting or circulation of written or printed matter exempted.
artisan primaries only.
raveling expenses exempted.

E: *Book of the States, 1964–1965*, pp. 26–29.

Have these sanctions proved effective? Generally, no, and for these reasons:

A. Unrealistically low limits, where maxima were specified, contribute to the evasion of law.
B. In more than one-half of the states the amounts spent on behalf of a candidate (but not by the candidate or under his direction) are not subject to any limits.
C. Report forms lack standardization.
D. County attorneys may be loath to proceed against members of their party and wash dirty linen in public.

E. Filing officers, secretaries of state, or auditors are not required by law to verify or investigate the reports submitted to them.

F. Nearly one-half of the states permit broad classes of exempted expenditures (personal travel, maintenance, correspondence, etc.) for which no reports need be made.

G. Many state courts have so interpreted the anti-corrupt practices statutes as to make it extremely difficult to fix effective responsibility on the candidate for violations of the law by committees or individuals working for his election, unless the prosecution could prove that these illegal campaign activities were either authorized or encouraged by the candidate personally.

Experimentation with strengthening and improving these laws continues. Preferring reliance on public disclosure, California, Florida, Nebraska, North Carolina, and Texas eliminated the meaningless fixed ceilings on total expenditures. To broaden the base of campaign contributors and at the same time to acknowledge the significance of legitimate sources of money for the effective operations of elections, Minnesota (1955), California (1957), Missouri (1961), and Hawaii (1963) enacted statutes which allow limited income tax deductions for political contributions. Minnesota additionally permits candidates for various offices to deduct from their gross incomes for personal campaign expenditures up to a maximum of $5,000 (for governor or United States senator).

The last decade's most basic revisions, however, were made in Florida. More clearly than any other anti-corrupt practices statute, the 1951 Florida law insists on centralizing responsibility for all campaign finances in primary and general elections in the candidate or in his personally designated agent, the campaign treasurer. No campaign contributions can be received and no disbursements authorized without the explicit and written approval of the treasurer. There is to be one single bank depository through which all funds are to be channeled. For one month preceding an election treasurers are to submit weekly reports of contributions and expenditures to the secretary of state or in case of countywide offices to the county clerk.

Among the other major provisions are the following:

A. No contributions can be received within five days of an election.

B. Within fifteen days after an election a complete accounting must be filed.

C. No limits are imposed on either contributions or expenditures although no individual can contribute more than $1,000 per election.

D. Corporations, labor unions, public utilities, holders of liquor licenses or horse or dog racing permits are prohibited from making campaign contributions.

E. No expenditures can be made without written authorization.

F. All reports, orders for payment, deposit slips, and vouchers must be completed on proper forms prescribed by law.

For determining a candidate's campaign finance operations—who contributed how much and for what purposes was the money spent—Florida relies primarily on careful public scrutiny of comprehensive, standardized, and published reports by the secretary of state of receipts and disbursements prepared by the candidate or by his agent.[16]

After the Florida law was successfully tested and widely acclaimed in four separate elections, the National Municipal League decided to incorporate its provisions, with some revisions, in a *Model State Campaign Contributions and Expenditures Law*. The strong public disclosure feature, to many commentators one of the major advances in this type of law, represents to some of the critics an undesirable interference by the state with a person's freedom to back his secret ballot with an equally secret contribution. Other critics are unwilling to further burden an already harassed candidate with the additional responsibilities that the *Model*'s centralized accounting provisions would necessitate.

Still very much at issue is the idea of a government subsidy to political campaigns, first proposed in this country by Theodore Roosevelt in 1907, as a positive measure to assure the electorate effective political alternatives and to free candidates and political parties from undesirable obligations to narrow or special interests. An indirect scheme of such subsidization is incorporated in such tax deductibility laws as those of Minnesota and California. Puerto Rico's Election Fund Act of 1957 on the other hand provides for major governmental assistance to parties and candidates in the belief that:

> [I]t is . . . in the public interest that political parties be free from the control of economic forces, private or governmental, which upon becoming necessary for the financing of the normal legitimate activities of political parties, might gain a control or influence over them that could be inimical to the democratic ideal. . . .

> [T]he Legislature thinks it wise that, on the one hand large monetary contributions to political parties be forbidden, and, on the other hand, that these democratic organizations be adequately provided the funds for the fulfillment of their most essential functions, independently of each citizen's duty to contribute toward the support of his political party small sums compatible with his income and with such standards as each party may set up. . . .[17]

Under the terms of this act the principal parties of Puerto Rico (those parties receiving at least 10 per cent of the vote for governor) may draw annually on the election fund for an amount not exceeding $75,000. In election years they are entitled to a grant of $150,000 plus a maximum of up to 50 per cent of its annual allotment that may not have been spent in a non-election year. Besides such subsidies parties may also solicit voluntary contributions from individuals. No person may contribute more than $200 to a local party organization nor more than $300 to the central organization in an election year. Party treasurers have the responsibility of keeping complete records and reports and

16 For an evaluation of the Florida law, see Elston Roady, "Ten Years of Florida's 'Who Gave It—Who Got It' Law," *Law and Contemporary Problems*, Summer, 1962, pp. 434–454.

17 The Election Fund Act of 1957, quoted in Henry Wells, *Government Financing of Political Parties in Puerto Rico* (Princeton, 1961), p. 35.

submitting proper vouchers to the commonwealth secretary of the treasury for payment directly to the creditors of the respective political parties for services rendered or supplies or equipment furnished. Section 5 of the act which enumerates a very large category of operating expenses towards which disbursements may be made includes the following:

> [R]ental of central offices; telephone and telegraph services in Puerto Rico; office supplies and equipment; light, water, and power service; radio broadcast, telecast and moving pictures for propaganda in Puerto Rico; travel expenses within Puerto Rico on political missions, and political advertisements in Puerto Rico newspapers; printing of party programs; postage, distribution and transportation of propaganda material in Puerto Rico relative to the political campaign or the election in Puerto Rico; expenses for general and special elections, referendums, primaries, conventions, assemblies, and registrations in Puerto Rico; printed matter, recordings, political propaganda material, symbols, flags, political propaganda films to be exhibited in Puerto Rico, including equipment, materials and machinery for the production thereof and such other expenses thereby incurred to implement and carry out in Puerto Rico the provisions of this act.[18]

While the act seemed to operate quite well between 1957 and 1959, "pressures of desperation" forced widespread violations during the 1960 election. "The basic trouble was that all three parties participating in the subsidy program . . . used up their allotments well in advance of the peak of the campaign [the one which included the unprecedented intervention of Puerto Rico's Roman Catholic bishop]. Their efforts to raise enough money from private contributors to make up the difference between allotments and expenses either failed to produce adequate results or aroused doubts and suspicions concerning the methods used." [19] It appeared that Puerto Rico's Popular Democratic party (Muñoz-Marin) proceeded to invoke the old "quota system" by which public employees "volunteered" a percentage of their salaries (in violation of the Civil Service law) while the Statehood party found wealthy Republicans who were willing to come to the aid of their cause even to the point of exceeding the law's limits on individual contributions.

United States congressional efforts to subsidize political parties and candidates directly have so far been unsuccessful. Under a fair election finance bill that was proposed in 1961 by Senators Neuberger, Douglas, Clark, Gruening, and Morse, the federal government would provide assistance in primary and general elections for broadcast and television time, for general campaign expenditures (in a total amount not exceeding 5 cents multiplied by the average vote in the state or congressional district for the contested office), for state voters' pamphlets, and for campaign correspondence. As a condition precedent for obtaining such subsidies, a candidate would have to certify that neither he nor his agents would receive "any gift, loan, or other contribution of money or property, exceeding $100 from any individual." Nothing came of this measure. Considerable pressure persists, however, in-

18 *Ibid.*, pp. 37–38.
19 *Ibid.*, p. 31.

side and outside of Congress to at least require television and radio stations to go beyond public service time now allotted equally to major candidates under the provisions of Section 315 (a) of the Federal Communications Act and to demand of these stations additional time for candidates or for their representatives as a condition of doing business under a federal license. As might be expected the response of the communications industry has been somewhat less than enthusiastic. Aside from considerations of costs, some of the industry's spokesmen have long based their opposition on the fear of excessive government involvement and on the likelihood of partisanship in the administration of such subsidies.

As campaign costs continue to climb, the search goes on to find new programs which might broaden the base of financing politics. Parties and candidates consider it increasingly necessary to persuade millions of additional small contributors to back their votes with their dollars. To devise methods which would attract these badly-needed funds, all sorts of suggestions have been advanced by scholars, journalists, practical politicians, and writers. Included among a wide range of suggestions are these: placing party membership on a dues-paying basis; national advertising campaigns which would dramatize the democratic imperative of having all citizens make a financial investment in politics; contests and competition to determine which party could attract the largest number of small contributors; a tax assignment subsidy plan which would "allot to political parties one-half cent out of every dollar of federal income tax, with each individual taxpayer allowed to choose for himself which party should receive *his* share of support." [20]

Strong concern for improving the fund-raising capabilities of political parties and for strengthening their fiscal responsibilities to the public also permeated many of the recommendations of the President's Commission on Campaign Costs (1962).

Among the more specific and controversial recommendations (most of which because of the nature of the commission's charge dealt only with the financing of *presidential* campaigns) are the following:

A. Tax incentives for contributors (maximum income tax credit of $10 per year, or as an alternative, a maximum total deduction for political contributions of not more than $1,000 per tax return);
B. Full and effective disclosure in place of unenforceable and ineffective limits on contributions and expenditures;
C. Prohibition of partisan campaign contributions and expenditures by corporations and labor unions;
D. Temporary suspension of Section 315 of the Federal Communications Act (on a continued, experimental basis) to make it possible for networks and radio-television licensees to bring to the public the campaign presentations of presidential and vice presidential nominees "without charge to them." [21]

[20] Herbert E. Alexander (ed.), *Money for Politics: A Miscellany of Ideas* (Princeton, 1963), p. 42; see also his *Tax Incentives for Political Contributions* (Princeton, 1961).
[21] President's Commission on Campaign Costs, *Financing Presidential Campaigns* (Washington, 1962), pp. 14, 17, 20, 24–27.

THE LEGAL SETTING OF ELECTIONS—CANDIDATES, VOTERS
CALENDARS, AND THE COUNTING OF VOTES

Qualifications for state officials are found either in state constitutions or in state statutes. For governors the age requirements range from a minimum of twenty-five in Arizona and Minnesota to a maximum of thirty-five in Hawaii, the typical age being thirty. Minimum age for members of the state Houses is usually set at twenty-one, and for state Senates at twenty-five. For the judiciary, the minimum age for trial justices tends to be 21 or 25, whereas members of the appellate courts would more likely be 30. Most states now specify that judges must "be learned in the law." In addition to setting out a minimum age, all states require candidates to be citizens of the United States and to satisfy certain residence requirements. Legislators ordinarily must have lived in their districts for one year before they are eligible to represent them. Seven states insist on two years; five, on five years; and seven years are required in Alabama and Pennsylvania.

To obtain a place on the primary ballot candidates for all major offices in most of the states must file their intent for office and pay a nominal filing fee within a sixty- to ninety-day period before the primary election. For statewide and congressional offices this filing process is usually transacted at the office of the secretary of state. County auditors or county or city clerks may serve as filing officers to candidates for county elective positions. In filing for primaries in connection with party-designated offices, the candidate may be required to prove his party affiliation.

A candidate nominated neither by convention nor by primary in a majority of the states can still have his name placed on the general election ballot through the device of a nominating petition with a fixed number of signatures which must be submitted generally at least a month before the election. How many citizens will have to sign the petition for such an "independent" candidate depends on the nature of the office and varies somewhat from state to state. For a statewide office it may require as many as a number equal to 1 per cent of the total vote cast for governor at the preceding election; for congressional office, 5 per cent of the preceding congressional total in the district and for county office an even higher percentage. For obvious reasons neither political party is very eager to smooth the path of candidates or new parties that seek to attain office via the nominating petition.

Voters must be citizens of the United States, must be twenty-one years old (except for Alaska, 19; Georgia and Kentucky, 18; and Hawaii, 20), and must meet certain residence and registration requirements. In nineteen states a voter may also be asked to take and pass a literacy test before he can be declared eligible to receive a ballot.

Voter residence requirements for state, county, and election district vary somewhat (see Table 4). The most common pattern prescribes a twelve-month period for the state, sixty to ninety days for the county, and thirty days for the precinct. Payments of poll taxes as a prerequisite to voting were still demanded by law in Alabama, Arkansas, Mississippi, Texas, and Virginia until 1964.

As to voter registration, the great majority of the states now employ a permanent system whereby voters remain on the rolls unless they fail to exercise their franchise at least once during a consecutive number of years, usually four. Only about a dozen states insist that voters re-register periodically.

Voters who cannot personally appear at the polls to cast their ballots due to such factors as illness, military service, physical disability or religious holidays, and in some states, for absence due to business travel, may apply for an absentee ballot in forty-four states. Generally, it is either the city clerk or county auditor who is required to process these applications and mail out absentee ballots a week or two ahead of the election. After marking the ballot in secret, the voter places it in an envelope, seals the envelope, inserts it in a larger envelope which he then signs in the presence of an attesting witness (postmaster or notary public) and mails the entire set back to the election office in time so that it can be counted on the day of election.

The fact that elections for federal office are held in November of the even-numbered years has left its impact on state election calendars. Although state legislatures have the power to schedule elections for state offices independently, only four states—Kentucky, Mississippi, New Jersey, and Virginia—decided to base their elections on the odd-numbered years. Louisiana, in a category by itself, votes for the state legislature and for such state-wide offices as governor, lieutenant governor, secretary of state and eight others in the spring of the even-numbered years, and for some of its judges on the appellate bench in November when ballots are cast for federal office.

Primary elections may come in April, May, June, August, or September—no single month being popular with more than 11 states. Despite these variations between states, the calendar of primaries within a state tends to be fairly stable and traditional. And when it is not, as was the case in New York in 1959, 1960, and 1961, where three different months were set for three successive primaries, the explanations are likely political. In 1961, for example, the legislative leadership of the majority party in Albany was convinced that a primary scheduled in September rather than in June would help to accentuate the family squabbles among the Democrats and would thus make more attractive and promising the Republican nomination for mayor of New York. It was not to work out this way, however.

Where it is necessary to conduct a run-off primary (see Table 1), three weeks is the common interval between it and the first primary. Election dates for local offices, city, town, and school board are either set by local charters or by state statute.

TABLE 4. VOTING RESIDENCE REQUIREMENTS

State	Requirements			
	State	County	Election district, precinct, or ward	Township, municipality, town, or city
Alabama	2 years	1 year	3 months [1]	
Alaska	1 year		30 days [2]	
Arizona	do.[3]	30 days	do.	
Arkansas	do.	6 months	do.	
California	do.[4]	3 months [5]	54 days	
Colorado	do.[6]	do.[5]	15 days	30 days.
Connecticut	do.[7]			6 months.[8]
Delaware	do.	3 months	30 days	
Florida	do.	6 months		
Georgia	do.	do.		
Hawaii	do.		3 months	
Idaho	6 months [7]	30 days		
Illinois	1 year [7]	3 months [5]	30 days	
Indiana	6 months		do.	2 months.[9]
Iowa	do.	2 months [5]		
Kansas	do.[10]		30 days	30 days.
Kentucky	1 year	6 months	2 months [9]	
Louisiana	do.	do.	3 months	4 months.[11]
Maine	6 months [12]	3 months [8][13]		3 months.
Maryland	1 year	6 months	6 months [8]	
Massachusetts	do.[12]			6 months.[8]
Michigan	6 months			30 days.
Minnesota	do.		30 days	
Mississippi	2 years		1 year [14]	
Missouri	1 year [7]	2 months [9]	2 months [9]	
Montana	do.	30 days		

[1] Otherwise qualified electors who have moved to a new precinct in the same county, town, or city may vote in their old precincts.
[2] In election district.
[3] New residents may vote for presidential electors if they were or would have been qualified to vote in State from which they moved.
[4] New residents in the State may vote for President and Vice President only, after 54 days of residence.
[5] 90 days.
[6] New residents may vote for presidential electors after 6 months in State if otherwise qualified.
[7] New residents in the State may vote for President and Vice President only, after 60 days of residence.
[8] No elector who has changed his residence from one county, precinct, or town to another loses his right to vote in his former county, precinct, or town until he acquires voting residence in the new one.
[9] 60 days.

THE VOTING PROCESS—THE PLACE, THE BALLOTS, AND THE ELECTION OFFICIALS

Votes are cast at a centrally-located public place—schoolhouse, fire station, or town hall—within an election precinct or district designated usually by city councils or county boards. Polling booths must assure the secrecy of the ballot and be sufficiently numerous to handle the flow of voters during a typical twelve-hour election period. Officials on duty at the polling place include election judges, clerks, and, in some states, party-appointed "watchers" or "challengers." These election officers who may be designated by their

State	Requirements			
	State	County	Election district, precinct, or ward	Township, municipality, town, or city
Nebraska	6 months [3]	40 days	10 days	3 months.
Nevada	do.	30 days	do.	
New Hampshire	do.		6 months	6 months
New Jersey	do.[15][16]	2 months [9]		15 days.[17]
New Mexico	1 year	3 months [5]		
New York	do.[18]	4 months	30 days	
North Carolina	do.		do.	
North Dakota	do.	3 months [5]	do.[9]	
Ohio	do.[3]	40 days [8]	40 days	
Oklahoma	do.	6 months	30 days	
Oregon	6 months [3]	30 days	do.	
Pennsylvania	1 year [19]		2 months	
Rhode Island	do.			6 months.
South Carolina	do.[3][20]	6 months	3 months	
South Dakota	do.	3 months [5]	30 days	
Tennessee	do.	do.		
Texas	do.	6 months	6 months	
Utah	do.	4 months	2 months [9]	
Vermont	do.			3 months.
Virginia	do.	6 months	30 days	6 months.
Washington	do.	3 months [5]	do.	
West Virginia	do.	2 months [5]		
Wisconsin	do.[21]		10 days	
Wyoming	do.	2 months	do.	
District of Columbia	do.			

[10] New residents with 45 days' residence in township or precinct may vote for presidential electors only.
[11] Municipality.
[12] New residents may vote for presidential electors after 30 days' residence in State.
[13] "Plantation."
[14] Ministers and wives may vote after 6 months' residence.
[15] 40-day residence requirement when voting for President and Vice President.
[16] State constitution amended but further legislative action necessary.
[17] In city of 4th class.
[18] New residents may vote for presidential electors after 90 days if otherwise qualified.
[19] 6 months if previously a qualified elector or native of Pennsylvania.
[20] Public school teachers and spouses may vote after 6 months' residence.
[21] 10-day precinct residence requirement when voting for President and Vice President.

SOURCE: *Congressional Record*, June 22, 1964, p. 14167.

local governmental units assist in checking voters against the registration lists, handing out ballots, operating the voting machines, counting of ballots, and perparing of reports showing the election returns for their respective precincts. In many states these officials are charged also with enforcing provisions against campaigning or distributing campaign literature in or near polling places.

About one-half of the electorate no longer casts paper ballots into a ballot box, but uses the more efficient and speedier voting machines. Costing approximately between $1,500 and $2,000 per unit, these machines are mechanically operated. Upon entering, the voter pulls a bar which closes the

TABLE 5. VOTING TURNOUT

1920	1940	1960	1964	State	Residence in state under 1 year	No literacy test	Permanent registration
63.8	80.3	80.1	77.0	Utah	—	+	+
53.3	69.9	77.0	76.3	Minn.	+	+	(+)
57.9	75.1	80.7	75.3	Idaho	+	+	+
67.8	81.4	77.3	74.5	W. Va.	—	+	+
71.0	79.8	76.9	73.3	Ind.	+	+	+
53.1	78.4	75.7	72.9	Ill.	—	+	+
56.6	72.4	79.4	72.9	N. H.	+	—	+
52.8	79.5	78.3	72.6	S. Dak.	—	+	—
63.7	74.1	76.5	72.0	Iowa	+	+	(+)
43.6	67.4	76.8	71.7	Conn.	—	—	+
45.9	69.6	73.4	70.5	Wis.	—	+	(+)
69.5	76.8	73.6	70.2	Del.	—	—	+
45.4	72.2	74.0	69.9	Wyo.	—	—	(+)
55.8	69.6	71.4	69.5	Mont.	—	+	+
47.3	61.8	72.4	68.8	Mich.	+	+	+
41.4	62.7	72.5	67.8	Vt.	—	+	—
63.7	75.2	78.5	67.3	N. Dak.	—	+	n o
48.0	69.6	71.8	67.2	N. J.	+	+	+
51.7	76.9	71.4	67.1	Colo.	—	+	+
41.2	69.5	76.1	67.1	Mass.	—	—	+
48.2	64.3	72.3	67.1	Oreg.	+	—	+
56.8	72.3	71.3	66.5	Ohio	—	+	(+)
47.3	67.4	75.1	66.3	R. I.	—	+	+
41.6	60.2	72.6	65.0	Maine	+	—	+
36.7	64.2	70.5	65.0	Pa.	—	+	+
46.5	66.5	72.3	64.6	Wash.	—	—	+
55.7	74.0	70.3	63.8	Kans.	+	+	(+)
56.9	64.4	62.1	63.6	N. Mex.	—	+	+
51.8	73.6	71.4	63.2	Nebr.	+	+	(+)
65.4	73.3	71.8	62.9	Mo.	—	+	(+)
40.7	66.9	67.4	62.7	Calif.	—	—	+
47.6	60.3	63.8	62.4	Okla.	—	—	+
44.5	67.4	67.0	61.9	N. Y.	—	—	(+)
49.7	55.7	57.2	56.6	Md.	—	+	(+)
35.4	52.0	54.5	54.6	Ariz.	—	—	+
52.1	70.6	61.2	54.5	Nev.	+	+	+
—	—	51.3	53.4	Hawaii	—	—	+
71.2	59.3	59.2	52.6	Ky.	—	+	+
44.5	42.6	53.5	52.2	N. C.	—	—	+
35.3	30.6	50.3	51.2	Tenn.	—	+	+
21.2	18.2	41.1	50.1	Ark.	—	+	n o
36.0	39.8	50.0	49.9	Fla.	—	+	(+)
13.6	27.1	44.8	47.1	La.	—	—	(+)
19.8	27.0	41.8	44.0	Tex.	—	+	n o
19.1	22.0	33.4	40.9	Va.	—	+	+
—	—	45.5	40.0	Alaska	—	+	n o
10.4	17.6	30.4	29.4	Ga.	—	—	+
8.6	10.1	30.5	38.5	S. C.	—	—	—
20.8	18.9	31.1	34.1	Ala.	—	—	+
9.6	14.7	25.5	33.2	Miss.	—	+	—

curtain behind him and readies the machine for action. The names of candidates and the wording of propositions are arranged across the face of the machine with levers above or below each which, when pulled, will register the vote on an enclosed tape. At the close of the polls, the machine will be un-

AND ELECTION LAW *

General civilian absentee registration permitted	Precinct registration	Registration closes within 1 month of election	Civilian absentee vote	Mere absence a ground for absentee vote	Absentee ballot application by mail	Polls open 12 hours or longer	Presidential voting by new residents	Presidential voting by former residents
+	+	+	+	+	+	+	−	−
+	−	+	+	+	+	+	−	−
+	+	+	+	+	+	+	+	−
+	+	−	+	−	+	+	−	−
−	−	+	+	−	+	+	−	−
−	+	+	+	+	+	+	+	−
−	−	+	+	+	+	(+)	--	−
−	−	+	+	+	+	−	−	−
+	+	+	+	−	+	+	−	−
−	−	+	+	+	+	+	+	+
+	−	+	+	+	+	(+)	+	+
−	+	+	+	−	+	+	−	−
+	+	+	+	+	+	−	−	+
+	+	−	+	+	+	(+)	−	−
+	+	+	+	+	+	+	−	−
−	−	+	+	−	+	(+)	−	+
registration			+	+	+	+	−	+
−	−	−	ǀ	+	+	+	+	+
−	(+)	+	+	+	+	+	+	−
−	+	−	+	+	+	(+)	+	−
+	+	+	+	+	+	+	+	−
+	−	+	+	−	+	+	+	−
−	(+)	−	+	+	+	(+)	−	−
−	−	+	+	+	+	+	+	−
−	+	−	+	−	+	+	−	−
−	+	+	+	+	+	+	−	−
+	−	+	+	+	+	(+)	+	−
+	+	+	−	−	−	+	+	−
+	−	+	+	+	+	+	+	−
−	−	+	+	+	+	+	+	−
−	+	−	+	+	+	(+)	−	−
+	(+)	+	+	−	+	+	−	−
−	+	−	+	+	+	(+)	−	+
+	−	−	+	+	+	+	+	+
−	+	+	+	−	−	−	−	−
+	+	+	+	+	+	−	−	−
−	+	−	+	+	+	+	−	−
−	(+)	+	+	+	+	+	−	−
−	−	+	+	+	+	−	−	−
registration			+	−	+	−	−	−
−	(+)	+	+	+	+	+	−	−
−	+	+	+	+	−	+	−	−
registration			+	+	+	(+)	−	−
−	+	+	+	−	+	+	−	−
registration			+	−	+	+	−	−
−	−	−	+	+	+	+	−	−
−	+	+	−	−	−	−	−	−
−	+	+	+	−	−	−	−	−
+	−	−	−	−	−	−	−	−

* The information in this chart has been checked with responsible officials in every state. In certain instances, it has not been feasible to show in detail specific exceptions to general provisions.

KEY: + = statewide, (+) = some areas only.

SOURCE: *Report of the President's Commission on Registration and Voting Participation* (Washington, 1963), p. 65. Data for 1964 taken from *Congressional Quarterly Weekly Reports*, November 13, 1964, p. 2670.

locked, the tape removed, and the running totals recorded on a precinct tally sheet.

Of particular interest to communities with rapidly expanding populations are recent developments in electronic voting equipment which promise faster, less expensive, and even more accurate tallies.

> Four systems have been developed to the point of actual production for use. Two, the Colemen Electronic Vote Tally System and the Votronics Vote Counter, are vote-tabulating devices using the customary paper ballot and tabulating them electronically. The other two are the Harris Votomatic System and the Coyle Electronic Voting Machines which are based upon a different principle, using a tabulating card as the ballot. Centralized counting, using conventional electronic tabulating equipment, in many cases already in use for other purposes, is an integral part of three of these systems and may also be used in the fourth.[22]

Ballots whether on paper or on a voting machine are usually of two main types; both types are sometimes called the Australian or secret ballot. The Party Column ballot which is used in Michigan and Indiana and in twenty-three other states, lists names of the nominees from president or governor to the lowest party-designated office in separate columns for each of the parties. A single mark on the paper ballot or moving of a single lever on a voting machine makes it possible for an elector to cast his vote for the entire state party ticket. Political forces that wish to discourage straight-party voting and stress the individual candidate rather than party association support the adoption of the office-type ballot, sometimes called the Massachusetts ballot. Under this arrangement voters must select their party preferences from among the various nominees who are grouped not according to party but according to office.

Supervision for the printing and distribution of ballots for statewide offices rests usually with the secretary of state; those for countywide offices with the county auditor, and those for citywide offices with the city clerk. As the key election officials for state and local government, these individuals may also have the statutory responsibility to convene city, county, and state canvassing boards for the purpose of compiling the official voting returns for their respective jurisdictions.

STATE ELECTION LAWS AND ELECTION ADMINISTRATION UNDER ATTACK

Excessively long or rigid residence requirements rank first among the many criticisms presently leveled at state election systems:

> Archaic state residence requirements, many adopted a century ago, are the greatest single barrier to voting. An estimated 8,000,000 voters out of the 33 million people who moved last year were unable to vote in the 1960 elections

---

[22] Harold T. Jones, "Electronics in Voting," *National Civic Review*, June, 1964, p. 306. This article goes into the costs and technical details of each of these devices.

because of inability to meet the state, county, or precinct residence requirements.[23]

Pressures for reform are coming from various sources: from congressmen who threaten federal action on behalf of uniform minimal standards unless the states act quickly, from wide segments of the press, radio and television, commenting editorially upon the appalling extent to which such residence requirements disenfranchise America's mobile population and not least from the disenfranchised voters themselves. A Gallup poll in 1959 showed 72 per cent of those queried favoring a law which would require not more than six months' residence to establish one's voting eligibility.

State officials themselves have become increasingly concerned with the need to liberalize their residence laws. Proposals to this effect were submitted by the Association of Secretaries of State, the General Assembly of the States, and the Governors' Conference, and a number of states actually adopted some changes either by constitutional amendment or by statutory enactment.

A. Nine states—California, Connecticut, Maine, Maryland, Massachusetts, Michigan, North Dakota, Ohio, and South Dakota —now permit otherwise qualified intrastate migrants to vote for a specified period of time (40 days to three months) at their previous local address if they cannot qualify for the ballot under the residence requirements of their new residence.

B. Six states—Arizona, Connecticut, New Jersey, Vermont, Wisconsin, and Wyoming—allow their former residents to vote for President by absentee ballot within a 24-month period after they have moved provided, of course, that they cannot qualify under the laws of their new residence.

C. Fifteen states approved provisions under which state residence requirements are waived so that newcomers can cast their ballots for the office of president and vice-president.

States that wish to re-examine their registration and voting laws with a view to enlarging their active electorate, can find a number of highly valuable suggestions in the Report of the President's Commission on Registration and Voter Participation (1963). In the judgment of the commission, millions of presently disenfranchised citizens could be brought to the polls if

A. Voter registration were easily accessible to all citizens;

B. State residence requirements did not exceed six months;

C. Local residence requirements before election did not exceed 30 days;

D. New state residents were allowed to vote for president;

E. Voter registration was extended as close to election day as possible, and ended not more than three or four weeks before election day;

F. Voter lists were kept current;

G. No citizens' registrations were cancelled for failure to vote in any period less than four years;

H. Voter registration lists were used only for electoral purposes;

I. States provided absentee registration for voters who could not register in person;

J. Literacy tests were not a requisite for voting;

[23] Brendan Byrne, *Let's Modernize Our Horse-And-Buggy Election Laws* (Washington, Conn., 1961), p. 3.

K. Election day were proclaimed a national day of dedication to our American democracy;
L. Polling places were so equipped as to eliminate long waiting periods;
M. Polling places were open throughout the day and remained open until at least 9:00 P.M.
N. Voting by persons 18 years of age were considered by the states;
O. Candidacy were open to all;
P. The right to vote were extended to those living on federal reservations;
Q. Absentee voting by mail were allowed for all who were absent from home on primary or general election day;
R. Poll taxes were eliminated as a qualification for voting.[24]

A second widespread criticism of state elections centers around the length and the complexity of the ballot itself. To cite only a few illustrations: voters in Denver were confronted in 1960 with seven constitutional amendments and 95 candidates for 45 offices; Georgia's ballot listed candidates for 43 offices, 19 constitutional amendments of statewide application, and 68 of local concern. Louisiana voters were presented with a total of 55 amendments of which only twenty-four were of a statewide nature.

In 1964 it was Illinois which offered voters the longest legislative ballot. Failure of the Republican-controlled legislature and of the Democratic governor to agree on a redistricting plan resulted in a three-and-one-half foot long paper ballot on which there was a total of 236 candidates for the 177 House seats. Nearly 10,000 workers were required to count and tabulate these ballots.

About three-fifths of the states use one long ballot crammed with names of all candidates, presidential, congressional, state, and local. Improper marking of ballots disqualifies thousands of votes nearly every election. Texas, for example, requires a voter to scratch out or mark out the names of all candidates except those of his choice. At the 1960 election, failure to follow these instructions invalidated an estimated 100,000 ballots.[25] The fact that an increasing number of states have adopted mechanical voting machines fortunately makes a major contribution not only to the speedier and more accurate reporting of election results but to the significant reduction of ballot spoilage as well.

Reducing the length of the ballot is, however, a much more difficult problem. Blamed for this must be the overly detailed language of state constitutional or charter provisions requiring frequent amendment, the excessively large number of elective officials in non-policy making positions, and the brevity of the terms of office for which these public officials are elected. All

---

[24] *Report of the President's Commission on Registration and Voting Participation* (Washington, 1963), pp. 2–3. Joseph P. Harris, a close student of the electoral process for many years, urges that state commissions be created "to inquire into all aspects of election administration and to draft revisions and codifications of the state election laws." See his "Modernizing Our Election Administration," *State Government*, Winter, 1963, p. 37.

[25] "Lost, Strayed or Stolen: Millions of Votes," *U. S. News & World Report*, March 6, 1961, p. 79.

of these represent fundamental and long standing characteristics of American state and local government not susceptible to easy reform. A slight improvement in the length of the ballot should, however, be noted. In over one-half of the states, laws now have been enacted making it possible to print a presidential "short ballot" which omits the long list of state presidential electors. This leaves only the names of each party's presidential and vice-presidential nominees which, of course, are all that is really necessary for a voter to register his choice for the nation's chief executive.

The third basic criticism hurled at the election apparatus by many—particularly following the 1960 presidential cliff-hanger in which a 1 vote shift per precinct would have changed the outcome—is its alleged failure to protect electors and ballots more effectively against fraudulent voting and corrupt election officialdom. One group of experts claimed that in the 1960 presidential election "a million and a half persons had their votes stolen by one party or the other." For example, many persons feel convinced that Kennedy's narrow victory in 1960 in Illinois would never have materialized had it not been for gross voting irregularities and outright ballot thefts in hundreds of Chicago's precincts. To be sure, many of the corrupt practices that were committed there had been used somewhere before at one time or another by one or the other party. When employed, such evil arsenals often include:

A. *"Tombstone voting"*—voter registration lists padded with the names of "ghosts."
B. *"Chain balloting"* whereby a corrupt election clerk will hand a marked ballot to a "bought" voter who casts the ballot and then hands back an unmarked ballot which will be marked by the official who gives it to another such voter to start the cycle all over again.
C. *Buying election judges* so that all judges are members of the same political party in fact though not in name.
D. Voting *"floaters,"* i.e., individuals who are transported to various polling places, using a different name in each, but voting as instructed.
E. *Rigging election machines*—opening the panel and setting artificial totals.
F. *Fixing registration lists* by removing names of opposition party members from the roster and so either delaying or precluding their voting altogether.

Quite obviously, then, there is still much that needs to be done to tighten and improve election laws. Registration lists must be kept current through careful and repeated scrutiny. More election judges should be recruited through examinations from the rosters of the Civil Service rather than from party volunteers. Yet even more than laws and gimmicks, the political parties themselves must be kept more viable and competitive so that they can serve as each other's most effective check and balance.

THE MINNESOTA RECOUNT—A GOVERNOR BY 91 VOTES

Following a strenuously fought campaign, the people of Minnesota after casting their ballots on November 6, 1962, did not know for 133 days who would be certified as their duly elected governor. On the basis of original returns from the canvassing boards of the state's eighty-seven counties, it appeared at first as if Lieutenant Governor Karl Rolvaag (D.F.L.), the challenger, had defeated Governor Elmer L. Andersen (R.), the incumbent, by a margin of 58 votes out of a total of over 1,265,000. In view of the narrowness of the vote and the widespread public uncertainty concerning its accuracy, both parties promptly demanded that some of the canvassing boards reaudit their tallies and reports. After nearly three weeks of checking and rechecking (with the press services reporting the candidates alternately leading and losing), the State Canvassing Board on November 29 decided to reverse itself on the basis of the amended returns and declare Governor Andersen the winner by 142 votes.

D.F.L. leaders quickly assailed the board's decision on the grounds that the newly-amended returns reflected a partial and biased selection of counties which tended to favor Andersen over Rolvaag. A few days later a state district court granted the D.F.L. petition for a complete recount of all gubernatorial votes. This nation's first experiment in physically reexamining nearly 800,000 ballots was about to be launched. Not subject to the recount were approximately 40 per cent of all gubernatorial votes—these were cast in the precincts where voting machines were used.

With practically no legal or historical precedents to guide this enormous undertaking, responsible leaders in both parties realized immediately the need for cooperation if the recount process was to be completed successfully and if public confidence in its outcome was to be assured. In the same spirit the chief justice of the state supreme court wisely gave both parties a voice in the selection of a three-member district bench which then served as the judicial tribunal for the entire recount. Under the direction of this court, both parties agreed to the rules and procedures which were to govern the operations of 100 three-member recount teams.

Composed of two members representing the candidates and a neutral (who had been approved by both parties and often included members of the League of Women Voters and even the clergy), the teams moved into each county scrutinizing ballots and tallies under the supervision of the county auditors. This canvass took approximately two weeks. Again, the results proved inconclusive. With over 97,000 ballots challenged by one or the other side, both candidates found it possible to claim victory. The battle now shifted to the court. In view of the massive total of disputed ballots, the court insisted that before beginning trial the parties would have to agree to reduce the contest to more manageable proportions.

Teams of party workers and attorneys were finally able to pare down to 1,300 the number of ballots in dispute after two more weeks of tedious sorting, sifting, patient negotiations, and mutual concessions.

The recount itself revealed no substantial evidence of intentional fraud or any actual theft of votes. That there was considerable laxity in the administration of election laws and in the reporting of election results became quite obvious. Exhaustion after long hours of counting votes or inadequate instruction in their duties were the explanations why some election officials failed to sign their tally sheets, why some improperly sealed or stored ballot boxes, and why some filed inaccurate reports of precinct totals. Of all the disputed ballots, nearly one-fifth belonged in the category of errors which arose because election judges had failed to initial them (a requirement of law) or because they were used as scratch paper for computational or similar purposes.[26] What also proved decisive in this extraordinarily close election was the great number of small human errors which were perpetrated in the marking of ballots. Most of these were due to either ignorance of the law or plain carelessness. For example, under Minnesota law, voters could spoil or invalidate their ballots by voting for two or even three candidates for governor (Andersen, Rolvaag and a third nominee who represented the Industrial Government, Socialist party) by mixing checks or indistinct marks with the required "X," or by doodles, erasures, or other ballot notations or defacements.[27]

It was now up to the recount court to determine judicially which of the 1,300 contested ballots were still admissable under the law and marked with sufficient clarity to discern the voter's intent and which were not. The most critical phase of the trial began on February 25 and was concluded on March 19. As a consequence of judicial rulings on the various categories of errors (in which the court admitted all but the most clearly invalid ballots), Rolvaag emerged with a 91-vote advantage. Four months of uncertainty had thus come to an official end; the court denied a motion filed by the Republicans to have the entire recount dismissed, and Andersen refused to avail himself of the opportunity to take an appeal from the decision of the district court to the state supreme court.[28]

[26] For a detailed statistical analysis of all phases of Minnesota's gubernatorial recount, see Ronald F. Stinnett and Charles H. Backstrom, *Recount* (Washington, 1964); a brief description of the recount is in Robert Forsythe, "The Recount Recounted," *Advance*, Summer, 1963, pp. 43–47.

[27] Following the recount, the Minnesota legislature, wishing to make sure that ballots with relatively minor irregularities would not lead to the disenfranchisement of voters in the future, amended the law as follows: "When a voter uses two or more distinct marks in expressing his vote on a ballot such as (X) and some other mark, the vote shall be counted for each candidate so marked, nonetheless, unless it is so marked by distinguishing characteristics so as to make the entire ballot defective. . . ." Sec. 204.22 (h), *Minnesota Statutes Annotated*, 1964. Most courts have held distinguishing marks will invalidate a ballot if they are of such a nature as to reveal a voter's intent to identify himself through their use. "A briber could demand a certain unusual mark and thereby assure a method of discovering compliance with the bargain. . . ." California furnishes the voter a rubber stamp for the symbol with which he may mark his individual choices. "The Role of the Courts in Election Contest Proceedings," *Minnesota Law Review*, May, 1964, pp. 1194–1197.

[28] Generally, under Minnesota law, the cost of a recount is assigned against the loser although a judge may, at his discretion, assess costs proportionately to the municipalities which have been found responsible for certain types of errors in election law administration. Sec. 209.06 (2), *Minnesota Statutes Annotated*, 1964. In the gubernatorial recount of 1963, the legislature appropriated $150,000 for the payment of ballot examiners ($15.00 per day), clerical help, court expenses, and other recount-connected costs. This

Throughout the recount, Governor-to-be Rolvaag worked in a small basement office under the state Capitol laying plans for his administration, while Andersen carried on as governor, and while the conservative leadership in the legislature confirmed the governor's appointments and continued to enact the governor's program. Most remarkable for a state known for its politically competitive climate was the positive attitude with which both parties cooperated during the trying months of uncertainty and with which the parties, the candidates, and the public accepted the outcome of the recount. Most Minnesotans viewed with considerable pride the dignity and poise that the two governors exhibited during the confusing and hectic months of the recount and the transition of government that followed. A *Minneapolis Morning Tribune* editorial "Recount in Retrospect" pointed up some of these sentiments:

> In a recent tongue-in-cheek editorial, the *Atlanta Journal* commented on the disposition of both Rolvaag and Andersen "to let the courts decide." It then harked back to Georgia's Arnall-Talmadge row when that state had two governors for a while, amid lots of shoving and pushing and with "two adjutants general bossing the troops around, and with everybody signing checks."
>
> "Minnesota may be all right," the editorial concluded, "but it must be an awfully dull place."
>
> Perhaps the readiness with which we resort to judicial processes and our willingness to abide by judicial decisions are characteristics bred in Minnesota —in contrast, say, to some southern states. But "awfully dull" or not, we have passed through the difficult trial of the recount with a becoming respect for the law, the courts and—we hope—each other.[29]

CASE PROBLEMS FOR CLASS DISCUSSION

1. A volunteer committee has been established to assist the campaign of your state senator. Your offer of service has been accepted and the candidate has selected you as chairman and campaign manager. During the course of a bitter campaign, the opposition alleges that some of your volunteers have approached certain liquor interests for campaign contributions. Your candidate wants to have nothing to do with those interests and disavows their support. You are asked to "straighten out the mess." What would you do?
2. Recent elections revealed evidence of sloppiness in the administration of election law. The secretary of state who is charged by law with the responsibility for enforcing the election code charges you, his assistant, with the responsibility of conducting training sessions throughout the state for the benefit of local election officials. Who should attend these sessions? Where would you hold them? What aspects of the law would you emphasize? What exhibits would you bring along?
3. The election committee of the legislature is considering a bill requiring the relatively detailed candidate disclosure of campaign contributions and expend-

---

amount was divided nearly evenly among the Rolvaag and Andersen recount committees. (Laws 1963, ch. 868, p. 1586.) Party sources insist that their respective sums covered less than half of the cash expenditures incurred and that large numbers of party volunteers have remained uncompensated for their efforts.

[29] *The Minneapolis Tribune,* March 26, 1964, p. 4.

itures. You covered all the committee hearings for one of the local papers and are now in the process of organizing your notes in preparation for writing a series of articles the paper wishes to publish on this issue. What was the central theme of the testimony given by the representatives for each of the following groups: Chamber of Commerce, AFL-CIO, Farm Bureau Federation, League of Women Voters, Democratic party, and Republican party?

4. Your local chamber of commerce has decided to organize an intensive voter registration drive. As chairman of the civic committee it is your responsibility to plan the drive. What would be your recommendations?

SELECTED BIBLIOGRAPHY

HERBERT E. ALEXANDER, "Paying the Politics Bill," *National Civic Review*, March, 1964, pp. 118–125.

GEORGE S. BLAIR, *Cumulative Voting: An Effective Electoral Device in Illinois Politics* (Urbana, 1960).

DOUGLAS CARLISLE, *Party Loyalty: The Election Process in South Carolina* (Washington, 1963).

WILLIAM G. CORNELIUS, "The County Unit System of Georgia: Facts and Prospects," *Western Political Quarterly*, December, 1961, pp. 942–960.

JOSEPH P. HARRIS, "Modernizing Our Election Administration," *State Government*, Winter, 1963, pp. 34–39.

ALEXANDER HEARD, *The Costs of Democracy* (Chapel Hill, 1960).

WALTER E. KALOUPEK and HENRY J. TOMASEK, *Administration of Election Laws in North Dakota* (Grand Forks, 1960).

FRANK MARINI, *Local Bond Elections in California: The Two-Thirds Majority Requirement* (Berkeley, 1963).

GEORGE B. MATHER, *A Preliminary Report of an Analysis of the Effects of the Use of Voting Machines in Voting on Special Questions in Iowa—1920–1956* (Iowa City, 1960).

DONALD R. MATTHEWS and JAMES W. PROTHRO, "Political Factors and Negro Voter Registration in the South," *American Political Science Review*, June, 1963, pp. 355–367.

DONALD R. MATTHEWS and JAMES W. PROTHRO, "Social & Economic Factors and Negro Voter Registration in the South," *American Political Science Review*, March, 1963, pp. 24–44.

LOUIS T. RIGDON, *Georgia's County Unit System* (Decatur, 1961).

HENRY ROSE, "A Critical Look at the Hatch Act," *Harvard Law Review*, January, 1962, pp. 510–526.

RICHARD M. SCAMMON, "The Electoral Process," *Law and Contemporary Problems*, Spring, 1962, pp. 299–306.

JOHN P. WHITE, *Voting Machines and the 1958 Defeat of Constitutional Revision in Michigan* (Ann Arbor, 1960).

JOHN P. WHITE and JOHN R. OWENS, *Parties, Group Interests, and Campaign Finance: Michigan '56'* (Princeton, 1960).

W. ROSS YATES, "The Functions of Residence Requirements for Voting," *Western Political Quarterly*, September, 1962, pp. 469–488.

Chapter X

THE CONSTITU-TIONAL AND LEGAL INTER-RELATIONSHIPS OF THE NATION AND THE STATES

What is the nature of the Union? Under our American system of federalism, what does the federal government constitutionally owe the states; what do the states owe the federal government; and what do the states owe each other?

Is cooperative federalism a steppingstone to national uniformity and political conformity, or the loss of state and personal individuality?

INTERGOVERNMENTAL relations in the United States must necessarily be complex. First of all, there is the relationship between the nation and the states. In this case political power is geographically divided on the basis of a *federal* principle. Second, there is a set of relationships between each of the states and their respective cities or local governmental units. The formula which is basic to these political arrangements is called *unitary,* i.e., subject to certain federal constitutional limitations, cities and local governmental units have only such powers as state constitutions and legislatures are willing to grant to them. Third, in addition to these two fundamental patterns, certain other types of legal relationships are in force between the states as well—interstate compacts and uniform state laws representing two examples. Fourth, there are what might be called interlocal relations. Much of what is presently labeled as metropolitan area government involves some form of agreement or consolidation between cities and other units of local government.

THE STATES UNDER THE FEDERAL CONSTITUTION

THE SUPREMACY CLAUSE—ARTICLE VI, SECTION 2 AND SECTION 3

The language of the United States Constitution leaves little doubt about the superior position of the federal government vis-à-vis the states. "This Constitution, and the laws of the United States which shall be made in pursuance thereof . . . shall be the supreme law of the land; and the judges of every State shall be bound thereby, anything in the Constitution or laws of any State to the contrary notwithstanding." Paragraph three makes it obligatory upon all state officials, legislative, executive, and judicial, to take the oath in support of the federal Constitution.

For a proper understanding and appreciation of the full scope of this article, one must add John Marshall's decisions in *McCulloch* v. *Maryland* (1819) [1]—perhaps the classic case enhancing the powers of the federal

[1] 4 Wheat. 316 (1819).

government. A Maryland statute which had placed a special tax on the notes of the Baltimore branch of the Bank of the United States was found by the Chief Justice to have represented an unconstitutional burden upon an instrument of the federal government and thus in view of the supremacy article, the statute was declared null and void. On the issue relating to the authority for establishing the bank, the federal government was found to possess not only the delegated powers enumerated in Article I, Section 8, but the implied powers as well—powers which the court held could be justly exercised by Congress under the "necessary and proper" clause found at the end of the section. As to what powers may be encompassed within such a broad enabling provision, Marshall had this to say: "Let the end be legitimate, let it be within the scope of the constitution, and all means which are appropriate, which are plainly adapted to that end, which are not prohibited, but consistent with the letter and spirit of the constitution, are constitutional. . . ."

As a result of this and a long list of other decisions handed down by the Supreme Court which taken together vastly expanded the authority of the federal government, the following set of propositions can now be advanced as describing in a general way at least the present interpretations given the supremacy article:

(1) In case of conflict, state policies and laws must not only defer to properly enacted federal policies and laws, but also must not frustrate or obstruct them to any substantial degree.

(2) In the absence of explicit congressional intent to the contrary, states may, however, exercise certain regulatory functions upon federal agencies and instrumentalities, as a legitimate function of their state police powers specifically reserved to them by the Tenth Amendment of the federal Constitution.

(3) While states may not use their powers of taxation to destroy an agency or instrumentality of the federal government, or subject federal possessions to property taxation, federal officials as citizens of the states may be forced also to pay franchise, occupation, excise, gross receipts, sales, use, and severance taxes. This narrower concept of immunity from state taxation developed only during the last thirty years and represents a clear reversal by the Supreme Court of a position which, in the tradition of the *McCulloch* precedent, consistently produced majority opinions insisting on a much more generous tax exemption of federal interests.

POWERS SPECIFICALLY DENIED TO THE STATES

I. *Article I, Section 10*

Article I, Section 10, of the Constitution prohibits states from entering into "any Treaty, Alliance, or Confederation," from granting Letters of Marque and Reprisal, from coining money, from emitting bills of credit, from making "any Thing but gold and silver Coin a Tender in Payment of Debts," from passing "any Bill of Attainder, ex post facto Law, or Law impairing the Obligation of Contracts," and from granting "any Title of Nobility."

Most of these provisions no longer have any great significance. They grew out of the historical settings which contributed to the constitutional shifts away from a loose compact among the states under the Articles of Confederation to establishing the federal Union which in turn led to a surrender by the thirteen states of many of such powers that were at one time attributes of their own sovereignty. Some of the constitutional restrictions imposed upon the states by the Philadelphia convention that are still relevant do, however, call for further clarification.

II. Laws "Impairing the Obligation of Contracts"

There can be no doubt that the sanctity of contracts and property represented to the Founding Fathers cardinal objectives tied to the very purpose of government itself. Here again it was John Marshall who initially gave judicial sanction to these widely-accepted Lockean principles. In *Fletcher* v. *Peck* (1810) [2] the Supreme Court upheld against an attempt at rescission the inviolability of a land grant issued by the legislature of Georgia "even though made under circumstances of the most scandalous corruption" and in the *Dartmouth College* case [3] it declared invalid an attempt by the New Hampshire legislature to change the terms of a charter issued originally by the Crown to a group of trustees for the establishment of a private college. Subsequent interpretations of this contract clause by the Supreme Court, briefly summarized, established the following qualifying principles:

A. Courts drew distinctions between grants of a corporate quality and mere licenses. Licenses or franchises could under some conditions be revoked or made subject to subsequent limitations (*Charles River Bridge Co.* v. *Warren Bridge Co.*, 1837).[4]

B. Officials elected to public office could not construe such positions generally to constitute contractual interests except to the extent that certain compensatable functions or services were already rendered entitling them to payment (*Butler* v. *Pennsylvania*, 1850).[5]

C. Corporation charters obtained from a state do not preclude the issuing state from regulating such a corporation within the scope of state police power—a power inherent in the state and reserved to it under the Tenth Amendment.

"It is settled law of this court that the interdiction of statutes impairing the obligation of contracts does not prevent the State from exercising such powers as are vested in it for the promotion of the common weal, or are necessary for the general good of the public though contract previously entered into between individuals may thereby be affected. . . . [I]n other

[2] 6 Cr. 87 (1810).
[3] 4 Wheat. 518 (1819).
[4] 11 Pet. 420 (1837).
[5] 10 How. 402 (1850).

words, that parties by entering into contracts may not stop the legislature from enacting laws intended for the public good" (*Manigault* v. *Springs*, 1905).[6]

D. In crisis situations arising out of military or economic disruptions, the court sustained also such regulatory measures affecting property rights as those brought about by rent control and mortgage moratorium statutes.

"The policy of protecting contracts against impairment," wrote Chief Justice Hughes in *Home Building and Loan Association* v. *Blaisdell* (1934), "presupposes the maintenance of a government by virtue of which contractual relations are worth while—a government which retains adequate authority to secure the peace and good order of society." [7]

E. States may withdraw legal powers they gave their own municipal corporations (as agencies of the state) without necessarily being subjected to the "impairment of contract" provision. Greater flexibility is permitted states under this clause when the municipal activities are of what the courts call "governmental" rather than "proprietary" quality. As in cases dealing with the public regulation of business, the courts have been unwilling to define rigidly or describe business activities as closed categories—as being either affected or unaffected with a public interest (*Munn* v. *Illinois*, 1877).[8]

Increasingly broad interpretations of the state police power by post-Civil War supreme courts have made it easier for state and local governments to expand their regulatory activities affecting property and contracts. Legislatures began to reflect a concept of social justice which conceived it to be the positive duty of the state to proceed against property rights when in the majority judgment of the electorate such interventions were necessary to protect the economically weak or the socially underprivileged. As a federal restriction on state power, the "impairment of contract" clause of Article I thus has lost much of its former importance. More and more when various interest groups within a state wished to challenge certain state laws for being violative of their economic or personal interests, their members, being also citizens of the United States, instead of basing their case on the language of Article I, began to assert their federal procedural and substantive rights on the provisions of the Fourteenth Amendment.

III. *Laws Denying United States Citizens "Due Process of Law" and the "Equal Protection of the Laws"*

Section 1, which contains the most critical language of the Fourteenth Amendment, includes, but also goes far beyond, matters of property and contract:

All persons born or naturalized in the United States, and subject to the jurisdiction thereof, are citizens of the United States and of the State wherein they reside. No State shall make or enforce any law which shall abridge the privileges or immunities of citizens of the United States; nor shall any State

[6] 199 U. S. 473 (1905).
[7] 290 U. S. 398 (1934).
[8] 94 U. S. 113 (1877).

deprive any person of life, liberty, or property, without due process of law; nor deny to any person within its jurisdiction the equal protection of the laws.

Long before the days of the Freedom Riders, of school desegregations, and of attempts at censoring movies, this amendment was invoked for nearly one hundred years against state civil and criminal laws and against state legal procedures at one time or another by nearly every segment of the population—by the rich, the poor, the alien, the citizen, and the corporation—by the politically radical, the liberal, and the conservative—by the states' righters and by the welfare staters.

Attorneys using the Fourteenth Amendment as a shield defended railroad companies and public utilities against state regulatory commissions and the rates and services they established, defended union organizers when anti-labor sheriffs and police chiefs attempted to obstruct their efforts, defended Jehovah's Witnesses when they preached publicly in city parks without a valid permit, defended Negroes seeking entry into the primaries of Southern Democratic parties, defended teachers who were fired by school boards for failing to sign loyalty oaths or anti-subversion affidavits, defended disseminators of birth control information in states where no such knowledge could legally be circulated, defended taxpayers against tax collectors where the levels of assessment or the nature of the brackets were deemed unreasonable or arbitrary. Urbanites relied on the Fourteenth Amendment in suits for more equitable legislative reapportioning; and counsels in criminal suits, to set aside convictions that involved forced confessions or invalid evidence. Racial and religious minorities claimed the amendment's assistance when they sought to enjoin the enforcement of restrictive real estate covenants; home owners, when they objected to city councils rezoning their streets for commercial purposes; and businessmen, when they contested Sunday closing laws as forms of religious and economic discrimination. Druggists, physicians, dentists, nurses, plumbers, accountants, peddlers, cab operators, electricians, lawyers, and representatives of hundreds of other specialized professional or occupational groups eagerly sought refuge in the Fourteenth Amendment whenever their activities were first made subject to license or inspection by the states or their political subdivisions.

Those who invoked the protections of the Fourteenth Amendment in their battles against the exercise of state police powers, or other similar state actions that they considered unwarranted or unreasonable interferences with personal civil or economic rights, were by no means rewarded with uniform success. With changing concepts of federalism, of economic liberty, and of civil rights, the Supreme Court's interpretations of the amendment and of its restraining force vis-à-vis the states have varied considerably.

Space does not permit a detailed review of the 200 pages of annotations which accompany the 80 words of the amendment's Section 1 in the official congressional edition of the United States Constitution. Yet for a proper understanding of the constitutional foundations of the complex pattern of federal-state relations, it is necessary to study in depth some of the milestone "due process of law" and "equal protection" cases that helped to shape the presently applicable principles however much they themselves may be in flux. Only those cases and principles that illustrate the amendment's effect upon the power of the state to regulate business, to tax, to exercise rights under eminent domain, and to deal with civil liberties guaranteed by the federal Bill of Rights are presented here.

THE FOURTEENTH AMENDMENT AND STATE REGULATION OF BUSINESS

During the last decades of the nineteenth century, it was traditional for businessmen to challenge substantively nearly every attempt of state legislatures to regulate economic life under the state police power through court litigation with the hope of having such state actions judicially declared to constitute a denial of due process of law. This is no longer possible. In the *Nebbia* case (1934) the Supreme Court, Mr. Justice Roberts writing the majority opinion, left little doubt about the enormous reservoir of regulatory power that is left to the states:

> The Constitution does not guarantee the unrestricted privilege to engage in a business or to conduct it as one pleases. Certain kinds of business may be prohibited; and the right to conduct a business, or to pursue a calling may be conditioned. . . . Statutes prescribing the terms upon which those conducting certain businesses may contract, or imposing terms if they do not enter into agreements, are within the State's competency.[9]

To earlier cases which had already established the right of states to regulate public utilities or businesses "affected with a public interest," the court now added that "there can be no doubt that upon proper occasion and by appropriate measures the state may regulate a business or any of its aspects, including the prices to be charged for the products or commodities it sells." What happened to the tests of due process of law? Left as the remaining bases for legal action were the procedural standards of due process of law—the question was not so much whether the idea of the law as such was sound or not but whether the law was fairly imposed and equitably administered.

"Price control, like any other form of regulation," the Court ruled in this Depression era case which involved the right of the New York Milk Control Board to fix retail prices, "is unconstitutional only if *arbitrary, discriminatory, or demonstrably irrelevant to the policy the legislature is free to adopt, and hence an unnecessary and unwarranted interference with individual liberty.*"

Also basically established and no longer subject to the charge of substantively denying due process of law is the right of the state to regulate maximum hours of work, minimum wages, and the conditions of work under which minors and women may be employed. As similarly compatible with the standards of due process, the Supreme Court sustained state laws which

[9] *Nebbia* v. *New York,* 291 U. S. 502 (1934).

regulated the exploitation of such natural resources as oil, coal, water, game, and fish and defined the conditions under which motor vehicles and carriers could operate on highways and streets.

Closely related to the reinforcing due process of law is the concept of equal protection of the laws. Its meaning like the meaning of all similar broad legal norms or formulae that are always in flux can only be described in general terms. Whatever else the "equal protection of the laws" clause demands, states certainly cannot enact or enforce laws which "favor . . . particular persons as against others in like conditions." [10] While it does not require "identical treatment for all persons without recognition of differences in relevant circumstances," [11] courts have made it quite clear that under this standard,

> equal protection and security should be given to all under like circumstances in the enjoyment of their personal and civil rights; that all persons should be equally entitled to pursue their happiness, and acquire and enjoy property; that they should have like access to courts of the country for the protection of their persons and property. . . .[12]

Again, it does not prevent a state from using its police power to establish reasonable classifications—not all corporations need be treated alike, not all property need be taxed equally, not all businesses need obtain licenses, and not all workers need be subjected to identical safety conditions. But when classes are established and property and persons are treated differently under the law, courts will inquire whether such acts of classifications

A. are based on substantial differences which make one class really different from another; [13]
B. have a "reasonable basis" and are not arbitrary; [14]
C. placed "greater burdens . . . upon one than are laid upon others in the same calling and conditions;" [15]
D. afforded "undue favor" or "class privilege." [16]

In general, courts have allowed state legislatures considerable discretion in the selection of classes and placed the burden on the attacking party to rebut the presumption that these classes were based on adequate and sufficient grounds.[17]

One of the most dramatic illustrations of the extent of such discretion that was left by the Supreme Court to the state legislatures under the Fourteenth Amendment is found in *Plessy* v. *Ferguson* (1896),[18] a case which was

[10] *Minneapolis and St. Louis Railway Co.* v. *Beckwith*, 129 U. S. 26, 28, 29 (1889).
[11] Edward S. Corwin (ed.), *The Constitution of the United States of America: Analysis and Interpretation* (Washington, 1953), p. 1144.
[12] *Barbier* v. *Connolly*, 113 U. S. 27, 31 (1885).
[13] *Lindsley* v. *Natural Carbonic Gas Co.*, 220 U. S. 61 (1911).
[14] *Watson* v. *Maryland*, 218 U. S. 173 (1910).
[15] *Barbier* v. *Connolly*, 113 U. S. 31 (1885).
[16] *Truax* v. *Corrigan*, 257 U. S. 312 (1921).
[17] Corwin, p. 1037.
[18] 163 U. S. 537 (1896).

to furnish the doctrine of segregation in public facilities with its judicial sanction.

Under attack was an 1890 Louisiana statute which required separate railway coaches for white and Negro passengers. In upholding this law over the dissent of Mr. Justice Harlan ("Our Constitution is color-blind, and neither knows nor tolerates classes among citizens"), Mr. Justice Brown, writing for the majority, argued that "Laws permitting, and even requiring [separation of the races] . . . in places where they are liable to be brought into contact do not necessarily imply the inferiority of either race to the other, and have been generally, if not universally, recognized as within the competency of the state legislatures in the exercise of their police power." Thus the majority viewed these segregation statutes as within the bounds of reasonable discretion and as thoroughly compatible with the "equal protection of the laws" clause of the Fourteenth Amendment.

Although the *Plessy* case involved railroad segregation only, its doctrine was in fact to become for nearly sixty years the controlling precedent for the defense of segregated public education. When the Supreme Court finally overruled *Plessy* in *Brown* v. *Board of Education of Topeka* (1954),[19] compulsory school segregation had been the law in seventeen Southern states and permissive practice in Arizona, Kansas, and New Mexico. Earlier cases had already found unequal the graduate school facilities of Missouri (*Gaines* v. *Canada*, 1938),[20] and a separate law school for Negroes at the University of Texas (*Sweatt* v. *Painter*, 1950).[21] But it was not until Mr. Chief Justice Warren delivered the unanimous opinion of the Court in the *Brown* case that the Court addressed itself to the central issue of the attempted reconciliation of the Fourteenth Amendment with the practice of segregation in all public schools. "In the field of public education," wrote the Chief Justice, "separate but equal has no place. Separate educational facilities are inherently unequal. Therefore, we hold that the plaintiffs and others similarly situated for whom the actions have been brought are by reason of the segregation complained of, deprived of the equal protection of the laws guaranteed by the Fourteenth Amendment."

THE FOURTEENTH AMENDMENT AND STATE TAXATION

State taxes may be high and even burdensome yet the Supreme Court sees nothing in the due process of law clause to permit a condemnation of such taxes on the sole basis of their being excessive. Nor does due process stand in the way of any particular form of taxation. Putting aside the more complex legal problems involving *situs* of property, a taxpayer's domicile, double taxation, and tax jurisdiction, as long as the levy is for a public purpose, legislatures are free to permit the taxing of incomes, inheritances,

[19] 347 U. S. 483 (1954).
[20] 305 U. S. 337 (1938).
[21] 339 U. S. 629 (1950).

corporations, sales, gifts, franchises, real estate, personal property, tangibles or intangibles. Persons who wish to challenge such taxes or test their validity must be given an opportunity to state their objections either before an administrative or judicial tribunal. In general, however, whatever the particular objection under due process of law to the fairness of a tax obligation or to its determination, the constitutionality of the "power to levy taxes . . . [cannot be made to] depend upon the enjoyment by the taxpayer of any special benefit from the use of the funds raised by taxation." [22]

Can differential tax treatments of persons and property be legally assailed on grounds of discrimination and as violations of the "equal protection of the laws" provision of the Fourteenth Amendment? Generally, unless these differences can be shown to constitute gross and intentional discriminations, federal courts have been loathe to interfere. In a major case, *Bell's Gap Railroad Co.* v. *Pennsylvania* (1890),[23] the Supreme Court held that a state may

> "if it chooses, exempt certain classes of property from any taxation at all, such as churches, libraries and the property of charitable institutions. It may impose different specific taxes upon different trades and professions, and may vary the rates of excise upon various products; it may tax real estate and personal property in a different manner; it may tax visible property only, and not tax securities for payment of money; it may allow deductions for indebtedness, or not allow them. All such regulations, and those of like character, so long as they proceed within reasonable limits, and general usage, are within the discretion of the State Legislature. . . ."

THE FOURTEENTH AMENDMENT AND THE POWER OF EMINENT DOMAIN

States or their local governmental units may under the power of eminent domain acquire private property upon payment of just compensation for highways, streets, housing projects and viaducts, for the public operation of utilities (water, rail, gas, electricity, etc.) or for any other purpose, provided only that it is a public purpose. Whether or not such purpose is of a public nature, while ultimately a judicial question, has in practice been left by the courts to the decisions of state legislature and city council. Closer judicial scrutiny was given to questions relating to the procedures involved in the exercise of eminent domain, to such factors as notice, hearing, and fair compensation. Elementary standards of due process require public notice of the proposed condemnation proceedings and the opportunity for the owner to challenge the fairness of the compensation awarded him. The price to be paid for the property can be determined by a special administrative tribunal or by a court; "[t]he general rule is that compensation 'is to be estimated by reference to the uses for which the property is suitable, having regard to the

---

[22] *Nashville C. & St. L. R. Co.* v. *Wallace,* 288 U. S. 249, 268 (1933).
[23] 134 U. S. 232 (1890).

existing business and wants of the community, or such as may be reasonably expected in the immediate future,' . . . [but] 'mere possible or imaginary uses, or the speculative schemes of its proprietor, are to be excluded.' " [24]

THE FOURTEENTH AMENDMENT, THE BILL OF RIGHTS, AND THE STATES' POLICE POWER

In the *Slaughterhouse* cases (1873) [25] the Supreme Court was able to see nothing in the wording of the Fourteenth Amendment to make applicable to the states any of the provisions of the federal Bill of Rights. To hold otherwise would be "so far-reaching and pervading, so great a departure from the structure and spirit of our institutions . . . ," wrote Mr. Justice Miller, as to "fetter and degrade the state governments by subjecting them to the control of Congress," and would in fact "radically change . . . the whole theory of the relations of the state and federal government."

Present critics of the centralizing trend in American federalism insist that nearly ninety years, and over a thousand cases later, much of what the Court then feared about the ascendancy of federal powers was, in fact, achieved through the subsequent interpretations of the Fourteenth Amendment. The "absorption" of the First Amendment, of its guarantees of freedom of speech, freedom of religion, freedom of the press, and the right to peaceful assembly into the Fourteenth Amendment's concept of liberty, began with *Gitlow* v. *New York* in 1925 [26] and was nearly completed with *Cantwell* v. *Connecticut* in 1940.[27] These basic liberties in Mr. Justice Cardozo's words, speaking for the majority of another Connecticut case, *Palko* v. *Connecticut* (1937),[28] "have been found to be implicit in the concept of ordered liberty." As such they were part and parcel of the privileges and immunities of citizens of the United States that could not be impaired by state action without constituting a denial of the due process of law clause of the Fourteenth Amendment. In accordance with this reasoning, the amendment has since 1937 been successfully invoked to strike down a wide variety of regulations which affected civil liberties and which were enacted by state or local governments under the authority of the state police power. Only a few major examples are cited here:

> A New Jersey City ordinance enabled the Director of Public Safety "to refuse a . . . [speaking] permit on his mere opinion that such refusal would prevent 'riots, disturbances . . . etc.' In *Hague* v. *CIO* (1939), the Supreme Court held that "the privilege of a citizen of the United States to use the streets and parks for communication of views on national questions may be regulated in the interest of all; it is not absolute . . . but it must not, in the guise of regulation, be abridged or denied." [29]

[24] *Chicago B. & Q. R. R. Co.* v. *Chicago*, 166 U. S. 226, 250 (1897).
[25] 16 Wall. 36 (1873).
[26] 268 U. S. 652 (1925).
[27] 310 U. S. 296 (1940).
[28] 302 U. S. 309 (1937).
[29] 307 U. S. 496 (1939).

A Texas law required that every labor union organizer who wished to operate in the state first had to obtain an organizer's permit from the secretary of state before he could recruit members for his union. The president of the United Automobile Workers, R. J. Thomas, had gone to Texas to address a union meeting without registering with the secretary of state and without securing the necessary permit. In *Thomas* v. *Collins* (1945) the Supreme Court declared the statute to be unconstitutional: "As a matter of principle a requirement of registration in order to make a public speech would seem generally incompatible with an exercise of the rights of free speech and assembly. Lawful public assemblies involving no element of grave and immediate danger to an interest the state is entitled to protect, are not instruments of harm which require previous identification of the speaker." [30]

West Virginia was one of a number of states in which school board regulations required all children to salute the flag of the United States regardless of their religious convictions. Failure to conform was considered insubordination and ground for expulsion. Jehovah's Witnesses whose children were expelled sought an injunction on the basis that their religious beliefs forbade them to salute "any graven image" and that their children should, therefore, not be compelled to violate their religion. In *West Virginia Board of Education* v. *Barnette* (1943) the Court overruled an earlier conflicting decision (*Gobitis* case) and asserted that "If there is any fixed star in our constitutional constellation, it is that no official, high or petty, can prescribe what shall be orthodox in politics, nationalism, religion, or other matters of opinion or force citizens to confess by word or act their faith therein. . . . We think the action of the local authorities in compelling the flag salute and pledge transcends constitutional limitations on their power and invades the sphere of intellect and spirit which is the purpose of the First Amendment to our Constitution to reserve from all official control." [31]

There were other cases and circumstances in which the Supreme Court was not at all willing to permit application of the newly-enriched Fourteenth Amendment to void restrictions on personal freedoms arising out of the exercise of state police powers.

Petitioner was addressing "an open-air meeting" in the city of Syracuse. There was no attempt of police officers to interfere with his speech. Then the speech about public officials and the American Legion became more impassioned, the crowd grew restless, derogatory remarks were exchanged between speaker and audience, finally the police decided to take steps in order to "prevent a fight." The speaker was asked to get down off the box and when he refused was placed under arrest. Courts below had found "that the officers in making the arrest were motivated solely by a proper concern for the preservation of order and protection of the general welfare. . . . [P]etitioner was . . . neither arrested nor convicted for the making or the content of his speech. Rather, it was the reaction which it actually engendered." In *Feiner* v. *New York* (1951) a divided court upheld the conviction, reasoning that "it is one thing to say that the police cannot be used as an instrument for the oppression of unpopular views, and another to say that, when as here the speaker passes the bounds of argument or persuasion and undertakes incitement to riot, they are powerless to prevent a breach of the peace." [32]

[30] 323 U. S. 516 (1945).
[31] 319 U. S. 624 (1943).
[32] 340 U. S. 315 (1951).

A Pennsylvania criminal statute enacted in 1959 "prescribing the Sunday retail sale of certain enumerated commodities" was assailed by appellants on the grounds that it violated the First Amendment since it "obliges everyone to honor . . . [a] basic doctrine of the major Christian denominations by abstaining from work and [encouraging] . . . Christian religious worship." A divided court, Mr. Chief Justice Warren writing the majority opinion, in *Braunfield* v. *Brown* (1961), upheld the Sunday Closing Law arguing that while the freedom to hold religious beliefs and opinions is absolute, "the freedom to act, even when the action is in accord with one's religious convictions, is not totally free from legislative restrictions . . . the Sunday law simply regulates a secular activity and, as applied to appellants operates so as to make the practice of their religious beliefs more expensive. . . . Fully recognizing that the alternatives open to appellants and others similarly situated— retaining their present occupations and incurring economic disadvantage or engaging in some other commercial activity which does not call for either Saturday or Sunday labor—may well result in some financial sacrifice in order to observe their religious beliefs, still the opinion is wholly different than when the legislation attempts to make religious practice itself unlawful." [33]

A Chicago city ordinance requires "submission of all motion pictures for examination prior to their public exhibition." Petitioner, a New York corporation, refused to submit the film to the office of the Commissioner of Police for examination. The ordinance made it clear that no permits could be issued until such examination was completed. Petitioner brought suit on the "sole ground that the provisions of the ordinance requiring submission of the film constitutes, on its face, a prior restraint within the prohibition of the First and Fourteenth Amendments. . . . Petitioner claims that the nature of the film is irrelevant, and that even if this film contains the basest type of pornography, or incitement to riot, or forceful overthrow of orderly government, it may nonetheless be shown without prior submission for examination." In *Times Film Corporation* v. *City of Chicago* (1961) a divided Court speaking through Mr. Justice Clark insisted that the courts have always recognized that in some "exceptional cases" previous restraints may be imposed on freedom of speech by a state under its police power in order to prevent "in the most effective fashion" the utterances of certain types of speech.[34] The court relied heavily on a 1942 case (*Chaplinsky* v. *State of New Hampshire*) in which it was held that there were "certain well defined and narrowly limited classes of speech, the prevention and punishment of which have never been thought to raise any Constitutional problem. These include the lewd and obscene, the profane, the libelous, and the insulting or 'fighting' words—those which by their very utterance inflict injury or tend to incite an immediate breach of the peace." [35]

To recapitulate, as far as freedoms of the First Amendment are concerned, the Fourteenth Amendment has now made these rights applicable to citizens of all the fifty states. State standards of civil liberty must comply with national standards if they are to meet the test of constitutionality. Thus when police chiefs, county attorneys, state judges, city councils, and state legislatures are called upon to balance the interests of the minority with the interests of the majority and its demands for public peace and order, they find that

[33] 366 U. S. 509 (1961).
[34] 365 U. S. 43 (1961).
[35] 315 U. S. 568 (1942).

their policies and actions are affected increasingly by the rulings of the Supreme Court of the United States. What this means in practical terms to the politics of various states and to the operations of the law enforcement machinery throughout the country will be developed in some of the following chapters.

NATIONAL POWER VERSUS STATES' RIGHTS—AN ONGOING
CONSTITUTIONAL DEBATE

From Thomas Jefferson to George Wallace, American constitutional and political history is replete with heated controversy concerning the proper spheres of federal and state activity. The task of discovering the precise intent of the Founding Fathers and the accurate meaning of the federal Constitution never ceases to confront the nation's courts and legislatures, governors and presidents, scholars and polemicists, conservatives and liberals. It is in the essence of American government that each generation is forced to face anew the dilemmas and complexities that necessarily inhere in the federal distribution of political power. It is also a well-known paradox of American government that modern liberals will often support their case for a strong central government with arguments taken from the writings of Hamilton and Madison—staunch protagonists of the sanctity of property, social stability, and the system of indirect elections—while modern conservatives find much that is congenial in the words of Thomas Jefferson, a strict constructionist of the Constitution, whose enthusiasm for majority rule never dimmed and whose absolute faith in direct democracy knew no bounds.

While political positions thus have been reversed, constitutional positions remain basically unchanged: old and new Hamiltonians would agree in their emphasis on national supremacy; old and new Jeffersonians would agree in their emphasis on the rights of the states. Rare are the occasions when today's Senate debates federal aid to education, poll tax legislation, the enforcement of civil rights, or the case for the strong presidency, that debaters on the one side of the issue do not confidently include repeated references to the constitutional views of Hamilton and Madison along with those of Marshall and Webster, and that those rebutting do not fail to enrich their case with the constitutional views of Jefferson, Calhoun, and Hayne.

During the last twenty-five years the partisans of the New Deal, of the Fair Deal, and of the New Frontier, and others who favored policies that required an increasingly elastic interpretation of the Constitution were more fortunate than their opponents. Not merely did they win more often at the polls—although this too helped to advance the cause—but their case for strong federal leadership and national support to the economy was based on certain explicit words and phrases of the Constitution itself if only the Supreme Court could be made to agree. And after 1937 the Court did so agree. At least a majority of the Supreme Court upheld as constitutional what some called "America's third Revolution." Some of the judges were persuaded by the logic of John Marshall (*McCulloch* v. *Maryland*), some agreed with the New Deal's social philosophy, some wished to adopt the doctrine of judicial self-restraint, and some approved the theory that the Supreme Court should watch the election returns. Throughout these years of controversy there were at least seven sections of the Constitution that proved most helpful to the cause of national supremacy and to the expanding powers of the national government:

A. Article I, Section 8, Cl. 1
The Congress shall have power to lay and collect taxes . . . and provide for the common defense and general welfare of the United States;

B. Article I, Section 8, Cl. 2
To borrow money on the credit of the United States;

C. Article I, Section 8, Cl. 3
To regulate commerce with foreign nations, and among the several States, and with the Indian tribes;

D. Article I, Section 8
To make all laws which shall be necessary and proper for carrying into execution the foregoing powers, and all other powers vested by this Constitution in the government of the United States, or any department or office thereof.

E. Article VI, Cl. 2
This Constitution, and the laws of the United States which shall be made in pursuance thereof; and all treaties made, or which shall be made, under the authority of the United States, shall be the supreme law of the land; and the judges in every State shall be bound thereby, anything in the constitution or laws of any State to the contrary notwithstanding.

F. Article VI, Cl. 3
The Senators and Representatives before mentioned and the members of the several State legislatures and all executive and judicial officers, both of the United States and of the several States, shall be bound by oath of affirmation to support this Constitution. . . .

G. Amendment XIV, Section 1
All persons born or naturalized in the United States, and subject to the jurisdiction thereof, are citizens of the United States and of the State wherein they reside. No State shall make or enforce any law which shall abridge the privileges or immunities of citizens of the United States; nor shall any State deprive any person of life, liberty, or property, without due process of law; nor deny to any person within its jurisdiction the equal protection of the laws.

Critics of Washington's new powers contended these constitutional clauses and sections furnished no evidence to justify the right of the federal government to regulate hours and wages, to require management to bargain collectively with union representatives, to compensate farmers for not growing crops, or to pay the unemployed. Moreover, did not the Tenth Amendment to the Constitution provide explicitly that:

The powers not delegated to the United States by the Constitution, nor prohibited by it to the States, are reserved to the States respectively, or to the people?

Three classic dissents entered in *Steward Machine Co.* v. *Davis* (1937),[36] one of the major cases sustaining the Social Security Act of 1935, illustrate an almost prophetic concern from members of the bench about the shrinking significance of the Tenth Amendment as an effective restraint on the expanding influence of the federal government.

MR. JUSTICE McREYNOLDS:

[So] far as we can see, the states are expected to function under federal direction concerning an internal matter. By the sanction of this adventure, the door is open for progressive inauguration of other of like kind under which it can hardly be expected that the states will retain genuine independence of action. And without independent states a Federal Union as contemplated by the Constitution becomes impossible.

MR. JUSTICE SUTHERLAND:

The effect of the dual distribution of powers is completely to deny to the states whatever is granted exclusively to the nation, and, conversely to deny to the nation whatever is reserved exclusively to the states. . . . The threat implicit in the present encroachment upon the administrative functions of the states is that greater encroachments, and encroachments upon other functions will follow.

MR. JUSTICE BUTLER:

The provisions in question, if not amounting to coercion in a legal sense, are manifestly designed and intended directly to affect state action in the respects specified. And, if valid as so employed, this "tax and credit" device [of the unemployment insurance system] may be made effective to enable federal authorities to induce, if not indeed to compel, state enactments for any purpose within the realm of state power, and generally to control state administration of state laws.

But a greater blow to the Tenth Amendment was yet to come. It was *Brown* v. *Board of Education* (1954) and the various desegregation cases initiated subsequently to carry out the Supreme Court's order for a show of "prompt and reasonable start toward full compliance" which helped to produce a clash of constitutional views unequaled since the Thirties in its intensity and ferocity. Many persons bitterly denounced the Court for breaking with precedents following *Plessy* v. *Ferguson* and for interfering with an educational system that had been traditionally viewed as clearly within the reserved powers of the states. Within three years of that decision every Southern legislature "had adopted interposition resolutions and manifestoes of various sorts varying from mild protests to outright declarations that the Supreme Court's decision is 'null and void.' " [37]

Many of these declarations reflected the spirit if not the letter of John C. Calhoun's concept of the Constitution:

[W]e must view the General Government and those of the States as a whole, each in its proper sphere independent; each perfectly adapted to its respective

[36] 301 U. S. 548 (1937).
[37] I. Hinderaker (ed.), *American Government Annual 1958–1959* (New York, 1958), p. 37.

objects; the States acting separately, representing and protecting the local and peculiar interests; and acting jointly through one General Government, with the weight respectively assigned to each by the Constitution, representing and protecting the interests of the whole; and thus perfecting, by an admirable but simple arrangement, the great principle of representation and responsibility, without which no government can be free or just. To preserve this sacred distribution as originally settled, by coercing each to move in its prescribed orbit, is the great and difficult problem on the solution of which the duration of our Constitution, of our Union, and, in all probability, our liberty depends.[38]

This federal-state constitutional debate was to be aggravated even further by additional decisions from the Warren Court which affected issues other than segregation and which went far beyond the South in their legal implications. Only a few can be noted.

The United States Supreme Court in

Griffin v. *Illinois* (1956) held that under the due process of law and the equal protection clauses of the Fourteenth Amendment an indigent defendant alleging errors at his trial in a criminal suit in a state court had to be provided with a transcript at public cost.[39]

Slochower v. *Board of Higher Education* (1956) invalidated the dismissal of a college professor for invoking his privilege of self-incrimination before a Congressional Committee.[40]

Koenigsberg v. *State Bar of California* (1957) ruled that the refusal of the California Bar to admit an attorney on the basis of his alleged moral unfitness violated the due process of law clause of the Fourteenth Amendment since there was no explicit showing in the record to have warranted such disqualifying interferences.[41]

Sweezy v. *New Hampshire* (1957) declared invalid a contempt citation issued under the New Hampshire Subversive Activities Act partly for statutory vagueness of such terms as "subversive person" and "subversive organization" and partly on the basis of procedures under which the legislature had authorized the Attorney General of the state to act as a one-man investigating committee.[42]

Mapp v. *Ohio* (1961) decided that evidence obtained in violation of the Fourth Amendment was inadmissible even in state courts under the due process of law standards of the Fourteenth Amendment thus applying the so-called federal exclusionary rule to the state judiciary as well.[43]

Baker v. *Carr* (1962) reversing, in effect, a long line of precedents now held that federal courts under the Fourteenth Amendment have the power and the duty to pass on the apportioning of state legislative districts.[44]

---

[38] John C. Calhoun, *The Fort Hill Address of John C. Calhoun* (Richmond, 1960), p. 8.
[39] 351 U. S. 12 (1956).
[40] 350 U. S. 551 (1956).
[41] 353 U. S. 252 (1957).
[42] 354 U. S. 235 (1957).
[43] 367 U. S. 643 (1961).
[44] 369 U. S. 186 (1962).

Engel v. *Vitale* (1962) adjudged New York's program of daily classroom prayers (prescribed by the Board of Regents) as incompatible with the "wall of separation" between Church and State demanded under the terms of the First Amendment.[45]

Abington School District v. *Schempp* and *Murray* v. *Curlett* (1963) struck down Pennsylvania and Maryland laws as violative of the First Amendment for stipulating the reading of verses from the Holy Bible and the recitation of the Lord's Prayer as required opening exercises for daily school work.[46]

Gideon v. *Wainwright* (1963), unanimously overruling a 1942 decision, held that states must provide legal counsel for indigent defendants who face "serious" criminal charges.[47]

Gray v. *Sanders* (1963) found Georgia's county unit system of voting to be unconstitutional on its face and explicitly rejected as totally inapplicable any analogy between this system and the federal electoral college. "The concept of political equality," wrote Mr. Justice Douglas for the majority, "can mean only one thing—one person, one vote." [48]

Malloy v. *Hogan* (1964) extended to defendants in state courts the privilege against compelled self-incrimination contained in the Fifth Amendment and heretofore held applicable to the federal proceedings only.[49]

Reynolds v. *Sims* (1964) decided for the first time that every state legislature —House as well as Senate—must be apportioned substantially equal in population.[50]

During the 85th Congress (1957–1959) "there were no less than 35 proposals to 'do something about the Supreme Court.' " [51] Led by a coalition of Southern Democrats and conservative Republicans, strong congressional pressures developed to deny the appellate jurisdiction of the court to certain types of cases, particularly in the field of subversion. Two of the relatively more moderate anti-Court measures, the Jenner-Butler bill and H.R. 3, both of which sought to incorporate some of these proposals, were narrowly defeated and even then only after Lyndon Johnson, at that time the Senate's majority leader, effectively applied some of his adroit delaying tactics.

Another major attack on the United States Supreme Court and the extension of federal power was launched in December of 1962 when a group of state legislators and officials working through the Council of State Governments urged the adoption of three critical states' rights amendments. One of these proposals called for the creation of a court of the Union composed of the fifty state chief justices with power to overrule decisions of the United States Supreme Court. A second proposal would have changed the United States

[45] 370 U. S. 421 (1962).
[46] 374 U. S. 203 (1963).
[47] 372 U. S. 335 (1963).
[48] 373 U. S. 368 (1963).
[49] 378 U. S. 1 (1964).
[50] 377 U. S. 533 (1964).
[51] Jack W. Peltason (ed.), *American Government Annual 1959–1960* (New York, 1959), pp. 57–58.

Constitution to the effect that any new amendment could be added by the states themselves without involving Congress in any phase of the process. The third change—by far the most popular—demanded that the federal judiciary be stripped of its power to compel a state legislature to reapportion or redistrict. This was accepted by the legislatures of Arkansas, Idaho, Kansas, Missouri, Montana, Nevada, Oklahoma, South Carolina, South Dakota, Texas, Utah, Washington, and Wyoming. All in all, by January 1964, at least sixteen states endorsed one or more of these amendments.

In addition, the Court came under serious attack from within the ranks of the judiciary itself. A conference of chief justices of state supreme courts on August 23, 1958, adopted by a vote of thirty-six to eight a report strongly critical of the decisions of the United States Supreme Court in the areas of federal-state relationships:

> [W]e think that the overall tendency of decisions of the Supreme Court over the last 25 years or more has been to press the extension of federal power and to press it rapidly.

> [T]he Supreme Court has too often tended to adopt the role of policy-maker without proper judicial restraint. . . .

> We do not believe that either the framers of the original Constitution or the possibly less gifted draftsmen of the Fourteenth Amendment ever contemplated that the Supreme Court would, or should, have the almost unlimited policy-making powers which it now exercises. . . .

> It is our earnest hope which we respectfully express, that that great Court exercise to the full its power of judicial self-restraint by adhering firmly to its tremendous, strictly judicial powers and by eschewing, so far as possible, the exercise of essentially legislative powers when it is called upon to decide questions involving the validity of state action, whether it deems such action wise or unwise. The value of our system of federalism, and of local self-government in local matters which it embodies, should be kept firmly in mind, as we believe it was by those who framed the Constitution.[52]

By way of rebuttal, supporters of the Supreme Court have contended that the critics tend to exaggerate and overgeneralize their case, ignoring a number of important decisions involving questions of subversion in which the Supreme Court actually sustained the states and their legal actions. For example,

> *Beilan* v. *Board of Public Education* (1958). The Supreme Court held that public employees could be discharged for their refusal to answer questions about alleged subversive activities on the basis that such lack of cooperation could reasonably be classed as constituting "incompetency." [53]

> *Uphaus* v. *Wyman* (1959). The Supreme Court held that the state legislature could properly authorize the attorney general of that state to question *Uphaus*, the defendant, about allegedly subversive connections involved in the activities

---

[52] "Report of the Committee on Federal-State Relationships as Affected by Judicial Decisions," *Harvard Law Record*, October 23, 1958, p. 6.
[53] 357 U. S. 399 (1958).

of a summer camp (World Fellowship) of which he was the executive director and force him to furnish the lists of speakers, participants, and employees.[54]

However, it must also be stressed that in most of these civil liberties cases affecting the relationship between the federal and state governments, whether the decisions favored the states or not, that the Court was deeply and narrowly split. In both *Beilan* and *Uphaus* the four libertarians of the Court, Justices Warren, Black, Douglas, and Brennan, for example, entered vigorous and consistent dissents. In both instances they criticized the states with the same vigor displayed earlier with respect to congressional investigations in *Watkins* v. *United States* (1957),[55] insisting that the Bill of Rights could not permit government "to expose for the sake of exposure." Put simply, these judges viewed the constitutional safeguards of civil rights to transcend the constitutional guarantees of states' rights.

Mr. Justice Black addressed himself specifically to this relationship in his dissent in a double jeopardy case, *Bartkus* v. *Illinois* (1959).

> Our Federal Union was conceived and created "to establish Justice" and to "secure the Blessings of Liberty," not to destroy any of the bulwarks on which both freedom and justice depend. We should, therefore, be suspicious of any supposed "requirements" of "federalism" which result in obliterating ancient safeguards. I have been shown nothing in the history of the Union, in the writings of its Founders, or elsewhere, to indicate that individual rights deemed essential by both State and Nation were to be lost through the combined operations of the two governments.[56]

And so, as the debate continues, it must be emphasized that the Supreme Court of the United States has weathered many a controversy, that conservatives and liberals have praised and damned the bench or its occupants, and that De Tocqueville was correct in his observation "that there is scarcely a political question in the United States which will not sooner or later be reconciled by the judiciary." Underlying the constitutional debates between centralists and states' righters are certain undeniable political realities—demands by the American Negro, demands for higher standards in state criminal justice, demands by urban residents for more equitable representation in state legislatures and in Congress. Reflected in these constitutional arguments are the most complex struggles between conflicting political interests and philosophies concerning the nature, direction and rate of socio-economic change that is needed in this country.

CONSTITUTIONAL GUARANTEES TO THE STATES AND FEDERAL AIDS

Relatively removed from the din of battle are a number of additional constitutional provisions under which the states are given certain specific federal protections and assurances.

[54] 360 U. S. 72 (1959).
[55] 354 U. S. 178 (1957).
[56] 359 U. S. 121 (1959).

Article IV, Section 3:

New States may be admitted by the Congress into this Union; but no new State shall be formed or erected within the jurisdiction of any other State; nor any State be formed by the junction of two or more States, or parts of States concerned as well as of the Congress.

While the Constitution thus sought to establish in express terms the doctrine of territorial integrity, the doctrine that the newly-admitted states ought to be on equal footing with the original states of the Union was a concept which developed only gradually out of specific congressional resolutions and judicial decisions. Nor did this development preclude Congress from imposing certain conditions precedent upon new states seeking admission. Ohio, for example, had to promise not to tax federally-sold lands for a period of five years; Utah was required to prohibit polygamous marriages; Arizona had to strike from its constitution a provision for the popular recall of its judiciary; and Oklahoma was to have its capital at Guthrie. When the citizens of that state later decided to move their capital to Oklahoma City, in direct conflict with the terms of the federal act of admission, the Supreme Court was called on to rule on the question whether the federal condition could in law override "any subsequent state legislation repugnant thereto."

"[W]hen a new state is admitted into the Union," the majority argued in *Coyle* v. *Smith* (1911) [57] which had posed the query, "it is so admitted with all the powers of sovereignty and jurisdiction which pertain to the original states [and] . . . such powers may not be constitutionally diminished, impaired, or shorn away by any conditions, compacts, or stipulations embraced in the act under which the new state came into the Union, which would not be valid and effectual if the subject of congressional legislation after admission." To hold otherwise, to deny the equality of the states, they reasoned, would disrupt the "harmonious operation of the scheme upon which the Republic was organized." With words such as these, the Court rejected the restriction which Congress attempted to attach to the act of admission.

Besides territorial integrity and legal equality, the federal government owes the states some additional guarantees:

Article IV, Section 4:

The United States shall guarantee to every State in this Union a Republican Form of Government, and shall protect each of them against Invasion; and on Application of the Legislature, or of the Executive (when the Legislature cannot be convened) against domestic Violence.

What is a republican form of government? As early as 1849, in a case growing out of a military contest between two factions in Rhode Island each claiming to be the legal government of the state, the Supreme Court speaking through Chief Justice Taney in *Luther* v. *Borden*,[58] decided that it was the

[57] 221 U. S. 559 (1911).
[58] 7 How. 1 (1849).

Congress and not the judiciary that would have to fulfill the guarantees as to a "republican form of government." Congress was given the power (1) to decide "what government is established," (2) which senators and representatives are to be admitted "into the Councils of the Union," and (3) "the authority of the government under which they are appointed." Once Congress made this determination "its decision is binding on every other department of the government and could not be questioned in a judicial tribunal." Also rejected as non-justiciable were subsequent attempts that would have had the Supreme Court decide such questions as whether a "republican form of government" was "compatible" with the initiative and referendum (*Pacific States Telegraph & Telephone Co.* v. *Oregon*, 1912),[59] with the invalidation of a state reapportionment law through a referendum (*Ohio ex rel. Davis* v. *Hildebrant*, 1916),[60] with the enactment of a workmen's compensation law (*Mountain Timber Co.* v. *Washington*, 1917),[61] or with statutes that restricted the franchise to male citizens only (prior to the adoption of the Nineteenth Amendment).

Actually it is not only the Congress but the president as well who is directly concerned with applying the standards of Article IV, Section 4. Under an act passed February 28, 1795, the president was specifically given the responsibility in cases "of insurrection in any State against the government thereof, on application of the legislature of such State or of the executive" to call out the militia "as he may judge sufficient to suppress such insurrection." Even beyond this, should it become necessary for the federal government to secure the rights entrusted to it by the Constitution, as was made clear in the *Debs* case (*In re Debs*, 1895),[62] the president has the authority to use "the entire strength of the nation . . . to enforce in any part of the land the full and free exercise of all national powers. . . ." Furthermore, should there occur within a state a breakdown of law and order accompanied by the likelihood of mass violence, a failure of the state governing authorities to request such presidential assistance or intervention does not at all preclude a president from taking action if he so decides. From Lincoln's Civil War actions to Eisenhower's use of troops in the Little Rock integration dispute, case and statutory authority have so construed the constitutional grant of powers given in Article II, Section 3, which declares that the president "shall take care that the laws be faithfully executed," that there can no longer be doubt about a president's legal authority to employ "the entire strength of the nation" on his own initiative if in his judgment the conditions of the moment demand it in order "to quell domestic violence . . . , to protect the property of the United States, to remove obstructions to the United States mails, or to protect interstate commerce from interruption by labor disputes. . . ."[63]

[59] 223 U. S. 118 (1912).
[60] 241 U. S. 565 (1916).
[61] 243 U. S. 219 (1917).
[62] 158 U. S. 565 (1895).
[63] Corwin, p. 705.

INTERSTATE RELATIONS UNDER THE CONSTITUTION

Constitutional relationships between the states may be far less dramatic than are those between the federal and state governments, but judicially they are in no way less complex. Some of the most difficult arbitral functions performed by the United States Supreme Court are those concerned with the attempts to reconcile detailed legal consequences arising out of the diverse and varying social policies, cultural traditions, statutory patterns, and economic interests which characterize the fifty states of the Union.

Here again only a few elementary constitutional principles can be pointed up for each of three major areas of interstate jurisdictional relations: (1) full faith and credit, (2) interstate rendition, and (3) interstate compacts.

Full Faith and Credit

Article IV, Section 1:

Full faith and credit shall be given in each State to the public acts, records, and judicial proceedings of every other State. . . .

Mr. Justice Robert H. Jackson, writing about this clause some years ago, insisted that "[i]t is doubtful if a century and a half of constitutional interpretation has advanced us much beyond where we would be if there had never been a [full faith and credit] clause. Local policies and balance of local interest still dominate the application of the federal requirement. . . ." [64] Put differently, the requirement that "Full faith and credit shall be given in each State to the public acts, records, and judicial proceedings of every other state" has as a matter of judicial practice not been interpreted despite its sweeping promise as demanding of one state the automatic and unqualified enforcement of legal orders issued in another. The reason for this development must be found in the deeply rooted traditions of Anglo-American common law which viewed each state jurisdiction as possessing considerable judicial autonomy. Thus a judicial civil order issued against a person in one state while recognized as competent and properly adjudged may call for yet another judicial process to force compliance in the sister state. "This conclusiveness is not automatic. A person who has secured a court order in one state and wishes to have it enforced against a person who has since gone to another state must bring a new legal action in the latter state. In this action the court will accept the original decree, examine it, and if it finds the order to be properly authenticated, will issue an enforcement order of its own. This must be done

---

[64] Robert H. Jackson, *Full Faith and Credit, the Lawyers Clause of the Constitution,* quoted in Francis H. Heller, *Introduction to American Constitutional Law* (New York, 1952), p. 152.

even if the public policy of the second state would not have permitted such a decision had the case originated there." [65] What is important to note here is that there is a difference between an original judgment or decree and a *suit to enforce* such through the application of the full faith and credit clause. In practical situations this distinction has meant that despite the potential of greater uniformity inherent in full faith and credit, courts have held enforceable in one state but unenforceable in a sister state gambling debts, penal judgments, and various types of contractual rights. Among the most dramatic illustrations of how decisions rendered by the courts of one state can be legally resisted in another state are those involving the validity of divorce decrees. Under full faith and credit the indispensable requirement for recognition of a divorce decree by the courts of the second state is the jurisdictional competency of the courts of the first state to issue it. Failure to have proper jurisdiction can be used to defeat the divorce and leave the affected parties legally married in one state and legally unmarried in another. For example, in *Williams* v. *North Carolina* (1945),[66] in the second *Williams* case, a divided Supreme Court held that since the power to grant a divorce rests on domicile, the courts of North Carolina were not to be precluded under full faith and credit to determine for themselves whether the Nevada domicile established by one of the spouses in fact did or did not constitute a *bona fide* domicile. Taking issue with the majority, Mr. Justice Rutledge stressed the enormously unsettling quality of this decision by insisting that "[e]very divorce, wherever granted . . . may now be reexamined by every other state, upon the same or different evidence, to redetermine the 'jurisdictional fact.' . . ." While this is still basically the law, subsequent decisions have somewhat modified its severity by judicial acceptance of the "divisible divorce" doctrine. Under this concept the courts of the second state can acquiesce to the dissolution of the marital status while at the same time reserving for their own redetermination such connected issues as alimony, child support, and the disposition of property. Far from satisfying demands for either clarity or certainty, this limited accommodation seeks to reconcile strongly differing laws embodying strongly-held views about marriage and divorce by the different states and sections of the country.

So far, full faith and credit has made only a very limited, if any, contribution to the solution of the many highly complex problems that have grown out of the inherent diversity and conflict of laws. Judged by expressions from its own members, the "arbitral functions" performed by the United States Supreme Court in these cases has done little to assure either an effective or an efficient administration of justice. While Congress has the constitutional powers to implement the full faith and credit clause, and to attempt a definition of uniform standards of jurisdiction or lay down rules governing the effect that should be given by the courts of one state to the statutes of another, political realities militate against the body's action. Strong legislative pres-

[65] C. Herman Pritchett, *The American Constitution* (New York, 1959), pp. 83–84.
[66] 325 U. S. 226 (1945).

sures against further federal aggrandizement in this direction promise to persist.

Whatever progress continues to be made towards more uniform state laws will more likely emerge from the states themselves in response to specific business and commercial needs. Considerable work on behalf of greater uniformity has already been done by the National Conference of Commissioners on Uniform State Laws. For seventy years this group composed of law professors, judges, practicing attorneys, attorneys general, legislators, administrative officers, and state research directors, working closely with the American Bar Association and the Council of State Governments, attempted to draft a great number of codes, uniform and model, which were designed to help establish or further the legal climate for a more truly cooperative federalism.

The following list of uniform acts, each adopted by at least thirty-five or more states since 1896, indicates something about the character of the problems that demanded attention and about the range on which interstate agreement could be reached:

Negotiable Instruments (1896)
Warehouse Receipts (1906)
Sales (1906)
Stock Transfer (1909)
Partnership (1914)
Limited Partnership (1916)
Declaratory Judgments (1922)
Veterans' Guardianship (1928)
To Secure Attendance of Out-of-State Witnesses (1931)
Narcotic Drug (1932)
Trust Receipts (1933)
Criminal Extradition (1936)
Simultaneous Death (1940)
Photographic Copies As Evidence (1949)
Reciprocal Enforcement of Support (Amendments, 1950)
Gifts to Minors (1956)
Simplification of Fiduciary Security Transfers (1958)

All in all, about 1,800 uniform and model acts have now been adopted by the fifty states, the District of Columbia, and Puerto Rico. Wisconsin ranks first with forty adoptions, and the rest of the states follow with a minimum of fifteen each.[67]

Laws dealing with such matters as interstate recognition of divorce, property, statute of limitations, criminal statistics, premarital blood tests, probate and rules of procedure have been found to be most difficult to adopt. Not met by the states with overwhelming response, so far at least, were the recommendations of model acts, begun in 1925, even though here uniformity was less explicit an objective. Two subjects stressed in thirty model acts were law enforcement and legal reforms.

[67] *Book of the States, 1964–1965*, pp. 103–107.

Interstate Rendition

The Founding Fathers did not envisage federalism as a design for obstructing justice or for encouraging criminals to escape lawful prosecution.

Article IV, Section 2:

A Person charged in any State with Treason, Felony, or other Crime, who shall flee from Justice, and be found in another State, shall on demand of the executive Authority of the State from which he fled, be delivered up, to be removed to the State having Jurisdiction of the Crime.

At first glance it might be presumed that the governor of the state of refuge would have no alternative but to turn over a fugitive from justice to the state demanding his return. This is not the case. Federal courts, interpreting this Article, have held (a) that the federal government cannot compel a governor to surrender a fugitive and return him to the state in which the offense was committed; [68] (b) that there can be no judicial inquiry into the motives "controlling the actions of the governors of the demanding and surrendering states;" [69] (c) that once a fugitive has been returned, courts of the receiving state may indict him for another offense than the one for which he was extradited; [70] and (d) that return of a fugitive even if carried out illegally will not preclude his trial and punishment by the state whose laws he offended.[71]

Hovering over these interpretations were the memories of fugitive slave laws and of constitutional concepts of interstate relations more indigenous to eighteenth and nineteenth century judicial thought about federalism than to those dominant during the twentieth century. As a practical matter, governors do generally extradite, and the Uniform Extradition Law of 1936 has standardized and facilitated the legal processes involved, nor has Congress remained entirely quiescent on this touchy subject.

In connection with certain major offenses, the Fugitive Felon Act (1934) enacted by Congress under its power over interstate commerce, has made it a crime, punishable by a fine of $5,000 or imprisonment of not more than five years or both, for a person to flee from one state to another with the intent of avoiding prosecution, custody, or confinement or for the purpose of avoiding giving testimony in such criminal proceedings. Legislative efforts to broaden the applicability of this law to make it applicable to all crimes punishable by terms of a year or more, so as to strengthen law enforcement authorities in their battles against organized crime and vice syndicates, resulted in the passage of the Fugitive Felon Act amendments of 1962 despite determined opposition from senators who stressed the diversity of state criminal statutes as well as the archaic quality of many of them.

[68] *Kentucky* v. *Dennison*, 24 How. 66 (1861).
[69] Corwin, p. 695.
[70] *Lascelles* v. *Georgia*, 148 U. S. 537 (1893).
[71] *Mahon* v. *Justice*, 127 U. S. 700 (1888).

Here again while federal assistance might well yield greater efficiency by requiring interstate conformity to certain legal norms, it poses considerations quite unacceptable to many people who treasure a pluralism that might tend to preserve and encourage local and sectional differences in approach to crime and punishment.

Interstate Compacts

Boundary disputes, between the American colonies and later between the states joined together under the Articles of Confederation, form the historical antecedents from which developed constitutional provisions governing interstate compacts or formal interstate agreements.

Article I, Section 10, Cl. 3:

No State shall, without the Consent of Congress . . . enter into any Agreement or Compact with another State, or with a Foreign Power.

Subsequent judicial interpretation of this section has somewhat modified the congressional consent requirement. There are types of interstate compacts not sufficiently affecting the federal power relationships which have been held valid without congressional approval. When Congress does consent, this may be in the form of a conditional consent; it may explicitly reserve to Congress "the right to alter, amend or repeal its consent." Constitutionally, every act of consent must always be subject to the plenary powers possessed by Congress over interstate commerce or over any other matter clearly delegated to it under Article I, Section 8. Three such recently concluded compacts involved interstate cooperation in the areas of social welfare and corrections:

New England Corrections Compact
Participating States: Rhode Island, Connecticut, Maine, New Hampshire, Vermont.
Purpose: To provide legal basis for the cooperative use of institutions for any type of correctional cases which the states concerned may wish to treat on a cooperative basis.

Interstate Compact on the Placement of Children
Participating States: New York and Maine.
Purpose: To provide procedures for interstate cooperation in the placement of children, for an exchange of information on adoption procedures, and to permit the institutionalization of juvenile delinquents in a cooperating state when the facilities of the state of origin are inadequate.

Interstate Compact on Welfare Services
Participating States: Maine and Connecticut.
Purpose: To eliminate residence requirements for receiving welfare services on a reciprocal basis.

While used to a minor extent throughout our earlier history, numerically and substantively interstate compacts have become significant only in the decades following World War I. It was during those years that legislators and governors became increasingly aware of the potential usefulness inherent in the compact clause. A now classic study by Felix Frankfurter and James M. Landis cogently stated its promise: "[t]he imaginative adaptation of the compact idea should add considerably to reserves available to statesmen in the solution of problems presented by the growing interdependence, social and economic, of groups of States forming distinct regions." [72] Since 1900, about one hundred various types of compacts have been concluded. Some established only study commissions; some, operating agencies with boards of commissioners appointed by the governor of each of the cooperating states supervising technical staffs and administrative personnel. With varying degrees of success, it has become possible for states to work jointly on problems affecting the conservation of natural resources, river basins, water pollution, toll bridge operations, port management, mass transportation, and fishing rights.

The compacts concluded during the last three years included an agreement between twelve Southern states to establish a Southern Interstate Nuclear Board to implement regional cooperation in the development of nuclear energy for peacetime purposes; a Washington Metropolitan Area Transit Regulation Compact designed to regulate fares, determine routes, and manage traffic patterns in the metropolitan area; a Vehicle Equipment Safety Compact to recommend safety equipment requirements to the states; a Driver License Compact to provide for exchange of out-of-state traffic conviction reports between the licensing state and the state in which the violation takes place; an Interstate Library Compact to provide a legal basis for extending cooperative library service across state lines; and a New England Health Services and Facilities Compact to coordinate programs and plan for improvement of health services and facilities in New England.

The recently completed Delaware River Basin Compact involves at least one new and unique development that will be watched closely by friends and foes of the compact idea. Established "to coordinate the work of the member jurisdictions in the development of the resources of the Delaware River including the planning and construction of flood prevention and water supply facilities and other water resource needs," the new commission was given broad authority to deal with such interrelated aspects as pollution control, watershed management, recreation, hydroelectric power, and the regulation of withdrawals and the diversion of Delaware River water. While varying forms of federal-interstate patterns of cooperation in the field of water resources administration have developed in the past throughout different sections of the country, what makes this compact unique is its formal setting—it is the first thoroughgoing interstate federal compact to be put into effect. The

[72] Richard H. Leach and Redding S. Sugg, Jr., *The Administration of Interstate Compacts* (Baton Rouge, 1959), p. 3. For background on interstate compacts, see also Council of State Governments, *Interstate Compacts, 1783–1956* (Chicago, 1956) and Frederick L. Zimmermann and Mitchell Wendell, *The Law and Use of Interstate Compacts* (Chicago, 1961).

United States government joining New York, New Jersey, Delaware, and Pennsylvania, decided to become one of the full partners to the compact.

To what extent this federal partnership will facilitate or deter future recourse to the interstate compact concept is as yet an open question. It may be contended that federal counsel, experience, and resources would be welcomed by the states and thus contribute to a more effective operation of projects which by their very nature must involve special federal interests— watershed management and conservation clearly belonging in this category. It is also true, however, that this same argument can be turned around to point up a threat of possible federal domination in an arrangement composed of supposedly equal partners. The states might wake up to discover that among equals some are more so than others.

Aside from the issue of federal partnership, at least two other developments have recently cast shadows of apprehension in the direction of existing as well as future compacts. As compacts multiplied, especially in the years following World War II, Congress began to take another long look at its consent power. Special stipulations were inserted in the general consent clause which required the compact authority to make periodic reports to Congress as well as resubmit any amendments to the compact which would substantially broaden the original scope of operations.

A furious and protracted battle between the New York Port Authority and the House Judiciary Committee was the other major development causing genuine concern among state legislators, governors, and compact officialdom. Legally at issue was the question of whether a congressional committee investigating the activities of the New York compact had the power under a consent clause—which explicitly reserved the right to "alter, amend or repeal"—to demand from the compact commissioners, and more specifically from its executive director, submission of certain documents relating to the external as well as internal operations of the agency. When the executive director refused to honor a congressional subpoena with respect to the second group of items (although he fully complied with the demand for information regarding such external matters as annual financial reports, rules, and by-laws), Congress, after some debate, voted to cite him for criminal contempt. In defense of his position, he challenged the constitutional ground on which Congress could "alter, amend or repeal" its consent and cited written orders from the governors of New York and New Jersey who had publicly protested the inquiry, instructing him not to obey the disputed sections of the subpoena.

To furnish Congress the internal memoranda, minutes, and correspondence constituted, in the judgment of these state officials, "an unconstitutional invasion of powers reserved to the states under the 10th Amendment to the Constitution." [73] In 1962 the defendant's cause was upheld by a unanimous decision from the United States Court of Appeals in Washington. Pointedly

[73] *Congressional Record,* June 22, 1962, p. 10610.

avoiding the constitutional dimension of the issue, the appellate court held on the narrowest grounds possible, that it could not believe that Congress "in the absence of any truly enlightening and informative floor discussion" could have wished to embark on so novel and "expansive" an investigation entailing most profound consequences for the entire pattern of federal-state relations without explicitly evidencing such an intent. Stressing that in its view the defendant was not "a criminal" and "no one seriously considers him one," the court felt persuaded "to read these authorizing resolutions to mean that the Judiciary Committee was empowered to conduct an investigation calling for documents relating to actual 'activities and operations' of the Authority rather than for all of the administrative communications, internal memorandums, and other intra-Authority documents demanded by the subpoena in question." [74] While the New York Port Authority and the governors rejoiced and hailed the decision, the final word may yet belong to Congress.

What assessment should be placed on the capacity of interstate compacts to revitalize American federalism by stimulating state initiative and imagination? Critics of the compacts have argued that the agencies established under them are operated by technicians and bureaucrats who are politically insensitive or at worst politically irresponsible inasmuch as they possess no electorate to whom accountability is due. The public knows little about the compacts, their problems, and their achievements or who the people are who make the decisions and why. Compact commissioners and their executives tend to prefer profitable enterprises to those which might render socially desirable and publicly-needed services but whose financial returns promise to be less favorable. Caught also between powerful local pressures, suspicious legislatures, competitive state economies, and preoccupied governors, the scope of compact operations and leadership will likely be technically narrow and devoid of genuine substantive innovations.

Protagonists of interstate compacts contend that these agreements "can play a tremendous role in the states' reassumption of power. For there are no necessary limitations on the nature of the assignments interstate compact agencies may be given, nor any arbitrary restrictions on the fields into which they may enter. They may be endowed with all the powers states ordinarily give to local governmental units or entrust to agencies within their several boundaries, including the power of eminent domain, the power to tax, and, if the states wish it so, the power to enforce their own orders." [75]

If the continued interest in developing new compacts can be taken as a realistic index of the popularity of this device among state officials, there can be little doubt that compacts will continue to multiply even more rapidly in the future as regional demands for interstate cooperation become more pressing for accelerating economic growth and for intensifying scientific and technological research.

[74] *Ibid.*, p. 10610.
[75] Leach and Sugg, p. 226.

TWO OTHER PATTERNS OF INTERSTATE COOPERATION—THE COUNCIL OF STATE GOVERNMENTS AND THE GOVERNORS' CONFERENCE

The Council of State Governments represents another major agency performing much of the preparatory work for interstate compacts. In this it is associated with the various state commissions on interstate cooperation—groups of state legislators and administrators especially designated for this function within each of the states. Established by the states themselves in 1933, as a successor organization to the American Legislators Association, the Council of State Governments forms a joint governmental agency which is controlled by the states and through which the fifty-member states can work cooperatively with each other and with the federal government on problems of common concern. Policy is set by a Board of Managers which includes delegates from each state. It meets annually and supervises the implementation of its directives through an executive committee and staff. In addition, it

Conducts "research projects on a broad variety of state programs and problems" and distributes "the research reports widely among the states."

Maintains "an inquiry-and-information service available to state agencies, officials, and legislators."

Serves "as a clearing house through which the states exchange their own information."

Holds national and regional meetings on particular questions.

"[P]rovides the staff for a number of affiliated interstate organizations."

Issues "publications on a broad gamut of state affairs," including a biennial standard reference work, *Book of the States,* a quarterly journal, *State Government,* a monthly newsletter, *State Government News,* a *Washington Legislative Bulletin,* and the *Legislative Research Checklist.*

Among the wide range of studies conducted by the council were the following: educational systems, highway safety, mental health, needs of the aging, problems of metropolitan areas, administration of water resources, state financing, legislative processes and procedures, central departments of administration, planning services, and judicial systems.

Affiliated with the council and using the organization as its secretariat are a number of professional associations whose members perform important state functions. These include the Governors' Conference, the National Legislative Conference, the Conference of Chief Justices, the National Association of State Budget Officers, the National Association of State Purchasing Officials, the National Conference of Commissioners on Uniform State Laws, the National Association of Attorneys General.

Special mention should be made of at least one additional council activity. Using this agency as its secretariat, the Committee on Suggested State Legislation, composed of legislators, attorneys general, members of state commissions on interstate cooperation, and other state officials, prepares an annual Program of Suggested State Legislation for submission to state legislatures. Containing formal drafts, uniform state laws, or other legislative suggestions, this project manifests an effort to provide all states with the best professional thinking and experience on the many complex subjects with respect to which laws may be needed and enacted. The 1963–1964 list of recommendations comprised, among others, such laws or topics of laws (other than uniform laws) pertaining to state concerns with radiation control, weights and measures, investment of idle funds, equal pay for women, review of sentences in criminal cases, loss of voting rights in presidential elections, and exchange of tax records and information. Not unexpectedly, in view of the problems faced by the states presently, the largest number of suggested measures involved the relationship of state to local governments.

Working in closest association with the council on many of the problems of state administration and of federal-state relations is the Governors' Conference. This institution, originally assembled in 1908 at the invitation of President Theodore Roosevelt as part of his campaign for federal legislation to protect and conserve the nation's natural resources, has become during the last thirty years one of the more significant extra-constitutional agencies for interstate cooperation. At the outset the annual Governors' Conference was largely devoted to social niceties and to the presentation of formal speeches on state administrative problems which pointedly avoided controversy and prolonged discussion of the broader issues of public policy. It took a series of state and national crises to activate the conference and reveal some of its potential power on the national scene. The great Depression, World War II, the postwar population explosion, and the accompanying social and economic changes confronted the states' chief executives with administrative and budgetary problems for which the conference seemed to offer a much needed forum in which harassed governors could exchange views and prepare for possible collective action by Congress and the presidency. Some governors viewed the conference as an ideal bastion of states' rights from which strong oratorical forays could be launched against steadily advancing federal encroachments. Some sought to apply the collective influence of the governors merely to modify rather than to blunt the impact of Washington's newly-expanding activities. Despite the obvious interest to preserve for their states as wide an autonomy as practicable, a majority of the governors generally proved willing to acknowledge the necessity of federal financial assistance for implementing those programs of the New Deal and Fair Deal where state resources were clearly inadequate and where the public demanded speedy action. Governors, too, watch election returns.

Yet even in those years of crisis, there were a number of instances when the governors were able to persuade the federal government that genuine federal-state cooperation cannot be equated with one-way accommodation.

Thus, for example, the governors succeeded after World War II in having the federal government return to the states the administration of employment services and the right to publish the names of public assistance recipients. Also, when it came to reducing the manpower strength of the National Guard or of the Army Reserve, the Department of Defense learned to take another look at its proposals in the light of impressive congressional opposition which governors marshalled to block such contemplated moves.

Recent Governors' Conferences, better attended and better briefed than ever on state problems, have continued to move aggressively into discussions not only of state but of national and international issues as well. No doubt, the presidential ambitions of some of its most prominent members have left their mark. The 1964 conference in Cleveland made this dramatically clear. Despite parallel efforts by others to minimize the role of politics and partisanship, neither can or perhaps should be avoided as the conference seeks to function more actively within the framework of a cooperative federalism which could be sufficiently flexible to permit a strong national government to be confronted with strong and viable state governments. Along these lines a former governor assessed the contributions of the Conference in the following terms: "The Governors' Conference is serving such a federalism in its search and leadership for more logic and order in federal-state relations; in its opposition to needless transfer of tasks to Washington; in the impetus it gives for interstate cooperation; above all in the studies and leadership through which it seeks to strengthen state government in structure and administration and to make state services more adequate for our times." [76] Commenting on the 1962 Governors' Conference, a *New York Times* columnist stressed the pioneer role of the American governor in solving the "new practical problems of the age." Means have to be devised through which separate state communities can come to grips with their ever-increasing needs for cooperative and interdependent effort in order to manage the rapid changes in technology, commerce, transportation, and education.

> Governors have to deal, not with ideological theories of political life but with facts. They may glorify "states' rights" in Fourth of July speeches, but if New York allows drinking at the age of 18 and New Jersey and Connecticut next door do not permit drinking until the age of 21, this is not a theory but a practical problem.
>
> In the same sense, if one city in a state tries to purify a river, but another city upstream pollutes the same river, the Governor has to try to figure out how to get the two cities together. . . .
>
> What they have been working on for years under the American Federal system, the new African, Asian and even the Common Market countries of Europe are just beginning to talk about.[77]

[76] Glenn E. Brooks, *When Governors Convene: The Governors' Conference and National Politics* (Baltimore, 1961), p. 165.

[77] James Reston, "The States of the Union and the World," *The New York Times*, July 4, 1962, p. 20.

THE FEDERAL GRANT-IN-AID PROGRAMS

THE SCOPE OF THE PROGRAMS

First, what is meant by federal grants-in-aid? As used in this chapter, and generally in political science text literature, the term denotes fiscal assistance given by the federal government to state and local governments for the purpose of applying and carrying out broad legislative objectives defined by congressional statute with the attached condition that the recipient governments are to share in varying ratios the costs and the administration of the programs. Reserved, however, to the federal government in these grants-in-aid enactments are such matters as the right of inspection, the right to specify minimum standards, and the right to approve the implementing actions undertaken by state and local governments.

These grants involve large amounts of money and constitute major items in the budgets of federal, state, and local governments. In fiscal 1963, for example, 14 per cent of all the revenues received by state and local govern-

FIGURE 1

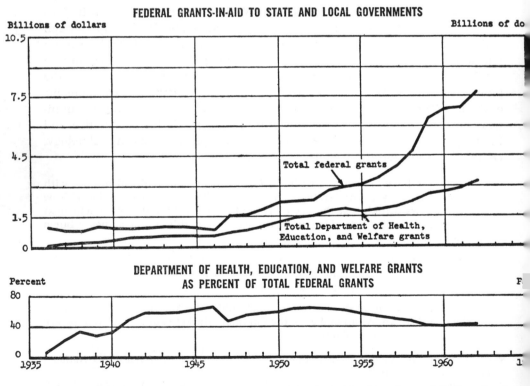

FEDERAL GRANTS-IN-AID TO STATE AND LOCAL GOVERNMENTS

DEPARTMENT OF HEALTH, EDUCATION, AND WELFARE GRANTS AS PERCENT OF TOTAL FEDERAL GRANTS

SOURCE: Department of Health, Education, and Welfare, *Health, Education, and Welfare Trends* (Washington, 1963), p. 109.

ments came from Washington where they represented about one-fifth of all federal, non-defense connected expenditures. Since 1948, federal grants-in-aid have been increased every year (see Figure 1); during the last ten-year period, for example, they almost tripled from $2.8 billion in fiscal 1953 to $10.5 billion (estimated) in fiscal 1965, averaging half a billion dollars per year (see Table 1).

To round out the picture, it must be emphasized that substantial amounts of such federal grants do not come directly out of each year's budget, but are chargeable against special trust funds congressionally established to support particular functions. Approximately 40 per cent of the fiscal 1965 total of $10.5 billion (estimated) comes, for instance, from the Highway and Unemployment trust funds.

Over the years the amounts dedicated to federal grants rose steadily and impressively. Recent enactments of the 89th Congress, particularly legislation in connection with the War on Poverty and fiscal supports for all levels of education, promise in the future to increase significantly the totals as well as the rate of expansion of federal grants-in-aid spending.

As may be expected, not all of the states share equally in federal aids. How much each state can receive under a particular program will vary with that state's population, needs, fiscal resources, and per capita income and

TABLE 1. FEDERAL AID EXPENDITURES IN
RELATION TO STATE-LOCAL REVENUE

	Total expenditures for aid to state and local governments	
	Amount (In millions)	As a per cent of state-local revenue *
1954	$ 2,657	10
1955	3,124	11
1956	3,753	12
1957	4,111	11
1958	5,072	12
1959	6,813	15
1960	7,174	14
1961	7,283	13
1962	8,167	14
1963	8,781	14
1964 est.	10,177	†
1965 est.	10,568	†

* Based on compilations published by Governments Division, Bureau of the Census. Excludes state-local revenue from publicly-operated utilities, liquor stores, and insurance trust systems.

† Not available.

SOURCE: *The Budget of the United States Government: Fiscal Year Ending June 30, 1965* (Washington, 1964), p. 430.

with the nature of the formula which Congress developed for the distribution of such funds.[78]

For example, overall federal grant-in-aid payments in 1962 constituted more than 24 per cent of state and local revenues in Alabama, Alaska, Arkansas, South Dakota, Vermont, and Wyoming but less that 12 per cent in Connecticut, Delaware, Florida, Illinois, Indiana, Maryland, Massachusetts, Michigan, New Jersey, New York, Pennsylvania, and Wisconsin (see Table 2). In this connection it might be interesting to note that aside from the Southern states, among the greatest beneficiaries of the grant-in-aid programs are six Western states—Idaho (21.8%), Montana (20.9%), Nevada (18.5%), New Mexico (22.4%), Utah (20.8%), and Wyoming (31.1%)— only two of which (Nevada and New Mexico) voted in 1960 for the Democratic presidential aspirant, a strong advocate of expanding federal grants-in-aid.

Actually, despite heavy increases in federal aid and the constantly expanding use of this pattern of intergovernmental assistance, considerable diversity persists as to the levels of state and local expenditures beyond the federally-required minimum for the different programs (see Table 3). This leaves a significant degree of freedom to state and local governments to adapt national goals to local resources and needs. A careful study of the political impact of these grants led one scholar to the following conclusion:

> The grant-in-aid system is by no means an undermining of federalism, but rather a refinement of it. It corresponds to a pragmatic pluralism, which has long been remarked as a characteristic of politics in the United States. It has built into it the characteristically different policy tendencies of states and of the

[78] "There are differences among Federal grant programs in the proportion of total program cost the State and their local governments, on the one hand, and the Federal Government, on the other, are required to bear. Forty-seven of the 60 Federal grant programs require the States (and/or local governments) to share in program costs. The remaining 13 grant programs have no specific matching requirements. Of those programs that do, the matching or cost sharing requirements are of two kinds: variable matching, whereby the proportion of total program cost borne by the State is determined on the basis of an index employed to measure relative State fiscal capacity; and fixed ratio matching, whereby each State and/or local government is required to share in the same proportion of program cost. . . ." Advisory Commission on Intergovernmental Relations, *The Role of Equalization in Federal Grants* (Washington, 1964), p. 39.

THE ROLE OF MATCHING PROVISIONS IN THE FEDERAL GRANT
EXPENDITURE FOR FISCAL 1962

Method	Amount (In millions)	Per cent
No matching	$ 870	12.4
Variable matching	1,193	17.0
Fixed ratio matching	4,951	70.6
	$7,014	100.0

SOURCE: *The Role of Equalization in Federal Grants*, p. 40.

TABLE 2. FEDERAL AID IN RELATION TO TOTAL GENERAL REVENUE
OF STATE AND LOCAL GOVERNMENTS, BY STATE, 1962

State & region	Amount (In millions)		Per capita		Revenue from federal government as % of total general revenue
	Total general revenue	Revenue from federal government	Total general revenue	Revenue from federal government	
United States	$58,214	$7,857	$313	$ 42	13.5
New England and Mideast	16,825	1,647	334	33	9.8
Maine	277	41	284	42	14.7
New Hampshire	178	32	287	51	17.8
Vermont	144	42	372	109	29.4
Massachusetts	1,798	200	346	39	11.1
Rhode Island	247	34	281	38	13.6
Connecticut	881	95	336	36	10.7
New York	6,837	484	391	28	7.1
New Jersey	1,922	168	302	26	8.7
Pennsylvania	3,116	340	274	30	10.9
Delaware	157	15	337	33	9.8
Maryland	977	118	302	36	12.0
District of Columbia	291	78	369	99	26.8
Midwest	16,085	2,013	307	38	12.5
Michigan	2,604	289	324	36	11.1
Ohio	2,818	359	281	36	12.7
Indiana	1,314	142	282	30	10.8
Illinois	3,189	357	316	35	11.2
Wisconsin	1,300	146	324	36	11.2
Minnesota	1,222	149	353	43	12.2
Iowa	882	108	318	39	12.3
Missouri	1,163	210	269	49	18.0
North Dakota	232	37	367	58	15.8
South Dakota	244	59	339	81	24.0
Nebraska	400	62	277	43	15.4
Kansas	716	94	323	42	13.1
South	14,143	2,464	256	45	17.4
Virginia	944	154	222	36	16.3
West Virginia	454	87	253	48	19.1
Kentucky	730	148	237	48	20.2
Tennessee	810	164	222	45	20.3
North Carolina	1,071	162	228	35	15.2
South Carolina	511	90	209	37	17.5
Georgia	1,003	196	246	48	19.5
Florida	1,541	166	284	31	10.8
Alabama	753	181	227	55	24.1
Mississippi	510	105	226	47	20.7
Louisiana	1,065	213	316	63	20.0
Arkansas	421	101	229	55	24.0
Oklahoma	752	162	307	66	21.6
Texas	2,734	375	270	37	13.7
New Mexico	345	77	346	78	22.4
Arizona	498	82	335	55	16.4
West	11,160	1,739	403	63	15.6
Montana	253	53	363	76	20.9
Idaho	214	47	306	67	21.8
Wyoming	160	50	483	151	31.1
Colorado	716	114	378	60	15.9
Utah	306	61	320	64	20.0
Washington	1,157	163	384	54	14.1
Oregon	654	124	362	69	18.9
Nevada	152	28	435	81	18.5
California	7,142	1,000	419	59	14.0
Alaska	135	46	557	190	34.0
Hawaii	271	52	391	76	19.4

SOURCE: Advisory Commission on Intergovernmental Relations, *The Role of Equalization in Federal Grants* (Washington, 1964), p. 20.

TABLE 3. REQUIRED STATE AND LOCAL MATCHING OF FEDERAL GRANTS-IN-AID IN RELATION TO STATE AND LOCAL TAX REVENUE AND GENERAL EXPENDITURE FROM OWN SOURCES FOR SELECTED FUNCTIONS

12 HIGHEST AND 12 LOWEST INCOME STATES, 1962

States (ranked from highest to lowest 1962 per capita income)	Required matching as % of tax revenue	Required matching as percent of general expenditure from own sources *				
		Total	Education	Highways	Public welfare	Health and hospitals
U. S. average	7.6%	6.1%	1.9%	12.8%	48.0%	2.6%

12 HIGHEST PER CAPITA INCOME STATES

Nevada	7.2	5.1	1.6	6.8	52.9	8.0
Delaware	5.9	4.7	1.8	3.6	25.0	16.5
Connecticut	5.3	4.1	1.3	7.4	29.3	1.2
New York	5.1	4.3	1.4	8.1	42.5	0.9
New Jersey	4.3	3.7	1.4	9.1	33.7	1.8
California	5.6	4.6	1.1	8.3	44.0	2.0
Illinois	6.6	5.7	1.7	14.0	34.9	2.2
Massachusetts	7.5	6.7	2.0	13.3	44.6	1.1
Maryland	5.6	4.4	1.7	9.5	48.7	1.5
Alaska	10.0	5.9	2.7	4.1	37.9	6.7
Washington	7.9	6.0	1.5	13.6	48.2	3.0
Michigan	6.7	5.1	1.6	10.5	41.9	2.0

12 LOWEST PER CAPITA INCOME STATES

Oklahoma	16.0	12.9	2.6	20.3	69.4	5.0
West Virginia	11.0	9.3	3.2	9.9	86.4	5.4
New Mexico	11.2	8.4	2.1	16.5	68.0	7.9
Louisiana	13.2	9.5	2.4	14.1	79.9	4.0
Georgia	12.9	9.4	3.4	18.0	†	4.3
North Carolina	9.7	7.9	3.1	14.8	90.0	5.1
Kentucky	12.1	7.4	2.6	12.1	74.4	6.8
Tennessee	11.5	8.6	3.4	14.2	69.1	4.3
Alabama	16.7	11.6	3.0	23.3	96.3	5.1
Arkansas	17.9	15.1	5.3	29.9	96.3	7.7
South Carolina	10.9	8.9	3.5	25.9	72.1	6.5
Mississippi	13.5	9.4	3.1	17.6	54.6	6.5

* The expenditure categories are as defined by the Bureau of the Census and include substantial amounts for activities for which there are no federal grant programs. "General expenditure from own sources" is defined as total general expenditure less amounts received from the federal government.
† Approximately 100%.
SOURCE: Advisory Commission on Intergovernmental Relations, *The Role of Equalization in Federal Grants* (Washington, 1964), p. 21.

national government. It is scarcely a means of enforcing similarity between them.[79]

Opponents to federal aid profess to see in the federal grants-in-aid technique an ill-concealed attempt to seduce states into surrendering their rights and autonomies. States join federal programs because they fear to let

[79] Philip Monypenny, "Federal Grants-in-Aid to State Governments: A Political Analysis," *National Tax Journal*, March, 1960, p. 16.

other states benefit from federal dollars paid out of funds to which their citizens had already been forced to make their tax contribution. Senator Goldwater had labeled these grants "in effect, a mixture of blackmail and bribery." [80] Similar sentiments were voiced some years ago in the following resolution adopted by the Indiana General Assembly:

> Indiana needs no guardian and intends to have none. We Hoosiers—like the people of our sister states—were fooled for quite a spell with the magician's trick that a dollar taxed out of our pockets and sent to Washington, will be bigger when it comes back to us. We have taken a good look at said dollar. We find that it lost weight on its journey to Washington and back. The political brokerage of the bureaucrats has been deducted. We have decided that there is no such thing as "Federal" aid. We know that there is no wealth to tax that is not already within the boundaries of the 48 states.
>
> So we propose henceforward to tax ourselves and take care of ourselves. We are fed up with subsidies, doles and paternalism. We are no one's step-child. We have grown up. We serve notice that we will resist Washington, D. C., adopting us.
>
> *Be it resolved by the House of Representatives of the General Assembly of the State of Indiana (The Senate concurring),* That we respectfully petition and urge Indiana's Congressmen and Senators to vote to fetch our county court-houses and city halls back from Pennsylvania Avenue. We want government to come home.
>
> *Resolved further,* That we call upon the legislatures of our sister States and on good citizens everywhere who believe in the basic principles of Lincoln and Jefferson to join with us, and we with them, to restore the American Republic and our 48 States to the foundations built by our fathers.[81]

As it turned out, neither Indiana's local pride nor that of her sister states were to prove sufficiently strong to reverse the stubborn trend towards greatly increased federal aid. Looking at a recent five-year span, between 1955 and 1960 alone, federal fiscal assistance to state and local governments in the form of grants-in-aid to hospital construction, vocational rehabilitation, and low-rent housing programs more than doubled. Federal grants in connection with expenditures for public health, federally-aided highways, and slum clearance and urban renewal multiplied three, four, and five times. Meanwhile, state and local airport developments topped even these—they increased their share of federal supports from $8,000,000 in 1955 to an estimated $58,000,-000 in 1962.[82]

There is really nothing very new or unique about the grant-in-aid device itself. As early as 1785, the Northwest Ordinance already provided that in every township one section was to be reserved for the purposes of public

---

[80] Barry Goldwater, *Conscience of a Conservative* (Shepherdsville, Ky., 1960), p. 26.

[81] William Anderson, *The Nation and the States: Rivals or Partners?* (Minneapolis, 1955), pp. 6–7.

[82] U. S. Department of Health, Education, and Welfare, *Health, Education, and Welfare Trends 1963* (Washington, 1963), p. 114.

education. Used throughout the nineteenth century to allow states to encourage railroad development and agricultural education, its heyday came during the great depression when the Roosevelt administration incorporated the grant-in-aid principle into various welfare measures. Proponents contend that the grant-in-aid concept is ideally suited for a federal state since it facilitates cooperation between center and circumference combining warranted diversity in administration with national uniformity in approach. Also, it facilitates the taxing of wealthier states for the benefit of the poorer so that all citizens regardless of the accident of birth or residence can share more equitably in a nationwide minimum standard of social welfare or service.

Those Americans, on the other hand, who perceive this country's collective role not in terms of what services the government can perform for its citizens, but in terms of maximizing individual freedoms against governmental interventions, will insist on a much stricter and much more literal interpretation of the Constitution. They will continue to register with varying degrees of political intensity their protests against federal involvements in the areas of public housing, urban renewal, and similar quasi-commercial activities through the operations of grants-in-aid or other similar measures. One of the current and most extreme manifestations of this reaction is the so-called "Liberty Amendment" which has been approved in Georgia, Louisiana, Nevada, South Carolina, Texas, and Wyoming. These are the key provisions:

> Section 1. The Government of the United States shall not engage in any business, professional, commercial, financial, or industrial enterprise except as specified in the Constitution.
>
> Section 2. The activities of the United States Government which violate the intent and purpose of this amendment shall, within a period of three years from the date of the ratification of this amendment, be liquidated and the properties and facilities affected shall be sold.
>
> Section 3. Three years after the ratification of this amendment the sixteenth article of amendments to the Constitution of the United States shall stand repealed and thereafter Congress shall not levy taxes on personal incomes, estates, and/or gifts.

CASE PROBLEMS FOR CLASS DISCUSSION

1. Assume that the Liberty Amendment has become the college debate topic of the year. You are the assistant debate coach at your school and have been asked to draw up a tentative outline of the arguments which the teams on both sides of the issue might wish to develop. Which Supreme Court decisions would have to be consulted? What other major sources would have to be included?
2. Have federal aids in fact impaired state and local governmental autonomy? Assume that it is your responsibility to draw up a research design which would throw some light on this question. Which type of aids could you select for study and why? How would you define and measure the federal impact? Which index of governmental "autonomy" would you attempt to isolate for the purpose of analysis?
3. As an administrative assistant to the governor, you have been assigned the duty of preparing staff papers in anticipation of the annual Governors' Con-

ference. The governor is very much concerned with strengthening interstate and regional economic cooperation and would like to be in the position of assuming leadership in this area at the conference. How would you proceed to organize your report for the governor? What type of data would you include?

4. Assume that North Dakota is considering the adoption of a drivers' license interstate compact for the purpose of furthering the cause of highway safety and law enforcement. Many Northwestern and Western states have already joined the compact. As a member of the North Dakota Legislative Research Committee you have been instructed to draw up a report which would offer the members of the legislature information that would prove helpful to the eventual enactment of the compact. What would you have to include concerning the nature of interstate compacts in general and the advantages of the pending proposal in particular?

SELECTED BIBLIOGRAPHY

Advisory Commission on Intergovernmental Relations, *Coordination of State and Federal Inheritance, Estate, and Gift Taxes* (Washington, 1961).

Advisory Commission on Intergovernmental Relations, *Intergovernmental Cooperation in Tax Administration* (Washington, 1961).

Advisory Commission on Intergovernmental Relations, *Intergovernmental Responsibilities for Mass Transportation Facilities and Services in Metropolitan Areas* (Washington, 1961).

Advisory Commission on Intergovernmental Relations, *Periodic Congressional Reassessment of Federal Grants-in-Aid to State and Local Governments* (Washington, 1961).

WILLIAM ANDERSON, *Intergovernmental Relations in Review* (Minneapolis, 1960).

WALTER P. ARMSTRONG, JR., "Uniform State Laws and the National Conference," *State Government,* Summer, 1962, pp. 185–190.

FRANK BANE, "Recommendations for Improving Intergovernmental Relations," *Public Management,* January, 1962, pp. 4–6.

JOHN E. BEBOUT, "The States' Best Friend," *National Civic Review,* February, 1964, pp. 70–73, 104.

WILLIAM D. CAREY and ABRAM M. VERMEULEN, "Intergovernmental Cooperation Through Budget Channels," *State Government,* Summer, 1963, pp. 166–171.

EMANUEL CELLER, "Congress, Compacts, and Interstate Authorities," *Law and Contemporary Problems,* Autumn, 1961, pp. 682–702.

O. HATFIELD CHILSON, "Federal-State Relations in the Field of Water Rights,"

State Government, Winter, 1960, pp. 32–38.

JACOB COHEN and MORTON GRODZINS, "How Much Economic Sharing in American Federalism," *American Political Science Review,* March, 1963, pp. 5–23.

"Congress and the Port of New York Authority: Federal Supervision of Interstate Compacts," *Yale Law Journal,* April, 1961, pp. 812–820.

JAMES M. COOK, "National-State Cooperation in Securities Regulation," *State Government,* Winter, 1962, pp. 57–61.

GEORGE S. DUGGAR, *Federalism and Self-Government in the United States: Urban Renewal as an Example* (Berkeley, 1961).

DANIEL J. ELAZAR, *The American Partnership* (Chicago, 1962).

ERNEST E. ENGELBERT, "Federal-State Relationships: Their Influence on Western Regional Growth," *Western Political Quarterly,* September, 1963, pp. 686–707.

ROBERT J. FRYE, *Federal-Municipal Relations: An Overview* (University, Ala., 1963).

SIDNEY GOLDSTEIN, "An Authority in Action —An Account of the Port of New York Authority and its Recent Activities," *Law and Contemporary Problems,* Autumn, 1961, pp. 715–724.

ROBERT A. GOLDWIN (ed.), *A Nation of States: Essays on the American Federal System* (Chicago, 1963).

W. BROOKE GRAVES, *American Intergovernmental Relations* (New York, 1964).

W. BROOKE GRAVES, "Maze of Governments," *National Civic Review,* May, 1960, pp. 230–237; June, 1960, pp. 293–301; and July, 1960, pp. 355–362.

HOWARD J. GROSSMAN and ROBERT A. COX, "Coordination: Teamwork in a Small

Community," *Public Administration Review*, March, 1963, pp. 35–39.

FRANCIS H. HELLER and DON R. BOWEN, *Uniform State Laws in Kansas* (Lawrence, 1962).

JAMES C. KIRBY, JR., "Limitations on the Power of State Legislatures over Presidential Elections," *Law and Contemporary Problems*, Summer, 1962, pp. 495–509.

RICHARD H. LEACH, "Interstate Agencies and Effective Administration," *State Government*, Summer, 1961, pp. 199–204.

RICHARD H. LEACH, "Interstate Authorities in the United States," *Law and Contemporary Problems*, Autumn, 1961, pp. 666–681.

JAMES A. MAXWELL, *Issues in Tax Credits and Intergovernmental Fiscal Relations* (Washington, 1962).

JAMES A. MAXWELL, "Recent Developments in Federal-State Financial Relations," *National Tax Journal*, December, 1960, pp. 310–319.

ELTON K. McQUERY, "Interstate Compacts for Traffic Safety," *State Government*, Spring, 1962, pp. 112–117.

ROBERT MONTGOMERY, JR., "Uniform Traffic Laws," *State Government*, Winter, 1963, pp. 54–57.

SELMA J. MUSHKIN, "Barriers to a System of Federal Grants-in-Aid," *National Tax Journal*, September, 1960, pp. 193–218.

KAN ORI, "Basic Ideas in Federal-State Relations: The Indiana 'Revolt' of 1951," unpublished Ph.D. dissertation, Indiana University, 1961.

JAMES K. POLLOCK, "Chronic Overlapping," *National Civic Review*, December, 1960, pp. 602–609.

DUANE W. RIGGERT, "Federal Grants-in-Aid and Shared Revenues Briefly Defined," *National Tax Journal*, March, 1961, pp. 104–108.

NELSON A. ROCKEFELLER, *The Future of Federalism* (Cambridge, 1962).

WILLIAM A. SCHNADER, "The Uniform Commercial Code: What is Accomplished —What Remains," *State Government*, Winter, 1963, pp. 49–53.

ROBERT H. SOLOMONS, III, "The Southern Interstate Nuclear Compact and Board," *State Government*, Winter, 1963, pp. 40–44.

REDDING S. SUGG, JR. and GEORGE H. JONES, *The Southern Regional Education Board: Ten Years of Regional Cooperation in Higher Education* (Baton Rouge, 1960).

JOSEPH A. VIEGES, JR., *Federal-State Relationships in Interstate Highway Administration: A Case Study of Florida* (Gainesville, 1963).

EDWARD W. WEIDNER, *Intergovernmental Relations as Seen by Public Officials* (Minneapolis, 1960).

DAVID WELBORN, "National-State Cooperation in Regulatory Administration," *State Government*, Summer, 1960, pp. 199–207.

MATTHEW E. WELSH, "The Hatch Act and the States," *State Government*, Winter, 1964, pp. 8–13.

FREDERICK L. ZIMMERMANN and RICHARD H. LEACH "The Commissions on Interstate Cooperation," *State Government*, Autumn, 1960, pp. 233–242.

FREDERICK L. ZIMMERMAN and MITCHELL WENDELL, "New Horizons on the Delaware," *State Government*, Summer, 1963, pp. 157–165.

Chapter XI

METROPOLITAN AREAS
TOWNSHIPS
SPECIAL DISTRICTS
AND COUNTIES

Who favors metropolitan reforms and who opposes them and why? Will counties or super cities emerge on top?

What are the patterns of inter-governmental cooperation in metropolitan areas, and what form are they likely to take in the immediate future? What can states do to help?

THE METROPOLITAN AREAS—THE SETTING AND THE PROBLEMS

The socio-economic significance of metropolitanism in contemporary America is strikingly impressive. A population which is 70 per cent urban, with nearly two-thirds living in 212 population clusters (classified by the Bureau of the Census as Standard Metropolitan Statistical Areas, S.M.S.A.) is not only crowded into such clusters but growing at a rate 50 per cent more rapidly than the country as a whole (see Figure 1). There can be little doubt that the effective and responsible governing of metropolitan areas constitutes one of this decade's most challenging problems.

As far back as 1958, these areas were credited with 76.8 per cent of the nation's economic value added by manufacture, with 67.2 per cent of all manufacturing establishments, with 73.8 per cent of total industrial employment, with 78.5 per cent of all manufacturing payrolls; in 1960, with 78.6 per cent of all bank deposits; and in 1959 and 1960, with 69 per cent of all housing starts.[1]

The largest of the population belts is encompassed now in a sprawling megalopolis, or super city, along the East coast from Lawrence-Haverhill, Massachusetts to Washington, D. C. It encompasses 31 million people (an increase of 16 per cent over 1950) in thirty-five large cities and suburbs. Within this area are nearly one-fifth of the nation's retail store business and over one-fifth of the nation's manufacturing business.[2] By the turn of the century an estimated 20 million people will live along the West coast in an urban strip reaching from Santa Barbara to San Diego. Clustered around Los Angeles City, in the County of Los Angeles are now seventy-one cities. In the East, fifty-seven cities surround Cleveland in Cuyahoga County, Ohio, and

[1] Advisory Commission on Intergovernmental Relations, *Alternative Approaches to Governmental Reorganization in Metropolitan Areas* (Washington, 1962), p. 5.

[2] Richard E. Mooney, "Population Soars Past 31 Million in East Coast City-Suburb Belt," *The New York Times*, August 13, 1961, pp. 1, 62.

357

FIGURE 1

STANDARD METROPOLITAN STATISTICAL AREAS OF THE UNITED STATES: 1962

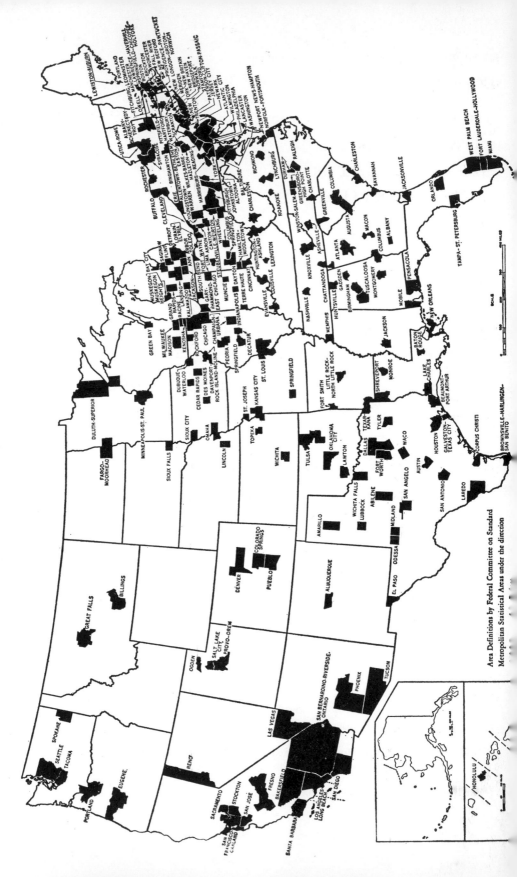

Area Definitions by Federal Committee on Standard
Metropolitan Statistical Areas under the direction

eighty-three municipalities have mushroomed around Pittsburgh in Allegheny County, Pennsylvania.[3]

This urban explosion represents mounting pressures on local governmental units which must provide their citizens with all types of services and protections. Financial resources are needed to build new schools and highways, to furnish law enforcement, fire protection, and public health and welfare, to construct sewage disposal plants, and rail, bus, and air terminals. Land has to be acquired for parks and recreational areas, ample water supplies assured, air and water pollution abated, and tax assessments equalized. A single governmental level alone cannot do this. The interests of cities, suburbs, and counties, of incorporated urban and unincorporated rural areas need to be coordinated and adjusted so that an area's fiscal basis is balanced with an area's service needs.

The weaknesses of local government in meeting these challenges since World War II became more and more apparent with the rapid population increases and major population shifts which characterized the postwar era. A well-known authority in the field of municipal government provides a cogent indictment of local governments for three basic failures:

> first, the failure to extend high standard government protections and services to the spreading settlements of homes and economic enterprises; second, the failure to produce area-wide goals and programs of action, including control plans, through the normal democratic process of debate, compromise and community-wide decision; and third, the failure to develop teamwork machinery for the metropolitan area, founded on a broad constituency and guided by local leaders and appropriate representative institutions.[4]

Behind these failures lie certain structural and legal peculiarities indigenous to the American system of local government. Of these, four major ones were stressed in a 1961 report by the Advisory Commission on Intergovernmental Relations to the Committee on Government Operations, United States House of Representatives:

A. Fragmentation and overlapping of governmental units.

In the 212 S.M.S.A.'s 18,442 local governmental units serve a population of 112.9 million persons—see Table 1. This includes 6,004 school districts. Twenty per cent of all local governments are located in the 212 S.M.S.A.'s.

B. Disparity between tax and service boundaries.

"Generally speaking, the larger the number of independent governmental jurisdictions within a metropolitan area the more inequitable and difficult becomes the process of financing those governmental services which by their nature are area-wide in character."

[3] Bureau of the Census, U. S. Department of Commerce, *Census of Governments: 1962*, I (Washington, 1963), pp. 108, 162, 176.

[4] Luther Halsey Gulick, *The Metropolitan Problem and American Ideas* (New York, 1962) p. 165.

C. State constitutional and statutory restrictions.

"They apply particularly to the organization and functions of county government, the under-representation of urban centers in state legislatures, antiquated annexation and incorporation laws, and the ability of local governments to tax and borrow money."

D. Metropolitan area problems frequently cross state lines.

"The twenty-six metropolitan areas that include territory in two or more states contain more than one-fifth of the Nation's people and almost one-third of its manufacturing activity." [5]

TABLE 1. METROPOLITAN AREAS: POPULATIONS AND LOCAL
GROUPS BY SIZE-GROUPS

SMSA size group (1960 population)	Number of SMSA's	Population, 1960 (000)	Local governments, 1962
All SMSA's	212	112,885	18,442
1,000,000 or more	24	61,582	7,227
500,000 to 999,999	29	19,215	2,857
300,000 to 499,000	28	10,373	2,146
200,000 to 299,999	41	10,182	3,141
100,000 to 199,999	68	9,772	2,540
50,000 to 99,999	22	1,761	531

SOURCE: Bureau of the Census, Department of Commerce, *Census of Governments: 1962*, Vol. I, "Governmental Organization" (Washington, 1963), p. 11.

Obstacles to an area-wide approach to local government are even more complicated than the already complex considerations of structure, statutes, and constitutions. Economic, social, and political factors and forces enter into the fray. Farmers and rural homeowners, for example, living in the suburban or unincorporated areas surrounding a central city often resent the intrusion by the city into governmental affairs they deem local in character and peculiarly suited to their minimal needs. This is especially true if they should be persuaded that a proposed area-wide water, sewage disposal, or law enforcement service would result in higher tax rates and assessments. Joining them will be suburban newspapers, suburban commercial interests, county leagues of municipalities, and local governmental officials and employees to whom an area-wide market or government constitutes a threat. Sometimes the conflict is further accentuated by long-standing political party alignments which divide the city from the surrounding country, Democrats from Republicans. Occasionally right-wing extremists see in the whole concept of metropolitanism "A socialist scheme to destroy local government . . . an American So-

[5] *Alternative Approaches to Governmental Reorganization*, pp. 8–10; for the California scene, see the excellent study by Winston W. Crouch and Beatrice Dinerman, *Southern California Metropolis: A Study in Development of Government for a Metropolitan Area* (Berkeley, 1963).

viet." [6] Moreover, since neither city nor suburbia constitute monolithic or homogeneous entities by themselves, reactions to a metropolitan area-wide approach may differ greatly between diverse groups of residents. Included in suburbia may be elegant subdivisions with impressive estates, older rural residences, or low-income fringe areas with newly-developed tracts accommodating large numbers of nearly identical and relatively inexpensive single-dwelling units, with different expectations and attitudes in each of these sections about the nature and extent of governmental services and about who should pay for them.

In the core city, downtown working-class residents may view any particular proposal for area-wide governmental consolidation with apprehension while it may be favored by chambers of commerce, real estate interests, city officials, League of Women Voters, industrial groups, the press, radio, television, and civic reform interests. Moreover, what the precise effect will be of voter apathy or ignorance when a proposal is actually submitted to the local electorate is, of course, nearly always a factor of great uncertainty in such elections.

PATTERNS OF GOVERNMENTAL REORGANIZATION IN METROPOLITAN AREAS

Proposals to reorganize local governments within metropolitan areas since World War II followed essentially five major approaches: city-county consolidation; metropolitan federation and the Lakewood plan and urban counties; city annexation; metropolitan special and multipurpose districts; and intergovernmental metropolitan cooperation.

CITY-COUNTY CONSOLIDATION

Which one of these patterns would be most adaptable to local circumstances must necessarily depend on many factors, not least among them the constitutional provisions under which the local units must operate. There are still about twenty states, for example, where it is nearly impossible to make basic structural changes in local government without first changing the state constitutions themselves. This is most difficult and expensive. Written into the basic charters have been such detailed matters as the boundaries of each county, the location of county seats, or the size of the electoral majorities that are required to merge units of local government. For this, as well as for many other political and socio-economic reasons, the consolidating of city with county governments represents, without doubt, the most ambitious pattern which could be recommended by reformers who sought to bring greater rationality and order to the present chaos of duplicated services, contradictory policies, and unplanned urban growth.

There is nothing especially novel about the idea of city-county consolidation as such. During the nineteenth century, Boston, Philadelphia, New Orle-

[6] Merrill Folsom, "Regional Council Surviving Attack," *The New York Times,* April 7, 1963, p. 76.

ans, and New York adopted varying forms of such mergers. Yet when this type of an approach was attempted in recent years it did not prove very successful at the polls. Thus since 1950, in only one out of nine attempts did the voters register their approval and that was in Davidson County, Tennessee, where in 1962 a majority of the voters of the county and of Nashville separately accepted a metro charter after having rejected a similar one four years earlier. In a subsequent judicial test the Supreme Court of Tennessee unanimously sustained the constitutionality of this consolidation. The nearly one-half million people in the Nashville area live under a single, consolidated city-county metropolitan government, "neither a city nor a county," headed by a mayor elected at-large with power to appoint all the major administrative department heads subject only to council confirmation.[7] The new metropolitan council of forty members, elected for four-year terms (the mayor too has a four-year term) from thirty-five districts ranging from 10,000 to 12,000 people, was designed to provide more equitable representation to large areas previously annexed and taxed but left without much of a voice in government and with few if any of the municipal services.

Nashville's successful governmental reorganization came after the city council—to the annoyance of suburbanites—had annexed significant industrial and residential properties and enacted a tax on automobiles using the city's streets (green sticker tax). An additional politically unpopular act of the mayor (who had opposed the second referendum) also contributed to strengthen the consolidationist forces. A recent student of the Nashville experience commented on the political aspects of the struggle to the effect that

> active involvement of rival professional political leaders in all stages of a metro reform movement . . . is not necessarily a kiss of death, does not prevent "radical reform," and may actually constitute a tactical advantage for metropolitan reformers.[8]

The eight defeats of city-county mergers occurred in Georgia (Macon-Bibb County, 1960); Missouri (St. Louis-St. Louis County, 1962); New Mexico (Albuquerque-Bernalillo County, 1959); North Carolina (Durham-Durham County, 1961); Tennessee (Nashville-Davidson County, 1958), (Knoxville-Knox County, 1959), (Chattanooga-Hamilton County, 1964); and Virginia (Richmond-Henrico County, 1961).

Without going into the detailed governmental arrangements that were contained in each of these defeated proposals, it is possible to outline a few of their major features. First, all of them provided for some sort of basic city-county charter which, not unlike a state constitution or city home-rule charter, defined the powers of a governing board or commission whose members are elected in the area and representative of the rural, urban, and suburban sections of the county. Second, most of the charters made provision for a

---

[7] Daniel R. Grant, "Consolidations Compared," *National Civic Review*, January, 1963, pp. 10–13, 29.

[8] Daniel R. Grant, "Metropolitics and Professional Political Leadership," *The Annals of the American Academy of Political and Social Sciences*, May, 1964, p. 72.

number of elected city-county officials such as mayor, city-county clerk, treasurer, assessor, police chief, and two even called for the position of a county manager who was to be given county-wide administrative powers. Third, the charters to varying degrees furnished legal authority for area-wide water, sewage, street maintenance, garbage collection, public health and welfare, library and hospital service, and police and fire protection, and for a more unified development of building codes, zoning ordinances, traffic controls, mass transport, and tax assessments.

The St. Louis proposals, defeated by heavy majorities both in the city and in the separate county, had specified an area-wide popular election of a comptroller and council president in addition to that of a mayor with significant appointive as well as veto powers. The two million residents of the city and surrounding county were to be governed also by a forty-four member metropolitan council including two representatives from the twenty-two boroughs "ranging in population from 46,000 to 98,000" into which the area was to be divided.[9] These boroughs were given smaller councils with the right to veto metro passed zoning ordinances which directly affected the territory in the borough. Also combined into one system were the formerly separate courts of the city and county, city and county offices, city and county property, public parks, and libraries.

Those who advocate the concept of city-county consolidation contend that it offers the best opportunity to reduce costs and enhance efficiencies through large-scale purchasing and through the elimination of duplicating efforts and districts. Stressed also are genuine advantages that could allegedly be gained by more central planning for a more intelligent utilization of resources, water, land, and fiscal, which are so basic to an orderly growth and development of the entire and often interdependent area.

Aside from the very serious and practical obstacles to such mergers in the form of necessary prior constitutional changes, some critics wish to emphasize what to them appear to be dangerous violations of the home-rule principle inherent in any scheme which imposes upon localities centrally enacted policies. What proponents consider as administrative logic and order, constitutes to localists an unwarranted submersion of plural patterns of local tastes, traditions, and interests.

METROPOLITAN FEDERATION AND THE LAKEWOOD PLAN AND URBAN COUNTIES

Metropolitan Federation

Despite this country's pride in having demonstrated to the world the viability of a most auspicious and successful experiment in federalism, it was not in the United States but in Toronto, Canada, in 1954, that this principle

[9] Richard D. James, "Missouri Votes Again Tomorrow on Uniting City of St. Louis and St. Louis County," *The Wall Street Journal*, November 5, 1962; see also Henry J. Schmandt, Paul G. Steinbicker, and George D. Wendel, *Metropolitan Reform in St. Louis: A Case Study* (New York, 1961).

was first applied to a North American metropolitan area. Under statutory authority from the Ontario Provincial Legislature, Toronto and its twelve suburban communities, all located in one county, were allowed to establish a metropolitan council composed of twenty-five members. Included in the group were the twelve mayors from the cities on the periphery, twelve representatives from Toronto, and a chairman designated by the provincial government. In this two-tier approach to the area's governmental needs, the Toronto Council was to handle such matters as water supply, sewage disposal planning, and control over arterial highways while such responsibilities as local law enforcement, fire protection, street maintenance, and education were left to the local communities. A similar pattern was adopted in 1960 by the Manitoba Provincial Assembly for the Greater Winnipeg Metropolitan Corporation.

In this country Miami-Dade County's Metro, operating under a county home-rule charter, granted by the state of Florida, represents probably the closest approximation to the federal formula used in Canada. Here, as there, political power in the metropolitan area is divided between a central governmental body and various city governments. The central unit possesses sufficient power to operate on area-wide problems as well as settle intergovernmental disputes within the metropolitan area, while the city governments possess (1) concurrent powers—powers exercisable by the central government as well as by themselves—and (2) residual powers—powers that are essentially local in range and effect.

As predictable, the Dade County experiment did not take shape overnight. It grew out of a set of conditions in which the population of the area nearly doubled between 1950 and 1960. People came to Miami's hospitable climate for various reasons: for play, recreation, retirement, or for newly-developing business and industrial opportunities. Whatever the personal motivations, the new influx of people presented the local governments with a vast challenge. Water supplies had to be increased, schools built, land acquired, highways constructed, and all the other customary governmental services provided. Local units soon discovered that they were neither structurally equipped or fiscally competent to respond to these challenges singly. Despite a few functional consolidations that did occur since 1943 in the areas of education, health, and hospitals, and in connection with the port authority, the basic problems persisted, finally causing important segments of civic leadership in Miami to demand and work for some form of federation which could furnish the area with a more comprehensive and effective government.

Metro came to Dade County by two major legal steps. First, the voters of the state ratified an amendment (1956) to the Florida constitution granting home rule to the county and then, one year later, the voters of the county approved a home-rule charter authorizing the establishment of Metro and defining the principal types of powers that were to be exercised by it, the new central government, and by the other remaining governmental units in the area.

The home-rule amendment set out at least four major purposes:

1. To free the county from legislative interventions through the enactment of special laws.
2. To permit the county to provide methods "for changing the boundaries of, merging, consolidating and abolishing from time to time all municipal corporations, county or district governments, special taxing districts, authorities . . . [etc.]."
3. To make it possible to devise methods of transferring to the new Board of County Commissioners "any and all of the functions or powers of any municipal corporation or other governmental unit in Dade County. . . ."
4. To declare that it was the intent of the legislature that the home rule provisions were to be liberally construed by the judiciary.

A home-rule charter, subsequently enacted and ratified by the voters, established the new Metro in the form of a county board of eleven commissioners (five elected at-large, five by districts, and one from the city of Miami) to which were entrusted the legislative functions, and a council manager who was to be the administrative head of the county.

Under the charter, Metro was given all the powers of a municipal character, powers that a county would perform in unincorporated areas, as well as a formidable reservoir of reserved powers reminiscent of the federal government's implied powers:

> No enumeration of powers in this Charter shall be deemed exclusive or restrictive and the foregoing powers shall be deemed to include all implied powers necessary and proper to carrying out such powers. . . . (Sect. 1.01 B)

The list of Metro's specified and enumerated responsibilities as a central municipal government is quite long and significant by itself, including

> provisions for regulation and control of arterial toll, and other roads, bridges, tunnels, parking facilities, traffic patterns; air, water, rail and bus terminals; post facilities; public transportation system; county-wide planning; hospital, health, and welfare programs; parks, playgrounds and recreational facilities; slum clearance and urban renewal; water, sewage collection and disposal; air pollution control; uniform building codes; zoning; utility franchises.

And yet there are some explicit guarantees to the cities which are important also in that they act as a limitation upon powers Metro might wish to exercise in pursuit of its broad mandate:

1. . . . No municipality . . . shall be abolished without approval of a majority of its electors voting in an election called for that purpose. The right to self-determination in local affairs is reserved and preserved except as otherwise provided in this Charter. (Sect. 5.01)
2. Each municipality shall have the authority to exercise all powers relating to its local affairs not inconsistent with this Charter. . . . (Sect. 5.02)
3. Revenues realized from franchise and utility taxes imposed by municipalities shall belong to municipalities. (Sect. 5.07)

So much for some of the legal aspects of the Miami experiment. Clearly, Metro's enabling provisions are as broad and unique as any that were contained in reorganization proposals recently adopted by a local electorate. Therefore, it is not surprising that neither Metro's birth itself nor the years since 1957 were free from doubt and controversy. Yet the experiment survived. Metro's charter won by a mere 51 per cent of the vote with only 26 per cent of Dade County participating in the election. The governing board was left strongly divided. The first county manager was forced to resign and board ordinances were subjected to bitter criticisms and protracted court tests. Controversy raged particularly around the traffic ordinance, building codes, county-wide law enforcement, and the financing of a seaport. The Miami Beach city council passed a resolution in 1960 requesting the right to secede and then submitted unsuccessfully a petition to the state legislature for permission to establish a separate county. A autonomy amendment, sponsored by the Dade County Municipal League, a determined foe of Metro, was designed to reaffirm municipal powers vis-à-vis Metro and was defeated in 1958 by 24,527 out of 124,313 votes. Another attempt at crippling Metro was turned back in 1961. This amendment would "have stripped Metro of control over such area-wide functions as sewage, water supply, transportation, traffic, and central planning." [10]

Throughout these battles the composition and leadership of pro-Metro and anti-Metro forces have been fairly constant and identifiable. Among the opponents to Metro, in addition to the Dade County League of Municipalities, were municipal and county employees groups, the Dade Central Labor Union, some of the mayors, nearly all of the municipal chambers of commerce, and the urban press (except in the City of Miami). The precincts in Hialeah and Miami Beach furnished much of the electoral backbone of the opposition.

Metro found its staunchest support among the members of the League of Women Voters, the Miami-Dade County Chamber of Commerce, the Dade County delegation in the Florida state legislature, in the editorials of the *Miami Herald* (especially the personal leadership of its Associate Editor, John Pennekamp), in the *Miami News,* and in such public bodies as the Metropolitan Miami Municipal Board and the Charter Commission. Both of these organizations and their memberships had been intimately involved in the preliminary research and drafting of the proposals that went into the actual establishment of the new governmental plan.

As in so many other local government reorganization campaigns, much of the literature and oratory centered around the claims advanced by the proponents that the Metro approach would bring about more effective government and a better balance between tax resources and service benefits and around the counter-claims by the critics that the new "super government" would destroy municipal home rule and lead to arbitrary decisions by central authorities unfamiliar with the peculiar needs and legitimate wishes of each separate locality.

What proved of decisive benefit to the "pro" forces in Miami was a population increment too recent in origin to have been able to develop strong

---

[10] Edward Sofen, *The Miami Metropolitan Experiment* (Bloomington, 1963), p. 165; Chs. 14, 15, and 16.

local attachments. Of advantage also were a favorable legislative climate at the state Capitol, competent and prestigious civic leadership, and effective newspaper support. Unlike St. Louis and Cleveland where powerful labor, ethnic, and political organizations were able to block governmental integration in terms of their own interests, in Miami they were not strongly enough entrenched to play an equally effective role.

There was still another factor of importance. What seemed to have helped the cause of Metro was its federal-type approach, which represented "an accommodation to both groups of antagonists: a shelter for localists against the 'terror' of total consolidation, and a half-way house towards integration for the centralists." [11]

The Lakewood Plan and Urban Counties

In 1960 there were 217 metropolitan counties with populations of over 100,000. Los Angeles County led all the rest with its 6 million residents. Up 2 million over 1950, it continues to increase at a weekly rate of about 5,000 immigrants. In its efforts to accommodate the enormous urban growth, its 3.5 million automobiles and 315 miles of freeways, this county under its home-rule charter of 1912 was able to devise a system of general service agreements with a large number of cities in the Los Angeles area. Named the Lakewood plan—Lakewood was one of the suburbs of Los Angeles and a prominent user of such contracts—the subjects of these agreements ranged from ambulance service and assessment of taxes to sewage disposal and water supply. These arrangements proved especially popular with the twenty-eight cities which were incorporated during the last ten years. Most of them would otherwise not have been financially affluent enough to afford, on their own, the capital outlays that would have been necessary had they wished to provide many of the services obtainable more conveniently and inexpensively from the county on a fee or rental basis. Substantial city-county functional consolidations in the furnishing of public health and welfare services continued additionally to reduce costs by eliminating duplication of administrative effort.[12]

Outside of California, many of this country's 263 urban counties with populations of 100,000 and over provide municipal-type services to incorporated localities. Where they do, about a third of the counties will serve their cities with police and parks, nearly a third with libraries, and about a fifth with street construction and recreation. Joint financing of county and city buildings is used in Chicago and St. Paul. Hospital facilities are jointly operated in Louisville and Chattanooga and in various Texas communities, sewage disposal plants in the metropolitan areas of Atlanta and Syracuse. Another of several illustrations that might be cited is North Carolina, where Winston-Salem and Forsyth County jointly finance the operation of a city-county tax collecting department, a city-county planning department, and a

---

[11] *Ibid.*, p. 85.
[12] Winston W. Crouch, "The California Way," *National Civic Review*, March, 1962, p. 143.

city-county court system. Promising city-county patterns of cooperation through service contracts or consolidations of functions also appear in Erie County, New York (Buffalo), Baltimore County, Maryland (Baltimore), Montgomery County, Maryland (Washington, D. C. area), and Monroe County, New York (Rochester). Rising costs in commuter transit have recently led to joint city-county operations of railroad stations in Westchester County, in the New York suburban area; to subsidies for commuter services in Bucks, Chester, Delaware, and Montgomery counties in the Philadelphia suburban area; and to enabling provisions for a county-operated transit system in Cuyahoga County to include Cleveland and its suburbs.[13]

Before any large number of urban counties can be expected to expand their services to cities, however, many obstacles will have to be overcome. First, about thirty of the state constitutions preclude such activities by express limitations on the powers of the county or its officialdom; second, many of the larger metropolitan areas transcend the boundaries of a single county (about one-third of all the S.M.S.A.'s); and third, inequitable representation, or more precisely, rural over-representation, in the majority of the states has created legislative climates often hostile to urban problems and needs.

CITY ANNEXATION

Historically, the most common method by which cities were permitted to extend their boundaries was that of annexing the surrounding territory and then incorporating it within the legal limits of the municipality. This is how most of the larger cities acquired new land during the nineteenth century. In more recent years, mushrooming suburbs and fringe areas frequently resented these annexation efforts and proceeded to fight them either with the ballot or through the courts. Yet annexation is still widely resorted to—so much so that during 1962 one out of five cities of 5,000 or more population employed it successfully.[14] Presently, the largest city area in the United States does not belong to Los Angeles as might have been presumed, but to Oklahoma City. Of its 620 square miles spread through four counties, 532 square miles have been acquired by annexation since 1959. Some other cities which expanded their boundaries significantly through this method during 1961 and 1962 were Norman, Oklahoma (its acquisition of 174 square miles represented the "second largest area ever annexed in a single year by a city in the United States"); [15] Phoenix, Arizona; Little Rock, Arkansas; Sacramento, California; San Diego, California; Gainesville, Florida; Macon, Georgia; Cedar Rapids, Iowa; North Las Vegas, Nevada; El Reno, Oklahoma; Nashville, Tennessee; Athens, Texas; Grand Prairie, Texas; and Houston, Texas. During the last fifteen years annexation has been most extensively used in Texas and Virginia, where its popularity has largely been due to legal factors such as the

[13] *Municipal Year Book, 1962*, p. 86.
[14] *Municipal Year Book, 1963*, p. 52.
[15] *Municipal Year Book, 1962*, pp. 51–52.

absence of veto powers by unincorporated areas, which have encouraged cities to engage in relatively quick land grabs.

There are various methods or approaches by which annexations can be carried out. Five basic patterns have been discerned: a proposed land annexation may be authorized by (1) a court, (2) a state administrative commission, (3) a referendum election on the question in the area to be annexed, in the annexing city, or in both, (4) a special or general law enacted by the legislature, and (5) a municipal ordinance. Some of the states make available to their local governments one or more or even a combination of these alternative approaches.[16]

How useful is the annexation process in meeting the needs of metropolitan growth? Its major value appears to be the relative ease with which unincorporated fringe areas can be absorbed into municipal boundaries and thus help form a more rational pattern of expansion in which due consideration can be given to metropolitan-wide considerations of governmental service and taxation. However, this advantage may be quickly overcome when unincorporated areas are given the right to vote and thus the potential power of vetoing their proposed annexation. Sometimes these areas, due to their fears of losing cherished autonomies, may attempt to avoid annexation by embarking on defensive incorporations. Such premature incorporation can greatly add to metropolitan woes by further proliferating governmental authority and jurisdiction and so fail to provide adequate plans, resources, and structures for the overall economic development of an interdependent area. A number of states have begun to weaken the veto potential of the areas to be annexed by permitting judicial determination or review which may in effect overrule an adverse electoral decision, should the annexation proposal seem otherwise sound and in harmony with legislative or administrative standards.

Some states—among them Indiana, Minnesota, and Wisconsin—have begun to insist that before villages may petition to incorporate as cities within a metropolitan area, they must be able to satisfy certain minimum standards of self-sufficiency. Under appropriate statutes administrators have been granted, for example, the power to ascertain that these communities can operate an effective governmental unit, that there is enough of a population density to warrant this step, that there is a compact and ample land area available for expansion, that there are adequate tax resources to furnish essential public services, that the incorporation will serve the public interest, and that it will not obstruct the orderly development of the metropolitan area as a whole.

Closely related to annexation is the presently rarely used process of inter-city consolidations. Despite likely savings due to larger scale operations and the elimination of one of two governments, voters are loathe to dilute their political power and forego established political loyalties. Sometimes it

---

[16] Frank S. Sengstock, *Annexation: A Solution to the Metropolitan Area Problem* (Ann Arbor, 1960), pp. 9–41. See also *Alternative Approaches to Governmental Reorganization in Metropolitan Areas*, p. 58.

does happen. In 1957, Newport News and Warwick, two cities in southeastern Virginia, consolidated themselves into the City of Newport News, merging their governments, their municipal services, their bonded indebtedness, and incidentally retaining most of their municipal employees.[17]

METROPOLITAN SPECIAL AND MULTIPURPOSE DISTRICTS

Simply defined, a metropolitan special district is a unit of government which has been given by statute the responsibility to perform a particular or limited function—usually a service function—that cuts across the jurisdic-

TABLE 2. SPECIAL DISTRICTS BY FUNCTION WITHIN AND
OUTSIDE METROPOLITAN AREAS

Type of special district	United States, total	Within SMSA's	Outside SMSA's	Per cent in SMSA's
Total_____	18,323	5,411	12,912	30
Natural resources_____	6,158	946	5,212	15
Other than natural resources_____	12,165	4,465	7,700	37
Fire protection____	3,229	1,174	2,055	36
Housing_____	1,099	391	708	36
Sewerage_____	937	570	367	61
Water supply_____	1,502	764	738	51
Other single-function districts_____	5,088	1,388	3,700	27
Multiple-function districts_____	310	178	132	57

SOURCE: Bureau of the Census, Department of Commerce, *Census of Governments: 1962*, Vol. I, "Governmental Organization" (Washington, 1963), p. 11.

tions of other established local governments situated within the metropolitan area. These metropolitan districts, which represented 30 per cent of all special districts in 1962, vary in detail (see Table 2). Commonly, they include a small governing board of officials appointed by the governor, by city councils in the area, by county commissioners, or by other district authorities that are functionally related. Governing boards are empowered by enabling legislation to determine the fees, rents, or tolls to be charged or to levy the tax assessments that need to be made in order to pay for the capital requirements and financing of the services for their territory. These districts also usually possess the corporate characteristic of being able to sue and be sued.

Historically, most special districts (other than school districts) constituted essentially rural units of government administering drainage, irriga-

[17] Advisory Commission on Intergovernmental Relations, *Factors Affecting Voter Reactions to Governmental Reorganization in Metropolitan Areas* (Washington, 1962), p. 58.

tion, water conservation, flood control, and fire protection functions. However, during the decade ending in 1962, it was primarily the urban or metropolitan special district or authority which registered a phenomenal rate of growth, an increase of nearly 50 per cent.

Reasons for this expansion can be found in at least five sets of circumstances which surround the operation of many existing units of local government: (1) they proved inadequate in terms of area and resources; (2) their expansion was hemmed in by legal restrictions; (3) their quality of service was poor; (4) certain interest groups wished special functions to be undertaken by new and independent units to obtain the best possible results; (5) the existing units themselves saw the value and needs in sponsoring special districts to handle functions they could not handle as well.[18]

Presently used with particular frequency in California, Illinois, Kansas, Missouri, Nebraska, New York, Oregon, Texas, and Washington, these districts provide a wide variety of services: in addition to "port facilities, sewage disposal, water supply, and parks, they also own and operate bridges, tunnels, airports, housing, libraries, and mass transit facilities; furnish public health services, regional planning, power, ice, gas, and coke; regulate navigation channels; and control water to prevent disasters." [19]

Among the most famous and powerful independent metropolitan special districts are the New York Port Authority, the Chicago Transit Authority, the Boston Transit Authority, the Hartford County (Connecticut) Metropolitan District, the St. Louis Bi-State Development District, the San Francisco-Oakland East Bay Municipal Utility District, the Cleveland Metropolitan Park District, the Golden Gate Bridge and Highway District (San Francisco), the Metropolitan Water District of Southern California, and the Washington Metropolitan Area Transit Commission. Three of these districts—New York Port Authority, the Bi-State Development District, and the Washington Metropolitan Area Transit Commission—operate services affecting a population of nearly 20 million people who reside in areas not merely comprising different cities and counties but more than one state as well. Under the federal Constitution these interstate metropolitan districts rest on charters which grew out of congressionally-approved interstate compacts.[20]

Special purpose districts have many attractive features. Much less ambitious in design than local government federation or consolidation, they rarely require state constitutional language or established governmental structures to be significantly changed. Given the multiplicity of local governments in a metropolitan area, these districts have definite appeal to those

[18] John C. Bollens, *Special District Governments in the United States* (Berkeley, 1957), pp. 6–15; a short study of the current status of special districts in Rhode Island is found in Frederick L. Bird, *Local Special Districts and Authorities in Rhode Island* (Kingston, 1962).

[19] *Ibid.,* p. 68.

[20] Robert W. Tobin, "The Interstate Metropolitan District and Cooperative Federalism," *Tulane Law Review,* December, 1961, pp. 67–90.

community interests that may wish to see a particular service performed with businesslike efficiency and performed quickly. It often has proved much easier to persuade a legislature of the need to provide the statutory authorization for the district than to embark on a highly risky campaign with a view of persuading a number of separate electorates or their city councils and county commissions that it is to their collective interest to undertake jointly the necessary service. Inasmuch as state constitutions and city charters have too frequently placed local governments in a fiscal strait jacket through rigid debt and tax limitations, special district authorities are given the distinct advantage of being able to finance their capital requirements much more flexibly and much more readily.

Despite these and other undeniable advantages, special districts can by no means be viewed as an unmixed blessing. They may, for example, contribute to a feast or famine type of financing by garnering public financial support and interest to the point of feasting the special district and its popular service, and by failing to obtain the essential public financial support and concern to the point of famine for the multitudinous but less spectacular duties remaining with the other local governments.

While special districts offer some real flexibility in an otherwise overly-rigid pattern of local government, they also introduce new inflexibilities of their own. This forces those interested in a metropolitan area-wide government to work around such districts or to reserve for them special status in any integrative scheme that may be proposed. The more successful the district, the more likely will the wind be taken out of the sails of those who advocate an overall approach to metropolitan reform. Demand may actually be intensified for the establishment of additional special purpose districts leading to a further fragmentation of an already fragmented local government map.

District authorities can make their decisions affecting the area's water supply, waste disposal, or transportation in an autonomous setting with little regard for cooperative effort with other related districts or governmental units. Rarely, if ever, does the area's electorate have a direct voice in the government of such districts. As a rule the mayors or councilmen who were appointed to the district's governing boards by the governor got there because their cities lay within the service territory rather than because they had campaigned on certain issues of policy that were before the district and on which voters had views that needed representation.

Metropolitan multipurpose districts, as the name might suggest, are empowered by the terms of their original legislative charters to perform more than a single or limited number of functions, should their governing boards or the areas' electorate so decide. To date, Seattle's Metropolitan Municipal Corporation established under statute in 1958 is the only such metropolitan-wide multipurpose district.

Sewage disposal and water pollution control represent the scope of its present operations. The district is governed by a board of sixteen members: fourteen are elected officials from the area's municipalities; one is designated by the King County board of commissioners; and one, the chairman, a non-elected official, is appointed by the metropolitan council itself. Although Seattle's Metropolitan Municipal Corporation is not granted the power of taxation, it may issue revenue bonds for capital needs, borrow from local governments, and obtain grants from the federal government. Current operations are financed by special charges assessed on each household served by the district. City and county governments in the Seattle area may also furnish the M.M.C. "supplemental income" based on the "proportionate share of the total assessed valuation of 'Metro' that is within its boundaries." [21]

A somewhat different form of multipurpose district, the Greater St. Louis City-County District was proposed but overwhelmingly rejected by the area's voters in 1959. Under this plan the district's government would have been composed of a fifteen-member board of supervisors elected for four-year staggered terms from city and county districts operating under the executive leadership of a president elected at-large on a partisan ballot with wide appointive power as general manager. The district was to be given area-wide responsibility for seven major functions: "establishment and control of a metropolitan road system; regulation of mass transit facilities; promotion of economic development; preparation for consideration of a comprehensive master plan; central control of police training and communication functions; civil defense; and sanitary powers and land drainage." [22]

INTERGOVERNMENTAL METROPOLITAN COOPERATION

Government officials in metropolitan areas along with their electorates may be reluctant to welcome reorganization moves towards consolidation, federation, or even functional district organization, and yet be fully cognizant of the benefits that could be obtained from some minimal forms of intergovernmental cooperation. Voluntary metropolitan councils have now been operative for nearly ten years. The best known and most effective are found in the areas around Baltimore, Detroit, New York, Philadelphia, Salem (Oregon), San Francisco, Seattle-Tacoma, and Washington, D. C.

One such council, the Association of Bay Area Governments (A.B.A.G.) around San Francisco (but not including the city of Oakland) now comprises seven of the area's nine counties, fifty-eight of its eighty-five cities, and 75 per cent of its population.[23] The association works through its General Assembly in which all member governments are represented, through an executive committee, and through a full-time professional director. General Assembly recommendations must be approved by a majority of the city and county representatives. Far from constituting a new government, the council's recommendations relate primarily to those functions in which cities and counties

21 *Factors Affecting Voter Reactions to Governmental Reorganization in Metropolitan Areas,* p. 67.
22 *Ibid.,* p. 65.
23 *National Civic Review,* May, 1962, p. 274.

can cooperate with "each acting within its own area and by means of its own employees and facilities." [24]

What are some of the major types of activities undertaken by metropolitan councils? Among other projects, A.B.A.G worked on a region-wide plan and for the congressional support of the Point Reyes National Seashore Bill. New York's Metropolitan Regional Council, including twenty-two counties from Connecticut, New Jersey, and New York, discussed air pollution control, regional public housing, and urban redevelopment needs along with commuter problems, traffic congestion, and other problems of regional concern. Williamette's Council (Oregon) conducted a regional transportation study, and Detroit's Supervisor's Inter-County Committee prepared reports on the area's problems with "roads, water, sewage and waste disposal, ports, and recreation." [25]

Metro councils can conduct studies, submit reports, urge the adoption of legislation, and provide a valuable forum for the exchange of views of city and county officials who are confronted with common problems. Still, this type of council is not a government. It can lay the foundations for achieving joint governmental actions, but it cannot act itself.

However overwhelming the consensus favoring an integrative step, no council majority vote can bind a stubborn minority which is unwilling to submit its more parochial interest to that of the region. Presently Metro councils may be viewed primarily as a stage and as an experiment in the development of greater metropolitan unity. As such, their major contribution may well lie in the future persuasiveness of their research or in the gradual articulation of consent among officials and voters for proposals which eventually involve structured changes of a more radical nature in the local governments of the metropolitan area.

IS THERE AN IDEAL PATTERN FOR THE GOVERNING OF
METROPOLITAN AREAS?

Before this question can be answered, if it is answerable at all, some standards or criteria might be explored with which to judge different approaches to reforming local government in the metropolitan areas. What characterizes most of these areas is an uneven clustering of special and general purpose governments with confusing jurisdictions, all struggling to balance fiscal resources with service demands without providing either the structure or the process through which area-wide decisions could be made and implemented. In essence then, the metropolitan area problem seems to be one of intergovernmental relations which call for

> A. [a] process of last resort to settle intergovernmental disputes and questions of jurisdiction . . .

[24] Crouch, p. 144.
[25] *National Civic Review*, January, 1962, p. 31.

B. [a] process [or processes] of intergovernmental cooperation . . .

C. [a] process by which the several governments may act separately and independently, as well as in cooperation . . .

D. [a] process of organic change which can neither be dictated nor stopped by a minority of components. . . .[26]

How best to achieve the structuring of these processes has been discussed for some time in the literature of American political science. One group of scholars contends that the federal approach to metropolitan woes is by far the most promising.

> Unless federation and representation are developed in metropolitan areas, compartmentalization of local government and fragmentation of public administration will continue. For lesser metropolitan areas currently in search of solutions to their needs, approaches like annexation and city-county consolidation [or separation and consolidation] may still prove workable when coupled with representative, democratic institutions. But for our colossal metropolitan regions, their central cities now ringed by potentially permanent satellite governments, neither annexation nor city-county consolidation has proved adequate. Metropolitan sprawl has over-reached our enlarged central cities and our city-counties in the great agglomerations. Only federation of governments and the building of an upper-tier metropolitan council, with legislative and administrative process to deal with various aspects of functions, will suffice.[27]

Another point of view is frankly critical of the notion that creating two-level governmental structures—local and metropolitan—would serve as a defensible tactic of reconciling suburban exclusiveness on the one hand with the legitimate claims of other area electorates on the other.

> Encouraging a scattering of communities and governments in the metropolitan area does not solve this problem; it intensifies it. . . . The small community is friendly and comfortable and it promises fraternity, but it is also intolerant, inquisitive, barren of privacy. It is at least an open question whether this creation of political boundaries around disparate groups and classes is an appropriate development in a democracy, or whether it truly frees the individual in the manner its advocates intend. . . . To the extent this proposition is true, there is something to be said for . . . gargantua—the creation of a single metropolitan government or at least the establishment of a regional superstructure which points in that direction.

> . . . Freedom of choice remains for the individual, for the entire variety of spectacles and experiences which a metropolis offers is open to him. But in a political sense, this freedom is accompanied by responsibility. A man cannot escape his neighbor by retreating to an exclusive suburb. . . .[28]

Aside from questions of political feasibility, *gargantua*, by applying the unitary rather than the federal principle, would sweep clean the metropolitan map of special districts, municipalities, and all other local authorities save

---

[26] Arthur Maass, *Area and Power* (Glencoe, 1959), p. 39.

[27] Stanley Scott, *Metropolitan Area Problems* (Berkeley, 1960), p. 19.

[28] Oliver P. Williams and Charles Press (eds.), *Democracy in Urban America: Readings on Government and Politics* (Chicago, 1961), p. 191.

one. Remaining would be a single all-purpose government large enough to meet the political, administrative, and service needs of the entire metropolitan area.

A third point of view hoping to avoid stress on major structural reforms places greater emphasis on the processes of policy formation and is more moderate in its expectation for the immediate future. Metropolitan areas will somehow continue to muddle through.

> The metropolitan citizen does not appear willing to pay in money or loss of local self-rule for a metropolitan government. He is willing to pay for special districts, area-wide in scope, to solve his most pressing problems. Sewage disposal can be such a pressing problem. Traffic and transportation may well become another interest which causes electoral turnstiles to ring. If so, there will be metropolitan transportation systems under coordinated management. But transport, crucial as it is to many other public tasks and basic to the emerging shape of the city, will then function even more freely outside the pressures of other competing and legitimate interests.[29]

> As problems press and action results, we do see a form of social invention taking place in the metropolis. Special district agencies, government by contract and subcontract, earnings taxes and public corporate enterprise, are ingenious and remarkable stopgaps. . . .[30]

> The metropolitan community is continuously improvised; its evolution is organic, not rational; change is crescive, not revolutionary; problems are solved by trial and error rather than by fiat. . . .[31]

> Our type of democracy does not permit an easy way out. We value the autonomy of local units and private groups and the separation of the legislative and executive functions. These values can continue to have vital meaning only if links are created between the units, groups, and functions . . . governmental reorganization will often come at the end of the process, not at the beginning.[32]

Still other approaches suggest that there are governmental resources, outside the metropolitan area, that could and should be called into action. For example, state legislatures could adopt laws which would endow cities with additional power to carry on planning and zoning activities that could more effectively control developments in the urban fringes. Proper regulations of this kind would contribute much to sound land, water, and space utilization which must be assured if the appearance of urban sprawl is to be avoided. Also, many states will need to adopt laws which would stimulate and encourage cooperative efforts among municipalities and local governments to pool their resources or join their efforts to meet particular functional needs. Many states could do a great deal more in the way of rendering expert staff services or in providing assistance to annexation and incorporation proceedings since

[29] Scott Greer, *Governing the Metropolis* (New York, 1962), pp. 145–146.
[30] *Ibid.*, p. 147.
[31] Scott Greer, *The Emerging City: Myth and Reality* (New York, 1962) cited in Greer, *Governing the Metropolis*, p. 148.
[32] Webb S. Fiser, *Mastery of the Metropolis* (Englewood Cliffs, 1962), pp. 129–130.

these are frequently of a highly technical nature and often carried out in a legal climate peculiarly detrimental to the interests of orderly urban expansion.

Then there are those who maintain that neither local nor state governments actually have sufficient means, willingness, or institutional adaptability to handle the population explosion in metropolitan areas. They insist that the federal government must be made to assume far greater fiscal responsibility and expand many of the existing loan and grant programs. Mentioned most prominently among the potential recipients of this federal largess are the following programs: city and regional planning, airport construction, small watersheds, public works, urban renewal, sewage treatment plants, hospitals, highways, land acquisition for parks and recreational areas, beach erosion control, mass transportation, open space and land preservation, and school construction.

SOME OF THE LESSONS OF METROPOLITAN REFORM

The substantial impetus to the vast amount of experimentation with different approaches to metropolitan reform came from the postwar urbanization of American life. Action seemed necessary to help accommodate significant population shifts, increasing birth rates, technological developments, and social changes. But what has emerged so far from all the action and inaction on the metropolitan front provides very few answers that can be considered anything but tentative. One thing is fairly certain. No single approach—be it city-county consolidation, federation, annexation, or any other—has proved politically feasible for all types of situations. Possibly, the metropolitan problem is far too complex to expect that a universally valid pattern can provide pat solutions for the intricate varieties of social and legal settings. It is not at all unlikely that metropolitan reformers for some time to come may have to eschew a search for overall solutions and be content with a piecemeal approach which combines diverse structural elements in an eclectic and pragmatic manner.

Results from the battle for reform have demonstrated so far, at least, that in general

A. The less drastic the reform proposal, the better is its chance of acceptance.
B. Public apathy towards reform is fundamental and often most difficult to overcome.
C. Reform proposals face rough going when their acceptance is conditioned on separate majorities in cities and suburbs or in incorporated and unincorporated places.
D. Governmental reforms cannot be separated from politics—attempts to ignore the political dimensions and realities in reorganization efforts nearly always end disastrously.
E. Popular acceptance of more basic changes usually require a tremendously intensive campaign utilizing all the media of communications and enlisting all levels of community leadership.

These then are some of the lessons that can be learned from a recent study of eighteen reform proposals which were submitted to public approval between 1950 and 1961, ten of which were rejected and eight accepted. More detailed analysis of these eighteen proposals revealed also that of the seven most drastic plans only one was successful, that of the six intermediate proposals three were adopted, and of the least drastic four were adopted.[33]

TABLE 3. NUMBER OF GOVERNMENTAL UNITS, 1942 AND 1962

| Type of government | Number of units | | Change in number |
	1964	1942	1942 to 1962
Total_____	91,236	155,116	−63,880
U. S. government_____	1	1	———
States_____	50	48	+ 2
Counties_____	3,043	3,050	− 7
Municipalities_____	17,997	16,220	+ 1,777
Townships_____	17,144	18,919	− 1,775
School districts_____	34,678	108,579	−73,901
Special districts_____	18,323	8,299	+10,024

SOURCE: Adapted from Bureau of the Census, Department of Commerce, *Census of Governments: 1962*, I, 1 and *1957 Census of Governments*, I, No. 1, 1.

THE LOCAL GOVERNMENT MAP OF THE UNITED STATES

In the United States local government may be divided into two main categories: general purpose and special purpose units. Based on the 1962 census enumeration of local governments, the former includes 3,043 county governments; 17,144 township and town governments (townships generally constitute the local subdivisions of counties outside of New England; towns assume the role of townships there); and 17,997 municipalities. The second category comprises 18,323 special districts and 34,678 school districts (for a state-by-state breakdown of the number of local governments, see Figure 2). A comparison of these figures with corresponding census data for 1942 (see Table 3) shows that special district governments more than doubled, that the number of municipalities increased about 10 per cent, that counties remained relatively stable, that townships decreased by about 10 per cent, and that school districts fell to less than one-third of the 1942 level. As educational costs and standards continue to rise, more and more states found it necessary

[33] *Factors Affecting Voter Reactions to Governmental Reorganization in Metropolitan Areas*, p. 8. For a highly stimulating exploratory discussion of theoretical models which might be constructed to ascertain statistically the extent of political integration of the large number of political communities operating within a particular metropolitan area (employing such concepts as "transaction flow analysis," "indicators of political cohesion," and "networks of influence" and research approaches suggested by Professor Karl W. Deutsch of Yale University), see Philip E. Jacob and James V. Toscano (eds.), *The Integration of Political Communities* (Philadelphia, 1964).

FIGURE 2

NUMBER
OF LOCAL GOVERNMENTS
BY STATES 1962

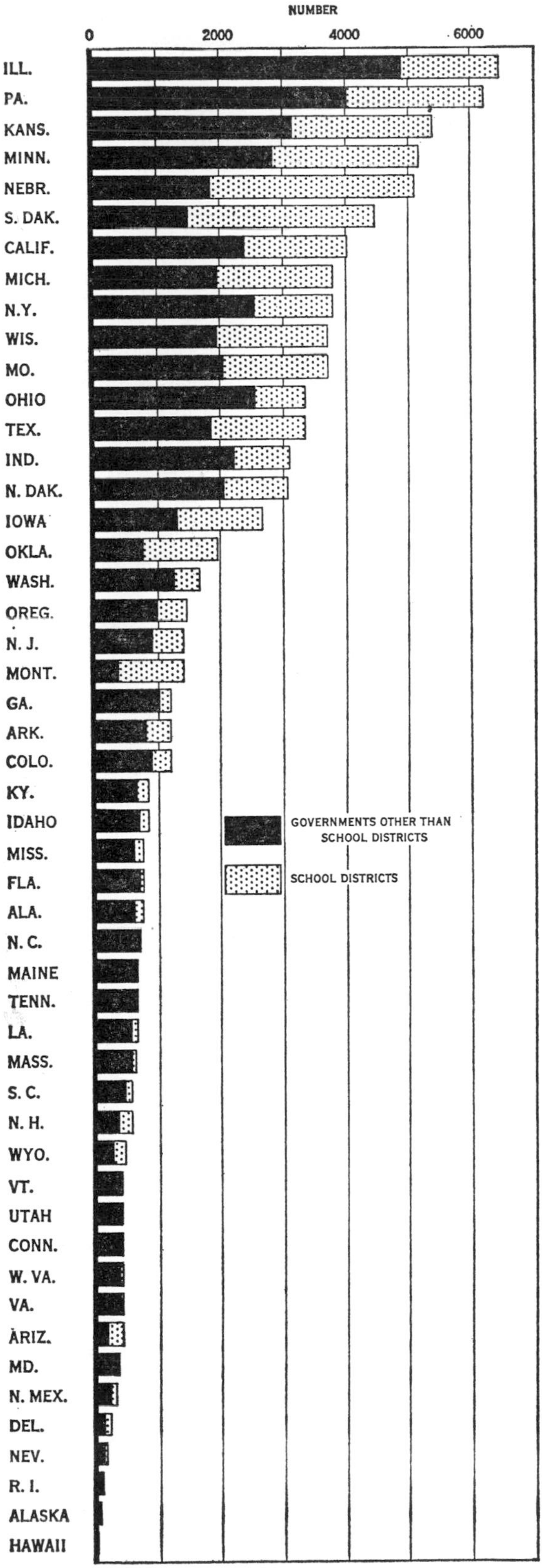

NUMBER

| | 0 | 2000 | 4000 | 6000 |

ILL.
PA.
KANS.
MINN.
NEBR.
S. DAK.
CALIF.
MICH.
N.Y.
WIS.
MO.
OHIO
TEX.
IND.
N. DAK.
IOWA
OKLA.
WASH.
OREG.
N. J.
MONT.
GA.
ARK.
COLO.
KY.
IDAHO
MISS.
FLA.
ALA.
N. C.
MAINE
TENN.
LA.
MASS.
S. C.
N. H.
WYO.
VT.
UTAH
CONN.
W. VA.
VA.
ARIZ.
MD.
N. MEX.
DEL.
NEV.
R. I.
ALASKA
HAWAII

GOVERNMENTS OTHER THAN
SCHOOL DISTRICTS

SCHOOL DISTRICTS

SOURCE: Bureau of the Census, Department of Commerce, *Census of Governments: 1962*, Vol. I, "Governmental Organization" (Washington, 1963), p. 19.

to eliminate or consolidate small school districts which had proved unable to provide adequate services. Still, nearly one-half of the remaining school districts operate schools which serve fewer than 150 pupils.[34]

COUNTIES

With the exception of Alaska, Connecticut, Louisiana, and Rhode Island, all of the states employ the county as a political subdivision. Although occasionally given some of the powers of a municipality, legally counties are creatures of the states, established "without the particular solicitation, consent, or concurrent action of the people who inhabit them." [35] Their size and significance vary greatly. They fulfill important governmental functions in the West and South, but are used little in the New England states. In size, they range from the 20,131 square miles of San Bernardino County, California, to the 25 square miles of Virginia's Arlington County, and in numbers they range from a low of three counties in Delaware to a maximum of 254 in Texas. In 1960, 277 counties had a population of 100,000 and over, the three most populous counties being Los Angeles County with 6 million; Cook County (Chicago), with 5.1 million; and Wayne County (Detroit), with 2.7 million. Obviously, the governmental role performed by these highly urbanized counties (and by the 50 per cent of all counties which are now in the 50,000–100,000 population range) is increasingly differentiated from that left to the 818 predominantly rural counties serving populations of 10,000 or less. Something of the extent of the migration from rural counties can be seen in the census figures which show that between 1950 and 1960 nearly two-thirds of the counties in eighteen mid-American farm states in the Western plains and deep South registered population losses. Along with population differences, county governments are quite naturally affected by such other factors as state constitutional provisions, statutes, economic resources, tax bases, social composition, political traditions, and by the numbers and character of other governmental units operating within the area. All of which helps to explain why it is impossible presently to speak of a single pattern of county government and county functions, be they urban or rural. This is so despite the historical fact that many contemporary county governmental powers and duties can be traced through the Northwest Ordinance and colonial experiences back to common origins in eleventh-century England.

County Functions and Governmental Organization

The constitutional position of the American county can be stated quite succinctly. It has such powers and only such powers as the state legislature is willing to grant to it. Over a hundred years ago, the Supreme Court of Ohio

---

[34] Norman Beckman and Marjorie Cahn Brazer, "Governments Galore," *National Civic Review*, March, 1963, p. 135.

[35] John F. Dillon, *Commentaries on the Law of Municipal Corporations* (Boston, 1911), Chs. 23–25; see also *Frederick* v. *Douglas County et al.*, 71 N.W. 798, (1897), at 799.

handed down an opinion, classic in its representativeness of numerous similar expressions found in the judicial reports of other states, to the effect that unlike a municipal corporation which "is created primarily for the interest, advantage, and convenience of the locality and its people," county government as an agent of the state

> is created almost exclusively with a view to the policy of the state at large . . . with scarcely an exception, all the powers and functions of the county organization have a direct and exclusive reference to the general policy of the state, and are, in fact, but a branch of the general administration of that policy.[36]

Traditionally, counties were concerned mostly with such matters as enforcing laws, administering justice, building highways, supervising county property, assessing and collecting taxes, directing poor relief, recording legal documents, and conducting elections. In the two decades following the end of World War II, the functions of counties have undergone considerable expansion. This is especially true of the more urbanized counties. An awareness that counties should have the opportunity to assume greater responsibilities in the increasingly urban matrix of American local government was given explicit recognition in the 1961 platform of the National Association of County Officials:

> County government has a decisive role to play in so-called metropolitan or urban area problems. Counties should take the lead in providing services in metropolitan areas where exploding populations have made it impossible for incorporated or unincorporated units to provide an adequate level of vitally needed services. . . . Counties are no longer merely local branches of the state government. . . .[37]

Recreational areas, flood control, water supply, sewage disposal, library services, airport facilities, and county-wide police and fire protection—these are the multiplying concerns of more and more counties today. Pressures persist to have counties take on quasi-municipal functions from smaller governmental units and from unincorporated localities, particularly those located in the suburban fringes of the larger cities (see Table 4).

Counties not only differ markedly in size and functions but in their governmental operations as well. Yet common to many counties are four basic types of governmental officialdom for which provision is made in state constitutions and statutes: (1) A group of county officials meeting jointly as one body named variously county board, board of county commissioners, county court, board of supervisors, etc., composed of three or more members elected by districts. In some states this county board is quite large (twenty-five members or more) and may even include township supervisors as, for example, in New York; a few of the Southern states give board membership to the county's justices of the peace; (2) a number of elected officials who hold separate county offices performing county-wide services as sheriff, county

---

[36] *Commissioners of Hamilton County* v. *Mighels,* 7 Ohio State Reports 109 (1857).
[37] "Editorial Comment: Counties on the Move," *National Civic Review,* March, 1962, p. 118.

TABLE 4. PERCENTAGE OF COUNTIES OVER 100,000 POPULATION
PROVIDING SERVICES TO ENTIRE COUNTY AND
TO UNINCORPORATED AREAS

Service	Percent of Counties providing services to	
	Entire county	Unincorporated areas
Police	33.0	68.8
Fire	5.4	24.4
Street construction	20.4	50.7
Street lighting	1.4	17.6
Recreation	21.3	37.5
Parks	33.0	42.9
Garbage collection	2.3	12.7
Public housing	1.4	6.8
Libraries	28.9	45.2
None	23.5	4.1
Not reporting	19.0	6.8

SOURCE: *Municipal Year Book, 1962*, p. 64.

attorney, auditor, recorder, surveyor, treasurer, coroner, assessor, judge, etc.;
(3) a larger number of appointive officials such as county engineer, health
officer, librarian, school superintendent, etc., many of whom are only partly
accountable to the county commissioners; and (4) certain special statutory
boards or committees such as county welfare board, county tax equalization
committee, and county civil service commission—the membership of which is
usually selected by the board of county commissioners and may even include
some of the commissioners in regular or in ex-officio capacity. No counties in
two states and rarely all counties within a single state will likely present an
identical table of organization or list of positions either elective or appointive.
Structure, positions, and functions in county government developed throughout the country as particular political needs were recognized and acted upon
by the legislature and not in accordance with an overall blueprint or design.

While county boards as a rule do not have inherent legislative powers of
their own, state laws have in fact devolved upon them significant ranges of
discretion in policy-making with respect to county taxation and finance and in
matters involving the management and supervision of county property, facilities, and institutions. A monthly county board agenda may thus have placed
on it items affecting the budget, personnel, and policies of the various county
departments. Contracts may have to be awarded, land conveyed, borrowing
authorized, sewage districts established, parks laid out, water supply systems
approved, the construction of highways, bridges, and airports sanctioned,
and the legality of land-use and zoning resolutions scrutinized.

The lack of an effective central executive authority has long been considered one of the genuine weaknesses in county government. In recent years
the heavy pressure of urban county business and the continuing demands for
greater efficiency persuaded some legislatures to permit the more populous
counties to provide for the appointment or election of a county manager or
chief administrative officer. Based on a 1961–1962 survey of urban counties

with a population of over 100,000, at least forty-five county boards were reported as having such an executive officer. Popularly-elected county executives were noted in Erie (Buffalo, N. Y.), Onondaga (Syracuse, N. Y.), Milwaukee (Milwaukee, Wisconsin), Nassau (New York, N. Y.), St. Louis (St. Louis, Mo.-Ill.), Suffolk (New York, N. Y.), and Westchester (New York, N. Y.).[38]

County boards and county executives notwithstanding, much of the governmental work of the county continues to be performed, as in the past, by a long list of officials elected in a majority of counties directly by the voters to positions of historic lineage and prestige. A short profile of such typical offices and duties would have to include the following:

A. *Sheriff:* County's chief law enforcement official; has major responsibility for the maintenance of the jail and for the care and security of prisoners; furnishes police protection to unincorporated areas of the county; as civil officer of the county court, he serves, processes, warrants, and auctions property; may also be required to collect delinquent personal property taxes.

B. *Auditor:* Maintains county financial and land records; computes tax rates; authorizes payment on county financial obligations through the issuance of warrants; may serve as filing and certification officer for national, state, and local elections.

C. *County Attorney:* Sometimes also designated as district attorney, state's attorney, solicitor, or prosecuting attorney, he functions as the county's chief legal officer; conducts criminal investigations, presents evidence, seeks indictments, and prosecutes law violators in the state courts on behalf of the public.

D. *Coroner:* Conducts or supervises medical investigation (so far only a minority of the states require this official to be a licensed physician to determine the cause of death of persons who died under unusual, violent, or suspicious circumstances; may be given the power to subpoena witnesses, administer oaths, and conduct formal hearings to ascertain the facts surrounding the person's demise.

E. *Treasurer:* Collects, disburses, and has custody of county funds; makes periodic reports about the fiscal activities of the county.

F. *County Clerk:* In some states named registrar or recorder; has responsibility for the preparation, issuance, and filing of such legal documents as deeds, mortgages, powers of attorney, plats, leases, marriage certificates, adoption papers, divorce records, and birth certificates; may also function as a filing or certification officer for federal, state, and local elections.

G. *Assessor:* Official is charged with the responsibility of determining the value of all taxable property in the county and of applying to it legislatively-defined tax rate classifications.

Some constitutions and statutes expand this list of elective officers to include the positions of land surveyor, probate judge, court commissioner,

---

[38] *Municipal Year Book, 1962*, pp. 75–81; on other county governmental developments, see Clyde F. Snider, "American County Government: A Mid-Century Review," *American Political Science Review*, March, 1952, pp. 66–80; Richard Bigger, Evan A. Iverson, Judith Norvell Jamison, James D. Kitchen, and Edward F. Staniford, *County Government in California* (Sacramento, 1958); and Matthew Holden, Jr., *County Government in Ohio* (Cleveland, 1958).

and county superintendent of schools. Other counties which are permitted to depart from this pattern appoint some or all of these officials.

Trends in County Government

Certain basic constitutional and political changes will have to materialize before counties can assume a more energetic stance in the future developments of American local government. Foremost at issue is the rigid constitutional status of the majority of counties. Restrictions abound in the form of detailed constitutional provisions governing the establishment, consolidation, and abolition of counties, the apportionment of debts, the designation of particular offices, the spelling out of powers that their occupants may exercise, the total of debts and expenditures that may lawfully be incurred, the location of the county seat, and the delineation of boundaries that cannot be altered—all substantive language which can only be changed through formal amendment of the constitutions themselves, a slow, expensive, and uncertain process at best.

Yet some progress has been made. Home-rule provisions under which legislatures could give powers to their counties to frame charters so that they might operate more independently as well as streamline their governmental structures to the extent, for example, of providing for a county manager or executive, were incorporated into the constitutions of Alaska (which uses boroughs in place of counties), California (1911), Hawaii (1959), Maryland (1915), Michigan (1963), Minnesota (1958), Missouri (1945), New York (1958), Ohio (1933), Oregon (1958), Texas (1933), and Washington (1948). Another group of states—Montana, North Carolina, North Dakota, and Virginia—have made available certain optional patterns of county organization from which interested counties might then select the one most suitable to their local conditions and needs.

To date very few, perhaps 3 per cent, of the approximately 500 counties which could frame these charters have actually done so. California leads the rest of the nation with ten of its counties having adopted home-rule charters. Understandably, there are many political reasons, besides voter apathy, for the failure of charter proposals to obtain the required majorities throughout a county. Some charter proposals, such as the one rejected in Cuyahoga County (Cleveland), Ohio in 1959, called not merely for the elimination of a substantial number of formerly elective county offices—clerk of courts, coroner, engineer, recorder, sheriff, and treasurer—but proposed a transfer to the county of important substantive service functions previously exercised by the various municipalities and smaller governmental units. The returns showed that a majority of the electorate proved unwilling to accept that much centralization and change. But even less ambitious proposals have run into trouble at the polls. In 1962, for example, two small Oregon counties, Benton and Sherman, turned down proposals which involved little more than the appointment of a county executive in one instance and the separation of a legislative county council from a three-member board of commissioners (as a county executive) in the other.

What is the nature of opposition to the model of county government under which county policy-making functions would be placed in the hands of the county board and county executive functions in the hands of a county manager or executive, or to plans which would seek to streamline county government through administrative reorganization, or to the consolidation of two thinly populated and economically poor counties so as to eliminate expensive duplication of functions and thus furnish a more adequate fiscal basis for county operations?

Officials whose positions are threatened represent one obvious and ready-made source of opposition. Another source may be the reluctance of rural voters to part with the anti-urban bias worked deeply into the apportionment formulas of most of the districts from which county commissioners are elected. A third source may be political parties which in the majority of the states look on county jobs, very few of which are under civil service, as necessary patronage for building campaign organizations (or machines). A fourth source may be conservative political interests which view any centralization of power in government—be it in the hands of the president, governor, mayor, or county manager—as a threat to the type of power diffusion which in their judgment best preserves or enhances a beneficial status quo.

THE GOVERNMENT OF TOWNS AND TOWNSHIPS

In the New England states the concept of "town" refers to particular urban places as well as to subdivisions of counties; towns "typically contain a concentration or concentrations of populations surrounded by relatively sparsely settled rural territory." [39] With powers derived from colonial legislatures, New England's traditional town meeting constituted this country's earliest and most significant form of local government cast in a near democratic mold. "New England town meeting. These words evoke the image of sober-faced Yankees filing silently into town hall to discuss the issues of the day." [40] Although their governmental needs were minimal, their taxes had to be assessed and collected, their roads built, land surveyed, schools established, and poor supported. The town meeting was and still is the central institution of town government. Open to all eligible voters, the annual meeting, a social as well as a political event, makes the important decisions and elects most of the town's key officials. Allowing for much variation, as noted earlier in the case of counties, today's list of elective officials would generally include from three to seven selectmen, a town clerk, assessors, justices of the peace,

[39] *Municipal Year Book, 1962,* p. 30.
[40] Benjamin W. Labare, "New England Town Meeting," *American Archivist,* April, 1962, p. 165.

constables, tax collector, treasurer, road commissioners, and members of the school and finance committees. Between town meetings the board of select-men, under statute and by law, supervises a large number of administrative officers and boards (health, engineering, utilities, and welfare, to mention only a few), and conducts the public affairs of the town. Selectmen also are charged with such duties as issuing licenses and authorizing bonds and with the overall management of all town property.

The New England town has long ceased being the compact, socially and religiously homogenous Calvinist community with stable agricultural popu-lations and well-established traditions, whose passing Henry Adams so deeply lamented and so well described. Immigrants and industry already changed much of its historic uniqueness by the turn of the century.

Local government in New England was in need of governmental reform, and three major structural innovations gradually won approval and support

TABLE 5. GEOGRAPHIC DISTRIBUTION OF
TOWNSHIP GOVERNMENTS, 1962

Area	Number of township governments	1960 population (000)
Total_ _ _ _ _ _ _ _ _ _ _	17,144	39,934
6 New England states_ _	1,424	5,085
3 Middle Atlantic states (New Jersey, New York, Pennsylvania)_	2,720	12,038
12 other states_ _ _ _ _ _ _	13,000	22,811

SOURCE: Bureau of the Census, Department of Commerce, *Census of Governments: 1962*, Vol. I,
"Governmental Organization" (Washington,
1963), p. 3.

in the legislatures and towns of Connecticut, Maine, Massachusetts, New Hampshire, and Vermont.

A. In some of the larger towns the pure democracy of the town meeting gave way to a smaller and limited one, through a system of indirect representa-tion in which town meeting members were elected and spoke for precincts into which the town electorate was now divided.

B. Much of the determination of the town's fiscal affairs, particularly the preparation of the budget, passed from the large and unwieldy town meet-ing and from the selectmen to a smaller committee specially constituted and charged with that responsibility.

C. Selectmen were given the authority to appoint a town manager to super-vise for them the day-to-day administration of town services and functions. (Based on a 1956 survey, 155 towns were operating under this plan.)[41]

Outside New England, it is the township government which constitutes in at least fifteen states the general civil subdivision of counties (see Table 5).

[41] Clyde F. Snider, *Local Government in Rural America* (New York, 1957), p. 211. See also Lashley G. Harvey, *The "Walled" Towns of New England* (Boston, 1964).

However, the extent of governmental functions which they now carry on varies considerably. In Kansas, Michigan, New Jersey, New York, Pennsylvania, and Wisconsin, general law has "vested [organized townships] with rather broad powers and where they include urbanized areas [they] perform many functions commonly associated with municipalities." [42] This is true especially in certain suburban areas of larger cities where long established residents prefer the traditional township structure to retain their area's distinct character within the enveloping metropolitan complex.

For many years township government played a significant part in the rural government of the Midwestern and Central Atlantic states, performing functions and services very similar to those of the New England towns. During the last thirty years, however, rural township government has lost much of its former vitality. Other civil entities such as municipalities and counties are increasingly called upon to act in the areas of education, welfare, health, highways, and law enforcement, areas formerly the concern of the organized township. Contributing to the township's decline were such factors as the improved means of communication, the failure to attract qualified candidates and professional personnel, the superior financial and governmental resources of city and county, the voter's apathy in township affairs, and the greater governmental flexibility which inheres in the municipal as contrasted with the township form of local government. For example, some of the restrictions operating on Michigan townships but not on cities were illustrated in a recent survey conducted in that state:

Cities can choose from various forms of governmental organizations, but townships cannot.

Townships, especially those that are heavily urban, tend to be underrepresented on county boards.

Cities can provide more public utility services than can townships.

Township peace officers do not have the same authority as possessed by city policemen.

Townships do not have the extent of control over their tax rates and expenditures as do cities. [43]

As far as can be generalized, the government of townships consists of (1) the annual township meeting (not too dissimilar in operation from the New England town meeting although less well attended) at which township officials are nominated and elected, taxes and expenditures approved, bonds authorized, and township bylaws enacted; (2) a township board composed generally of from three to five members—sometimes called township board of

[42] *Municipal Year Book, 1962*, p. 18.

[43] Kenneth Verburg, *A Study of the Legal Powers of Michigan Local Governments: Comparing Cities, Townships, and Charter Townships* (East Lansing, 1960), pp. 5, 6, 14, 16, 23. For a short political profile of a South Dakota township, see Alan L. Clem, *Spirit Mound Township in the 1960 Election* (Vermillion, 1961).

trustees or supervisors—elected for two or four-year terms at the annual township meeting, with powers to prepare budgets, supervise township administration, and manage the business of the township between township meetings; (3) a township executive designated chairman of the township board, trustee, or supervisor; (4) township administrative officers, in some states elected, in others appointed, including the township clerk (possibly the township's single most important official), treasurer, assessor, overseer of the poor, highway overseer, weed inspector, and fence viewer. It is not at all unusual in the more rural townships for one officer to be called on to perform a variety of functions and in many townships, rural or urban, for the more important township officials also to be members ex-officio of the township board.

THE STATES AND THEIR LOCAL GOVERNMENTS

Constitutionally the position of counties, boroughs, towns, townships, villages, and cities is quite clear. These units of government have such powers and only such powers as state constitutions and state laws permit. Their legal independence, their authority, and their duties are bestowed by the states under a unitary rather than federal arrangement. This means that states can give and take away such powers as their constitutions, and the laws enacted pursuant to them, may provide. In this pattern of state-local relationships, the role of the legislatures thus becomes focal. Counties must come to them when they wish to raise the salaries of their officials, abolish a county office, build an airport, add to their judiciary, or authorize a bond issue. Similarly, cities also must normally go to the legislature when they want to raise money, establish a housing and redevelopment authority, allow joint operations of a city-county facility, raise the pay of mayor and aldermen, build new fire stations, or change the majority of the vote that shall be required to amend their charters.

Every session thousands of bills reach the state legislatures that affect the structure of local government as well as the policies enacted by them with respect to such matters as highway safety, law enforcement, intergovernmental relations, education, taxation, conservation, liquor control, welfare, banking, zoning, and housing.

State courts are second only to the legislatures in their great influence over local governments and over the policies which these units are allowed to pursue. Since nearly every bond issue, zoning ordinance, building code, license, or traffic and health regulation is tested in a state court for its substantive and procedural validity, the judiciary has in fact become a major source of direction for local government. In general, it has been a conservative force, favoring precedent and property. Unless statutes clearly ordered it or constitutions authorized it, many courts were reluctant to enlarge the area of authority under which local units might, for example, engage in economic activity traditionally reserved to private enterprise or for which they might be permitted to tax and spend. Where, on the other hand, legislatures, in response to social and economic changes, did pass statutes enabling local governments to involve themselves in certain types of business functions, courts relied on the "public purpose" doctrine to uphold these grants. In recent years, local governments were sustained, for example, in supporting with appropriations or credit slum clearance and urban renewal, the construction and operation of parking facilities, the construction and leasing of commercial recreational facilities, and the building or acquisition of plants for use by private industry.[44]

States also exert varying degrees of administrative supervision and control over the activities of local government. There is first the matter of standards. Before local governments can obtain state financial aid, they are normally required to live up to certain state established standards of service or performance—their highways must pass state inspection, their teachers must meet statewide minimum educational qualifications, their welfare recipients must prove that they are entitled to support under the policies of the state (and federal government).

Related to the maintenance of standards is the right of supervision and inspection. The state department of correction may wish to inspect the conditions of local jails; the health department, the local water supply and sewage system; the welfare department, the homes for the aged; and the state auditor or public examiner, the city and county accounts.

Second, state administrative departments may wish to come to the assistance of local governments with professional advice and technical resources. The state crime bureau may assist local officials with a major crime investigation; the department of education may provide consultative services to public school libraries; the governor's Human Rights Commission may aid a county or city with an intergroup race problem; the highway department may offer its legal staff to a county in its dealings with the United States Bureau of Public Roads; the livestock and sanitary division of the state health department may help counties with their brucellosis eradication program; and the state liquor control department may send its agents to a county or city to assist in the scrutiny of liquor license applications and the enforcing of regulations.

Third, state governments exercise important fiscal powers over local governments. The financial dependence of local governments on state aid greatly increased during the last twenty years when local expenditures nearly quadrupled while revenues only tripled. Whereas local governments were left with the already overburdened property tax as their major source of revenue, states turned mostly to the more lucrative sales and income taxes for their needs. As cities and counties were faced with steeply rising costs in welfare, education, and highway construction, they were forced to look to state (and national) Capitols for help, thus further strengthening the strategic position of the states in local affairs.

[44] *University of Pennsylvania Law Review,* November, 1959, p. 95.

WHAT STATES MIGHT DO ADDITIONALLY TO HELP LOCAL
GOVERNMENTS AND THE METROPOLITAN AREAS—
THE RECOMMENDATIONS OF THE FEDERAL ADVISORY
COMMISSION ON INTERGOVERNMENTAL RELATIONS

The problem of intergovernmental relations has always constituted a challenge in American federalism. During the last fifteen years, various prominent executive and congressional commissions and committees devoted much effort to develop recommendations that sought to strengthen the effectiveness of intergovernmental cooperation, eliminate expensive administrative duplications, and examine possible reallocation of "functions, responsibilities, and revenues among the several levels of government." To go beyond the initial findings of such groups as the Hoover Commission, the Kestnbaum Commission, and the House Intergovernmental Relations Subcommittee (the Fountain Committee), Congress in 1959 established the Advisory Commission on Intergovernmental Relations as a "permanent, bipartisan body of twenty-six members to give continued study to the relations among local, state and national levels of government."

Composed of governors, state legislators, members of the United States Congress, mayors, county officials, and three citizen members appointed by the president, the commission is assisted in its work by an executive director, a ten-member research staff, and a group of consultants which includes some of the nation's leading scholars in political science, economics, and taxation. Commission studies in the fields of intergovernmental taxation and finance, metropolitan area problems, and local governmental structures and functions have already been widely praised for their objectivity and professional competence.

According to a 1961 report on "suggested actions by local, state and national governments," there were at least ten major steps that the states could take to help their local governments, their metropolian areas, as well as themselves. For example, states might wish to

A. impose certain limitations on the traditional concept of home rule "as applied to political subdivisions located within metropolitan areas . . . [and] reserve sufficient authority in the legislature to enable legislative action where necessary to modify responsibilities of and relationships among local units of government located within the metropolitan areas in the best interests of the people of the area as a whole."

B. authorize municipal annexation of unincorporated areas without the consent of areas annexed to make possible the "orderly and equitable extension of municipal boundaries" where urban development is under way or in prospect.

C. permit "two or more units of local government . . . [particularly within metropolitan areas] to exercise jointly or cooperatively any power possessed by one or more of the units concerned and to contract with one another for the rendering of governmental services."

D. enact legislation which would allow "local units of government within metropolitan areas to establish . . . metropolitan service corporations or authorities for the performance of governmental services necessitating areawide handling, such corporations to have appropriate borrowing and taxing power, but with the initial establishment and subsequent broadening of functions and responsibilities being subject to voter approval on the basis of an areawide majority."

E. authorize "the legislative bodies of municipalities and counties located within metropolitan areas to take mutual and coordinate action to transfer responsibility for specified governmental services from one unit of government to the other."

F. establish a unit of state government, an executive department for local affairs or a state commission on metropolitan area problems or similar agencies for "continuing attention, review, and assistance with respect to the metropolitan areas of the state and associated problems of local government, planning, structure, organization and finance."

G. establish programs for financial and technical assistance to metropolitan areas "in such fields as urban planning, urban renewal, building code modernization, and local government organization and finance."

H. ". . . enact legislation providing rigorous statutory standards for the establishment of new municipal corporations within the geographic boundaries of metropolitan areas. . . ."

I. adopt legislation to ". . . provide for acquisition by the State of conservation easements designed to remove from urban development key tracts of land in and around existing and potential metropolitan areas and . . . authorize local units of government to acquire interests and rights in real property within existing metropolitan areas for the purpose of preserving appropriate open areas and spaces within the pattern of metropolitan development."

J. authorize their governors to assist in the resolution of disputes among local units of government in metropolitan areas.[45]

THE FEDERAL GOVERNMENT—THE CITIES—AND THE METROPOLITAN AREAS

In American government the day is long past when cities look to state Capitols as their only source of aid and comfort whenever the public's demands for service and assistance exceeds locally available resources. Cities began to turn to Washington for help during the Depression of the 1930's, when skyrocketing expenditures for relief and work projects proved fiscally beyond the reach of local and state government. When the post-World War II population explosion came along, it merely accentuated a well-established trend. In the course of the last fifteen years, federally-supported programs grew and multiplied to the extent that their dollar impact alone is estimated to have reached in 1962 a total of $20 billion annually. Included in this are over

[45] Advisory Commission on Intergovernmental Relations, *Governmental Structure, Organization, and Planning in Metropolitan Area* (Washington, 1961); on the extent of restrictions on local government, see also Advisory Commission on Intergovernmental Relations, *State Constitutional and Statutory Restrictions upon the Structural, Functional, and Personnel Powers of Local Government* (Washington, 1962); and Verburg, *A Study of the Legal Powers of Michigan Local Governments: Comparing Cities, Townships, and Charter Townships.*

TABLE 6. SUMMARY OF MAJOR FEDERAL PROGRAMS

	Amount in millions	
	1962	1963
A. Transportation:		
(1) Roads and highways:		
Interstate highways (BPR)_____	$2,100.0	$2,819.0
Primary roads grant (BPR)_____	379.0	451.0
Secondary roads grants (BPR)_____	259.0	301.0
Urban roads grants (BPR)_____	253.0	250.0
Highway research and planning (BPR):		
Direct research_____	2.7	2.9
Cooperative—grants_____	.8	1.2
Thousands		
Advanced planning_____ $82–$98		
Current planning_____ 211–255		
Urban planning____ _____ 317–383		
National planning_____ 106–128		
(2) Mass transit:		
Mass transit grants (HHFA-OA)_____	15.8	9.1
Mass transit loans (HHFA-OA)_____	26.5	23.5
(3) Airports:		
Design and development grants (FAA)_____	6.7	6.7
Facilities and equipment (FAA)_____	125.0	145.0
Airport construction grants (FAA)_____	81.0	76.0
(4) Ports: Navigation development (C of E)_____	341.6	362.5
B. Water, sewerage, and sanitation:		
(1) Sewer and water service facilities:		
Waste treatment facility grants (HEW-PHS)_____	45.0	55.0
Water and sewerage facilities loans (HHFA-OA)___	95.0	100.0
(2) Water resources:		
Water supply and pollution control grants (HEW-PHS)_____	17.1	20.5
Water resources investigation (DI-GS)_____	14.1	14.5
Water resources research (DI-GS)_____	_____	2.8
Water resource planning (C of E)_____	13.4	15.9
Saline water research (DI-OSW)_____	5.3	7.7
(3) Water and air pollution:		
Air pollution research (HEW-PHS-BSS)_____	6.0	9.0
Environmental engineering—waste disposal grants (HEW-PHS-BSS)_____	.2	.3
C. Schools and hospitals:		
(1) School construction:		
Grants to impacted areas (HEW-OE)_____	60.0	60.0
College housing loans (HHFA-CFA)_____	300.0	300.0
(2) Hospital construction:		
Hill-Burton grants (HEW-PHS-BSS)_____	166.0	192.0
Hospital construction (VA)_____	53.0	70.0
D. Land acquisition, protection, and improvement:		
(1) Open space and parks:		

sixty different grants and matching funds, direct federal expenditures, as well as federally-operated insurance programs.[46]

Among the various programs of federal assistance aimed at cities and metropolitan areas (see Table 6), those encouraging private and public developments in housing and urban renewal now reaching nearly 2,000 com-

[46] Senate Committee on Government Operations, *Role of the Federal Government in Metropolitan Areas,* Hearings, December 13, and 14, 1962, before the Subcommittee on Intergovernmental Relations, 87th Cong., 2nd Sess. (Washington, 1963), p. 66.

	Amount in millions	
	1962	1963
Construction and park acquisition (DI-NPS)	40.6	44.0
Open space grants (HHFA-URA)	34.9	14.8
Parkland rehabilitation (DI-NPS)	17.9	20.0
(2) Protection of land:		
River basin investigations (DI-BR)	7.0	8.1
Flood protection (C of E)	132.5	128.6
Flood control and multipurpose projects (C of E)	404.8	467.0
Flood plain information (C of E)	.5	.7
Tidal damage (C of E)	4.0	7.4
Beach erosion control (C of E)	1.2	1.5
E. Urban renewal and planning:		
Urban planning assistance grants (HHFA-URA)	18.3	18.0
Urban renewal grants (HHFA-URA)	800.0	600.0
Urban studies research (HHFA-OA)	.3	.3
Public works planning grants (HHFA-CFA)	13.0	12.0
F. Housing:		
Housing for elderly loans (HHFA-CFA and FHA)	152.5	100.0
Low-income demonstration grants (HHFA-OA)	2.0	3.0
Public housing loans (HHFA-PHA)	171.3	193.0
Insured veterans loans (VA)	5,088.7	5,250.0
Direct veterans loans (VA)	19.7	25.0
Rural housing loans (DA-FHA)	75.0	75.0
Farm labor housing loans (DA-FHA)	1.0	1.0
Home improvement loan insurance (HHFA-FHA)	847.9	930.0
Housing for military (HHFA-FHA)	121.3	136.4
Urban renewal housing insurance (HHFA-FHA)	305.1	1,090.4
Home and rental insurance programs (HHFA-FHA)	5,492.3	6,704.8
G. Business aids:		
Disaster loans (SBA)	3.0	6.0
Loans to development companies (SBA)	31.5	17.0
Development of power reactors (AEC)	191.8	191.3
H. Rural-urban programs:		
Telephone system loans (DA-REA)	97.3	165.0
Electric facilities loans (DA-REA)	195.8	360.0
Enlargement loans (DA-FHA)	1.7	7.8
Family farm direct loans (DA-FHA)	105.0	105.0
Soil and water conservation loans (DA-FHA)	71.6	25.0
Economic research (DA-ERS)	3.3	3.9
I. Federal installations:		
(1) Public buildings:		
National Guard and Reserve buildings (DOD)	66.1	46.3
Post office planning and lease-back contracts (POD)	91.4	150.0
Public buildings (GSA)	72.0	150.0
Planning of facilities (GSA)	.6	.6
(2) Defense installations: National Guard and Reserve		
installations (DOD)	66.1	46.5

SOURCE: Senate Committee on Government Operations, Subcommittee on Intergovernmental Relations, Hearings, December 13 and 14, 1962, *Role of the Federal Government in Metropolitan Areas*, 87th Cong., 2nd Sess. (Washington, 1963), pp. 71–72.

munities have assumed first-rate significance. They were given even greater impetus by the Housing Act of 1961. Aside from a $2 billion increase, which doubled the capital grants available to the Urban Renewal Administration, the act emphasized the following seven program needs: (1) moderate income families (long-term, no down payment mortgages and long-term, low-interest rate loans for rental and cooperative housing financed from federal funds); (2) the "financially disadvantaged families at the bottom of the economic ladder" (approximately 100,000 additional low-rent public housing units); (3) housing for the elderly (authorization for direct loans was increased from $50 to $125 million); (4) financing the construction of college dormitories, faculty housing, dining halls, and student unions (Housing and Home Finance Agency's [H.H.F.A.] revolving fund was increased from $50 to $125 million); (5) aid to communities requiring more adequate public facilities such as water and sewer (an increase from $150 to $600 million); (6) aid to communities seeking to acquire permanent open space to prevent urban sprawl ($50 million); and (7) mass transportation demonstration grants and mass transportation facility loans for urban areas ($50 million).

The Housing Act of 1965, signed August 10, 1965, increased appropriations for established housing programs and added several new features, the most prominent of which are:

A. The subsidization of rental payments over and above 25 percent of family income for certain low income or handicapped families living in housing financed by non-profit or limited-dividend corporations.
B. Subsidization of rentals for low-income families entitled to public housing for apartments in privately owned facilities.
C. Provision for grants up to $1500 for rehabilitation of housing in blighted areas to enable residents to upgrade their properties.

These new provisions of the law are aimed not only at providing more public housing, but also at encouraging private investors to provide housing and at diffusing public housing throughout the community in order to avoid possible creation of public housing "ghettos."

Further attention needs to be given to the Federal Urban Renewal Program as a pattern illustrative of federal-local relationships and as a crucial factor in the economic, physical, and social development of America's cities. Stated simply, the purpose of urban renewal is to permit the federal government to come to the assistance of a community's private and public resources in order to "prevent and correct urban blight and decay and to set in motion long range, planned redevelopment."

The actual planning of a renewal project is done by the cooperating community, by its public housing authority or department of city government, as the state may provide. Normally such a plan calls for the acquisition of blighted areas and the disposition of the cleared land for particular industrial, commercial, or residential redevelopment purposes. It may also include provisions for the rehabilitation of existing buildings and existing but inadequate public facilities.

In order to qualify for a redevelopment grant or loan through the Housing and Home Finance Agency (the federal government's arm administering the urban renewal program), the local plan submitted must also provide details on the proposed execution of the project. Included in the request must be such data as method of financing, extent of land acquisitions, and arrangements for the relocation of present site occupants. If the local redevelopment plan meets federal specifications and standards, the federal government will supply two-thirds, sometimes three-fourths, of the difference between what it costs the local authorities to acquire and clear redevelopment land and what this land will bring when resold.

Generally, urban renewal projects are financed by:

A. local contributions taking "the form of cash or noncash grants-in-aid, such as donations of land, demolition and removal work, project improvements, certain expenditures by colleges, universities, and hospitals or public facilities."
B. federal capital grants, loans, and advances; depending on size of the community and the economic conditions of the areas involved. These federal loans and advances are available for the planning of projects, as clearing sites, and for other related expenses.
C. federal capital and relocation grants are available also (⅔ or ¾ of the difference) to communities so that they may conduct comprehensive long-range plans for community renewal and improvement, for urban transportation surveys and studies, and for the relocation of individuals ($200 for moving costs) and business establishments ($3,000 and more in some special cases.)[47]

While most of the funds for rehabilitation of buildings must come from private sources, low-income displaced families may be assisted in their re-housing in low-rent federally-supported public housing units (Public Housing Administration, H.H.F.A.) or by liberalized mortgage insurance arrangements made possible through the programs of the Federal Housing Administration or the Federal National Mortgage Association, both constituent agencies of the H.H.F.A.

Constitutionally, cities cannot, of course, accept federal aid for their

[47] "The Urban Renewal Program," *Federal Housing Administration Fact Sheet*, February, 1962, pp. 2–3; on federal assistance for municipal planning, see Urban Renewal Administration, Housing and Home Finance Agency, *Urban Planning Assistance Program: Project Directory* (Washington, 1963). Under the urban renewal program Congress has authorized financial assistance to relocation efforts of the elderly. The problem of the aged is often accentuated by such factors as poor health, low incomes (50% of the aged have incomes of less than $3,000 a year), widowhood (6 million widowed persons among the aged), and residential concentration in decaying areas of cities. "Even under ideal circumstances relocation is a disrupting force creating an abiding sense of crisis over the loss of a home, a neighborhood, friends, and a community. For the aged the difficulties are compounded manyfold as the disruption affects life-preserving relationships to the past, the present, and the immediate future. It comes at a time when income is lowest, health problems greatest, and when emotional attachment to a home and a way of life is most intense and necessary." Sidney Spector, Assistant Administrator, Office of Housing for Senior Citizens, Housing and Home Finance Agency, in Senate Special Committee on Aging, Relocation of Elderly People, Subcommittee on Involuntary Relocation of the Elderly, Hearings, Pt. 1, 87th Cong., 2nd Sess. (Washington, 1963), p. 4. See also Senate Special Committee on Aging, *Housing for the Elderly*, Report of the Subcommittee on Aging, August 31, 1962, 87th Cong., 2nd Sess., (Washington, 1962).

renewal efforts unless state law authorizes them to do so. Enabling statutes for such projects were in force (as of December, 1961) in all of the states except Idaho, Louisiana, South Carolina, Utah, and Wyoming.[48] Wishing to speed up and encourage slum clearance and urban renewal, the legislatures of Connecticut, Massachusetts, New York, and Pennsylvania even "extended or authorized grants or loans to assist municipalities in paying the local share of federally aided renewal projects." [49]

Since its inception in 1949, urban renewal has been highly controversial. Its supporters can demonstrate an impressive record of activity and achievement. Participating are 702 communities in forty-two states. Nearly half of all urban renewal projects are located in cities of less than 25,000 population. Despite the involvement of the federal government, all projects must first be given local hearings and local government approval. Over 150,000 families have been relocated, 92 per cent of them in "decent, safe and sanitary housing." Of all land disposed of under urban renewal, 75 per cent (exclusive of streets and alleys) has been bought "by private persons and organizations" and the remainder "will be devoted to commercial, industrial or institutional purposes." Surveys comparing property assessments in the area before and after redevelopment reveal values that are "averaging more than five times the value prior to slum clearance." [50]

Among the various types of projects, most of which have been completed, are the following:

Nashville, Tennessee—Capitol Hill Project
This 96-acre project surrounds the Tennessee State Capitol Building in downtown Nashville. Before renewal, the area was a mass of slum residences mingled with run-down, marginal businesses. Truck traffic was heavy, police and fire calls were abnormally high.

Cleared project land has been devoted to new public, commercial, and residential uses. Included are new public buildings (a municipal auditorium, for example), office buildings, high-rise apartments, motels, and a parking garage. A new parkway through the area has greatly improved traffic flow.

Anticipated federal capital grant—$3,590,000.

Minneapolis, Minnesota—Gateway Center Project
This 72-acre project northwest of the Minneapolis central business district was the local skid row. It was characterized by an incompatible mixture of residential, commercial, industrial uses, by overcrowding of structures, run-down buildings, and all the ills associated with skid rows.

Renewal plans called primarily for clearance and redevelopment, with a handful of commercial buildings scheduled for retention and rehabilitation. Re-

[48] *Housing and Home Finance Agency 15th Annual Report, 1961* (Washington, 1962), p. 295.

[49] *Municipal Year Book, 1962*, p. 350.

[50] Statement by William L. Slayton, Commissioner, Urban Renewal Administration, H.H.F.A., before House Committee on Banking and Currency, *Urban Renewal,* Subcommittee on Housing, Hearings, November 19–21, 1963, Pt. 2, 88th Cong., 1st Sess. (Washington, 1963), pp. 410, 421, 425.

development involves new residential, public, and commercial structures. In residential, 1,500 dwelling units are planned. Public buildings include city, state, and federal. Commercial re-use includes a hotel and several office buildings.

Federal capital grant—$12,080,004.

New Haven, Connecticut—Wooster Square Project
This is a 235-acre project in southeast New Haven. Before renewal it was a run-down, mixed residential, commercial, and industrial area, characterized by noxious commercial and industrial installations, overcrowding, and poor traffic circulation.

This residential section of the renewed area involves both new construction and rehabilitation. New construction includes three multi-family developments, one of which is housing for the elderly. In rehabilitation, more than 1,000 dwelling units have been upgraded. The industrial-commercial portions of the area embrace thirty new structures, completed or under way.

Anticipated federal capital grant—$19,000,000.

Chicago, Illinois—Illinois Institute of Technology Project
This 38-acre area adjoins the institute campus. Predominantly residential before clearance, it contained 135 structures of which more than 85 per cent were dilapidated or had inadequate sanitary facilities.

Redevelopment of the area as part of the campus is in line with institute campus expansion begun in 1940. The expansion program includes laboratories, dormitory and apartment buildings, classrooms, and maintenance and athletic installations.

Federal capital grant—$2,359,423.[51]

In his address to the United States Conference of Mayors (1964), Mayor Tucker of St. Louis, Missouri, one of the strong supporters of his city's massive renewal program, emphasized that urban renewal

In its concentrated attack on slums . . . did more to expose the ugliness and squalor of the poverty stricken among us than any other program. . . .

[Has exposed] the deplorable housing of the urban slum [and] made the public generally more aware of the need to provide adequate housing for the forgotten fifth of our population. . . .

[51] *Ibid.*, pp. 389–526. On the urban renewal controversy, see also Peter Rossi and Robert A. Dentler, *The Politics of Urban Renewal: The Chicago Findings* (New York, 1959); Edward J. Wynne, Jr., "Ensuring Proper Land Re-Use in Urban Renewal: An Analysis of Present Federal and Local Policies and Practices," *New York University Law Review,* November, 1962, pp. 882–915; Institute for Community Development and Services, *Urban Renewal in Private Enterprises* (East Lansing, 1962); Robert B. Mitchell (ed.), "Urban Revival: Goals and Standards," *The Annals of the American Academy of Political and Social Sciences,* March, 1964; Sidney Z. Searles, "Bulldozers at Your Door," *Reader's Digest,* September, 1963, pp. 83–87; Beverely Duncan and Philip Hauser, *Housing A Metropolis—Chicago* (Glencoe, 1960); and John A. Logan, Paul Oppermann, and Norman E. Tucker (eds.), *Environmental Engineering & Metropolitan Planning* (Evanston, 1962).

[H]as starkly exposed the shame of the slum—the indignities man must suffer if he is poor; and urban renewal was the first Government program, at any level of government, which said if you take a family out of the slum through a publicly sponsored clearance program, you must, if possible, relocate him in standard housing.[52]

Criticism of the urban renewal program ranges all the way from an outright denunciation of its underlying concept of social engineering to a mere disapproval of particular phases of the program's administration.

A. Urban renewal, like other forms of government intervention in the business activities of the people, is Marxism. Its object is redistribution of wealth. Its result is wider impoverishment along with the destruction of freedom. It is one of the tools by which Marxists deceive good people and induce them to speed up the process of their own communization.[53]

B. The impact of the urban renewal program on small business establishments can be disastrous. According to a recent study of some of the economic consequences of this program in Providence, R. I., of a group of 292 small service and neighborhood shops (mostly owned and operated by the elderly), 22% failed to reopen their doors in new locations either due to lack of money or desire.[54]

C. Where renewal has taken place, it has demonstrated it can indeed disrupt neighborhoods and dislocate people but by no means necessarily improve the urban scene or the people on it. A lot of public housing is an architectural fright to begin with; a lot of it degenerates into new slums. In many cases crime rates are high. . . . The assumption [is] that better housing, when it actually is that, will automatically make better people. Some it will undoubtedly help; a good many others, unfortunately not.[55]

D. Red tape, politics, inexperience and construction difficulties are a few of the factors bogging down projects. And many tenants and small businessmen in blighted areas are aggravating delays by resisting the cities' efforts to relocate them . . . despite a measure of progress, most of the property cities have acquired for urban renewal purposes hasn't yet been developed.[56]

Members of the Negro community have registered strenuous objections to what they saw to be the ghetto-making consequences of the urban renewal program. Chicago's Hyde Park Project has come under particularly heavy attack. To make room for the bulldozers, masses of Negro citizens were evicted upon short notice. Properties were underevaluated and federal relocation assistance was found to be entirely inadequate. Housing for the dislocated was all too frequently either of an inferior quality or priced beyond their reach. Segregation instead of being reduced grew, in fact, worse and more rigid.

---

[52] *Congressional Record*, February 25, 1964, p. 3333.

[53] "Renewal In, Prosperity Out," reprinted from *Christian Economics* in the *Congressional Record*, April 10, 1963, p. 5836.

[54] See Basil G. Zimmer, *Rebuilding Cities* (Chicago, 1964); an intensely critical view of urban renewal is found in Martin Anderson, *The Federal Bulldozer* (Cambridge, 1964).

[55] Editorial, *The Wall Street Journal*, January 30, 1964.

[56] Stanley Penn, "Urban Renewal Ills," *ibid.*, January 28, 1964.

Initially touted as a national model [Hyde Park] for racially integrated urban renewal, the federally-assisted "nondiscriminatory" pilot project has served to roll back the ghetto border, generating pressures that deliver displaced residents into the hands of greedy landlords and ruthless speculators.[57]

Still other critics of the federal urban redevelopment program insist that cooperative efforts by local banks, business establishments, real estate interests, and public-spirited groups, if given the opportunity, can be sufficiently effective to carry out most of the needed rehabilitation and rejuvenation in most of the nation's cities. Whether such a self-help approach can succeed or not (aside from the question of attracting the necessary capital) would depend in no small measure on the willingness and ability of city government to enforce municipal construction codes, to update city zoning regulations, and to encourage the activities of private redevelopment corporations.

Pressures for urban renewal activities of some type will persist throughout the 1960's. Economic, social, and political forces demanding action are too strong to be ignored. In such a setting, the precise forms of private and public involvement that will distinguish the emerging programs in the burgeoning urban areas cannot be discerned at this moment. As noted earlier in this chapter, local conditions, experiences, and traditions are too diverse to permit the use of uniform patterns or approaches either towards governmental reorganization or towards the additional services that might be rendered the public. Unwilling to accept the complexities of broadened intergovernmental relations plans and lacking a consensus regarding the need for a metropolitan, area-wide government, cities, districts, and towns continue to muddle through by making only minor structural adjustments or more often by shifting to the next higher level of government those functions or problems that they cannot or will not handle themselves. Whether sufficient countervailing power can be mobilized to preserve areas of significant local governmental control and policy self-determination remains to be seen.

CASE PROBLEMS FOR CLASS DISCUSSION..

1. Political forces operating out of the major city in a large metropolitan area (population, 500,000), have been able to advance the cause of a Metro government to the point where voter approval throughout the area appears imminent. Municipal leagues of the smaller municipalities which surround the major city have strongly opposed the Metro proposal. Representatives of these leagues have come to you for help. They persuade you to organize an effective campaign to defeat Metro. What would be your strategy? Who would be your political allies? How would you organize your campaign?
2. You are the chief planning officer of a city of 350,000 which is in the process of developing a long-range capital improvement program. There is considerable

---

[57] Elinor Richey, "Splitsville, U. S. A.: An Ironic Tale of Urban Renewal and Racial Segregation," *The Reporter*, May 23, 1963, pp. 35–38. As a matter of law and Urban Renewal Agency directive, renewal developers must promise to comply with all federal, state, and local law prohibiting discrimination or segregation by reason of race, religion, color, or national origin in the sale, lease, or occupancy of the property.

opposition to the rezoning of certain tracts which in your judgment need rebuilding. Hearings before the planning board and city council indicate the need for a well-organized campaign to gain support of the community for the improvement program. The mayor is calling a strategy meeting. Which departments of the city would have to be represented?

3. You are the executive secretary of the local mosquito control district. The legislature calls you before its committee on municipal affairs which is considering a bill disestablishing the district and transferring its duties to the city public health department. In your opinion this would severely cripple your program. What would be the nature of your argument, and what evidence would you provide to prove your case?

4. Your local housing authority has acquired land for redevelopment purposes with the aid of a grant under the Federal Housing and Redevelopment Program. Considerable opposition has now developed throughout the community against the proposed destruction of a number of older homes located in the redevelopment area. Foes of the program insist that the city council hold a referendum on the issue and let the people decide. Supporters of the plan fight the referendum and stress the economic benefits which would accrue to the city as a result of these redevelopment activities. You are a reporter working on the local paper. Your editor wants you to write a series of articles on this controversy. Before going deeply into the issue, you decide that you must have answers to five questions: Legally, can there be a referendum on this issue? May the city condemn private homes for the purpose of providing land for new industry? Can the city back out of its contract with the federal government under which some aid had already been received? Which groups favor the referendum and which oppose it? Is new housing to be provided for those displaced?

SELECTED BIBLIOGRAPHY

CHARLES R. ADRIAN, Governing Urban America (New York, 1961).

Advisory Commission on Intergovernmental Relations, Intergovernmental Responsibilities for Water Supply and Sewage Disposal in Metropolitan Areas (Washington, 1962).

Advisory Commission on Intergovernmental Relations, Performance of Urban Functions: Local and Areawide (Washington, 1963).

BENJAMIN BAKER, "Municipal Autonomy: Its Relationship to Metropolitan Government," Western Political Quarterly, March, 1960, pp. 83–98.

EDWARD C. BANFIELD, "The Political Implications of Metropolitan Growth," Daedalus, Winter, 1960, pp. 61–78.

EDWARD C. BANFIELD (ed.), Urban Government: A Reader in Politics and Administration (New York, 1961).

PETER BARRY, "Cooperation Pays Off," National Civic Review, April, 1960, pp. 179–183, 188.

ALAN BIBLE, "Uncle Sam's Metro Job," National Civic Review, December, 1960, pp. 595–601.

RICHARD BIGGER and JAMES D. KITCHEN, "City Managers and Metro," National Civic Review, March, 1960, pp. 120–126.

GUTHRIE S. BIRKHEAD (ed.), Metropolitan Issues: Social, Governmental, Fiscal (Syracuse, 1962).

JOHN C. BOLLENS (ed.), Exploring the Metropolitan Community (Berkeley, 1961).

DAVID A. BOOTH, Metropolitics: The Nashville Consolidation (East Lansing, 1963).

JERRY C. BOSWORTH, How the Huron-Clinton Metropolitan Authority Responds to Its Public (Ann Arbor, 1961).

FRANKLIN M. BRIDGE, Metro-Denver: Mile High Government (Boulder, 1963).

ARTHUR W. BROMAGE, Political Representation in Metropolitan Agencies (Ann Arbor, 1962).

WILLIAM G. COLMAN, "Old Neglect Subsiding?" National Civic Review, January, 1964, pp. 10–13.

ROBERT H. CONNERY and RICHARD H. LEACH, "Southern Metropolis: Challenge to Government," Journal of Politics, February, 1964, pp. 60–81.

PATRICK G. CULLEN and ROBERT J. NOE, "Progress Through Metropolitan Annexation," *Notre Dame Lawyer,* December, 1963, pp. 56–95.

DONALD J. CURRAN, "The Metropolitan Problem: Solution From Within," *National Tax Journal,* September, 1963, pp. 213–223.

KINGSLEY DAVIS and ELEANOR LANGLOIS, *Future Demographic Growth of the San Francisco Bay Area* (Berkeley, 1963).

GEORGE H. DEMING, "Metro and Little Places," *National Civic Review,* June, 1961, pp. 304–308, 317.

THOMAS R. DYE, HAROLD HERMAN, CHARLES S. LIEBMAN, and OLIVER P. WILLIAMS, "Differentiation and Cooperation in a Metropolitan Area," *Midwest Journal of Political Science,* May, 1963, pp. 145–155.

JEAN GOTTMANN, *Megalopolis: The Urbanized Northeastern Seaboard of the United States* (New York, 1961).

SAMUEL K. GOVE, *The Lakewood Plan* (Urbana, 1961).

DANIEL R. GRANT and LEE S. GREENE, "Surveys, Dust, Action," *National Civic Review,* October, 1961, pp. 466–471.

SCOTT GREER, *Metropolitics: A Study of Political Culture* (New York, 1963).

SCOTT GREER, "The Rational Model, the Sociological Model, and Metropolitan Reform," *Public Opinion Quarterly,* Summer, 1963, pp. 242–249.

LUTHER GULICK, "Goals for Metropolis," *National Civic Review,* December, 1960, pp. 586–594, 609.

CLARENCE J. HEIN, "Metropolitan Government: Residents Outside the Central Urban Areas," *Western Political Quarterly,* September, 1961, pp. 764–769.

SAMUEL HUMES, "Organization for Metropolitan Cooperation," *Public Management,* May, 1962, pp. 105–107.

THEODORE M. HUTCHISON, *Metropolitan Area Problems: the Role of the Federal Government* (Ann Arbor, 1961).

"Intergovernmental Approach to Metropolitan Areas," *Public Management,* July, 1961, pp. 152–156.

RUTH ITTNER, *Special Districts in the State of Washington* (Seattle, 1963).

VICTOR JONES, "Cooperation Pattern," *National Civic Review,* June, 1962, pp. 302–308.

T. J. KENT, JR., *City and Regional Planning for the Metropolitan San Francisco Bay Area* (Berkeley, 1963).

RICHARD H. LEACH, "New Urban Challenge," *National Civic Review,* October, 1961, pp. 480–484, 518.

DUANE LOCKARD, "Balancing of Weights," *National Civic Review,* October, 1963, pp. 482–488.

C. DAVID LOEKS, "Taming Urban Giant," *National Civic Review,* July, 1962, pp. 354–360.

JOSEPH M. McKENNA, *The Growth and Problems of Metropolitan Wyandotte County* (Lawrence, 1963).

JOSEPH M. McKENNA, *The Topeka Metropolitan Area: Its Political Units and Characteristics* (Lawrence, 1962).

IRVING G. McNAYR, "All Pulling Together," *National Civic Review,* March, 1962, pp. 135–138.

ALLEN D. MANVEL, "The States' Concern," *National Civic Review,* February, 1962, pp. 70–74, 85.

ROSCOE C. MARTIN, FRANK J. MUNGER, and OTHERS, *Decisions in Syracuse* (Bloomington, 1961).

EDMUND W. MEISENHELDER III and ROBERT A. LOVELACE, *Laws for City-County Cooperation in Tennessee* (Knoxville, 1960).

GORDON E. MISNER, "Recent Developments in the Metropolitan Law Enforcement," *Journal of Criminal Law, Criminology and Police Science,* January–February, 1960, pp. 497–508 and July–August, 1960, pp. 265–272.

ROBERT J. MOWITZ and DEIL S. WRIGHT, *Profile of a Metropolis: A Casebook* (Detroit, 1962).

ROBERT T. NORMAN, "The Harvard Plan for Metropolitan Boston," *Western Political Quarterly,* September, 1963, pp. 708–721.

JAMES A. NORTON, *The Metro Experience* (Cleveland, 1963).

JAMES A. NORTON, "Referenda Voting in a Metropolitan Area," *Western Political Quarterly,* March, 1963, pp. 195–212.

VINCENT OSTROM, CHARLES M. TIEBOUT and ROBERT WARREN, "The Organization of Government in Metropolitan Areas: A Theoretical Inquiry," *American Political Science Review,* December, 1961, pp. 831–842.

JOHN K. PARKER, "Cooperation in Metropolitan Areas Through Councils of Governments," *Public Management,* October, 1963, pp. 223–225.

WILSON RECORD, *Minority Groups and Intergroup Relations in the San Francisco Bay Area* (Berkeley, 1963).

THOMAS H. REED, "A Call for Plain Talk," *National Civic Review,* March, 1962, pp. 119–128.

Research and Policy Committee of the Committee for Economic Development, *Guiding Metropolitan Growth* (New York, 1960).

LLOYD RODWIN and KEVIN LYNCH (eds.), *The Future Metropolis* (New York, 1961).

ROBERT H. SALISBURY, "The Dynamics of Reform: Charter Politics in St. Louis," *Midwest Journal of Political Science,* August, 1961, pp. 260–275.

HENRY J. SCHMANDT, "The Area Council— Approach to Metropolitan Government," *Public Management,* February, 1960, pp. 30–32.

HENRY J. SCHMANDT, "The City and the Ring: The Two-Way Street of Metropolitan Reorganization," *American Behavioral Scientist,* November, 1960, pp. 17–19.

MEL SCOTT, *Partnership in the Arts: Public and Private Support of Cultural Activities in the San Francisco Bay Area* (Berkeley, 1963).

STANLEY SCOTT and WILLIS CULVER, *Metropolitan Agencies and Concurrent Office-Holding: A Survey of Selected Districts and Authorities* (Berkeley, 1961).

FRANK S. SENGSTOCK, *Extraterritorial Powers in the Metropolitan Area* (Ann Arbor, 1962).

EDWARD SOFEN, "Problems of Metropolitan Leadership: The Miami Experience," *Midwest Journal of Political Science,* February, 1961, pp. 18–38.

EDWARD SOFEN, *A Report on Politics in Greater Miami* (Cambridge, 1961).

PAUL STUDENSKI, "Metropolitan Areas, 1960," *National Civic Review,* October, 1960, pp. 467–473 and November, 1960, pp. 537–542, 548.

KENNETH C. TOLLENAAR, "A Home Rule Puzzle," *National Civic Review,* September, 1961, pp. 411–416.

RAYMOND VERNON, *Metropolis 1985; An Interpretation of the Findings of the New York Metropolitan Region Study* (Cambridge, 1960).

ROBERT WARREN, "Changing Patterns of Governmental Organization in the Los Angeles Metropolitan Area," unpublished Ph.D. dissertation, University of California, 1964.

RICHARD A. WATSON, "Metropolitan Government for Metropolitan Cleveland: An Analysis of the Voting Record," *Midwest Journal of Political Science,* November, 1961, pp. 365–390.

JOHN M. WINTERS, *Interstate Metropolitan Areas* (Ann Arbor, 1962).

ROBERT C. WOOD (with Vladimir V. Almendinger), *1400 Governments* (Cambridge, 1961).

ROBERT C. WOOD, "Metropolitan Government, 1975: An Extrapolation of Trends," *American Political Science Review,* March, 1958, pp. 108–122.

ROBERT C. WOOD, "There are Many Roads," *National Civic Review,* March, 1962, pp. 129–134, 174.

THOMAS J. WOOD, "Dade County: Unbossed, Erratically Led," *The Annals of the American Academy of Political and Social Science,* May, 1964, pp. 64–71.

CATHERINE BAUER WURSTER, *Housing and the Future of Cities in the San Francisco Bay Area* (Berkeley, 1963).

RICHARD M. ZETTEL, *Urban Transportation in the San Francisco Bay Area* (Berkeley, 1963).

✔ *Chapter XII*

MUNICIPAL
GOVERNMENT

In analyzing city politics is it possible to determine scientifically where the key decisions are made?

What should be the working relationship between city hall and state Capitol?

AMERICA'S CITIES AND THE 1960 CENSUS

Based on the 1960 census returns, there were in the United States a total of 5,445 urban communities—cities, towns, and villages with populations of 2,500 and over, in which lived nearly 70 per cent, or 125.3 million, of the

TABLE 1. COMPONENTS OF URBAN POPULATION FOR THE
UNITED STATES, 1960

Component	United States	Inside urban- ized areas	Outside urban- ized areas
Total	179,323,175	95,848,487	83,474,688
Urban	125,268,750	95,848,487	29,420,263
Incorporated places of 2,500 or more	106,308,257	79,487,607	26,820,650
Unincorporated places of 2,500 or more	5,106,083	2,679,492	2,426,591
Urban towns and townships	3,313,559	3,140,537	173,022
Other urban territory	10,540,851	10,540,851	
Incorporated places of under 2,500	689,746	689,746	—
All other	9,851,105	9,851,105	—
Rural	54,054,425	—	54,054,425

SOURCE: *Municipal Year Book, 1963*, p. 27.

nation's people (see Table 1). Census figures for the decade then concluded revealed also that,

A. Of the country's five largest cities, New York, Chicago, Los Angeles, Philadelphia, and Detroit, all but one—Los Angeles—encountered small decreases in the population of the core city while the metropolitan areas surrounding each city showed enormous gains, from 46 per cent to 80 per cent over 1950. Of the nation's twenty largest cities, in only eight did the population of the central city score any advances.

B. Greater Los Angeles now including Orange and Los Angeles counties housed seven million persons "in an 85-by-125 mile sweep of coastal plain and mountains" and continued to gain at a rate of 5,000 per week.

C. The nation's population living in suburbs grew from 22.9 million to 41.6 million, an upswing of 82 per cent.

D. Aided by sunshine and mild climate, the fastest growing cities were found in the West and South: Orlando, Florida, up 442.7%; Tucson, up 368.4%;

403

FIGURE 1. PER CENT CHANGE IN URBAN POPULATION, BY STATES, 1950–1960

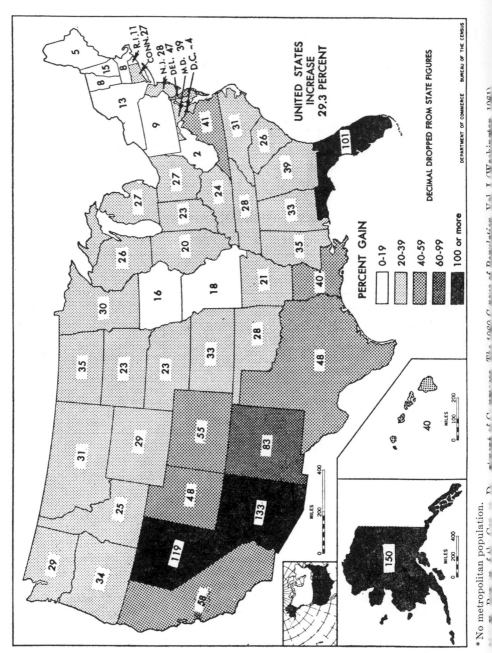

R.I. 11
CONN. 27
N.J. 28
DEL. 47
M.D. 39
D.C. −4

5
8 15
8
13
9
2
27
27
23
24
28
33
35
21
40
48
28
33
23
23
16
18
30
26
20
26
39
35
31
29
55
83
133
48
119
25
34
29
58
41
31
26

UNITED STATES
INCREASE
29.3 PERCENT

PERCENT GAIN

0-19
20-39
40-59
60-99
100 or more

DECIMAL DROPPED FROM STATE FIGURES

DEPARTMENT OF COMMERCE   BUREAU OF THE CENSUS

MILES
0   200   400

40

MILES
0   100   200

150

MILES
0   200   400

* No metropolitan population.

Jacksonville, Florida, up 357.9%; Phoenix, up 311.1%; Spokane, up 217.4%; Tampa, up 120.5%; San Jose, up 114.3%; El Paso, up 112.0%; Albuquerque, up 107.8%; and San Diego, up 71.4%. (For state figures on metropolitan population growth, see Figure 1.)

E. Between 1950 and 1960, a very significant influx of Negroes occurred in a number of Northern cities. For example, in Newark, New Jersey, the percentage of Negroes nearly doubled in ten years, reaching a total of 34% in 1960; Detroit's Negro population rose from 16.2% to 28.9%; Chicago, from 13.6% to 22.9%; and in Philadelphia, from 18.2% to 26.4%. The contrast between the 1940 and the 1960 picture is even more striking (see Table 2).

F. Racial segregation tends to sharpen as white residents move to suburbia while Negroes remain in the center of the city (see Table 3). A recent study noted that "white populations in outlying regions of the nation's twelve largest metropolitan areas climbed from 93 per cent in 1930 to 99 per cent in 1960." [1]

TABLE 2. NEGRO POPULATION IN SIX NORTHERN
CITIES AND IN WASHINGTON, D. C.

City	1940	1960
New York	458,000	1,088,000
Chicago	278,000	813,000
Los Angeles	64,000	344,000
Philadelphia	251,000	529,000
Detroit	149,000	482,000
Cleveland	85,000	251,000
Washington, D. C.	187,000	412,000

SOURCE: Bureau of the Census, Department of Commerce, *United States Census of Population: 1960*, Selected Area Report on Standard Metropolitan Statistical Areas (Washington, 1963).

Over one-half of the nation's retail trade is carried on in thirteen urban belts composed of a group of cities built along major arterial highway systems extending from

Boston to Washington	San Francisco to San Diego
Albany to Erie	Seattle to Eugene
Cleveland to Pittsburgh	Kansas City to Sioux Falls
Toledo to Cincinnati	Fort Worth-Dallas-San Antonio-Houston
Detroit to Muskegon	Miami-Tampa-Jacksonville
Chicago-Gary to Milwaukee	Atlanta to Raleigh.[2]
St. Louis to Peoria	

These urban belts, sometimes called "spread cities," will continue to expand in the years to come as the land between them, in the absence of adequate planning or zoning, is used for homes, shops, industries, and municipal facilities in patterns which often defy any rational design which would balance land requirements for recreation, residence, jobs, and highways.

[1] Mitchell Gordon, "Doomed Cities?," *The Wall Street Journal*, October 16, 1962, p. 14.
[2] "Sprawling 'Strip Cities'—They're All Over U. S.," *U. S. News & World Report*, September 18, 1961, pp. 74–75.

Serious concern for such developments has been repeatedly expressed by governmental officials, professional planners, and many other private and public groups that are conscious of the need for orderly urban growth and for more intelligent utilization of the remaining open space.

A major study, the New York metropolitan survey, completed in 1962 disclosed, for example, that in the course of the next twenty years, that area would probably extend "fifty miles from Times Square upstate and into New Jersey and Connecticut,"

> that it would add six million people to its present total of sixteen million . . .
>
> that New York City's population (core city) would perhaps decrease by one-half million . . . ;
>
> that the land available per household in suburbia would probably be one-fourth of that available in the boom years following World War II;
> that the number of automobiles would increase by 78%, but population by only 38% as residents find themselves farther and farther away from their places of employment;
>
> that state and local governments would have to spend an additional 1.6 billion dollars annually in capital outlays to furnish "transportation, water, education and other facilities";
>
> that by 1985 the area will be one continuous city "about 100 miles across, as far as Riverhead, Long Island; Danbury, Connecticut . . . and Lakewood, New Jersey." [3]

TABLE 3. PERCENTAGE OF NEGROES IN CENTRAL CITY
AND IN SUBURBIA IN NINE NORTHERN CITIES, 1960

City	Per cent in central city	Per cent in suburbia
Detroit	28.9	3.7
Cleveland	28.6	0.7
Chicago	22.9	2.9
Cincinnati	21.6	3.4
Los Angeles	12.2	3.1
New York City	14.0	4.8
Philadelphia	26.4	6.1
Pittsburgh	16.7	3.4
St. Louis	28.6	6.1

SOURCE: Bureau of the Census, Department of Commerce, *United States Census of Population: 1960*, Selected Area Report on Standard Metropolitan Statistical Areas (Washington, 1963).

Neither this survey nor any other has so far proposed easy solutions to the dangers of urban sprawl. While metropolitan experts disagree on many technical facets of this problem, there is a viable consensus to the effect that if future generations are to be saved from the excessive costs of mismanaged resources and unwise public investments, regional planning will have to be

[3] Peter Kihss, "Regional Planners Score Trend to a 'Spread City,'" *The New York Times,* September 4, 1962, p. 1.

strengthened, zoning regulations updated and enforced, and the cooperative relationships between federal, state, local, and inter-local governments made more meaningful, as indicated in the previous chapter.

As upper-income and upper-middle class Americans left the core city for the suburbs and the open country, they left behind them an everexpanding urban blight. At the congested center of the troubled metropolis remained the dilapidated dwellings, poorly-heated and lighted, and equipped with substandard sanitary facilities, that housed the influx of rural immigrants, Southern Negroes, Puerto Ricans, or Mexicans, the semiliterates, the unskilled laborers, the aged, the infirm, the unemployed or the underemployed.

The real estate which these people occupied was quite profitable to its owners, yet the crime, delinquency, and social needs which all too frequently characterize slum or near-slum neighborhoods constituted burdens which few of the large cities were prepared to assume. After rural-dominated state legislatures proved unsympathetic to their pleas for financial assistance, and after local voluntary efforts failed to measure up to the task of social and physical rehabilitation, mayors and councilmen descended on Washington with demands for aid. Beginning in 1949, a number of measures were enacted to help cities with low-cost housing and urban renewal. In the judgment of some experts, urban blight continued to increase at a rate too rapid for it to be overtaken by such federal redevelopment and slum clearance programs. As reported in 1962, "New York City, whose activities in this field have been more extensive than those of any other city in the nation, has cleared less than three of its 315 square miles over the past quarter century with all its publicly supported removal projects put together," insisted one such critic.[4]

A more optimistic view comes from United States Senator Joseph S. Clark of Pennsylvania, under whose leadership the city of Philadelphia has had a distinguished record of civic accomplishments. Basing his position on studies conducted by the Senate Banking and Currency Committee, he noted that between 1940 and 1960

A. substandard [housing] inventory dropped from 18,369,000 to 11,501,000 with the substandard per cent dropping from 49.2 to 19.2;
B. over 200,000 slum dwellings [were] being destroyed or rehabilitated at a total federal cost of one billion seven hundred million dollars, and at a total local cost of half that amount.[5]

LEGAL BASIS OF CITY GOVERNMENT

In local government there are few canons of law that have been cited with greater regularity or authority than Dillon's Rule (1872) on the power of municipalities:

[4] Quoted in Gordon, p. 14.
[5] Elizabeth Geen, Jeanne R. Lowe, and Kenneth Walker (eds.), *Man and the Modern City* (Pittsburgh, 1963), p. 79.

> It is the general and undisputed proposition of law that a municipal corporation possesses, and can exercise, the following powers, and no others: First, those granted in express words; second, those necessarily or fairly implied in, or incident to, the powers expressly granted; third, those essential to the declared objects and purposes of the corporation—not simply convenient, but indispensable.

This restrictive rule of interpretation emphasizes one central legal fact about the status of American cities—they, like other local governments, have such powers and only such powers as state constitutions and state legislatures are willing to grant to them. Unlike other local governmental units which can only act as administrative agents of the state, the distinguishing feature of a municipal corporation is its ability to serve the interests of its residents as an instrument for local self-government. What these powers of self-government are to be, is found generally in the city's basic charter or law of incorporation and in the amendments, judicial interpretations, and rulings which have been added over the years.

Although the source and nature of city charters varies considerably among the states and within states, many of the topics with which these charters must deal are fairly similar. Usually included are provisions—some governmental, some quasi-governmental—relating jointly to such matters as the city's name, boundaries, structure of government, ordinance-making powers, finances, contracts, purchasing, bonds, courts, municipal elections, property assessments, zoning, building codes, licensing, initiative and referendum, franchises, law enforcement, education, health, streets, parks, and utilities. Legal distinctions as to which of these activities are governmental and which merely corporate and non-governmental involve such issues as what standards of liability should be imposed on cities and for what purposes may the cities tax and spend. In recent years court decisions have tended to blur this distinction as cities were permitted, under police powers delegated to them, to engage in activities on behalf of public welfare traditionally reserved to private corporate enterprise exclusively.

Authorities in the field discern at least four main types of city charters:

(1) *Special Charters:* Historically the oldest and most common form of grant, they are still operative in New England and in some of the Southern states. Cities having such charters remain directly under legislative control to the extent that specific legislative approval must be obtained before a municipality may make changes in its government or before it may engage in any new service or function.

(2) *General Charters:* Cities in this category operate within the framework of one general and uniform charter. Inasmuch as city governmental needs vary greatly due to size of population, economic resources, social composition, and rate of development, legislatures found it necessary to supplement general charters with general laws applicable to different cities, based on a system of population classification. While no doubt useful in offering some needed flexibility of approach, these classification efforts were, however, sometimes little more than ill-concealed devices for overcoming constitutional prohibitions against special legislation.

Such barriers against special legislation had been incorporated into constitutions during the last century by many states as a result of widespread and brazenly unwarranted legislative interventions into strictly local affairs.

(3) *Optional Charters:* Over one-third of the states now permit their cities within the various population classes to elect governmental structures from a variety of options which their residents deem most appropriate to local conditions.

(4) *Home-rule Charters:* Still greater pressures for local self-determination led municipal reformers to demand home-rule charters under which cities could adopt governmental forms and services suitable to themselves without legislative interference. Beginning with Missouri in 1875, twenty-six state constitutions now include provisions allowing the issuance of such charters. Alaska's home-rule provision clearly embodies the relatively novel principle of residual powers; Article X, Sect. 11 "A home-rule borough [taking the place of counties] or city may exercise all legislative powers not prohibited by law or by charter." This, of course, enables the courts of that state to ignore Dillon's Rule altogether. Five additional states authorize home rule on statutory basis. Whether constitutional or statutory in origin, home rule usually calls for elective or appointive charter commissions to draw up the basic instrument which proposes to outline the governmental structure, define the powers, and establish the legal framework within which municipal officials are to make and execute their policies. After proper filing and notice, these charters are then submitted to the municipal electorate for approval or rejection at the polls.

A SECOND LOOK AT HOME RULE

Despite the availability of the home-rule principle, its use in at least two-thirds of the nation's larger cities (200,000 and over), and its political attractiveness to cities where legislatures were unsympathetic to their needs, there are nonetheless a number of obstacles which have prevented an even wider adoption. Constitutional grants in some of the states are often vague and unworkable. Smaller cities are rarely included in the original enabling provisions. Also, legislatures often are unwilling to enact the necessary statutes to authorize home rule in those states where it is constitutionally otherwise not self-executing, i.e., effective without further legislative action. Courts as well as legislatures have discovered that it is difficult to draw a clear line of demarcation between governmental functions that are primarily local in character and thus properly left to local discretion within the framework of home rule, and those that transcend the purely local by overriding statewide interests that legislatures could not, even if they wish, devolve upon their cities. Aside from these factors which may help explain the lag in the adoption of home rule, a more fundamental issue is posed by the realities of modern American government which make it no longer possible to view federal, state, and local governments as a three-layer cake composed of distinct and separate levels of government. A better analogy would be that of a marble cake in which all three levels of government are thoroughly mixed and integrated one into the other. In an address to the Local Government Section of the American Bar Association (1962), an authority in the field reflected quite well the contemporary position of many students of home-rule government:

> The principal drive for home rule was established in an era when a city represented a separately organized, social and economic community. A city was a practical and natural self-contained settlement. Now, it is clear that in our great metropolitan regions this is no longer true. Most of the cities in our metropolitan areas are not separate organic self-contained communities, with a life and destiny which they can shape and control. Instead, they are but a part of a much larger community, whose parts are inextricably bound up in a myriad of social and economic ties.[6]

Home rule as such is not to be repudiated. What is questioned here is the appropriateness of home rule for cities which lack the economic and political resources to function effectively under it, and where the concept of home rule is a rationalization of the city's basic unwillingness to join or cooperate with other stronger local units in the formation of a wider-based community that could, in fact, work successfully under a home-rule government.

THE THREE MAJOR FORMS OF CITY GOVERNMENT

American city government consists, with local adaptations and variations, of three main patterns of organization: mayor-council, commission, and council-manager.

MAYOR-COUNCIL

This is the oldest, the most congenial to this country's tradition of separating legislative from executive power, and the most widely-used—by 52.8 per cent of all cities with populations of 5,000 or more, by 80 per cent of the cities in the 500,000 and up category, and by 65.0 per cent of the cities in the 5,000 to 10,000 group (see Table 4). There are strong and weak mayor-council systems, with the distinction arising from the range of powers which the charter places in the hands of the mayor over such matters as appointments, removals, and budgetary controls. Two and four-year terms are most common for mayors under this system. In the strong mayor-council cities the electorate votes for the mayor, the councilmen (see Table 5), and in some of the cities, for one or more additional key officials such as treasurer, clerk, or city attorney. As the city's chief executive, the mayor is given the responsibility of appointing and supervising the heads of such city departments as police, fire, health, welfare, public works, parks, playgrounds, personnel, and planning. In some of the larger cities, notably Philadelphia, New Orleans, San Francisco, and New York, the mayor is assisted by a professional chief administrative officer (C.A.O.) or managing director with supervisory responsibilities for certain essential staff or line functions.

[6] Eugene C. Lee, "Home Rule Appraised," *National Civic Review*, October, 1962, p. 487.

Council members, ranging from three to fifty—with the larger councils usually found in the more populous cities—are elected typically at-large for terms of either two or four years (see Table 5), at salaries from $12 to $12,000 annually. As the city's legislative organ, the council works through committees conducting hearings, investigations, and studies preparatory to its plenary sessions at which it enacts budgets and taxes as well as the city ordinances. Policies are set with respect to licensing, zoning, and planning and guidelines for the city's administrative departments are drawn up. In over half of the cities where the mayors are directly elected, they are given the power to veto all or some types of council-passed ordinances which, if they are to be re-enacted over this veto, must then obtain higher and specified council majorities. The office of mayor, not unlike that of governor, can be molded by the occupant into a powerful instrument of political and administrative

TABLE 4. FORM OF GOVERNMENT IN CITIES OVER 5,000 POPULATION

Population group	Total number of cities	Total number of cities in table	Mayor-Council Number	Per cent	Commission Number	Per cent	Council-Manager Number	Per cent
Over 500,000	21	20	16	80.0	0	0.0	4	20.0
250,000 to 500,000	31	31	15	48.4	4	12.9	12	38.7
100,000 to 250,000	79	79	30	38.0	10	12.6	39	49.4
50,000 to 100,000	194	192	70	36.4	23	12.0	99	51.6
25,000 to 50,000	406	393	141	35.9	46	11.7	206	52.4
10,000 to 25,000	1,031	1,013	484	47.8	101	10.0	428	42.2
5,000 to 10,000	3,291	1,284	835	65.0	62	4.8	387	30.2
All cities over 5,000	5,053	3,012 *	1,591	52.8	246	8.2	1,175	39.0

* Not included in this table are Washington, D. C., 13 cities with town meeting government, 19 with representative town meeting government, and eight other cities for which no information was received.
SOURCE: *Municipal Year Book, 1964*, p. 84.

leadership. A list of mayors who did just that in large cities and achieved remarkable success in wresting control from the city council and city hall would have to include the following:

Fiorello La Guardia and Robert Wagner in New York
Charles P. Taft in Cincinnati
Richard Daley in Chicago
Albert Cobo in Detroit
Raymond Tucker in St. Louis
Frank Zeidler in Milwaukee
DeLesseps Morrison in New Orleans
Richardson Dilworth in Philadelphia
David Lawrence in Pittsburgh
Hubert Humphrey in Minneapolis

Mayor Wagner, for example, won his battle for greater executive power in 1961 only after he and a broadly-based civic reform coalition were able to overcome entrenched party opposition and bring about the amendment of

New York's 1938 city charter. The newly-added provisions greatly enhanced the mayor's powers over the budget (at the expense of the formerly influential Board of Estimate and Taxation), gave him the direction of street maintenance and sewer construction which had formerly been under the five borough presidents, and assured his office the necessary centralized power in the overall administrative and fiscal management of city affairs.

In the weak mayor-council system, which is most characteristic of but not restricted to smaller cities, the council's powers loom large indeed. Aldermanic committee chairmen often are in the position to compete effectively with the mayor for administrative leadership, as department heads go to them, rather than to the city's chief executive, for conferences and decisions on budget, personnel, and policy.

TABLE 5. TYPE AND METHOD OF COUNCILMANIC ELECTIONS IN CITIES OVER 5,000

Form of government or population group	Type of election			Method of election			
	Number of cities reporting	Per cent of reporting cities		Number of cities reporting	Per cent of reporting cities		
		Partisan	Non-partisan		At large	By wards	Combination of wards and at large
Form of government							
Mayor-Council	1,533	51	49	1,534	44	31	25
Commission	241	37	63	237	95	5	0
Council-Manager	1,165	16	84	1,161	76	13	11
Town Meeting	13	46	54	13	92	0	8
Rep. Town Meeting	17	24	76	18	83	17	0
Population group							
Over 500,000	20	40	60	20	40	25	35
250,000 to 500,000	30	23	77	31	64	10	26
100,000 to 250,000	79	38	62	78	65	13	22
50,000 to 100,000	194	32	68	192	58	21	21
25,000 to 50,000	400	30	70	398	62	19	19
10,000 to 25,000	1,010	38	62	1,000	62	20	18
5,000 to 10,000	1,237	38	62	1,244	60	25	15
All cities over 5,000	2,970	36	64	2,963	61	22	17

SOURCE: *Municipal Year Book, 1964*, p. 88.

The mayor's appointment powers are minor. In Minneapolis, for example, which operates under a weak mayor-council charter, there is left to the mayor one major appointment only—that of the city police chief. Inevitably, that city's ballot has grown painfully long—thirty-six positions on the average—as voters struggle each election day to identify and pass judgment on members to three separate boards, library, parks, and estimate and taxation, as well as on the thirteen aldermen, the treasurer, and the comptroller. It is the city council and not the mayor, then, which appoints such administrative officials as the city attorney, city engineer, city assessor, and city clerk. Some of the more successful mayors who were faced with such obstacles to their concept of political or administrative leadership found it necessary to go outside the formal framework of government by establishing volunteer citizens' committees composed of prestigious members of the community and then asking these committees to serve as their lobbyists before the council.

Not surprisingly then, the literature and forces of municipal reform are practically unanimous in condemning the weak mayor-council pattern for confusing the voter by diffusing the executive power and for inviting corruption by stripping those in nominal authority of the powers necessary to insure public accountability and policy direction.

Often arrayed against the reformers are city hall bureaucrats and councilmen who share the apprehension that any strengthening of the office of mayor will entail mayoral arbitrariness, bossism, or dictatorship. Such sentiments are frequently echoed and reinforced by socio-economic interests throughout the city to whom any further centralization in government is an anathema—a move inextricably tied to increased taxation and welfarism. Other groups may oppose such developments in city hall for no other reason than that established channels of access and influence may be blocked or destroyed by a new managerial point of view which might prove insensitive to hard-won favors and privileges.

COMMISSION

Whereas the mayor-council pattern endeavors to maintain some distinction between legislative and executive functions, the commission repudiates this principle and combines policy-making and policy-executing functions in one council. Its antecedents do not go back to the political theories of the Constitutional Convention but to the organizational experience of America's efficient business corporation where a board of directors sets managerial policies.

First introduced in Galveston, Texas, in 1901, and then refined by the Des Moines plan in 1907, commission government, although fairly popular before World War I, never did attain the wide popular acceptance of either the mayor-council or the council-manager systems. Less than 10 per cent of all cities of 5,000 and over use the commission system; the greatest number of cities using the system is found in the 5,000 to 25,000 category (see Table 4).

The organization and structure of the commission is quite simple. Voters elect at-large (95 per cent of the cities) on nonpartisan ballots (63 per cent of the cities) an average of five commissioners for two or four-year terms, each of whom must then function in a dual capacity—as a member of the city's legislative council and also as administrative head of one of the city's major departments.

The mayor in a few of the commission cities, such as in St. Paul, is elected separately for a two-year term, is given the veto power, and in addition to appointing minor officials and commission committees, has the authority to assign commissioners to the six departments of the city—department of finance, department of public works, department of public safety, department of parks, recreation, and public buildings, department of public utilities, and department of libraries, auditorium, and civic buildings. In other commission cities, either the commissioners as a group will designate one of their colleagues as presiding officer (mayor), or the commissioner who had received the highest number of votes will automatically be designated mayor.

Among the undeniably attractive features of the commission form of city government are the compactness of the commission, which permits the use of a short ballot, the relative ease with which responsibility can be fixed for a particular administrative decision, and the avoidance of some of the procrastination and buck-passing which all too frequently characterizes the mayor-council system. And yet the number of cities which are governed under this plan has decreased consistently and significantly since World War I, to the point where today only approximately fifteen cities over 100,000 in population still employ it.

Three major factors may account for this. First, the weakness in the office of mayor tends to inhibit any energetic action on a city-wide basis affecting problems requiring a community consensus or the services of more than one department. Second, it is hard to attract competent and imaginative administrators to head the commissions on a full-time basis at salary levels which city charters, public opinion, or state legislatures are willing to offer. Third, commissioners find it most difficult to campaign in support of particular programs when they themselves do not know for certain which one of the commissions will be theirs to administer.

COUNCIL-MANAGER

The commission form had been popular with the governmental reformers of the early nineteen hundreds. Since they had attributed the prevalence of widespread corruption in American state and local politics to the long ballot, the "bedsheet" ballot, which they believed badly confused the voters and aided the bosses in the mayor-council system, they were eager to support the council-manager plan, which developed out of an early adaptation of the commission pattern and had proved highly successful in Staunton, Virginia, in 1908.

The council-manager plan is in force today in over a third of all cities with populations of 5,000 and over and in more than half of all the cities between 25,000 and 100,000. With the exception of Cincinnati, Dallas, San Antonio, and San Diego, there is no other city above 500,000 which presently operates under the plan (see Table 4). All in all there were, as of January 1, 1964, over forty-four million people living in 1,926 city-manager and 28 county-manager governed communities.[7] Fifty years ago there were only 49 such communities.[8]

[7] *Municipal Year Book, 1964*, p. 263.
[8] Charles R. Adrian, *Governing Urban America* (New York, 1961), p. 220.

The central concept of the council-manager system is the division of city government into a policy-making phase which is to be the major concern of a small, part-time, non-partisanly (84 per cent of the cities) elected council, and an administrative phase which is placed under the central direction of a council-appointed professional city manager. This manager in turn appoints the city's department heads and supervises the overall administrative operations of the city. He "runs" the city. His tenure, however, is dependent entirely upon his ability to retain the council's confidence and support for the manner in which he executes their general policy decisions. That managers have been able to solidify their positions despite such hazards is no longer in doubt. For evidence on tenure, the 1964 annual report from the International City Manager's Association varies little from that rendered by the association in previous years.

TABLE 6. SALARIES FOR CITY MANAGERS AND MAYORS FOR CITIES BETWEEN 10,000 AND 500,000 POPULATION, 1964

Population	Number of cities reporting	Lowest		Salaries (Median)	Highest
250,000–500,000	11	CM	$22,500	$25,000	$30,000
	11	M	9,600	16,000	25,000
100,000–250,000	37	CM	15,000	21,500	29,340
	21	M	6,500	15,000	25,000
50,000–100,000	89	CM	9,000	17,500	27,028
	45	M	1,500	11,800	17,000
25,000–50,000	186	CM	8,400	15,000	25,000
	89	M	100	7,500	20,000
10,000–25,000	372	CM	6,000	12,000	22,000
	278	M	20	2,600	12,000

SOURCE: Adapted from *Municipal Year Book, 1964*, pp. 160–162.

The average tenure of the 35 managers who died in office or retired during 1963 was 15.6 years for all cities served and 7.3 years per city. . . . The average tenure of the 95 managers who resigned or were removed from office during 1963 was 6.7 years per manager for all cities served. . . .[9]

Comparative salary data illustrate (see Table 6) how successful city managers have been in climbing above the pay levels for chief executives under the mayor-council systems. To be sure, these comparisons have to be qualified by the facts that the responsibilities of city managers are inherently much heavier, that their tenures are more precarious, and that most of the smaller cities do not have full-time mayors.

In terms of occupational background, the majority of the managers who are presently sought out by city councils for appointment are professionals who have some graduate training in public administration or political science, men who have served as managers or as assistant city managers, and to a somewhat lesser degree, men who come to the profession from a career in engineering, business, or government.

[9] *Municipal Year Book, 1964*, p. 496.

The mayor in the council-manager system, as was the case in the commission form, may be selected by the council members themselves, may be a council member who is so designated because of his having led the ticket, or may be elected at-large for either a two or four-year term of office. Irrespective of the manner of election, mayors are given few powers beyond presiding at council meetings and doing the honors as the city's ceremonial head.

After the council has selected a manager and invested him with the administrative responsibilities and powers of serving as its agent in the day-to-day operations of city government, its own continuing obligations involve action upon the manager's budgetary recommendations, the adoption of city ordinances and resolutions, the raising of taxes, and the making of departmental appropriations.

City-manager governments are not restricted to any one region of the country; aside from Indiana and Hawaii, all of the states report some adoptions. Their greatest popularity, however, is reserved to a dozen states which comprise nearly 70 per cent of all adoptions: California (242), Texas (160), Maine (143), Michigan (143), Pennsylvania (129), Florida (100), North Carolina (80), Virginia (78), Oklahoma (67), Illinois (57), Ohio (54), and Tennessee (53).

There is much in the nature of the council-manager system that recommends itself to efficiency in local government. Responsibility can be focused on a representative council which is accountable to the voters for the broad outlines of public policy and on its professionally-trained administrator who has been given power to implement this policy. Confusion and obstruction can be held to a minimum in a system which draws as clear a line as this between those who are empowered to spend the taxpayer's money and those who appropriate it, between those who determine what municipal services shall be rendered and those who actually render them. Under this system, the ballot can be kept short enough for voters to make effective choices and the campaign sharp enough to concentrate on the issues. Finally, should the city's customers no longer approve of their municipal services, new members of the council are in the position to carry out their freshly-acquired mandate without delay; they can fire the old manager and hire a new one.

The case of those who favor the council-manager form as a cure for many of the structural ills of American local government seems to be a strong one. Still, some stubborn questions remain. Why, for example, have the nation's largest cities (with the exception of Cincinnati, Dallas, San Antonio, San Diego, and for awhile, Cleveland) despite pressing demands for governmental efficiency, refused to turn to the city manager plan in which efficiency represents one of the pivotal values? Also, studies have shown that larger cities—cities with populations of 100,000 and over—abandoned the plan at a rate over four times as often as did cities under 100,000.[10] It is quite possible that the explanation for this lack of enthusiasm may point up at least one

[10] Table 2 in Arthur W. Bromage, *Manager Plan Abandonments*, 4th ed. (New York, 1954), p. 8.

major weakness that goes to the heart of the council-manager arrangement—its failure to furnish effective political leadership. Cities with deep political cleavages require the skills, the training, and the experience of professional politicians who can build the areas of agreement without which effective action and central direction of municipal administration becomes impossible. Not many city managers can fill this bill.

By personality, background, or conviction, these men often tend to avoid or minimize the political dimensions of their city's problems and instead concentrate on the administrative dimensions, on the assumption that politics can and ought to be separated from administration, that municipal services affecting a city's housing, streets, parks, water supply, or libraries, or the operation of its police and fire departments, should be rendered in a climate as politically sterile as possible. This has proved at times to be an unrealistic expectation.

There are other criticisms to which the council-manager plan has been subjected and factors which may have contributed to its abandonment. Some possibly were inherent in the system, some arose out of its practical operation, some were due to the community's failure to understand its objective.

Traditions against the experts running the government go deep in America's political culture and cut across wide segments of the public. Beyond this, labor and low-income groups have at times strongly resented what they saw as the businessman's point of view in the city manager's office, a point of view which, they believed, ignored the legitimate distinction between the role of government and the function of a private corporation organized for profit.[11] Well-entrenched administrative officialdom has fought new managers and programs that threatened their tenures. Mayors resented the prominence of the manager in the community and councils begrudged the manager's influence over policy decisions which may have grown out of his superior knowledge of departmental operations and experiences.[12]

On balance it must be noted, however, that the number of cities adopting city manager plans continues to increase and that in the years ahead it promises to "become the principal type of urban government."[13]

POLITICAL PARTIES IN MUNICIPAL GOVERNMENT

"There is no Republican or Democratic way to pave a street; all the citizens want is 'good' government." This has been the battle cry of municipal reformers since the first decade of this century.

[11] On the various attitudes of unions, see Adrian, pp. 228–230, and National Municipal League, *Labor Unions and the Council-Manager Plan* (New York, 1948).

[12] A comparative study of city-manager tenure and terminations in eight Florida communities ranging from 5,000 to 60,000 in population is found in Gladys M. Kammerer, Charles D. Farris, John M. DeGrove, and Alfred M. Clubok, *The Urban Political Community: Profiles in Town Politics* (Boston, 1963).

[13] Herbert Kaufman, *Politics and Policies in State and Local Governments* (Englewood Cliffs, 1963), p. 49.

"When the ballot is short with only five (or less) really important offices at one time," argued a former president of the National Municipal League and one of the nation's most effective spokesman for the council-manager plan, "the voter can get along nicely without the politician and his asparagus string. . . . Under these conditions nonpartisan ballots become feasible. . . . Essentially our complaint against politicians is not that they are sometimes corrupt or extravagant, but that they pervert the processes of democracy and tap the public purse to entrench themselves in power. . . ." [14]

C. E. Merriam, who served as president of the American Political Science Association, expressed views about the involvement of national political parties in municipal politics which were representative of the dominant attitude shared for many years by the majority of local government experts. "The lines that divide men in national affairs do not run [in] the same direction in local questions, and the attempt to force them to do so has been a conspicuous failure in this country." [15]

Governmental reform groups, chambers of commerce, realtors, and taxpayer's associations blamed political party influences for city hall's inefficiency, lack of economy, corruption, and incompetence, for causing most of those conditions which a generation before had led James Bryce to label city government as "the most conspicuous failure of the American people."

When city politics are kept apart from state and national politics, so the argument went, it is much easier to attract honest and independently-minded men to run for office and to give the city the kind of businesslike administration which the electorate deserves. For figures on concurrently-held elections, see Table 7. Over the years the campaign against the political parties has progressed to the point where party labels are now no longer shown on the municipal ballots of 84 per cent of the council-manager cities, of 63 per cent of the commission cities and of 49 per cent of the mayor-council cities. A recent study summarizes four election systems that appear to have resulted from the wider acceptance of the nonpartisan ballot:

A. A system of elections in which the only candidates who normally have any chance to win are those supported by a major political party organization. In these cities, a short ballot is used, candidates are easily identifiable by party, and the result is not much different from partisan elections. Chicago is an example of this type of "nonpartisan" city. . . .

B. A system of elections in which slates of candidates are supported by various groups, including political party organizations. Here the voters perceive nonpartisan elections as being a distinctive type, but the political party groups are able to compete against slates of candidates presented by nonparty groups. The politics of Albuquerque, Cincinnati, and Wichita, along with other cities, appear to fit this pattern.

C. A system of elections in which slates of candidates are supported by various interest groups, but political party organizations have little or no part in campaigns. In these cities, candidates may have no party affiliation, or

[14] Richard Spencer Childs, *Civic Victories: The Story of an Unfinished Revolution* (New York, 1952), pp. 38–42.

[15] Charles E. Merriam, *Chicago: A More Intimate View of Urban Politics* (New York, 1929), p. 99.

it may be unknown, or the voters may consider it to be irrelevant. This pattern appears to be far more common than the two listed previously. Kansas City (since the fall of the Pendergast machine), Dallas, Fort Worth, and many California and Michigan cities appear to fit this category.

D. A system of elections in which neither political parties nor slates of candidates are important. This type appears to be very common, possibly even more so than the third type. It is especially important in small cities, for in these communities what Eugene Lee has called "the politics of acquaintance" is often the decisive factor. . . .[16]

What is clearly discernible from this summary is that the removal of the party designation has by no means signaled the end of all party influence. On

TABLE 7. PER CENT OF CITIES HOLDING ELECTION CONCURRENTLY WITH OTHER ELECTIONS OR INDEPENDENTLY IN CITIES OVER 25,000

	No. of cities reporting	Independently	With other local election*	With state or national election
Form of election				
Partisan	137	51	22	27
Nonpartisan	391	71	19	10
Form of government				
Mayor-council	170	59	20	21
Commission	53	72	19	9
Council-manager	306	68	20	12
Population group				
Over 500,000	15	40	47	13
250,000 to 500,000	25	64	20	16
100,000 to 250,000	69	64	17	19
50,000 to 100,000	142	66	20	14
25,000 to 50,000	278	67	19	14
All cities over 25,000	528	66	20	14

* Excluding cities also holding election concurrently with state or national election.
SOURCE: *Municipal Year Book, 1963*, p. 82.

the contrary, political parties formally or informally still play a role in the governing of some cities, especially the larger cities. Where they continue to function, they mostly recruit or endorse candidates and assist with their campaigns by canvassing voters, conducting rallies, scheduling coffee parties, providing party workers, and activating the electorate. Moreover, while "old style" urban party organizations as such are disappearing, many cities which are turning into "lower class, non-white enclaves" persist to offer "a continuing market for the services of the service-oriented old style politician." [17]

[16] Adrian, p. 101. Copyright © 1961. Used by permission of McGraw-Hill Book Company.

[17] Fred I. Greenstein, "The Changing Pattern of Urban Party Politics," *The Annals of the American Academy of Political and Social Science,* May, 1964, p. 13; see also David Gold and John R. Schmidhauser, "Urbanization and Party Competition: The Case of Iowa," *Midwest Journal of Political Science,* February, 1960, pp. 62–75. An excellent discussion of urban politics is found in Edward C. Banfield and James Q. Wilson, *City Politics* (Cambridge, 1963). The uniqueness of suburbia is discussed in Robert C. Wood, *Suburbia: Its People and their Politics* (Boston, 1958).

Where political parties have become quiescent or where they have disappeared altogether, an alderman or mayor may have to seek campaign support from interest groups directly, or build his own personal following with interest group support operating on a more indirect basis. While either of these alternatives may be made to give the appearance of nonpartisanship, partisan overtones can rarely be avoided entirely. Outside the South, not many chambers of commerce are known for their strong Democratic leanings and not many union locals for their Republican predilections. Facts such as these have caused some political scientists who are eager for more responsible and programmatic municipal politics, to reassess the traditional canons of nonpartisanship and to question both the possibility and the desirabilty of keeping municipal and party politics separate.

Is it really possible, they argue, to approach such municipal concerns as public housing, taxation, urban redevelopment, economic growth, highways, and slum clearance as issues apart and isolated from state and national politics when state and national party platforms contain planks and promises with respect to each of these? Even if it should be possible to separate out the municipal dimensions of such issues, it might well have an undesirable effect upon the political parties themselves. Nonpartisan municipal politics can weaken the parties by removing them from the local rung of the structure where leaders and followers are recruited, trained, and tested. Moreover, it can deprive state parties of an organizational level particularly well-suited to involve large numbers of citizens in efforts to solve the problems that affect them directly and immediately.

POLITICAL POWER AND DECISION-MAKING IN THE CITIES

Among students of local government, Los Angeles, for example, is known as a city in which political power is widely diffused; where political parties play no major role either in the city's decision-making process or in the recruitment of its candidates for city offices; where population mobility and vast diversities in social and economic setting have as yet precluded the coalescence of disciplined organizational factors or elites. The fabric of its politics is exceedingly well-described in the following passage:

> There are almost no general-interest groups seeking to influence formulation or execution of policy at either the municipal level or the metropolitan area level. The grouping of aggregates of political interest is made according to a different pattern. The pattern is more nearly a grouping of interests according to functional concerns. Influence groups, composed of clusters of public and private representatives, tend to form around programs; for example, planning and zoning, harbors, air pollution control, flood control, indigent aid, and public health protection.

> Although there is some overlap in the membership of the interest groups concerned with several functions at the local and regional levels alike, there is no common aggregate. Because the membership of the influence groups

surrounding functional organizations tends to vary, a pluralistic system has developed in which competition exists among groups who covet the prizes to be bestowed through the allocation of political and economic resources. . . .[18]

Although political parties are very much in evidence in New York City, and although precinct and borough organizations do serve as steppingstones for state and national office and influence (despite Tammany's present impotence) in the decision-making process concerning New York City affairs, parties must share political power with other forces.

> No single group of participants in the city's political contest is self-sufficient in its power to make decisions or require decisions of others. Every decision of importance is consequently the product of mutual accommodation. Building temporary or lasting alliances, working out immediate or enduring settlements between allies or competitors, and bargaining for an improved position in the decision centers are the continuing preoccupations of all leaders—whether party leaders, public officials, leaders of organized bureaucracies, or leaders of nongovernmental groups.[19]

How interest groups tend to coalesce and the context in which this occurs in a large city is well brought out in a study of St. Louis politics:

> St. Louis . . . displays two broad configurations of interests. On one side are the locally oriented labor unions, Negroes, neighborhood businessmen, and lower income people generally. This grouping focuses its attention primarily on the specific bread-and-butter issues of jobs, stop signs, spot zoning, and the like, and exhibits a sharper antipathy toward any suggestion of increased tax rates. Downtown business interests and the middle and upper middle income residents, on the other hand, are primarily interested in broader policy questions—economic growth, urban renewal—and their approach to problems of fiscal solvency is more sympathetic to the needs for more tax revenue.[20]

It can by no means be assumed that politics in all large cities is necessarily diffused and pluralistic in nature. A community in the 500,000 and over population category which exhibits a very different type of power configuration is that of Dallas, Texas. Here is a city which according to a recent study appears to be under the control of a tightly-structured power group with a continuing and readily identifiable membership drawn from a narrow socio-economic base.

In an attempt to discover the key decision-makers, the author of the

---

[18] Winston W. Crouch and Beatrice Dineman, *Southern California Metropolis* (Berkeley, 1963), p. 17.

[19] Wallace S. Sayre and Herbert Kaufman, *Governing New York City: Politics in a Metropolis* (New York, 1960), p, 712; on New York City, see also Nathan Glazer, "Is New York City Ungovernable?" *Commentary*, September, 1961, pp. 185–193; Coleman Woodbury, "Great Cities, Great Problems, Great Possibilities?," *Public Administration Review*, Autumn, 1958, pp. 332–340; John E. Bebout, "Management for Large Cities," *Public Administration Review*, Summer, 1955, pp. 188–195; and Henry F. Graft, "The Kind of Mayor LaGuardia Was," *The New York Times Magazine*, October 22, 1961, pp. 46, 51–52, 56.

[20] Robert H. Salisbury, "St. Louis Politics: Relationships among Interests, Parties, and Governmental Structure," *Western Political Quarterly*, June, 1960, p. 500.

Dallas study employed the so-called Reputational Technique (by which local residents were interviewed to identify and nominate the persons and groups that in their judgment "have a reputation for leadership and power"). While the validity of findings based upon the Reputational Technique is not free from criticism, the study nevertheless did reveal a group of sixty-seven all-white males who were rated as most powerful and prominent in the ruling of the city. Here are a few of the salient findings about the leaders and the Civic Committee which seem to share the responsibility for the governance of Dallas:

> Persons in business make up about 73 per cent of the leaders, compared to 16.4 per cent from industry. Financial leaders alone—banking and insurance executives—comprise a striking 31.3 per cent of these decision-makers. . . .

> None of the city governmental offices were represented on the list except in the person of one of the highest ranking Key Leaders who, without doubt, was a man of top power long before he accepted his position as mayor of the city. . . .

> [T]here is no labor leader among the inner circle of Dallas decision-makers. . . .

> There is a definite, although informal, process by which potential leaders are selected for the power system and one by which their qualifications for advancement within it are tested and evaluated . . .

> The "Civic Committee". . . [more powerful than any other organization] was chartered to be concerned with and act upon vital issues involving Dallas, and does so function. Its membership is highly selective, limited to company presidents and board chairmen.

> It is evident that the City Council plays a much less central and powerful role in community decision-making than does the Civic Committee. . . .

> "Devotion to Dallas" and unselfish service were frequently stressed as essentials for achieving power status, together with personal integrity. Another important personal characteristic is having a reasonably conservative businessman's philosophy. . . .[21]

No two cities are politically ever alike. Leadership, interest group alignments, governmental structures, and issues vary due to historical, social, economic, regional, and population factors. Where mayors are weak and party designations absent from the ballot, as in Minneapolis, the politics of the city council may take the center of the stage when it comes to city appointments and city favors. In the politics of Detroit and Wayne County, the Committee on Political Education (C.O.P.E.), the political arm of the AFL-CIO, plays a major role which is by no means always victorious. There, working with and through the Democratic party, labor helps get out the vote, organizes the precincts, endorses candidates, drafts resolutions, and recruits candidates.

---

[21] Carol Estes Thometz, *The Decision-Makers* (Dallas, 1963), pp. 31, 34–35, 70, 71. (This book was published in October, 1963). Reprinted with the permission of Southern Methodist University Press.

In St. Louis, labor's political effectiveness is severely blunted by a deep split between the AFL-CIO and the Teamsters, and in Houston, Texas, labor is forced to avoid any major involvement in the dominantly conservative climate of local politics in order to conserve what little strength it does have to support the liberal wing of the Democrats in their state and national efforts.

Politics in the larger cities differs markedly from politics in town and village in terms of leadership, process, and climate. In rural towns it is typical, for instance, for elected officials to be local businessmen primarily owners and operators of retail stores. These men know each other well; they are long-time residents; their interests and experiences are similar; their knowledge of governmental details and law is limited. For technical advice they rely heavily on the town's counsel. In outlook they tend to be conservative. Any increases in taxes and governmental expenditures are eschewed whenever possible. To perpetuate their office and influence they seek to maintain an image of public unanimity through the avoidance of actions and issues which are likely to be controversial and which might sharpen the electoral contests.

Unlike the highly personalized and closed politics of the small town where leadership is fairly homogeneous, where interest groups are few and stable, and where the community consensus is clear and disinclined to change, the politics of the larger cities are increasingly characterized by their impersonal nature, by the interplay of powerful interest groups with conflicting demands, by the persistent search for managerial talent and professional personnel to administer public office, and by the need to discover the governmental institutions and processes which might best accommodate social and technological changes without major disruptions and dislocations.

The governance of America's exploding cities represents one of the nation's major political tasks. Fortunately, during the course of the last fifteen to twenty years, great progress has been made to erase from city halls some of the worst blight of corruption, graft, inefficiency, bossism, and machine politics. In cities of various sizes charters have been amended or reformed, better fiscal controls added, zoning, licensing, and planning procedures and policies overhauled, municipal services improved, excesses of patronage curbed, civil service expanded, and more competent leadership elected. For example, among the twenty-three largest cities (500,000 and over), the most encouraging advances were noted in Cincinnati, Milwaukee, Philadelphia, San Francisco, New York, Pittsburgh, Baltimore, and Detroit. In a number of communities public apathy is giving way to increased voter participation and interest in city affairs. (Table 8 indicates that voter participation tends to be higher in cities holding partisan elections concurrently with national, state, or other local elections.)

Notable gains were registered where good government leagues, neighborhood improvement associations, chambers of commerce, Leagues of Women Voters, or other reform-minded groups, including political party activists moved aggressively to enlist wide civic support for programs of municipal betterment. Commercial areas are slowly being rebuilt, slums

TABLE 8. PER CENT OF ADULTS VOTING IN CITIES OVER 25,000

	No. of cities reporting	Lower quartile	Median	Upper quartile	No. of cities reporting	Lower quartile	Median	Upper quartile
	All city elections				Held concurrently with state or national elections			
Form of election								
Partisan	109	37	50	57	31	47	51	65
Nonpartisan	350	21	30	43	32	31	43	59
Form of government								
Mayor-council	137	38	50	57	31	47	51	65
Commission	41	29	38	47	3	28	33	61
Council-manager	281	20	27	39	29	29	43	60
Population group								
Over 500,000	15	26	39	47	2	46	—	47
250,000 to 500,000	25	21	37	48	4	45	56	76
100,000 to 250,000	54	24	32	50	9	30	50	55
50,000 to 100,000	124	21	33	51	17	20	51	62
25,000 to 50,000	243	23	33	47	31	35	47	64
All cities over 25,000	461	22	33	48	63	35	50	62
	Held concurrently with other local elections *				Held independently of any other election			
Form of election								
Partisan	22	48	53	58	56	26	41	53
Nonpartisan	65	27	35	47	246	19	27	39
Form of government								
Mayor-council	28	40	50	55	78	34	44	56
Commission	5	28	57	71	32	28	38	47
Council-manager	54	26	35	47	193	18	23	32
Population group								
Over 500,000	7	33	39	50	5	19	20	39
250,000 to 500,000	5	24	35	54	16	18	34	41
100,000 to 250,000	9	31	46	50	36	21	29	46
50,000 to 100,000	24	30	51	55	82	20	29	44
25,000 to 50,000	42	28	41	50	164	20	29	41
All cities over 25,000	87	29	44	51	303	20	29	41

* Excluding cities also holding election concurrently with state or national election.

SOURCE: *Municipal Year Book, 1963*, p. 83.

reduced, traffic conditions improved, service standards raised, park and recreational facilities improved. However, like all other reform movements, the momentum of upgrading city government and services travels in cycles of alternating enthusiasm and disinterest, of achievement and failure—as noted earlier in the discussion of the metropolitan area problems, much indeed still needs to be done before the cities of the 1960's and 1970's can begin to provide urbanized America with the types of governmental and political institutions that the voter demands and deserves.

To obtain a better understanding of how some of these future political changes and adaptations should proceed, an increasing number of political and social scientists, believing that they must first come to grips more systematically with the actual processes of policy formation, have pressed their research studies far beyond the mere describing of the various formal structures of local government. Their objective is to gain a more realistic understanding of basic political power configurations and of the men and groups who actually make the critical decisions.

Among the many questions posed by these scholars, two seem to be central: (1) To what extent are city officeholders—mayors, councilmen, and other elected officials—the makers of policy, or to what extent do they merely reflect or carry out decisions made by the less visible leaders of the important economic, social, and political interests that are active in the community? (2) Is political power in any given community structured pyramidically, with much discretion left in the hands of a very small number of individuals at the top who can act authoritatively without much check and balance from below, or is power highly decentralized and pluralized among many groups whose leaders are then forced to build different coalitions of interests when confronted with different policy issues? [22]

While answers to these highly complex questions may well vary from community to community, findings to date do permit at least five generalized observations which, however tentative, can usefully serve as starting points for further study and verification:

[22] In their excellent study, *Four Cities, A Study in Comparative Policy-Making* (Philadelphia, 1963), Professors Oliver P. Williams and Charles R. Adrian compared policy-making in four Michigan cities (50,000 to 70,000 class) with respect to such matters as (1) promoting economic growth; (2) providing or securing life's amenities; (3) maintaining (only) traditional services; and (4) arbitrating among conflicting interests.

    Some other highly significant research studies in the area of municipal power structure and civic leadership are the following: Floyd Hunter, *Community Power Structure* (Chapel Hill, 1962); Herbert Kaufman and Victor A. Jones, "The Mystery of Power," *Public Administration Review,* Summer, 1954; Nelson W. Polsby, "How to Study Community Power: The Pluralist Alternative," *Journal of Politics,* August, 1960; Peter H. Rossi, "Community Decision-Making," *Administrative Science Quarterly,* June, 1956; William V. D'Antonio and Eugene C. Erickson, "The Reputational Technique as a Measure of Community Power: An Evaluation Based on Comparative and Longitudinal Studies," *American Sociological Review,* June, 1962; Robert Presthus, *Men at the Top: A Study in Community Power* (New York, 1964); Ernest A. T. Barth and Stuart D. Johnson, "Community Power and a Typology of Social Issues," *Social Forces,* October, 1959, pp. 29–32; Robert C. Hanson, "Predicting a Community Decision: A Test of the Miller-Form Theory," *American Sociological Review,* October, 1959, pp. 662–671; Donald W. Olmsted, "Organizational Leadership and Social Structure in a Small City," *American Sociological Review,* June, 1954, pp. 273–281; Delbert C. Miller, "Decision-Making Cliques in Community Power Structures: A Comparative Study of an American and an English City," *American Journal of Sociology,* November, 1958, pp. 299–310; Paul A. Miller, "The Process of Decision-Making Within the Context of Community Organization," *Rural Sociology,* June 1952, pp. 153–161; and Robert E. Agger, "Power Attributions in the Local Community: Theoretical and Research Considerations," *Social Forces,* May, 1956, pp. 322–331. The most comprehensive survey of the periodical literature in this field may be found in Charles Press, *Main Street Politics: Policy-Making at the Local Level* (East Lansing, 1962).

First, there is little evidence that American cities are ruled by tightly knit elites which can be readily identified as belonging to any one particular economic, social, or political group.

Second, decision-making in communities is often shared by representatives from various socio-economic groups, none of which has sufficient monopolistic power to dominate all phases of the governing process.

Third, decision-makers may not be officeholders at all but may be leaders who operate from executive positions of influence and prestige in such fields as business, finance, and industry.

Fourth, the political values of the policy-makers are strongly reflective of middle and upper-class values of American society.

Fifth, the influence of organized labor and ethnic minorities in the decision-making process appears to be disproportionately weak, although these groups do possess an effective veto power over decisions which they hold to affect their particular interests directly.

HOW ABOUT A FEDERAL DEPARTMENT OF URBAN AFFAIRS?

For some years now, the increasingly complex scope of the problems with which urban America is confronted, as well as the obvious prominence of Washington's rule in the future development of cities and metropolitan areas, has led various political interests in and out of Congress to call for the establishment of an integrated federal department of urban affairs. A plank in the 1960 Democratic party platform explicitly provided for it. Congressional hearings on legislation creating such an executive department with cabinet status had been conducted since 1955. Three separate committees, one in the House and two in the Senate, acted favorably on such a proposal, yet until 1965 the House was not willing to complete action on the matter.

President Kennedy had first recommended it in a special message on housing in 1961. One year later he again included it in his State of the Union message. When the Rules Committee blocked action on it, the President resorted to his administrative reorganization powers and transmitted his proposal to Congress on January 30, 1962, in the form of Reorganization Plan No. 1.

Favoring the proposal were such groups as the American Municipal Association, the United States Conference of Mayors, the American Federation of Labor and Congress of Industrial Organization, mayors of New York, Chicago, and St. Louis, and the governors of Ohio, Illinois, California, and Connecticut. Testimony in opposition to the new department came from the United States Chamber of Commerce, the National Association of Manufacturers, the National Association of County Officials, and the Home Builders' Association. Three weeks later, the reorganization plan was defeated overwhelmingly.

What was the nature of the argument? Proponents of the department of urban affairs contended (1) that the enormous growth of cities and metropolitan areas throughout the United States created problems and tensions which required the kind of leadership and decision-making which could come only from a cabinet level position; (2) that such a department would greatly simplify the task of coordinating various federal agencies presently operating in the housing, urban development, and urban redevelopment fields; (3) that the extent of money and manpower already invested in these federal programs was of such scope as to justify a separate department for their most efficient administration; (4) that it was only fair to give to cities which housed nearly three-fourths of the nation's population a departmental voice equal in strength to that already possessed by the farmer, the businessmen, or the worker; and (5) that the burdens of mayors and other urban officials would be lightened, as their requests for federal counsel and assistance would henceforth be directed to one department and answered within the framework of one policy instead of multiple agencies, each operating under separate and even conflicting policies.

Critics of the urban affairs department stressed (1) that there was no need to further increase the already much too powerful federal government —"If Washington pays the bill, Washington will direct the action . . .";[23] (2) that the entire proposal was essentially politically motivated—a device for attracting city voters; (3) that such local issues as repairing streets and water mains should remain local and not become subjects of cabinet level pressures; (4) that the establishment of such a department would constitute a dangerous precedent for organizing federal departments on geographic rather than functional bases; (5) that the relationship between the states and their local governmental units would be detrimentally affected by encouraging cities to go around counties, state legislatures, and governors, and deal directly with the federal government; and (6) that even the most outspoken supporters of such a department were not able in the course of the congressional debate to point to a single substantial federal administrative activity which would in fact be transferred into the new department which was not already located in H.H.F.A., which made somewhat academic the claims of administrative consolidation and streamlining.

On February 21, 1962 by a 264 to 150 vote the House defeated the President's reorganization plan, which would have created a cabinet-level department of urban affairs.[24] Judging by the decisiveness of the bill's defeat, one of the issues receiving considerable public attention, namely, Southern reluctance to see a Negro, Dr. Robert Weaver, head of the H.H.F.A., elevated to cabinet rank, did not seem to have played a major role in the final outcome. Non-Southern defections from the Democratic voting strength combined with heavy Republican opposition to defeat the measure. A very different result was reached in the summer of 1965 when heavy Democratic majorities in the

---

[23] Senate Committee on Government Operations, *Department of Urban Affairs and Housing*, Report to accompany S. 1633, September 6, 1961, 87th Cong., 1st Sess. (Washington, 1961), p. 25.

[24] *Congressional Quarterly Weekly Report*, February 23, 1962, pp. 310–311.

House and Senate contributed to the passage of substantially similar bills establishing a cabinet-level department of urban affairs.

While primary responsibility for solving many of the problems of local government will undoubtedly remain with these units, it is equally certain that in the years to come the pressure for federal action will continue to persist if not to increase. Reasons for that must be found in certain stubborn realities—political, economic, technological, social, and defense—which sharply point up state and local dependence on out-of-state resources and services. What direction the pattern of assistance will take cannot be predicted with certainty, nor can it be the function of a text such as this to offer dogmatic solutions in the midst of lively partisan controversy.

Yet, based on findings published by Congress, by competent professional researchers, and by private and public institutions conducting studies in this field, any minimum and moderate program of improving federal cooperation with states, cities, and metropolitan areas would have to include some of the following:

A. Increased federal financial and technical assistance to state and local governments for metropolitan area-wide planning.
B. Improved coordination of various federal programs "which impact upon orderly planning and development within the large urban areas." [25]
C. Periodic review by state and metropolitan area agencies (along with Congress) of particular applications for specific federal grants-in-aid for highway, hospital, and waste treatment plant construction, for urban renewal and public housing, or for any of the other major aid programs.
D. Periodic review and study by federal and state governments of the actual effects of federal programs in the various metropolitan areas.
E. Creation within the Executive Office of the President of a special Metropolitan Area Advisory Council "with power to collect data, ask questions, and make recommendations to the President." [26]

None of these recommendations is likely to provide quick or facile answers to the more basic problems of intergovernmental relations which are indigenous to American federalism as well as to the metropolitan areas. At best, they may assist in clarifying alternative policies or courses of action for parties and politicians, laymen and technicians, legislators and executives.

CASE PROBLEMS FOR CLASS DISCUSSION

1. You have been asked to serve as an election consultant to a candidate campaigning on a nonpartisan ballot for alderman (middle-class area) in a city of 300,000 population. The candidate is a local attorney who has been active in various civic efforts. This is his first campaign for public office. What would your suggestions be with respect to such matters as campaign budget, composition of volunteer committee, use of communications media, campaign organization, and campaign literature?

[25] Advisory Commission on Intergovernmental Relations, *Governmental Structure, Organization, and Planning in Metropolitan Areas* (Washington, 1962), p. 52.
[26] Robert H. Connery and Richard H. Leach, *The Federal Government and Metropolitan Areas* (Cambridge, 1960), p. 229.

2. You are a member of your city's charter commission. A proposal has been made to your group to exchange the present commission form of government for the stronger mayor-council pattern. Assume that limited research funds can be obtained. What types of information should be made available to the charter commission to assist its deliberations?

3. Your political science department just received a grant to study decision-making in local government. What kind of research design would you suggest to determine who or which groups make the politically major decisions in your community?

4. Based on your knowledge of local government and politics, you have been given the responsibility of composing a checklist of duties that should be assigned to the executive secretary of mayor serving a medium-size city. What would you have to include in such a list?

SELECTED BIBLIOGRAPHY

MARK K. ADAMS, A Report on Politics in New Castle, New York (Cambridge, 1961).

MARK ADAMS and GERTRUDE ADAMS, A Report on Politics in El Paso (Cambridge, 1963).

HAROLD F. ALDERFER, American Local Government and Administration (New York, 1956).

THOMAS F. ANTON, "Power, Pluralism, and Local Politics," Administrative Science Quarterly, March, 1963, pp. 423–457.

EDWARD C. BANFIELD (ed.), Urban Government (New York, 1961).

RUTH BAUMANN, The County in Wisconsin (Madison, 1962).

CHARLES W. BENDER, A Report on Politics in Seattle (Cambridge, 1961).

DAVID A. BINGHAM, Constitutional Municipal Home Rule in Arizona (Tucson, 1960).

ROBERT H. BINSTOCK, A Report on Politics in Manchester, New Hampshire (Cambridge, 1961).

GEORGE S. BLAIR, American Local Government (New York, 1964).

ROBERT P. BOLAN, Fundamentals of Home Rule (Kingston, 1960).

DAVID A. BOOTH and CHARLES R. ADRIAN, "Power Structure and Community Change," Midwest Journal of Political Science, August, 1962, pp. 277–296.

RONALD R. BOYCE, "Commercial and Industrial Development in Smaller Cities," Public Management, August, 1963, pp. 174–178.

BEVERLY L. BROWNING, North Kingstown Selects Two Managers—A Case Study (Kingston, 1962).

SEVERYN T. BRUYN, Communities in Action: Pattern and Process (New Haven, 1963).

KENNETH G. BUECHE, Incorporation Laws: One Aspect of the Urban Problem (Boulder, 1963).

JEPTHA J. CARRELL, "The City Manager and his Council: Sources of Conflict," Public Administration Review, December, 1962, pp. 203–208.

JEPTHA J. CARRELL, The Role of the City Manager (Kansas City, 1962).

JEPTHA J. CARRELL, "The Role of the City Manager: A Survey Report," Public Management, April, 1962, pp. 74–78.

F. STUART CHAPIN, JR., and SHIRLEY F. WEISS (eds.), Urban Growth Dynamics in a Regional Cluster of Cities (New York, 1962).

RICHARD S. CHILDS, "Quest for Leadership," National Civic Review, November, 1961, pp. 526–529, 539.

ROBERT H. CONNERY and RICHARD H. LEACH, "Do We Need a Department of Urban Affairs?" Western Political Quarterly, March, 1960, pp. 99–112.

County Government Activities in Wisconsin (Madison, 1961).

ROBERT A. DAHL, Who Governs? Democracy and Power in an American City (New Haven, 1961).

WILLIAM R. DAVLIN, "The Urban Redevelopment Program in Pennsylvania," State Government, Winter, 1960, pp. 23–27.

MARTHA DERTHICK, City Politics in Washington, D. C. (Cambridge, 1962).

EDWARD T. DOWLING, Administrative Organization in Massachusetts Towns (Amherst, 1960).

GEORGE S. DUGGAR, "The Relation of Local Government Structure to Urban Renewal," Law and Contemporary Problems, Winter, 1961, pp. 49–69.

GEORGE H. ESSER, JR., "Next Steps in Improving Local Government," *Public Management,* January, 1962, pp. 7–11.

SETHARD FISHER, "Community-Power Studies: A Critique," *Social Research,* Winter, 1962, pp. 449–466.

JOHN ANSON FORD, *Thirty Explosive Years in Los Angeles County* (San Marino, 1961).

WILLIAM H. FORM and WARREN L. SAUER, "Organized Labor's Image of Community Power Structure," *Social Forces,* May, 1960, pp. 332–341.

LINTON C. FREEMAN, THOMAS J. FARARO, WARNER BLOOMBERG, JR., and MORRIS H. SUNSHINE, "Locating Leaders in Local Communities: A Comparison of Some Alternative Approaches," *American Sociological Review,* October, 1963, pp. 791–798.

ROBERT J. FRYE and JOHN A. DYER, *The City Manager System in Alabama* (University, Ala., 1961).

STANLEY T. GABIS, "Leadership in a Large Manager City: The Case of Kansas City," *The Annals of the American Academy of Political and Social Science,* May, 1964, pp. 52–63.

JOHN F. GALLAGHER, *Supervisorial Districting in California Counties: 1960–1963* (Davis, 1963).

FRANK K. GIBSON and EDWARD S. OVERMAN, *County Government in Virginia* (Charlottesville, 1961).

WILLIAM I. GOODMAN, "Urban Planning and the Role of the State," *State Government,* Summer, 1962, pp. 149–154.

DAVID GREENSTONE, *A Report on the Politics of Detroit* (Cambridge, 1961).

DAVID GREENSTONE, *A Report on Politics in San Diego* (Cambridge, 1962).

SCOTT GREER, "The Social Structure and Political Process of Suburbia," *American Sociological Review,* August, 1960, pp. 514–526.

VICTOR GRUEN, "Who is to Save Our Cities?" *Harvard Business Review,* May–June, 1963, pp. 107–115.

JOHN G. GRUMM, "Do We Need a State Agency for Local Affairs?" *Public Management,* June, 1961, pp. 129–133.

JOHN G. GRUMM, *A State Agency for Local Affairs?* (Berkeley, 1961).

A. CLARKE HAGENSICK, *Municipal Home Rule in Wisconsin* (Madison, 1961).

A. CLARKE HAGENSICK, "Wisconsin Home Rule," *National Civic Review,* July, 1961, pp. 349–355.

STUART C. HALL, *County Supervisorial Districting in California* (Berkeley, 1961).

BERTIL HANSON, *A Report on the Politics of Milwaukee* (Cambridge, 1961).

PHILIP M. HAUSER, *On the Impact of Population and Community Changes on Local Government* (Pittsburgh, 1961).

LAWRENCE HAWORTH, *The Good City* (Bloomington, 1963).

LAWRENCE J. R. HERSON, "In the Footsteps of Community Power," *American Political Science Review,* December, 1961, pp. 817–830.

IRVING HOWARDS, "Rural Progress Step," *National Civic Review,* June, 1960, pp. 286–292.

ROBERT J. HUCKSHORN and CHARLES E. YOUNG, "Study of Voting Splits on City Councils in Los Angeles County," *Western Political Quarterly,* June, 1960, pp. 479–497.

DIXIE S. HUEFNER, *A Report on Politics in Salt Lake City* (Cambridge, 1961).

HUBERT H. HUMPHREY, "To Aid the Small City," *National Civic Review,* December, 1961, pp. 582–586, 600.

JOHN M. HUNGER and EDWARD V. SCHTEN, *Constitutional Changes Concerning the Milwaukee County Executive—1962 Referendum* (Madison, 1963).

M. KENT JENNINGS, "Public Administrators and Community Decision-Making," *Administrative Science Quarterly,* June, 1963, pp. 18–43.

RUSSELL D. JONES, "The Changing Role of the City Manager," *Public Management,* June, 1962, pp. 122–126.

VICTOR JONES, RICHARD L. FORSTALL, and ANDREW COLLVER, "Economic and Social Classification of Cities," *Public Management,* May, 1963, pp. 98–101.

GLADYS M. KAMMERER, *The Changing Urban County* (Gainesville, 1963).

GLADYS M. KAMMERER, "Is the Manager a Political Leader?—Yes," *Public Management,* February, 1962, pp. 26–29.

GLADYS M. KAMMERER and JOHN M. DE-GROVE, *Florida City Managers: Profile and Tenure* (Gainesville, 1961).

GLADYS M. KAMMERER and JOHN M. DE-GROVE, "Urban Leadership During Change," *The Annals of the American Academy of Political and Social Science,* May, 1964, pp. 95–106.

GLADYS M. KAMMERER, CHARLES D. FAR-RIS, JOHN M. DEGROVE, and ALFRED B. CLUBOK, *City Managers in Politics: An Analysis of Manager Tenure and Termination* (Gainesville, 1962).

HAROLD KAPLAN, *Urban Renewal Politics:*

Slum Clearance in Newark (New York, 1963).

JEROME KEITHLEY, "Advancement in Annexation Methods," *Public Management,* July, 1960, pp. 146–149.

RICHARD H. LEACH, "Federal Urban Renewal Program: A Ten-Year Critique," *Law and Contemporary Problems,* Fall, 1960, pp. 777–792.

EUGENE C. LEE, "The City Manager and the Sixties," *Public Management,* December, 1960, pp. 269–272.

DUANE LOCKARD, "The City Manager, Administrative Theory, and Political Power," *Political Science Quarterly,* June, 1962, pp. 224–236.

JACKSON M. MCCLAIN and ROBERT B. HIGHSAW, *Dixie City Acts: A Study in Decision-Making* (University, Ala., 1962).

STUART A. MacCORKLE, "Tenure of City Managers," *Public Management,* July, 1962, pp. 150–153.

ROSCOE C. MARTIN, "Manpower for Cities," *Public Management,* February, 1963, pp. 26–30.

STEVE MATTHEWS, "How Manager Leads," *National Civic Review,* June, 1961, pp. 294–297.

WARNER E. MILLS, JR., and HARRY R. DAVIS, *Small City Government: Seven Cases in Decision-Making* (New York, 1962).

FRANK C. MOORE, "Cities Look to the State," *National Civic Review,* February, 1960, pp. 71–76.

FRANK C. MOORE, "New York State's New Office for Local Government," *State Government,* Autumn, 1960, pp. 227–231.

Municipal Government in the State of Washington (Seattle, 1962).

Municipal Manpower Commission, *Governmental Manpower for Tomorrow's Cities: A Report of the Municipal Manpower Commission* (New York, 1962).

ORIN F. NOLTING and DAVID S. ARNOLD, in *Municipal Yearbook, 1963* (Chicago, 1963).

ROBERT J. M. O'HARE, "Cradle of Liberty," *National Civic Review,* November, 1962, pp. 543–549.

PHILLIP F. PALMER, *The Allouez Study: Governmental Organization for the Town of Allouez* (Madison, 1961).

LOIS M. PELEKOUDAS (ed.), *Illinois Local Government* (Urbana, 1961).

JOHN M. PFIFFNER, "The Job of the City Manager," *Public Management,* June, 1961, pp. 122–125.

JEWELL CASS PHILLIPS, *Municipal Govern-*

ment and Administration in America (New York, 1960).

H. G. POPE, "Is the Manager a Political Leader?—No," *Public Management,* February, 1962, pp. 30–33.

HENRY REINING, "The City Manager as Urban Coordinator," *Public Management,* June, 1961, pp. 126–129.

HARRY W. REYNOLDS, JR., "Local Government Structure in Urban Planning, Renewal, and Relocation," *Public Administration Review,* March, 1964, pp. 14–20.

CHARLES S. RHYNE, "State Action Needed for Municipal Ordinance Codification," *State Government,* Winter, 1960, pp. 28–31.

PETER H. ROSSI, "Power and Community Structure," *Midwest Journal of Political Science,* November, 1960, pp. 390–401.

ELMER R. RUCO, *Municipal Home Rule: Guideline for Idaho* (Moscow, 1960).

TERRANCE SANDALOW, "The Limits of Municipal Power under Home Rule: A Role for the Courts," *Minnesota Law Review,* March, 1964, pp. 643–721.

LYLE E. SCHALLER, "Home Rule—A Critical Appraisal," *Political Science Quarterly,* September, 1961, pp. 402–415.

E. E. SCHATTSCHNEIDER and VICTOR JONES, *Local Political Surveys* (New York, 1962).

HENRY J. SCHMANDT, *The Municipal Incorporation Trend, 1950–1960* (Madison, 1961).

LEO F. SCHNORE and ROBERT R. ALFORD, "Forms of Government and Socio-Economic Characteristics of Suburbs," *Administrative Science Quarterly,* June, 1963, pp. 1–17.

STANLEY SCOTT, *California Legislation Governing Municipal Incorporation: A Criticism and Suggested New Policies* (Berkeley, 1960).

STANLEY SCOTT, LEWIS KELLER, and JOHN C. BOLLENS, *Local Governmental Boundaries and Areas: New Policies for California* (Berkeley, 1961).

EDGAR L. SHERBENOU, "Class, Participation, and the Council-Manager Plan," *Public Administration Review,* Summer, 1961, pp. 131–135.

WILLIAM L. SLAYTON, "State and Local Incentives and Techniques for Urban Renewal," *Law and Contemporary Problems,* Fall, 1960, pp. 793–812.

HARRY R. SMITH, *Home Rule for Iowa?* (Iowa City, 1962).

CLYDE F. SNIDER and IRVING HOWARDS, *County Government in Illinois* (Carbondale, 1960).

EDWIN O. STENE, "Short-Term City Managers," *Public Management*, July, 1961, pp. 146–152.

"Surveys of New York City Government, 1948–1960," *Municipal Reference Library Notes*, March, 1960, pp. 272–287.

DANIEL C. THOMPSON, *The Negro Leadership Class* (Englewood Cliffs, 1963).

ROBERT F. WAGNER, "Cities with Hands Tied," *National Civic Review*, July, 1960, pp. 346–350, 362.

ROBERT F. WAGNER, "Help for Our Cities," *National Civic Review*, January, 1960, pp. 6–10, 21.

EDWIN W. WEBBER, *Rhode Island Local Government and Administration* (Kingston, 1963).

CHARLES P. WEIKEL, *How Park Hills Moved the County Line: A Self-Study in Citizen Action* (Berkeley, 1961).

RUTH Y. WETMORE, *Council and Commission Manager Government* (Lawrence, 1960).

OLIVER P. WILLIAMS, "A Typology for Comparative Local Government," *Midwest Journal of Political Science*, May, 1961, pp. 150–164.

CLYDE J. WINGFIELD, "Power Structure and Decision-Making in City Planning," *Public Administration Review*, June, 1963, pp. 74–80

RAYMOND E. WOLFINGER, "Reputation and Reality in the Study of 'Community Power,'" *American Sociological Review*, October, 1960, pp. 636–644.

✎ Chapter XIII

EDUCATION

Can public funds be given to private primary and secondary schools without violating the constitutional principle of separation of church and state?

How much educational opportunity and equality does the public owe the nation's children? Can local government do the job? Is state help adequate?

CONCERN for public education goes deep into the heart of the American ethos. Around the middle of the seventeenth century, New England already had compulsory school attendance laws which insisted that the colonial government could require children to be educated, that towns establish schools, and that public funds could properly be used to pay for public education. In short the support, management, and control of educating children was deemed a public and governmental undertaking.

True to the Puritan conscience and pattern of life, the "battle against Satan" was to go beyond reading and writing and beyond knowing the capital laws. A proper knowledge of scripture was central to the Puritan concept of education.

> It being one chiefe project of ye ould deluder, Satan,
> to keepe men from the knowledge of ye Scriptures. . . .[1]

Despite such fervor for education, geographic distance and social and economic factors combined to hold back the growth of the common school in New England's towns and districts. Apprenticeship training rather than formal school attendance remained the predominant pattern of education for the majority of the people. Children acquired the rudiments of their learning as a by-product of training given them by parents or masters in field, shop, store, or home. Among the upper classes, parents either hired private tutors or sent their children to the newly-emerging Latin grammar school which offered the required classical preparatory work for college. In the South and in the middle colonies, where the Puritan influence was less pronounced, public education proceeded at an even slower pace. Thus at the time of the Revolution, the overall progress of formal, institutionalized mass education was not particularly noteworthy. "Even in school-conscious New England," it was estimated, "perhaps one youngster in ten even attended a school, and often this youngster attended intermittently and for very brief periods of time." [2] And still, the

---

[1] Quoted in E. P. Cubberley, *Readings in Public Education in the United States* (Boston, 1934), pp. 18–19. On current educational controversies, see Henry Ehlers (ed.), *Crucial Issues in Education: An Anthology* (New York, 1955).

[2] R. Freeman Butts and Laurence A. Cremin, *A History of Education in American Culture* (New York, 1953), p. 236.

relevance of public education for orderly progress remained clearly uppermost in the minds of those who were instrumental in the founding of the nation and in the writing of the early state constitutions.

Three examples may be cited. First, the Land Ordinance of 1785 enacted by the Continental Congress provided that in each township one section, the sixteenth, should be set aside for the support of public school education; secondly, Article 3 of the Northwest Ordinance of 1787—the charter which laid out the basic governmental framework for that vast territory out of which five Western states were eventually formed—declared that "Religion, morality and knowledge, being necessary to good government and the happiness of mankind, schools and the means of education shall be forever encouraged"; and thirdly, explicit provisions for public schools were incorporated into the constitutions of Delaware, Georgia, Massachusetts, New Hampshire, Pennsylvania, and Vermont. The constitution of Massachusetts, for instance, employed the following words:

> Wisdom, and knowledge, as well as virtue, diffused generally among the body of the people; being necessary for the preservation of their rights and liberties; and as these depend on spreading the opportunities and advantages of education in the various parts of the country, and among the different orders of the people, it shall be the duty of Legislatures and Magistrates, in all future periods of the Commonwealth, to cherish the interests of literature and the sciences, and all seminaries of them; especially the university at Cambridge, public schools and grammar schools in the towns. . . .

Not until the Jacksonian movement helped democratize American life, through its emphasis on egalitarianism and populism, did the concept of tax-supported, secular free public school receive the necessary social impetus to transform legal intent into educational reality.

Friends of the public schools, led by men like Horace Mann, Henry Barnard, Thaddeus Stevens, and Lyman Beecher, struggled patiently and finally won out over the determined opposition from rural interests, from many of the wealthy, and from some of the churches. Around the middle of the nineteenth century the common elementary school had at last attained its essential character. It was now ready to throw its doors open to all classes, all religions, to natives and immigrants alike. Along with the development of the English high school (successor to the old academy) and the newly-founded state university, elementary schools began to represent the primary level of a three-level public educational system designed to provide the widest possible educational opportunities for this country's fast-growing population.

In such an educational pyramid, primary schools were to remain for some years by far the most typical and popular school. By 1900, for example, while 14.5 million students attended primary schools, only about one half million went on to high school, and less than 250,000 entered all public and private colleges and universities. Then, over the next two generations, social and economic conditions made it possible for masses of students to climb the educational ladder. During the 1963–1964 academic year, almost 42 million children enrolled in public schools, almost 27 million were taught in the elementary grades, and about 15 million in high schools. For the same period, public colleges and universities reported about 3.4 million full-time students.

THE STATE PUBLIC SCHOOL SYSTEM

It is, of course, impossible to describe in a few pages the educational machinery through which fifty states and their local governments attempt to educate almost 42 million young Americans with the aid of 1.5 million teachers who teach in 1.3 million classrooms within the nation's 100,000 schools. At an annual cost of over $21 billion, education not only represents the largest single state and local budgetary item, but exceeds in its magnitude all of the moneys appropriated by all of the states for highways, welfare, and public health.

LOCAL SCHOOL DISTRICTS

Without doubt, local and decentralized control over education expresses one of the distinguishing characteristics of the American public school system. Responsibility for the education of more than three-fourths of all students is placed in not less than 31,000 separate school districts—units of local government endowed by state law with considerable administrative, curricular, and fiscal independence—although constitutionally the task of education is inherently a state function.[3]

Much less of such autonomy is granted to the so-called "dependent districts" which function as adjuncts or agencies of town, city, county, or state government and which now enroll one-fourth of all public school children. This type of organizational pattern is used exclusively in Hawaii, Maryland, North Carolina, and Virginia and to a significant extent in Tennessee and five of the New England states.

The number of independent school districts operating today while still impressively large totals but one-third of that in existence twenty years ago. Since 1942, state school consolidation and annexation laws have greatly facilitated the elimination of thousands of financially weak districts that were incapable of providing an effective education in the face of steeply rising costs for instruction and school construction.

Kansas, Minnesota, Nebraska, Pennsylvania, and South Dakota are five states which still report 2,000 or more independent school districts. However, in each of these states the totals include hundreds of so-called "non-operating districts" which do not provide instruction but do furnish transportation and tuition for students residing in their areas but attending schools in neighboring or newly-consolidated districts.

Many factors lie behind the determined reluctance or outright refusal of smaller school districts, many of them rural, to lose control over their systems.

[3] *NEA Research Bulletin,* February, 1964, p. 4.

There may be strong objections by parents that their children might be sent to schools dominated by an urban point of view, by teachers advocating newer educational philosophies, or by different social groups. Parents may fear that their children would lose their sense of identity and locality or that they would absorb social values incompatible with or hostile to the traditional standards of the community from which they came. Other times, a battle may obfuscate issues much more mundane—loss of prestige yielding local school board positions and power. Whatever the precise reasons, the struggle to close or combine districts has not been entirely successful.

According to the 1962 Census of Governments, over four-fifths of all school systems still enroll 600 or less students. In the judgment of many professional experts this reflects the continued prevalence of many schools too small in size to afford necessary specialization and to secure teachers, laboratories, and library facilities held indispensable to meet the demands of a well-rounded and scientifically updated educational process.

THE LOCAL SCHOOL BOARD

A recent survey of about 4,000 school boards heading systems including 1,200 or more students conducted by the Department of Health, Education, and Welfare (in cooperation with the National School Board Association) permits at least these generalizations:

A. Over four-fifths of all school board members were elected; when appointed (more in the South than in any other region) this may be by action of a city council, county commission, mayor, governor, or judge.

B. Although there were differences, a majority of the boards had a membership of five with terms of office of either three or four years.

C. Half of the school board members had graduated from college.

D. Women were represented on less than half of all school boards.

E. Among occupations represented on boards, the single largest category (over one-third) was that of business owners, officials, and managers; this was followed by persons engaged in professional and technical services (28 per cent) and by farmers (12 per cent).

F. Although 47 per cent of the board members had been in office for five years or more, some turnover in membership was not unusual; half of the boards reported at least one or more persons with service of less than one year.

G. Except for executive sessions, nine-tenths of the boards always conducted open meetings.

H. Over three-fourths of the boards made it a policy to compensate or reimburse their members for travel and other incidental expenses incurred in connection with official business; among school systems enrolling 25,000 students or more, 57 per cent of the boards paid their members a fixed annual rate; $1,200 was the median amount for these larger systems. In 1958–1959, of all the boards reporting, over half expended less than $500 for their members.[4]

4 U. S. Department of Health, Education, and Welfare, *Local School Boards: Organization and Practices* (Washington, 1962).

Policy and tradition have vested great power and responsibility in the hands of local school boards. Subject to state law, to voter approval, and to professional advice from its superintendent and other administrative officials, this group must decide whether to consolidate partially-used schools or to build new ones; how school construction and transportation are to be financed; what the building priorities shall be; what is to be taught; who is to teach it; and how much those who teach and those who administer shall be paid.

To carry out these functions a newly-elected board will organize itself, select its officers, determine the structure of its committees, agree on basic educational policies, and work out patterns that will guide its relationship with the superintendent and the community. If boards found their responsibilities heavy in the past, the immediate future promises responsibilities even heavier. Climbing educational costs, changing curricula, shifting populations, desegregation problems, rising enrollments, and the demands for greater educational excellence constitute challenges that will strain as never before, a local board's competence and leadership as it seeks to rally community support for its program.

Such support, especially financial support, is of course, not easily obtained. A study of voter turnout at special school bond and tax elections between 1948 and 1959 revealed no groundswell of public interest.[5]

While participation varied a great deal, on the average only a little more than one out of three of a district's eligible voters was sufficiently interested to cast a ballot. Perhaps even more significant than that was the finding which indicated that a larger voter turnout more likely than not actually spelled defeat for the proposals. Thus school boards wishing to secure a district's approval for greater financial investments in education will have to work not so much for an enlarged as for a better informed and more favorably inclined electorate.

STATE BOARDS AND DEPARTMENTS OF EDUCATION

The fact that most public schools operate under decentralized control must not be taken to mean that state governments are left without any educational responsibilities of their own. On the contrary, state constitutions and legislatures (and to some extent federal law as well) impose on their respective state boards and departments of education important duties of supervision and leadership.

All states but three—Illinois, Michigan, and Wisconsin—provide for a state board of education. Board members are directly elected in nine states (to terms generally of from 2–4 years) and appointed by the governor in thirty-one states. Among the remaining states, board membership varies but is so

---

[5] Richard F. Carter and William G. Savard, *Influence of Voter Turnout on School Bond and Tax Elections* (Washington, 1961).

structured as to include, along with the chief state school officer, a combination of two or three high executive officials whose duties are not primarily concerned with education. This may include the governor, secretary of state, or attorney general. New York is different; here the Board of Regents of the University of the State of New York—a constitutionally established board of thirteen members elected by the legislature—also acts in the capacity of a state board of education.

In addition to boards of education, all states make provision for a chief educational officer variously designated state commissioner of education, state superintendent of public instruction, or head of the state department of education. Twenty-one states elect this official usually to terms of from two to four years, twenty-four let their state boards select him, and five states place the choice in the hands of the governor.

Within the framework of law, state boards of education formulate policies and set standards for the guidance of their administrative agent, the department of education, and for the local school boards. How detailed these policies, how close the supervision, and how severe the consequences for a non-complying local board are matters that differ greatly from state to state.

Granted such diversity, there are nevertheless a number of policy concerns common to a majority of state boards and departments. For example, what minimum educational qualifications should be made applicable to teachers and administrators? Should the curriculum of instruction contain a fixed number of subjects and how much time should be devoted to each? What types of reports should be required from local school boards regarding enrollments, textbooks, fiscal operations, utilization of plant, or future school construction plans? Actually, most of the day-to-day work of a typical state department of education has to do with matters much more prosaic—research and planning and rendering special advice and services to teachers, librarians, administrators, school boards, and legislators. Within the department:

a legal section will interpret newly-enacted statutes, the rulings of the attorney general, or relevant decisions from federal and state courts;

a statistical section will assist in calculating and distributing state and federal aid in compiling data showing costs per pupil unit in average daily attendance, tax rates, and assessed valuations;

a school lunch section will provide information for schools and institutions entitled to special milk and food assistance under federal law; it will also process applications and supervise the distribution of such aid;

instructional sections for elementary and secondary schools will assist with the distribution of suggested course outlines and curricular guides and help with planning special workshops for teachers and administrators;

a teacher certification and accreditation section will evaluate, issue, or renew teaching credentials or help place teachers;

a library section provides rural library and traveling library services and assists in the administration of appropriate federal aid;

a vocational education section has responsibility for the development and for the supervision of programs in the areas of agricultural, homemaking, business, trade, industrial, and distributive education;

a vocational rehabilitation section will provide guidance and other services for the handicapped and assists in referring those in need of rehabilitation to special educational and training centers.

Among other sections there may be those furnishing consultative services and information to local school systems concerning the latest developments in audio-visual education, safety education, physical and health education, school bond markets, or school reorganization procedures. Beyond these more traditional functions, in recent years some of the state departments of education participated in major long range studies. The search for measures leading towards early identification and discernment of the needs of gifted and retarded children by the departments of California, Connecticut, Minnesota, Ohio, and Oregon illustrates only one of many such projects. Pressing problems for nearly all departments currently are the educational impact of urban renewal, desegregation, the frightening rate of dropouts, and the undereducation of the unemployed youth.

How much of a ripple these departmental staff efforts cause in the educational pond and how much they contribute to the raising of educational standards depends greatly on the caliber of the departmental leadership, on the scope of legal powers granted the department by state law, and most of all, on the degree of the department's public acceptance.

STATE UNIVERSITIES AND STATE CAPITOLS

In 1900, sixty-one per cent of all college and university students were enrolled in privately supported institutions, the so-called independent or church connected colleges and universities. Today, the ratio is nearly reversed. Of the 5 million students (both full and part-time) presently in higher education, 3.2 million are enrolled in public and 1.8 million in private institutions. Twenty-five years hence, it is estimated that the public sector will enroll 80 per cent of the anticipated students.[6] To provide enough professors, academic facilities, and housing for the "war babies" of the 1940's and for this country's rapidly growing college-oriented generations represents awesome organizational and fiscal challenges to both campus and state.

If "decentralization" was the appropriate concept characterizing the relationship predominant between Capitol and schoolhouse, then "centralization" is a far more appropriate term describing the relationship of state government to state university. Reasons that underlie a different development of higher education go to the very nature of the American university's legal

[6] Sidney G. Tickton, *Letter to a College President on the Need for Long Range Planning* (Fund for the Advancement of Education, 1963) as found in Hearings of the Senate Committee on Labor and Public Welfare, Subcommittee on Education, *Education Legislation 1963*, 88th Cong., 1st Sess. (Washington, 1963), VI, 3474–3475.

basis, its role in the public mind, and its position as an arm of state government.

By the time the first American state universities were founded—Georgia (1785), North Carolina (1789), and Vermont (1791)—the pattern of how such institutions of higher learning should be governed had already taken shape. It was derived from seventeenth and eighteenth century legal precedents first developed for the governance of private colleges in Holland and then in the colonies. Colleges like Harvard, Yale, William and Mary, and Princeton were chartered as educational corporations under boards of trustees with legal powers to acquire and sell property, employ teachers, set salaries, determine curricula, define admission standards, administer funds, and adopt all such rules and regulations as were necessary to the internal management of the institution.

In the nineteenth century when most state universities were established in the belief that higher education was a proper public concern, legislatures proceeded to create boards of regents to manage the affairs of these new institutions as agencies of state government. Unlike the universities of France which were under the immediate control of a state ministry, and unlike the British universities of Oxford and Cambridge which were largely administered by the professors themselves, the people of this country struck a pattern of limited internal university autonomy combined with clear-cut responsiveness to the public will as expressed by the political branches of state government. The regents—either elected by the people, appointed by the governor, or selected by the legislature—and the university were viewed as a department of government. More protected from detailed central supervision or intervention by the legislature or by the governor than any ordinary administrative department, most state universities, nevertheless, were not permitted to forget that their budgets, personnel, and policies were as a matter of public law ultimately subject to legislative oversight and control. Slightly more insulated against "outside" influences were the state universities in California, Colorado, Georgia, Idaho, Michigan, Minnesota, and Oklahoma where authority of the regents and institutional independence were surrounded with certain explicit constitutional safeguards. But neither these universities nor most of the others found it easy to maintain their managerial autonomy as the efficiency and economy in government movement gained momentum during the decades following World War I.

As state after state, in order to strengthen overall financial control (and the governorship), adopted the concept of a single department of finance or administration and charged this agency with the responsibility for centralized budgeting, procurement, and maintenance of public property, instances of conflicts between the commissioners of administration and university officials multiplied. The influence of such state budget officers over the university's operation became more noticeable and controversial.

Along with these interventions has come the growth of the centrally-administered civil service. Nearly half of the states now extend their state personnel regulations to the non-academic employees of the university—the secretaries, technicians, custodial and service personnel.[7] Differences between government employment in general and the demands of an educational setting have caused their share of problems.

While educators and budgeteers work out their internal administrative accommodations and while the system of higher education begins to experience its most rapid expansion in history, there are on the horizon as yet no basic changes in the overall relationship between the state and the university.

A few of the states, Florida and Georgia are two such examples, continue to place some general policy supervision over all university-level education in the hands of one central board.[8] Others, among them, notably, Minnesota, Wisconsin, and Texas, left the regents in charge of the state university but created additional boards to direct the four-year state colleges, institutions formerly known as state normal schools and teachers' colleges.[9] Still another group of states, Arizona and Minnesota among the most recent members, established a third type of central state board to guide the activities of the newest, most rapidly growing institutions, the junior or community colleges.

States lacking one central governing board for their entire system of higher education, but sensing keenly the need to avoid expensive duplication of effort and anxious to give to their educational goals and resources a sharper focus, have been experimenting recently with the organization of inter-institutional coordinating councils and committees. Illinois, Indiana and Ohio are three states which employ a voluntary pattern of coordination, while Texas and Wisconsin represent a group of states which by law transferred to a central coordinating agency for centralized determination selected staff functions such as purchasing or budgeting.

California's 1960 Master Plan for Higher Education deserves special attention.[10] Faced with continually vast increases in population (70 per cent during the last ten years), with enormous industrial and urban growth, and with college enrollments of staggering proportions, the people of California insisted that their state must not fail to provide a system of higher education that was second to none.

With 58,000 students, the University of California, now the largest in the nation, plans to add three additional branches each with a proposed maximum capacity of 27,500 students, although already in 1964, it operated six separate campuses along with seventy research and extension stations, two

---

[7] Malcolm Moos and Francis E. Rourke, *The Campus and the State* (Baltimore, 1959), p. 179. Also note the Committee on Government and Higher Education, *The Efficiency of Freedom* (Baltimore, 1959). A brief discussion of recent political and administrative problems besetting the Colorado State College system and the University of Colorado is found in *The New York Times*, April 14, 1963.

[8] Alexander Brody, *The American State and Higher Education* (Washington, 1935), p. 148.

[9] See Lyman A. Glenn, *Autonomy of Public Colleges: The Challenge of Coordination* (New York, 1959) for further information on methods of cooperation.

[10] Ben Hibbs, "California Builds Big for Education," *Reader's Digest*, July, 1963, pp. 164–171.

atomic research installations, fifty farm advisory offices, and adult education courses in 179 communities. In addition to the university, California's sprawling higher education complex, currently includes seventeen state colleges (some with enrollments of over 10,000) and sixty-nine junior or community colleges to which the state makes major financial contributions.

Within this context of transition and accelerated change, some of the junior colleges pressured for permission to become state colleges and some of the four-year state colleges aspired to the status of a university preferably under the supervision of the board of regents which, so they contended, would assure them greater independence than the state board of education could or was willing to grant. As competition for the educational tax dollar intensified, and confusion abounded, the need for some form of inter-institutional coordination became blatantly self-evident to the colleges themselves as well as to the legislature.

The plan that finally emerged and was found acceptable by the 1960 legislature (1) placed the state colleges under a newly-created State Board of Trustees (but at the same time granted to each institution greater autonomy than it possessed heretofore), (2) promulgated general policies governing the admission of students, the employment of faculty, and the overall educational functions for each of the three segments of the system, and (3) established the California Coordinating Council for Higher Education, an agency of considerable stature and potential power.[11]

Council membership includes representatives from the university, the state colleges, the junior colleges, the private colleges, and the public at large. Provided with a staff and with authority to require cooperation from all public institutions, the council is charged with responsibilities that encompass:

A. Rendering advice to the three governing boards of higher education and to state officials.
B. Reviewing budget requests from the university and the state system.
C. Approving plans for future developments and sites.
D. Reporting their recommendations to the governor and to the legislature.

There is obviously much in this Master Plan that could prove useful to a state that must currently meet the educational needs of nearly 400,000 students, a figure only two-thirds of what experts project it will likely run up to in 1975. But while Californians are thus forced to "think big" they are apparently not all willing to create a system of "giantism" which would concentrate large masses of students in similar campuses with similar curricula and purposes.

One such concrete expression of this, other than the Master Plan itself, is the proposed university branch at Santa Cruz. What is planned for that 2,000 acre campus overlooking Monterey Bay, is not a single university serving 20,000 students, but a group of up to twenty small and distinctive four-year liberal arts colleges, each authorized to experiment with courses,

[11] *Book of the States, 1962–1963*, p. 321.

curricula, and programs, and each having its own faculty, classrooms, and residence quarters. Each would be encouraged to develop its own traditions and emphases on courses. Shared, however, by the entire group would be laboratory facilities, science buildings, the library, and some of the more specialized courses and faculty.[12] That other less wealthy states than California could or would copy such a model is, of course, somewhat doubtful.

THE JUNIOR AND COMMUNITY COLLEGES—

INCREASED ENROLLMENTS AND STATE SUPPORT

No other segment of post-high school education received a greater impetus in recent years than the junior or community college. Offering non-professional general credit courses for either terminal purposes or for transfer to regular four-year colleges, nearly seven hundred of such public and private institutions enroll now almost one million students (90 per cent of them in public colleges). This is close to twice the number that attended such schools in 1950, and still further expansion is indicated. An estimate by the American Association of Junior Colleges foresees "that by 1970 three out of four students entering college will enroll in a junior college." [13] During the last five years alone, of the ninety new colleges founded, sixty-five were junior colleges.

There are many explanations for the popularity of this type of college. Tuition is low. Compared to four-year colleges (with their more expensive and specialized faculties and facilities), it costs only about half as much to educate students at junior colleges. Also, students who might not be able to meet the higher college and university standards of admission can now be given the opportunity to try themselves out. Perhaps even more significant, low tuition combined with the possibility of residing at home while attending college brings a college education within the reach of qualified students, an estimated one-quarter to one-third of which are presently barred from it merely because of financial reasons.[14]

Among the fourteen states having twenty or more junior or community colleges, California, New York, and Florida clearly lead the movement. California now enrolls 125,000 students in its seventy junior colleges, and by 1975, it expects that about 70 per cent of all of its lower division students will be registered in these colleges.[15] By then, New York also expects to have as

[12] Lawrence E. Davies, "California Plans a Cluster of 20 Small Colleges," *The New York Times,* November 18, 1962, p. 57.

[13] Mitchell Gordon, "Two-Year Institutions Play An Expanding Role in Higher Education," *The Wall Street Journal,* December 26, 1963, pp. 1, 9.

[14] Statement by Edmund J. Gleazer, Jr., Executive Director of the American Association of Junior Colleges, *ibid.,* pp. 1, 9.

[15] Statement by Dr. Donald E. Deyo, President of the American Association of Junior Colleges, in May 14–17, 1963, hearings of the Senate Committee on Labor and Public Welfare, Subcommittee on Education, *Education Legislation 1963,* 88th Cong., 1st sess. (Washington, 1963), II, 1067.

many as 50 per cent of its first-year students in higher education enrolled in two-year community colleges. In Florida, over three-fifths of its high school seniors live "within reasonable commuting distance" of its twenty-nine junior colleges.[16]

Something of the spectacular rate of growth in Florida's system is illustrated by Miami-Dade Junior College which started out in 1960 with 1,300 students and a staff of forty-six and "now has more than 6,000 students and a staff of 250." [17]

Legislative interest in the development of the junior college continues to be in evidence among other states as well. Laws authorizing additional local districts to establish such colleges were enacted since 1960 in Connecticut, Maryland, Minnesota, Ohio, Rhode Island, Washington, and West Virginia. State aid for students attending such institutions was increased in Colorado, Georgia, Kansas, Maryland, and Minnesota.[18]

FEDERAL AID TO SCHOOLS, COLLEGES, AND UNIVERSITIES

THE RECORD OF LEGISLATION

Prior to 1900, most of the educational aid provided the states by the national government took the form of land grants. This was true of the acts of 1785, 1787, as well as of the Morrill Act of 1862 which by turning over to the states some seventeen million acres fathered the land-grant colleges and universities now totalling sixty-eight, and enrolling at least 20 per cent of all students. Regular annual appropriations to institutions of higher learning began with the Hatch Act of 1887 which furnished funds for agricultural extension stations and experimental work. Aid for instruction in home economics was initiated with the Smith-Lever Act of 1914, and vocational education received its first federal boost three years later under the Smith-Hughes Act which extended similar aid to educational institutions below the college level.

Federal aid multiplied during the Depression years of the 1930's. Funds were made available through various federal agencies for adult education, school lunch programs, nursery schools, vocational rehabilitation, retraining of the unemployed youth, and part-time employment for needy college students. States and cities also received loans and grants for the construction of schools and colleges. Viewed only as temporary and crisis induced, most of these programs were terminated by 1940.

During World War II, the War Manpower Commission developed a variety of programs to provide the necessary training facilities for thousands of defense production workers, and under the Lanham Act hundreds of towns and cities, crowded with servicemen, military bases, and new industrial

[16] *Ibid.*, p. 1067.

[17] *Miami Herald*, March 22, 1963, as cited in *Education Legislation 1963*, II, 1076.

[18] *Book of the States, 1960–1961*, p. 300 and *Book of the States, 1962–1963*, p. 322.

establishments, were entitled to apply for grants to help finance school maintenance, construction, and expansion. Aid to these federally-affected localities, the so-called "impacted school districts," has been continued.

Although the federal government had previously assisted with the education of certain special groups—Indians, military dependents, veterans of World War I, nurses, public health workers, and the physically disabled—it was not until after World War II that Washington gave direct and massive financial support to millions of students enrolled in colleges and universities all over the country. According to the provisions of the Servicemen's Readjustment Act of 1944, nearly all World War II veterans who wished to pursue their education could obtain federal funds for subsistence allowances as well as for tuition, books, and supplies as they enrolled in private or public accredited institutions of their choice. Depending on the veteran's length of service, the maximum entitlement ran to a period of four years.

When the enrollment under the G. I. Bill of Rights reached its peak in 1947–1948, an average number of 2,450,000 veterans availed themselves of such educational opportunities at a cost to the federal government of $2.8 billion. For all the various educational benefits to veterans, Washington spent nearly $12 billion. Nor was this the final total. Through subsequent congressional amendments, some of this type of federal educational beneficence was also extended to the veterans of the Korean campaign—though on a more moderate and limited basis.

The phasing-out of veterans did not put an end to demands from many other sources for a more permanent role of federal financial support to both higher and general education. Congress was bombarded with information that too many school districts were financially embarrassed by record enrollments and an insufficient number of available classrooms, that too many teachers were leaving the profession because of lagging salaries, that too many colleges and universities were inadequately financed to meet the projected increases in oncoming student generations, that too many laboratories were lacking in facilities necessary to furnish this nation's required physicians, scientists, and engineers, and that the Russians had achieved too many successes in the areas of science and technology to allow the American educational system to remain unaffected or unchanged in a highly competitive race for scientific and industrial advances.

While such considerations caused many people to turn to Washington for help, this did not, of course, represent the thinking of all segments of the public or of all educators or of the Congress itself. Strong reluctance to move away from the deeply-rooted traditions of locally or, at most, state-financed and controlled primary and secondary education was evidenced by the National School Board Association, local taxpayers' associations, chambers of commerce, and other conservatively inclined groups. Also opposed were those to whom federal aid constituted but one more instrument of leverage in the hands of radicals bent on accelerating the process of desegregation. Finally, there were those who viewed with genuine apprehension any possible weakening in the constitutional doctrine separating church and state which might come about as a legal by-product of any public aid measure in which private and parochial schools were permitted to share.

Still, pressures persisted. So much so in fact (especially after the Soviet Union launched her Sputniks), that the friends of federal aid to education were able to score a major breakthrough in 1958. This followed two minor victories in 1950 when Congress passed a small-scale program of long-term, low-interest loans for public as well as private college housing, and when it expanded aid for school construction in areas affected by federal activities.

The National Defense Education Act (1958)

This measure was designed to help the nation identify and assure for itself an adequate supply of trained professional manpower and leadership. Educational benefits granted under the National Defense Education Act, and its amendments as administered by the United States Office of Education, affect all levels of education from primary school through graduate school.

> A. *Loans to Students in Institutions of Higher Education:* Under this provision graduate and undergraduate students who need financial assistance may borrow up to $1,000 per academic year or a total of $5,000 for their entire college education. Special consideration in given to students who wish to teach in elementary and secondary schools and to those who evidence a superior capacity for professional work in science, mathematics, engineering, and modern foreign languages. The federal government will match funds from cooperating colleges and universities on a nine-to-one basis.

A 1961 survey of students who borrowed funds under this provision revealed that "two out of every five borrowers came from families whose annual incomes were $4,000 or less, and five out of seven from families whose incomes were $6,000 or less." [19] Since the beginning of the student loan program in 1958, about 490,000 students in 1,534 colleges and universities have borrowed approximately $330 million under the program. "Ninety per cent of the student borrowers reported that they could not have begun or continued their college studies without the assistance." [20]

> B. *Financial Assistance for Strengthening Science, Mathematics and Foreign Language Instruction:* This involves federal aids, on a fifty-fifty matching basis, to state approved elementary and secondary schools for the acquisition of laboratories and special equipment in order to improve and make more attractive the classroom teaching of these subjects. Nonprofit private schools are entitled to obtain low interest, ten-year loans rather than grants.
>
> C. *National Defense Fellowships:* Up to 1,500 fellowships ranging from $2,000 to $2,400 for each year of graduate study (three-year maximum) plus a $400 annual allowance for each dependent is made available to students engaged in a course of study leading to a Ph.D or equivalent degree. No matching is required.

[19] U. S. Department of Health, Education, and Welfare, Office of Education, *Report of the National Defense Education Act: Fiscal Years 1961 and 1962* (Washington, 1963), p. 8.

[20] U. S. Department of Health, Education, and Welfare, *Health, Education, and Welfare Indicators,* December, 1963, p. xviii.

A four-year survey for this type of grant indicates the following distribution in the major areas of academic specialization:

NUMBER AND PERCENTAGE OF GRADUATE FELLOW-
SHIPS ALLOTTED BY ACADEMIC AREA, FISCAL YEARS
1959–1962

Area	Number	Percentage
Social Sciences	1,463	26
Humanities	1,377	25
Physical Sciences	943	17
Biological Sciences	797	14
Engineering	536	10
Education	422	8

SOURCE: Department of Health, Education, and Welfare.

D. *Guidance, Counseling, and Testing: Identification and Encouragement of Able Students.* To receive fifty-fifty matching grants under this title, states must submit testing programs for their secondary schools devised to identify students with outstanding aptitudes and abilities as well as plans for guidance and counseling services aimed at encouraging students to finish school, and if they are found academically promising to urge them to enter a college or university so that they may continue their education.

No matching is stipulated for federal funds provided for the support of short-term counseling and guidance training institutes designed for secondary school counselors or for teachers preparing for counseling. Participants in such institutes receive weekly stipends of $75.00 and a $15.00 weekly allowance for each dependent.

Mention should be made of the additional provisions of this important act. The federal government supplies funds for language and area centers at colleges and universities for teaching and research in modern languages not commonly studied, for research and experimentation in the more effective utilization of television, radio, motion pictures, and related media for educational purposes, for area vocational education programs, and for the improvement of statistical services of state education agencies.

Since the passage of the Morrill Act, no Congress in United States history was quite as education conscious as was the 88th. Among the various measures enacted in 1963, under strong prodding by the Kennedy administration, were those offering aid to

A. *College Construction:* The nation's 1,298 public and 842 private and church connected four-year colleges, technical institutes, and junior colleges were authorized to apply for outright grants of up to one-third of the costs of constructing new science, mathematics, engineering, modern languages and library buildings or facilities ($540 million over three years). Public junior colleges can apply for similar grants but up to 40 per cent of construction costs of all types of academic facilities ($150 million); grants given for graduate school construction, not limited to any field, were based on the same matching ratio as that applicable to undergraduate institutions ($145 million); also made available were loans for the construction of both graduate and undergraduate college facilities ($120 million each year for three years).

B. *Student Loans:* The National Defense Education Act loan program was expanded and helped to finance between 70,000 and 90,000 additional students each year ($304 million).

C. *Vocational Education:* Additional funds were furnished existing programs of vocational education, and under a new amendment communities wishing to operate residential vocational schools for full-time vocational training could qualify for federal assistance for the construction, equipment, and operation of such schools ($731 million over four years); also added was a "work-study" program especially addressing itself to communities having a substantial number of youths who dropped out of school and who need earnings from part-time employment in order to pursue their vocational training courses ($849 million over three years).

D. *Impacted Areas:* More money was provided public school districts in communities crowded with children of servicemen or of employees of federal installations now educating approximately one-third of all the nation's school children ($527 million over three years).

E. *Medical Education:* Private and public dental and medical colleges were entitled to construction grants for new buildings and facilities with the federal government paying two-thirds of such costs ($175 million); provisions were inserted to benefit from 7,500 to 9,000 medical students with loans of up to $8,000 each for their four-year graduate courses. ($1.4 million over three years.) It is estimated that this measure will increase from 12,500 to 19,000 the number of students entering medical and dental schools.[21]

In 1965, the House of Representatives passed an amendment to the 1963 act which proposed doubling funds available for construction of college academic facilities ($290 million) and which would establish federal scholarships through advances to state scholarship loan funds (or directly to students in states which are unwilling to establish such funds). The bill also provided for grants to upgrade college libraries and train librarians ($70 million), to encourage colleges to institute community service programs which seek solution to the problems of urban and suburban areas ($50 million), and to aid smaller and newly-developing colleges ($30 million).[22]

It took the momentum of the 1964 presidential election to force a congressional breakthrough on the subject of federal aid to schools. Passed into law during the first 100 days of the 89th Congress was one of Mr. Johnson's high priority pieces of legislation—the $1.3 billion Elementary and Secondary Education Act of 1965 designed to assist schools and students in low-income areas.

Among the major provisions in this complex statute are the following:

A. 3-year grants to school districts and counties for the purpose of encouraging and supporting the establishment, expansion, and improvement of special programs, including the construction of minimum school facilities where needed to meet the special requirements of educationally deprived

[21] *Washington Post*, December 23, 1963, p. A12.

[22] H. R. 9567 passed the House on August 26, 1965. A similar version was passed by the Senate on September 2, 1965.

children of low income families (annual income of less than $2,000); President is to appoint a 12-member National Advisory Council on the Education of Disadvantaged Youth to review the administration of the program ($1.06 billion) in fiscal 1966.

B. 5-year grants to make available to all school children (public and non-profit private) "school library resources, textbooks, and other printed and published instructional materials" subject to state promulgated plans, policies and provisions for the allocation of such resources. Title and control of books and other printed matter must remain in a public agency and none of these resources may be used in religious worship and instruction. ($100 million in fiscal 1966)

C. 5-year grants for the establishment of supplementary educational centers and services and experimental pilot projects. Plans must have the approval of state educational authorities and of representatives from cooperating agencies and institutions (non-public schools, museums, art galleries, educational television stations and other cultural non-profit agencies). Among projects included are these: guidance and counseling, remedial instruction, school health, psychological and social work services, adult education, specialized instruction and "related services for persons who are in or from rural areas who are or have been otherwise isolated from normal educational opportunities. . . ." An Advisory Committee on Supplementary Educational Centers and Services is to be established in the U. S. Office of Education to assist the Commissioner in the review of grant applications and in the development of general policy regulations ($100 million in fiscal 1966).

D. 5-year grants "to public and other nonprofit universities and colleges and other public or nonprofit agencies to assist them in providing training in research in the field of education . . . ;" contracts and cooperative arrangements are authorized with universities, professional associations, and other research agencies covering research traineeships, internships, fellowships, as well as surveys and demonstrations. "No grant may be made . . . . for training relating to sectarian instruction." ($100 million for fiscal 1966).

Title VI offers these major sets of restrictions:

". . . [N]othing contained in the act will be construed to authorize any department, agency, officer, or employee of the United States to exercise any direction, supervision, or control over the curriculum, program of instruction, administration, or personnel of any educational institution, or school system, or over the selection of library resources, textbooks, or other printed or published instructional materials by any educational institution or school system."

". . . [N]othing in the act may be construed to authorize the making of any payment for religious worship or instruction."

FEDERAL AID TO PRIMARY AND SECONDARY EDUCATION—

THE PROS AND CONS

Debate on this issue had been raging for years. Recent enactments of the large-scale college and vocational aid bills only served to intensify the controversy. It will be the purpose of this section to stress a few of the more focal and cogent arguments which were advanced by proponents and opponents in hearings before congressional committees, in the press, in books and journals, and on public platforms.

Are There Persuasive Precedents Authorizing the Federal Government to Aid Education?

Yes, said the proponents. Beginning with the enormous land grants by Congress under the Articles of Confederation and then later through the Morrill Act, the national government has given clear expression of its interest and legitimate concern for education. Subsequent legislation of major import —the Smith-Hughes Act, the Servicemen's Rehabilitation Act, the National Defense Education Act, the Aid to Medical Education Act, and the College Academic Facilities Act—all of these simply expanded legal and policy precedents readily accepted by the courts and by the public as proper application of the federal power of taxation exercised on behalf of the national interest and welfare.

No, said the opponents. The purpose of the early land grants was not primarily to aid the cause of education but to induce immigrants and settlers to bring land under cultivation and to populate the West.

> Neither railroads, nor homesteaders nor other beneficiaries who in the aggregate received 92 per cent of all federal land grants ever claimed that the grants established a precedent for continued support from the federal government.[23]

It is one of the oldest principles of American education that responsibility for the support and control of public elementary and secondary schools belongs to local and state government and not to the federal government.

Will State and Local Governments be Able to Finance Education Adequately in Future Years?

No, said the proponents. Heavy reliance on property taxes (fifty-four percent in 1960 of all educational revenues), a tax already exceedingly high and regressive in its effect upon farmers and lower income groups, raises serious doubts that these governmental levels can effectively finance the necessary improvements and expansions which are demanded of our educational system now and in future years.

> In 1961–1962, total expenditure for these public schools per year was $18.1 billion. It is estimated that increasing enrollments will require new staff, buildings, and other instructional costs that will drive annual expenditures to nearly $25.9 billion by 1970–1971.[24]

[23] Roger A. Freeman, *Taxes for the Schools* (Washington, 1960), II, 41.

[24] A staff memorandum of the Department of Health, Education, and Welfare, included in testimony by Senator Joseph S. Clark in hearings of the Senate Committee on Labor and Public Welfare, Subcommittee on Education, *Education Legislation 1963*, 88th Cong., 1st Sess. (Washington, 1963), I, 262.

In order to meet their fiscal responsibilities to education, state and local authorities have already heavily mortgaged their communities. Whereas the federal debt increased by about 12 per cent between 1950 and 1961, that of state and local government rose by 213 per cent.[25]

Yes, said the opponents. State and local governments have already demonstrated that they can efficiently manage their educational finances.

> [F]rom 1900 to 1961, enrollment multiplied 2.4 times . . . current school expenditures per pupil have multiplied 8.4 times in terms of the same constant dollar, an increase more than three and one-half times as great as the increase in enrollment.[26]

People at the local level are perfectly willing to pay for their education and that of their children.

> At school bond elections in 1960, voters approved more than $1,756,975,000 of additional bonds for elementary and secondary schools. This represents approval of over 81 per cent, by value, of the school bonds submitted for approval at bond elections.[27]

Should this prove insufficient Senator Goldwater, among others, suggests that taxpayers be permitted to deduct the full amount of their school taxes from their *net* federal income tax liability.

Is There Really a Classroom Shortage?

Yes, said the proponents. The United States Office of Education placed the shortage of public elementary and secondary school classrooms at 142,000 (fall, 1960). This figure includes 66,100 classrooms required to accommodate the 1,868,000 students still housed in excess of normal capacity.[28] In 1954, 18.7 per cent of all secondary school pupils were in excess of normal classroom capacity; six years later the figure rose to 36.8 per cent, nearly double.[29]

No, said the opponents. Based on projections furnished by the United States Office of Education, 610,000 new classrooms need to be built during the next ten years. Since the average annual rate of construction during the past

[25] *Education Legislation 1963*, I, 265, (based on U. S. Department of Commerce Bureau of the Census, *Statistical Abstract of the United States 1962* and *Summary of Governmental Finances in 1961*).

[26] *Education Legislation 1963*, I, 287. Testimony by Senator Barry Goldwater. Recommendations for a moderate position on federal aid, taken by various Republican members of the House, are found in the *Congressional Record*, June 29 and 30, 1961.

[27] Statement of the American Farm Bureau Federation presented by John C. Lynn, Legislative Director in Senate Committee on Labor and Public Welfare, Subcommittee on Education hearings, *Public School Assistance Act of 1961*, Pt. 2, 87th Cong., 1st Sess. (Washington, 1961), p. 1172.

[28] Statement of the U. S. Office of Education, *ibid.*, Pt. 2, pp. 998–999.

[29] Statement by Abraham Ribicoff, Secretary of Health, Education, and Welfare, *ibid.*, Pt. 1, p. 95.

five years yielded 67,360 such units, no future shortages should develop and no federal aid is required. Nor was there a classroom shortage between 1950 and 1960 when

> the unprecedented influx of children . . . swelled public school enrollment by 10.8 million. The presence of those children required a net addition of 370,000 classrooms. Actually, 567,000 classrooms were completed in the years 1949–1950, 1958–1959. That left about 200,000 classrooms for the replacement of old buildings, and for the reduction of whatever shortage existed in 1950.[30]

Is There Really a Teacher Shortage or Salary Problem?

Yes, said the proponents. In classrooms throughout the nation, there are now some 90,000 teachers who fail to meet full professional certification requirements and in thirty-five states only 40 per cent or less of secondary school teachers possess an M.A. degree.[31]

According to a United States Department of Labor study, an urban family with two children needed a salary in 1959 of "at least $6,130 per year for a modest but adequate standard of living." [32] Three years later, in 1962–1963, sixty per cent of the states paid average salaries below $5,940.[33] Thus in three-fifths of the states teachers had as yet not even attained this minimum standard of living. All of which means that without federal aid teachers will still be forced to moonlight (take secondary jobs) and to work during the summer to obtain an essential income instead of continuing their education as most of them should and would prefer to do for professional growth and for the benefit of their students.

No, said the opponents. There may be a shortage in a few specialized teaching fields, in mathematics and science, but even that is nearly solved. Between 1954 and 1959, "the number of all college graduates prepared to teach increased 47 per cent, [and] the number of those prepared to teach science or mathematics jumped by 100 per cent." [34] Admittedly, teacher salaries vary throughout the nation, but even in the lower income states, the teacher's *relative* salary position is superior to that of his colleague in the higher income states. Moreover, any salary comparisons with different professions and occupations must, of course, take into consideration the fact that no other group is granted as much vacation time as are teachers. At that, teacher salaries did improve significantly in recent years (see Table 1).

[30] Statement of the American Farm Bureau Federation, *ibid.*, Pt. 2, p. 1174.

[31] Statement of the U. S. Office of Education, *ibid.*, Pt. 2, pp. 998–999 and *Education Legislation 1963*, VI, 3234.

[32] Testimony by Peter T. Schoemann, AFL-CIO Vice-President and Chairman of the Education Committee, *ibid.*, Pt. 1, p. 392.

[33] *Education Legislation 1963*, VI, 3235.

[34] Statement of the American Farm Bureau Federation, *Public School Assistance Act of 1961*, Pt. 2, p. 1172.

TABLE 1. CLASSROOM TEACHER SALARIES,
1952–1964

| Year | Percentage of salaries | | |
	Below $3,500	$3,500–4,499	$4,500 and over
1952–53	62.0%	25%	13.0%
1960–61	9.6%	27%	62.3%
1963–64	2.5%	14.8%	82.7%

SOURCE: *National Education Association Research Bulletin*, February, 1964, p. 5.

Does Federal Aid Necessarily Entail Federal Control Over Education?

No, said the proponents. Thousands of "federally impacted" school districts have been aided, millions of school luncheons served, and hundreds of thousands of students vocationally trained with funds supplied by Washington, all of which has been accompanied by such evident lack of federal intervention into matters of local policy, administration and personnel for twenty-one United States senators to have been eager to co-sponsor President Kennedy's School Assistance Act of 1961, and for forty-nine United States senators to have voted for its approval on May 25, 1961. That even strong supporters of such federal aid found it necessary to insist on clear assurances against federal interference in schools was given expression in the bill itself. The second section of Title I (S. 1021) provided

> In the administration of this title, no department, agency, officer or employee of the United States shall exercise any direction, supervision, or control over the policy determination, personnel, curriculum, program of instruction, or the administration or operation of any school or school system.

But the tenor of the support remained clear throughout the debates. Without such federal aid, inequalities of educational opportunities within and between states will persist, and the lack of state and local fiscal resources will continue to make it impossible for state and local systems to make the substantial improvements in instructional methods and standards which this nation has a right to expect if its people are to live effective and productive lives in the difficult years ahead.

Yes, said the opponents. Their case is most lucidly advanced in a Senate minority report submitted by Senators Barry Goldwater and Everett M. Dirksen.

> It is plain to see that the citizens, the taxpayers, and their legally elected representatives, both State and local, are not demanding Federal aid to education. The professional educationists and their allies, fully aware of this, realize that their complete control of our educational system can come about only if education is federalized. It is much easier for pressure groups to influence a single legislative body like the Congress, and a single executive,

the President, than it is fifty State legislatures, fifty Governors, and 50,000 local school boards.

The fight over Federal aid to education has been commonly viewed as a battle over money for the schools. It is conceivable that the real issue is not just money. The crucial issue may well be a power struggle over the control of the schools between the organized profession and the lay public. Federal funds would strengthen the hand of the educational bureaucracy—but it would weaken the authority of the citizens and their communities.[35]

FEDERAL AID TO PAROCHIAL PRIMARY AND

SECONDARY SCHOOLS

No discussion of federal aid to education can be complete if it leaves out consideration of the issue of federal support to private and parochial schools. These schools represent an influential, and to some, a controversial segment of American education. During 1961–1962, nonpublic schools enrolled an estimated 6,500,000 students from kindergarten through the twelfth grade. Of this group nearly one million secondary students were denominationally distributed over 3,266 church-related schools as shown in Table 2.

Of the nonpublic primary as well as secondary schools, the Catholic

TABLE 2. NUMBER OF STUDENTS IN CHURCH-
RELATED SECONDARY SCHOOLS *

Baptist	4,713	Presbyterian	2,740
Christian Reformed	9,765	Protestant Episcopal	16,180
Friends	5,041	Roman Catholic	887,481
Jewish	7,597	Seventh Day Adventist	15,800
Lutheran	14,680	Other sectarian	10,442
Methodist	2,923		

* By denomination.

SOURCE: Senate Committee on Labor and Public Welfare, Subcommittee on Education, *Education Legislation 1963*, 88th Cong., 1st Sess. (Washington, 1963), III, 1638–1641.

system is by far the largest and most important, enrolling 90 per cent of all students in about 60 per cent of all nonpublic schools.[36] In each of four states—California, Illinois, New York and Pennsylvania—Catholic schools enroll over 200,000 students, and in New York alone, the number of pupils in such schools exceeds the entire school population of thirty-four states and the District of Columbia. Increases in enrollments, heavy enough in the public sector, are hitting Catholic schools even more heavily. Between 1950 and 1960, enrollments in elementary public schools, for example, rose by 42 per cent, that of elementary Catholic schools by 71 per cent. Beset by such growing pains and consequent financial stresses and as a matter of justice

[35] Senate Report No. 225, *Public School Assistance Act of 1961*, pp. 26–29.

[36] Department of Education, National Catholic Welfare Conference, "Catholic Schools U.S.A.: A Significant Element in the Educational Scene," *Education Legislation 1963*, III, 1656.

and morality, Catholic leadership has found it impossible to approve any proposed pattern of federal aid which would bar their privately-financed system from sharing "equitably" in tax-supported benefits.

As Catholic spokesmen see it, the moral and religious teachings of the Church provided in parochial schools offer students an increment of character education which is in addition to, and in no way detracts from, the basic academic subjects already in the curriculum and meeting state standards for accreditation.

With respect to the constitutional issue of federal aid to parochial schools, those who favor it make frequent reference to language found in the major First Amendment cases decided by the United States Supreme Court:

A. *Pierce* v. *Society of Sisters* (1925). The fundamental theory of liberty upon which all governments in this Union repose excludes any general power of the state to standardize its children by forcing them to accept instruction from public teachers only. . . .

B. *Cochran* v. *Board of Education* (1930). (Upholding a state law providing free textbooks for children whether attending public or parochial schools.) The schools, however, are not the beneficiaries of these appropriations. . . . The school children and the states alone are the beneficiaries.

C. *Everson* v. *Board of Education* (1947). (Upholding transportation aid.) The "wall of separation between church and state" does not prohibit the state from adopting a general "program to help parents get their children, regardless of their religion, safely and expeditiously, to and from accredited schools."

D. *Zorach* v. *Clauson* (1952). (Upheld the "released time program.") We are a religious people whose institutions presuppose a Supreme Being. . . . When the state encourages religious instruction or cooperates with religious authorities by adjusting the schedule of public events to sectarian needs, it follows the best of our traditions.

A brief drawn up by the Legal Department of the National Catholic Welfare Conference on "The Constitutionality of the Inclusion of Church Related Schools in Federal Aid to Education," concluded that:

A. Education in church-related schools is a public function which, by its nature, is deserving of governmental support.

B. There exists no constitutional bar to aid to education in church-related schools in a degree proportionate to the value of the public function it performs. Such aid to the secular function may take the form of matching grants or long-term loans to institutions, or of scholarships, tuition payments, or tax benefits.

C. The parent and child have a constitutional right to choose a church-related educational institution meeting reasonable state requirements as the institution in which the child's education shall be acquired.

D. Government in the United States is without power to impose upon the people a single educational system in which all must participate.

E. Massive spending solely for public schools would in time result in a critical weakening of church-related schools, presaging the ultimate closing of many of them.[37]

[37] Legal Department, National Catholic Welfare Conference, "The Constitutionality of the Inclusion of Church-Related Schools in Federal Aid to Education," *ibid.*, III, 1764–1765.

Traditionally opposed to any form of federal aid for parochial schools were the powerful National Education Association, the National Congress of Parents and Teachers, and such groups as the National Council of the Churches of Christ, the six major Baptist conventions, and the American Jewish Committee. Their "public aid to public schools only" position is predicated on the conviction that (1) such aid would contravene the "genius" and spirit of the American principle of separation of church and state, (2) it would violate the United States Constitution, and (3) it would inaugurate a public policy both unwise and dangerous to the welfare of the nation.

(1) Most frequently cited in support of the separation principle are the Founding Fathers themselves:

> I contemplate with sovereign reverence that act of the whole American people which declared that their legislature should "make no law respecting an establishment of religion, or prohibiting the free exercise thereof," thus building a wall of separation between church and state.
>
> Thomas Jefferson, *Letter to the*
> *Danbury Baptist Association*, 1802.

> It is proper to take alarm at the first experiment on our liberties. . . . Who does not see that the same authority which can establish Christianity, in exclusion of all other religions, may establish with the same ease any particular sect of Christians, in exclusion of all other sects? That the same authority which can force a citizen to contribute three pence only of his property for the support of one establishment, may force him to conform to any other establishment in all cases whatsoever?
>
> James Madison, *Memorial and*
> *Remonstrance Against Religious*
> *Assessments*, 1785.

Such also were the principles which some years later guided those leading the battle for free public schools and textbooks. To give further legal support to this idea, every state admitted into the Union after 1876 was required to incorporate into its constitution the concept of a public school system that was to remain free from sectarian control.

> If a man is taxed to support a school where religious doctrines are inculcated which he believes to be false, and which he believes that God condemns, then he is excluded from the school by the divine law, at the same time that he is compelled to support it by the human law. This is a double wrong.
>
> Horace Mann, *Final Report to the*
> *Massachusetts State Board of*
> *Education*, 1848.

(2) As to the unconstitutionality of such aid, opponents stress the *McCollum* decision and restrictive language contained in the opinions of the *Everson* and *Zorach* cases:

Both religion and government can best work to achieve their lofty aims if each is left free from the other within its respective sphere.

> *McCollum* v. *Board of Education*, 1948.
>
> (In this case the Supreme Court struck down a church sponsored released-time program in religious instruction carried out on school property.)

No tax in any amount, large or small can be levied to support any religious activities or institutions, whatever they may be called, or whatever form they may adopt to teach or practice religion. Neither a state nor the Federal Government can, openly or secretly, participate in the affairs of any religious organization or groups and vice versa. . . .

> *Everson* v. *Board of Education*, 1947.
>
> (Here, however, the Supreme Court did uphold the right of the state to supply free school bus service to students attending parochial schools.)

Government may not finance religious groups nor undertake religious instruction nor blend the secular and sectarian education nor use secular institutions to force one or some religion on any person.

> *Zorach* v. *Clauson*, 1952.
>
> (This released-time program was sustained since it did not involve the use of public school facilities for religious instruction.)

While *Everson* and *Cochran* (and even *Zorach*), in the opinion of some, may have smoothed the constitutional paths for further accommodations, opponents are able to find sufficient grounds to construe these cases narrowly and as in no way authorizing public aid to parochial schools. It is contended that

A. The aid went directly to the child or to the parent. No public funds went to the parochial schools directly or indirectly. *No religious organization or school acquired new property because of state action.* . . .
B. None of the books or the process of transportation could be *adapted or used for the teaching of religion.*
C. *The state kept complete control of the administration of all state funds.* In *Cochran,* the state chose the books and lent them to the children, making no special arrangements for those books used by children attending parochial schools. In *Everson,* the local public authority made the rules and contracts for transportation and the children rode on "regular buses operated by the public transportation system." It is a different matter entirely to suggest that the Court would allow public funds to be turned over to the church schools to buy books or buses.[38]

[38] George R. LaNoue, *Public Funds for Parochial Schools* (New York, 1963) pp. 20–21; see also his *A Review of Church-State Legal Developments 1961–62* (New York, 1962).

(3) A resolution passed in 1961 by the National Council of the Churches of Christ illustrates some of the policy reasons advanced by those who object to all public aid to parochial schools by federal, state, or local government and irrespective of whether such aid takes the form of loans, grants, tuition, scholarships, tax credits, tax forgiveness, or school tax exemptions.

> Thus, while supporting as Americans the public system of elementary and secondary schools with a host of our fellow citizens, as Christians we stand for the right of all parents, all citizens, and all churches to establish and maintain non-public schools whose ethos and curriculum differ from that of the community as a whole. . . .
>
> We do not, however, ask for public funds for elementary or secondary education under church control. If private schools were to be supported in the United States by tax funds, the practical effect would be that the American people would lose their actual control of the use of the taxes paid by all the people for purposes common to the whole society. We therefore do not consider it just or lawful that public funds should be assigned to support the elementary or secondary schools of any church. The assignment of such funds could easily lead additional religious or other groups to undertake full scale parochial or private education with reliance of public tax support. This further fragmentation of general education in the United States would destroy the public school system or at least weaken it so gravely that it could not possibly adequately meet the educational needs of all the children of our growing society.[39]

SOME OTHER CRITICAL ISSUES FACING AMERICAN PUBLIC EDUCATION IN THE SIXTIES

FREEDOM AND CENTRALIZATION IN HIGHER EDUCATION

Strong concern has been expressed by leaders in American higher education concerning the growing tendency of state governments to exert restrictive administrative supervision and control over state university or college budgeting, personnel policies, purchasing practices, and building programs. While this is done in the name of greater managerial efficiency and economy, all too often it leads to the kind of interference with university affairs that contributes to stifling an institution's educational independence and growth.

Dependence on public support unavoidably brings a state university close to the legislature and governor. As enrollments expand and costs increase, the institution's need for a politically friendly climate is enhanced even further. This makes it more important than ever for legislatures to restrain themselves from using their powers over appropriations to affect the content of the curriculum, the direction of research, or the composition of the faculty. More than ever, governors should guard themselves against pressuring regents or permitting partisan influences to dictate university policies,

[39] Cited in *Education Legislation, 1963,* VII, 3880.

and state budget officers should be kept from using their fiscal controls to determine details of internal university management.

A group of prominent educators who recently completed a careful study of present trends in the relationships between government and the universities concluded that the freedom and independence of public institutions of higher learning is best preserved if the responsibility and authority for the management of such institutions is placed "in the hands of an able, independent lay board of trustees, who themselves are held accountable to the people of the state for wise and effective action." [40]

SCHOOL DROPOUTS AND THE LABOR MARKET

Overly-limited educational attainments of millions of American youths and adults represent one of the most serious social and economic problems of the 1960's. Despite the enormous scientific and technological progress projected for this decade, significant unemployment of unskilled and semi-skilled workers promises to be a persistent depressant and retarding influence in the nation's economic future. Still further aggravating this picture, of course, is the wider and more intensive use of automation and mechanization. Manpower estimates for the Sixties anticipate a 22 per cent reduction in the demand for farmers, farm managers, laborers, and foremen and no increases whatever in the job opportunities for most unskilled and semi-skilled workers. Professional, technical, and skilled personnel on the other hand will likely register the most substantial employment advances of any of the major occupational groups.

What is all the more shocking against the background of an economy that eagerly absorbs the more highly-trained and clerically proficient, but casts out the unskilled, are statistics which continue to reflect a high rate of school dropouts and low levels of schooling for large segments of the nation's youth and potential job seekers.

It is estimated that during the decade of 1960 to 1970,

A. There will be 7.5 million young people entering the labor market without a high school diploma.
B. Almost 75 per cent of all new workers will have twelve years or less of schooling.
C. Twenty-six million teen-agers, an increase of 40 per cent over the 1950's, will look for jobs.
D. During only one school year alone (1962), between 600,000 and 800,000 teen-agers were out of school looking for employment.
E. Twenty million youths will require vocational education by 1965 before they can be employed.[41]

[40] The Committee on Government and Higher Education, *The Efficiency of Freedom* (Baltimore, 1959), p. 44.
[41] U. S. Department of Labor, Division of Manpower Requirements and Reserves, *Manpower Research Bulletin No. 3, 1963* and the testimony of Anthony J. Celebrezze, Secretary of Health, Education, and Welfare, in *Education Legislation, 1963*, I, 220.

These data represent a threat of economic and social waste of staggering proportions. The millions of young people, who want a job but can neither find nor keep one, represent an indefensible loss in self-respect and demoralization. There are now over twenty million adults with an eighth grade education or less. An additional undereducated labor force, unless quickly returned to further schooling or vocational training, cannot help but compound and multiply all the problems of hard-core poverty which have so far stubbornly defied solution.

PRAYER AND RELIGIOUS EXERCISES
IN THE PUBLIC SCHOOLS

In order to reinforce the moral and spiritual training of its school children, a New York school board adopted a nondenominational prayer composed by the New York State Board of Regents for just such a purpose. To be said aloud by each class in the presence of a teacher at the beginning of each school day was this prayer:

> Almighty God, we acknowledge our dependence upon Thee, and we beg Thy blessings upon us, our parents, our teachers and our country.

In a six-to-one decision (two of the justices did not participate in the deliberations), the United States Supreme Court in *Engel* v. *Vitale* (1962) ruled that this prayer written by a governmental agency was "wholly inconsistent" with the Establishment Clause, that it constituted a "religious activity" and that it clearly breached the wall of separation of church and state in violation of the First Amendment made applicable to the states by the Fourteenth Amendment. Reactions to this decision found the churches divided. Generally speaking, the Protestant groups represented in the National Council of Churches favored it, as did most of the Jewish spiritual leadership. Most critical were spokesmen for Roman Catholicism and those of Protestant churches which were inclined to be fundamentalists.

Some segments of the clergy reacted quite vehemently and denounced the decision as an attempt by the Supreme Court to take God out of the schools and put a materialistic creed in its place. Most bitter were the reactions of leading Southern senators and representatives in Congress. Here is what Representative L. Mendel Rivers of South Carolina had to say:

> What is wrong with this prayer? Only a court composed of agnostics could find its defects . . . the Court has now officially stated its disbelief in God Almighty. This, to me, represents the most serious blow that has ever been struck at the Constitution of the United States. I know of nothing in my lifetime that could give more aid and comfort to Moscow than this bold, malicious, atheistic and sacrilegious twist of this unpredictable group of uncontrolled despots. . . .[42]

[42] *Congressional Record*, June 26, 1962, p. 10897.

Despite similar speeches criticizing the Supreme Court, and although a number of resolutions—including one by Congressman Becker of New York —were actually introduced to amend the Constitution which would permit prayer in public schools, and although hearings have been held to date on a number of them, no national legislation is considered likely. Undaunted by the voices of protest, the following year the Supreme Court further extended and elaborated its position in two cases that touched on closely related questions; one case came from Pennsylvania (*Abington School District* v. *Schempp*) and the other from Maryland (*Murray* v. *Curlett*). In a eight-to-one vote, it ruled that neither states, nor local governments, nor school boards could force their public schools to require the recitation by their pupils of the Lord's Prayer or Bible verses.

While in no way opposing the study of the Bible or of religion "when presented objectively as part of a secular program of education," the Court insisted again that the practices of prayer here challenged "were religious exercises required by the states in violation of the First Amendment."

Before the United States Supreme Court came to act on these issues, the extent to which formal religious activities were sanctioned or practiced in public schools varied widely among the states. Bible reading and prayer were upheld by state courts in ten states and struck down in seven.[43] A pre-*Engel* survey showed twelve states required Bible reading by law; specific judicial decisions or statute had made it "permissive" in thirteen states; in another group of thirteen states, it had become so "under general terms of the law or by reason of silence." In only eleven states were there clear cut constitutional or statutory provisions against it. All in all, over two-thirds of the states with or without explicit legal sanction permitted Bible reading along with a host of other religious practices—baccalaureate services, Christmas observances, non-denominational weekly chapel services, or the distribution of Gideon Bibles or religious literature.[44]

What this survey also revealed were notable differences between regions. For example, to the question, "Is Bible reading conducted in the schools of your system?" of the respondents in the East, 68 per cent replied "Yes" compared to a mere 11 per cent for the Western states (see Figure 1).

In view of such strong commitment to infuse formal religious activities into the public schools of a relatively large number of states, it becomes most difficult to predict the extent to which an early compliance with the Supreme Court decisions may be expected. Based on findings during the summer of 1963, a few states insisted on ignoring or defying the court. The Alabama Board of Education continued to make Bible reading a part of the required curriculum. Kentucky took a similar position and South Carolina's Superintendent of Education was quoted as informing teachers that they "could feel free" to continue classroom exercises.[45]

---

[43] *Engel* v. *Vitale*, 191 N. Y. S. 2d 453 (1959), at 488.
[44] R. B. Dierenfield, *Religion in American Public Schools* (Washington, 1962), p. 21.
[45] "Schools Ignoring Court on Prayer," *The New York Times*, August 7, 1963, p. 35.

FIGURE 1

Is Bible reading conducted in the schools of your system?

By sections of the country

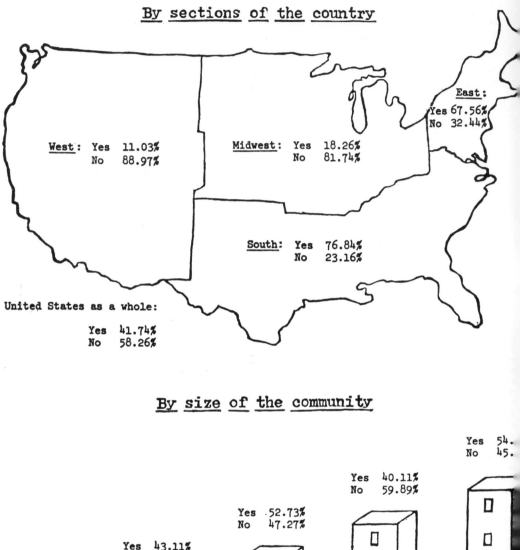

West: Yes 11.03%
No 88.97%

Midwest: Yes 18.26%
No 81.74%

East:
Yes 67.56%
No 32.44%

South: Yes 76.84%
No 23.16%

United States as a whole:
Yes 41.74%
No 58.26%

By size of the community

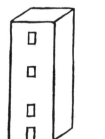
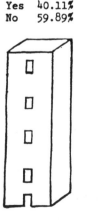
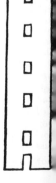

Yes 30.84%
No 69.16%

Yes 43.11%
No 56.89%

Yes .52.73%
No 47.27%

Yes 40.11%
No 59.89%

Yes 54.
No 45.

500-2500   2500-5000   5000-25,000   25,000-100,000   Over 100

SOURCE: Richard H. Dierenfield, *Religion in American Public Schools* (Washington, 1962), p. 51.

DESEGREGATION, 1954–1964, A PROGRESS REPORT

Ten years after the Supreme Court of the United States had ruled that segregated schools cannot be considered equal under the standards of the Fourteenth Amendment, only 1.18 per cent, or 34,110 of the South's 2,894,563 Negro students attended primary and secondary schools with white students in the eleven states of the Confederacy. Based on surveys conducted by the highly responsible Southern Education Reporting Service, there was not a single integrated school district in Mississippi, only one such district in South Carolina, two in Louisiana, and four each in Georgia and Alabama. Of the remaining Southern states, Texas made the best record. (See Table 3.)

The border states and the District of Columbia, as was expected, integrated their schools at a much faster rate. With the exception of Washington, D. C. (where nearly all schools are integrated) and of Oklahoma (where only one-fifth of the Negroes were in mixed schools), about half of all Negro students in Delaware, Kentucky, Maryland, Missouri, and West Virginia attended biracial schools in 1963–1964. Thus, in the seventeen Southern and

TABLE 3. PUBLIC SCHOOL DESEGREGATION

	School districts			Enrollment		In desegregated districts		Negroes in schools with whites	
	Total	With Negroes & whites	Deseg.	White	Negro	White	Negro	No.	% †
bama	114	114	4	539,996 **	287,414 *	106,199 **	70,896 **	21	.007
ansas	415	228	13	328,023 **	112,012 **	66,752	18,643	366	.327
rida	67	67	16	964,241	237,871 *	669,375	130,667	3,650	1.53
rgia	197	181	4	689,323	337,534	95,731	77,599	177	.052
isiana	67	67	2	460,589	301,433 **	68,700	79,077	1,814	.602
sissippi	150	150	0	304,226 **	291,971 **	0	0	0	0
th Carolina	171	171	40	820,900 *	347,063 *	367,764 *	133,164 *	1,865	.537
th Carolina	108	108	1	368,496 *	258,955 *	3,108	9,539	10	.004
nessee	154	143	45	687,902	164,940 *	380,321	120,447	4,486	2.72
as	1,421	899	263	2,045,499	326,409 *	1,300,000 *	200,000 *	18,000 *	5.52
inia	130	128	55	710,176	228,961	486,231	145,658	3,721	1.63
TH	2,994	2,256	443	7,919,371	2,894,563	3,544,181	985,690	34,110	1.18
aware	86	86	86	78,730	18,066	68,321	13,976	10,209	56.5
rict of Columbia	1	1	1	19,803	117,915	19,803	117,915	98,813	83.8
tucky	204	165	163	611,126 *	54,874 *	492,701 *	54,874 *	29,855	54.4
ryland	24	23	23	540,667	160,946	535,691	160,946	76,906	47.8
souri	1,597	212 *	203 *	793,000 *	95,000 *	NA	90,000 *	40,000 *	42.1
ahoma	1,160	241	197	541,125 *	43,875 *	324,023 *	35,596 *	12,289 *	28.0
t Virginia	55	44	44	417,595 *	23,449 *	417,595 *	23,449 *	13,659 *	58.2
DER	3,127	772	717	3,002,046	514,125	1,858,134 ††	496,756	281,731	54.8
ION	6,121	3,028	1,160	10,921,417	3,408,688	5,402,315 ††	1,482,446	315,841	9.3

stimated.
962–63.
o. of Negroes in schools with whites, compared to total Negro enrollment.
issouri not included.
RCE: *Southern School News*, May, 1964, p. 1A.

border states, 9.3 per cent of the area's 3,408,688 Negro students are now enrolled in desegregated schools.

At the level of higher education, Arkansas, North Carolina, and Tennessee "have opened all their colleges and universities to both races in practice or in policy." For the South as a whole, a little more than one-half of the 212 colleges and universities have so far been desegregated while in the border states, Negroes are no longer barred from any of the public institutions of higher learning.[46]

Negro impatience with the slowness of integration, especially in primary and secondary schools, is not difficult to understand. It seemed as if non-compliance with the edict of the Supreme Court has been the rule rather than the exception throughout most of the South. While the obstructionist tactics of Governors Faubus, Barnett, and Wallace, and the closing of all public schools in Prince Edward County, Virginia, made headlines, some of the more subtle tactics were found to have proved actually much more effective. Without ever mentioning the word "race," pupil placement and restrictive transfer laws in the hands of reluctant boards were often so administered as to make tokenism, the admission of a few carefully selected Negroes, the legally sanctioned equivalent to integration.

Designed to avoid trouble and maintain law and order, this was the strategy of gradualism. But to a Negro community eager for America to make payment now on its "promissory note for equal citizenship regardless of color," it meant continuing frustration and anger. It was a travesty of justice. One of the most articulate and prominent Negroes in the United States chose these words with which to underscore his indignation:

> [O]f course everybody's against trouble! But does any American know of any great social advance in the history of mankind that was not accompanied by "trouble"? When we Americans reach the point of soft indifference where we hate trouble more than injustice, we shall have reached the dawning of our era of greatest troubles.[47]

The battle against segregation is by no means confined to the South exclusively. Socio-economic factors and discriminatory housing practices have long reinforced the kind of de facto segregation and black ghettos which continue to plague quite a few Northern metropolitan areas. Negro leaders charge that instead of adopting positive measures to correct this situation, municipalities, school authorities, or neighborhoods prefer the use of obstructionist devices in order to block school biracialism. Included on the offending roster are such large cities as New York, Cleveland, Chicago, and Philadelphia, as well as such smaller cities as Englewood, New Jersey, New Haven, Connecticut, Freeport, Long Island, Malverne, Long Island, and New Rochelle, New York. In these and other communities, Negro parents wishing to have their

[46] *Southern School News*, December, 1963, pp. 1, 16.
[47] Carl T. Rowan, "The Travesty of Integration," *Saturday Evening Post*, January 19, 1963, p. 8.

children attend racially-balanced schools found themselves outmancuvcred by:

A. Gerrymandering of school zone lines.
B. Transfer policies and practices.
C. Discriminatory feeder pattern of elementary to secondary schools.
D. Overcrowding of predominantly Negro schools and underutilization of schools attended by whites.
E. Selection of building sites to create or perpetuate segregation.
F. Discrimination in vocational and distributive education and in the employment and assignment of Negro teachers.[48]

Beginning in 1962, the N.A.A.C.P. and other civil rights groups launched a major effort to bring about a better racial balance to the Northern schools. The campaign centered on eighty-one school systems in seventeen states and included mass protests, picketing, demonstrations, boycotts, and litigation.[49]

Involved in a number of these communities was one of the most difficult issues of all. How far can or should a state or its local subdivisions go in transporting children to schools located out of their own neighborhood for the primary purpose of achieving a more equitable classroom distribution between the races? In New York, when, for example, the state commissioner of education attempted to force a school district to correct a serious imbalance which he labeled "a deprivation of equality for educational opportunity," a state court enjoined his action on the basis that the corrective measures themselves constituted discriminatory practices.[50] Subsequent court decisions appeared, however, to sustain his action.

THE STEEPLY RISING COSTS OF EDUCATION

Expenditures for primary and secondary education almost tripled during the last decade. There is nothing to indicate that the trend will be reversed in the immediate future. With competition for professional manpower becoming keener, teachers are bound to intensify their demands for higher salaries (average was about $6,000 in 1963–1964), and approximately two-thirds of every school dollar expended goes towards paying teachers. Other costs too promise to rise—administrative, maintenance, and construction. Nor is this all. Library resources are notably inadequate. About 10,600,000 students, estimates the American Library Association,[51] are without regular school

[48] United States Commission on Civil Rights, *Civil Rights U.S.A.: Public Schools in the North and West 1962* (Washington, 1962), pp. 1–2; note also the following: United States Commission on Civil Rights, *Civil Rights U.S.A.: Public Schools, Southern States 1962* (Washington, 1962); Hubert H. Humphrey (ed.), *School Desegregation: Documents and Commentaries* (New York, 1964); and Jim Leeson (ed.), *A Statistical Summary, State By State, of School Segregation-Desegregation in the Southern and Border Area from 1954 to the Present* (Nashville, 1963–1964).

[49] *The New York Times,* January, 16, 1964, p. 82.

[50] *Ibid.,* January 16, 1964, p. 82.

[51] Fred M. Hechinger, "No Place To Read," *The New York Times,* April 21, 1963, p. E7.

libraries, and 47,000 schools have "no qualified school library as such." [52] Also, far too many laboratories are still woefully unequal to the minimum needs of updated courses in modern science. Most of all, however, curricula need to be improved, instructional standards upgraded, and counseling services significantly expanded before quality education can begin to meet the demands of all students—the talented, the average, and the below average. Thus education will not come cheaply in a world of exploding knowledge and rigorous requirements for skilled competence.

In 1963–1964, school expenditures for current operations and capital outlays of all fifty states came to about $20 billion. Of this amount approximately 56 per cent was raised by local units, 40 per cent by state governments, and 4 per cent came from Washington in the form of federal aids.[53] With 96 per cent of all primary and secondary school revenues derived from state and local sources, annual educational expenditures mirror wide sectional variations in fiscal capacity. (See Figure 2.) For example, New York, Alaska, New Jersey, Illinois, Connecticut, California, Wyoming, Oregon, and Delaware, the highest among the states, were able to spend more than $500 per pupil in average daily attendance, whereas Alabama, South Carolina, and Mississippi, at the other end of the continuum, could only afford about $250 (the average for the twelve Southeastern states was about a third below that for the nation as a whole). At that, Alabama and Mississippi, fully aware of their educationally disadvantaged position, had already boosted local and state financial efforts by 125 per cent during the past decade. However, with a per capita income half that of the top group, the prospects for most of the Southern states (except Florida and Texas) bridging the spending gap in the foreseeable future obviously do not appear very bright.

In terms of accelerating economic, social, and educational progress, it is all the more tragic, for this is the one region which pays the lowest instructional salaries, which has the highest student dropout rate, and which contributes the largest number of the functionally illiterate, i.e., adults twenty-five years and over with less than five years of schooling.[54] In the Appalachian soft coal mining area, now a belt of poverty and unemployment that reaches from Maryland to Alabama, there are rural counties in which as many as 60 per cent of the boys fail to complete the eighth grade.[55]

How to increase the flow of revenue for public education in the years ahead constitutes a gigantic challenge to all regions and all fifty states. Property taxes which now finance over one-half of all primary and secondary schools have already been used excessively. How much more can be added to

[52] *Education Legislation 1963*, II, 1124.

[53] *NEA Research Bulletin*, February, 1964, p. 4.

[54] U. S. Department of Health, Education, and Welfare, Division of Educational Statistics, Bureau of Educational Research and Development, *Digest of Educational Statistics* (Washington, 1963), pp. 27, 96–98.

[55] Homer Bigart, "Education to Aid Depression Area," *The New York Times*, November 20, 1963, p. 34.

FIGURE 2

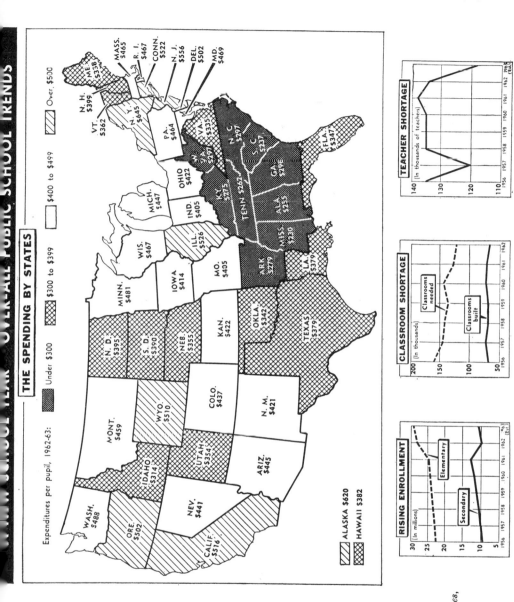

THE SPENDING BY STATES

Expenditures per pupil, 1962-63:

Under $300 $300 to $399 $400 to $499   Over $500

TEACHER SHORTAGE
(In thousands of teachers)

CLASSROOM SHORTAGE
(In thousands)
Classrooms needed
Classrooms built

RISING ENROLLMENT
(In millions)
Elementary
Secondary

SOURCE: *The New York Times*, September 1, 1963, p. E 7.

them is a matter of heated controversy among the experts. The search for alternate tax sources is becoming more frantic. In 1958, sales and excise taxes already furnished about 25 per cent and income taxes 8 per cent of all school funds collected.[56] Still other sources are tapped every year. To illustrate a few: New Hampshire, in furthering the cause of education, decided to enact a lottery law; Philadelphia imposed a 2 per cent tax on pari mutuel betting at its harness race track at the Liberty Bell; and Baltimore places a 1 per cent tax on certain real estate transactions.[57]

Bonded indebtedness continues to rise also as voters approve approximately 70 per cent of the school bond referenda submitted to them annually. State and local government debt nearly doubled over the last eight years (see Table 4).

As capital outlays for new buildings and facilities continue at the rate of $2 to $3 billion annually, debt service payments become more burdensome. During the last ten years, interest payments on such debts multiplied nearly five times.

TABLE 4. PER CAPITA PUBLIC DEBT

Year	State	Local	Federal
1946	$ 18	$102	$2,034
1954	61	185	1,713
1962	118	325	1,630

SOURCE: Tax Foundation, Inc., *Facts and Figures on Government Finance, 1962–1963*, 12th ed. (Englewood Cliffs, 1963), p. 26.

As more and more communities are faced with heavy property tax rates, or as they reach state or charter-imposed borrowing limits, they turn to their state legislatures for additional aid. On a national average such aid since 1930 has risen from 17 per cent to 40 per cent, although here too, state practices vary considerably.[58] States that pay 60 per cent or more of the local school bill include Alabama, Delaware, Georgia, Louisiana, North Carolina, South Carolina, and Washington. At the other extreme, paying 10 per cent or less, are Nebraska, New Hampshire, and South Dakota. Most of the remaining states fall into the 20 per cent to 50 per cent category.[59]

State aid to education takes many forms. Three patterns at least can be distinguished. (1) A flat sum given local districts on a per pupil in average daily attendance basis; (2) equalization payments in which an effort is made to balance the varying fiscal capacities of different school districts; (3)

---

[56] Table 63: "Sources of Public School Revenue in 1958," in *Public School Assistance Act of 1961*, Pt. 1, p. 662.

[57] Roger B. May, "Rising Education Costs Touch Off Tax Boosts for Property Owners," *The Wall Street Journal*, January 15, 1964, p. 1.

[58] Table 59: "School Revenue and State Support in Selected Years 1890 to 1950," in *Public School Assistance Act of 1961*, Pt. 1, p. 659.

[59] *Book of the States, 1962–1963*, p. 315.

matching grants which support programs benefitting particular groups of children such as aids to emotionally-disturbed children, children from under-privileged homes, or children in need of remedial reading.

Pressure for state aid cannot always be traced to either the unwilling-ness or the fiscal inability of local governments to absorb rising educational costs. In many states, constitutions and statutes impose arbitrary and rigid debt or tax limitations which cannot be changed through local action. Then, too, there is the tendency in a number of states to exempt significant cate-gories of property from property taxation altogether or to ignore wide diver-gences in local tax assessment policies and procedures. Until such obstacles to effective local and state revenue raising efforts are removed, tax equity cannot be attained, and the needed funds for educational improvements are not likely to be produced. Perhaps even with such reforms some of the states, because of their inadequate per capita income and economic development, will simply not be able to afford the type of education that the 1960's and 1970's call for. This at any rate was one of the central contentions of those who argued for federal aid to primary and secondary schools.

Whatever the impact of the newly provided federal aids, one thing is clear. Education must be viewed as a major economic investment in the fu-ture, aside from the cultural and esthetic values that inhere in it. In view of this country's high population mobility, it is a fact, for example, that no state can any longer consider itself educationally an island unto itself.

> Nearly one-third of the American people live in a State other than the one in which they were born. According to the 1960 census southern Negroes, too often victims of poor school systems, leave the South at an average rate of 12,000 a month. The poorly educated child of today in one State becomes the unemployed worker of tomorrow in another State.[60]

CASE PROBLEMS FOR CLASS DISCUSSION

1. You have just been appointed by the president of the state university to assist in presenting the budgetary needs of the university to the appropriate com-mittees of the state legislature. Your role is that of an assistant lobbyist and you have a few weeks to prepare yourself for this new responsibility. Where would you begin? What type of reports would you have to study? With whom would you wish to consult?

2. You have been asked to structure a one-day workshop centering around the problems created by the newly enacted Elementary and Secondary Educa-tion Act of 1965 in the area of church-state relations. How would you divide the subject; how would you staff your panels; if you were to prepare some questions for each speaker to guide him in the preparation of his remarks, what would they have to include to assure the best coverage of the subject?

3. Assume that you are a member of the legislature representing a community of 20,000 which is eager to obtain a new junior college. It is your responsibility to persuade your fellow legislators, a state junior college board, and the governor of the wisdom of establishing the college in your city. What data would you

[60] Andrew J. Biemiller, Legislative Director, AFL-CIO, in *Education Legislation 1963*, III, 1405.

need, what type of arguments would you use, and from where might come some of the major objections?

4. You have just been elected to the local school board in a city of 100,000. A local school bond campaign is in the offing in order to provide funds for a new senior high school. School board members are invited to defend the need of this new school before civic and neighborhood groups. You have very little time to acquaint yourself with background information and, although you are a member of the local bar, your knowledge of the schools is quite limited. What sort of questions must you anticipate, where would you go for answers, and what kinds of data would you need to have with you?

SELECTED BIBLIOGRAPHY

HERMAN R. ALLEN, *Open Door to Learning: The Land-Grant System Enters Its Second Century* (Urbana, 1963).

HOMER D. BABBIDGE, JR. and ROBERT M. ROSENZWEIG, *The Federal Interest in Higher Education* (New York, 1962).

STEPHEN K. BAILEY, ROBERT C. WOOD, RICHARD T. FROST, and PAUL E. MARSH, *Schoolmen and Politics: A Study of State Aid to Education in the Northeast* (Syracuse, 1962).

WARNER BLOOMBERG, JR., and MORRIS SUNSHINE, *Suburban Power Structures and Public Education: A Study of Values, Influence, and Tax Effort* (Syracuse, 1963).

DONALD E. BOLES, *The Bible, Religion, and the Public Schools* (Ames, Iowa, 1961).

WILLIAM W. BOYER, "Sectarian Teachers in Wisconsin Public Schools: A Study in Administrative Decision-Making," *Religious Education*, May–June, 1962, pp. 195–202.

WILLIAM W. BRICKMAN and STANLEY LEHRER (eds.), *Religion, Government and Education* (New York, 1961).

JESSE BURKHEAD, *State and Local Taxes for Public Education* (Syracuse, 1963).

JAMES B. CONANT, *Slums and Suburbs: A Commentary on Schools in Metropolitan Areas* (New York, 1961).

WERNER Z. HIRSCH, "Determinants of Public Education Expenditures," *National Tax Journal*, March, 1960, pp. 29–40.

H. THOMAS JAMES, "School Aid Apportionment: State Action Needed on the Property Tax," *State Government*, Autumn, 1960, pp. 256–262.

BOYD R. KEENAN, "The Midwest's CIC: Experiment in Regional Cooperation," *Public Administration Review*, March, 1963, pp. 40–44.

DOUGLAS M. KNIGHT, CHARLES A. QUATTLEBAUM, JAMES MCCORMICK, VINCENT A. FULMER, JOHN A. PERKINS, and

DANIEL W. WOOD, *The Federal Government and Higher Education* (Englewood Cliffs, N. J., 1960).

I. M. LABOVITZ, *Aid for Federally Affected Public Schools* (Syracuse, 1963).

J. KENNETH LITTLE, "Higher Education and the Federal Government," *Higher Education*, October, 1963, pp. 3–6, 21–23.

JOSEPH O. MCCLINTIC, "California's Ability to Finance Higher Education," *National Tax Journal*, June, 1962, pp. 170–183.

ROSCOE C. MARTIN, *Government and the Suburban School* (Syracuse, 1962).

LOUIS S. MEYER, *Federal Aid to Education: Its Impact on Arizona* (Tempe, 1962).

JERRY MINER, *Social and Economic Factors in Spending for Public Education* (Syracuse, 1963).

EDGAR L. MORPHET and JOHN G. ROSS, *Local Responsibility for Education in Small School Districts* (Berkeley, 1961).

FRANK J. MUNGER and RICHARD F. FENNO, JR., *National Politics and Federal Aid to Education* (Syracuse, 1962).

BENJAMIN MUSE, *Virginia's Massive Resistance* (Bloomington, 1961).

HAROLD ORLANS, *The Effects of Federal Programs on Higher Education* (Washington, 1962).

THEODORE POWELL, *The School Bus Law: A Case Study in Education, Religion, and Politics* (Middletown, Conn., 1960).

CHARLES E. RATLIFF, JR., "Centralization, Ability, and Effort in School Finance," *National Tax Journal*, March, 1960, pp. 41–44.

H. CLYDE REEVES, "Higher Education and State Tax Policy," *National Tax Journal*, September, 1962, pp. 291–296.

THEODORE L. RELLER, *Problems of Public Education in the San Francisco Bay Area* (Berkeley, 1963).

ALICE M. RIVLIN, *The Role of the Federal Government in Financing Higher Education* (Washington, 1961).

SIDNEY C. SUFRIN, *Administering the N.D.E.A.* (Syracuse, 1963).

SIDNEY C. SUFRIN, *Issues in Federal Aid to Education* (Syracuse, 1962).

ROGER C. VAN TASSEL, "Conditional Grants-in-Aid for School Construction in Massachusetts," *National Tax Journal*, September, 1960, pp. 219–231.

FORREST P. WHITE, "Tuition Grants: Strange Fruit of Southern School Integration," *South Atlantic Quarterly,* Spring, 1961, pp. 226–229.

PHYLLIS R WIENER, "Doorbell Ringing for a State Education Measure," *Western Political Quarterly,* June, 1962, pp. 345–352.

YORK WILLBERN, "Municipal Government, and the Schools," *Public Management,* May, 1963, pp. 107–109.

✔ *Chapter XIV*

PUBLIC TRANSPOR-
TATION AND
CONSERVATION

Are cities irrevocably destined to become cement labyrinths of superhighways, restricted access roads, and parking lots?

Who should manage this nation's natural resources—federal government, state government, private interests—and what should be the major policy objectives with respect to the disposition of water, forests, minerals, parks, and lands?

HIGHWAYS, STREETS, AND THE AUTOMOBILE—AN OVERVIEW

Among the most stubborn challenges facing state and local governments in the 1960's—next to the population explosion itself—is a closely-related problem, that of the fantastic volume of automobile and truck traffic that plagues most of the nation's major streets and highways.

A few statistics provided by the Automobile Manufacturers' Association will serve to illustrate the magnitude of the problem. Three-fourths of all families in the United States own an automobile. In households with incomes of $10,000 and over, the figure rises to 95 per cent. For many families, one car is clearly no longer sufficient. Between 1954 and 1964 multi-car ownership increased by 100 per cent to a point where now over one-fifth of all car-owning households drive two automobiles (see Table 1). There are now operating on this country's streets and highways sixty-nine million automobiles and thirteen million trucks and buses. Such totals represent a 50 per cent increase in registration over 1950.

Americans consider their cars indispensable for work, shopping, travel, and recreation. Nearly two-thirds of the 27 million workers who reside in the country's 190 largest metropolitan areas drive their automobiles to and from work either singly or in car pools. Cars are used heavily for short as well as for long-distance travel. Three-fifths of all trips involve distances of less than five miles; 92 per cent of all intercity travel is done by car, and millions use automobiles and buses for vacation outings or long journeys. During 1963, for example, 32,600,000 persons visited the national parks and 122,582,000 visited the national forests. Almost all the visitors came by car or bus.[1]

The highway system of the United States encompasses a network of surfaced and nonsurfaced roads totalling 3.6 million miles of which over 95 per cent are still under the control of state or local governments. Within this massive system, state governments are charged with direct administrative responsibilities for over 700,000 miles while local governments (with varying degrees of state assistance) are given primary control over the remaining 2.3

[1] Automobile Manufacters' Association, *Automobile Facts and Figures, 1964* (Detroit, 1965), pp. 18, 39, 41, 42, 46, 61.

472

million miles of the largely rural highways of which 70 per cent are now surfaced.[2]

Administrative authority over the 115,000 miles not incorporated in

TABLE 1. CAR OWNERSHIP HIGHEST IN SUBURBS AND IN WEST

Car ownership by income groups, city size, and regions

CITY SIZE	Per cent of households owning cars within each group	Distribution of households	INCOME	Per cent of households owning cars within each group	Distribution of households
Met. Area Centers:					
500,000 or over	59.1%	11.9%	Under $4,000	57.3%	19.1%
Under 500,000	80.7	16.1	$4,000–4,999	68.7	10.2
Met. Area Suburbs	87.8	34.3	$5,000–6,999	84.3	31.1
Outside Met. Area			$7,000–9,999	89.7	21.7
(Non-Farm)	76.8	30.3	$10,000 or more	95.2	17.9
All Farms	78.3	7.4			100.0%
		100.0%			
REGIONS					
Northeast	73.1%	24.2%			
North Central	82.2	30.0			
South	75.3	29.1			
West	84.1	16.7	U. S. Total	78.1%	100.0%

AUTOMOBILE OWNERSHIP WITHIN INCOME GROUPS, EARLY 1961–64

Percentage distribution of spending units

	OWNS								DOES NOT OWN			
	1 Automobile				2 or More							
	1961	1962	1963	1964	1961	1962	1963	1964	1961	1962	1963	1964
All spending units	60%	58%	59%	56%	14%	14%	18%	19%	26%	28%	23%	25%
Money income before taxes:*												
Under $1,000	16	17	22	28	1	1	2	2	83	82	76	70
$1,000–$1,999	35	34	41	32	2	2	1	3	63	64	58	65
$2,000–$2,999	53	51	53	59	3	3	6	6	44	46	41	35
$3,000–$3,999	64	66	58	58	6	6	10	8	30	28	32	34
$4,000–$4,999	73	68	67	62	7	7	15	10	20	25	18	28
$5,000–$5,999	75	67	74	66	15	11	12	19	10	22	14	15
$6,000–$7,499	69	71	72	71	19	20	18	17	12	9	10	12
$7,500–$9,999	67	69	65	63	23	23	30	31	10	8	5	6
$10,000 and over	51	54	49	51	42	42	47	45	7	4	4	4

* Money income for previous year.

NOTE: A "Spending Unit" consists of all persons living in the same dwelling and related by blood, marriage, or adoption, who pooled their income for major items of expenses. Some families contain two or more spending units.

SOURCE: Automobile Manufacturers' Association, *Automobile Facts and Figures, 1964* (Detroit, 1965), p. 42.

[2] U. S. Department of Commerce, *Statistical Abstract of the United States, 1963* (Washington, 1964), pp. 556–557.

either state or local networks is exercised by the federal Bureau of Public Roads. This includes the 41,000 mile national system of interstate and defense highways authorized by Congress in 1956 and scheduled for completion in 1972. The cost of the $37 billion project will be financed on a 90 to 10 or 95 to 5, federal-state matching basis. Under the Federal Aid Highway Act of 1958, states may be entitled to an additional one-half of 1 per cent of the federal share of the cost for building their portions of the interstate system if they enter into an agreement with the secretary of commerce regulating outdoor advertising on such highways.

"Highway Beautification," an enactment of federal legislation to improve the landscaping of United States highways through control of outdoor advertising and junkyards along federally-aid highways, was strongly urged by the Johnson administration and became the substance of a bill (S 2084) passed by the Senate on September 16, 1965.

Actually, federal financial assistance to highways began with the Federal Aid Highway Act of 1916, when Congress enacted a program of providing funds, subject to equal matching, which was designed to help the states with the construction of their major highways. Under laws enacted in 1944 and subsequent years, this aid was broadened to cover both primary and secondary roads as well as the urban extensions of the state highway network. Known as the ABC roads, the system includes today 830,000 miles, receives an annual federal subsidy of nearly $1 billion, and accommodates almost half of the nation's total traffic.[3]

The following discussion will indicate some of the effects that the automobile and highway have had and continue to have on the nation's economy and way of life.

The automobile and trucking industry—including the production, sale, servicing, and operation of vehicles—ranks as the largest and wealthiest in the United States. It represents a $69 billion share of the gross national product. It employs nearly 12 million persons, buys 22 per cent of the steel output, 61 per cent of the rubber, and 44 per cent of all the radios produced, absorbs between 15 per cent and 20 per cent of all the patents, and exports its products at a rate of $1.5 billion annually.[4] In 1962, states disbursed almost $8.1 billion for the construction and maintenance of highways and for interest and principal payments on highway bonds.[5] Washington's share came to almost $2.8 billion (see Figure 1). This share has been projected at almost $3.7 billion for fiscal 1965.[6]

Superhighways and supermarkets have radically changed consumer habits; they have helped suburbs to mushroom while bringing economic

---

[3] House Committee on Public Works, Subcommittee on Roads, Hearings, *Federal Highway Act of 1960*, March 1, 2, and 3, 1960, 86th Cong., 2nd Sess. (Washington, 1960), pp. 3, 69. See also Rex M. Whitton, "Profiles of the Future: The Interstate Highway System," *Business Horizons*, Winter, 1962, pp. 5–6.

[4] Philip H. Burch, Jr., *Highway Revenue and Expenditure Policy in the United States* (New Brunswick, 1962), p. 9 and *Automobile Facts and Figures, 1964*, pp. 12, 14, 30, 66.

[5] *Book of the States, 1964–1965*, p. 363.

[6] *Ibid.*, pp. 361, 365.

FIGURE 1

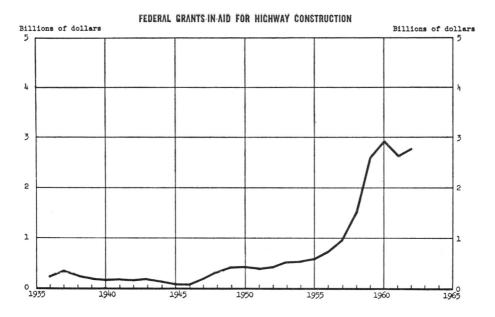

FEDERAL GRANTS-IN-AID FOR HIGHWAY CONSTRUCTION

SOURCE: Department of Health, Education, and Welfare, *Health, Education, and Welfare Trends* (Washington, 1963), p. 114.

stagnation to many small towns and small-town businesses. Freeways have reduced travel time and brought the farm closer to the city, and better education to outlying areas. Commerce and industry have found new and cheaper ways of transporting their commodities and of reaching new markets. Masses of people have become more mobile, more travel-conscious, and more enthusiastic for outdoor life and recreation.

And with all of these blessings have come new problems and new costs. Every year between 30,000 and 40,000 persons are killed and between three and four million injured in automobile-connected accidents.[7] Social pressures related to car ownership and operation have figured prominently in juvenile delinquency and family tensions. Strangulating traffic patterns and inadequate parking facilities slow city traffic to a snail's pace. The exhaust from thousands of cars, trucks, and buses constitutes a health hazard in most of the larger cities. New urban freeway construction runs into fiery opposition from businesses and persons about to be displaced or dispossessed. Urban mass transportation systems are in deep economic trouble and the commuter's problems grow worse every year.

STATE AND LOCAL HIGHWAY FINANCE, ADMINISTRATION, AND POLITICS

Historically, the building and maintaining of highways in this country was viewed as a strictly local responsibility. Able-bodied men were required by law or custom to give a certain number of specified days, usually during the

[7] *Statistical Abstract of the United States, 1964* (Washington, 1965), pp. 63, 85.

summer, hauling materials and working with pick and shovel to provide needed town and township roads. Even after road taxes were imposed, it was not uncommon to have local residents work off their tax obligations by personal labor. But as communities grew and stagecoach traffic multiplied and loads increased, the traditional and crude methods of road construction were forced to give way to technically more proficient labor and more highly-specialized equipment. Even so, excepting major thoroughfares and turn-pikes, rural roads on the whole continued to be poorly constructed and often impassable. An 1893 account of a bicycle enthusiast is illuminating:

> A bicycle trip through Iowa is a succession of discomforts; in the spring the mud renders the trip somewhat impossible; in summer the roads, having no foundation, become a perfect sand bar, through which the wheels slip in all directions, giving the devoted rider many a fall, while the wind whirls the dust about his devoted head, filling his eyes, nose and ears, preventing his opening his mouth even to call down blessings on the man who made the road. . . . But woe be he who wanders far from home, for the least rain ruins the roads for a week, the soft dirt absorbing the moisture readily and the wagons cutting ruts that make cycling a torment.[8]

Modern highways are a product of the twentieth century, a Siamese twin to the automobile. In 1910, there were only 400,000 cars registered in the entire country; ten years later the figure rose to eight million. Today over eighty-six million cars, trucks, and buses crowd the roads of the nation.[9] It did not take long for towns and townships to discover how unprepared they were in terms of finances and engineering skill to build or maintain the kind of hard-surface roads that automotive traffic demanded. Most of the roads that were built by the smaller units of local government were poor in design and construction and proved prematurely obsolescent as traffic volume and road wear exceeded all expectation and planning. Soon even the counties (outside of the New England states) to which townships were surrendering local highway responsibilities found it difficult to cope with the increasing costs and complexities of a modern highway system. In many state legisla-tures there were strong pressures to have the state government itself shoulder a larger share of the administrative and fiscal burdens of rural mileage. "In 1920," according to a recent study of American highway revenue and expendi-ture policies, "the local units of government occupied a dominant position in the over-all highway picture. Approximately 70 per cent of all road work was undertaken by the political subdivisions of the state. Today over three quar-ters of highway funds are channeled through state authorities." [10]

---

[8] Donald E. Boles and Karl A. Fox, *Welfare and Highway Functions of Iowa Counties* (Ames, 1961), p. 373.

[9] *Automobile Facts and Figures, 1964*, p. 19.

[10] Burch, p. 81. An excellent discussion of modern electronic and mechanical devices used in highway construction is found in an address by H. A. Radzikowski, Chief, Division of Development, Office of Operations, Bureau of Public Roads, U. S. Department of Com-merce, presented at the annual meeting of the American Road Builders' Association in Atlanta, Ga.; see *Congressional Record,* January 30, 1961, p. A 560.

Not only have state government and the state highway department become more significant in the picture, but important changes have also occurred in the methods of paying for highways. Before 1910, most highway construction was financed with funds obtained either from property taxes or from special bond issues. After World War I, gasoline taxes and automobile registration fees, the road user taxes, became the chief source of highway revenue. Federal, state, and local taxes on highway users in 1964, for example, amounted to $10 billion, while property taxes and assessments totalled not more than $993 million.[11] Motor fuel and vehicle taxes alone have doubled during the last ten years and now have reached a point where they constitute around 25 per cent of all state tax revenues.

Responsibility for disbursing the major share of these funds is placed in state highway departments. By state and federal law, these agencies are generally given charge of a wide variety of functions: (1) administering federal and state aids to county and municipal highways: (2) supervising the design, construction, and maintenance of major state roads and the interstate highway system; (3) providing technical and engineering services to county and local highway departments; (4) approving local governmental highway plans and projects; (5) maintaining cooperative relations with the Bureau of Public Roads; (6) assisting the state and its local subdivisions in acquiring right of way necessary for the construction of new and improved highways; (7) assuring compliance with national and state standards of highway construction and traffic engineering; and (8) carrying out various highway safety measures throughout the state.

Highway departments in the fifty states are headed either by a single or by a plural executive; the latter arrangement is predominant in the South.[12] As a rule, such highway commissioners are appointed by the governor with the advice and consent of the state Senate for four-year terms; longer terms are, however, not uncommon. Although fourteen states do give governors the power to remove highway commissioners at will, traditional distrust of gubernatorial power still characterizes most state government in this as it does in so many other areas of executive management. Fear of the strong governor is expressed in many forms: in staggered terms for commission members, in statutory requirements that governors must select their commissioners from specified districts, or in legislative practices which reserve to the lawmakers the actual control of locating and classifying particular routes.

Nearly unrestricted appointive power, however, is reserved to some of the governors in connection with naming members to independent toll road authorities. Fifteen of these agencies operate under special state enabling statutes in the Eastern states. They administer 3,000 miles of turnpikes, most of which were built at a fast rate after World War II, in order to help high-density population centers in Illinois, Indiana, Massachusetts, New Jer-

[11] *Automobile Facts and Figures, 1964,* p. 53.

[12] Highway Research Board, *State Highway Administrative Organizations: An Analysis,* Special Report 51 (Washington, 1959); p. 5. Also, Burch, p. 166.

sey, New York, and Pennsylvania expedite their vast volume of high-speed, intercity traffic.[13]

Rural interests have long held disproportionate power in most state legislatures. It should come as no surprise, therefore, that the formulas designed to distribute state aids to local governments, and the classification process under which rural roads were brought into the state aid system did, in fact, reflect more noticeably the interests of rural than of urban America. For example, it was shown as late as 1959 that:

A. Seven states—Florida, Kentucky, Missouri, North Dakota, South Carolina, Texas, and West Virginia—channeled no aid whatever to their city streets and highways.
B. Although nearly three-fifths of the American people lived in cities of 10,000 and over, aid to urban highways constituted, on an average, only 25 per cent of total state road disbursements.
C. While state highway departments absorbed approximately one-fourth of the "essential rural mileage," only a "little more than 10 per cent of all city streets received like treatment." [14]

"I was busy looking for the exact change."

SOURCE: *The Wall Street Journal*, July 3, 1964.

More than a mere anti-urban slant or rural "conspiracy" is involved. Highway construction and right-of-way acquisition in urban areas are not only much more expensive, but also politically more explosive. Admittedly,

[13] Charles L. Dearing, "Turnpike Authorities in the United States," *Law and Contemporary Problems,* Autumn, 1961, p. 747.
[14] Burch, pp. 123, 124–125, 152.

urban freeways may facilitate safer, speedier, and more economic transportation, but their construction frequently necessitates serious and politically unpopular dislocations of people, business establishments, neighborhoods, and widely-treasured landmarks. Rural representatives in quest of state aid can speak and lobby before legislative committees and state highway departments with a solidarity and unanimity of opinion that can rarely be matched by their less fortunate city cousins.

As a matter of fact, the urban road picture, though far from bright as yet, nevertheless has improved considerably since World War II. States spent nearly three times as much in percentage for these roads in the late fifties as they did in the late forties.[15] This upward trend was encouraged, no doubt, by federal aid to the urban extensions of state primary and secondary highways which rose in dollar volume "from $137.5 million for fiscal 1954 to $243.7 million for fiscal 1965." [16]

GOVERNMENTAL CONCERNS FOR HIGHWAY SAFETY

Fortunately both federal and state authorities are beginning to demonstrate a heightened awareness of the carnage on the nation's highways which has resulted in loss of life to thousands and in injury to millions year after year. Operating on the federal level are the President's Committee for Traffic Safety, the Interdepartmental Highway Safety Board, and the Office of Highway Safety (Bureau of Public Roads). Working cooperatively with other public and private groups, these agencies attempt to rally wide public support for various aspects of highway safety. Under special congressional authority, financial and technical assistance can be provided for programs which seek to raise highway engineering standards, further research in accident prevention and traffic control, or assure greater uniformity in traffic laws and their enforcement. In this connection should be mentioned also the National Driver Register Service, "a voluntary, cooperative Federal-State driver record exchange on individuals whose driving privileges have been withdrawn for driving while intoxicated or for involvement in a traffic fatality." [17]

State governments have not been inactive either. Here are but a few illustrations of the many measures enacted by the states in 1961, 1962, and 1963 which were designed to strengthen highway safety in one way or another:

    A. Half of all states entered into the newly-inaugurated Vehicle Equipment Safety Compact which aims to make more uniform state regulations dealing with safety equipment on cars, buses, and trucks and seeks to encourage interstate cooperative research in highway safety.

    B. At least twelve states—Arizona, California, Idaho, Illinois, Maine, Missis-

[15] *Ibid.,* p. 171.
[16] U. S. Department of Commerce, Bureau of Public Roads, *Highway Progress: Annual Report of the Bureau of Public Roads Fiscal Year 1962* (Washington, 1963), p. 21.
[17] *Ibid.,* p. 47.

sippi, Montana, Nebraska, Nevada, New Mexico, Oregon, and Washington —joined the Driver License Compact. This is an agreement between the states (1) to facilitate interchange of information concerning violations of traffic laws by drivers' license holders, and (2) to bring about greater uniformity in the legal status and consequences of particular violations.

C. Seat belt installation on new cars was made mandatory in twenty states and the District of Columbia.

D. Implied consent laws for drivers driving under the influence of alcohol were adopted in Connecticut, Minnesota, North Carolina, and Virginia.

E. New York now requires that drivers undergo an eye examination every nine years; Maine insists on annual inspection of cars; and Rhode Island authorizes the Registrar of Motor Vehicles to suspend or revoke drivers' licenses at his discretion.[18]

Considerations of safety, in addition to those of national defense and economic growth, play an important role in the justification of the 41,000 mile interstate highway system. From a 1961 study, the Bureau of Public Roads estimates that the 11,000 miles of the system already completed and opened to traffic during that year alone, saved the nation 2,000 lives, 25,000 injuries, 60,000 accidents, and $100 million in accident costs.[19] This salutary record is attributed largely to the system's controlled access roads, planned interchanges, and separated roadways, as well as to many other features of modern highway design incorporated into these high-speed freeways.

THE URBAN TRANSPORTATION MESS

While interurban vehicular travel has undoubtedly become safer, speedier, and more convenient, the nation's new freeways and expressways have contributed little, if anything, to reduce downtown traffic congestion and parking problems. The automobiles that are funneled into the center of the city slow traffic to a crawl, pollute the air, discourage potential shoppers, and disrupt the flow of pedestrians as they attempt to move from their places of residence, employment, or entertainment. Every additional mile of a multi-million dollar freeway which was designed to unsnarl traffic also eliminates more taxable property, reduces city revenues, and forces businesses to relocate and people to be rehoused.

How much more appropriation of urban land to accommodate city traffic can be economically justified? Already two-thirds of the Los Angeles downtown land area is devoted to highways, streets, and parking facilities. And still more suburban-to-core-city traffic is predicted for the years ahead. Population experts insist that in the 1980's almost half of this country's 280 million people will live in forty major metropolitan areas, which would increase the number of commuters by at least 50 per cent. City planners, transportation specialists, and nearly all who have studied the modern city's traffic picture

---

[18] Based on "Action by the Legislatures: 1961," *State Government*, Autumn, 1961, pp. 269–273 and *Book of the States, 1964–1965*, pp. 367–368.

[19] *Highway Progress*, p. 12.

readily agree that highways and automobiles alone will never be able to do the job. They must have help from public mass transit. This is especially true for areas of high population density. Chicago, for example, discovered that even after the completion of three enormously expensive superhighways—the Outer Drive, the Congress Expressway, and the Northwest Expressway—it increased its ability to move cars in and out of the downtown district at peak loads by a mere 1–1.5 per cent.[20] Los Angeles has spent nearly $1 billion on freeways; more than 300,000 people travel on the Hollywood Freeway on an average day; and the city's traffic congestion remains unsolved.[21] As more and more traffic-burdened cities are compelled to take another look at urban mass transportation systems, they find that many such systems have been experiencing serious financial reverses in recent years. Since 1954, for instance, passengers on buses and street cars have declined by 22 per cent; of the approximately 1,200 privately owned transit companies and commuter roads, an estimated 243 transit companies have been sold and 194 abandoned, leaving 70 cities of 25,000 population or more without any public transportation system whatever.[22] Some of the major factors explaining this crisis in urban mass transit were highlighted in a 1963 report submitted by the Senate Banking and Currency Committee:

> Many private bus, transit, and rail carriers are finding it extremely difficult to meet operating expenses of existing facilities and almost prohibitive to finance new capital improvements to meet expansion requirements. Caught in the squeeze of rising capital and operating costs, and declining patronage, many private bus and rail carriers must resort to raising fares, trimming service, and deferred maintenance—which simply drives away more riders and accelerates the downward spiral.[23]

Despite such depressing findings, there is much solid evidence, technological and economic, that points to rail transit as the most reasonable way of balancing out the multiple transportation requirements of millions of suburban commuters. Based on peak load capacity studies, automobiles on expressways can move 2,000 people per lane, per hour; buses can handle between 6,000 and 9,000, but rail systems can carry up to 60,000 per hour. The potential passenger capacity of one rail line is estimated to be equal to that of twenty expressway lanes of automobiles or seven expressway lanes of buses.[24]

Quite naturally, these statistics do not show what most commuters know all too well. Too many suburban railroads are presently in deplorable operat-

---

[20] Senate Committee on Banking and Currency, *Urban Mass Transportation—1963,* Subcommittee Hearings, February 28, March 1, 4, 5, 8, and 11, 1963, 88th Cong., 1st Sess. (Washington, 1963), p. 200.

[21] See "Revolt Against Big City Freeways," *U. S. News & World Report,* January 1, 1962, p. 50.

[22] Senate Committee on Banking and Currency, *Urban Mass Transportation Act of 1963,* Senate Report No. 82, 88th Cong., 1st Sess. (Washington, 1963), pp. 4–8.

[23] *Ibid.,* p. 4.

[24] Testimony by Senator Abraham Ribicoff in *Urban Mass Transportation—1963,* Hearings, p. 239.

ing conditions. Service is poor and rolling equipment is unreliable, inefficient, uncomfortable, and occasionally even dangerous. Passengers broil during the summer months and freeze during the winter. Excessive stops reduce speeds and inconvenient schedules drag out the time spent en route or in waiting.

"The fault is not ours," spokesmen for the railroads insist. Mounting deficits, high labor costs, increasing tax burdens, sprawling suburbs and poorly-planned real estate developments, unfair competition from buses, trucks, and cars which operate on publicly-subsidized multimillion dollar expressways, public and private resistance to raising fares to levels consonant with profitable operations, as well as the peculiar reluctance of the average American to part with his beloved automobile and the privacy and status that he believes it assures him—these are the real villains that must shoulder the blame for the deterioration of the suburban rail systems.

Given these conditions, can the suburban commuter be lured back into taking the train on his way to and from work? The answer appears to be a qualified "Yes;" the Chicago and Northwestern Railway, to give one example, claims considerable success in having raised its passenger totals. Beginning slowly in 1956, the company turned mounting deficits on its commuter routes into respectable earnings by making a number of major changes. It furnished new, speedier, more comfortable, air-conditioned, high-capacity trains, reduced the number of stops, and conducted an intensive $100,000-a-year advertising campaign telling the public that it could ride the trains for about 40 per cent of what it would cost to drive a private car. A favorable revision of railroad property tax assessments also helped the company's cause.[25]

Other metropolitan areas, like New York, Philadelphia, San Francisco, and Boston, found it necessary to provide even more direct forms of public subsidies. Aid was given in the form of cash, credit, tax benefits, or outright tax relief, lest their commuter rail systems slip into bankruptcy and thus further complicate an already impossible traffic situation. At best, most of these were stopgap measures. The basic needs of commuter service could only be met by a coordinated approach which viewed the mass transportation requirements of the entire urban complex as an interdependent network of rail, bus, and rapid transit.

Significant steps towards this type of regional approach were taken recently in the San Francisco and New York areas. In 1962 voters in San Francisco, Alameda, and Contra Costa Counties approved a $792 million bond issue for a transit system, part of which "will be below ground, part in the air and part on the surface."[26] Plans call for:

[25] Todd E. Fandell, "Coddling Commuters: How North Western Turns a Profit Without Subsidies," *The Wall Street Journal*, February 18, 1964, p. 16.

[26] *Municipal Year Book, 1963*, p. 61. Considerable interest in the possibility of developing subway systems to supplement other means of urban transportation is reported from Los Angeles, Washington, D. C., and Atlanta; see Mitchell Gordon, "Going Underground," *The Wall Street Journal*, June 8, 1964.

Lightweight modern electric trains governed by a centrally located electric computer . . . to run . . . at an average speed of 45 miles an hour. Each of five lines would carry 60,000 seated passengers an hour, five times as many as a six-lane freeway. Fares would be tabulated by computer using a charge account plate system, and billing customers on a monthly basis.[27]

After long and protracted negotiations by the governors and legislative leaders of New York, Connecticut, and New Jersey, and under strong pressure from the Bureau of Public Roads, these three states finally approved in 1964 a Tri-State Transportation Commission

[with] the authority to take over and operate transit facilities in serious financial difficulty, but only after returning to the Legislatures of the states involved and receiving express approval for each project.[28]

Regional and metropolitan area-wide transportation studies received a major impetus and stimulus from federal grants made available under the Housing Act of 1961. Section 701 of this act authorized financial assistance for comprehensive urban transportation surveys, studies, and plans which would aid in solving problems of traffic congestion and "facilitate the circulation of people and goods in metropolitan and other urban areas."

Here are a few examples of the types of projects which the Home and Housing Finance Agency approved in 1962 and 1963:

Washington, D. C.: "Minibus Study"; To test whether suitably designed small buses circulating within a central business district on a fixed route and frequent schedule will attract enough riders to facilitate the movement of people, reduce traffic congestion, and stimulate business activity.

Southeastern Pennsylvania Transportation Compact: To determine the effect of service improvements and fare reductions on the public's use of railroad commuter service.

Memphis Transit Authority: To determine how the pattern and volume of ridership is affected by establishing full-scale mass transit service in the early stages of the development of representative types of suburban areas, as compared to the normal situation where full service is deferred until an area has been substantially developed.

Mass Transportation Commission, Commonwealth of Massachusetts: To determine the effects of service improvements and fare reductions, alone or in combination, on the public's use of railroad commuter, rapid transit, and bus facilities.

City of Detroit: To demonstrate the effects on patronage of substantial increase in bus service and the effects of such increased service on other street traffic.

University of Washington, Seattle Monorail: To secure factual data on the operation of the monorail installed at Seattle in connection with the Century 21 Fair.

---

[27] Joe Alex Morris, "Can the Commuter Survive?," *The Saturday Evening Post,* May 6, 1961, p. 85.

[28] George Cable Wright, "3 States Agree on Transit Body," *The New York Times,* February 6, 1964, p. 31.

Tri-State Transportation Committee (New York, New Jersey, Connecticut) *Long Island Railroad Fare Collection Project:* To test, through actual use, equipment designed for automatic fare collection and ticket validation . . . also for the "New Brunswick Project": To demonstrate the effects upon the use of existing railroad commuter service of providing a specialized commuter patron station, with convenient vehicular access and ample parking space, outside the congested central business district of a suburban city.[29]

Most of the preliminary reports on the results of these pilot projects were highly encouraging. Supporters of federal aid succeeded in obtaining passage of the Transportation Act of 1965 (P.L. 89–220) authorizing the secretary of commerce to conduct a 3-year $90 million research, development, and demonstration project in high speed ground transportation.

THE URBAN MASS TRANSPORTATION ACT OF 1964

Requests for more substantial federal assistance to state and local governments to help relieve the fiscal crisis in urban mass transportation have been before Congress for at least four years. An administration-sponsored bill was passed by the Senate on April 4, 1963. Costing about half a billion dollars, it included four main features: (1) long and short-term loans and grants for mass transportation facilities and equipment: (2) grants for greatly expanded research and demonstration programs; (3) grants to assist in the relocation of families and business concerns displaced by such aided projects, and (4) provision for mandatory coordination in planning and programming between federal agencies assisting highways and those assisting urban mass transportation facilities.

Organizational support for this bill came from groups like the AFL-CIO, the American Municipal Association, the American Transit Association, the Association of American Railroads, and the United States Conference of Mayors. Among those testifying in opposition were spokesmen for the United States Chamber of Commerce, the Investment Bankers' Association, and the powerful American Farm Bureau Federation.

The case for federal aid to urban mass transportation was supported by at least four major arguments. They recurred with some frequency in committee hearings, in the committee's report accompanying the bill, and in the senatorial floor debate preceding its passage:

A. Cities and states are either unwilling or incapable of providing sufficient capital resources with which to come to the aid of their deteriorating urban mass transportation systems.
B. The effects of inadequate urban mass transport transcend local boundaries; "one-fourth of the metropolitan areas either border or cross over state lines."
C. Clogged streets, traffic congestion, and an excessive number of delay-causing stops burden the arteries of commerce—local, intrastate and inter-

---

[29] Statement of activities of Housing and Home Finance Agency relating to Transportation Demonstration Grant and Loan Programs under the Housing Act of 1961, February 27, 1963, *Urban Mass Transportation—1963,* Hearings, pp. 55, 56, 57, and 58.

state; "it has been estimated that traffic jams cost the nation about $5 billion a year in time and wages lost, extra fuel consumption, faster vehicle depreciation, lower downtown commercial sales, and lower taxes. . . ." [30]

D. Too many privately-owned public mass transportation companies fail to show profits at levels sufficient to attract investment capital; lacking such capital, they are not in the position to make the improvements in equipment, facilities, and service at fare levels which would appeal to growing numbers of patrons.

Senators Bennett of Utah, Tower of Texas, Simpson of Wyoming, Dominick of Colorado, and all Republican members of the Senate Banking and Currency Committee with the exception of Senator Javits of New York, who had strongly supported the bill, jointly spelled out a stinging dissent for inclusion in the committee's report. [31] Among the various reasons why they objected to this measure, the following were stressed:

A. State and local governments are equally as capable of financing their transportation needs as is the federal government.

B. The bill would give excessive power to the federal government, especially to the administrator of the Housing and Home Financing Agency who would have a blank check in give-aways at the expense of all taxpayers.

C. The true and total cost of aid to urban transportation would run into many more billions of dollars of which the proposed appropriations constitute but a small down payment.

D. There does not exist a national crisis in mass transportation ". . . to the extent the entire country should be asked to sacrifice in these times of high taxes and deficit federal spending, in order to almost completely relieve the large cities of their responsibilities." [32]

E. There is no substantial evidence to the effect that improvements in mass transportation facilities will, in fact, cause individual commuters to give up the use of their automobiles. "It is not economically feasible to duplicate the versatility and convenience of the automobile in any known type of mass transit system." [33]

A slightly modified version of the Urban Mass Transportation Act did finally pass the Congress in June of 1964. One of the changes demanded by the House involved the elimination of a revenue bond guarantee section which had been included in the earlier Senate-passed bill.

AIRPORTS AND AVIATION

Among the various forms of interurban transportation, air-passenger traffic now assumes a major role. (see Table 2).

Freight and express carried by aircraft increased between 1954 and 1962 by nearly one million ton miles and even more spectacular gains are

---

[30] *Urban Mass Transportation Act of 1963*, p. 13.

[31] Senator Proxmire, Democrat of Wisconsin and a committee member, also opposed the bill. His major objection centered on the conviction that the cities could handle their own transportation problems. Senator Muskie, Democrat of Maine, likewise a committee member, voted for sending the bill to the floor although he doubted the wisdom of the priority of spending that much money at a time of an anticipated federal deficit.

[32] *Urban Mass Transportation Act of 1963*, p. 46.

[33] *Ibid.*, p. 52.

projected for the future. According to estimates of the Federal Aviation Agency, by 1970 air cargo traffic is expected to be twice that of 1962; the number of air passengers will have risen from 59.9 to 85 million; the number of passenger miles traveled from 33.0 to 51.0 billion miles; and the number of hours flown in general aviation for business, commercial, personal, and instructional purposes (other than in scheduled air carriers) will have climbed from 13.3 to 18.5 million hours. For general aviation, in particular, the future looks promising. Already nearly twice as many miles are flown in general aviation as by domestic certificated airlines.[34]

In terms of economic importance, aviation ranks high among the most important industrial and commercial enterprises. "It employs 650,000 people in the manufacture of aircraft and aircraft parts, a figure that exceeds the number employed in any other manufacturing industry except the motor vehicle and associated equipment industry." [35]

TABLE 2. INTERURBAN TRANSPORTATION *

Year	Domestic air carriers	Railroads	Buses
1944	2,200	95,500	27,400
1962	33,600	19,800	21,000

* In millions of passenger miles.

SOURCE: Adapted from *Book of the States, 1964–1965*, p. 374.

After 1946, when the federal government began its airport assistance programs, about a half a billion dollars of federal funds were channeled into the states under grant-in-aid arrangements which sought to provide "a system of public airports adequate to anticipate and meet the needs of civil aeronautics." In 1962 the Federal Airport Act was extended for an additional five years with an annual appropriation raised from $62 million to $75 million. President Johnson has urged an extension of the program at a somewhat reduced figure ($62.5 million).

Under the Federal Airport Act of 1946, 75% of the annual appropriations available were apportioned among the states according to a formula which allocated one-half on the basis of population and one-half on the basis of area. The remaining 25% of the annual appropriations were reserved for the discretion of the F.A.A. administrator, to pay for projects throughout the nation, especially those which would service national parks, monuments, forests, and recreational areas. A 50% matching requirement was also included in the apportionment formula.[36]

[34] Federal Aviation Agency, *National Airport Plan, Fiscal Years 1965–1969* (Washington, 1964), pp. 6–9.

[35] Federal Aviation Agency, *National Airport Plan, Requirements for Fiscal Years 1963–1967* (Washington, 1963), p. 3.

[36] W. Brooke Graves, *American Intergovernmental Relations* (New York, 1964), pp. 955–956.

Federal participation in airport construction and development was restricted by statute to particular projects. Costs incurred in the construction of public parking lots, restaurants, and passenger terminal facilities, for example, were declared ineligible. Items for which federal contributions could be used included the following:

> field surveys; preparation of plans and specifications; supervision and inspection of construction work; procurement of work contracts; acquisition of land easements; and interests in air space. . . .[37]

The largest share of federal aid was absorbed by costs connected with land acquisition, site preparation, and paving.[38] One of the responsibilities of the federal government under the provisions of the Federal Airport Act was to assist the states in the planning of future airport development within a national system. Revised annually, this National Airport Plan (which encompasses all airports receiving federal assistance under the act) offers each state and each airport within each state, an estimate of their financial, construction, and equipment requirements for the ensuing five years. Cost projections cover suggested additions or improvements which should be undertaken, in the judgment of F.A.A. technical experts, if the national airport system is to meet the growing demands imposed on it and on all civilian aviation by an expanding economy and population.

Among major policy issues involving future airport development is the question of environmental zoning and the degree of authority that should be vested in the federal government in connection with it. When the Senate Commerce Committee urged the extension of the Federal Airport Act in 1963, it called for an amendment which would give to the F.A.A. administrator the power to see to it through "assurances in writing satisfactory to him, that

> appropriate action, including the adoption of zoning laws, has been or will be taken, to the extent reasonable, to restrict the use of land adjacent to or in the immediate vicinity of the airport to activities and purposes compatible with normal airport operations including landing and take-off of aircraft. . . ."[39]

Critics assailed the proposed amendment in committee hearings as being vague, impractical, and lacking standards or criteria of enforcement.[40] It was pointed out that since most airports were already surrounded by residential properties, the necessity of obtaining agreement from multiple zoning authorities would greatly delay airport construction or expansion, while increasing the cost by millions of dollars. Testimony by the administrator of the F.A.A. stressed the amendment's moderate language—"to the extent reasonable"—as well as a principle of constitutional law which insists that

[37] 60 Stat. 170, 49 U.S.C. 1011, Sec. 2 (6).

[38] *National Airport Plan, Fiscal Years 1965–1969*, p. 5.

[39] *Amendments to the Federal Airport Act*, Committee on Commerce, Senate Report No. 446, August 20, 1963, 88th Cong., 1st Sess. (Washington, 1963), p. 3.

[40] *Federal-Aid-To-Airports Program*, Hearings, Subcommittee on Aviation, Committee on Commerce, April 9, 10, and 23, 1963, 88th Cong., 1st Sess. (Washington, 1963).

the federal government should leave to the states and their political subdivisions the exercise of their zoning powers over the land surrounding airports.

> If the airport sponsor lacks this authority because the airport is located outside the city limits, the neighboring city or the county does not lack the authority.

> Because airport sponsors do have a voice in community affairs, and the community has a substantial stake in the airport, working jointly they can assure zoning where feasible; they can assure that schools are not built in approach paths; they can use these areas to locate parks and recreational facilities; they can discourage if not prevent, erection of apartment or housing developments in noise-critical areas. Such influence and persuasion constitutes "appropriate action" fully as much as does zoning.[41]

Spokesmen for the American Municipal Association, the National Association of Counties, and the Airport Operators Council expressed particular concern in hearings before the Senate Commerce Committee that the federal government should assume full responsibility and custodianship for the public right of freedom of transit through the navigable airspace of the United States. If such a public easement of transit for the landing and taking-off of aircraft were to result in damage to the rights of an adjacent landowner, then compensation should be determined and paid by the federal government and neither persons exercising such rights of transit, airport operators, nor owners should be held liable.

What had alarmed these representatives of local government groups was not so much the amendment to the Federal Airport Act as such, but a decision of the United States Supreme Court handed down on March 5, 1962, *Griggs* v. *Allegheny County*.[42] In this case the Court held that the county as promoter, owner, and lessor of the airport had taken an air easement from Griggs, over whose house planes passed at low altitudes when landing and taking off. Under the Fourteenth Amendment the defendant county was held liable for compensation by reason of such flights, although the aircraft were neither owned nor operated by the county and although the county neither controlled their flight patterns nor their methods of operation. The fact that federal statute has made it abundantly clear since 1958 that it was the intent of Congress that the airspace needed to insure safety in landing and take-off of aircraft was navigable airspace and belonged to the United States, apparently did not persuade the Court to deny recovery to Griggs. "Without the 'approach areas,'" wrote Mr. Justice Douglas, "an airport is indeed not operable. Respondent in designing it had to acquire some private property. Our conclusion is that by constitutional standards it did not acquire enough."

The pressure for the federal government to delegate greater financial responsibilities to owners of land adjoining airports will no doubt continue, especially as hundreds of new airports need to be developed in areas relatively

[41] *Amendments to the Federal Airport Act*, pp. 21, 22.
[42] 369 U. S. 84 (1962); on this case, see also "Griggs v. County of Allegheny," *Comments, Northwestern University Law Review*, July–August, 1962, pp. 346–354.

densely populated or surrounded by valuable residential and industrial land. Whether state and local governmental units will be willing to limit some of their zoning power in exchange for an enlarged federal role in airport development remains to be seen.

Perhaps Mr. Justice Black's dissent in the *Griggs* case offers yet a third alternative—a sharing of liability between federal and state government.

> The planes that take off and land at the Greater Pittsburgh Airport wind their rapid way through space not for the peculiar benefit of the citizens of Allegheny County but as part of a great, reliable transportation system of immense advantage to the whole Nation in time of peace and war. . . .

> [I]t would be unfair to make Allegheny County bear expenses wholly out of proportion to the advantages it can receive from the national transportation system.

CONSERVATION OF NATURAL RESOURCES—

THE NATIONAL SETTING

In a nation blessed with a superabundance of natural resources neither federal nor state governments displayed much interest in conservation efforts prior to the beginning of this century. For over one hundred years, this country's soil, wildlife, forests, minerals, gas and petroleum, streams, and lakes seemed to have been placed here for all comers to use or abuse according to the individual's interest and conscience. In their eagerness to build a new and better life for themselves and their families, men exploited this natural wealth at a fantastic pace. It was not until after 1890 when conservationists of the stature of Charles R. Van Hise, Gifford Pinchot, and Theodore Roosevelt helped to dramatize the cause, that the American people became sufficiently concerned about how immorally and utterly unwisely they were wasting their nearly inexhaustible gifts of nature. A change in attitude began to crystallize. If what was left of the national domain was to be preserved, the federal government had to act and act promptly.

Congress responded favorably to this emerging consensus and the conservation movement secured a number of important legislative victories. Among these milestones in conservation were the Forest Reserve Act of 1891 (beginning the establishment of the forest system), the Reclamation Act of 1902 (safeguarding the distribution of water in the arid states of the West), and the Mineral Leasing Act of 1920 (regulating the exploitation of mineral wealth). Collectively, these statutes constituted a significant beginning to a wiser use and management of United States water, forest, and mineral resources.

That much was left undone was tragically underscored again by the disastrous duststorms of the 1930's, when dust bowl and Depression combined to scourge this nation's land and people. Out of this emergency setting grew the Tennessee Valley Authority, the Civilian Conservation Corps, the Soil Conservation Service, and the Taylor Grazing Act, to mention some of the more important conservation efforts undertaken in the New Deal era. Whatever the other objectives that these programs and activities may have represented, significant progress was achieved in fighting soil erosion, in irrigating arid lands, in controlling floods, and in safeguarding the Western grazing ranges.

Now, a generation later, this country is confronted with yet another set of problems in managing its resources prudently and economically. The conservation crisis of the 1960's is much less overt, certainly not as dramatic, but chemically, technologically, economically, socially, and politically equally as complex and as demanding in farsightedness as any of the previous challenges.

In addition to strengthening the already established and more traditional programs, conservationist-minded groups, with strong support from President Kennedy, Secretary of Interior Udall, and Senator Anderson (New Mexico), stressed for this decade the urgency of adopting measures which would:

A. Lead to the establishment of a National Wilderness Preservation System.
B. Facilitate the creation of conservation funds with which to acquire "key conservation lands."
C. Make possible the most effective control and avoidance of water and air pollution.
D. Assure the acquisition, development, and protection of land, water, and shoreline resources for use in outdoor recreation by the residents of our teeming metropolitan areas.
E. Come to the assistance of local governments seeking to preserve open space for playgrounds, parks, golf courses, and similar public use, against the threats of enveloping housing developments, shopping centers, highway constructions, and parking lots.
F. Expand prominently the visitor accommodating capacity of national and state parks, forests, camping grounds, and picnic facilities.

The Wilderness Act of 1964, placing 9.1 million acres of government land into a wilderness conservation system, incorporated a number of these objectives. Overcoming the objections of certain lumber, oil, mining, and ranching interests, the act provides that these lands be kept in a primitive state. Automobile travel and commercial establishments are prohibited, although grazing and limited prospecting are permitted. Subject to inclusion into the system are 6,998,014 acres of areas already classified as wilderness districts and 1,355,034 acres now categorized as wild in Arizona, California, Colorado, Montana, Nevada, New Hampshire, New Mexico, North Carolina, Oregon, and Washington; and an 886,673-acre canoe area in Minnesota.

Closely related to these conservation needs are certain important changes which are occurring in agriculture. Increased farm output as a result of greater efficiency, heavier capitalization, and more intensive specialization makes it now possible and even necessary to relegate larger areas of crop land to conservation and recreational purposes. Compared, for example, with 1920, crop production per acre has risen by 70 per cent and output per breeding animal by 90 per cent; one farm worker then produced enough food, fiber, and other agricultural products to meet the needs of eight people; he is now able to so supply twenty-seven persons.[43] According to estimates furnished by the secretary of agriculture, in 1980 when our population will have increased by 45 per cent, "we can meet all the needs for crop products with fifty million fewer acres" than were available in 1962.[44]

In view of developments such as these, the question, then, of how to strike the most socially-desirable balance in the multiple uses of land for agriculture, recreation, highways, conservation, and urban growth will for many years be the overshadowing concern of all those who are charged with the orderly management of private and public land.

Administratively, major conservation activities in state government are often centered in a single department of conservation, although some important conservation programs may also involve the activities, personnel, and services of other closely related departments such as agriculture and public health or the state agricultural extension service.

Within such a conservation department, assumed for the moment to be fairly typical, separate divisions or bureaus would be given managerial responsibilities for the different natural resource areas—forestry, public lands, minerals, state parks, game and fish, and waters. How strong each of these divisions would be or what organizational combination of bureaus may be encountered in one or the other states depends, of course, on various factors. It may depend on the wishes of the legislature, on the magnitude of the resource itself, or on the strength of a division's public clientele throughout a particular state.

Although considerable variation exists in law and practice from state to state, here very briefly are a few illustrations of major functions that would most likely be performed by such a department of conservation:

> *Forestry Division* manages the state-owned forest lands; operates state tree nurseries; conducts sales of state-owned timber; has responsibility for state forest planting program, forest insect and disease control, and for the administration of state-established forest land management procedures; has charge of state forest fire prevention and protection program on private as well as on public products operations; administers flood prevention program and technical assistance in all woodland management.

> *Public Lands and Minerals Division* administers all lands owned by the state which may include forest lands, agricultural lands, mineral lands, grazing ranges, or swamp lands; has responsibility for leasing or sale of all public lands or minerals; conducts surveys, research, and exploration with respect to the availability and potential of mineral resources; enforces state policies affecting mineral exploitation and the conditions of mine safety.

---

[43] U. S. Department of Agriculture, *Fact Book of U. S. Agriculture: Revised 1963* (Washington, 1963), p. 3.

[44] *White House Conference on Conservation: Official Proceedings May 24 to May 25, 1962* (Washington, 1963) p. 15.

State Parks Division administers and has responsibility for all state parks and recreational areas; camping facilities and picnic grounds; processes land acquisitions, improves sites, provides sanitation and water supply systems; conducts naturalist interpretations and information programs.

Game and Fish Division is charged with the management of the state's wildlife resources and with the enforcement of laws and regulations provided for their protection; operates programs for the acquisition of wetlands and hunting grounds; fisheries section has responsibility for the operation of state fish hatcheries, stream and lake improvements, spawning and rearing areas, public access sites; conducts conservation education and liaison programs with civic groups interested in wildlife preservation; under supervision of the division, state game wardens post refuges, check hunting, fishing, and trapping laws, and enforce the state's firearms safety program; the fisheries section also conducts research in problems connected with wildlife resource management and control.

Waters Division has administrative control over the use and distribution of surface and underground waters throughout the state; after investigation, issues permits to those seeking public water acquisition rights or wishing to make encroachments on lake beds or streams; constructs, maintains, and operates state dams; conducts mapping and topological surveys and studies of water conditions and availability; assists in the establishment of watershed districts and assists in water conservation measures.

At the grass-roots level of all state and federal conservation activities are the nation's 2,900 conservation districts (Soil Conservation Service). Operating in nearly every county in every state, these districts extend their coverage over more than 1.7 billion acres of farm and ranch land and include 97 per cent of all farms and ranches.

Under federal and state laws, conservation districts are entitled to receive technical and financial assistance which will help them plan and carry out watershed and flood protection programs and soil erosion control practices. Conservation methods applied to crop land and range by such districts include contour farming, strip cropping, range land seeding, tree planting, drainage improvements, and irrigation projects.

Local districts also assist the United States Department of Agriculture's Soil and Conservation Service with a nationwide survey, begun in 1956, which seeks to inventory the entire country's soil and water conservation needs. This inventory will then serve as a basis for all future national and state watershed planning and development.

Emphasis is placed by more and more conservation districts on multiple land uses and on the withdrawal of surplus crop lands from production. In the Great Plains states this involves conversion into grass from feed grains, wheat, and cotton, and in the South "shifts from row crops to pasture or to managed woodland, especially for pulpwood. . . ." [45]

[45] U. S. Department of Agriculture, *1962 Report of the Secretary of Agriculture* (Washington, 1962), p. 51 and U. S. Department of the Interior, *1961 Annual Report of the Secretary of the Interior* (Washington, 1961).

In recent years state governments also have been strengthening the fiscal powers of soil conservation districts. Some authorize them to borrow money, others to issue bonds, and still others permit counties, cities, and other units of local government to purchase crop land turned into conservation reserves for recreational or park purposes.[46]

It is only natural that urban redevelopment projects, massive highway building, and rising industrial demands for urban land in densely-settled areas, all combine to intensify awareness in state and local government that planning authorities need to be given more effective tools with which to guard present as well as future uses of urban land. Whenever public officials and federal, state and local, or private interests fail to work in close cooperation in the area of urban land planning and development, serious waste of land resources and of other social capital as well is unavoidable. Thus when private real estate developments or subdivisions "leap frog" vacant and less desirable tracts, they always add greatly to the expense of future streets and utility services. "A far wiser course," contends a careful study, *Land for the Future,*

> would have been to plan the area in advance; bought the future park, school, and other public sites while the land was still at a price reflecting its undeveloped character; and then to have built roads and streets in locations to have influenced if not directed urban expansion along the lines planned.[47]

Perhaps this was too much to expect in a country with abundant land and a profoundly treasured freedom of individual economic choice. In the absence of an overwhelming visible crisis, the scope of public action and social discipline which such long-range planning requires could not have been mobilized.

STATE AND LOCAL GOVERNMENT IN WATER RESOURCE

MANAGEMENT

Since World War II, problems of water conservation and pollution control have concerned all levels of American government to an extent previously unknown. A number of factors help to account for this. First, urban population in 1960 was 55 per cent above that of 1940. Second, almost no municipal or industrial waste treatment facilities were constructed during the war years. Third, post-war industrial growth placed additional strains on available water resources. Fourth, newer technological processes greatly complicated the water pollution control problem not merely in terms of the actual volume of

---

[46] "Soil Conservation," *Book of the States, 1962–1963,* p. 467. For an illustration of a local survey, see John Quay, "Lake County Uses Soil Survey In Planning Its Urban Areas," *Soil Conservation,* December, 1963, pp. 99–102.

[47] Marion Clawson, R. Burnell Held, and Charles H. Stoddard, *Land for the Future* (Baltimore, 1960), p. 119; Papers of the Land Economics Institute, *Modern Land Policy* (Urbana, 1960); and Sidney M. Willhelm, *Urban Zoning and Land-Use Theory* (New York, 1962).

water discharged, but more critically because of the type of synthetic chemicals and radioactive contaminants which were permitted to enter into the
nation's streams and lakes (see Figure 2).

FIGURE 2

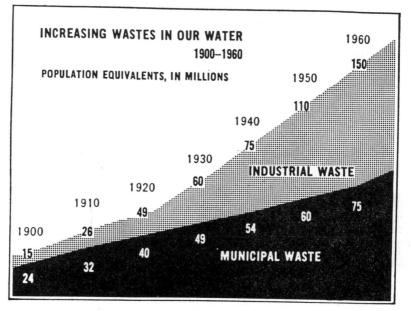

SOURCE: *Protecting Our Water Resources: The Federal Water Pollution Control Program*
(Washington, 1962), p. 2.

Within this common framework of problems, states will differ somewhat
in their priorities of needs. This emerges clearly from a survey conducted in
1960 by the Senate Select Committee on National Water Resources. The
following illustrations were drawn from this survey:

Washington: "Increased per capita consumption, rapid growth of small
               communities, building of roads, increased recreational ac-
               tivity, and logging of our watersheds have multiplied the
               problems of keeping our water supplies in safe clean con-
               ditions."

Tennessee: A number of the towns and cities of the State have flood
               control problems. There are 272 public water systems in the
               State serving 68 per cent of the total State population. Many
               of these systems are in need of major improvements. Of the
               192 sewer systems, 111 are considered satisfactory. . . .

New Jersey: ". . . New Jersey has a primary interest in the multiple-
               purpose development of the water resources of the Delaware
               River Basin. . . . Interstate cooperation appears to be the
               best means for realizing these objectives. . . ."

New Hampshire: "The major difficulty to be resolved lies in the fact that in most instances the easily available, low-cost water-supply developments have taken place. Communities will now have to contemplate the additional higher costs occasioned by the investment needed to develop the more remote sources of water supply. This is particularly true of the seacoast area where surface sources are limited and ground-water reserves have been developed to a high degree."

Maryland: "Maryland will always have adequate water resources—at a price. The problem is to supply the water in the quantity needed when needed and where needed by the consumers."

Louisiana: Louisiana stands alone among all the States in the magnitude and variety of its water problems. Foremost among these problems is that of flood control, for all of the drainage from 41 per cent of the United States passes through the State and reaches the sea within its borders. Heavy rainfall on the extensive areas of low, flat lands creates many local drainage problems, and periodic droughts bring severe water deficiencies, particularly in the rice-growing sections dependent upon irrigation.

California: "The fundamental physical problem of water resources development in California is the extreme geographical and seasonal maldistribution of the state's water resources. . . . With approximately 72 per cent of the water resources occurring in the northern one-third of the State, and approximately 75 per cent of the annual demand, present and future, found in the southern two-thirds of the State, the problems of conservation and distribution of water supplies for beneficial uses are readily apparent." [48]

Some themes recur, however, in nearly all of the fifty reports. Unless certain actions are taken soon by government, it will become increasingly difficult in the years ahead to provide sufficient quantities of usable water at reasonable costs. Although progress was made after this survey, the Surgeon General of the United States underscored the urgency of the situation when he reported in 1963 that 13 million Americans lived in 1,500 communities which permitted untreated water to be discharged into their streams; that another 17 million people lived in cities possessing inadequate sewage systems; and that "more than 2,700 small towns serving almost 6 million people did not even have sewer and treatment facilities." [49]

In 1975, a population of 225 million Americans will need 450 billion gallons of water per day; in 1980, consumption will have risen to 650 billion

[48] Senate Select Committee on National Water Resources, *Water Resources Activities in the United States: Views and Comments of the States*, Committee Print No. 6, January, 1960, 86th Cong., 2nd Sess. (Washington, 1960), pp. 369, 333, 226–227, 211, 111, 88, and 14.

[49] "Pollution of U. S. Air and Water—How Serious?" *U. S. News & World Report*, September 16, 1963, p. 99; see also "Let's Stop Poisoning Our Waters," *This Week*, December 3, 1961; and U. S. Department of Health, Education and Welfare, Public Health Service Publication No. 958, *The Struggle for Clean Water* (Washington, 1962).

daily. Based on current estimates, this is the optimum of usable water available in this country.[50]

The heaviest demand for water will, of course, occur in urban areas where population growth and industrial development are concentrated. Only about one-half of the urban areas consider their present water supplies sufficient for their 1971 demands and only a little more than one-fourth predict sufficient supplies for their areas by 1981.[51]

ISSUES IN STATE POLLUTION CONTROL

State water pollution control activities are administered either by a state department or board of health (in twenty states), or by an independent agency within a state health department (in ten states).

With varying degrees of effectiveness, these pollution control programs attempt to promulgate tolerable pollution standards and investigate the extent

TABLE 3. PERCENTAGE OF WATER USED
BY CATEGORY *

	West	East
Irrigation	82	3
Industrial	13	84
Municipal	4	11
Rural	1	2

* 17 Western and 31 Eastern states.

SOURCE: Council of State Governments, *State Administration of Water Resources* (Chicago, 1957), pp. 9–10.

to which public waters have already been polluted. After hearings, the agency may then have the authority to issue orders demanding that violators—cities, industries, or other private parties—cease and desist with their undesirable and dangerous sewage discharge practices. When the law makes provision for a review and approval of a proposed sewage treatment disposal facility, it is generally the state water pollution control agency which is authorized to issue or deny the necessary construction permits.

Closer analysis and study of such agencies and of the laws under which they operate reveal notable differences in approach between regions and states. In the Eastern states, for example, concern for water quality and distribution ranks high, while in the arid West greater stress is placed on the

[50] U. S. Department of Health, Education and Welfare, *Proceedings of the National Conference on Water Pollution*, December 12–14, 1960 (Washington, 1961), p. 282.

[51] Advisory Commission on Intergovernmental Relations, *Intergovernmental Responsibilities for Water Supply and Sewage Disposal in Metropolitan Areas* (Washington, 1962), p. 7; see also Richard D. Duke and Paul Nickel, *An Annotated Bibliography on Water Problems* (East Lansing, 1962).

regulation of water rights and on the availability of sufficient quantities of water (see Table 3).

Also, the West, under the doctrine of *prior appropriation*, places surface and underground water rights under the state, while in the East the *riparian system* gives property owners adjacent to the rivers and lakes the "non-consumptive use of the water," subject only to the exercise of the state police power. Inasmuch as the state police power approach necessitates a case adjudication, the Eastern states find it more difficult to give central direction to the future planning and use of their overall water resources.[52] Aside from such regional differences, the pollution authorities of the Central states also differ considerably with respect to the scope and range of power given them by their legislatures. For instance, there is the problem of water standards and classification.

States differ, for example, as to how much discretion is placed in the water pollution control agency with respect to fixing water quality standards and classification. Even when the agency is authorized to fix standards, there is considerable disagreement among the experts as to what is meant by "clean water," what the chemical, biological, or biochemical yardsticks should be, what standards should be applied to the different users of water, or which type of treatment has proved most efficacious for the different sewage and industrial wastes. Should standards be based on considerations of public health primarily (as certain affected industrial groups contend), or should the public interest be construed more broadly so as to encompass the protection of wildlife, the preservation of aesthetic values, and the expanding needs of recreation (as many of the conservation-conscious would insist)? As of 1963, about one-third of the states failed to adopt a statewide system of minimum water standards or classification. This leaves matters of quality objectives to be determined on a case-by-case basis.[53]

States differ also as to the extent and effectiveness of their monitoring or sampling systems and as to how much control their central agency may exercise over local pollution standards and classification practices.

Only about a dozen states have laws under which financial assistance in the form of loans or grants can be made available to municipalities that wish to construct a water or sewage treatment facility. States differ most significantly in the degree to which central pollution control agencies can enforce their directives and assure effective abatement. Voluntary cooperation is the typical pattern of securing compliance; about a third of the states have brought not a single pollution control offender, public or private, to court in five years or more.[54] There are at least two major obstacles to a more vigorous

---

[52] *Ibid.*, ch. 5.

[53] Summary of state actions to establish water quality criteria or standards: *Congressional Record*, October 16, 1963, p. 18682.

[54] House Committee on Public Works, *Federal Water Pollution Control*, Hearings of March 14, 15, 16, and 29, 1961, pursuant to H.R. 4036, 87th Cong., 1st Sess. (Washington, 1961), p. 249.

enforcement in this field. First, states in their efforts to attract industry are fearful of offending present or potential taxpayers and employers; and secondly, state agencies may not have sufficient financial resources and professional staffs to provide the research and conduct the investigations which would be required to prove their case against violators in commission hearings or court adjudications.

To strengthen anti-pollution measure procedures, pressures have been building up in nearly all states to enact broader enabling laws under which cities, counties, or special water control districts could increase their own organizational and financial resources to prevent, abate, or control undesirable local waste discharge practices.

Most instructive in this connection are some of the findings and recommendations of the Advisory Commission on Intergovernmental Relations that deal with the responsibilities of the states for water supply and sewage disposal in the metropolitan areas.

In the financial realm, such measures would include:

> State purchase or guarantee of local bonds, the waiving of debt restrictions to permit issuance of general obligation bonds to finance water and sewerage improvements ordered by a state agency, and authorization for local units to float bond issues to finance water and sewerage improvements without submitting the question to a referendum. . . .

Even more important, however, in the judgment of the commission would be provisions which increased technical assistance to local governmental units for waste disposal, planning, and construction, authorized joint action by local units to meet an area's water and sewage needs, and strengthened local governmental regulatory authority over individual wells and septic tank installations. Inasmuch as effective water resources management depends on state leadership in intergovernmental relations, the states themselves would first of all have to improve their own anti-pollution programs.

THE ROLE OF THE FEDERAL GOVERNMENT
IN FIGHTING WATER POLLUTION

The active and large-scale involvement of Washington in the battle against water pollution is a relatively recent one. Although the United States Public Health Service did conduct some surveys and technical studies of the health-endangering aspects of pollution beginning in 1912, major federal assistance to the states and their local governments was not provided until 1956. Under the Federal Water Pollution Control Act passed at that time, Congress for the first time furnished funds for the construction of municipal waste treatment facilities, for research, and for a broader enforcement program. Incentive grants were provided for 2,746 municipalities which were building $12 billion worth of treatment plants. The federal grants-in-aid share came to 13% for communities over 50,000 and 87 per cent for those below. When completed, this program will have brought about "the improvement of

33,000 miles of rivers and streams and will serve 27 million people." [55] The act was amended in 1961 to include authorizations of $570 million to combat pollution. Among the principal changes were these:

A. Increased federal support for the construction of municipal waste treatment facilities;
B. Broadened and strengthened federal enforcement powers;
C. An intensified program of research "looking forward to more effective methods of pollution control, with special emphasis on regional variations";
D. Provision for federal support of state and interstate pollution control programs.[56]

In supporting this legislation, the majority of the House Committee on Public Works stressed the urgency of increasing drastically the reuse of water resources through improved pollution control if the nation's water needs are to be met in the future. The minority, while insisting that they favored water conservation and the prevention of water pollution, saw "no indication that municipalities, or the States, generally are unable to finance the costs of constructing waste treatment works." [57] Late in 1965 the House and Senate passed substantially similar legislation relating to the disposal of solid wastes. The proposed act would provide for a federally-financed research and development program for improved methods of solid waste disposal and for technical aid to state and local entities for developing or establishing solid waste disposal programs. The federal facility would be the joint responsibility of the Departments of Health, Education, and Welfare and Interior. In addition, grants would be made available to private research agencies and to state and interstate agencies for research and surveys.

As a result of the federal financial support already furnished states and cities and as a consequence of steps taken cooperatively by the three levels of government and by private industry, a significant beginning has been made. Pollution in the Missouri and Ohio Rivers has been cut down, over 4,000 projects have been added throughout the country, enforcement procedures have become more effective, and cities are spending about twice as much each year on their water and sewer treatment facilities. During fiscal 1962 alone, 754 projects were approved, to which the federal government contributed $65 million and local governments, $332 million, making it approximately a one-to-five federal to local ratio. During 1963, spending for sewage treatment facilities proceeded at an estimated rate of $600 million annually.

Much, of course, remains to be done. Industry still needs to build about 5,000 treatment plants for its own waste disposal. The backlog in new and enlarged municipal facilities is still close to $2 billion, and in thousands of

[55] U. S. Department of Health, Education, and Welfare, *Building for Cleaner Water: A Progress Report on Five Years of Federal Incentive Grants for Municipal Waste Treatment* (Washington, 1962), pp. 2–4.
[56] U. S. Department of Health, Education, and Welfare, *Protecting Our Water Resources: The Federal Water Pollution Control Program* (Washington, 1962), p. 6.
[57] House Committee on Public Works, *Federal Water Pollution Control Act Amendments of 1961*, House Report No. 306, 87th Cong., 1st Sess. (Washington, 1961), p. 19.

suburban communities and smaller towns septic tanks are overburdened, creating serious health hazards and widespread economic losses. More research will be necessary to probe the toxic effects of pollutants, radioactive wastes, and the presence of live viruses in treated sewage effluent. Pollution treatment processes and plants (many of them more than thirty years old) must be modernized and refined in order to screen out wastes which are produced by the manufacture of thousands of new synthetic fibers, plastics, detergents, and medicines.

Even more important, there should be a goal for pollution abatement that government, private industry, and householder could follow in the years ahead. The 1960 National Conference on Water Pollution Control suggested this credo:

A. Users of water do not have an inherent right to pollute.
B. Users of public waters have a responsibility for returning them as nearly clean as is technically possible.
C. Prevention is just as important as control of pollution.[58]

WATER RESOURCE DEVELOPMENTS IN THE WEST

On November 8, 1960, the voters of California approved a $1,750,000,-000 general obligation bond issue to finance one of the most gigantic and ambitious water conservation and distribution programs in the world. State Water Project, a twenty-year undertaking, is designed to transport the huge water surplus of the Sierra Nevada and of Northern California through the San Joaquin valley down into the fast-growing but arid coastal areas of the southern part of the state. Work on the intricate system of dams, levees, pumping stations, aqueducts, diversion tunnels, master drains, and reservoirs has already begun. Based on careful projections, this complex conveyor system should be completed, if present construction schedules are maintained, in time to meet the sharply-rising needs of the state for the remainder of the century. Involved in this project is more than the distribution of California's water. For example, Big Oroville Dam (it will be the world's highest when completed), will not only store water for flood control and power purposes but also will irrigate over a quarter million acres in the Feather River basin. Five upstream dams along the river will serve important recreation objectives, while in the North Bay aqueduct industrial needs are given a high priority.

California's State Water Project (along with the already federally-assisted Central Valley project and other federal flood control and reclamation works) thus constitutes a Herculean effort to manage water resources so as to balance regional interests as well as urban and rural needs for the benefit of the entire state. Without such a comprehensive plan and scheme of control, California, with its population increasing at a rate two and one-half times faster than the national average, would consider its present and future economic growth seriously jeopardized.

Water and power problems have always plagued the Western and Southwestern states—Arizona, California, Nevada, New Mexico, and Utah (see Figure 3). Key to the area's rapidly-expanding population and unprecedented

[58] *Proceedings of the National Conference on Water Pollution,* p. 564.

FIGURE 3

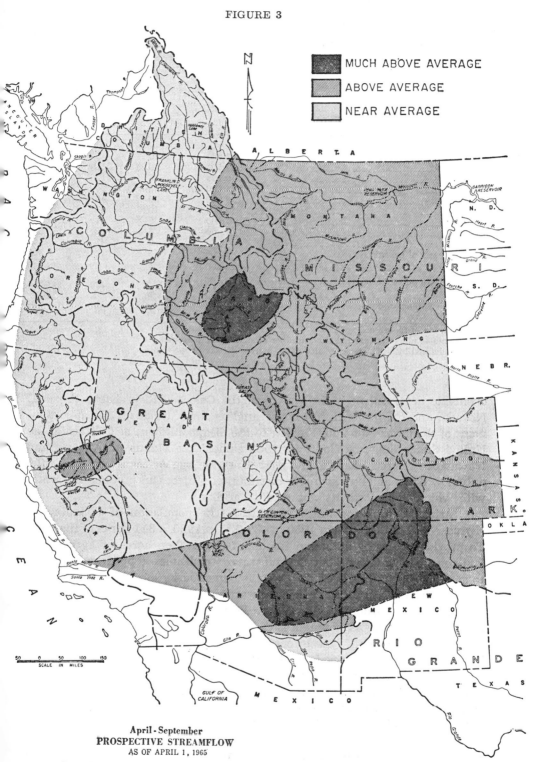

MUCH ABOVE AVERAGE

ABOVE AVERAGE

NEAR AVERAGE

April - September
PROSPECTIVE STREAMFLOW
AS OF APRIL 1, 1965

SOURCE: Compiled by the United States Soil Conservation Service, in *The New York Times*, July 5, 1961 p. 26.

TABLE 4. ESTIMATED [1] NUMBER OF PLACES WITH AIR POLLUTION PROBLEMS

Population class	All urban places		Major problems		
			Places		
	Number in class	Approximate population	Per cent	Number	Approximate population
Urban places:					
1,000,000 or more	5	17,500	100	5	17,500
500,000 to 1,000,000	16	11,100	70	11	7,800
250,000 to 500,000	30	10,700	45	13	4,800
100,000 to 250,000	81	11,600	25	20	2,900
50,000 to 100,000	201	13,800	20	40	2,800
25,000 to 50,000	432	14,900	10	43	1,500
10,000 to 25,000	1,134	17,600	8	91	1,400
5,000 to 10,000	1,394	9,800	3	42	290
2,500 to 5,000	2,152	7,600	2	43	150
Unincorporated parts of urbanized areas	--	9,900	--	--	3,800
Subtotal	5,445	124,500	5	308	42,940
Urban and rural places under 2,500	14,345	11,100	--	--	--
Grand total	19,790	135,600	5	308	42,940
Per cent of total U. S. population [4]	--	76	--	--	24

NOTE: 1960 population in thousands.
[1] Accuracy of estimates not to be inferred from number of significant digits reported.
[2] Urban places as defined by U. S. Department of Commerce, Bureau of the Census.

economic development is the waters of the Colorado River basin. Arizona, Nevada, and California have been wrangling for years about the apportionment of the lower Colorado. Finally, to the disappointment of California, the United States Supreme Court in 1963 upheld the claims of Arizona and Nevada for a larger share of the river. But although Arizona won the battle, only new dams and an expensive distribution project can produce the water with which it can win its war against aridity.

Arizona's need for water is critical. The population of Phoenix has skyrocketed from 106,000 in 1950 to 439,000 in 1960, a 311 per cent increase. To provide necessary irrigation for about one million acres of agricultural lands north of Phoenix, underground water supplies are tapped and depleted to such an extent that the water table is dangerously lowered. As a result of the recent Supreme Court decision awarding the state a 2.8 million acre-feet allotment, Arizona finds itself now legally entitled to triple its diversions from the Colorado. (An acre-foot is the quantity of water required to cover an acre of land to a depth of one foot.) But lacking sufficient capital, the state has decided to turn to the federal government to found its Central Arizona Project. This is to be a partially self-liquidating (from power revenues over a period of fifty years) $1 billion federally-aided multiple project including reclamation, flood control, irrigation, recreation, and power. Clouding the future time table and priority of this development somewhat, is the federal government's emphasis on a regional approach which seeks to solve the water problems of the West by taking from the water-rich North and giving to the water-poor South. A $4 billion Pacific Southwest Water Plan advanced by

ND POPULATION EXPOSED TO AIR POLLUTION "

| Moderate problems | | | Minor problems | | | All problems | | |
| Places | | Approximate population | Places | | Approximate population | Places | | Approximate population |
Per cent	Number		Per cent	Number		Per cent	Number	
0	0	0	0	0	0	100	5	17,500
30	5	3,300	0	0	0	100	16	11,100
45	14	4,800	10	3	1,100	100	30	10,700
50	40	5,800	25	21	2,900	100	81	11,600
35	70	4,800	45	91	6,200	100	201	13,800
25	108	3,700	45	194	6,700	80	345	11,900
20	227	3,500	37	420	6,500	65	738	11,400
12	168	1,200	35	487	3,400	50	697	4,890
10	215	760	28	602	2,100	40	860	3,010
--	--	2,300	--	--	2,300	--	--	8,400
15	847	30,160	33	1,818	31,200	53	2,973	104,300
--	--	--	--	--	--	[3] 30	4,300	3,300
15	847	30,160	33	1,818	31,200	37	7,273	107,600
--	--	17	--	--	17	--	--	60

Problems are mostly minor.
Total U. S. population in 1960 was 179,323,000.

SOURCE: *A Study of Pollution—Air: A Staff Report to the Committee on Public Works*, United States Senate, 88th Cong. 1st Sess. (Washington, 1963), p. 9.

Secretary of the Interior Udall envisaged, for example, a diversion of some of northern California's water to meet Arizona's needs, 1,000 miles to the south.

As might be expected, this plan has already aroused considerable antagonism in California as well as in certain other states of the Pacific Northwest. What is feared is an unwarranted interference with states' rights and states' resources, and the accumulation of dictatorial powers in the hands of Washington officialdom—more particularly the United States Bureau of Reclamation. Moreover, any proposed further alteration in the Western water picture must ovecome strong objections of certain conservationists (the "bug and bunny" people), and recreation interests which oppose the construction of additional dams and waterworks on the basis that these impair the natural beauty and wilderness status of the canyons.

THE FIGHT FOR FRESH AIR

According to United States Public Health Service estimates, over 100 million Americans live in cities which have an air pollution problem. In as many as 308 urban communities comprising 43 million people, the problem has reached major proportions (see Table 4). That excessively polluted air, especially when given an opportunity to combine with certain meteorological conditions, can even cause serious damage to human life has been known for years. For example, smog reached catastrophic proportions in London in 1952 and again in 1962 when 340 deaths were officially attributed to it. In this country, concentrations of heavily polluted air over Donora, Pennsylvania in

1948 is charged with having killed seventeen persons and causing illness to over 4,000 others. More than 200 may have died in New York City in 1953 as a consequence of "unusually high levels of sulfur dioxide and smoke shade" which stagnated over the city for ten days.[59]

There is now considerable medical evidence to the effect that continued or excessive exposure to highly-polluted air can play a significant and often dangerous role in certain types of respiratory ailments. Breathing in polluted air may increase susceptibility to or may aggravate such diseases as chronic bronchitis, pulmonary emphysema, bronchial asthma, and even lung cancer.

The economic losses due to air pollution add another dimension to the problem. Senator Abraham Ribicoff of Connecticut, former Secretary of Health, Education, and Welfare, and one of the main supporters of more effective measures for pollution control, summarized the cost picture as follows:

> "[P]olluted air" makes our livestock ill and so reduces meat and milk production, stunts and sometimes destroys our crops. It corrodes buildings, bridges, monuments, and structures of all kinds. By reducing visibility, it creates traffic hazards and poses a threat to air navigation.
>
> Expert estimates of the high price we are paying for the filth in the air today run into billions of dollars a year. Some of our metropolitan centers suffer damages of up to $100 million a year. The daily average of airborne pollutants in one of our largest cities is 25,000 tons. The U. S. Public Health Service . . . estimates that polluted air costs every man, woman and child in this country something like $65 a year—and the cost is going up. Increased cleaning and laundry bills, the destruction of stone and metal building materials, depressed property values, higher home maintenance expenses, and a host of other economic losses contributed to the ever-rising cost.[60]

A national authority at the University of California estimates the field and vegetable crop damage due to air pollution in that state alone to amount annually to about $8 million. He places primary blame for this contamination on oxidates, ozone, ethylene, fluoride, and sulfur dioxide—oxidized hydrocarbon pollutants that come from uncontrolled combustion devices. In such highly-urbanized areas as Los Angeles, San Francisco, and San Diego, motor vehicles are thought to emit as much as 80 per cent of such contaminants.

STATE AND LOCAL GOVERNMENTAL ACTIVITIES IN

AIR POLLUTION CONTROL

What is the current status of air pollution control? Based on official replies from forty-seven state governments to inquiries addressed to them by the United States Senate Committee on Public Works during 1963, the following picture emerges:

[59] Senate Committee on Public Works, *A Study of Pollution—Air,* Staff Report of September, 1963, 88th Cong., 1st Sess. (Washington, 1963), p. 13.

[60] Abraham Ribicoff, "We Are Poisoning the Air," *Look,* October 22, 1963, p. 132. For a discussion of the problem of air pollution in the light of recent Congressional actions, see Will T. Johns "Conservation's Last Frontier," *Conservation News,* February 15, 1964.

A. "Some type" of air pollution control laws have been enacted in thirty-three states.
B. Of these thirty-three states, fifteen provide "some" control authority; twelve states have no central state control authority but have laws enabling local units to enact appropriate control measures; six states provide only for "research and technical assistance."
C. About a dozen states have worked out formal or informal procedures for handling interstate pollution problems.
D. Spending $5,000 or more per year (in 1961) were seventeen states, and eighty-five local governmental units—cities, counties, or special district authorities. The total for all state and local units came to around $10 million. However, nearly half of this total was expended by one state, California, and its political subdivisions, and of all eighty-five local governmental units, about 60 per cent spent less than $25,000 annually.[61]

Closer scrutiny of state laws reveals that California appears to have developed the most comprehensive and effective anti-air pollution program enacted by any state to date. Among the major provisions of the law are these: First, all of the counties are authorized to adopt pollution control districts; second, to such districts are then given "broad powers to adopt and enforce rules and regulations on the control of pollutants from stationary sources"; third, the state's Department of Public Health is charged with studying the "health effects and the nature and occurrence of air pollution," with assisting "local agencies to monitor air pollutants," and with "adopt[ing] standards for air quality and for motor vehicle emissions"; fourth, responsibility for testing pollution control devices, for approving them, and for scheduling their adoption has been given to the State Motor Vehicle Control Board (which was established at a special session of the 1960 legislature); fifth, placed in the State Department of Motor Vehicles is the licensing and supervision of motor vehicle pollution control device inspection stations; and last, amendments to the state tax laws permit the deduction from income tax of costs incurred in the installation of air pollution control equipment; also built into the law is a five-year amortization period for the cost of such equipment.[62]

Under California's air pollution control law, as now administered, all new cars must be equipped with special crankcase devices which are so designed as to eliminate the "blow by" gases and other vapors. It is estimated that these devices will help to reduce the emission of hydrocarbons by approximately 30 per cent by recirculating such gases and precluding their entry into the atmosphere through the crankcase.

According to present plan, by 1965, when 90 per cent of nearly all motor vehicles old and new have been covered by the control system, 500 tons of smog-producing pollutants will be eliminated each day from the Los Angeles area alone. In the metropolitan counties (with five million cars and 80 per cent of the state's population) mandatory installations on old cars began January 1964, at prices ranging from about $13 to $20 per car, bus, or truck. To insure compliance, motor vehicle registration in California from then on was made

[61] *A Study of Pollution—Air*, pp. 31–34.
[62] *Ibid.*, pp. 58–59.

dependent on evidence that cars had been properly equipped with one type or another of a state-approved crankcase device.[63]

No metropolitan area in California is more eagerly anticipating positive results from all these new measures than is Los Angeles. Although its district has already spent $45 million since 1949 in the war against smog, pollution control program activities for 1963 alone required an annual budget of $3.5 million, and the labor of 262 employees.[64] The city's fresh air problem is still far from being solved. Peculiarities of geography and meteorology help to make the problem of Los Angeles extremely difficult and expensive. Here is an enormous urban and industrial complex that is penned in between the mountains and the ocean. Exhaust from the hundreds of thousands of cars and trucks, hot gases from industries, and escaped chemicals from oil refineries, unless blown out to the sea, push against a low layer of warm, immovable air which hovers above the city. As pollutants interact and concentrate in this low ceiling toxic chamber, they cause a condition which experts call thermal inversion and which most everyone else calls smog, thus results the most unwanted and dangerous by-product of California's unusual urban and economic growth.

Federal assistance to state and local governmental efforts in air pollution control began in 1955. Grants from the United States Public Health Service were made available to governments, private agencies, and universities for studies, surveys, research, and technical aid. Also established was a national air monitoring network, including 250 stations and equipped with sampling and recording instruments to facilitate the collection of pollution data from both rural and urban areas.

Still, additional legislation is sought by the administration. Congress completed action in 1963 on the Clean Air Act which increased federal financial and technical assistance to state and local air pollution control agencies for research, training, and demonstration projects. In 1965, the House of Representatives and the Senate passed similar bills amending the Clean Air Act of 1963 by directing the secretary of health, education, and welfare to establish standards limiting the emission of pollutants from gasoline-powered or diesel-powered vehicles, to establish a federal air pollution laboratory, and finally to support research programs relating to the development of low-cost techniques which would reduce emission of sulfur dioxide from the combustion of sulfur-containing fuels.

Testimony in opposition comes from representatives of such groups as the American Paper and Pulp Association, the National Association of Attor-

---

[63] Report to Governor Edmund G. Brown and the State Legislature by State of California Motor Vehicle Pollution Control Board, January, 1963, in House Committee on Interstate and Foreign Commerce, *Air Pollution*, 88th Cong., 1st Sess. (Washington, 1963), pp. 147–162.

[64] Senate Committee on Public Works, Special Subcommittee on Air and Water Pollution, *Air Pollution Control*, Hearings, September 9, 10, and 11, 1963, 88th Cong., 1st Sess. (Washington, 1963), p. 141.

neys General, the American Petroleum Institute, the Western Oil and Gas Association, American Mining Congress, the American Iron and Steel Institute, the National Association of Manufacturers, and the American Medical Association. Support for the administration-backed proposals is given by the American Public Health Association, the United States Conference of Mayors, the American Municipal Association, the National Association of Counties, and the American Federation of Labor and Congress of Industrial Organizations.

STATE PARKS AND OUTDOOR RECREATIONAL AREAS

The search for fresh air, the love of outdoor life and outdoor sports, increasing amounts of leisure time, and higher standards of living have drawn America's rapidly-expanding population to recreation spots as never before. Since World War II, for instance, the number of visitors crowding the state parks has nearly tripled and attendance in the national parks increased from 22 million in 1946 to over 72 million in 1960.

In the New York–Philadelphia complex, "a recent survey of recreation areas, other than ocean beaches, within 120 miles [of these cities] . . . indicated a capacity to serve 375,800 persons staying one time. Yet these facilities were called upon in 1960 to serve 32.6 million visitors. On a summer weekend day these facilities have to handle about 552,000 people on the average and about 233,100 visitors are served on weekdays." [65]

In another generation, by the year 2000, this country's recreational facilities will have to meet the needs of 350,000,000 Americans. To study this problem in depth, Congress in 1958 established the Outdoor Recreation Resources Review Commission to be made up of a bipartisan group of four senators, four representatives, and seven citizen-members appointed by the president. When this commission, chaired by Laurance S. Rockefeller, submitted its report four years later, it offered the nation the first detailed survey of

> what the public does in the out-of-doors, what factors affect its choices, what resources are available for its use, what are the present and future needs, and what the problems are in making new resources available.

In its recommendations the commission urged the establishment of a federal Bureau of Outdoor Recreation (in the Department of Interior), which would be called on to perform certain staff functions and cooperate with the states.[66] In its general tenor, however, the report left no doubt that the pivotal role in enlarging recreational opportunities would have to be assumed by the states themselves or by their local subdivisions, and not by Washington. Nor was this to be a governmental affair only. As at present, private initiative and

[65] Outdoor Recreation Resources Review Commission, *The Future of Outdoor Recreation in Metropolitan Regions of the United States*, Study Report 21, I (Washington, 1962), p. 24.
[66] *The New York Times*, February 1, 1962, p. 16; see also *The Future of Outdoor Recreation in Metropolitan Regions of the United States*.

enterprise were seen to bear the major share of the responsibilities for furnishing to millions who seek pleasure, physical exercise, or mental relaxation, the vast recreational opportunities and services that will be needed in the future. When Congress in 1963 enacted Public Law 88–29, the Outdoor Recreation Act, it relied heavily on the pioneer work of this commission. The Department of Interior was given the responsibility to

> inventory the nation's recreation needs and resources; to classify outdoor recreation resources; to formulate and maintain a national outdoor recreation plan; to furnish technical assistance to states and their local subdivisions—including private interests and non-profit organizations; to encourage regional cooperation; to sponsor and engage in research relating to outdoor recreation; to advance federal interdepartmental cooperation in this field; and to accept and use donations or money, property, services, and facilities for carrying out the purposes of the act.

In the years ahead state governments should, in the opinion of the commission, encourage and assist the private sector of the recreation industry to acquire land and develop sites, as well as to expand and improve existing facilities. To their cities, state governments will have to furnish special assistance for the acquisition of open spaces within or as close to the urban complex as possible. In fact, recreation consciousness and recreation activities have already increased notably among the states during the 1960's. This development was encouraged, to be sure, by federal aids made available under such acts as the Area Redevelopment Act of 1961 (loans to help launch industries, including recreation industries, in economically-depressed areas), the Agricultural Act of 1962 (authorizing recreation activities in small watershed projects), and the Housing Act of 1961 (Title VII, authorizing grants to states and local governments for the acquisition of open space lands and Title V, providing public facilities loans). For example

> *Pennsylvania* voters approved a program which included a $70 million bond issue for recreation, scenic grandeur, and tourism. Forty million dollars were earmarked for regional parks and for water development in counties without adequate recreation facilities. Also, counties and cities were authorized to share on a grant-in-aid basis in a $20 million fund which makes possible open space acquisitions for parks and recreational areas. The state's Game and Fish Commission received $10 million with which to buy sites to strengthen wildlife, fish, and water sports resources.[67]

> *New York* in 1960 approved a $75 million bond issue with which (among other purposes) to acquire recreation lands, stream easements, forest preserves, and access strips for the launching of boats. The park acquisition program alone is proposed to enlarge the state's public lands by 25,000 acres.[68]

Among other developments, New Jersey adopted a $60 million "Green Acres" program; Wisconsin, Minnesota, and Michigan added a one cent a pack

---

[67] "70 Million Program for Parks Is Acclaimed in Pennsylvania," *The New York Times,* January 28, 1962, p. 49.

[68] John C. Devlin, "Purchase of 25,000 Acres for State Parks Outlined," *The New York Times,* December 19, 1960, p. 1.

cigarette tax to finance their state recreation area programs. Special tax levies for such purposes were also authorized in Nebraska, Texas, and Vermont. Other than Pennsylvania, state matching provisions for local recreational developments were included in the laws of Massachusetts and Wisconsin. California proposed a five-year $100 million bond issue with which to finance purchases of land for parks and beaches.[69]

Without cataloguing any additional state and local activity in this field or supplying more detail, this brief run-down of projects should prove sufficient to support a modest note of optimism concerning the future of outdoor recreation. Appropriating money and laying out plans, of course, is only a beginning. Programs for expanded recreational opportunity necessarily bring into focus complicated intrastate governmental and political relationships. Problems of intergovernmental relations are always perplexing. But even more disturbing are the findings of the Outdoor Recreation Resources Review Commission which point up how thousands of underprivileged and disadvantaged residents of the inner city in a large metropolis are almost completely deprived of recreational facilities:

> [T]o a very large extent they are members of minority groups—Puerto Ricans and Negroes in New York, Negroes and southern whites in Chicago, Negroes and Mexicans on the Pacific Coast. . . .
>
> Typically they do not own cars and also they have the large families of rural people. They probably possess only rudimentary recreational skill, yet the children and adolescent members of these slum dwellers would probably benefit from outdoor recreation, both as an environmental factor in making life more pleasant, and also as a technique of acculturalization. . . .
>
> In New York City it is estimated that there are 180,000 children who would be unable to pay for a day camp because of poverty, and upwards of a half million additional New York City children could only attend camp if the cost were defrayed by substantial subsidies.[70]

Planning for public recreational programs in the years ahead will occupy all governments at all levels. As the work week and day are shrinking, as retired people live longer, as paid vacation time is increasing at an astounding rate, more people than ever are enabled to enjoy genuine leisure. Vacation leisure alone has doubled from 1900 to 1950 and it is estimated to increase fivefold in the second half of the century. To create the best possible climate for the intelligent, morally sound, and creative use of leisure constitutes a most unusual challenge to all aspects of social life. Government also will have to be prepared to make its contribution.[71]

---

[69] Book of the States, 1962–1963, pp. 486–488, and speech by Ira N. Gabrielson, former Director of the U. S. Fish and Wildlife Service, before North American Wildlife Conference, Denver, Colorado, March 1962, in the Congressional Record, March 23, 1962, p. A 2255.

[70] The Future of Outdoor Recreation in Metropolitan Regions of the United States, I, 10–11.

[71] Marion Clawson, "How Much Leisure, Now and in the Future?" in James C. Charlesworth (ed.), Leisure in America: Blessing or Curse? (Philadelphia, 1964), p. 13.

CASE PROBLEMS FOR CLASS DISCUSSION

1. Your state is considering a new formula for apportioning highway user tax revenues to the state trunk highway system, to county roads, and to city streets. As research director to the state highway commissioner, it is your task to come up with recommendations which the commissioner can present to the next legislature. What criteria would you employ in the make-up of the ratios? How would you justify the new formula against critics who prefer the present arrangement?
2. A proposal banning billboards from the national defense highway system in your state is before the legislature. It has passed the Senate, but stiff opposition in the House highway committee clouds the future of the measure. You are the legislative representative of the state automobile association which strongly favors the enactment of the bill. In your judgment it seems necessary to call together all other lobbyists who work for the highway billboard proposal for an exchange of views concerning the best ways of rallying legislative support. Which interest groups would be represented at the conference? What plan would you suggest?
3. Assume that your state includes an area of great natural scenic beauty traversed by a river. It is proposed to construct a hydroelectric power plant which would tap this river for the supply of electricity urgently needed in a nearby metropolitan complex. While urban interests strongly favor the project, conservationists and other groups associated with them in this essentially rural state are opposed to it with equal fervor. You are asked to predict, as scientifically as you can, the outcome of this conflict. What would be your research design?
4. A community of 50,000 in your state is about to pass a tough anti-smoke ordinance. One of the local industries (employment, 5,000) insists that it cannot abide by this ordinance and that it would have to move its operations out of town if the proposed measure were enacted. Smoke control devices are available but the directors of the plant are unwilling to expend the necessary funds. Some groups in the community have urged that the city subsidize the installation of controls. You have been asked to serve as mediator. How would you proceed?

SELECTED BIBLIOGRAPHY

ELTON R. ANDREWS and WILLIAM F. LIPMAN, "Open Space for Recreation," State Government, Autumn, 1960, pp. 222–226.

ALFRED BALK, " 'Progress' and Parks," National Civic Review, October, 1960, pp. 474–476, 483.

HARVEY O. BANKS, "The Bases of an Adequate State Water Program," State Government, Spring, 1960, pp. 133–139.

WILLIAM J. BLOCK, The Separation of the Farm Bureau and the Extension Service; Political Issue in a Federal System (Urbana, Ill., 1960).

KENNETH G. BUECHE and MORRIS J. SCHUR, Air Pollution Control—Selected Governmental Approaches: Possibilities for Colorado (Boulder, 1963).

WESLEY CALEF, Private Grazing and Public Lands, Studies of the Local Management of the Tayler Grazing Act (Chicago, 1960).

RICHARD A. COOLEY, Politics and Conservation: The Decline of the Alaska Salmon (New York, 1963).

HARRIET H. COOTER, "To Stay Out of Floods," National Civic Review, November, 1961, pp. 534–539.

PETER FARB, "Let's Plan the Damage," National Civic Review, May, 1960, pp. 238–241.

PHILLIP O. FOSS, Politics and Grass (Seattle, 1960).

IRVING K. FOX and HENRY P. CAULFIELD, JR., "Getting the Most Out of Water Resources," State Government, Spring, 1961, pp. 104–111.

ROBERT S. FRIEDMAN, State and Local Relations in Highway Finance in Louisiana (Baton Rouge, 1962).

Land Use in 33 Oregon Cities (Eugene, 1961).

DEAN E. MANN, "The Law and Politics of Groundwater in Arizona," *Arizona Law Review*, Winter, 1960, pp. 241–267.

ROSCOE C. MARTIN, *Water for New York* (Syracuse, 1960).

ROSCOE C. MARTIN, GUTHRIE S. BIRKHEAD, JESSE BURKHEAD, and FRANK J. MUNGER, *River Basin Administration and the Delaware* (Syracuse, 1960).

GAYLORD A. NELSON, "Planning and Developing our Resources: A Critical Task for State Action," *State Government*, Autumn, 1961, pp. 220–225.

VINCENT OSTROM, "The Political Economy of Water Development," *American Economic Review*, May, 1962, pp. 450–458.

Outdoor Recreation Resources Review Commission, *The Future of Outdoor Recreation in Metropolitan Regions of the United States*, 3 vols. (Washington, 1962).

SAMUEL M. ROGERS, "Air Pollution Legislation—A Review of Current Developments," *Journal of Public Health*, May, 1960, pp. 642–648.

ERNEST F. ROSS, *State Supervision of Michigan Local Governments: The Water Pollution Problem* (Ann Arbor, 1960).

MEL SCOTT, *The Future of San Francisco Bay* (Berkeley, 1963).

GORDAN S. SMITH, "Drying Wet Lands," *National Civic Review*, December, 1963, pp. 591–592, 614.

CHARLES A. SULLIVANT, *The Kansas Watershed District* (Lawrence, 1960).

JOHN T. THOMPSON, *Public Administration of Water Resources in Texas* (Austin, 1960).

DOROTHY C. TOMPKINS, *Water Plans for California: A Bibliography* (Berkeley, 1961).

CHARLES K. WARRINER, "Public Opinion and Collective Action: Formation of a Watershed District," *Administrative Science Quarterly*, December, 1961, pp. 333–359.

EDWARD J. WYNNE, JR., "Ensuring Proper Land Re-Use in Urban Renewal: An Analysis of Present Federal and Local Policies and Practices," *New York University Law Review*, November, 1962, pp. 882–915.

Chapter XV

HEALTH
AND WELFARE

What are the politics of medicine, welfare, and poverty?

Are state and local relief rolls loaded with "chiselers," "loafers," and "social parasites"?

PUBLIC HEALTH

In most states administrative control over essential public health functions is lodged in a state board or department of health appointed by the governor. Among the oldest and least controversial of health activities carried on either by the states themselves or by their local governments are those dealing with the collection of vital statistics—birth, death, marriage, divorce, adoption—and those which are concerned with the detection, prevention, and control of communicable or occupational diseases. State laws define procedures and regulations to effectuate such controls as compulsory vaccination, immunization, and quarantine. Also established by statute are certain minimum standards of sanitation affecting the production and processing of milk and other foods and the safeguarding of water supplies. In more recent years state operations in environmental sanitation have been concerned with problems of air and water pollution, accident prevention, and with measures designed to afford protection against the effects of radiation.

While the federal government assisted state and local health units to some extent in the nineteenth century (battling infectious epidemics), the major growth in federal aid did not occur until 1935, when the Social Security Act was passed. Under this law and its subsequent amendments, the national government began to furnish significant financial grants-in-aid to strengthen and enlarge state and local health services. Funds were made available, usually on a matching basis, for medical, surgical, and corrective aid to crippled children and for maternal and child care (see Table 1); for medical

TABLE 1. FEDERAL, STATE, AND LOCAL EXPENDITURES
FOR MATERNAL AND CHILD WELFARE SERVICES,
FISCAL 1962

Program	Federal	State and local
Child welfare services	$17,811,076	$228,200,000
Crippled children services	24,591,692	53,915,713
Maternal and child health services	24,406,943	70,073,171

SOURCE: Department of Health, Education, and Welfare, *Grants-in-Aid and Other Financial Assistance Programs* (Washington, 1963), pp. 252, 258, 271.

TABLE 2. FEDERAL, STATE, AND LOCAL EXPENDITURES
IN THE BATTLE AGAINST MAJOR DISEASES, FISCAL 1961

Disease	Federal	State and local
Venereal disease	$2,379,805	$12,707,377
Tuberculosis	3,082,055	28,116,758
Cancer	3,313,568	8,220,994
Mental health	5,941,888	70,640,190
Heart disease	3,300,482	8,161,628

SOURCE: Department of Health, Education, and Welfare, *Grants-in-Aid and Other Financial Assistance Programs* (Washington, 1963), pp. 35, 61, 98, 129, 135.

assistance of those on relief (1950); and for improvements in research and control of venereal disease (1938), tuberculosis (1944), mental health (1946), cancer (1948), and heart disease (1948). (For federal aid for disease control, see Table 2.)

Federal aid for hospital surveys and construction was initiated in 1946 with the passage of the Hill-Burton Act (see Table 3). This law and its amendments afforded assistance not only to general hospitals but to certain specialized hospitals—tuberculosis, mental health, chronic diseases—as well as to nursing homes, public health centers (diagnostic and rehabilitative), and state health laboratories.

The "medically" indigent aged came in for special attention when Congress enacted the Kerr-Mills Bill in 1960. Under this measure, which had been strongly supported by the American Medical Association and found inadequate by the Kennedy-Johnson administration, federal government grants were made available to states to help them pay for medical expenses of citizens over sixty-five years of age who were neither eligible nor willing to apply for relief but who were, nevertheless, unable to meet medical expenses by themselves. Left to each state were such important determinations as what medical benefits to include (hospitalization, nursing homes, medical fees,

TABLE 3. FEDERAL AND LOCAL EXPENDI-
TURES FOR HOSPITAL AND MEDICAL
FACILITIES CONSTRUCTION

Fiscal year	Federal	Local (Est.)
1950	$ 56,926,035	$138,338,000
1955	73,564,726	179,139,000
1959	135,134,696	384,298,000
1960	143,461,588	365,990,000
1961	156,974,121	363,696,000
1962	164,395,064	307,031,000

SOURCE: Department of Health, Education, and Welfare, *Grants-in-Aid and Other Financial Assistance Programs* (Washington, 1963), p. 65.

etc.), the extent of the funds to devote to this program, and the basis constituting medical indigence.

In an effort to meet the severe shortages of medical personnel, Congress
in 1963 passed the Health Professions Educational Assistance Act which
authorized aid for three years totalling almost a quarter of a billion dollars.
This measure was designed primarily to increase the training opportunities
for physicians, dentists, and other professional health workers by providing
federal grants for the construction of medical and dental teaching facilities.
Also made available were liberal loans to students pursuing full-time courses
in such schools as medicine, osteopathy, or dentistry. This act was extended
and considerably expanded by the House in September, 1965.

What the states accomplished by way of implementing the Kerr-Mills
(Medical Assistance for the Aged) Program during its first eighteen months
emerges from a report to the Senate Special Committee on Aging.[1] In general,
the tenor of the staff report was quite critical—not entirely surprising in view
of the fact that the committee's chairman, Senator McNamara, a Michigan
Democrat, had long favored the administration approach of placing medical
care for the aged under the Social Security Act. Under that approach all
persons sixty-five or over who were covered by Social Security (O.A.S.I.)
would as a matter of right regardless of earnings be eligible for medical
assistance financed through an increase of one-fourth of 1 per cent in social
security tax for employers and employees.

The report noted that the congressional intent of providing medical
services to the many medically indigent aged was not realized. This was held
due to the fact that

A. Only 24 states [2] and three territories as of June 1, 1962, had established
Medical Assistance for the Aged (M.A.A.) Programs. (During fiscal 1962–
1963, only 2 per cent of the country's 18 million aged received aid under
this program.)
B. Every state with such a program required applicants to submit to a means
test which "apart from any degrading qualities, excluded from help many
of the aged who are desperately in need of assistance." [3]

[1] Senate Committee on Labor and Public Welfare, *Performance of the States*, Report to the
Special Committee on Aging, June 15, 1962, 87th Cong., 2nd Sess., (Washington, 1962).
For an even better report, see Senate Special Committee on Aging, *Medical Assistance for
the Aged: The Kerr-Mills Program 1960–1963*, Report by the Subcommittee on Health of
the Elderly, October, 1963, 88th Cong., 1st Sess. (Washington, 1963); see also Senate
Committee on Labor and Public Welfare, *The Aged and the Aging in the United States:
A National Problem*, Subcommittee on Problems of the Aged and Aging, Senate Report
No. 1121, February 23, 1960, 86th Cong., 2nd Sess. (Washington, 1960). A discussion of
the various health insurance proposals is found in Special Senate Committee on Aging,
Comparison of Health Insurance Proposals For Older Persons, 1961–1962, prepared
by the Staff, May 10, 1962, 87th Cong., 2nd Sess. (Washington, 1962).
[2] *Book of the States, 1964–1965*, p. 424 reports that other states have entered the program
since June 1, 1962, and that eleven more have enacted enabling legislation to permit
joining later.
[3] Editorial, *The New York Times*, November 5, 1963, p. 30.

C. The quality of medical aid was adversely affected by the unwillingness of a number of hospitals and physicians to accept M.A.A. payments and rates.

D. The formula under which the grants were distributed tended to favor the wealthier and more populous states at the expense of the smaller and lower per capita income states.

E. A number of states because of insufficient financial resources already found it necessary to restrict benefits drastically.

F. "Complex limitations on eligibility and benefits" contributed to making the administrative costs of the program unavoidably high.

Spokesmen for the American Medical Association and other groups favoring the Kerr-Mills Act, lauded the states for their achievements and labeled the criticisms of the Medical Assistance for the Aged Program premature and biased. In congressional and public debate on M.A.A. and on administration proposals for so-called socialized medicine, their arguments stressed that

A. Based on public opinion polls and congressional sentiment, there is no strong public demand in this country for the federal government to assume comprehensive, socialized medical insurance programs of a type adopted in Western Europe and Scandinavia.

B. If the present rate of enrollments in private medical insurance plans is permitted to continue, 75 per cent of the aged would be covered adequately by 1965.

C. Private surveys have shown federal health statistics to be excessively pessimistic regarding the actual medical condition of aged citizens.

D. Freedom of choice of physicians and hospitals can be preserved more effectively if medical assistance is provided outside the social security framework.

E. The costs of a comprehensive medical assistance program as outlined by the administration would be enormously high, way beyond the given estimates, and would thus have to be supported by the steepest increases in social security taxes.

F. Even if the social security approach were to be adopted, 4 million citizens not subject to O.A.S.I. would still be excluded from medical benefits altogether.[4]

Before the reader is swayed excessively one way or another, it seems appropriate at this point to emphasize a few of the basic socio-economic and medical characteristics (see Figure 1) of the aged on which there is little dispute among the disputants:

A. Persons aged 65 and over now number about 18 million and constitute 9 per cent of the population. In another decade they will exceed 20 million.

B. Seven out of ten live alone or in two-person family units.

C. Fewer than 20 per cent have any paid employment.

D. Should serious illness strike, O.A.S.I. benefits will prove insufficient to pay for major medical bills. The monthly maximum for a retired worker is $125 and $187 for a couple.

[4] Senator Wallace Bennett, "Medical Care For The Aged," *Congressional Record*, April 3, 1961, p. A2304. A New York State Joint Legislative Committee recently completed a study of 100 Health Insurance Plans. Dr. Leroy K. Young, of the Sloan Institute of Hospital Administration at Cornell University Graduate School of Business Administration directed the survey; see *The New York Times*, July 5, 1964.

E. The aged are twice as likely as younger people to have one or more chronic medical conditions, and six times as likely to be subject to debilitating physical conditions.
F. Hospital care is likely to be twice as long as for younger people.
G. Presently, no more than 50 per cent of those 65 and older have hospital insurance.
H. Families where the head is 65 or older show a median income of less than $1,920, and a third reported no earnings.
I. Of those 65 and over, two-thirds have less than $500 in liquid assets although almost two-thirds of them own their own homes (80 per cent of which are mortgage free).
J. Although the majority of private insurance companies now do enroll the aged, rates may be from 50 per cent to 100 per cent higher than for younger people, the benefits usually more limited, cancellation provisions more frequently exercised, and enrollment periods more restricted.[5]

Supporters of the Kennedy-Johnson approach to medical assistance scored their major victory in the spring of 1965 when Congress finally enacted a historic $6 billion comprehensive medical care act for persons 65 and older (whether under Social Security or not).

There are essentially two distinct phases of this newly enacted "medicare" measure: (1) a compulsory basic health insurance plan covering hospital costs which is to be financed through payroll taxes and administered by the social security system and (2) a voluntary and supplementary medical program which will pay doctor bills and additional medical expenses financially supported by contributions from participants and general tax revenues.

Under the basic insurance plan persons eligible will be entitled (after paying the first $40) to hospitalization benefits (up to sixty days), to nursing home care (up to 100 days), and to outpatient hospital diagnostic services (subject to a $20 deductible charge), and to posthospital home health services (up to 100 visits when patient is under care of a physician).

Those over 65 who elect to join the supplementary medical plan may receive a wide variety of additional services for a monthly premium of $3, matched equally by federal government out of general revenues. After the patient pays the first $50, the program will then cover 80% of his bills for physicians' and surgical services furnished in a hospital, clinic, office or in the home; hospital care for 60 days in a spell of illness in a mental hospital (180-day lifetime maximum); home health services (up to 100 days per calendar year); and for such additional medical and health services as diagnostic X-ray and laboratory tests, electrocardiograms, basal metabolism

[5] Senate Special Committee on Aging, *Background Facts on the Financing of the Health Care of the Aged*, May 24, 1962, 87th Cong., 1st Sess. (Washington, 1962) pp. 1–3, 36; note also Senate Special Committee on Aging, *Developments in Aging 1959 to 1963*, Senate Report No. 8, February 11, 1963, 88th Cong., 1st Sess. (Washington, 1963); *The Aged and the Aging in the United States: A National Problem*, Senate Report No. 1121; and Senate Special Committee on Aging, *Increasing Employment Opportunities for the Elderly*, Hearings, Subcommittee on Employment and Retirement Incomes, December 19, 1963, Pt. 1, 88th Cong., 2nd Sess. (Washington, 1964).

FIGURE 1

AS THE U.S. DEBATES MEDICAL CARE FOR THE AGED

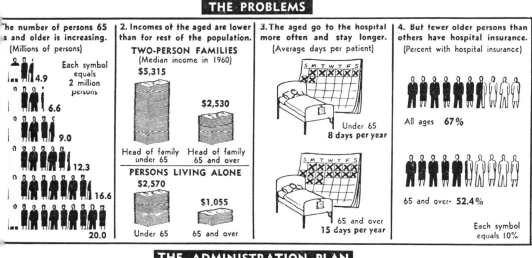

THE PROBLEMS

he number of persons 65 s and older is increasing. (Millions of persons)	2. Incomes of the aged are lower than for rest of the population.	3. The aged go to the hospital more often and stay longer. (Average days per patient)	4. But fewer older persons than others have hospital insurance. (Percent with hospital insurance)
Each symbol equals 2 million persons 4.9 6.6 9.0 12.3 16.6 20.0	TWO-PERSON FAMILIES (Median income in 1960) $5,315 $2,530 Head of family under 65 Head of family 65 and over PERSONS LIVING ALONE $2,570 $1,055 Under 65 65 and over	Under 65 8 days per year 65 and over 15 days per year	All ages 67% 65 and over 52.4% Each symbol equals 10%

THE ADMINISTRATION PLAN

The Administration's King-Anderson bill would provide for: (1) up to ninety days in a hospital with all costs paid for in excess of $10 for each of the first nine days; (2) up to 180 days in a skilled nursing home; (3) payment for out-patient diagnostic services in excess of $20; and (4) visiting nurse services for up to 240 visits a year. The program would be financed by an additional one-quarter of 1 per cent of the Social Security tax for both employe and employer and three-eighths of 1 per cent for self-employed persons on the first $5200 earned.

SOURCE: *The New York Times*, May 20, 1962, p. 10E.

readings, radium and radioactive isotope therapy, ambulance services, surgical dressings, splints, casts, iron lungs, oxygen tents, artificial limbs, etc. Dental work, drugs, and medicines, on the other hand, are, as yet, not included in the program.

MIGRATORY FARM LABOR—A STORY OF NEGLECT

Of no small concern in many of the states has been the plight of the medical conditions surrounding the 500,000 to 900,000 foreign and domestic migratory farm workers and their families as they follow the major crop seasons through a thousand counties in thirty states. Generally speaking efforts to date by state and local health authorities (with some assistance from the United States Departments of Health, Education, and Welfare and Labor and Agriculture) have simply not been able to keep up with the pressing medical needs of this population segment. Despite considerable expenditures, rural counties, where many of these people live and work, in California, Florida, Idaho, Michigan, New York, Texas, and Washington, find it extremely difficult financially to provide adequate medical facilities, clinics, or trained personnel. Living in crowded and unsanitary conditions, migratory workers are particularly vulnerable to dysentery, smallpox, and typhoid. Their children frequently fail to receive proper immunization against whooping cough, diphtheria, and tetanus. Prenatal and postnatal care are often woefully inadequate, and dental care nonexistent. Further aggravating these problems are such factors as the temporary and seasonal nature of the work, low annual family incomes, and barriers of culture, language, and education.

A series in the *Raleigh Times* conveys some of the color and tragedy of migratory life:

> An army of despair is again making its wretched odyssey through North Carolina. At its peak now, it will number 12,000 before October. . . . The state employment security commission which arranges to bring them here and assigns them to growers paints a rosy picture of the camps. But ministers of the North Carolina Council of Churches on their weekly, often daily visits, see the worst of them as they are: blighted, stinking hovels, filthy and overcrowded. . . . Of the four camps the Raleigh *Times* reporter-photographer team visited, one fulfilled the minimum sanitation standards required by the Carteret County Health Department. There are 15 camps in the county, and people close to the picture say that one camp is the only decent one there.

> The picture the *Times* saw was this: open piles of refuse, crumbling outhouses used by men and women; filthy unscreened rooms, occupied by as many as 10; unsanitary water supplies; no bathing or washing facilities; and flies crawling over food left in the open because there was no place else to put it. . . .

> "It is a terrible problem," says a minister.
> "There is no plan for these migrant laborers in trouble," says one county worker.

> "They don't appreciate what the growers do for them. We are dealing with the scum of the earth." "Animals," said another county official.[6]

A federal Migrant Health Act, which was passed in 1962, authorizes Public Health Service grants of up to $3 million a year for three years to public and private nonprofit agencies to pay part of the cost of projects for setting up and operating family health service clinics for migratory farm workers and their families. With Congress appropriating matching funds in its first year, thirty-five projects in twenty-two states have been undertaken.

It is to be hoped that the series of measures outlined in President Johnson's "war on poverty" would also address themselves to these truly desperate conditions characterizing the life of thousands of migrant workers and their families.

---

[6] House Committee on Interstate and Foreign Commerce, Hearing before a subcommittee on Health Clinics for Migratory Farmworkers, February 15, 1962, 87th Cong., 2nd Sess. (Washington, 1962), pp. 73–74.

MENTAL HEALTH—THE NUMBER 1 HEALTH

PROBLEM IN THE STATES

There is increasing evidence of heightened public awareness that there must be a substantial expansion in governmental action (as well as in private and in voluntary community effort) if the sharply rising demand for mental health services is to be met and met adequately. In 1961, a Special Governor's Conference on Mental Health was called. The group adopted a policy statement which emphasized a broader approach to mental health, one which would not only include treatment but prevention, early identification, and rehabilitation as well. Also stressed was the need for more specialized services to deal with the related problems of drug addiction, alcoholism, mental retardation, and mental deterioration associated with old age.

To assist in these various dimensions of mental health work, all levels of government would have to significantly enlarge their appropriations for scientific research and for professional staffs. While there are obviously neither cheap nor easy solutions to complex mental health problems, implicit in these and other similar recommendations is the promise that better care will result in speedier recovery for an ever-growing number of individuals who can be returned to their communities to pursue normal lives and productive careers.

Federal grants to state mental health programs began in 1946 with the passage of the National Mental Health Act which established the National Institute of Mental Health. Under this act the federal government supports the development of community mental health clinics, encourages research into the nature and causes of mental disorders and into methods of treatment, and provides grants for advanced training for psychiatrists, psychologists, social workers, and other mental health professional personnel. Among the research grants, the largest share (more than a third) dealt with schizophrenia "which accounts for more than half of all patients hospitalized for mental disorders in the United States." [7]

With federal assistance and without, states moved ahead to make important advances in the mental health field. An abridged summary of activities for 1960–1963, for example, reveals a continued expansion of the community health service act concept under which states provide matching grants to local mental health clinics. Such laws were enacted in Michigan, New Hampshire, North Carolina, Oregon, Rhode Island, South Carolina, and Wyoming. New York increased its state aid for local mental health services by nearly 50 per cent over the 1959 level and also greatly expanded its aftercare services. State research grants to help identify the emotionally-disturbed child were reported in Alabama, California, Colorado, Florida, and Maine, and grants facilitating the establishment of research training centers were

[7] U. S. Department of Health, Education, and Welfare, *Annual Report 1962* (Washington, 1963), p. 216.

reported in California, Connecticut, Florida, Georgia, Indiana, Michigan, New Jersey, New York, Ohio, Washington, and Wisconsin.

Since 1950, improved methods of treatment tended to reduce the overall number of patients in mental hospitals. In Maryland, for example, the length of a patient's stay in a mental hospital averaged around fifty months. Ten years later the figure had been reduced to twenty-four months.[8] Undoubtedly contributing to this downward trend in Maryland and elsewhere, were the successful applications of newer psychotherapeutic methods—electroshock treatment, insulin shock treatment (for schizophrenia), psychosurgery, and most promising of all, chemo-psychiatry (anti-depression drugs).

Despite undeniable improvements in state mental health services, progress has been uneven. A 1961 article from the *St. Louis Globe Democrat* illustrates the point:

> Tomblike rooms with concrete floors and bars on the windows. Rows of silent, lonely people swaying back and forth in rocking chairs. These are the things you remember most after a look behind the walls of Missouri's mental institutions where patients are stacked like cordwood.
>
> It makes your flesh creep.
>
> Some patients, especially the mentally retarded and the more hopeless psychotics, live in conditions of squalor. At one hospital, rats recently gnawed the fingers of three patients.
>
> Many buildings are old and are firetraps. There is overcrowding to an absurd degree. Beds are placed head to head. Privacy is unknown.
>
> Worst of all, there are nowhere near enough doctors, nurses, psychologists, and other professional people. This means that many of the 14,000 patients in Missouri's public mental institutions receive no treatment other than tranquilizer pills to keep them passive.
>
> We toured the hospitals and we talked to the devoted people, many of them people with a missionary zeal, who work in our mental institutions. . . .
> All of what we saw wasn't bad, of course. . . . Here and there you get a sense that something is really being done in the way of treatment.
>
> But the plain, unvarnished truth is that Missouri's institutions are, taken as a whole, only storage vaults for the mentally ill.[9]

Missouri is by no means unique in its shame. President Kennedy's 1963 message on Mental Illness and Mental Retardation noted that:

> Nearly one-fifth of the 279 state mental institutions are fire and health hazards; three-fourths of them were open prior to World War I.
>
> Nearly half of the 530,000 patients in our state mental hospitals are in institutions with over 3,000 patients, where individual care and consideration are almost impossible.

---

[8] Dr. Frank J. Ayd, Jr., address to the New Jersey Association for Mental Health, in the *Congressional Record*, September 15, 1961, p. 18449.

[9] Marsh Clark, "Inside Missouri's Mental Hospitals—Patients Live in Squalor," *St. Louis Globe-Democrat,* in the *Congressional Record*, June 26, 1961, p. A4800.

Many of these institutions have less than half of the professional staff required, with less than one psychiatrist for every 360 patients.

Forty-five per cent of their inmates have been hospitalized continuously for ten years or more.[10]

A comprehensive five-year study of this country's mental health needs costing over $1.5 million was completed in 1961. The Joint Commission on Mental Illness and Health, author of the study, included over thirty professional associations, representatives from three federal executive departments, distinguished leaders from the medical profession and the universities, state commissioners of mental health, and interested civic organizations. Among other recommendations, the commission's report called for:

A. Doubling of federal, state, and local expenditures for mental patient services in the next five years, and tripling in the next ten;

B. Launching of a national manpower recruitment and training program . . . to stimulate the interest of American youth in mental health work as a career;

C. Converting existing state hospitals of more than 1,000 beds gradually and progressively into centers for the long-term care of persons with chronic conditions;

D. Investing a much larger proportion of total funds for mental health research in basic research as contrasted with applied research;

E. Aiming at a mental health program which would make available one fully staffed full time mental health clinic to each 50,000 of population;

F. Including in the staffing of mental health services not only professionally trained medical personnel—physicians, psychiatrists, neurologists—but non-medical health workers with aptitude, sound training, practical experience and demonstrable competence to do general, short-term psychotherapy.[11]

Leaning heavily on these recommendations, the President in his message referred to previously, urged federal assistance to state mental health activities which would support research into new methods of treatment and new drugs, contribute to the decentralization of mental health services to local clinics and outpatient treatment, and develop demonstration pilot projects. He also sought support for a more effective program of community mental health diagnostic and treatment centers in which the federal government would share from 45 per cent to 75 per cent of the project costs. Special emphasis was reserved in this message for the battle against mental retardation:

Mental retardation ranks as a major national health, social, and economic problem. It strikes our most precious asset, our children. It disables ten times as many people as diabetes, twenty times as many as tuberculosis, twenty-five times as many as muscular dystrophy, and 600 times as many as infantile paralysis. About 400,000 children are so retarded they require constant care or

[10] President John F. Kennedy, message to Congress on mental illness and retardation (H. Doc. No. 58), in the *Congressional Record*, February 5, 1963, p. 1745.
[11] *The New York Times*, March 24, 1961, p. 20.

supervision. . . . There are between 5 and 6 million mentally retarded children and adults, an estimated 3 per cent of the population. Yet despite these grim statistics, and despite an admirable effort by private voluntary associations, until a decade ago not a single state health department offered any special community services for the mentally retarded or their families.[12]

The President termed "fragmentary and inadequate" the over $500 million spent annually on mental retardation and special education by federal, state, and local governments. In view of the close statistical relationship of mental retardation to premature birth and early childhood diseases, the program also envisaged a substantial expansion in federal aid for comprehensive maternity and infant care.

Congress responded in the fall of 1963 to his message by passing The Mental Retardation Planning Amendments of the Social Security Act and The Mental Retardation Facilities and Community Mental Health Centers Construction Act. The first act authorized a grant of $2.2 million to the states during fiscal 1964 for planning comprehensive state and community action to combat mental retardation. The second authorized grants of $329 million over a four-year period for construction of community mental health centers and research centers related to mental retardation. In addition, Congress included in the appropriation for the Department of Health, Education, and Welfare $4.2 million for grants to prepare community and state plans for community-based mental health programs and $6 million for grants to improve inpatient care in state mental hospitals.

SOME PROBLEMS AND SOME PROGRESS IN STATE
AND LOCAL HEALTH ADMINISTRATION

From what has been observed so far, it must be apparent that among the many difficulties which state and local governments face in the field of public health administration, the problem of proliferating functions is certainly one.

Beyond the more traditional disease-fighting functions and beyond mental health and mental retardation, maternal and child care, and medical aid for the indigent aged and migratory labor, greater attention than ever must be paid to accident prevention, to air and water pollution control, and to radiological and occupational health. While it is true, of course, that maternal and child mortality rates have gone down, and while more people live longer (a man now 65 has a life expectancy of 78) and death from tuberculosis and other infectious diseases occurs much less frequently, other diseases and injuries are definitely on the increase. This is particularly noticeable in our aging population where 78 per cent of those over 65 were shown to have at least one chronic condition and where accident rates take a high toll.[13] Persons

[12] Kennedy message, *Congressional Record*, February 5, 1963, p. 1745.
[13] *The Aged and the Aging in the United States: A National Problem*, Senate Report No. 1121, p. 86.

65 and over, while constituting only 9 per cent of the population, "accounted for 28 per cent of all accidental deaths and 20 per cent of all serious disabling injuries." [14] In addition, infectious venereal disease among young persons has registered alarming advances. In 1961, for example, the number of syphilis cases was three times that of 1959 and twice as large as in 1960. New York City listed 635 cases in 1957 and 3,374 cases five years later.

In administering public health, state and local governments are confronted with a second problem of note—the unevenness of the distribution of the aged among the several states, and the varying extent of medical care available. By way of illustration, New York has 193 physicians per 100,000 population and 10.1 per cent of its population is in the sixty-five and over age category. Iowa, with 11.9 per cent of its population in the aged category, must meet its medical needs with a physician to population ratio one-third less favorable than that of New York's. Among other states whose population of aged ranges about 20 per cent above the national average are Arkansas, Florida, Kansas, Maine, Massachusetts, Missouri, Nebraska, New Hampshire, and Vermont. In a majority of these states the supply of doctors is substantially below that of the national norm, 132 to 100,000 population.[15]

Third, states for a variety of reasons find it extremely difficult to offer an integrated system of tax-supported medical care. There are the usual institutional conflicts—general hospitals versus specialized hospitals, and hospitals versus nursing homes. At issue frequently are different approaches to medical care, standards of service, and costs; separate governing boards and budgets may aggravate these differences. Also, in nearly every community, leaders of the local medical association, men of significance in the local power structure, will view questions of medical care, medical social policy, and medical economics somewhat differently than will the professional public health workers. Many doctors believe that:

> Questions of public policy should be determined predominantly by the doctors as a group through their medical society. The professional health worker sees the situation differently. To him, the application of mass measures for prevention of disease is most important, and local government is the logical focus of power. Individual medical and allied practitioners are regarded as the manpower necessary to cope with disease in individuals but not to determine or control social policy. The health department should be the logical authority over matters affecting the public health and should coordinate the multiple agencies concerned.[16]

Complicating matters further is the fragmentation of medical programs which grew out of efforts to meet the needs of special groups of patients such as youth, the aged, or the veterans. Pleas by and for such groups resulted in

[14] *The New York Times*, March 12, 1961, p. 81.

[15] U. S. Department of Health, Education, and Welfare, *Health, Education and Welfare Trends* (Washington, 1963), p. 121; note also Clark, p. A4800.

[16] Milton I. Roemer, "Changing Patterns of Health Service: Their Dependence on a Changing World," *Annals of the American Academy of Political and Social Science*, March, 1963, p. 55.

federal and state laws and financial support favoring particular rather than undifferentiated public health services, thus taking away from local authorities important decision-making functions as to how best to utilize available professional resources.

Much work remains to be done in the field of public health administration in order to improve operating relationships and communications between local governmental agencies and state and federal levels. While existing statutes may force higher governmental echelons to lay down general policy guidelines, while state departments of health may be given the responsibility to review and inspect local standards of service, it is often a local community rather than Washington or the state Capitol which is in the best position to determine local needs and to adapt general policies to local circumstances. New York City can appropriately serve as an illustration of a community which during the last few years made major gains in the areas of public health. The city's annual health budget is over $300 million. Over 40,000 persons are employed in the operation of twenty-seven health centers, twenty-two hospitals, and several medical centers. The sanitation code has been revised; a large municipal health research program is in process; full-time physicians are employed as chiefs of service for all municipal hospitals; a central health board was created in order to coordinate city-wide efforts in mental health; salaries were raised significantly for all employees; and over $200 million was expended during the last eight years alone for the construction of new hospital facilities.[17]

Significant shortages of medical, dental, and nursing personnel constitute a fourth area of concern in public health administration (see Figure 2). With the ratio of one physician per thousand of population usually accepted as the norm for reasonably adequate medical care, nearly one-third of all the counties in the United States (many of them rural and Southern) presently find themselves with twice as many persons per physician. As professional research and specialization become the absorbing interests of more and more medical school graduates, resulting personnel shortages have been particularly evident in the ranks of general practitioners, small-town doctors, and hospital staffs. For example, currently one-fourth of all United States hospital residents and interns are graduates of foreign medical schools. In Arizona, Delaware, New Jersey, North Dakota, Rhode Island, South Dakota, and West Virginia, the ratio is even higher—one-half of such personnel having received their medical education abroad.[18]

It has been estimated, on the basis of publicly and privately-financed surveys, that if the medical picture is not to deteriorate even more drastically in view of population growth, the United States by 1975 must increase its supply of physicians by 50 per cent, of dentists by 100 per cent, of nurses by at least 20 per cent. What remains to be seen is whether or not federal aid

[17] *The New York Times,* September 10, 1961, p. 83.
[18] U. S. Department of Health, Education, and Welfare survey, cited in "Shortage of Doctors —What's Causing It," *U. S. News & World Report,* March 25, 1963, p 73.

FIGURE 2

HEALTH MANPOWER

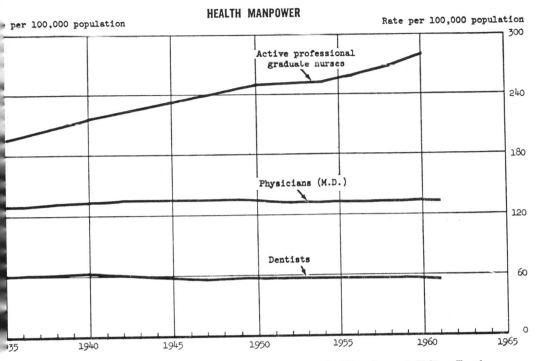

per 100,000 population   Rate per 100,000 population

SOURCE: Department of Health, Education, and Welfare, *Health, Education, and Welfare Trends* (Washington, 1963), p. 27.

under the newly-enacted Health Educational Assistance Act can stimulate state and private non-profit efforts to build and support a minimum of twenty new medical and dental schools, and whether or not a sufficiently large number of qualified students can actually be attracted to these fields. Still left unsettled are the issues of the uneven geographic distribution of medical personnel and the proper balance between specialist, researcher, and generalist.

A NOTE ON THE POLITICS OF MEDICAL CARE

During the last twenty years medical spending, private and public, multiplied nearly eight times (see Figure 3). These rising costs can in no way detract from the enormous contribution that American medicine and pharmacology are making to a longer, healthier, and happier life—truly one of the marvels of contemporary science. Yet despite these achievements or because of them, significant segments of the public and leading liberal politicians from Truman to Johnson have urged recourse to collective action, govern-

FIGURE 3

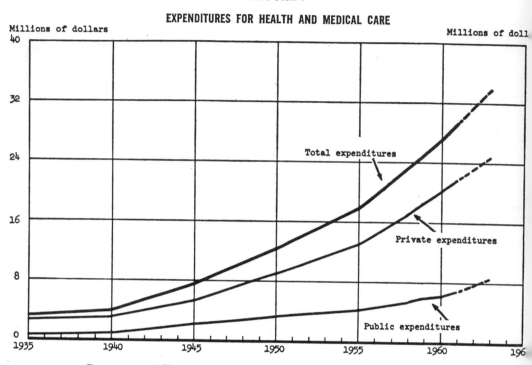

EXPENDITURES FOR HEALTH AND MEDICAL CARE

SOURCE: Department of Health, Education, and Welfare, *Health, Education, and Welfare Trends* (Washington, 1963), p. 26.

mental and cooperative, in order to assist financially-burdened individuals or families to defray their medical bills.

Advocates of a larger federal role insist that the time has come for the United States to study and apply some of the European practices where governments have long aided in the process of diffusing and spreading the costs of medical care among the entire working population. In Scandinavia and Great Britain, where individuals are insured through government-sponsored programs, comprehensive medical attention and care are obtained as a matter of right and not of charity. Such measures are held justified on the basis of social ethics as well as on economic considerations. Without such measures, it is contended by those favoring this approach, adequate medical attention will become increasingly difficult for a large percentage of low-income Americans whose present voluntary insurance policies offer insufficient protection against arbitrary cancellations, and whose coverage is characterized all too frequently by small benefits, broad exemptions, and excessively high rates for those least able to afford them.

Spokesmen for the 175,000 member American Medical Association appearing before congressional and state legislative committees vociferously, and largely successfully, objected to any further governmental intervention into the realm of medicine—more particularly into what they consider the primary doctor-patient relationship. Utilizing all the media of communications and even going to the point of establishing a Medical Political Action Committee (1962), the strongly individualistic A.M.A. was and is prepared to do spirited battle against any and all forms of "socialized medicine."

American free enterprise medicine, so they maintain, built the best medical schools, developed the finest drugs, maintained the highest standards of medical care, and advanced research beyond that of any country in the entire world. Such progress can only be continued if medicine remains free and dynamic.

Recent A.M.A. pronouncements stress the usefulness of voluntary surgical, medical, and hospital insurance policies which now include over 70 per cent of the population, the wide scope of philanthropy through which some $1.5 billion is annually collected by thousands of voluntary agencies (such as Red Cross and Heart Association), and the over $600 million of free medical care given every year by doctors to private patients, hospitals, and clinics.[19]

Least favored by the A.M.A. is the somewhat recently developed prepaid comprehensive insurance which thus far includes, however, a mere 2 to 3 per cent of all health insurance policyholders.[20] Sponsored by certain unions (e.g., United Mine Workers Welfare and Retirement Plan), industries (e.g., Kaiser Foundation Health Plan), consumer cooperatives (e.g., Group Health Cooperative of Puget Sound), or communities (e.g., Ross-Loos Medical Group of Los Angeles), such policies provide for unusually broad coverage of medical needs including the services of physicians, dentists, and nurses as well as drugs and appliances. Other than the obviously heavy costs of initiating such programs, opposition from the medical profession has been a major factor in slowing their growth.

Hostility centered on a variety of arrangements—the group practice pattern of medicine (employed by a number of such plans), the limitation of fees, the auditing of medical services, or the general concept of permitting doctors to be "controlled" by non-doctors. Discrimination practiced by a number of hospitals against physicians participating in such groups further contributed to slow down wider adoption of this type of policy.

PUBLIC WELFARE—BASIC CONCEPTS AND PROGRAMS

Self-discipline, self-reliance, and hard work were important ingredients in the Puritan ethic and in the American ethos. By following righteous ways individuals should be able to avoid poverty and avoid becoming dependent

[19] House Committee on Interstate and Foreign Commerce, *Health Professions Educational Assistance*, Hearings, February 5, 6 and 7, 1963, 88th Cong., 1st Sess. (Washington, 1963), p. 280.

[20] Anne Ramsay Somers, "Comprehensive Prepayment Plans as a Mechanism for Meeting Health Needs," *Annals of the American Academy of Political and Social Science*, September, 1961, p. 81.

upon others. With premises such as these, the poor laws of England and early America were understandably hard and expressive of aroused moral indignation for indigence and the indigent. When individuals faltered in their battles with life, their families were expected to assume the responsibilities for succor and benevolence. Should this prove impossible, private philanthropy and church charity would supplement individual and family efforts. Aided by the setting of a rural society and the open frontier, it was generally not too difficult to absorb many of the fallen brothers and sisters.

As far as government was concerned, the traditional unit charged with the administration of poor relief was the local township or county and its poor farms and almshouses. Generally, it was not before the nineteenth century that state and local governments found it necessary to maintain asylums, charity hospitals, orphanages, and similar institutions in order to perform public welfare functions on a larger and more formal scale.

A major revolutionary shift in public opinion occurred during the Depression decade of the 1930's, not merely with respect to basic concepts of public welfare as such, but also with regard to the roles that government—federal, state, and local—should play in the administration of welfare programs. Put simply, conditions of poverty were no longer to be viewed as primarily personally induced, but as impersonal consequences of social and economic forces and circumstances over which the individual had little control and for which the individual could no longer be held accountable.

Filled with a sense of frustration and insecurity, many Americans began to look to government for help in overcoming the results of the Depression—loss of jobs, incomes, savings, homes, shops, and farms. From now on, society collectively was to assist with shouldering the economic burdens of the aged, the unemployed, and those on relief. When local and state governments proved that they could or would not by themselves handle the scope and staggering costs of the new mass demand for public aid, pressures multiplied for Washington to assume a major share of the responsibility. This then was the political climate in which the Social Security Act was born in 1935.

What evolved from the Depression era was a complex of welfare programs intertwining the activities of federal, state, and local governments and combining the principle of social insurance with that of direct aid for certain categories of indigence.

Left entirely to the federal government was the operation of the old-age survivors and disability insurance system, and left entirely to the states and their local governments was the operation of public relief (general assistance). A third approach was taken to provide public support for certain needy groups—old age assistance, aid to dependent children, aid to the blind, aid to the permanently and totally disabled, and (since 1960) medical assistance to the aged. Here, subject to certain conditions, the federal government furnished funds matching state appropriations but reserving to the states responsibilities for the actual administration of such aided programs. (For federal, state, and local expenditures for public assistance since 1937, see Table 4.)

TABLE 4. FEDERAL, STATE, AND LOCAL
EXPENDITURES FOR PUBLIC
ASSISTANCE SINCE 1937

Fiscal year	Federal (000)	State and local (000)
1937	$ 142,568	$ 167,326
1946	446,048	572,663
1948	722,527	757,041
1950	1,095,788	1,020,600
1952	1,209,076	1,111,222
1956	1,463,618	1,244,893
1958	1,757,078	1,387,376
1959	1,972,918	1,426,885
1960	2,055,226	1,493,152
1961	2,191,225	1,568,146
1962	2,465,562	1,720,756

SOURCE: Department of Health, Education, and Welfare, *Grants-in-Aid and Other Financial Assistance Programs* (Washington, 1963), p. 281.

During the nearly thirty years that the Social Security Act has been in operation, Congress has added numerous amendments to increase social security taxes, expand coverage, and liberalize benefits. Although space does not permit a review of the many changes and amendments, it is necessary to point out a few of the major developments that have occurred since 1960, more particularly those which reveal something of the direction in which public welfare policies and administration are presently moving.

Amendments added in 1961–1962 made federal funds available to families of dependent children, to children of unemployed parents, and to state and local governments to make "protective" payments to third parties interested in the welfare of children; these funds were to facilitate the development of day care services (for working mothers) and the placement of children in suitable homes or institutions should local authorities deem this advisable in order to prevent the exploitation, abuse, or delinquency of children.

Greater flexibility as well as administrative efficiency were the twin objectives of a new provision, Title XVI of the Social Security Act, under which states were finally permitted to consolidate their formerly separate adult public assistance programs—aid to the aged, the blind, and the disabled and medical assistance for the aged—into a single, integrated plan.

Additional federal aids were provided for special research grants, experimental pilot projects, advance training of state and local personnel working in the various public welfare fields, and administrative costs for state programs designed to help families and individuals attain self-sufficiency. States were encouraged to provide work incentives for those on public assistance and to develop more effective welfare methods and policies in order to reduce and prevent dependency.

Under the 1965 amendments to the Social Security Act, all old-age, survivors, and disability insurance benefits were increased by 7%; children's insurance benefits were continued until the person reaches age 22 (instead of 18) if the child is attending an accredited school or college as a full-time student; and widows were given the option of receiving social security benefits at age 60 (instead of 62). Provisions were liberalized with respect to eligibility requirements for the disabled; for certain persons over 72 not now eligible for social security benefits; and for those receiving benefits but wishing to earn a supplementary income. Also, social security coverage was made available to self-employed physicians and interns.

ADMINISTRATIVE FRAMEWORK OF PUBLIC WELFARE

Federal law stipulates the conditions for federal participation in state-operated public assistance programs. Among the major provisions set out in the law are the following: (a) these programs must be statewide in operation; (b) states must make financial contributions to these programs; (c) there must be a single state agency which either directly administers the programs or which supervises local agencies to which certain responsibilities may have been delegated subject, however, to statewide minimum standards and general rules; (d) names and addresses of recipients and the amounts of assistance may (if the state so decides) be made a matter of public record and declared open to interested persons under appropriate state law, although commercial and political use of this information is prohibited; (e) application must be open to all United States citizens who consider themselves entitled to assistance, and proper appeal procedures must be established to hear and determine cases if claims are denied; (f) the Social Security Administration has the right to demand special and periodic reports; (g) residence requirements for entitlement may not exceed five years in the last nine years and one year immediately preceding application; in the case of aid to dependent children, one year is held sufficient; (h) in staffing all such federally-supported programs, states are required to establish merit personnel systems.

As noted earlier, while public assistance receives federal support, general assistance is left entirely in the hands of state and local governments. It is these governments which furnish

> financial assistance to needy families or individuals primarily in their homes. Assistance may be given in the form of money payments, assistance in kind provided directly to recipients, vendor payments for medical or remedial care, or vendor payments for either goods and services. . . .[21]

In fifteen states general assistance is administered directly by a state agency; in nineteen states, by local agencies under state supervision; and in

---

[21] Senate Special Committee on Unemployment Problems, *Characteristics of General Assistance in the United States*, prepared by the Bureau of Public Assistance, Social Security Administration, Department of Health, Education, and Welfare, November 30, 1959, 86th Cong., 1st Sess. (Washington, 1959), p. 1.

twenty six states, by a local agency operating under city, county, or township governmental control.

ELIGIBILITY RESIDENCE, AND FORMS OF ASSISTANCE

In the administration of general assistance, standards of eligibility, residence, types of assistance, and methods of payment vary considerably from state to state. As a rule, all states will come to the assistance of needy families and individuals on an emergency or temporary basis but will qualify with considerable restrictions and conditions any extension of such aid for longer periods of time.

In seventeen states applicants to be awarded general assistance must not have an employable person in their family; six states specify that the couples and non-family persons are eligible only if non-employable; and in Oregon, the non-availability of employment is one of the conditions of entitlement. Single, employable, unemployed males under fifty years of age will be given assistance by the State of Washington only at the discretion of local administrators in the light of local employment conditions.

Willingness to work as evidenced by registration with either the state or the United States Employment services is a condition precedent for obtaining general assistance in most of the states. Missouri and North Carolina go beyond this by declaring employable persons generally ineligible altogether.

As to amount and length of payment, most of the states do not impose a fixed maximum but leave this matter to local discretion. Twenty-one states authorize money payments to recipients, ten states provide vendor payments to suppliers of goods and services, and nineteen states leave this to be decided by local officials.

WHO ARE THE PEOPLE ON RELIEF AND

WHAT ARE THE COSTS?

Four per cent of the population or approximately 7.8 million persons in the United States—most of them living in cheap and crowded housing near the centers of our large cities, in economically-depressed areas or in rural slums—received some form of relief in 1963. The total bill came to about $4.6 billion of which more than half came from the federal government. Included in this figure were payments for 3 million children ($1.1 billion), 2.3 million aged ($2.3 billion), 1 million mothers ($300 million), 500,000 permanently and totally disabled ($40 million), 100,000 blind ($100 million), and 900,000 ($400 million) recipients of general assistance (see Figures 4 and 5).[22]

Monthly benefit payments (June 1963) varied considerably. Averages for a family with dependent children ranged from a high of $203.22 in Illinois to a low of $35.41 in Mississippi with $135.00 representing the average

[22] U. S. Department of Health, Education and Welfare, *Health, Education, and Welfare Indicators,* May, 1964, pp. 41–42.

FIGURE 4

PUBLIC ASSISTANCE RECIPIENTS

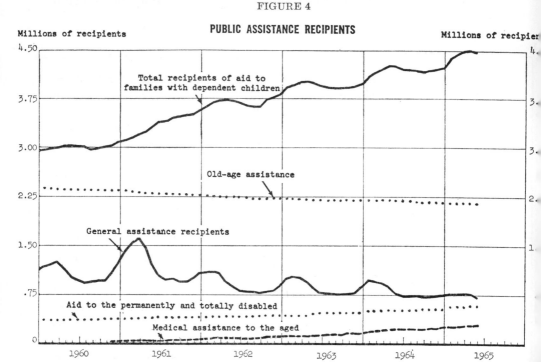

SOURCE: Department of Health, Education, and Welfare, *Health, Education, and Welfare Indicators*, August, 1965, p. S-24.

among the states. Most of these families were without fathers, without employment, or without both.

Massachusetts offered the highest monthly average amount for both the blind, $136.95, and for the permanently and totally disabled, $131.89, while Mississippi offered the lowest with $37.98 and $34.23 respectively; in old-age assistance, Minnesota took the honors with a high of $109.28, and Mississippi was at the other end of the scale with a monthly average payment of only $35.20. Of the twenty-five states providing medical assistance for the aged, Illinois paid the highest average benefit, $387.26, and West Virginia paid the lowest, $36.25.

Still lower were the benefit payments awarded under general assistance (see Table 5). New Jersey was at the top with $121.52 per case, while Alabama stood at the other end of the scale with $13.22 per case.

And yet despite such minimal levels of aid, the annual costs of welfare—public assistance and general assistance—continue to rise impressively. They increased by 102 per cent between fiscal 1950 and fiscal 1962.

With all relief spending coming under attack in varying degrees, the public Aid to Dependent Children Program (A.D.C.) experienced its most

FIGURE 5

TOTAL PAYMENTS TO PUBLIC ASSISTANCE RECIPIENTS

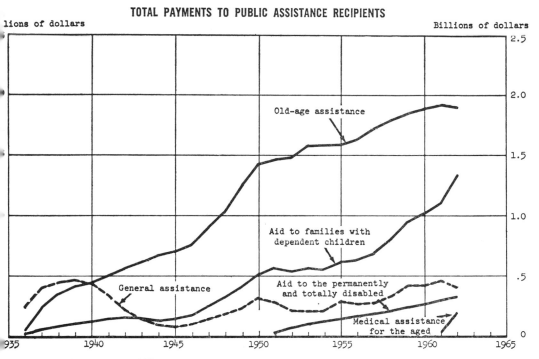

SOURCE: Department of Health, Education, and Welfare, *Health, Education, and Welfare Trends* (Washington, 1963), p. 91.

pointed criticism during the early 1960's. Charges multiplied that the program is actually abetting illegitimacy, that it encourages irresponsibility and desertion among fathers, that chiseling is widespread, and that some women seem to view their aid checks as a fiscal inducement for futher promiscuity. Criticisms of A.D.C. are buttressed with reports from major cities reporting sharp upturns in costs as well as in the number of recipients.

What these statistics of rising costs cannot reveal at sight is the stubborn persistence of poverty among even the assisted families. For example, a recent Detroit study of 93 mothers and 334 children receiving A.D.C. funds noted that:

A. Two-thirds of the mothers who did not use food stamps [a pilot program of the U. S. Department of Agriculture under which about $225 million worth of surplus food was made available to needy families at greatly reduced prices] said [that] they did not have enough cash to buy them.

B. Half of the families depend on gifts from relatives, friends or school teachers.

C. Eighty per cent of the boys and 50% of the girls had only one pair of shoes, 50% of the children had no rubbers or boots and 75% had no raincoats.[23]

[23] *The New York Times,* November 3, 1963, p. 49.

TABLE 5. GENERAL ASSISTANCE:

(Except for expenditures for assistance and administration,

| | | Number of recipients, June, 1963 | | | |
| | | Persons | | | |
State or other jurisdiction	Cases	Total	Number per 1,000 persons under 65 years of age (a)	Average payment per case, June, 1963	Expenditures for assistance and administration, calendar year 1962 (in thousands)
Total	329,000(b)	775,000(b)	4.7(c)	$65.55	$461,538(d)
Alabama	95	95	(e)	13.22	31
Alaska	192	548	2.6	55.95	898
Arizona	2,437	5,164	3.6	58.31	2,519(f)
Arkansas	255	945	.6	14.95	597
California	30,074	68,543	4.4	63.32	32,983
Colorado	1,249	4,256	2.4	39.85	3,992
Connecticut	4,403	10,814	4.5	66.28	6,242(g)(h)
Delaware	1,274	2,274	5.3	53.81	1,248
District of Columbia	663	721	1.0	72.52	1,499
Florida	8,400(i)	(j)	(j)	------------	3,085(g) (h)
Georgia	2,195	4,934	1.3	31.27	993
Guam	4	4	.1	(k)	2
Hawaii	1,064	1,481	2.5	63.57	1,542
Idaho	(j)	(j)	(j)	------------	28(l)
Illinois	26,108	52,925	5.8	80.02	58,849
Iowa	3,500(i)	7,500(i)	3.1	------------	6,205(l)
Kansas	3,027	8,434	4.3	66.68	4,309
Kentucky	1,836	5,537	2.0	40.07	1,020(h)
Louisiana	7,732	8,487	2.7	52.06	5,939
Maine	2,330	7,986	9.4	42.61	3,434(l)
Maryland	5,160	5,739	1.9	70.37	4,491
Massachusetts	6,924	14,174	3.1	67.44	9,329
Michigan	29,888	105,596	14.2	95.50	75,838(m)
Minnesota	8,619	24,731	8.0	75.78	17,192(l)
Mississippi	1,169	1,557	.8	14.11	177(h)
Missouri	9,220	11,958	3.2	66.40	7,588
Montana	1,076	3,148	5.0	41.98	5,097
Nebraska	759	2,163	1.7	49.11	1,729(l)

* Prepared by the Welfare Administration, U. S. Department of Health, Education, and Welfare. All data subject to revision.

(a) Based on population estimated by the Social Security Administration as of July 1, 1963.

(b) Partly estimated; does not represent sum of state figures because totals exclude for Indiana and New Jersey estimated number of cases and persons receiving only medical care, hospitalization, and/or burial; recipient count also includes an estimate for states not reporting such data. Excludes Idaho and Indiana; data not reported.

(c) Average for forty-seven states. See footnote (j).

(d) Excludes data on administration for ten states. See footnote (h).

(e) Less than 0.05.

(f) Data for administration partly estimated.

SELECTED DATA ON RECIPIENTS, PAYMENTS AND FINANCING *

excludes vendor payments for medical care and recipients receiving only such payments)

| State or other jurisdiction | Number of recipients, June, 1963 | | | Average payment per case, June, 1963 | Expenditures for assistance and administration, calendar year 1962 (in thousands) |
| | Cases | Persons | | | |
		Total	Number per 1,000 persons under 65 years of age (a)		
Nevada	288	472	1.4	59.59	2,346(h)
New Hampshire	882	2,958	5.4	54.34	909(h)
New Jersey	8,957(n)	28,670(n)	4.9(n)	121.52(n)	15,653
New Mexico	433	758	.8	42.17	533(l)
New York	34,725(o)	79,461(o)	5.0(o)	84.04	42,212
North Carolina	1,566	4,282	1.0	26.87	2,429
North Dakota	316	1,206	2.1	51.66	816
Ohio	30,634	109,019	11.8	71.09	58,066
Oklahoma	8,437	(j)	(j)	14.09	1,235(h)
Oregon	4,594	(j)	(j)	51.64	5,343
Pennsylvania	38,545	46,857	4.6	58.77	32,356
Puerto Rico	2,365	2,365	1.0	7.64	213
Rhode Island	2,459	5,121	6.7	52.46	2,853
South Carolina	1,413	1,636	.7	31.57	851(l)
South Dakota	291	970	1.5	32.97	1,323(l)
Tennessee	1,824	4,962	1.5	16.32	449(h)
Texas	10,000(i)	(j)	(j)	------------	2,609(g) (h)
Utah	1,375	3,309	3.6	61.72	1,289
Vermont	900(i)	(j)	(j)	------------	425(g) (h)
Virgin Islands	166	172	5.2	31.81	115
Virginia	2,382	5,778	1.5	45.32	1,961
Washington	8,068	17,208	6.4	72.22	15,315
West Virginia	1,616	2,548	1.6	34.02	795
Wisconsin	7,523	22,881	6.3	86.30	13,539(l)
Wyoming	309	1,168	3.8	70.44	1,046

(g) Data for assistance partly estimated.
(h) Represents assistance payments only; data on administration not available.
(i) Estimated.
(j) Data not reported.
(k) Average payment not computed on base of fewer than fifty recipients.
(l) Data incomplete.
(m) Includes administrative costs for programs other than general assistance.
(n) Includes an unknown number of recipients of only medical care, hospitalization, and/or burial and payments for these services.
(o) Includes recipients of medical care only.

SOURCE: *Book of the States, 1964–1965*, p. 420.

Prominent among those who viewed the criticisms of A.D.C. and other welfare programs and their administration as highly exaggerated and distorted was the former Secretary of Health, Education, and Welfare, Abraham Ribicoff, presently the junior Senator from Connecticut. He emphasized that:

A. An average payment per child of $1.00 per day could hardly be considered an "inducement" for mothers "to take on the costs and problems of raising another child."
B. During the last ten years, despite higher dollar costs, the actual share of the gross national product directed into public assistance did in fact decline by 11 per cent (see Table 6).
C. Studies [of relief recipients] have shown that fraud and outright chiseling amount to less than 2 per cent.[24]

During his administration, Ribicoff initiated a number of directives under which states were urged to strengthen their procedures for locating

TABLE 6. SOCIAL WELFARE EXPENDITURES

Fiscal year	Gross national product (in billions)	Social welfare expenditures as percent of gross national product						
		Total [1]	Insurance	Public aid	Health and medical services	Other welfare	Veterans' programs	Education [2]
1889–90	$13.0	2.4	([3])	[4] 0.3	0.1	([4])	0.9	1.1
1912–13	39.9	2.5	([3])	[4] .3	.4	([4])	.5	1.3
1928–29	101.6	4.2	0.3	[4] .5	.4	([4])	.5	2.4
1934–35	68.7	9.3	.6	4.4	.6	0.1	.7	3.0
1939–40	95.9	9.1	1.3	3.8	.7	.1	.6	2.8
1944–45	212.5	4.2	.7	.5	1.1	.1	.4	1.4
1949–50	264.0	8.7	1.8	.9	.8	.2	2.4	2.5
1954–55	377.5	8.5	2.6	.8	.8	.2	1.2	3.0
1955–56	409.5	8.5	2.6	.8	.8	.2	1.1	3.0
1956–57	432.9	9.1	2.9	.8	.9	.2	1.1	3.3
1957–58	440.2	10.3	3.6	.8	.9	.2	1.1	3.6
1958–59	466.8	10.7	3.9	.9	.9	.2	1.1	3.6
1959–60	493.9	10.6	3.9	.8	.9	.2	1.0	3.7
1960–61	504.6	11.5	4.4	.9	1.0	.3	1.0	3.9
1961–62	539.2	11.5	4.4	.9	.9	.3	1.0	3.9
1962–63 [5]	568.6	11.7	4.5	.9	1.0	.3	1.0	4.0

[1] Includes public housing, not shown in distribution.
[2] Beginning 1954–55, includes basic research and training grants; data for earlier years not available.
[3] Less than 0.05 percent.
[4] "Other welfare" included with public aid.
[5] Preliminary estimates.
SOURCE: *Social Security Bulletin*, November, 1963, p. 8.

[24] Abraham Ribicoff, "It's Time For A New Look At Relief," *This Week*, February 11, 1962, p. 14.

deserting parents and for reducing even further the possibilities of fraud through improved supervision and control. But what concerned the Secretary still more was the necessity for Congress and the states to adopt a constructive legislative approach which would encourage relief recipients to seek jobs or training and which would facilitate the expanded development of state services for family restoration. While such measures might even lead to a temporary increase in welfare expenditures, in the long run this country's taxpayers would discover that helping individuals back on the road to self-respect and productive employment constitutes both an immensely humane and wise investment. Many of these suggestions were finally enacted into law and formed the substance of the Public Welfare Amendments of 1962 which were discussed earlier in this chapter.

"RELIEF À LA NEWBURGH"—A CASE STUDY

OF CONFLICTING CONCEPTS OF PUBLIC WELFARE

In public welfare, interrelationships between federal, state, and local governments take many forms. Both federal and state governments make financial grants to local governments. They also issue directives, conduct field surveys, and assert supervision. Both federal and state governments demand from local welfare officials statistical reports, periodic accounting, and the maintenance of specified minimum standards. That such intergovernmental cooperative relationships should at times experience serious stresses and strains must be expected. Also not difficult to understand, despite arrangements for interpersonal and interoffice communications, workshops and consultations, is the tendency of local officials to resent particular actions and policies of higher echelons. Nor is it rare, moreover, for them to charge state and federal agencies with excessive centralized bureaucratic behavior, with unreasonable demands for uniformity, and with a conspicuous failure to appreciate the peculiarities of local setting, sentiment, and conditions. Occasionally such conflicts are aggravated by socio-philosophical disagreements between state Capitol and city hall which come to the very essence of the meaning and role of public welfare. The Battle of Newburgh offers a vivid illustration of just such a conflict—bitter, personal, professional, philosophical, and political.

Until recently, few people in this country had ever heard of Newburgh, a city of 31,000, sixty miles from New York City in the Hudson Valley. This changed suddenly in 1961. In the spring of that year City Manager Joseph M. Mitchell, strongly backed by four Republican council members (and equally strongly opposed by the mayor, a Democrat), decided to remove from the city's relief rolls "chiselers," "loafers," and "social parasites." With relief expenditures constituting about one-third of the city budget, the Mitchell group believed that radical measures were called for especially since the community—classified as an area of substantial labor surplus—was already faced with declining property values, low industrial wages, business

departures, and a dangerously spreading waterfront blight. Further aggravating the relief picture, it was argued, were migratory workers, mostly
Negro, who had been moving into the area since World War II to help pick
fruit during the summer and who then decided to remain when they found
Newburgh's welfare administration a soft touch during the long winter
months.

To meet this crisis, the council adopted a 13-point program to go into
effect in July which ordered that certain conditions would first have to be met
before welfare recipients could be considered for continued support.

Among the major provisions were these: All able-bodied men on relief
were to work a forty-hour week for the city maintenance department; instead
of cash, relief recipients were to be issued vouchers for their food, clothing,
and rent; individuals who were physically capable and available for employment but who refused to accept a job, were to be denied relief; mothers of
illegitimate children were to be advised that they would be refused relief
should they have any more children out of wedlock; applicants for relief who
left a job voluntarily, who were not fired or laid off, were to be denied relief;
no family was to be allotted relief in excess of the take home pay of the lowest
paid city employee with a family of comparable size; all applicants who were
new to the city had to show evidence that their purpose for coming to
Newburgh was in response to a concrete job offer; with the exception of aids
to the blind, the aged, and the disabled, assistance was to be limited to a
maximum period of three months within any one year.[25]

As to the compatibility of such regulations with state and federal law,
Mitchell insisted: "The point here is not whether the welfare money comes
from the state or Federal Government. The point is that it is taxpayers' money
that is being misspent. Also, there is the question of home rule. Can Newburgh work out its own destiny or must it be saddled with regulations that are
placing the welfare of the whole community in jeopardy?"[26]

State officials disagreed with this interpretation of welfare law. If put
into effect, New York State's share of $150–$200 million under the public
assistance programs would clearly have been put into jeopardy. After a
special hearing by a five-man committee of the New York State Department of
Public Welfare, Governor Rockefeller's Commissioner of Welfare, Raymond
W. Houston, ordered Newburgh to drop its relief plan. "These proposals,"
wrote the Commissioner, "if carried out would set up an illegal program to
push around unfortunate men, women and children; and even if not carried
out, they constitute psychological warfare against the needy and helpless."[27]

Due to state-obtained injunctions, twelve out of the thirteen points of
the code were actually never implemented; the city was, however, upheld in
its demand that able-bodied men be required to check in monthly about

---

[25] Representative Katharine St. George, extension of remarks on the Newburgh welfare
plan. *Congressional Record*, July 12, 1961, p. A5183.
[26] *The Wall Street Journal*, July 10, 1961, p. 10.
[27] *The New York Times*, July 13, 1961, p. 37.

possible employment prior to being given relief. While these legal measures were taken, investigations by state officials revealed that:

  A. Instead of the allegedly large number of "loafers," there was only one able-bodied welfare recipient reporting under the city's work demand who had to be excused subsequently in order to take care of his five children while his wife was away at the hospital.
  B. Throughout 1960, only $205 was paid out to newcomer applicants and the city of Newburgh was reimbursed by the state for these payments.
  C. Newburgh's welfare caseload was below that of five comparable cities and below that of the state average.
  D. Not a single case of fraud was ever substantiated.[28]

Based on newspaper reports and interviews, Mitchell and the council had the enthusiastic support from a substantial majority of the city. There were, of course, some local critics, among them the mayor, Newburgh's welfare commissioner who testified against the code (and was later replaced), the city's N.A.A.C.P. chapter, the ministerial association, Catholic charities, and some local unions. But most of the vocal segments of the community considered Mitchell's program thoroughly justified and reasonable. Newburgh's battle quickly became a national issue. Apparently it helped crystallize a common problem and a widespread popular dissatisfaction with the relief system.

The Gallup poll in August of 1961 reported that 85 per cent of the respondents favored the policy that physically-fit relief recipients (male) be put to work on city projects; 84 per cent favored the requirement that those physically fit must take any job at going wages; 74 per cent favored requiring proof of relief applicants that they came into the area because of a definite job offer; and 75 per cent favored limiting relief of men with large families to what they could earn if they took a job.[29]

"It's a fine commentary on public morality in this country," editoralized the *Wall Street Journal*, "when a local community's effort to correct flagrant welfare abuses is declared illegal under both state and federal law." [30] Senator Goldwater was enthusiastic in his support of the Newburgh plan. "I'm tired of professional chiselers walking up and down the streets who don't work and have no intention of working. I would like to see every city in the country adopt the plan." [31]

Opposition to Newburgh's code came from certain leading public figures like Secretary Ribicoff and Governor Rockefeller, from liberal journals and most of all from the professional workers in the public welfare field. It was emphasized in varying ways that welfare abuses were minimal, and that Newburgh's approach was negative, degrading, vindictive, heartless, violative

---

[28] Eve Edstrom, "Newburgh is a Mirror Reflecting on Us All," *Washington Post*, August 6, 1961, p. E1.
[29] *The Minneapolis Tribune*, August 13, 1961, pp. 1, 8A.
[30] *The Wall Street Journal*, July 10, 1961, p. 10.
[31] *The New York Times*, July 19, 1961, p. 1.

of human dignity and self-respect. Representative of many of the critical statements was that issued by the New York State Charities Aid Association:

> The Newburgh crusade is not justified by the facts. The public has been misinformed and misled. . . . Public welfare is the tangible evidence of the conscience and the heart of America. . . .

> [W]e recognize that the generally favorable reaction to the Newburgh crusade reflects widespread misgivings about welfare. The readiness of the public to accept a get tough policy reveals a deeply rooted suspicion of public welfare. . . .

> A basic fallacy is the idea that public welfare measures are of purely local concern. Actually State and Federal Governments have a large stake in how all children everywhere are nurtured physically and emotionally. Indeed, the health and well-being of the entire population are a State and national concern.

> Lack of minimum uniform standards could only lead to a return to the period of punitive treatment of defenseless people in which each community competes to give the least possible help in order to expel harassed unfortunates from its borders. . . .[32]

What has happened in Newburgh has not been forgotten by either friend or foe. The debate continues between those who wish to stress the elimination of chiselers and those who wish to stress the need to rehabilitate and regenerate. "The heart of the difference between the Mitchell and Ribicoff schools," noted one commentator on the Newburgh episode, "lies in whether the main object of relief reorganization should be saving money or saving people."[33]

A LOOK AT STATE UNEMPLOYMENT INSURANCE SYSTEMS

Laws governing unemployment insurance—its coverage, finances, benefits, and administration—are technically quite complex and vary a great deal from state to state. A few of the major outlines of such laws and some of their common characteristics are explained here.

Generally excluded from compulsory coverage are such groups as agricultural workers, workers in firms employing less than four employees, domestics, employees of religious, charitable, and educational institutions, and the self-employed.

Workers in the covered occupations are usually entitled to certain amounts of unemployment benefit payments derived from payroll taxes imposed on their employers. Only three states—Alabama, Alaska, and New Jersey—also collect contributions from employees. While the standard payroll tax is 3 per cent on the first $3,000 (fourteen states now have a tax base above $3,000) earned by an employee in each calendar year, states are left

---

[32] "Newburgh: Symbol of Unrest—Statement by the New York State Charities Aid Association," in the *Congressional Record*, February 8, 1962, p. A1009–11.

[33] A. H. Raskin, "Newburgh's Lessons for the Nation," *The New York Times Magazine*, December 17, 1961, p. 59; see also "Newburgh: Symbol of Unrest—Statement by the New York State Charities Aid Association," pp. A1009–A1011.

with wide discretion to experiment with different rates based on the unemployment experience and risks of different employers and industries. Under the terms of federal law (the Social Security Act of 1935), up to 90 per cent of such payroll tax if channeled into an approved state unemployment trust fund may then be used by the employer as a credit against his federal unemployment tax liability. Ten per cent, the federal share of the payroll tax, goes back to the states in the form of grants to pay for the administrative costs incurred in the operation of the unemployment insurance system.

In order to qualify for unemployment benefits, most states stipulate that a claimant must have earned a specified minimum amount of wages over a minimum period of time, and that he is ready, willing, and able to perform suitable work should such become available.

After a waiting period of one week, claimants may be entitled to benefit payments the level of which varies with the worker's past earnings, the number of his dependents, whether he is partially or fully unemployed, and the different state-enacted maximum and minimum limits. Weekly minimum benefit payments range among the states from $3.00 (Missouri) to $25.00 (California) and maximum payments from $30.00 (Mississippi) to $70.00 (Alaska), with $40.00 the most representative payment. The maximum number of weeks for which benefit payments may be collected ranges from 22 to 39; thirty-nine states set 26 weeks as the outer limit.

That benefit payments such as these can at best only represent a temporary and partial replacement of the wage losses suffered by the unemployed workers is, of course, widely acknowledged. Thus in all but six states (Maine, New Hampshire, New Mexico, South Carolina, South Dakota, and Virginia), it is now possible for the unemployed to receive supplementary pay checks from special funds established under contract between union and management similar in nature to those negotiated at Ford and General Motors.

Among grounds for disqualifying a claimant may be his failure to register at a local employment office, his discharge for a job-connected misconduct, his voluntary separation from employment, or his unwillingness to accept suitable employment. A determination of what constitutes "suitable employment" involves such elements as a claimant's physical fitness, prior training, length of unemployment, and earning experience. Claimants whose entitlement is questioned or whose claim for compensation is denied must then be given a fair hearing before an impartial tribunal and afforded the opportunity to press their appeal before a reviewing authority.

Officials who make these and the many other decisions affecting the status of claimants are charged with the responsibility of interpreting and applying state-enacted unemployment insurance laws. Operating under a merit system (a federal requirement), these officials work under the direction and supervision of state administrative agencies which are organized either as independent boards or commissions, as separate departments of employment security, or as employment security divisions within a state department of labor.

To insulate further the administration of unemployment insurance against political pressure and partiality and to assure the fiscal integrity of the system, special advisory councils appointed by the governor are provided with representatives drawn from labor, employers, and the public.[34]

PROBLEMS AND ISSUES

IN STATE UNEMPLOYMENT INSURANCE

When Congress passed the Temporary Extended Unemployment Compensation Act in 1961, attention was focused once again on certain limitations inherent in the entire unemployment insurance system. For one, it was estimated then that without additional help from the federal government (financed by a temporary increase in the federal payroll tax), approximately 1.5 million unemployed workers would have exhausted their regular state benefits. What had become increasingly evident in the various extensive hearings which Congress conducted in connection with unemployment problems in recent years was the inadequacy of any approach which treats the jobless as a single, homogeneous group and which views unemployment as a uniform phenomenon.[35]

Unemployment may be due to automation or to foreign competition. Unemployment may be seasonal or structural, nationwide or sectional. Whatever its precise nature and cause, unemployment tends to affect differently the different segments of the working force. Particularly vulnerable to any slowdown in business growth and to the general underemployment of resources in economically-depressed areas are certain categories of workers: the aged, youth, unskilled, women, and Negroes. Not only are these groups distributed unevenly among the states (and within the states), but quite often the areas of the country which show the least rapid economic expansion are the very places financially least able to address themselves constructively to the consequences of unemployment.

Critics of the present unemployment compensation program see in this a fundamental argument in favor of a national rather than state-operated system. Were the national government to be entrusted with major responsibility for unemployment insurance, the risks of unemployment could be spread more widely and the fiscal stability of the system strengthened; costs could be reduced through the elimination of administrative duplication inevi-

[34] U. S. Department of Labor, Employment Security Bureau, *Comparison of State Unemployment Security Laws as of January 1, 1962* (Washington, 1962) and "Unemployment Insurance Legislation in 1963," *Monthly Labor Review*, February, 1964, pp. 168–172.

[35] House Committee on Ways and Means, *Extended Temporary Unemployment Compensation Benefits*, Hearings, August 22–24, 1962, 87th Cong., 2nd Sess. (Washington, 1962) and Senate Special Committee on Unemployment Problems, *Unemployment Problems*, Hearings pursuant to S. Res. 196 in eight parts, 86th Cong., 1st Sess. (Washington, 1960).

tably present in the operation of fifty separate systems; worker mobility could be enhanced which would further reinforce the advantages of a truly national market; employers and states would be freed from unfair payroll tax competition; above all, public acknowledgement could finally be given to the fact that unemployment is a national problem and not a state problem and that efforts to ameliorate the condition of the unemployed must, therefore, be largely national rather than state.

This is wrong and dangerous, argue the supporters of the present pattern. To entrust the federal government with the power of defining eligibility standards or with determining the levels and duration of benefit payments would constitute an unwarranted intrusion into state affairs. Also, it would mean that the states would no longer be in the position to experiment with different approaches to the problem, to adapt unemployment compensation to local needs, resources, and conditions. Doors would be opened to national political pressures and chicanery that might result in overly-generous benefit payments which could easily destroy a worker's incentive to seek employment. Since state legislatures are more privy than Congress to the local economic setting—more knowledgeable than Washington about the character of the local labor market and business conditions, about wage rates, and about cost of living differentials—let the decision be made on the state level as to what should constitute reasonable compensation for workers temporarily out of employment and as to what should constitute reasonable payroll tax burdens for the employers in the state.

Beyond arguments of those favoring and those opposing the nationalization of the unemployment insurance system are the often repeated concerns about the sufficiency and reliability of federal statistics of total unemployment. For example, are federal figures unwarrantedly inflated because definitions of unemployment are so broad as to include those partially employed, those temporarily laid off and those merely wanting a secondary or supplementary job? Is it possible to base sound policy decisions regarding unemployment problems on figures which fail to distinguish adequately between those workers wanting to work and going out after a job and those not actively seeking employment out of the belief that no suitable jobs were available for them to take? Should not further distinctions be drawn in reporting overall unemployment data between the unemployed who constitute heads of families and those who only round out or improve the family budget with incidental or supplementary earnings—women and children looking for part-time or occasional employment?

A special United States Senate Committee on Unemployment Problems (1959) concluded that more data and measurements were needed on:

A. The total number of the unemployed, including those who are involuntarily working part time and those who have withdrawn from the labor force because they have been unable to find work.
B. Family responsibilities of the unemployed and the impact of unemployment on their living standards.

C. The estimated number of persons unemployed from frictional, structural and cyclical causes.

D. The rural labor force, and unemployment and underemployment in rural areas.

E. The composition of the labor force, conditions under which youth enter the labor force and workers leave it.

F. The role of women in the labor force and the adjustments necessary because of their changing role.

G. The work history of the unemployed and data on those who suffer frequent periods of unemployment.[36]

Meanwhile enough data are already available to leave little doubt in the minds of state and federal officials working on these problems that during the next decade unemployment will persist and continue to be felt keenly among the young and unskilled, among the non-whites and the technologically displaced, and among those living in depressed areas. Throughout 1962, 146 such areas located in thirty-one out of fifty states, encompassing a population of 21.4 million people, registered substantial unemployment—a range from 6 per cent to 14 per cent of the labor force.[37]

While the overall rate of unemployment for the entire nation was pegged at 5.7 per cent (during 1963), the following data from the Department of Labor indicates that joblessness struck the diverse segments of labor quite differently:

Total unemployment	5.7%
Non-white workers	10.9%
Married men	3.4%
Teen-agers—white	13.4%
Teen-agers—non-white	29.8%

Pressures for federal assistance to states burdened with pockets of persistent unemployment have led to the enactment of five major pieces of legislation:

Area Redevelopment Act (1961): Authorizes federal financial assistance by the Department of Commerce for industrial projects, public facilities, urban renewal and occupation retraining in designated areas of chronic unemployment and underemployment. Secretary of Health, Education, and Welfare is enabled to enter into contracts with state vocational educational agencies for occupational retraining of persons referred to him by the Department of Labor.

Public Works Acceleration Act (1962): Designed to provide immediate useful work for the unemployed and underemployed in those communities in which projects assisted under the act must be located, and to help communities to meet longstanding public needs, improve community services, etc. The act authorizes Federal Housing and Home Finance Agency to make grants and

[36] Senate Special Committee on Unemployment Problems, *Report on Unemployment Problems,* Senate Report No. 1206, 86th Cong., 2nd Sess. (Washington, 1960) pp. 125–126; for background papers, see Senate Special Committee on Unemployment Problems, *Studies in Unemployment,* 86th Cong., 2nd Sess. (Washington, 1960).

[37] Senate Committee on Public Works, *Public Works Acceleration,* Hearings of April 12 and 13, 1962 pursuant to S. Res. 196, 87th Cong. 2nd Sess. (Washington, 1962), pp. 210–231.

loans to areas of substantial unemployment or to areas currently designated by the Secretary of Commerce as "redevelopment areas."

Manpower Development and Training Act (1962): Secretary of Labor is empowered to determine the skill requirements of the economy, encourage the development of programs, including on-the-job training, to equip the nation's workers with the new and improved skills that are required; Secretary of Health, Education, and Welfare is charged with the responsibility of entering into agreements with the states to provide occupational training to unemployed and underemployed persons referred to him by the Secretary of Labor.

The Economic Opportunity Act (1964): This nearly one billion dollar package includes establishment of a job corps for unemployed youth aged 16–21 (first year accepting 40,000—second year, 100,000) in residential conservation camps and job training centers with facilities for a coordinated program of vocational education and work experience. Conservation camps will stress the attainment of an eighth grade literacy level through intensive training in fundamentals—reading, writing, and arithmetic (essential requirements for subsequent vocational training). Title I of the Act also includes a work training program for part-time jobs for boys and girls, 16–21, through grants to state and local governments or to non-profit organizations to pay for them, and a work study program with grants to colleges and universities to pay up to 90 per cent of the costs of part-time employment for students of low income families. Title II of the Act—Community Action Programs—authorizes $315 million in federal grants to local public and private agencies for projects which aim at the elimination of the causes of poverty such as adult illiteracy, lack of training, and poor or unsanitary living conditions. Title III provides programs to combat rural poverty. This includes grants (up to $1,500), loans (up to $2,500) to low-income rural families, and assistance for migrant agricultural employees. Title IV authorizes 15-year loans (up to $25,000) to strengthen small business concerns, to improve their managerial skills, and help further the cause of employment. Title V authorizes $150 million to support experimental pilot or demonstration projects designed to help unemployed fathers and other needy persons to find and keep jobs. Title VI provides for the establishment of a 5,000-member ($10 million) Volunteers in Service to America Service Corps (VISTA) to work with federal, state, local, and private agencies in the "war on poverty." Volunteers would serve in migrant labor camps, mental hospitals, Indian reservations, community action programs, and Job Corps Camps. (VISTA has been likened to a domestic Peace Corps.)

Appalachian Regional Development Act (1965): Establishes Appalachian Regional Commission consisting of 11 governors and 1 federal representative to prepare plans and programs for the economic development of economically depressed Appalachia and to coordinate federal-state-local efforts in 360 counties (all of West Virginia and portions of Alabama, Georgia, Kentucky, Maryland, North Carolina, Ohio, Pennsylvania, South Carolina, Tennessee, and Virginia). Over $1 billion is authorized (to the end of fiscal 1971) to include grants and aids for the construction of highways and access roads, for multi-county health facilities (including hospitals and diagnostic and treatment centers), for soil conservation, erosion control, and land and timber improvement and management, for water resource development and pollution control, for vocational education, and for assistance to economic development districts and facilities.

"I don't know how you feel about this 'War on Poverty,' but I'm fightin' back!"

SOURCE: Jim Berry, from NEA in the *St. Paul Sunday Pioneer Press*, May 31, 1964.

Although it obviously is too soon to assess with any degree of objectivity how successful past legislation (especially the "anti-poverty" act of 1964) has been, some shortcomings and problems emerged from experience with the Manpower Act that deserve further attention.

A. There has been a tendency among state employment agencies to eliminate from retraining the truly disadvantaged workers among their unemployed. This may be partially due to the legislative stipulation inserted into the Manpower Act that there must be a "reasonable expectation" of a job as a condition precedent for retraining. Whatever the precise reason, the very groups most urgently in need of occupational retraining—Negroes, older workers, youth, the handicapped, and those with very limited educational background—such people do not appear to have received their proportionate share of benefits under the program.[38]

[38] U. S. Department of Labor study reported in *The New York Times*, December 1, 1963, pp. 1, 48.

B. An estimated 500,000 of the nation's 4.5 million unemployed were found to lack the minimum education "necessary to undertake regular federal training programs." [39]

C. The program started off quite slowly. At the end of the first fiscal year the number of workers actually retrained in the 1,075 projects was disappointingly small; only 6,300 actually finished their training.[40]

D. Completion of training did not uniformly assure employment. In West Virginia, for example, a state beset by serious unemployment, only approximately one-half of the trainees were able to secure a job. On the other hand, Massachusetts and Connecticut reported excellent results. Nearly all of their carefully selected "graduates" obtained employment. [41]

A NOTE ON POVERTY

America's enormous prosperity and affluence constitute an undeniable fact. Yet despite an impressive growth rate in profits, wages, investments, housing, population, and technology, an equally undeniable fact is the persistence of a significant sector of poverty.

While it is true that no middle class in the world ever lived better or in greater comfort and while the percentage of family incomes of between $7,500 and $14,999 more than quadrupled since 1935, it is also true that during the last few years the reduction in poverty slowed down considerably.[42] In 1953, 26 per cent of this country's families received an income of under $3,000 (adjudged by the Department of Health, Education and Welfare as the cut-off point for poverty); yet nine years later the percentage of all families at the bottom of the income category was not less than 20 per cent.[43]

If the total number of individuals living in families receiving incomes of less than $3,000 is combined with the total number of individuals living alone and receiving incomes of less than $1,500 (the H.E.W. cut-off for this group), it becomes possible to obtain an overall estimate of the number of people in the United States who live in varying degrees of poverty. These estimates range from a low of 33,000,000 to a high of 35,000,000.[44] Thus despite the wealth of this nation and its rapidly expanding economy and despite the efforts of the "welfare state," labor unions, and private charity to reduce poverty, one-fifth of the nation continues to exist on a standard of living substantially below that held necessary to enjoy the essentials of the American style of life. (For an area breakdown of percentages of families living in poverty, see Figure 6.)

[39] Estimate of Seymour L. Wolfbein, Director, Office of Manpower, Automation and Training (Department of Labor) in *The New York Times*, April 14, 1963, p. 47.

[40] *Book of the States, 1964–1965*, p. 548.

[41] *The Wall Street Journal*, March 25, 1963, p. 14.

[42] Conference on Economic Progress, *Poverty and Deprivation in the U. S.*, a study cited in *The New Yorker*, January 19, 1963, p. 110.

[43] Wilbur J. Cohen and Eugenia Sullivan, "Poverty in the United States," *Health, Education and Welfare Indicators*, February, 1964, p. ix.

[44] *Ibid.*, p. ix.

FIGURE 6

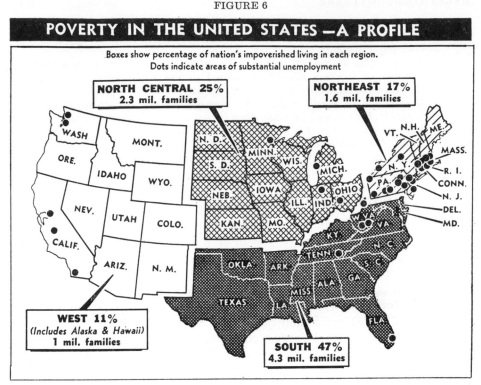

POVERTY IN THE UNITED STATES — A PROFILE

Boxes show percentage of nation's impoverished living in each region.
Dots indicate areas of substantial unemployment

NORTH CENTRAL 25%
2.3 mil. families

NORTHEAST 17%
1.6 mil. families

WEST 11%
(Includes Alaska & Hawaii)
1 mil. families

SOUTH 47%
4.3 mil. families

SOURCE: *The New York Times*, August 16, 1964, p. E10.

Who are these people who have been left behind, and who remain outside the mainstream of American prosperity? As a rule, they are the families with the poorest housing, least education, intelligence, health, skills or energy.

Many of them have a long history of poverty behind them. They reside in the old and new slums, in the ethnic ghettos or even in skid row. Many of them come from the ranks of the non-whites, the unskilled, the sharecroppers, the cotton pickers, or the migrant workers. When they do find employment, their work record is generally erratic and unsatisfying. Whatever drive they may have had was long ago thwarted by failure, or incompetence, or inadequate persistence. They, and all too often their children, represent a large segment of America's alienated citizens—this country's disillusioned, frustrated, and above all helpless and unwanted remnant.

Alongside these are nearly half of all the aged (many of the physically handicapped), the emotionally sick, and the recipients of welfare stipends too small to keep body and soul together. Together with the poor, these "other Americans"

are those who, for reasons beyond their control, cannot help themselves. . .
The individual cannot usually break out of this vicious circle. Neither can the group, for it lacks the social energy and the political strength to turn its misery into a cause. Only the larger society, with its help and resources, can really

make it possible for these people to help themselves. Yet those who could make the difference too often refuse to act because of their ignorant, smug moralism. They view the effects of poverty—above all, the warping of the will and spirit that is a consequence of being poor—as choices.[45]

Poverty's challenge to the rest of the nation is not only a moral one but a social and economic one as well. Too many of the poor do not consume enough of the industrial output, do not eat enough of the farmer's produce, and do not provide enough of the skilled and professional manpower that is required to keep the economy growing at an ever-increasing rate. Nor is it ever possible to overestimate the cost of poverty in terms of crime, delinquency, and disease to all levels of government, to the communal life as a whole, and to each of the individuals concerned.

Hard core poverty in the midst of prosperity constitutes a paradox as well as a challenge.

CASE PROBLEMS FOR CLASS DISCUSSION

1. Assume that you are the administrative director of a migratory labor camp accommodating nearly 300 agricultural workers and their families. It is late at night and you have just been informed that at least ten children have come down with "some sort of typhoid fever." The nearest town, the county seat (2,500 population), is twenty miles away. There is no clinic or medical personnel at the camp. What would you do?
2. As director of public welfare in a city of 30,000, you are faced with a serious cut in the welfare budget. The community has long been critical of the welfare program and there is no chance of obtaining additional appropriations. You are concerned that serious hardships will result unless more funds are provided and that state and federal welfare standards cannot be met under the downward revisions of your city's welfare budget. What measures would you adopt?
3. The commissioner of public welfare in your state has just published a directive authorizing state and local welfare officials to distribute birth control information whenever requested. As the department's legislative liaison officer, you have been "summoned" to explain the highly controversial order to an irate legislative committee. You are personally opposed to the directive on religious grounds. Should you refuse to testify, resign, or support the departmental order? If you do decide to testify, what would be the nature of the departmental case, and how would you substantiate it?
4. Assume that your state includes a coal mining area now characterized by underemployment, unemployment, and generally-depressed economic conditions. A disproportionately large segment of the work force is over forty-five and most of the older workers are unemployed miners. You have been designated local retraining officer by your state department of employment security. After you arrive at the county seat, which is located near the center of the area, you call a public meeting to acquaint the local people with state and federal programs designed to help them. What would you tell the group, and what would be the actual retraining procedures that would have to be established? Would you retrain first those with low literacy and few skills, or those with higher literacy and greater skill convertability?

[45] Michael Harrington, *The Other America: Poverty in the United States* (New York, 1962), p. 15.

SELECTED BIBLIOGRAPHY

Advisory Commission on Intergovernmental Relations, *Modification of Federal Grants-in-Aid for Public Health Services* (Washington, 1961).

JOSEPH M. BECKER, "Twenty-Five Years of Unemployment Insurance," *Political Science Quarterly*, December, 1960, pp. 481–499.

DONALD BRIELAND, "Community Mental Health: The Illinois Program," *State Government*, Spring, 1963, pp. 112–117.

EARL F. CHEIT, "Workmen's Compensation, O.A.S.D.I.: The Overlap Issue," *Industrial Relations*, February, 1964, pp. 63–80.

EARL F. CHEIT and MARGARET S. GORDON (eds.), *Occupational Disability and Public Policy* (New York, 1963).

ELIAS S. COHEN, "An Aging Population and State Government," *State Government*, Summer, 1962, pp. 168–175.

JAMES A. CRABTREE, "A Decade of Public Health in Pennsylvania: Prelude to the Future," *Journal of Public Health*, July, 1960, pp. 942–947.

JAMES A. CRABTREE, "Plans for Tomorrow's Needs in Local Public Health Administration," *Journal of Public Health*, August, 1963, pp. 1175–1182.

ERNEST R. D'AMOURS, "State Supervision of Charities: Present Status," *State Government*, Summer, 1962, pp. 191–200.

RICHARD E. DAWSON and JAMES A. ROBINSON, "Inter-Party Competition, Economic Variables, and Welfare Policies in the American States," *Journal of Politics*, May, 1963, pp. 265–289.

WILLIAM S. DEVINO, *Exhaustion of Unemployment Benefits During a Recession: A Case Study* (East Lansing, 1960).

ADDISON M. DUVAL, "Public Mental Health: A Look Backward and Forward as a Decade Passes," *State Government*, Autumn, 1960, pp. 243–250.

KATHRYN D. GOODWIN, "Twenty-Five Years of Public Assistance," *Social Security Bulletin*, August, 1960, pp. 31–39.

MARGARET GREENFIELD, *Social Dependency in the San Francisco Bay Area: Today and Tomorrow* (Berkeley, 1963).

HENRY C. HUNTLEY, *Intergovernmental Responsibilities for Public Health* (Kingston, R. I., 1962).

SOL LEVINE, PAUL E. WHITE, and BENJAMIN D. PAUL, "Community Interorganizational Problems in Providing Medical Care and Social Services," *Journal of Public Health*, August, 1963, pp. 1183–1195.

EDGAR MAY, *The Wasted Americans* (New York, 1963).

SAMUEL MENCHER, "Newburgh: The Recurrent Crisis of Public Assistance," *Social Work*, January, 1962, pp. 3–11.

HERMAN P. MILLER, *Rich Man, Poor Man* (New York, 1963).

KEITH F. MULROONEY, "Community Responsibility for Mental Health," *Public Management*, June, 1962, pp. 127–130.

ROBERT M. NORTHROP, *Organizing for Public Health: Recommendations for New Jersey* (New Brunswick, 1962).

JOHN R. PHILP, "Government Programs on Alcoholism," *State Government*, Winter, 1962, pp. 49–52.

DONALD ROMERO, "Nature's Way with Waste," *National Civic Review*, July, 1960, pp. 351–354.

WILLIAM RYAN, "Urban Mental Health Services and Responsibilities of Mental Health Professionals," *Mental Hygiene*, July, 1963, pp. 365–371.

ALVIN L. SCHORR, *Slums and Social Insecurity* (Washington, 1963).

LEE SCHREIBEIS, JOHN J. GROVE, and HERBERT R. DOMKE, "Air Pollution Control in Urban Planning," *Journal of Public Health*, February, 1961, pp. 174–181.

FRANK TETZLAFF, SAMUEL M. ROGERS, and SIDNEY EDELMAN, "Guiding Principles for State Air Pollution Legislation," *Journal of Public Health*, February, 1961, pp. 182–189.

ROBERT D. TOMASEK, "The Migrant Problem and Pressure Group Politics," *Journal of Politics*, May, 1961, pp. 295–319.

DAVID J. VAIL, "Administration of Mental Health Research in a State Program," *State Government*, Summer, 1962, pp. 162–167.

R. GORDON WAGENET, "Twenty-Five Years of Unemployment Insurance in the United States," *Social Security Bulletin*, August, 1960, pp. 50–59.

ALONZO S. YERBY, "The Provision of Drugs in Public Welfare Medical Care Programs," *Journal of Public Health*, May, 1961, pp. 655–658.

Chapter XVI

BUSINESS,
LABOR, AND ECONOMIC
DEVELOPMENT

With nothing in any of the state constitutions relating to fair trade or Sunday closing laws, how can a government assume the right to tell a merchant that he must sell his commodities at a certain price and that he may not stay open on Sunday regardless of his religion?

Should state government be permitted to use tax-collected funds for the purpose of inducing business to come into the state and help relieve unemployment?

PROPERTY AND CONTRACT RIGHTS UNDER THE LAW—

SOME BASIC CONCEPTS

To acquire and own property, to manage or dispose of it—these are economic rights which Americans cherish highly. They are considered soundly protected by state and federal constitutional guarantees to the effect that no person shall be deprived of property without due process of law and that contracts must not be impaired. These concepts are deeply anchored as civil liberties in all of the fifty state constitutions, in the United States Constitution of 1787, as well as in the Fifth and Fourteenth Amendments. None of which means, of course, that property rights (or for that matter any of this country's other basic freedoms) constitute absolute rights which no government may limit or regulate regardless of circumstances or conditions. For equally solidly based are those legal foundations which authorize government to regulate the ownership of property and the conduct of persons, should requirements of public welfare and public order make this necessary. "Under our form of government," said the United States Supreme Court in *Nebbia* v. *New York,*

> the use of property and the making of contracts are normally matters of private and not of public concern. The general rule is that both shall be free of governmental interference. But neither property rights nor contract rights are absolute; for government cannot exist if the citizen may at will use his property to the detriment of his fellows, or exercise his freedom of contract to work them harm.[1]

[1] *Nebbia* v. *New York,* 291 U. S. 502 (1934), at 523. For an excellent discussion of the relationship between business and government in the U. S., see Clair Wilcox, *Public Policies Toward Business,* rev. ed. (Homewood, Ill., 1960).

In state government, which is the primary concern of this book, all property and contractual rights are subject to at least three great powers that are constitutionally inherent in the state: First, the state police power; secondly, the power of eminent domain; and, thirdly, the power of taxation.

Unquestionably, the state police power, a power specifically reserved to the states by the Tenth Amendment to the United States Constitution, is the most comprehensive of such powers and the one under which all state and local governments have been allowed to impose significant controls on personal property and on business activities.

Definitions of the state police power vary in detail from state to state and from court to court, yet the essential meaning of the state police power emerges with some clarity. It is the valid exercise of regulatory power by state government on behalf of public health, safety, morals, order, and welfare. Within this enormously broad concept, courts throughout the country have upheld, as being in the public interest, thousands of regulatory measures against challenges that government was unwarrantedly interfering with individual freedoms.

STATE REGULATORY COMMISSIONS

Under the state police power, most comprehensive regulation is reserved in all states for businesses which are by nature monopolistic in character and at the same time directly affected with the public interest. To protect the public nearly all fifty states entrust to utility or service commissions the regulation of privately-owned companies which furnish electricity, gas, water, telephone and telegraph services or which operate rail, trucking, and bus transport. In most of the states members of such commissions are appointed by the governor for staggered terms of six years, although longer and shorter terms are not unusual; in fifteen states commission members reach their office through popular election rather than through appointment.

By statute public utility commissions are given the right to prescribe accounting practices to businesses subject to their control, and to require from them periodic reports of operations. Additional duties include the right to conduct quasi-judicial hearings, to carry out investigations, to inspect facilities, to publish regulations, and to issue certificates of public convenience, the enabling charters or franchises which permit a utility to perform its service for the public.

The commission's most critical and strategic role has to do with its statute-imposed responsibility to fix "reasonable" rates and to determine what constitutes sound standards of safety, service, or equipment. This, of course, places the commission in the unenviable position of having to work out an equitable balance between the interests of the utility owners who naturally wish to maximize their profits and the interests of the consumers or users who want the commission to secure for them, the public, utility services or rates at the lowest possible cost.

After the Civil War, when most legislatures began to establish regulatory commissions, private utility interests at first fought public regulation with all the powers at their command. They viewed the commissions as their mortal enemies bent on destroying private profit and enterprise. Actually most commissions, with their memberships drawn from backgrounds friendly to business, preferred to follow rather conservative rate-making practices instead of crusading for concepts of egalitarian social justice as had been feared by the opponents of regulation.

Nor, as a rule, were legislatures sufficiently eager to make the kind of appropriations which would have been necessary for the commissions to obtain the best size and quality of staff. This proved to be quite crucial since the regulated enterprises rarely lacked professional and legal resources when contesting rate decisions in the courts for fairness or due process of law. Public apathy concerning the often technical work of the commission and the lack of consumer organization constituted a third factor which pulled some of the teeth from the regulatory process.

Businesses such as banking, insurance, securities, or liquor, while usually not subject to control by regulatory commissions, are considered in most states to be so closely associated with the public interest as to justify special administrative supervision. States again differ as to whether the laws governing this supervision are to be administered by a single commissioner, a department head, a director, a group of commissioners, or an executive director responsible to such a commission or department. Concentrating on a few of the major areas of state regulation of business, and leaving aside the considerable variations of administrative patterns, it may be noted that typically a

State Banking Commission will examine financial and lending institutions, scrutinize their assets and enforce state banking laws which are designed to protect investors, savers, and borrowers.

State Insurance Commission will review and examine the policies and rates of insurance sold in the state, issue or cancel agents' licenses, conduct hearings, and audit annual statements. (In some of the states an insurance commissioner may also perform the functions of state fire marshall with responsibilities for the enforcement of state fire prevention laws.)

State Securities Commission will register, license, and supervise dealers, brokers, and investment firms; and seek to protect the public from fraudulent investment practices.

State Liquor Control Commission will oversee and inspect the local enforcement of liquor laws, the collection of liquor excise taxes, the licensing and certification of establishments selling liquor, the registration of brand labels, and conduct periodic auditing of reports and accounts of distillers, brewers, and wholesale liquor distributors.

The brevity given to this discussion of the commissions and their duties must not, however, lead to the conclusion that their work is always routine in nature or generally beyond controversy. Far from it. Few are the states in which one or the other of such commissions do not find themselves at one time or another embroiled in public controversies (sometimes scandalous) of major magnitude and consequence. Corrupt inspectors fail to enforce the laws; crime syndicates work their tentacles around a commission member; influence peddlers purchase favorable decisions; fraudulent records and accounts are permitted to camouflage financial conditions or ownership of a business; or crooked legislators are allowed to use legislative blackmail in order to obtain favorable decisions from a commission.

Often it is most difficult to place the blame for corruption exclusively on the commission or its staff. Recent disclosures in New York's liquor scandals made this abundantly clear.

In an editorial entitled "A Rocky Political Road," *The Wall Street Journal* had this to say:

> What the present law actually supports is vice. The bribery, the extortion and all the other scandals recently uncovered in the New York liquor control system stem directly, and almost inevitably, from the law itself. Each retail liquor license is a little neighborhood monopoly which a state bureaucrat can give or take away; once obtained, it's practically a license to coin money since the prices are fixed and no competitor can undersell you.[2]

What also became quite apparent, as Governor Rockefeller was to discover to his political embarrassment, is the difficulty involved in persuading a legislature to tighten the law. When he urged the legislature to adopt the liquor law recommendations of a special blue ribbon commission, the Moreland Commission, which had studied and investigated the problem thoroughly, he found himself bitterly opposed. "The lobbies, halls and galleries of the legislature," he exclaimed in a special message to the legislature, "are jammed with liquor lobbyists presenting their special interests."[3] However candid this description of the legislative setting, the general tone of the message did little to calm legislative resentments.

In nearly each state then, there are also laws which give to certain boards or officials the duty to examine and issue certificates to

> accountants, architects, engineers, land surveyors, amateur and professional boxing promoters, barbers, physicians, dentists, chiropractors, osteopaths, teachers, hairdressers, beauty culturists, attorneys, optometrists, pharmacists, physical therapists, psychologists, veterinarians, watchmakers, and others.

City and other local governments may, under the state police power delegated to them, issue licenses upon payment of fees (and fulfillment of other stipulated requirements) to

> employment agencies, awning hangers, hotels, cigarette and candy vendors, peddlers, merchants, solicitors, junk yards, secondhand dealers, parking lot operators, auto repair garages, trailer camps, auto rentals, house movers, storers of bulk oil, gasoline filling stations, billposters, ice cream processors

[2] Editorial, *The Wall Street Journal*, March 30, 1964, p. 12.
[3] "Message on Liquor Bills," *The New York Times*, March 26, 1964, p. 31.

and distributors, radio and television repairmen, well drillers, mercantile brokers, druggists, sellers of Christmas trees, beauty shops, photographers, laundries and cleaning plants, newsstands, pawn shops, window cleaners, electrical repair businesses, hardware stores, opticians, food warehousemen, auctioneers, carnivals, amusement rides, baseball parks, roller skating rinks, handbill distributors, movie theaters, taxicabs, motor buses, restaurants

and many other types of businesses or activities which state law or city ordinance requires to maintain certain minimum standards of operations for the purpose of safeguarding the public health, safety, morals, order, or welfare.

City building codes are filled with detailed regulations defining standards and affecting such subjects as

general construction requirements (i.e., electrical work, oil burners, plumbing and gas piping, warm air heating, elevators and moving stairways, refrigeration, sheet metal work, lathing and plastering, thickness of structural steel and cement, etc.); width of aisles in places of assembly, ventilators, enclosures for motion picture projectors; number and location of exit ways in dwellings, assembly halls, churches, and theaters, etc.; mandatory fire safety features in private and public construction, etc.

In order to control not only the construction but the location of trades and industries as well, state law or city charter gives to the zoning board of a city considerable power and discretion to interpret and apply the zoning codes. These govern the use to which buildings or premises may be put within the boundaries of the city. Thus neighborhoods or use districts may be classified as residential, commercial, light industrial, or heavy industrial. Quite obviously, a person's property rights and economic interests may be profoundly affected by such public action which the city exercises within the framework of its police power. But unless zoning board classifications are found to be arbitrary, discriminatory, or illegal, complainants rarely find a court that is willing to reverse the board's decision. Nor does the law grant to property owners a vested right in the consequences of a zoning ordinance. Thus if the public interest should dictate a change in the classification of a neighborhood—as made necessary in hundreds of the urban renewal projects—and if the zoning board can substantiate this by proper and sufficient evidence, courts will generally consider rezoning a legislative prerogative inherent in the city, and it will not be judicially denied.

Closely related to the state police power is the *power of eminent domain*. This is a power inherent in the state but delegable by it to cities, counties, and other political subdivisions. Under this power state constitutions allow the taking of private property for a public purpose at fair compensation. Left primarily to legislative determination, but certainly not precluded ultimately from judicial review, are such questions as what property is to be taken, what is meant by "taking," what purpose constitutes a public purpose, and what can be considered a fair compensation.

What has brought the governmental exercise of eminent domain into prominent and often highly controversial focus in recent years is the public's acute need for land. The demand for land grows out of such developments as slum clearance, urban renewal, area redevelopment, open space land programs, defense highway construction, power and pipe line right of way, and airports or harbor terminals.

To take but one example, by 1962, not less than 45 states adopted enabling statutes which authorized their local governments to take an active part in federally-assisted large-scale urban renewal and slum clearance programs under the terms of the Federal Housing Act of 1949 as amended. Much of this construction occurs in densely-populated areas. Of the nearly 700 cities participating in these programs, two-thirds had populations of 50,000 and over.

During the Sixties, urban renewal proceedings in these communities, for instance, will involve billions of dollars in land values. It is estimated that the highway program alone will require the acquisition of 700,000 parcels of land, much of it in exceedingly expensive settings.

> The flood of lawsuits is beginning to overwhelm the courts. Former Presiding Judge Fred Young of the New York State Court of Claims recently reported that eminent domain cases increased from 52 per cent of the court's calendar in 1960 to "the truly alarming proportion of 68 percent" two years later. Last year a single New York Supreme Court Justice . . . tried more than 5,000 cases involving upwards of 42 million dollars.[4]

As a result of large-scale condemnation proceedings, protests against inadequate and outdated eminent domain statutes have become louder throughout the country. This is particularly true for areas of dense population and high land value. Much of the resentment centers around the general failure of eminent domain statutes to provide adequate and prompt compensation for expenses incurred when a home owner or business is evicted or forced to move to a new location. Too many condemnation awards despite federal financial assistance simply do not realistically account for such factors as loss of good will or decreases in business earnings due to the uncertainties and delays which may have preceded the actual taking of title.

FAIR TRADE LAWS

Nearly half of the states, many of them in the East, continue to have laws on their books which facilitate the maintenance of retail prices at a level fixed by the manufacturer or wholesaler of brand products. Under these laws, fair trade agreements are held to bind all dealers, signers or non-signers alike, as soon as one of them agrees to follow the minimum resale prices fixed by the manufacturer. Violation of such merchandising (mostly in the major appliance field) will result in a dealer's loss of franchise or in a suit for an injunction forcing him to conform to the required pricing practice.

[4] Sidney Z. Searles, "Bulldozers at Your Door," *Reader's Digest*, September, 1963, p. 86.

Proponents of such legislation, among them the powerful National Association of Retail Druggists, maintain that retail price maintenance

A. Assures the retailer a fair profit;
B. Provides the consumer with a stable and reliable market free from deceptive merchandising practices;
C. Will prevent ruinous price cutting.

Opponents of such pricing practices insist that it

A. Interferes with a retailer's economic freedom to sell his goods at a price which will increase his volume;
B. Makes it impossible for consumers to reap the benefits of effective competition;
C. Keeps retail prices in states with such laws above the level found in states without such restrictions.

Both retail price maintenance laws as well as minimum markup laws (in force in about half of the states prohibiting the sale of goods below cost with the intent of destroying competition) have been found difficult to enforce. For one, there are the discount houses which successfully persist in selling standard brands at prices considerably below those of other retailers. Then there are price-cutting practices which regular retail establishments engage in but which are difficult to prove. They may involve such practices as the giving of gifts, stamps, coupons, or the offer of special bargains or trade-in allowances.

SUNDAY CLOSING LAWS

Historically, there can be little doubt that the sanctions underlying present-day laws prohibiting business activities and bodily labor on Sunday were religious in origin. Ecclesiastic authority for them can easily be traced back through parliamentary statutes of the seventeenth and eighteenth centuries, through ordinances and edicts issued by English kings during the thirteenth and fourteenth centuries, through the decrees of Constantine in 321 A.D. and finally to the Fourth Commandment itself. Quite naturally, Puritan America accepted such laws as properly reinforcing the Christian faith. "Keeping holy the Lord's day is a principal part of the service of God," proclaimed the law of Georgia in language typical of the colonial era.

Beginning with the nineteenth century, however, Sunday closing laws were forced to conform to a more distinctly secular character in view of the Bill of Rights and its doctrine of separation of church and state. Increasingly, considerations of rest and recreation, rather than church attendance, became the rationale for shutting down stores, shops, and plants.

Sunday took on a new face and character as the pace of urban life and trade quickened, as traditional Puritan precepts weakened and as mass sports became popular forms of entertainment. In such a setting the list of economic activities and services and the items for sale by druggists and vendors grew from year to year, and few were the legislative sessions where demands could not be heard to further broaden existing exemptions or to add new ones.

At the present time 38 states have Sunday closing or blue laws banning regular weekday labor, business, commercial or industrial activities; 21 states provide limited exemptions for Jews, Seventh Day Adventists, and those who observe their Sabbath on Saturday rather than on Sunday; an additional group of states leaves the enactment of Sunday closing measures to local governments.

The constitutionality of such closing laws has been assailed over the years in hundreds of cases; yet state and federal courts have held rather consistently that these laws represent proper civil regulations and that they are "not repugnant to religious freedom." This also was the position that the United States Supreme Court took in 1961 when called on to review cases involving Sunday closing laws from Massachusetts,[5] Pennsylvania[6] and Maryland.[7]

Speaking for the majority of the Court in the *McGowan* case, Chief Justice Warren wrote:

> Sunday Closing Laws, like those before us, have become part and parcel of this great governmental concern [for public health and welfare] wholly apart from their original purposes or connotations.

> People of all religions and people with no religion regard Sunday as a time for family activity, for visiting friends and relatives, for late sleeping, for passive and active entertainments, for dining out, and the like. . . . It would seem unrealistic for enforcement purposes and perhaps detrimental to the general welfare to require a state to choose a common day of rest other than that which most persons would select of their own accord. For these reasons, we hold that the Maryland statutes are not laws respecting an establishment of religion.

Mr. Justice Douglas entered a vigorous dissent:

> The question is not whether one day out of seven can be imposed by a state as a day of rest. The question is not whether Sunday can by force of custom and habit be retained as a day of rest. The question is whether a state can impose criminal sanctions on those who, unlike the Christian majority that make up our society, worship on a different day or do not share the religious scruples of the majority. . . .

> The "establishment" clause protects citizens . . . against any law which selects any religious custom, practice, or ritual, puts the force of government behind it, and fines, imprisons, or otherwise penalizes a person for not observing it. . . .

> The issue of these cases would, therefore, be in better focus if we imagined that a state legislature, controlled by orthodox Jews and Seventh Day Adventists, passed a law making it a crime to keep a shop open on Saturdays. Would a

[5] *Gallagher* v. *Crown Kosher Market,* 366 U. S. 617 (1961).
[6] *Braunfeld* v. *Brown,* 366 U. S. 599 (1961).
[7] *McGowan* v. *Maryland,* 366 U. S. 423 (1961).

Baptist, Catholic, Methodist or Presbyterian be compelled to obey that law or go to jail or pay a fine?

Actually much of the present widespread agitation for strengthened Sunday closing laws, for more vigorous enforcement and stiffer fines, derives from forces and sentiments somewhat more mundane than alluded to by the distinguished bench. At issue frequently are aggressive merchandising practices by discount department stores. Located near the outer fringes of the great cities, these newer establishments have discovered that by staying open on Sundays they are able to attract large numbers of customers who find it convenient to combine a leisurely Sunday drive into the country with a profitable family shopping expedition. In 1962, the value of such Sunday sales was estimated to have risen to nearly a billion dollars.[8]

Reaction came quickly. Successfully denouncing the emergence of a seven-day week and the threatened disappearance of a common day of rest before city council and state legislature were representatives from downtown department stores, chambers of commerce, commercial clubs, retailers' associations, as well as spokesmen from organized labor and the churches. In the face of such pressures, Sunday closing laws are experiencing a new won popularity. Intensive efforts to tighten the noose around Sunday sales are reported from Colorado, Florida, and Kansas.

STATE LEGISLATION GOVERNING THE EMPLOYMENT OF LABOR

Long gone are the days of the common law which considered labor to be nothing more than a commodity the price of which was to be determined in the economic market place by the impersonal interplay of demand and supply. Particularly since 1908 when the United States Supreme Court in *Muller* v. *Oregon* upheld a maximum hours law, legislatures of nearly every state have enacted a vast number of statutes under the authority of the state police power affecting the employment and conditions of labor.

In addition to provisions which attempt to reduce the economic burdens of unemployment discussed earlier in this book, states have adopted laws which

A. Regulate minimum wages and maximum hours and occupational health and safety conditions for various segments of the work force;
B. Provide disability benefits for injured workers;
C. Aim to stabilize management-labor relations;
D. Attempt to eliminate or reduce discrimination in employment.

The purpose of the following discussion is to stress briefly some of the recent emphases and directions which these statutes reflect.

---

[8] James C. Tanner, "Blue Law Battle Pits Discounters Against Conventional Retailers," *The Wall Street Journal*, November 14, 1962, pp. 1, 22 and Clarence Newman, "Sunday Closing Laws: Their Foes Base Legal Attack on Unequal Enforcement," *The Wall Street Journal*, January 16, 1963, p. 18.

MINIMUM WAGES AND MAXIMUM HOURS

Millions of workers employed in enterprises neither covered by the provisions of the Federal Fair Labor Standards Act nor by union contracts continue to find their wages lagging behind the federal minimum. In 1961, for example, the hourly wage for most of such workers in agriculture, hospitals, hotels, restaurants, retail stores, laundries, and domestic or service occupations failed to reach $1.00 an hour. This figure was at least 15 per cent below the required federal minimum wage for workers in employment connected with interstate commerce.

Fortunately for some of the federally-exempted groups, twelve states— Alaska, Connecticut, Hawaii, Maine, Massachusetts, Nevada, New Hampshire, New York, Pennsylvania, Rhode Island, Vermont, and Washington—provide for a statutory hourly minimum wage of $1.00 or more; seven other states with minimum wage laws fall below that figure.[9] Compared with a total of only seven states reporting minimum wage laws in 1950, the fact that there are now nineteen such states seems to offer notable evidence of an increased legislative concern about the depressive effects of low wages. There are also now at least a dozen states which require that labor employed on public works and buildings be paid a wage at least equal to that prevailing in the locality for similar work under private contracts. What cannot be ignored is the existence of a significant number of workers who are still excluded from all coverage in even some of the more recently enacted minimum wage laws.

Public solicitude for the health, safety, and morals of women and minors has led all states to enact elaborate codes for their protection. In half a dozen states, for instance, women may not be required to work from two to four weeks before and for four weeks following childbirth. Certain occupations such as mining, tending bar, and those peculiarly injurious to health or morals are also barred to them.

Among the major changes in the employment status of women has been the rapid growth of the equal pay for equal work concept. In 1950, ten states had laws prohibiting discrimination in rate of pay because of sex. Thirteen years later twenty-four states had adopted such provisions.

In addition to federal child labor provisions already applicable to business and industry engaged in interstate commerce, all fifty states have laws prescribing the conditions under which children and minors may be employed. Although, as in all other aspects of state labor laws, such regulations vary in detail and scope from state to state, some provisions are common to nearly all jurisdictions:

> A. As a condition of employment nearly all states require that a minor must obtain a certificate or permit of employment from the state department of labor, industrial commission or school indicating his physical fitness and regular school attendance;

[9] *Monthly Labor Review*, December, 1961, p. 1357.

B. Most states impose a maximum daily and weekly hour limit on a minor. For children under sixteen, an eight-hour day and a forty-hour week is customary; night work between 7:00 P.M. and 6:00 A.M. is generally prohibited;

C. Practically all states list special occupations which because of their hazardous or health-endangering character are unsuitable for the employment of minors.

Laws enacted in recent years in a number of states—California, Colorado, Connecticut, Florida, Hawaii, New York, North Carolina, Ohio, Utah, Vermont, Washington, West Virginia, and Wyoming—attempt to strengthen on-the-job training and vocational education programs in order to help reduce school dropout rates and to lift the level of skill among young job seekers. Wyoming finally adopted sixteen as the minimum age for the employment of minors, and Texas raised to fourteen the age at which a needy child may obtain a work permit. The curfew hours during which a minor could be employed were liberalized to 9:00 P.M. in at least half a dozen states.[10]

New York's migrant labor program—along with that of Colorado—one of the most advanced in the nation, was specifically designed to improve the social and economic conditions of the 25,000 migratory workers who annually come into the state. Essential elements of the program include:

> prohibition of child labor (fourteen is the minimum when school is not in session; sixteen otherwise); child care centers operated by the Growers and Processors Federation subject to state inspection by the department of agriculture; at most camps public health services are made available through state and local governmental health and nursing services; all farm labor contractors of crew leaders must register with the industrial commission; migrant workers are subject to the same welfare services and payments as are New York State residents; migrant labor camps must conform to the State Sanitary Code; wage rates must meet the minimum set out in application filed with the industrial commissioner; contractors, crew leaders must keep detailed pay records; migrant labor may be covered by workmen's compensation law (70 per cent are); New York State pays for summer schools operated by local school districts for the benefit of migrant children.[11]

DISABILITY BENEFITS—WORKMEN'S COMPENSATION

Among the harshest principles of the common law of labor brought over from Britain were those concepts under which a worker by accepting employment was held to have assumed all the risks of injury that he might sustain in the course of his employment. Redress for injury or damages could only be obtained upon complicated proof that the worker did not himself in any way contribute to the events leading to his injury or that the accident was not

---

[10] Based on *ibid.*, December, 1961, December, 1962, November, 1963, *State Government,* Autumn, 1962 and 1963, and *Book of the States, 1962–1963, 1950–1951.*

[11] Memo prepared by Robert D. Helsby, Executive Deputy Industrial Commissioner of New York State, entered by Senator Jacob Javits (R–N. Y.) in the *Congressional Record,* June 11, 1963, pp. 10019–10020.

attributable to either his negligence or to that of his fellow workers. Beginning in 1902, with Maryland, all of the states gradually adopted laws, over the determined opposition of many employers, which required employers to insure their workers either with a private insurance company or with a state insurance fund against injuries that employees might incur in the performance of their jobs.

A majority of today's workmen's compensation laws cover most employers (except for agriculture and domestics), specify weekly maximum benefits for temporary or total disability, provide death benefit payments for survivors, and establish procedures for filing and settling claims. Appeals from an administrative determination of such a claim can generally be taken to a state workmen's compensation board or to an industrial commission which is empowered by statute to conduct investigations and hearings and to act in the capacity of a quasi-judicial tribunal.

As legislatures continue to amend their workmen's compensation laws, the resulting changes tend to increase cash and medical benefits, extend coverage to formerly exempted groups (such as farm workers and public employees), include rehabilitation expenses of injured workers, and lengthen the periods during which applications may be filed for benefits compensating for disabling effects of radiation diseases.

LABOR-MANAGEMENT RELATIONS

State governmental activities in the realm of labor management relations still bear the imprint of many bitter legislative controversies and struggles for power. Long a political fact of life has been organized labor's profound sense of frustration with state legislatures dominated by rural or small-town interests whose leaders made no secret of their intense antagonism to national unions, collective bargaining, and the principle of the union shop. This experience on the state level formed part of the background which persuaded labor to turn to the federal government to protect its interests and to respond to its grievances. The Wagner Act of 1935 enabled organized labor to gain a degree of economic and political power that few, if any, state legislatures would have permitted. But after Congress passed the Taft-Hartley Act in 1947, which outlawed the closed shop, the pendulum began to swing away from a public policy which stressed the rights of organized labor. What now received emphasis again were the rights of employers vis-à-vis a union's unfair labor practices and, under Section 14-b, the right of the states to prohibit contracts between union and employers requiring all workers to join and support the union.

As the Taft-Hartley Act was interpreted by the National Labor Relations Board and by the courts, the role and voice of the states in the field of labor-management relations were further strengthened. For example, in 1949, there were only a dozen states which had enacted laws under their police power forbidding the closed shop or similar types of union security agreements; all of them except Arizona were Southern or Midwestern states—Florida, Georgia, Iowa, Nebraska, North Carolina, North Dakota, South Dakota, Tennessee, Texas, and Virginia.[12] Yet fourteen years later, not less than twenty states had adopted the right-to-work laws under which it became illegal to have union membership constitute a necessary condition of employment. The list of right-to-work states now includes

> Arkansas (1944); Florida (1944); Arizona (1946); Nebraska (1946); Georgia (1947); Iowa (1947); North Carolina (1947); South Dakota (1947); Tennessee (1947); Texas (1947); Virginia (1947); North Dakota (1948); Nevada (1952); Alabama (1953); South Carolina (1954); Mississippi (1954); Utah (1955); Indiana (1957); Kansas (1958).

Both state and federal courts have upheld such laws as a proper exercise of the state police power, as compatible with the Taft-Hartley Act, and as non-violative of the United States Constitution.

The political battles fought for and against such laws are always exceedingly bitter and vehement. So much so in fact, that the right-to-work issue's lack of popularity and the bitterness that it engendered in the Ohio election of 1958 overshadowed all other candidates and contests. It was blamed for having contributed directly to the disastrous showing that the Republican party made at the polls at that time.

Those who favor the right-to-work laws—and there is a national Right To Work Committee (a registered lobby) operating in Washington furnishing literature and leadership—stress some of the following arguments:

> A. Under this country's concept of freedom no man should be forced to join a union in order to earn his daily bread and hold a job of his choice;
> B. Right-to-work laws have proven highly beneficial to the states which have adopted them; by attracting new business, these states were able to attain a faster rate of economic growth—sales climbed higher, bank accounts increased more rapidly, payrolls grew faster, and industrial wealth was added more quickly—than were states which did not enact such laws;
> C. Right-to-work laws are aimed at the monopolistic power of unions and not at the individual worker who actually welcomes such a measure as an effective weapon against the coercive and irresponsible tactics of union hierarchies.

Spokesmen for organized labor and other critics of the right-to-work laws counter these contentions by insisting that

> A. Economic progress of the economically less developed states was achieved despite and not because of right-to-work laws.
> B. The real objective of such laws is to attack the entire labor movement and the principle of collective bargaining and to return to the pattern of industrial relations characterizing the pre-New Deal Era.
> C. The position of the so-called "free rider"—men who want to share in the benefit of union-won wages without sharing in the responsibilities and costs without which such benefits could not have been obtained—is not only immoral but will inevitably undermine the union's bargaining power

[12] *Book of the States, 1950–1951*, p. 455.

and necessarily lead to industrial instability and labor-management warfare.

Fortunately, from the point of view of organized labor, the enforcement of right-to-work laws does not appear to have been too effective.[13] The older and more powerful unions have not been hurt to any substantial extent. Smaller unions, on the other hand, especially those involving unskilled labor and the building and construction trades have found the effect of these laws to be more burdensome. Concentrated efforts by labor to repeal Section14-b of the Taft-Hartley Act were partially successful in the summer of 1965 when the House voted to strike the section.

The range of governmental concern in labor-management relations obviously finds many other applications beyond the right-to-work issue. For example, laws in twenty-six states (modeled closely after the Wagner Act) restrict court injunctions in connection with labor disputes. Mass picketing, secondary boycotts, and strikes by public employees are illegal in most jurisdictions, but the recruitment of strike breakers is prohibited in at least six states—Delaware, Hawaii, Maryland, New Jersey, Rhode Island, and Washington. Private employment agencies are regulated as to fees or referral practices in all states but Alaska, Mississippi, New Mexico, South Carolina, and Vermont.[14]

DISCRIMINATION IN EMPLOYMENT

Mandatory fair employment laws enacted in twenty-five states—Alaska, California, Colorado, Connecticut, Delaware, Hawaii, Idaho, Illinois, Indiana, Iowa, Kansas, Massachusetts, Michigan, Minnesota, Missouri, New Jersey, New Mexico, New York, Ohio, Oregon, Pennsylvania, Rhode Island, Utah, Washington, and Wisconsin—make it illegal to discriminate on basis of race, color, or national origin.[15] Discrimination on the basis of age unless clearly made necessary by the nature of the occupation is prohibited in seventeen states—Alaska, California, Colorado, Connecticut, Delaware, Hawaii, Louisiana, Massachusetts, Nebraska, New Jersey, New York, Ohio, Oregon, Pennsylvania, Rhode Island, Washington, and Wisconsin.[16]

Most anti-discrimination statutes place administrative responsibility in a fair employment practices commission or in a state commission against discrimination, although Hawaii, which passed such a law in 1963, decided to give the task of the enforcement to the State Department of Labor and Industrial Relations. Commissions are generally authorized to receive complaints, investigate alleged charges of discrimination, conduct hearings, and

[13] William James Lee, *"Right to Work Laws": Some Economic and Ethical Aspects*, Ph.D. dissertation, The Catholic University, 1961.

[14] *Monthly Labor Review*, November, 1963, p. 1300.

[15] Commission or Law and Social Action, American Jewish Congress, *Summary of 1962 and 1963 State Anti-Discrimination Laws* (New York, 1963), p. 2.

[16] *Monthly Labor Review*, November 1963, p. 1299.

attempt "by means of education, conference, conciliation, and persuasion to eliminate unfair discriminatory practices" in all types of employment.

As to sanctions or methods of enforcing decisions, the earlier laws, such as the Indiana Fair Employment Act of 1945, relied exclusively on voluntary compliance. Gradually, more and more states moved in the direction of permitting their commissions to apply to the courts, after a hearing and upon a finding of an unlawful employment practice, for a judicial enforcement of their rulings. In Minnesota, however, the legislature placed an intermediary review between the commission and the courts. On failing to eliminate an unfair employment practice, the Minnesota State Commission Against Discrimination must notify the governor who in turn will then select three persons from a special panel to serve as a board of review for the commission. Should this group, after conducting its own hearings, agree with the commission, it can issue a cease and desist order. If the respondent then fails to comply with the order, the review board is entitled to institute proceedings in the district court.[17]

Recently-adopted changes and the newer fair employment statutes tend to facilitate a more vigorous enforcement than that. Under provisions effective in Delaware, Hawaii, Idaho, Iowa, and Vermont, for example, willful violation of a commission's cease and desist order is held to constitute in itself a criminal offense punishable by fine or imprisonment for up to ninety days. Actually, in the majority of the cases, commissions find that conciliation efforts will prove adequate to dispose of most complaints.

The following case, fairly typical of most employment dispositions, is taken from the pages of a report submitted to the governor and legislature of one of the states by its State Commission Against Discrimination:

> The complainant alleged that he was discriminated against because of his race.
>
> The investigation uncovered, through interviewing of the local manager of the department, that his department and some seven others in the state of . . . are leased from department stores and managed and owned by a single company. He indicated that the applicant was well qualified for the position but he did not hire Negroes and that it was company policy not to hire Negroes. A finding of probable cause of discrimination was made by the Commission on the basis of this information. Since the local manager indicated he was implementing the company's discriminatory policy, the conciliation proceeded with the owner of the chain of stores leasing departments throughout the state. The conciliation revealed that the local manager had been in error in his interpretation of company policy and, after discussion with the Commission staff, the non-discriminatory policy of the company was interpreted to each of the local managers and a position was offered to the young man who had brought this complaint.[18]

Of 205 complaints received by this commission during the year, 32 were satisfactorily adjusted in this manner; 81 were dismissed for no probable

[17] *Minnesota Statutes Annotated*, Ch. 363 (St. Paul, 1963).
[18] State Commission Against Discrimination, *Seventh Annual Report (1962)* (St. Paul 1963), p. 5.

cause; 68 complaints were resolved informally; 9 were dismissed for lack of jurisdiction; 3 were withdrawn; 4 were dismissed for insufficient evidence; and 3 were processed for probable cause.

While it is undeniable that the fair employment practices laws may be credited with some progress against the most flagrant denials of equal opportunities in employment, it would be sheer folly to claim that they have substantially overcome the problem of discrimination. Nothing could be further from reality. Discrimination in employment against Negroes and other racial and religious minorities goes far beyond the level of hiring practices; it extends with varying degrees of formality, to apprenticeship training programs, restrictive union practices, and employment service referrals—most of which are way beyond the effective reach of either state law or, because of budgetary considerations, a state's fair employment practices commission.

In its study on discrimination in employment, the United States Civil Rights Commission pointed to still another dimension of the problem. Its findings concluded with this observation:

> The vicious circle of discrimination in employment opportunities was clear: The Negro is denied, or fails to apply for, training for jobs in which employment opportunities have traditionally been denied him; when jobs do become available, there are consequently few, if any, qualified Negroes available to fill them; and often, because of lack of knowledge of such newly opened opportunities, even the few who are qualified fail to apply.[19]

A much more significant federal effort on behalf of fair employment practices can be expected as a consequence of the passage of the Civil Rights Act of 1964, especially in those states which fail to enact anti-discrimination statutes of their own. Title VII of this federal law provides for a five-member Equal Employment Opportunity Commission (E.E.O.C.) with power to investigate complaints of alleged discrimination, to conduct hearings (assuring confidential proceedings), and to seek the elimination of unlawful employment practices "by informal methods of conference, conciliation and persuasion." In carrying out these activities, the E.E.O.C. is specifically authorized to cooperate with appropriate state and local public or private agencies. The act declared discrimination against individuals on basis of race, color, religion, sex, or national origin in interstate commerce, industry, or trade to constitute an unlawful employment practice. Employers, employment agencies, apprenticeship committees, and unions were prohibited, for example, from discriminating

A. With respect to hiring or firing;
B. With respect to compensation, terms, conditions or privileges of employment;
C. With respect to limiting, segregating, or classifying employees in any way which would deprive or tend to deprive any individual of employment opportunities or otherwise adversely affect his status as an employee;

[19] United States Commission on Civil Rights, 1961 Report, Book 3, *Employment* (Washington, 1961), pp. 153–154.

D. With respect to excluding any individual from union membership or segregating union members;

E. With respect to the admission of an individual to apprenticeship, retraining, or on-the-job training programs.

In order to encourage local initiative and to give to state agencies additional opportunity to eliminate discriminatory employment practices, the 1964 act (a) made provision for a year's delay before the full force of the federal law could be called into effect and (b) barred the E.E.O.C. from allowing petitions to be filed with it until the local agency has had a period of time (120 days) to act on the complaint. Full coverage was to proceed gradually. At first only firms with 100 or more employees would be affected; firms with twenty-five workers will only be reached during the fifth year. Exempted altogether from coverage are certain employees of religious and educational institutions and those of state and local governments. The law also specifically permits "an employer to apply different standards of compensation, or different terms, conditions, or privileges of employment pursuant to bona fide seniority or merit systems . . . or a system which measures earning by quantity or quality of production. . . ." Furthermore, there was nothing in the law that could require employers or unions "to grant preferential treatment to any individual, or to any group . . . on account of an imbalance which may exist with respect to the total number or percentage of persons of any race, color, religion, sex or national origin. . . ."

Should the conciliar and informal methods of the E.E.O.C. fail to bring about compliance with the law, at least three additional sanctions are available: (1) the aggrieved party may bring civil suit against the respondent in a federal district court (with the aid of a court-appointed attorney); (2) the United States attorney general may bring civil action when he "has reasonable cause to believe that any person or group of persons is engaged in a pattern or practice of resistance to the full enjoyment of any of the rights secured . . ."; or (3) the district court itself may, upon finding of intentional discrimination, issue an injunction restraining respondent "from engaging in such unlawful employment practice. . . ."

ANTI-DISCRIMINATION LAWS IN HOUSING AND PUBLIC
ACCOMMODATIONS

Laws against discrimination in the sale, rental, and leasing of privately-owned residential property have been enacted in eleven states (Alaska, California, Colorado, Massachusetts, Michigan, Minnesota, New Hampshire, New Jersey, New York, Oregon, and Pennsylvania). Their enforcement is lodged either in a state commission against discrimination (which may have also been charged with carrying out provisions of the state's fair employment practices code) or in a separate statutory tribunal with similar powers to hear complaints and demand compliance.[20]

[20] *Summary of 1962 and 1963 State Anti-Discrimination Laws*, p. 2.

Under the fair housing law of Massachusetts, which is fairly typical in its prohibitions, it is unlawful

> For the owner, lessee, sublessee, licensed real estate broker, assignee, or managing agent of publicly assisted or multiple dwelling or contiguously located housing accommodations or other person having the right of ownership or possession or right to rent or lease . . . such accommodations . . . (a) to refuse to rent or lease . . . or otherwise to deny or to withhold from any person or group of persons such accommodations because of the race, creed, color, or national origin of such person or persons; (b) to discriminate against any person because of his race, creed, color, or national origin in the terms, conditions or privileges of such accommodations . . . or in the furnishing of facilities or services in connection therewith. . . .[21]

The path of these laws has not been a smooth one. Supporters of such civil rights measures have generally encountered determined opposition in state legislatures and in city referenda. During the first six months of 1964 alone, a housing anti-discrimination bill was defeated in the Rhode Island House of Representatives on a 61 to 32 roll call vote; open housing ordinances were turned down by the voters of Seattle, Washington, by a ratio of more than 2 to 1, and by the voters of Tacoma, Washington, by better than 3 to 1. In 1963, Berkeley, California, defeated a similar proposal (for the second time in three years) by 22,720 to 20,323.[22] On November 3, 1964, California's electorate nullified the state's fair housing law, the Rumford Act, by adopting overwhelmingly (with a margin of 1,587,205) Proposition No. 14 which stated:

> Neither the state nor any subdivision thereof shall deny, limit, or abridge, directly or indirectly, the right of any person who is willing or desires to sell, lease or rent any part or all of his property, to decline to sell, lease or rent such property to such person or persons as he, in his absolute discretion, chooses.[23]

In the course of these battles for the acceptance of anti-discrimination laws, civil rights organizations, minority spokesmen, clergymen, and reform groups have insisted that moral and democratic principles required public action to assure greater equality in housing for all citizens. Opponents—real estate interests and home owners' associations among others—have contended that such laws violate constitutionally-protected rights of owners of private property to rent or sell freely to whomever they pleased and that the adoption of such measures would unfairly jeopardize property and neighborhood values.

When challenged through litigation, anti-discrimination laws have, in recent years, generally been sustained as proper applications of the state

---

[21] *Annotated Laws of Massachusetts*, Ch. 151B, Sect. 4, Subsect. 6, 1963 Cumulative Supplement (Charlottesville, Va. and Rochester, N. Y., 1964).

[22] Associated Press, April 10, 1964; *Seattle Post-Intelligencer*, March 11, 1964; *Tacoma News Tribune*, February 12, 1964; and *San Francisco Chronicle*, April 3, 1963, cited in *Congressional Record*, June 12, 1964, p. 13178.

[23] *Congressional Quarterly*, November 13, 1964, p. 2706.

police power in both state and federal courts. Starting with the central premises made classic in *Nebbia* v. *New York,* a majority of courts have held that since neither property rights nor contract rights are absolute, and since government cannot exist "if the citizen may at will use his property to the detriment of his fellows," government must have the right to regulate property in the common interest and for the general welfare as determined by legislatures or city councils. Thus, when, for example, the Massachusetts Supreme Judicial Court upheld the state's fair housing law, it conjectured that the legislature could easily have arrived at a finding that

> A. Discrimination in multiple dwelling and contiguously located housing might tend to restrict Negroes to a relatively small area and perhaps to encourage slum conditions through density of population. . . .
> B. Housing discrimination could impede the relocation of families affected by urban redevelopment programs. . . .
> C. There might be a shortage in housing from which Negroes could suffer more than other groups.[24]

When a taxpayer of the city of Oberlin, Ohio, sought a declaratory judgment to strike down the city's fair housing ordinance as "an infringement of constitutionally guaranteed property rights," the majority of the Ohio Court of Appeals ruled

> that the ordinance, designed and enacted to prevent discrimination in the field of private housing, bears a substantial and reasonable relation to the health, comfort, safety, convenience, and welfare of the residents of the city of Oberlin, and is not an unreasonable, arbitrary or oppressive exercise of the police power.

Considerably less resistance (at least outside of the South) has been shown in laws aimed at eliminating discrimination in hotels, restaurants, meeting halls, places of business, transportation facilities, and other public accommodations based on race, color, religion, or national origin. Even before the enactment of the federal Civil Rights Act of 1964, there were at least thirty states which had outlawed such forms of discrimination. The list included

> Alaska, California, Colorado, Connecticut, Idaho, Illinois, Indiana, Iowa, Kansas, Maine, Maryland, Massachusetts, Michigan, Minnesota, Montana, Nebraska, New Hampshire, New Jersey, New Mexico, New York, North Dakota, Ohio, Oregon, Pennsylvania, Rhode Island, South Dakota, Vermont, Washington, Wisconsin, and Wyoming.[25]

Title II of the 1964 act attempts to bar discrimination "on the ground of race, color, religion, or national origin" in a place of public accommodation if "its operations affect commerce, or if discrimination or segregation . . . is supported by State action. . . ." The act covers

> any inn, hotel, motel or other establishment which provides lodging to transient guests, other than an establishment located within a building which contains

[24] *Massachusetts Commission Against Discrimination* v. *Colangelo,* 182 N.E. 2d 595 at 599–600 (1962).
[25] *Summary of 1962 and 1963 State Anti-Discrimination Laws,* pp. 2–3.

not more than five rooms for hire and which is actually occupied by the proprietor of such establishment as his residence . . .

any restaurant, cafeteria, lunch room, lunch counter, soda fountain, or other
facility principally engaged in selling food for consumption on the premises, including, but not limited to, any such facility located on the premises of any retail establishment; or any gasoline station;

any motion picture house, theater, concert hall, sports arena, stadium, or other
place of exhibition or entertainment. . . .

Not included within the provisions of the law were small retail establishments
and specifically exempted were bona fide private clubs unless their facilities
had been made available to the customers or patrons of a covered establishment.

Enforcement of the act was to be achieved through civil actions for
preventive relief including temporary or permanent injunctions. In states
which had barred discrimination in public accommodations through laws of
their own, cases of alleged violations can be referred to state or local agencies
for a thirty-day period (and even longer if proceedings are pending) so that
local remedies might first be exhausted. In the other states courts were
empowered to refer complaints to a newly-established federal Community
Relations Service which was given an opportunity (up to 120 days) to seek
voluntary compliance with the law. Suits for injunctions may be instituted by
an aggrieved person or by the attorney general whenever he "has reasonable
cause to believe that any person or group of persons is engaged in a pattern or
practice of resistance to the full enjoyment of any of the rights secured by this
title. . . ." To reinforce sanctions even further, the act authorizes courts to
appoint an attorney to aid the complainant and also to allow "the commence-
ment of the civil action without the payment of fees, costs or security."

ECONOMIC DEVELOPMENT

AND THE PROBLEM OF DISTRESSED AREAS

During the last twenty years more and more states and local governments proceeded to help finance private industrial and business enterprises in
areas of persistent unemployment through the issuance of loans, guarantees
of credit, or through exemptions from taxation. By 1963, the number of
states providing such authority for their local governments had reached
twenty-three. Laws in thirteen states permitted such subsidies to be furnished
directly by the state itself. A growing number of states have decided to leave
behind certain memories of the nineteenth century when public credit, land,
and money were made available freely to aid railroads or other utilities. After
experiencing disastrous consequences due to business reverses, overspecula-
tion, and instances of corruption, constitutions in quite a few states were so
amended as to prohibit in the most explicit of terms any such governmental
partnership with business. Pennsylvania's constitutional provision exempli-
fied this policy:

> The General Assembly shall not authorize any county, city, borough, township or incorporated district to become a stockholder in any company association, or corporation, or to obtain or appropriate money for, or to loan its credit to, any corporation, association, institution or individual. (Art. IX, Sec. 7.)

What has helped to create the present legal basis which enabled states to render such public aid to private enterprise are constitutional changes that came about through amendments, through a more liberal judicial interpretation of relevant constitutional or statutory language or through a combination of all of these. Also helpful along this line, was the willingness of courts to construe much more broadly than ever the concept of public purpose in cases involving the application of the powers of eminent domain, taxation, and police.

A recent Maryland case, *City of Frostburg* v. *Jenkins,* illustrates quite well how a court, if it wishes, can get around restrictive constitutional language.

> Plaintiff Jenkins sought an injunction to prevent the holding of a special election under a Maryland statute which had authorized the city of Frostburg to issue certain municipal bonds. The proceeds of these bonds were to be devoted to the acquisition of a site and towards the cost of constructing a building which was to be used by a privately-owned manufacturing company. Maryland had a constitutional provision to the effect that "the credit of the State shall not in any manner be given or loaned to, or in aid of, any individual, association, or corporation."

A majority of the court contended that (a) Maryland's constitutional provision restricted the state from engaging in such a scheme but not its local subdivision; (b) the attraction of new industries by means of tax exemptions had already been judicially approved before—"We see no real difference between the tax exemption . . . and . . . [the benefit given] in the instant case"; and (c) other states, notably, Alabama, Arkansas, New Mexico, and Tennessee also had successfully adopted similar schemes. The final paragraph of the opinion concluded on this note:

> The Constitution does not guarantee a static condition of society, or write into our basic law the economic doctrine of laissez-faire. So long as the legislation has a substantial relation to the public welfare and can fairly be said to serve a public purpose, it is not the court's function to strike it down, merely because we fear it may lead to unwise and unfortunate results. We think the legislation in the instant case is not beyond the bounds of legislative power.

Relying on decisions handed down in Florida, Nebraska, and New York, the dissent rejected the view that political subdivisions such as cities were not bound by credit restraints constitutionally imposed on the state. Central to the reasoning of the dissent was the following argument from a New York case including a similar set of facts:

> It is true, of course, that the city may be benefited by the location of the company in the city. It may produce employment for citizens of the community. It may tend to balance a locally restricted economy. But general benefit to the

economy of a community does not justify the use of public funds of the city unless it be for a public as distinguished from a private purpose. This is simply a case where the city is attempting to use the powers, credits and public moneys of the city to purchase land and erect industrial buildings thereon for the use of a private corporation for private profit and private gain.[26]

The issues were thus resolved in favor of newer concepts of public policy and governmental roles.

An excellent report of the Advisory Commission on Intergovernmental Relations (1963) addresses itself to the closely-related policy questions. "The industrial development bond," concluded the commission, "tends to impair tax equities, competitive business relationships and conventional financial institutions out of proportion to its contribution to economic development and employment." Two members of the commission, Senator Muskie of Maine and Speaker Lowman of Kentucky, disagreed. They urged that state and local governments "should be encouraged—not discouraged—to attack problems of economic stagnation and underemployment." They likened industrial development bond financing as not "materially differ[ent] from the provision of water, sewage disposal, roads, parks, swimming pools and the other facilities provided by government to encourage economic activity . . . [which are] frequently financed through public borrowing." [27]

The majority of the commission while not favoring these developments felt reasonably sure, however, that state and local governments would continue to engage in such credit activities for many years to come. On the basis of this assumption and as a result of their investigations, the commission felt it prudent to suggest a number of guidelines which would help to safeguard and "minimize intergovernmental friction" and which would insure that governmental resources deployed for this purpose "bear a reasonable relationship to the public purpose served. . . ." A partial summary of their recommendations follows:

A. Local programs are best adapted to rural areas with a surplus of farm labor and a dearth of capital and property leasing resources; . . . State programs lend themselves most effectively to the needs of urban and industrial areas with surplus labor. . . .

B. [I]f States elect to permit their political subdivisions to issue industrial development bonds, they [should] require that all such bonds be approved by an appropriate state agency as a condition of issuance.

C. Rather than creating special districts, authority to extend such aid should be limited to "general units of government, i.e., counties, municipalities and organized townships."

D. States should "place a limitation on the total volume of such bonds which may be outstanding at any one time, and to the extent practicable, relate

---

26 *City of Frostburg* v. *Jenkins*, 136 A. 2d 852 (1957); in this connection see Samuel Mermin, *Jurisprudence and Statecraft: The Wisconsin Development Authority and Its Implications* (Madison, 1963) and Advisory Commission on Intergovernmental Relations, *Industrial Development Bond Financing* (Washington, 1963).

27 *Industrial Development Bond Financing,* p. 15.

such limitation to meaningful criteria, such as the personal income of the population."

E. Provisions should be included to "restrict the 'pirating' of industrial operations by one community from another." [28]

DISTRESSED AREAS

In certain areas of substantial and critical long-term unemployment, economic redevelopment efforts involve increasingly the cooperation between all three levels of government—federal, state, and local. This is especially true of such severely depressed states as West Virginia (where approximately 9.6 per cent of the state's labor force is unemployed), and such areas as the mining counties in the Appalachian and Cumberland Mountains (particularly eastern Kentucky), and in the group of counties comprising the iron range of northeastern Minnesota, northern Wisconsin, and western Michigan. Often in these and several other severely-affected areas, stark poverty had already reached such levels of intensity as to call for more immediate measures of welfare—food, clothing, and other essentials of life—while public and private efforts sought the necessary capital for more basic measures of economic rehabilitation. When local and commercial resources proved inadequate or unavailable, Washington became an important source for this new seed capital.

Federal assistance (for stimulating economic self-help) in the form of loans to businesses and industries which would locate or expand and create new jobs in the over 1,000 distressed areas are now channeled principally through the Area Redevelopment Administration. Some loans to small establishments and to local development corporations are made available also by the Small Business Administration. Public bodies such as state and local governments may obtain funds for job-creating projects in depressed areas under provisions of the Public Works Acceleration Act.

For an area to be officially entitled to assistance under the Area Redevelopment Administration, the unemployment rate must be substantially above that of the national average as provided in the law:

Section 5 (a) Unemployment is currently 6% or more of work force, discounting seasonal or temporary factors. . . . The annual average rate of unemployment has been at least:

A. 50% above the national average for three of the preceding four calendar years, *or*

B. 75% above the national average for two of the preceding three calendar years, *or*

C. 100% above the national average for one of the preceding two calendar years . . . or the median farm family income fell below $1,887.00 a year.

Before a business applicant in an area so designated can actually receive an Area Redevelopment Administration loan, a number of conditions have to

[28] *Ibid.*, pp. 19, 20, 21, 24, and 26.

be met. A local economic development program has to be prepared and approved by agencies of all three levels of government; there must be evidence that local and state sources are able to supply at least 35 per cent of the costs of the project; at least 5 per cent of the cost has to be provided by non-governmental sources; and lastly, an applicant who wishes to purchase land, equipment, or machinery, must be able to show that financial assistance for this purpose was not otherwise available from private lenders on reasonable terms.

Throughout its short existence (1961), much of the Area Redevelopment Administration's work has been subject to serious political controversy. This is how the Chamber of Commerce evaluates the agency and its program:

> We feel that the ARA has been unsuccessful and will continue to be so. There are many causes which can be listed among those creating an economically depressed area: changes in consumer demand; depletion of resources; changes in defense procurement or in location of defense facilities; decentralization of production; lack of industrial diversification; and technological changes, among others. The Area Redevelopment Administration has done nothing to change any of these causes of depressed areas. It cannot. No federal program can.[29]

Some Republican congressmen on and off the floor dubbed ARA the "Area Reelection Administration," accusing it of pork barrelism, political favoritism, and maladministration. Far from creating additional employment, the agency stands accused by the critics of "pirating" industrial plants, of "creating an incredible variety of local boondoggles," and of using taxpayers' moneys for "happiness projects like golf courses, bowling alleys, ski resorts, fishing camps, marine playgrounds, resort hotels and motels."[30]

In 1963, when the administration requested Congress to double the appropriations for the Area Redevelopment Administration and extend its life, the Senate went along with the proposals, but the House rejected them by five votes. Congressman Wright Patman of Texas, one of the powerful Area Redevelopment Administration supporters in the House, thinks that much has been accomplished:

> The area development program has brought hope to hundreds of communities and rural areas which have suffered for years from heavy unemployment. Already some 800 areas, accounting for 78 per cent of all eligible places, have submitted overall economic development plans analyzing the problems which face them and blueprinting the steps to be taken to restore prosperity and full employment. The Agency has approved 700 individual projects which will create 34,000 jobs and help 18,000 worker-trainees. The benefits of this program will go far beyond those directly involved by helping to stimulate the

[29] Statement of Edward P. Neilan, President, U. S. Chamber of Commerce, in Senate Committee on Banking and Currency, *Area Redevelopment Act Amendments 1963*, Hearings before a subcommittee, April 30–May 6, 1963, 88th Cong., 1st Sess. (Washington, 1963), p. 270.

[30] Robert Dietsch, "Taxpayers Build Ski Lifts: U. S. Area Redevelopment Helps Finance the Good Life," *Washington Daily News*, September 30, 1963.

growth of the entire area and, in fact, helping to raise production and incomes nationally.[31]

Among senators who have strongly endorsed the Area Redevelopment Administration and believe its activities to have been largely successful, are Douglas of Illinois, Randolph of West Virginia, Fulbright of Arkansas, Muskie of Maine, McIntyre of New Hampshire, Hartke of Indiana, and Sparkman of Alabama.

Whenever the Area Redevelopment Administration is subject to debate whether in or out of Congress, political lines are quickly drawn. Those who are willing to assign to the federal government a responsibility to come to the direct assistance of economically-depressed areas tend to favor the type of program which the ARA represents. Others who insist that balanced budgets, reduced taxes, and free competitive market operations can be relied on to produce the necessary self-regenerative economic momentum within the needy area have strongly rejected any such interventionist roles for the federal government in the past and will probably continue to do so in the future.

CASE PROBLEMS FOR CLASS DISCUSSION

1. Your state legislature is considering a bill establishing procedures for accrediting and certifying bookkeepers similar in nature to those presently applicable to C.P.A.'s. You are an attorney retained by the state association of bookkeepers to represent them before the legislature. In your presentation to the committee on civil administration, which arguments would you stress, and what would be the nature of your evidence submitted to the group?
2. The liquor control committee of your legislature has before it a proposal to permit municipalities to acquire liquor stores and to conduct retail operations in packaged liquors. You have been retained as counsel by the liquor interests in the state to defeat this bill. Your employers ask you to submit a plan detailing your strategy, budget, and estimate of success.
3. The business development department of your state has decided to establish a Washington office representing the state and assisting its congressional delegation to obtain a larger share of defense contracts. You have been appointed to this new position and are asked to prepare a brief brochure providing information on the state's natural resources, industrial establishments, labor supply, educational facilities, and tax structure. The department is willing to cooperate fully; time is short; the data must be as current as possible. How would you proceed?

SELECTED BIBLIOGRAPHY

Advisory Commission on Intergovernmental Relations, *Industrial Development Bond Financing* (Washington, 1963).

MONROE BERKOWITZ, *Workmen's Compensation: The New Jersey Experience* (New Brunswick, 1960).

W. PAUL BRANN, "Mississippi Emphasizes Research for State Development," *State Government*, Spring, 1960, pp. 122–127.

PHILLIP H. BURCH, JR., *Industrial Safety Legislation in New Jersey* (New Brunswick, 1960).

[31] Remarks offered March 6, 1963, *Congressional Record*, March 19, 1963, p. A1579; also see U. S. Department of Commerce, *Annual Report on the Area Redevelopment Administration 1962* (Washington, 1963).

"Compensation for a Partial Taking of Property: Balancing Factors in Eminent Domain," *Yale Law Journal,* December, 1962, pp. 392–405.

EDWARD F. COOKE, "Research: An Instrument of Political Power," *Political Science Quarterly,* March, 1961, pp. 69–87.

MARVIN A. FAIR, "Port Authorities in the United States," *Law and Contemporary Problems,* Autumn, 1961, pp. 703–714.

ROBERT E. FIRTH, *Public Power in Neraska: A Report on State Ownership* (Lincoln, 1962).

ROBERT J. FRYE, *Government and Labor: The Alabama Program* (University, Ala., 1960).

JAY KRAMER, "Law and Policy in State Labor Relations Acts: The New York Board as Innovator," *The Annals of the American Academy of Political and Social Science,* January, 1961, pp. 59–75.

JAMES W. KUHN, "Right-to-Work Laws— Symbols or Substance?" *Industrial and Labor Relations Review,* July, 1961, pp. 587–594.

JOSEPH LAZAR, "Tripartitism in Minnesota," *Industrial Relations,* February, 1963, pp. 119–126.

STANLEY MOSK, "Subdivision Promotions in the West," *State Government,* Summer, 1963, pp. 142–147.

DWIGHT R. PALMER, "State Government and Transportation," *State Government,* Summer, 1962, pp. 144–148.

NATHANIEL S. PRESTON, "Public Authorities Today," *State Government,* Summer, 1961, pp. 205–211.

"The 'Public Purpose' of Municipal Financing for Industrial Development," *Yale Law Journal,* April, 1961, pp. 789–905.

BARRIE RICHARDSON, "State Regulation of Retail Revolving Credit," *State Government,* Summer, 1963, pp. 172–177.

WILLIAM J. RONAN, "State Help for Railroads," *State Government,* Autumn, 1961, pp. 233–236.

LEO SANDON JR., "When Kansas Said Yes to 'Right to Work,'" *Midwest Quarterly,* Spring, 1963, pp. 269–281.

BENJAMIN T. SHUMAN and EDWARD S. JAFFRY, "Government and the Installment Land Sales Contract," *State Government,* Summer, 1963, pp. 148–151.

ROBERT J. SICKELS, *The Public Utility Franchise in Maryland: Scope and Limitations* (College Park, Md., 1963).

JAMES H. SWANTON, "The Municipal Quest for Industry," *Public Management,* April, 1962, pp. 79–83.

NED L. WALL, "Developments in Municipal Housing Codes," *Public Management,* May, 1960, pp. 107–109.

What is a good tax structure—a healthy state tax climate, and what should be the standards of judgment?

How desirable is interstate tax uniformity?

EXPENDITURES AND REVENUES IN STATE AND LOCAL GOVERNMENT

GENERAL CONSIDERATIONS

Among the most striking developments in state public finance since World War II has been the fact that state and local government expenditures not only grew enormously but that they increased more steeply than did federal expenditures (see Figure 1).

As shown in Table 1 spending by state and local governments since 1946 rose by about 400 per cent while that of the federal government did not quite double. Reflected in these rapidly growing expenditures are, of course, the heavy outlays which state and local governments were called on to make in the post-war years on behalf of highway construction, education, and public welfare. During this period, for example, school enrollments rose by over 12 million students; the number of persons sixty-five and over climbed from nearly 10 million to 16.6 million, and over 40 million people were added to this country's total population.

Educational needs alone will demand sustained fiscal attention. Based on Census Bureau findings and estimates between 1960 and 1965, the number of grade school children will continue to increase by about 600,000 each year and high school enrollment by 1965 will be nearly one-fourth above that of 1960.

TABLE 1. FEDERAL, STATE, AND LOCAL EXPENDITURES
FOR SELECTED YEARS *

Year	Federal	State	Local
1946	66,534	6,162	7,011
1954	77,692	15,803	17,836
1958	86,054	23,338	25,539
1962	112,217	29,200	33,000

* In millions.

SOURCE: Based on figures of the Bureau of the Census, Department of Commerce in Tax Foundation, Inc., *Facts and Figures on Government Finance, 1962–1963*, 12th ed. (Englewood Cliffs, 1963), p. 20; these data do not include spending from government trust funds for social security, highways, etc.

FIGURE 1

GENERAL GOVERNMENTAL EXPENDITURES

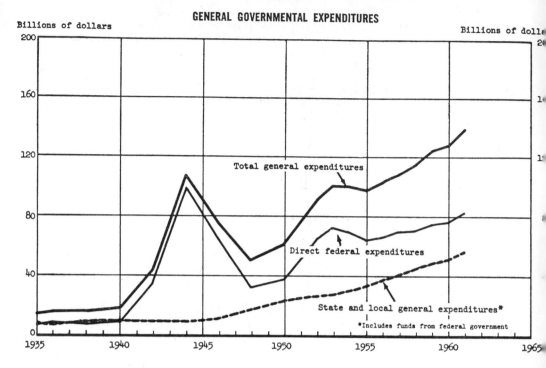

* Includes funds from federal government.
SOURCE: Department of Health, Education, and Welfare, *Health, Education, and Welfare Trends* (Washington, 1963), p. 103.

To interpret the rising costs of state and local government merely as a response to population increases or shifts would be quite inaccurate. Other factors must also be considered. There can be little doubt, for instance, that the public demanded and expected not only more but better services from its governments. What was wanted were not only schools and teachers but better school buildings and better-trained teachers, not just highways but high-speed freeways, not only remedial welfare but preventive and rehabilitative welfare as well. Broader programs and greater professionalization of public services represented policy decisions which were determined by electorates and legislatures as a matter of democratic choice. By paying higher taxes, excises, or fees, the public proved its willingness to assume the necessary fiscal burdens which these policies entailed.

Whether in the light of these developments government spending has already reached dangerous levels constitutes a highly controversial question. Involved in it are issues of social justice, tax policy, economics, and partisan politics each of which is often treated in a single text.

What can and should be pointed out here, however, are two sets of qualifications which, if ignored, tend to obscure the picture. First, any comparisons of present relatively high levels of government spending with those of earlier years need to acknowledge the significant changes which have taken place in the value of the dollar. To illustrate: whereas governmental purchases in current dollars increased by about 64.8 per cent between 1956 and 1962, such increases if measured in constant dollars and adjusted to the fluctuations in prices come to only about half that figure.[1] Second, if governmental expenditures are to be judged by their relationship to the Gross National Product (G.N.P.), as some authorities insist they should, then the rate of spending by state and local governments has been remarkably stable. In 1929 these levels of government spent 7.3 per cent or $7.6 billion of a total G.N.P. of $104 billion. Thirty-two years later in 1961, expenditures by state and local governments amounted to 10.4 per cent or $54 billion of a G.N.P. of $519 billion. This represents an increase of only 3.1 per cent during the course of an entire generation.[2]

STATE AND LOCAL GOVERNMENTAL EXPENDITURES BY FUNCTIONS

Spending by all state and local governments in 1962 ran up a total of $70 billion. This was more than two and one-half times the amount spent in 1950. The five major functional items included in the 1962 total were expenditures for education ($21.9 billion), highways ($10.3 billion), public welfare ($5.1 billion), health and hospitals ($4.3 billion), and police and fire ($3.2 billion).[3] Table 2 compares the spending for these functions by high- and low-income states.

What is shown here are notable variations of expenditures for different functions both between and within these two groups of states. As may be expected, most of the high-income states tend to spend more on all of their major functions. But there is no uniformity. With reference to nationwide averages, three of the high-income states spend less on education, six less on public welfare, and five less on highways. By contrast and despite obvious needs, all of the lowest income states fall below the national averages in their expenditures for education. All but one spend less than the national average on health and hospitals. Outlays for highways, on the other hand, appeared to be least affected by wealth differentials between the states. Federal matching and geographic considerations partially explain this phenomenon.

Public concepts change over the years as to what type of service or roles state and local governments should perform. For example, at the beginning of this century, neither state nor local governments were expected to invest their funds in housing or community redevelopment. Similarly unknown were such

---

[1] *Book of the States, 1964–1965*, p. 225.

[2] Tax Foundation, Inc., *Facts and Figures on Government Finance, 1962–1963*, 12th ed., (Englewood Cliffs, 1963), p. 27.

[3] *Book of the States, 1964–1965*, p. 215; for further statistical compilations, see also Bureau of the Census, U. S. Department of Commerce, *Compendium of State Government Finances in 1962.* (Washington, 1963); and Bureau of the Census, U. S. Department of Commerce, *Compendium of City Government Expenses in 1962* (Washington, 1963).

TABLE 2. HIGH AND LOW INCOME STATES—STATE AND LOCAL
EXPENDITURES BY FUNCTION, 1962

Ten highest-income states *

State	Education	Highways	Public welfare	Health & hospitals
Alaska	$174.14	$133.52	$20.39	$40.69
California	166.78	56.03	38.34	29.03
Connecticut	130.68	63.61	25.98	21.12
Delaware	136.26	59.16	18.84	20.31
Illinois	112.83	49.64	32.52	20.36
Maryland	119.13	51.76	15.07	27.03
Massachusetts	103.84	47.86	40.58	32.89
Nevada	150.44	95.40	19.73	37.89
New Jersey	111.89	42.08	15.73	21.05
New York	123.30	51.86	30.97	38.89

Ten lowest-income states *

State	Education	Highways	Public welfare	Health & hospitals
Alabama	$ 89.29	$ 49.34	$30.47	$16.22
Arkansas	80.19	51.49	27.21	17.27
Georgia	87.71	51.07	24.21	27.52
Kentucky	95.77	68.06	25.63	14.94
Louisiana	107.59	60.83	52.81	18.96
Mississippi	87.76	54.35	26.71	21.24
North Carolina	98.85	39.79	18.16	16.55
South Carolina	83.23	38.28	13.79	18.56
Tennessee	78.44	58.02	18.34	19.36
West Virginia	96.36	54.13	34.81	14.57
United States (average)	$117.97	$ 55.65	$27.43	$23.37

*Per capita expenditures.

SOURCE: *Book of the States, 1964–1965*, p. 219.

social insurance programs as workmen's compensation, unemployment compensation or sickness insurance. Yet in 1962 state and local government expenditures directed into such insurance trust funds came to almost $5 billion, an amount in excess of what was spent during that year for such traditional purposes as welfare, health, police, or fire protection. Housing and community redevelopment projects absorbed more than an additional $1 billion.[4]

Views also changed as to which level of government would be best qualified to support new or expanding social services. For instance, state financial assistance to local governments (for schools and public welfare) did not become significant until after World War I. Since then state aids constantly increased to the point where in 1961 one out of four dollars of revenue received by local government came from the states.

Federal aids to state and local governments first hit the $1 billion mark during the depression in 1934; a generation later federal grants-in-aid totalled

[4] *Book of the States, 1964–1965*, p. 215.

over $7 billion. This figure included funds for such major categories as veterans' services and benefits; health, welfare, and labor; education and general research; agriculture and agricultural resources; other natural resources; highways and transportation; housing and urban renewal. Presently, nearly 11 per cent of all current state and local revenue comes from the federal government in the form of intergovernmental aids. Just how much the relative positions of federal, state, and local governments have changed with respect to spending since the turn of the century emerges clearly from Table 3.

TABLE 3. FEDERAL, STATE, AND LOCAL
EXPENDITURES SELECTED FISCAL
YEARS, 1902–1962 *

Year	Federal	State	Local
1902	34.5	10.8	54.8
1922	40.5	13.6	46.0
1940	49.3	22.3	28.5
1952	71.7	13.4	15.0
1962	64.3	16.7	18.9

* Figures will not add up to 100 per cent due to rounding off.

SOURCE: Based on figures of the Bureau of the Census, Department of Commerce in Tax Foundation, Inc., *Facts and Figures on Government Finance, 1962–1963*, 12th ed. (Englewood Cliffs, 1963), p. 21.

THE PROBLEM OF INTERSTATE TAX COMPARISONS AND TAX EFFORT

Rare are the elections in state and local government where campaign oratory and exhortations do not decry a grossly unfavorable tax climate of the home state. Charts and statistics are produced which allege that the beneficial tax treatment given business and citizens in other states makes it much more attractive for people to live and work there, and that the home state's lack of economic growth can be directly attributed to a competitively disadvantageous tax structure. Whether a particular business or industry will prefer to locate in state A or in state B is actually dependent on many factors. Tax policies and burdens represent only one of many considerations. Of equal or sometimes even of greater significance than taxes may be questions which relate to the proximity of natural resources, to the availability of skilled labor, to the adequacy of truck and rail transportation, to the nearness of major markets, to the level of prevailing wage rates, or to the overall attractiveness of the particular community—its educational facilities, cultural opportunities, housing, and climate. In connection with these variables one of the best state tax studies concluded that:

[W]e are not able to attach a specific weight to state and local taxes as a locational factor. . . . Among . . . [the many] factors taxation has its place, and "other things being equal," a lower tax load or one more conducive to economic growth undoubtedly adds to the attractiveness of a state as a place within which to expand or locate. However, other non-tax factors are never quite equal.[5]

Nor, it may be added, are two state tax systems ever exactly alike. While it is accurate to assert that property, sales, and income taxes constitute the three largest sources of state and local tax collections (see Figure 2), the tax systems of the states differ greatly in a number of ways. Leaving further details to a subsequent section, the following general propositions will support the argument here.

First, states do not employ the same combination of taxes. Corporation income taxes have been adopted in 38 states, individual income taxes in 33 states, and sales taxes in 38 states. In 23 states both personal income and sales taxes were used, while Nebraska has adopted neither a personal income nor a sales tax (see Figure 2).

Second, where the personal income tax is in effect, wide variations exist as to the possibility of deducting federal income taxes, as to rates of progression, and as to personal exemptions for dependents. Differences in policies governing deductibility profoundly affect the divergence between the statutory rate and the effective rate of taxation.

Third, sales taxes may be general (both wholesale and retail) or selective (imposed on selected tangible personal property). Some sales taxes exempt food generally, others only farm produce sold directly to the consumer.

Fourth, although nearly 90 per cent of local governmental revenues for the country as a whole come from property taxes, there are important differences here which complicate interstate comparisons. States, and even counties, differ considerably with regard to their assessment policies, homestead deductions, equalization procedures, and categories of constitutionally or legislatively exempted properties.

These are only a few of the reasons which make it difficult to compare the tax systems of two or more states without going into considerable technical detail and without subjecting statistical comparisons to the most careful professional scrutiny before meaningful conclusions can be drawn. Caution also must be exercised with reference to the interpretation of what may be called interstate differences in tax effort. A staff report from the Advisory Commission on Intergovernmental Relations makes this point abundantly clear:

A high tax effort . . . does not necessarily mean that taxes are diverting too large a share of resources to State and local governmental programs. Nor does a low tax effort . . . necessarily point to the need for tax increases. The underlying differences in the States' economic structure preclude such automatic in-

[5] *Report of the Governor's Minnesota Tax Study Committee* (Minneapolis, 1956), p. 135.

FIGURE 2

1962

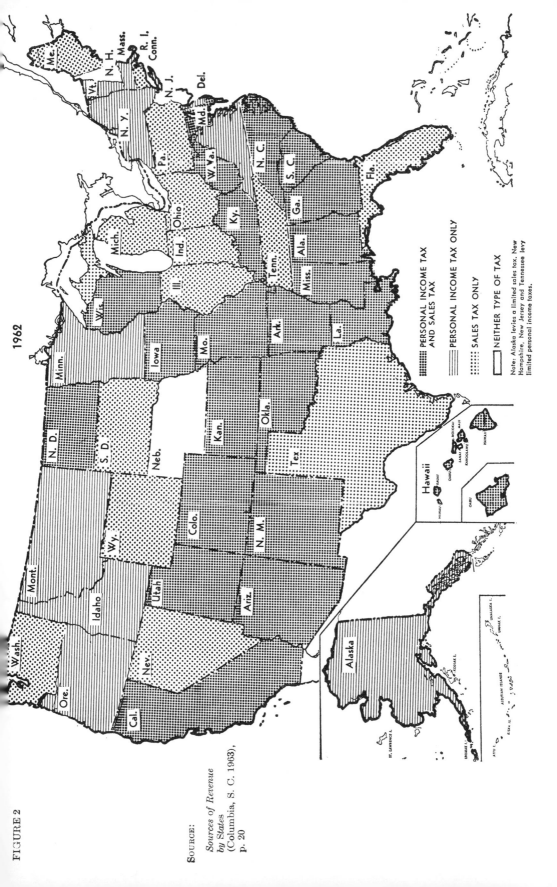

PERSONAL INCOME TAX
AND SALES TAX

PERSONAL INCOME TAX ONLY

SALES TAX ONLY

NEITHER TYPE OF TAX

Note: Alaska levies a limited sales tax. New
Hampshire, New Jersey and Tennessee levy
limited personal income taxes.

SOURCE:

*Sources of Revenue
by States*
(Columbia, S. C. 1963),
p. 20

terpretation of tax effort. . . . States at varying stages of economic development and experiencing different growth rates may elect to allocate their resources differently between public and private uses. Quite apart from differences in attitudes toward public versus private purposes, one State may allocate a small share of its resources to public purposes in an effort to encourage industrial development. . . . States, moreover, may choose different routes to identical objectives. While one may hope to stimulate private industrial development by keeping taxes low, others may seek to do so by providing a high level of public facilities and services, reflecting a view that the newer electronic and chemical industries place a high value on the availability of good quality school, hospital, library, higher educational, recreation, water, and sanitary facilities. Investments in these facilities would be reflected in tax effort indexes.[6]

SOME CRITERIA FOR JUDGING STATE AND LOCAL
SYSTEMS OF TAXATION AND TAXES

From what has been said already, it must be quite obvious that there exists no simple or single standard of judgment against which the appropriateness or desirability of a tax system can be authoritatively measured. State and local governments not only differ in their economic resources and needs, in their legal setting and political composition, but also in the dominant conceptions of what constitutes a good tax climate. After all, there are not many issues in government which involve more deeply one's political philosophy than those which bear on the power that should be granted to the public to take, dispose, and invest private wealth or income.

Many of the considerations which are applicable to the tax system as a whole have relevance also to individual taxes. First of all, is there such a thing as a fair tax? While there may be ready agreement on the proposition that the wealthier should pay higher taxes than the less wealthy, agreement tends to dwindle rapidly when the question is reduced to specific rates or to the precise share of the total tax burden that different income groups should be prepared to bear. What is a fair tax base? How much of the tax should come out of income, how much out of consumer spending, and how much from property ownership? Should benefits derived from public service figure prominently in the selection of the tax base or in the determination of rates for taxes so selected? How should government proceed to apportion to the different groups of taxpayers such tangible or intangible values as good libraries, well-equipped museums, ample recreational facilities, attractive parks, and clean rivers and air? Is it fair to burden an elderly couple living on a small pension on their modest homestead with ever-increasing property tax rates because the educational services of the community must keep up with the population

---

[6] Advisory Commission on Intergovernmental Relations, *Measures of State and Local Capacity and Tax Effort* (Washington, 1962), p. 73; on the peculiar fiscal problems of the South, see James W. Martin and Kenneth E. Quindry, *Southern States: New Revenue Potentials* (Atlanta, 1960).

explosion? At what point does a particular tax become so burdensome as to invite large-scale evasion or avoidance and when do rates reach levels so excessively high that they in fact do depress the economy by punishing private initiative or a potential investor's willingness to assume economic risks?

There are, of course, no simple answers to any of these questions. Yet among the many guidelines or criteria which scholars and writers in the field of public finance offer for the evaluation of taxes and tax systems, the following may serve as a point of departure:

A. A tax should provide revenue *sufficient* for the purpose for which it was adopted.
B. A tax should be fairly *stable* in order to assure the continuance of basic governmental operations not only during normal times but also during periods of economic recessions.
C. Taxes should be *equitable*. This means at least that the tax would treat equally individuals or corporations found in similar circumstances or situations.
D. "Ability to pay" should be an important consideration in any tax system; therefore, taxes should as far as possible be *progressive* rather than regressive.
E. Taxpayers should be reasonably *certain* as to their future tax liability.
F. To enhance compliance, *convenience* in collection represents a desirable tax quality.
G. In some taxes there should be a positive relationship between tax payment and *benefit derived* from the public service supported by the tax.

No single tax can possibly live up fully to any or all of these criteria for any or all of the groups which it affects. *Sufficiency, stability, equitability, progressivity, certainty, convenience,* and *benefit derived* constitute standards which vary considerably from tax to tax and which are also weighed differently by voters from state to state.

In the subsequent discussion of the more widely-employed taxes, an attempt will be made to project the character and operation of each tax against one or more of these suggested standards of evaluation.

STATE AND LOCAL TAXES

PROPERTY TAXES

While only 3 per cent of state tax collections come from this source— cities, counties, townships—nearly all local units of government continue to rely on this tax as their principal form of revenue (see Figure 3). Of the $21 billion of taxes collected by local governments in 1962, $18 billion came from property tax collections.

The general property tax comprises two major types of levies: (a) a tax

FIGURE 3

PERCENT OF ALL TAX REVENUE OF STATE AND LOCAL GOVERNMENTS
PROVIDED BY PROPERTY TAXES, BY STATES: 1961

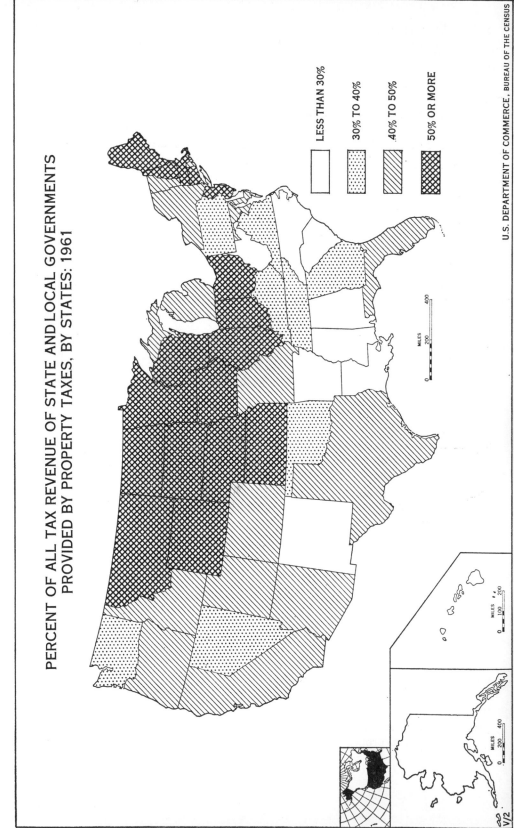

LESS THAN 30%

30% TO 40%

40% TO 50%

50% OR MORE

U.S. DEPARTMENT OF COMMERCE, BUREAU OF THE CENSUS

on real estate land and buildings and (b) a tax on personal property—tangibles (business inventories, automobiles, furniture, jewelry, etc.) and intangibles (stocks, bonds, notes, and mortgages). Intangibles as a basis for property taxation have become less important, as other forms of taxes, especially income taxes, have become more prominent.

The levels at which parcels of property or personal property are to be taxed are usually set by the local units of government within whose jurisdiction such property is situated. What the actual rate will be, that is how many units per dollar of assessed valuation, depends generally on two factors: the amount of money that the unit of government needs to raise and the total assessed value of property in its area. Once the rate is determined each property owner's personal share of the total tax bill can then be computed by applying the unit rate to the assessed value of his property.

Many states for reasons of social or economic policy will not assess all types of property at uniform rates based on market value. In some states where constitutions prohibit classifications as violative of their uniformity clauses, different types of property will receive different treatment either as a result of varying tax rates or of customary assessment practices. In other states, notably Minnesota, Montana, Ohio, and Virginia, statutory classification schedules spell out ratios at which different types of property are to be assessed. In Minnesota, for example, the assessor's full and true value for different realty such as residential, multiple dwelling, commercial, industrial, public utility, lake shore, and farm averaged in 1955 about 36 per cent of the market value for such properties.[7]

In nearly all states aggrieved taxpayers who wish to challenge the fairness or accuracy of an assessor's decision are given an opportunity to have their original assessment reviewed upon notice and hearing before boards of review or equalization at either local or state levels. To guard against the tendency of local districts or governmental units to underevaluate property and thus create unequal tax burdens between different communities within the state, a number of states including Wisconsin and Illinois have given to their state departments of taxation or finance or to their agents, the power to equalize or revise assessments centrally. Central assessment may also be made applicable by law to certain types of property, such as railroads, mines, and public utilities, the kinds of properties which are difficult to assess on a local basis where most assessors lack the necessary professional training skills and staffs.

There are some categories of property that are exempt from taxation in nearly all of the states. These are properties used for non-profit, charitable, educational, religious, and public purposes. Authority to exempt from taxation a part of the value of a homestead (dwelling and land occupied by the owner) may also be found in the constitutions of Alabama, Arkansas, Florida,

[7] *Report of the Governor's Minnesota Tax Study Committee*, p. 168.

Georgia, Louisiana, North Carolina, Oklahoma, Texas, and Utah as well as in the statutes of a number of other states including Minnesota, Mississippi, and Wyoming.

Among exemptions presently arousing the greatest controversy are those given by state and local government in an effort to attract new business and industry or to induce existing industries to expand. Where constitutions fail to prohibit the lending of public credit or the extending of tax benefits in the most explicit of terms, courts have generally permitted legislatures and city councils wide discretion as to whether such aid to private economic enterprise as a method of relieving unemployment could, in fact, be justified as promoting a public as distinguished from a private purpose.

What's Right and What's Wrong with the Property Tax?

Property taxes constitute the backbone of the revenue system in American local government. While the public may not like any taxes, property taxes are accepted as traditional and as necessary incidents to ownership of forms of wealth that must contribute their share to the cost of operating the government and its services. Assuming reasonably fair administration, the tax possesses the quality of subjecting property of similar situation and character to rates which are relatively uniform, certain, and equitable. If it is desirable to relate taxes to benefits received, what could be wrong with having those who own property help pay for the services that government renders property and its owners in the form of police and fire protection, sewage disposal, and street maintenance? Those with more property, the presumably more affluent, would also be expected to possess a greater ability to pay than would those with less property. Thus this tax combines to some extent at least, the principle of proportionality with that of benefits received.

Lastly, the property tax generally is a locally-collected tax, with locally-set rates, with locally-determined assessments for purposes and projects locally-resolved. All of these represent qualities which defenders of localism in an age of rapid centralization in American government value as highly important.

Property taxes have come under severe attack for the theories upon which they rest as well as for the manner in which they are administered. They are considered to be a regressive type of tax correlating poorly with tax-paying ability and with taxable wealth. Since the poor nearly always spend a larger share of their income on housing than do the rich, the property tax is regarded as burdening those with lesser means more heavily than those in more fortunate circumstances. This is true whether they are home owners who cannot shift the incidence of the real estate tax or whether they are apartment dwellers in which case the landlord will tend to pass the tax on to them in the form of higher rents. Moreover, inasmuch as the lower- when compared with the higher-income group usually devotes a larger share of its disposable income on consumption, those with more modest incomes once again will be adversely affected as business establishments proceed to shift their real and personal property taxes on to the consumer.

In an earlier, agricultural America, property may have been a fairly reliable measure of wealth but this is no longer so. Today, it is income and intangible forms of wealth that represent a more accurate measure of tax-paying ability. Therefore, if the goal of tax equity is to be served, income particularly rather than property should increasingly become the basis of a modern democratically-oriented tax policy.

It is the administrative phase of the property tax even more than its philosophy which is subject to sharpest criticism. With the exception of urban areas most tax assessors are part-time officials with little if any professional training. Rarely do they find themselves adequately equipped to assess property with the necessary scientific skill, accuracy, or frequency. At best all assessing is but a crude process of approximating a standard of market value for a particular piece of property; in the case of industrial and business properties there may be no readily available standard to which reference could be made. Being elected officials, assessors are understandably sensitive to the complaints of the politically and economically influential and to incurring widespread public disfavor for evaluating property at realistic but painful levels. Consequently, most of the property in the United States is chronically, and maybe unevenly, assessed below its full and true value.

Assessment of personal property involves administrative problems of still greater complexity. Least satisfactory is the tax on intangibles. While it is difficult to conceal an automobile or livestock, too many taxpayers fail to report such intangible property as stocks and bonds; when it is reported, assessors find it difficult to classify and evaluate it properly. (Realities such as these have caused more and more states to subject this type of wealth to the income rather than to the property tax.)

Tangible personal property on the other hand, especially business inventories and livestock, is still very much on the property tax rolls. The problem here centers on the fact that such property is usually assessed on one particular day of the year, usually May 1. In practice, this often tends to work hardships on those taxpayers who, on that day, find themselves with an unusually large inventory due to the peculiarities of their business, seasonal factors, or slow inventory turnover.

In recent years a growing number of states and cities have attempted to reform their systems of property tax administration along some of the following lines: assessors may be required to pass civil service examinations, to attend state-conducted training courses or to give evidence of professional qualifications; appraisal of industrial property may be placed in the hands of a central assessment agency rather than left to local assessors; the powers of tax equalization boards have been strengthened in order to reduce the extent of competitive underassessment and thus bring about a more equitable balance of tax burdens between counties. A well-known authority in the field of public finance concludes his discussion of the property tax with this note:

[A]lthough constantly under attack and although cracking badly in places, the general property tax is probably destined to continue for many years as a major source of support for important public services.[8]

Meanwhile, the search goes on for substitute or supplementary taxes which might aid in spreading the growing tax burdens more equitably and more progressively.

SALES TAXES

Next to the property tax, the sales tax now represents the single largest source of revenue in state and local taxation (see Figure 4). If tax sources of state government are viewed separately from those of local government, general sales, use, or gross receipts taxes in 1962 ranked actually first among the ten broad tax categories. In one form or another thirty-eight states have adopted these taxes. While lacking a uniform pattern, there are among these states at least four major types of sales taxes that can be readily discerned:

"There's no such thing as standard cheating!"

SOURCE: *The Wall Street Journal*, April 3, 1964.

---

[8] Harold M. Groves, *Financing Government* (New York, 1964), pp. 113–114; see also Seymour Sacks and William F. Hellmuth, Jr., *Financing Government in a Metropolitan Area: The Cleveland Experience* (New York, 1961); W. D. Knight, *Property Taxation and the Wisconsin Tax System* (Madison, 1960); and G. Ross Stephens and Henry J. Schmandt, "Revenue Patterns of Local Governments," *National Tax Journal,* December, 1962, pp. 432–437.

A. *Retail Sales Taxes* "imposed on sales of tangible personal property at retail or for consumption; in most states also on admissions, restaurant meals, public utility sales, and hotel rooms."

B. *General Sales Taxes* "applies to wholesaling, extractive industries, and/or manufacturing, in addition to sales at retail."

C. *Gross Receipts Taxes* "includes sales of personal and professional services in addition to transactions and receipts under [A.] and [B.]."

D. *Selective Sales Taxes* "[refers to] retail sales and use taxes imposed upon selected tangible personal property." [9]

Significant differences prevail not only between types of sales taxes but also to the exemption policies that the various states have adopted. For example, food purchases are exempted from sales tax in such states as California, Connecticut, Maine, Maryland, Ohio, Pennsylvania, Rhode Island, Texas, and Wisconsin but taxed in Illinois, Indiana, and North Carolina. Prescription medicines are exempted in California, Florida, Illinois, Maryland, North Carolina, Pennsylvania, Rhode Island, Texas, and Wisconsin. While twenty-five states preclude the taxing of sales to schools, churches, hospitals, and other similar institutions, thirteen states do not; and while thirty-

FIGURE 4

PERCENTAGE DISTRIBUTION OF GENERAL STATE AND LOCAL GOVERNMENT REVENUES BY SOURCE

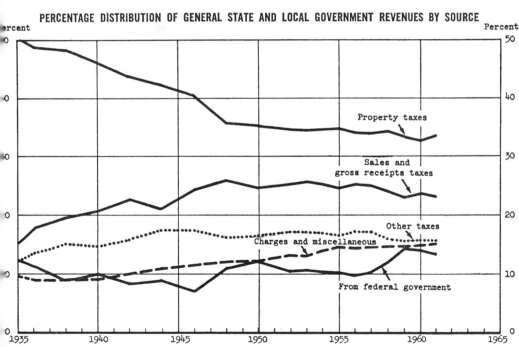

SOURCE: Department of Health, Education, and Welfare, *Health, Education and Welfare Trends* (Washington, 1963), p. 102.

[9] *Facts and Figures on Government Finance*, p. 195.

four states exempt sales to state and local governments, this is not the case in Arkansas, California, Louisiana, and Washington.

States with the fewest exemptions and broadest sales tax coverage include Arizona, Hawaii, Indiana, Mississippi, New Mexico, Washington, and West Virginia.[10]

Other states in which sales and use tax collections rank high when related to a per capita population basis are California, Illinois, Michigan, and Nevada.

California also permits its local govermental units, cities, and counties to impose an additional one per cent sales tax which is to be returned to them in addition to the three per cent state tax bringing the total levy collected by the state to four per cent. Alaska and Virginia on the other hand have left the entire field of retail sales taxation to their local governments. In fact, sales taxes have proved so popular on the local level that they are now employed by approximately 1,800 communities in twelve states with rates generally of either ½ per cent or one per cent. The leading city sales tax states are Illinois (1,171 cities), California (361 cities), and Mississippi (138 cities). County-wide sales taxes are imposed in Alabama (21 counties), California (all 58 counties), Colorado (4 counties), Illinois (66 counties), Louisiana (4 counties), and New York (7 counties).[11]

Sales taxes first came into prominence during the Depression years of the 1930's as a response to widespread property tax delinquencies. Another wave of adoptions followed World War II when state and local governments required heavy revenues in order to pay for their rapidly-expanding services. Since 1946 the volume of sales taxes collected has multiplied more than five times, rates have increased from two per cent and three per cent to four per cent and five per cent, twelve additional states have accepted the sales tax, and a number of jurisdictions which had previously adopted this tax have reduced their exemptions in order to further increase revenues.

Why sales taxes have proved so popular with legislatures and city councils is easy to understand. (1) The tax yield can be quite large. From this source alone, for example, California collects annually over three quarters of a billion dollars; the take in Illinois, Michigan, and Pennsylvania comes to nearly half a billion dollars. (2) Sales taxes provide a relatively stable source of revenue since people must buy their necessities of life regardless of business cycle fluctuations. (3) It is a convenient tax. Taxpayers are able to discharge their tax liability in small amounts on a current, installment basis. (4) In an affluent society such as ours, it is only fair, proponents of this tax insist, that the middle and lower-income groups, which benefit proportionately more from such governmental services as education, health, and welfare, should also make a proportionately heavier contribution for the financial

---

[10] Alfred G. Buehler, *Tax Study: State of Connecticut* (Hartford, 1963), p. 101 and the University of Wisconsin Tax Impact Study Committee, *Wisconsin's State and Local Tax Burden: Impact, Incidence and Tax Revision Alternatives* (Madison, 1959), p. 83.
[11] *Facts and Figures on Government Finance*, p. 244.

support of such services than should those in the higher-income brackets. From Minnesota, for instance, where there is no sales tax, comes a study which estimates that taxpayers in the $2,000 to $3,000 group who paid $178 in state and local taxes received $422 in benefits from state and local government expenditures while those in the $10,000 and over group received $686 worth of benefits for a combined state and local tax bill of $1,622. This means that the top groups had to pay nearly ten times as much in taxes for a little more than 50 per cent of additional governmental benefits.[12] (In studies of this kind, obviously much depends on the definition of "benefits.")

(5) Since sales taxes are visible taxes they serve to remind the electorate, in most unmistakable terms, that there is a price tag on all governmental services, that they can't get something for nothing. Anything, many supporters of sales taxes contend, that helps to make the public more tax- and cost-conscious will thus tend to slow down the race towards the welfare state.

(6) Sales taxes are particularly useful for reaching this country's highly mobile population—tourists, commuters, transients—persons who derive certain benefits from the host state in the form of fire and police protection and similar public services. Were it not for these taxes, millions of people might otherwise escape from making any direct financial contribution whatever towards these operations of state and local government.

Critics of sales taxes advance at least two major arguments: (1) Sales taxes are essentially regressive, i.e., they place an inequitable tax burden on those who are least able to assume it. Clearly disadvantaged are families with large numbers of children, the unemployed, and those whose low earnings force them to spend a significant share of their disposable income on consumer goods. Per $1,000 of income, sales tax levies will typically "collect about twice as much . . . at the $1,000–$2,000 level as at the level of $10,000." [13] Attempts by sales tax states to exempt expenditures for food and medicines while, of course, reducing the regressivity of the tax necessarily reduces its overall yield. This would also be true if states were to decide to adopt a per capita income tax credit system which has been urged by some tax authorities. Under such a system a $15 per capita credit if combined with a 3 per cent sales tax, would be the equivalent of allowing each person an exemption of $500 of taxable sales.[14]

(2) Administrative and enforcement problems adversely affect the extent of sales tax compliance. A recent survey conducted by the Tax Foundation sheds some additional light on the nature of these problems:

> Left to themselves, some retailers will not report and pay, except, perhaps, after long delay. Unless there is effective follow-up when an account becomes delinquent, loss of revenue is to be expected. . . .

[12] O. H. Brownlee, *Estimated Distribution of Minnesota Taxes and Public Expenditure Benefits* (Minneapolis, 1960) in *Retail Sales and Individual Income Taxes in State Tax Structures* (New York, 1962), p. 34.

[13] Groves, p. 291.

[14] *Ibid.*, p. 292.

Over one-third of the states reporting put the seller's failure to keep adequate records high on the list of difficulties. Continuing supervision is required. . . .

Less than half of the states attempt field audit on what might reasonably be considered a large scale. California has devoted extensive effort to sales tax administration. It maintains nearly a third of a million accounts and almost 800 auditors. Pennsylvania had almost 500 auditors, Michigan 250, and Illinois over 200. . . .

Statutory exemptions further complicate the picture. Buyers and sellers are often inadequately informed as to which items are covered by the sales tax and which are not. Legal definitions of excluded articles tend to be arbitrary and confusing, and the legal status of interstate sales introduces additional elements of uncertainty. Factors such as these cannot help but lead to substantial tax evasion and avoidance.[15]

INCOME TAXES

Income taxes now form an integral part of the tax structure in over three-fifths of the states. Adopted mostly during the 1920's and 1930's when the property tax proved insufficient, personal and corporate income tax collections have grown immensely—to the point of doubling during the past twenty years. Of the two types of income taxes, those on individual income are by far the more productive. In 1963 individual income tax collections in thirty-five states totaled $3 billion which was about twice that collected by states from corporations.[16] Among all state tax sources, the $4.5 billion total for both forms of income taxes represents, next to sales taxes, the largest category.

Revenue demands made it necessary for twenty-four states to enact both sales and income taxes. Some states—including Connecticut, Florida, Illinois, Michigan, Ohio, Pennsylvania, and Texas—found their sales taxes adequate; others preferred the income tax to the sales tax. With the exception of Virginia, all of these states represent a northerly tier: Idaho, Massachusetts, Minnesota, Montana, Oregon, and Vermont.

Even among income tax states there are wide differences as to how significant a share of their tax revenues comes from this source. Ten high income states are Alaska (38.4%), Colorado (33.1%), Idaho (37.2%), Massachusetts (38.4%), Minnesota (39.1%), New York (55.3%), Oregon (52.6%), Vermont (30.7%), Virginia (33.9%), and Wisconsin (43.1%). Most of the states where the income tax provides less than 10 per cent of the total tax revenue are found in the South—Louisiana (8.7%), New Mexico (9.3%), Tennessee (8.5%), and West Virginia (9.8%). To this, New Hamp-

---

[15] *Retail Sales and Individual Income Taxes in State Structures,* p. 39.

[16] *Book of the States, 1964–1965,* p. 242. Most states that have adopted a personal income tax also levy corporate income taxes, but not all. New Hampshire and West Virginia, personal income tax states, do not have a corporate income levy and Connecticut, Pennsylvania, and Rhode Island enacted the latter tax but not the former; on tax incidence, see Emanuel Melichar, *State Individual Income Taxes: Impact of Alternative Provisions on Burdens, Progression, and Yields* (Storrs, Conn., 1963).

shire (3.6%) and South Dakota (.8%) furnish the exception.[17] Corporate net income taxes yielding $1.5 billion have been enacted in thirty-eight states. While most of them operate on the principle of a flat percentage rate, small graduations are incorporated into the laws of seven states (see Table 4). The tax is usually supported on the principle that corporate profits—stockholders' equities—should not be exempt from taxation and that non-resident stockholders should be compelled to pay for state services from which they derive business benefits. Critics of the corporate income tax point out that subjecting corporate profits, whether distributed or not, to this tax constitutes a form of burdensome double taxation which is economically unsound and morally indefensible and that heavy corporate tax rates invite a shifting of taxes to the consumer, in effect not unlike that of a sales tax.

Another type of corporation tax which has been attacked for the similar ease with which its tax incidence may be passed on to the consumer, is Michigan's *value-added* tax. Enacted in 1953 as the lesser of two evils (in place of a bitterly-fought corporation income tax), the value-added tax is defined as "one based on the dollar value of the contribution of the business, farm, or professional enterprise to the output of economic goods and services in the community, state or nation." [18] The tax base consists of gross receipts minus the cost of operating the business enterprise, excepting however, wages, salaries, bonuses, dividends, depletion, and depreciation allowances. Amendments to the law include provisions which permit minimum optional deductions of up to 60 per cent of gross receipts. Highly productive of revenue (Michigan collected $78 million from this single source in 1963), the tax has been lauded for its flexibility, allowing close correspondence with fluctuating values in business output.

A few of the main features of the income tax require further emphasis. State individual income taxes are ordinarily graduated (not as steeply as the federal income tax) ranging from one per cent or two per cent in the lowest brackets to 10 per cent and 11 per cent in the highest. Provisions are made for personal exemptions for married or single persons and for dependents. Here again, the states tend to be slightly more generous than the federal government. Unique among the states is the Alaskan plan under which that state imposes a flat 16 per cent of the federal tax payable upon net income derived from sources in Alaska. In 1961 West Virginia adopted a similar pattern but preferred a lower rate of six per cent. All in all, a dozen states have integrated various aspects of their income tax structures with that of the federal pattern. One serious problem of tying state income taxes to the federal tax is that any reduction in the latter causes an immediate effect upon the former. Alaska, for example, was recently forced to call a special session to address itself to

[17] New Jersey's income tax applies only to New York residents who derive income from New Jersey sources and vice-versa (footnote u, Table 142, *Facts and Figures on Government Finance*, pp. 190–191).

[18] *Report of the Governor's Minnesota Tax Study Committee*, p. 480; see also Richard E. Slitor, "The Value-Added Tax as an Alternative to Corporate Income Tax," *Tax Policy*, October-November, 1963, pp. 3 10.

TABLE 4. RANGE OF STATE

State or other jurisdiction	Tax rate (per cent)	Federal income tax deductible
Alabama		
Business corporations	5(a)	x(a)
Banks and financial corporations	6	x
Alaska		
Business corporations	18 per cent of federal tax	
Banks and financial corporations	16 per cent of federal tax (b)	
		—
Arizona		
Business corporations:		
$0 to $1,000	1	
Over $6,000	5	
Banks and financial corporations	5	
Arkansas		—
$0 to $3,000	1	
Over $25,000	5	
California		—
Business corporations	5.5(c)	
Banks and financial corporations	5.5–9.5(d)	
Colorado		—
Business corporations	5	
Banks and financial corporations	6	
Connecticut	5(e)	—
Delaware	5	—
Georgia	4	—
Hawaii		—
Business corporations:		
$0 to $25,000	5(f)	
Over $25,000	5.5	
Banks and financial corporations	10	
Idaho	10.5(g)	x
Indiana	2	—
Iowa	3	x
Kansas		x
Business corporations	3.5	
Banks and financial corporations	5	
Kentucky		x
$0 to $25,000	5	
Over $25,000	7	
Louisiana	4	x
Maryland	5	—
Massachusetts		
Business corporations	6.765(h)	
Banks and trust companies	Not to exceed 8	
Utility corporations	4.92(i)	

* Prepared by the Federation of Tax Administrators.
  (a) The 1963 legislative session eliminated the federal tax deduction, but submitted a constitutional amendment to the voters, which they approved, restoring the federal deduction and raising the rate from 3 to 5 per cent.
  (b) In addition, banks and other financial institutions are subjected to a license tax of 2 per cent of net income.
  (c) Minimum tax is $100.
  (d) Rate adjusted annually; maximum, 9.5 per cent, minimum, 5.5 per cent; minimum tax is $100.
  (e) Tax paid shall not be less than $25, or 2.5 mills per dollar of asset value.
  (f) Capital gains are taxed at 2.75 per cent.
  (g) An additional tax of $10 is imposed on each return.
  (h) Total rate is composed of the following: permanent tax, 2.5 per cent; temporary additional excise of 3 per cent; temporary surtax of 20 per cent of taxes assessed; additional surtax for old-age pensions, 3 per cent of taxes assessed.
  (i) Total rate is composed of a 4 per cent permanent tax plus a 23 per cent surtax.
  (j) The permanent rate is 7.5 per cent. A temporary 1.8 per cent tax is in effect for tax years beginning before January 1, 1965. The permanent and temporary rates are increased 10 per cent for tax years beginning before January 1, 1965. The minimum tax is $10.

CORPORATE INCOME TAX RATES (As of January 1, 1964) *

State or other jurisdiction	Tax rate (per cent)	Federal income tax deductible
Minnesota		x
Business corporations	10.23(j)	
Banks	12.54(k)	
Mississippi		—
$0 to $5,000	2	
Over $10,000	4(l)	
Missouri		x
Business corporations	2	
Banks and trust companies	7	
Montana	4.5	—
New Jersey	1.75	—
New Mexico	3	x
New York		—
Business corporations	5.5(m)	
Banks and financial corporations	4.5(n)	
North Carolina		—
Business corporations	6	
Banks	4.5(o)	
North Dakota		x
Business corporations:		—
$0 to $3,000	3	
Over $15,000	6	
Banks and financial corporations	4(p)	
Oklahoma	4	x
Oregon		—
Business corporations	6(o)	
Banks and financial corporations	8(o)	
Pennsylvania	6	—
Rhode Island	6(q)	—
South Carolina		—
Business corporations	5	
Banks	4.5	
Financial associations	8	
South Dakota		x
Banks and financial corporations	4.5(r)	
Tennessee	4	—
Utah		x
National banks	4	
Business corporations and state banks	4(s)	
Vermont	5	—
Virginia	5	—
Wisconsin		x(t)
$0 to $1,000	2	
Over $6,000	7	
District of Columbia	5	—

(k) The permanent rate is 9.5 per cent. A temporary 1.9 per cent tax is in effect for tax years beginning before January 1, 1965. The permanent and temporary rates are increased 10 per cent for tax years beginning before January 1, 1965.

(l) Maximum rate is scheduled to be reduced one-half per cent annually until it reaches 3 per cent in 1966.

(m) Or $25, 1 mill per dollar of capital, or 5.5 per cent of 30 per cent of net income, plus salaries and other compensation to officers and stockholders owning more than 5 per cent of the issued capital stock less $15,000 and any net loss if any of these is greater than the tax computed on net income.

(n) Minimum tax is $10 or 1 mill per dollar of capital stock.

(o) Minimum tax is $10.

(p) Minimum tax is $50.

(q) Or, for business corporations, 40 cents per $100 of corporate excess is collected if greater than the tax computed on net income. For banks, if a greater tax results, the alternative tax is $2.50 per $10,000 of capital stock. For both business corporations and banks, the minimum tax is $10.

(r) Minimum tax is $24.

(s) State banks and corporations pay 4 per cent of net income or $\frac{1}{20}$ per cent of value of tangible property, whichever is greater, but not less than $10.

(t) Limited to 10 per cent of net income before federal tax.

SOURCE: *Book of the States, 1964–1965*, p. 236.

this problem. Ten states permit income splitting in computing taxes on joint returns and twenty-seven states provide for the withholding of salaries and wages. Tax withholding has proved not only of convenience to taxpayers but has contributed measurably to improving compliance. Tax record-keeping has been improved (at some slight expense to the businessman), collections have been greatly facilitated, and tax loss due to population mobility is now reduced to a minimum.

A word of caution is again in order before attempting qualitative interstate comparisions of income tax systems. The effective tax liability to which a person in state A may be subjected to can be quite different from what he might face in state B in spite of the fact that the statutory rates of the two states seem on the surface to be identical.

That this should be so results from the interplay of a number of variables. Statutory tax rates may be identical, yet state A adopts the principle of community property, under which half of the income automatically belongs to the other spouse, and permits separate returns to be filed, while state B does not allow this type of income splitting; this may amount to a tax differential of as much as 35 per cent between taxpayers of equal income. State A may authorize the deduction of exemptions before the tax rate schedule is applied while state B in lieu of exemptions uses a system of personal credits applicable only after the tax is computed; persons in top income brackets may benefit considerably under state A's arrangement. Under the laws of state A, the amount of federal income taxes paid by the taxpayer may be deducted from his state income tax—this may not be the law in state B; federal income tax deductibility alone can so radically affect statutory rates that the marginal effective rate at the top of a state income tax bracket will in fact be only as little as 2.27 per cent of a publicized statutory rate of 11 per cent.[19]

State A and state B may have graduated income taxes equally steep, but due to shrinkage of its tax base (owing to under-reporting of income, heavy personal exemptions, and preferential deductions), state A on the basis of collections per $1,000 of personal income may rank far below state B whose tax base had not similarly eroded.[20]

Proponents of the personal income tax contend (1) that this tax, more than any other state tax, rests on the principle of "ability to pay," and that it therefore introduces a progressive element into an otherwise highly regressive tax structure; (2) that income is the most appropriate base upon which to impose taxation in a modern industrial society in which intangible property plays such a major role; (3) that exemption and deduction policies can be framed so as to adapt to the particular domestic circumstances of each

---

[19] *Report of the Governor's Minnesota Tax Study Committee*, Ch. VII.
[20] "For example, in 1957 North Dakota and Colorado had the highest and most steeply graduated tax rate structures in the nation, but on the basis of collections per $1,000 of personal income received that year they ranked 20th and 14th respectively, among the 24 personal income tax states for which data were available." Reuben A. Zubrow, "The Erosion of a State Income Tax," *National Tax Journal*, March, 1960, p. 59.

taxpayer; (4) since tax liability fluctuates with the economy, it will not cause an undue burden on taxpayers in periods of business downturns and reduced earnings as would, for example, the general property tax.

Resistance to personal income taxation has been heavy. This partially explains why, compared with the federal model, state income taxes allow higher exemptions and stipulate lower rates. As noted earlier, over a dozen states have so far been unwilling to adopt it, preferring reliance on other taxes, mostly sales taxes, to make up for their rising revenue requirements. Standard objections to the income tax include the charge (1) that income taxes act as a depressant on the economy by penalizing personal effort, risk-taking, and incentive; (2) that income taxes are difficult to compute especially if the taxpayer's income is derived from multiple sources; (3) that the concept of net income is a highly complicated one involving questions concerning the tax treatment that should be afforded income splitting, gratuities, capital gains and losses, deductions, inventory valuations, and personal trusts—all concepts equally baffling to taxpayers, legislators, courts, and most of all to tax administrators and auditors who are charged with keeping tax avoidance to a minimum; (4) that income taxes pose enormously complex jurisdictional problems (often resulting in double taxation) since states follow different policies with respect to how income earned in another state should be treated or whether a taxpayer's domicile or *situs* should be considered determinative.

LOCAL INCOME TAXES

Where local communities impose personal income taxes, as for example in Kentucky, Michigan, Missouri, Ohio, and Pennsylvania, they generally employ a flat .5%, 1%, or 1.5% tax in place of the graduated rate schedules characteristic of personal income taxes levied by state or federal government.[21] Pennsylvania (which does not have a state income tax) leads the nation in the local income tax field. Orginating with Philadelphia in 1939, there are now over 800 Pennsylvania cities, boroughs, townships, and even school districts which have adopted this tax. Ohio follows with seventy-three cities, Illinois with nine, and Missouri with one (St. Louis). Under the Pennsylvania law, tax liability extends generally to salaries, wages, commissions, bonuses, and other personal compensations as well as to net profits of unincorporated businesses and to the professions. It does not apply to corporations. Residents and nonresidents alike are subject to the tax whether the source of their income is derived from sources within the city or without. Collected mostly through withholding, no provisions are made for personal exemptions or for deductions (although some cities such as Louisville, Kentucky, do exempt the income of domestic servants and ministers).

While this tax certainly does not as yet constitute a major revenue

[21] On municipal income taxes, see Robert A. Sigafoos, *The Municipal Income Tax: Its History and Problems* (Chicago, 1955).

source for cities nationwide ($308 million in 1962), local income taxes where applied do constitute a very important supplementary form of municipal earnings. It can be used to keep property taxes from rising; it is a certain and a broadly-based tax; it is productive of revenue, fairly convenient for tax-payers, and not too difficult to administer. Its failure to utilize a graduated rate scale and its exemptions of unearned income such as stocks, bonds, and annuities expose the tax to the criticism of regressivity—of ignoring the ability to pay principle. Taxpayers who work in the city but reside in the suburbs object to the tax on the grounds that it subjects them to taxation without representation or to double taxation albeit under a different label. Municipal critics express apprehension that a decline in business activities will quickly result in reduced tax earnings at the very moment when com-munity needs for revenue are most critical.

This debate not withstanding, it is a matter of record that during the past twenty years local governments have been able to double their collection of taxes from sources other than property. Taxes on sales and to a smaller extent on income, liquor, amusement, motor fuels, and cigarettes represented the kind of levies with which more and more local units proceeded to meet the fiscal challenge of the ever-rising costs of public service. This mushrooming of local taxes has not been entirely an unmixed blessing. Local firms found it difficult to compete with suburban establishments outside the tax limits; tax collection and administrative costs rose as tax levies and jurisdiction pyra-mided; major variations in tax approach between governments comprising a metropolitan area or market tended to stifle optimum economic development as well as to complicate taxpayer compliance.

A special study of the Advisory Commission on Intergovernmental Rela-tions which addressed itself to possible contributions that state government might render local government in the area of non-property taxation came up with a series of recommendations, two of which are given below:

A. The case for most non-property taxes is strongest in the large urban places. Even here, these taxes are best imposed cooperatively by a group of eco-nomically interdependent jurisdictions. Therefore, the city and the other jurisdictions comprising an economic area should be provided with (a) uni-form taxing powers and (b) authority for cooperative tax enforcement. The states should take active leadership in promoting the pursuit of coor-dinated tax policies and practices by these economically interdependent jurisdictions.

B. In states where a particular tax, such as the sales or income tax, is in widespread use by local governments and is simultaneously used also by the state, the most promising coordinating device is the local tax supple-ment to the state tax. It gives local jurisdictions access to the superior enforcement resources of the state and eases taxpayer compliance but leaves the decision to impose the tax to local initiative. [22]

---

[22] Advisory Commission on Intergovernmental Relations, *Local Nonproperty Taxes and the Coordinating Role of the State* (Washington, 1961), p. 6.

MOTOR FUEL TAXES

Next to sales and income taxes, motor fuel taxes (totaling 17.4 per cent of all state tax collections in 1963) make up the third largest source of state levies. Actually, special motor user taxes came to over $5 billion and constituted 25 per cent of all state tax revenues. Included in this $5 billion package were state taxes on motor vehicle fuels ranging from five to eight cents per gallon ($3.8 billion), state license taxes on motor vehicles ($1.6 billion), and state license taxes on vehicle operators ($137 million). Nearly all (over 93 per cent) of these tax proceeds were directed toward state and local highway construction and maintenance. The underlying theory of such taxes is that those who benefit from the highway system should contribute towards its support and that those who drive should pay for the privilege of operating their vehicles on public roads and streets. How much of a license tax the operator of a particular vehicle may have to pay varies somewhat from state to state as well as with the type or classification of vehicle. Generally, state legislatures will promulgate rate schedules which give differential tax treatment to buses, passenger cars, and trucks and to vehicles used for private as distinguished from commercial purposes. License rates may be additionally refined by such considerations as a vehicle's weight, age, value, or horsepower.

Motor user taxes are ordinarily judged to be stable, reliable, highly productive of revenue, and reasonably related to the purposes for which they are imposed. Yet a number of basic questions of policy continue to remain at issue among experts, legislators, and affected interest groups. Considering the fact that the benefits of good highways accrue to not only their more immediate users but to the entire community and economy, how much of a fiscal burden should, therefore, be placed on the shoulders of motorists and how much on the public at-large? How should license rates be adjusted to balance equitably the wear and tear caused by domestic as contrasted with interstate trucking? What comparative assessment should be given to weight and distance traveled by each vehicle; what formula should be adopted to distribute state-collected motor user taxes among the various units of government that are charged with the maintenance of highways?

ALCOHOL TAXES

Alcoholic beverage excise taxes ($794 million in 1963) furnished states only about one-fifth of the revenue they received from their motor fuel taxes. Yet, if to this tax are added the license and special permit fees on manufacturers, wholesalers, and distributors of alcoholic beverages, the total for all units of government is estimated at $4 billion annually. Cities alone collected $80 million in 1962 in net profits from their municipally-owned liquor stores— a one-third increase over the 1958 figure.

Excise taxes on distilled spirits range upward (per gallon) from $1.15 in Delaware to $4.00 in Alaska (most states charging between $1.00 and $2.00); on wines the levies range from a low of $.01 in California to a high of $1.08 in South Carolina; on beer there is a spread from $.02 in Wyoming to $.45 in South Carolina.

In the thirteen states which have established a liquor monopoly—Idaho, Maine, Michigan, New Hampshire, North Carolina, Ohio, Oregon, Pennsylvania, Vermont, Virginia, Washington, West Virginia, and Wyoming—excise taxes on alcohol are ordinarily computed into the retail markup of the beverage.

Another group of states use a tax formula which is based on the wholesale or sales price of the beverage; this group includes Hawaii (16 per cent of the wholesale price of all alcoholic beverages), Montana (16 per cent of the sales price of distilled spirits and wines), Pennsylvania (10 per cent of the sales price of distilled spirits and wines), and Utah (4 per cent of the sales price of distilled spirits and wines).

While the collection of license fees from manufacturers, wholesalers, and distributors is ordinarily placed in the hands of the state, licenses for retailers are usually reserved to local governments. Such fees may range from a low of $100 to well into thousands of dollars per establishment depending on the category of alcoholic beverage (distilled spirits, wines, or beer) and on the population classification of the city issuing the license.

High markups and the well-known profitableness of the liquor business has made the obtaining of liquor store licenses enormously attractive to the criminal syndicates and to other socially suspect interests. More cities appear to be turning to municipal ownership as a method of safeguarding proper law enforcement while simultaneously assuring to the public at-large its full share of profits from the sale of liquor.

TOBACCO TAXES

Tobacco taxes, yielding over a billion dollars in 1963 (5.1 per cent of all state collections), represent another type of highly productive sumptuary taxes. In addition to special taxes on wholesalers or retailers, all fifty states now levy taxes on cigarettes (usually from two to eight cents per package of twenty), eleven states tax smoking tobacco (generally between 10 per cent and 25 per cent of the wholesale or retail price), eleven states tax cigars ($1.00 and up per thousand), and twelve states tax chewing tobacco and snuff (either on weight or as a percentage of the wholesale or retail price). Hawaii taxes all forms of tobacco on the basis of 20 per cent of wholesale price. In New Hampshire, the tax amounts to 15 per cent of the tobacco's retail price.

As was true in the case of taxes on liquors, wines, and beer, excises on tobacco are passed on directly to the consumer whether levied on the manufacturer, wholesaler, distributor, or retailer. What makes these taxes clearly regressive in character is the fact that people with lower incomes spend proportionately larger amounts of their earnings on "demon" alcohol and tobacco than do people with higher incomes. However, this type of regressivity finds ready justification on the ground that unhealthy and socially undesirable consumer habits are particularly worthy subjects for taxation. The case for sumptuary taxes becomes even more persuasive when it can be demonstrated that the proceeds from these taxes are used to build better schools, aid the indigent, and generally pay for governmental services which might otherwise atrophy.

BUSINESS TAXES

In the absence of a single, equitable, and uniform tax on business and industry, the states over the years have been experimenting with gross earnings and special business taxes.

Originally designed to force monopolistic or special types of business ventures (such as banks and insurance companies) to make their fair contribution to the financing of the states, these taxes taken together still bring in over a billion dollars annually.

Presently, gross earnings taxes are imposed in addition to certain local *ad valorem* taxes by about half of the states on railroads, telephone, telegraph, and other utility companies. Among the distinct advantages claimed for this approach is that of administrative effectiveness and of tax responsiveness to changes in company earning power; avoided also is the need of leaving to untrained assessors the complex task of handling elaborate business enterprises which defy simple valuation processes or formulae.

Special business taxes are imposed in nearly all of the states although interstate comparisons are extremely difficult due to differences in policies and administrative practices. Most of the states which tax banks and insurance companies do so on the basis of their capital stocks, gross premiums, or dividends rather than on their earnings. This method is traditionally defended in view of the fiscal structure of such businesses which makes it very difficult to ascertain and measure net earnings with clarity and reliability. Underlying these special taxes is the simple rationale that, complexities notwithstanding, these businesses are so profitable that they should be brought within the reach of the state tax collector in order to pay for the privilege of transacting business within the state. From their side, banks and insurance companies insist that their property is already taxed locally and that special business taxes make their intangible holdings (stocks, notes, mortgages, and bonds) subject to double taxation. Further complaints are raised against alleged tax discriminations which result from the exemptions of mutual funds, building and loan associations, and non-profit cooperative or benevolent societies. Insurance companies further emphasize that they perform socially significant services for which the state should not exact a tax penalty and that in the absence of such a tax, excess earnings would routinely be returned to policy-holders in the form of reduced premiums or increased protections.

MISCELLANEOUS TAXES

Only the briefest attention can be given here to a whole host of state taxes which, taken together, total about one billion dollars a year. Prominent among these are *estate, inheritance,* and *gift* taxes with an annual yield of al-most $600 million which represents 2.8 per cent of all state tax collections. With the exception of Nevada, all states now levy a tax on property transferred at death. Under most of these state laws, property bequests to charitable, edu-cational, scientific, religious, and public institutions or purposes are exempted; inheritance tax schedules (less steeply graduated than on the federal plane) are provided allowing lower rates and larger exemptions for spouse, child, or parent than to other relatives; estate taxes, as distinguished from inheritance taxes, are imposed on the undistributed estate in which the relationship of heirs and a beneficiary's personal exemption are given less preferential recog-nition.

As to taxes on gifts of property, their level and their incidence appears to be affected considerably by whether the gift was made in contemplation of death, whether the gift was to take effect upon death, or whether the gift was between living persons and not at all in contemplation of death. Redistribu-tion of wealth, the fact that the tax incidence cannot be shifted, and the avoidance of concentrated economic power in the hands of the few—these are given as among the most desirable social objectives of inheritance taxes. Advocates of these taxes hold these objectives to be much more important than the possible loss of economic incentive (wishing to leave a substantial estate to one's heirs), the possibility of breaking up well-established family enterprises, or wider recourse to elaborate tax-avoiding trust devices.

Severance taxes are collected in twenty-nine states where they produced $465 million in 1963. Included among the major resources so taxed are iron ore, forest products, oil, gas, and petroleum. Severance taxes sometimes supplemented by *ad valorem* levies play a significant role in Louisiana, Min-nesota, New Mexico, Oklahoma, and Texas. Underlying the theory of such taxes is the notion that the public should be recompensed for the depletion of an irreplaceable natural resource that belongs to all the people—to present as well as to future generations. The mining and oil companies, on the other hand, which must pay these taxes tend to view them as politically inspired, as insensitive to the speculative character of their business ventures, as unappre-ciative of the risk and capital investment which these operations demand, and as ignoring the extent of foreign competition which is eager to enter the American market.

In twenty-five states legalized gambling on races returns about a quarter of a billion dollars through *pari-mutuel taxes* which are based on a percentage of the "total daily handle" and "breakage." Among states in which they have proved unusually productive are California ($41 million), Florida ($28 million), Illinois ($22 million), Massachusetts ($14 million), New Jersey ($29 million), and most of all New York ($111 million). In 1963, over objections that gamblers and criminal interests would be attracted to New Hampshire, the voters of the Granite State overwhelmingly approved a referendum which authorized the state to sell lottery tickets on races at Rockingham Park Race Track with the proceeds earmarked for the support of education. Governor King signed a lottery bill on May 1, 1963. Tickets ($3.00 apiece) for prizes ranging from a few hundred dollars to $100,000 were sold only at the tracks and in state liquor stores. As of the summer of 1964, $1.3 million worth of tickets had been sold in the state which boasts of having neither a sales nor an income tax. Most of the tickets were actually not even purchased by the citizens of New Hampshire, but by residents of neighboring New England States.[23]

By contrast with pari-mutuels, *amusement taxes*, although in effect in twenty-nine states, provide only less than one-tenth as much revenue. The only state relying heavily on this tax is Nevada which collected $13 million from this source in 1963.

DEVELOPMENTS IN STATE AND LOCAL GOVERNMENT DEBTS

Considering the population explosion of the post-World War II era and the pent-up demand for public construction during the war years, sharp increases in state and local debt were to be expected. Building the new schools, highways, toll roads, hospitals, bridges, and universities made necessary not only additional taxes but capital outlays of major magnitude by both state and local governments (see Table 5).

Explicit and detailed constitutional restrictions on borrowing in all but eight of the states necessitated numerous formal amendments or popular

TABLE 5. GROSS DEBT OF STATE AND LOCAL
GOVERNMENTS FOR SELECTED YEARS *

Year	State	Local
1946	$ 2,353	$13,564
1956	12,890	35,978
1962	22,023	58,779

* In millions.

SOURCE: Bureau of the Census, *Historical Statistics on Government Finances and Employment*, pp. 41–42, 44–45.

[23] "New Hampshire Sweepstakes Tickets Move at Galloping Pace," *Minneapolis Sunday Tribune*, June 21, 1964, p. 15B. On June 30, 1964 the electors of North Dakota turned down by a nearly 2 to 1 vote a proposal to permit betting on horse and dog races subject to a pari-mutuel tax, *The Minneapolis Star*, July 1, 1964.

referenda before such states could legally proceed to finance long-term obligations for their capital needs.

Whatever merits state constitutional barriers to state borrowing may possess, they did not prevent states from engaging in building programs which substantial segments of the public and legislature were willing to authorize. Where proposed amendments or referenda failed to obtain the extraordinary majorities (specified in the constitution) or where greater fiscal freedom and discretion were held essential, state legislatures turned to the issuance of revenue bonds. This development has reached a point where "most states now find themselves able to borrow for public improvements of any nature, constitutional restrictions notwithstanding." [24]

Unlike general bonds which are backed by the full faith and credit of the state, revenue bonds, rated somewhat less secure, carry a higher interest rate and extended-period maturities. This, of course, raises the cost of debt management correspondingly. That states are willing to pay this price for the privilege of casting off their constitutional shackles is demonstrated clearly by the speed with which this form of financing has taken hold. Of the total long-term state debt of $21.6 billion in 1962, over half or $11.2 billion was of the non-guaranteed type. Twelve years ago less than one-fifth of state debts were financed in this manner.

In the name of fiscal responsibility and safety, state constitutions and state law curtail the debt-incurring powers of local governments even more thoroughly than they do those of state government. Such provisions take at least four principal forms: (1) Local government debt may not exceed a specified percentage ratio of its property tax base; (2) constitutions or laws enumerate the purposes for which debts may be incurred; (3) the manner in which a local bond referendum is to be submitted to the electorate and what type of majority vote constitutes approval will be spelled out in detail; (4) local governments may be restricted with respect to the tax levels that may be imposed in order to service the debt.

As was true in the case of the states, economic circumstances and political pressures forced local governments to devise methods of working their way out of the fiscal strait jacket. Large-scale public constructions were considered essential, and the law had to adapt itself—again at a price. Under the *special fund doctrine,* a number of courts finally permitted cities to issue revenue bonds outside of their debt limits for the purpose of financing certain facilities, such as the building or acquiring of a sewage plant, where the debt could be discharged directly from fees charged the public for services rendered by the plant.

Sometimes state legislatures came to the assistance of their cities by creating *special districts* or *corporate authorities* with powers to sue and be sued and with the right to issue full faith and credit obligations.

[24] A. James Heins, *Constitutional Restrictions Against State Debt* (Madison, 1963), p. 83.

Lease-purchase agreements represent another pattern of adjustment to excessive local debt restraints. Cities adopting this judicially-sanctioned formula enter into a lease with a private builder of a waterworks that it wishes to acquire under the terms of which the rent is applied to the eventual purchase of the facility.

Most of the borrowing which was thus made possible resulted in greater recourse to revenue bond financing which in turn contributed to raising debt servicing costs at a time when cities could least afford such extra burdens (see Table 6).

TABLE 6. OUTSTANDING LONG-TERM DEBT OF
LOCAL GOVERNMENTS AT END OF SELECTED FISCAL YEARS *

Year	Total	Full faith and credit	Nonguaranteed
1952	$22,080	$17,509	$ 4,571
1956	34,424	25,895	8,529
1960	48,673	32,738	15,935
1962	55,728	37,792	17,936

* In millions.

SOURCE: Bureau of the Census, *Compendium of Government Finances;* adapted from Advisory Commission on Intergovernmental Relations, *State Constitutional and Statutory Restrictions on Local Government Debt* (Washington, 1961), p. 25 and *Book of the States, 1964–1965,* p. 215.

Aside from the costs of debt management, restrictions on local government further accentuated the proliferations of special districts, the diffusion of governmental accountability, the search for avoidance of constitutional mandates (however unrealistic their nature), and, what is probably most critical of all, it led to greater reliance by local government on state and federal financial aid.

What cities and other local units need if they are to live up to their public responsibilities—in the judgment of the Advisory Commission on Intergovernmental Relations—is to be "granted maximum powers with respect to local government indebtedness." More specifically, the commission recommended

A. That authority to issue bonds should be legally vested in the governing bodies of local governments, subject to a permissive referendum only, on petition, and with participation in any such referendum available to all eligible local voters and the results determined—except under unusual circumstances—by a simple majority vote on the question.
B. The repeal of constitutional and statutory provisions limiting local government debt or debt service by reference to the local base for property taxation.

The role of state government as envisaged in these recommendations is one limited to making available "technical and advisory assistance" and to prescribing the minimum content of official statements prepared by local governments in connection with their issuance of long-term debt, in order to provide prospective investors with data needed to evaluate the security offerings.[25]

INTERGOVERNMENTAL AID, IMMUNITY, AND AREAS OF

TAX CONFLICT AND COOPERATION

Since the late 1940's, federal aid to state and local governments increased from around $1 billion to nearly $10 billion. Most of this increase went to the support of education, public health, highways, housing and community development, and public assistance. State governments in

FIGURE 5

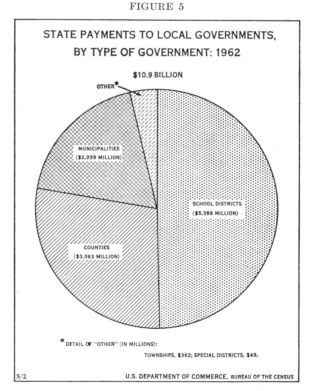

STATE PAYMENTS TO LOCAL GOVERNMENTS,
BY TYPE OF GOVERNMENT: 1962

$10.9 BILLION

OTHER*

MUNICIPALITIES
($2,039 MILLION)

SCHOOL DISTRICTS
($5,386 MILLION)

COUNTIES
($3,063 MILLION)

*DETAIL OF "OTHER" (IN MILLIONS):
TOWNSHIPS, $362; SPECIAL DISTRICTS, $49.

5/2   U.S. DEPARTMENT OF COMMERCE, BUREAU OF THE CENSUS

SOURCE: Bureau of the Census, Department of Commerce, *Census of Governments: 1962*, Vol. VI, No. 2, "State Payments to Local Governments," (Washington, 1963), p. 6.

turn came to the assistance of their local governments to the point where in 1962 their almost $11 billion contribution amounted to 35 per cent of their total expenditures. For the amount of state aid given to various local govern-

[25] Advisory Commission on Intergovernmental Relations, *State Constitutional and Statutory Restrictions on Local Government Debt* (Washington, 1961), pp. 4–5; for a case illustration, see Kenneth E. Beasley, *State Supervision of Municipal Debt in Kansas: A Case Study* (Lawrence, 1961).

FIGURE 6

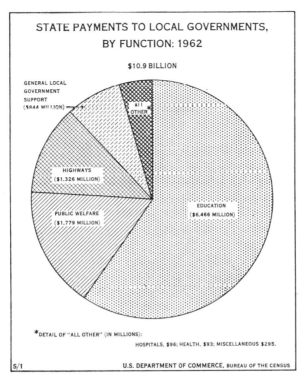

STATE PAYMENTS TO LOCAL GOVERNMENTS, BY FUNCTION: 1962

$10.9 BILLION

GENERAL LOCAL GOVERNMENT SUPPORT ($844 MILLION)

ALL OTHER*

HIGHWAYS ($1,326 MILLION)

PUBLIC WELFARE ($1,779 MILLION)

EDUCATION ($6,466 MILLION)

*DETAIL OF "ALL OTHER" (IN MILLIONS):
HOSPITALS, $96; HEALTH, $93; MISCELLANEOUS $295.

S/1   U.S. DEPARTMENT OF COMMERCE, BUREAU OF THE CENSUS

SOURCE: Bureau of the Census, Department of Commerce, *Census of Governments: 1962*, Vol. VI, No. 2, "State Payments to Local Governments," (Washington, 1963), p. 6.

ments in 1962, see Figure 5. Figure 6 summarizes the purposes for which state aid was given. Education with $6.5 billion ranked first; public welfare with $1.8 billion, second; highways with $1.3 billion, third; and general local government support with $844 million, fourth. Viewed from the point of view of local government, 25 per cent of all intergovernmental aid came from the states and 1.6 per cent from the federal government.

These intergovernmental aids do not merely show the dependence of local governments on federal and state funds, but also bring into focus anew the complex problems of intergovernmental revenues. *McCulloch* v. *Maryland* (1819) [26] first authoritatively elucidated the constitutional relationship between the powers of the national government and the powers of state government to tax a federal agency. "If the states may tax one instrument employed by the [federal] Government in the execution of its powers," wrote Chief Justice Marshall in striking down Maryland's law (which had imposed a tax on the notes of the Bank of the United States), "they may tax any and every other instrument. . . . This was not intended by the American people. They did not design to make their [federal] Government dependent on the states. . . ."

[26] 4 Wheat. 316 (1819), at 432.

Subsequent decisions broadened this doctrine and granted reciprocal tax immunity to the operations of state and local government, their securities, their officers, and their employees.

Then, under the impact of the Depression and the intensive search for new sources of revenue which accompanied these years of stringency, a number of decisions and federal statutes combined to narrow substantially the areas of intergovernmental immunity. Federal, state, and local government bonds and properties in private hands are still clothed in tax immunity. Recent efforts in various states and municipalities to issue tax-exempt bonds for the purpose of building or acquiring industrial properties (to attract business and aid in economic development) cast a serious doubt on the ability of the immunity concept to survive in its present form. Critics of the immunity concept insist that in its present operation it tends to distort tax equity as well as benefit unfairly those cities and states which have allowed their governments to become involved in business activities of a "socialistic" nature.

Judicial attempts to draw a line between activities historically conceded to be "governmental" and those "proprietary" have been found wanting in clarity and consistency. A somewhat different test was applied in *New York* v. *United States* [27] which upheld a federal tax under the United States Revenue Act of 1932 on the sale of bottled mineral water sold by the Saratoga Springs authority, a New York public benefit corporation. "[S]o long as Congress generally taps a source of revenue by whomsoever earned and not uniquely capable of being earned only by a state," wrote Mr. Justice Frankfurter for the majority, "the Constitution of the United States does not forbid it merely because its incidence falls also on a state." Mr. Justice Douglas defended tax immunity with this strongly-worded dissent:

> A tax is a powerful, regulatory instrument. Local government in this free land does not exist for itself. The fact that local government may enter the domain of private enterprise and operate a project for profit does not put it in the class of private business enterprise for tax purposes. Local government exists to provide for the welfare of its people, not for a limited group of stockholders. . . . Many state activities are in marginal enterprises where private capital refuses to venture. Add to the cost of these projects a federal tax and the social program may be destroyed before it can be launched. . . . If the truth were known, I suspect it would show that the activity of the States in the fields of housing, public power and the like have increased the level of income of the people and have raised the standards of marginal or submarginal groups.

Far more difficult than the issue of tax immunity are the problems of intergovernmental tax coordination. With the federal government presently accounting for 68 per cent of all tax collections, the shrinking share of taxes

[27] 326 U. S. 572 (1946); see also the discussion by Rudolph V. Parr in "State Condemnation of Municipally-Owned Property: The Governmental-Property Distinction," *Syracuse Law Review,* Fall, 1959, pp. 27–35.

still left to state and local governments is subjected to the keenest of interstate and interlocal competition.

Tax duplication and pyramiding abound as federal, state, and local governmental authorities are free to impose taxes on individual incomes, corporate income and profits, gasoline and fuels, alcoholic beverages, cigarettes and tobacco, estates and inheritances, and gifts.

As a by-product of federalism, this overlapping system of taxes makes compliance more difficult, loopholes more numerous, taxpaying problems more vexatious, tax incidence more uncertain, and tax administration more costly.

Various recommendations to improve this situation have been submitted by private and public tax commissions, governors' conferences, presidential committees and joint federal-state councils. Despite such efforts, no acceptable method has as yet been developed which could either separate tax sources or reserve particular types of taxes to one or the other level of government.[28]

This lack of progress is not too difficult to understand. Changes in tax jurisdictions involve more than mere administrative questions—they go beyond considerations of efficiency, matters of convenience, or structural symmetry. Taxation deals with profound issues of public policy. Questions like "Who should pay how much and why?" are matters not easily reconciled. They are thoroughly political in nature and susceptible to political solutions in which expert testimony is only one of many ingredients. In these deliberations the various segments of the taxpaying public, especially the more organized and articulate, will be slow to exchange the known for the unknown.

Closely connected to the problem of tax duplication is that of state-imposed taxes on non-resident corporations engaged in interstate commerce. How complex a situation may be faced by a corporation doing business in more than one state—the so-called multi-state corporation—is well described by the following report on interstate income tax apportionment practices:

> Thirty-six States, including the District of Columbia, use an apportionment formula in levying their corporate income taxes. In determining the apportionment formula, thirty-three States use the property, thirty-six States use receipts (sales), twenty-four States use payrolls (an additional seven States use payrolls in figuring cost factors), and twenty States include other factors (usually relating to items of income that are to be specifically allocated). Unfortunately the diversity among the States does not end here. All thirty-six States use receipts in their tax formulas, but seventy-five items or definitions are used, either singly or in combination, to determine receipts in the apportionment formulas. . . .[29]

---

[28] On intergovernmental fiscal relations, the best discussion is found in W. Brooke Graves, *American Intergovernmental Relations* (New York, 1964), pt. IV; see also the findings of Advisory Commission on Intergovernmental Relations, *Intergovernmental Cooperation in Tax Administration* (Washington, 1961).

[29] Council of State Governments, *Washington Legislative Bulletin*, November, 1960, p. 4, cited in Graves, p. 464.

The right of a state to levy use taxes on an out-of-state vendor (who need not even maintain an establishment in the taxing state) for sales made to a purchaser subject to its tax jurisdiction has been acknowledged by the United States Supreme Court in the *Scripto* case. Subsequent developments have done little to smooth the flow of interstate commerce:

> The result is that manufacturers are currently receiving thousands of demands from all of the thirty-six sales and use-tax states, and from many local governments, to register as sellers and to collect their sales and use taxes. Under the *Scripto* decision, it is clear that states have the legal right to make such demands, if the seller has "some minimum connection" with the state; specifically, if he solicits business there through his own employers or through independent manufacturer's representatives. A growing number of states are claiming that they have this right to the use of the U. S. mails. . . .[30]

If greater tax uniformity represents an important economic objective, it could be attained in one of three ways: through congressional legislation in pursuance of the federal government's power over interstate commerce, through a uniform state law suggested by the National Conference of Commissioners on uniform state laws, or through an interstate compact on interstate taxation.

The goal of such tax uniformity is favored by many commercial interests; it is opposed with equal enthusiasm by state and local tax collectors most of whom perceive these developments as endangering revenues their governmental levels could ill afford to lose.

BUDGETS AND BUDGETARY PROCESSES

In the most fundamental sense, budgets determine what projects the government decides to support, who is to receive what and who is to pay for what the government has to give. Struggles for what is to go into the budget —which items are to be reduced, which increased, which removed—involve enormously complex considerations of policy and principle for those who prepare and act upon the budget. Pressures within and without government converge on every aspect of the decision-making process. In this battle each dollar represents a building block in the construction of expenditure and revenue programs which will finally determine how many people may be employed in a particular agency, which contracts negotiated, which services performed, which goods purchased, which salaries raised, and which pensions denied or granted. All of this makes the budget process an intensely political process operating in a political climate, under political rules, with consequences often profoundly political for those major participants who must proceed to make the critical and visible decisions.

No two state governmental budgets will ever be alike in either structure or content. They vary in length, make-up, comprehensiveness, and accounting

[30] House Committee on the Judiciary, *Sales and Use Taxes,* Hearings before the Special Committee on State Taxations of Interstate Commerce, June, 1962, 87th Cong., 2nd Sess. (Washington, 1962), p. 14.

practices; some cover one fiscal year at a time, others a biennium. Regardless of differences such as these, most budgets necessarily include sections detailing expenditure requests by departments and agencies, for salaries, equipment and supplies (usually in line-item form), projected capital outlays for institutional building programs (hospitals, prisons, educational facilities), anticipated tax revenues, fees, and trust fund earnings, and scheduled repayments on outstanding debts. Then for the guidance of the legislature, some budgets may also specify separate entries showing levels of authorized spending in previous years, along with current departmental requests and gubernatorial recommendations.

Budget-making authority is placed in the hands of the governor except in these seven states: Arkansas, Florida, Indiana, Mississippi, North Dakota, South Carolina, and West Virginia. Moreover, in the great majority of the states, the actual task of preparing the budget is carried out under the

THE PATIENT'S DILEMMA.

SOURCE: Marcus in *The New York Times*, April 7, 1957. © 1957 The New York Times Company. Reprinted by permission.

supervision and with the assistance of an official appointed by the governor who is designated variously as Commissioner of Administration and Finance, Director of Finance, or Budget Director.

In states with notoriously weak governorships that lack centralized executive control, budget-making authority is usually the reserve of a budget commission. Such commissions may be composed either of a group of executive officials—governor as chairman, budget officer, secretary of state, comptroller, treasurer, attorney general, commissioner of agriculture, and superintendent of public instruction (as in Florida) or of a commission which in addition to key executive officers includes such important leaders of the legislature as the chairman, House Ways and Means Committee, chairman, House Appropriations Committee, chairman, Senate Finance Committee, and president pro tem of the Senate (the Mississippi pattern).

The pre-legislative phase of the budget cycle begins ordinarily in the spring of the year when each governmental agency and department is asked to determine its requirements in the light of its needs and within broad directives promulgated by the chief executive or his budget officer. In September or October, after the requests have been submitted to the state finance director, the serious task of consolidating thousands of projections and the actual building of the state budget begins. Individual departmental requests will have to be reviewed, revised, and often scaled down; revenue estimates must be obtained from the tax department, and balances struck. How much power the finance director possesses, in connection with these critical decisions, differs from state to state not only as a variable of law but also of the personal relationship that exists between the governor and his finance director.

What further restricts a budget director's choices is the fact that in at least thirty-one states there is some form of constitutional earmarking of funds. Eleven states dedicate over a third of all their revenues to particular funds and purposes thus placing these outside the budget-building process.[31]

Ultimately, of course, it is the governor who must make the final decisions—the passing of the buck stops here.[32] From among the numerous factors which enter into the decision-making process, at this point a few need to be stressed. The governor must decide whether his budget is to be balanced within existing revenues or not; whether a particular departmental request should be increased in order to insure the success of a program he considers important to his administration; whether he should override the strenuous objections which may have come to him from a department head whose requests were denied or revised downward by the finance director in the

[31] Constitutional Earmarking of State Tax Revenues, Memorandum No. 207 (Lansing, 1962), pp. 12–13; in this connection see Advisory Commission on Intergovernmental Relations, State Constitutional and Statutory Restrictions on Local Government Debt (Washington, 1961).

[32] For an excellent discussion of the governor's role in connection with the budget, see Thomas Flinn, "Governor Freeman and the Minnesota Budget," in Edwin A. Bock (ed.), State and Local Government: A Case Book (Birmingham, 1963), pp. 457–491.

course of an earlier review; whether he should insist on stringent economies which might involve overall budget trimming or merely whittling down particular sections; whether he should recommend to the legislature the raising of new taxes (and what types of taxes), the elimination of certain tax exemptions, or the submission of a constitutional amendment authorizing additional state borrowing and debt.

Obviously, these decisions are not made by a governor in splendid isolation. On the contrary, most governors before submitting their budgets will consult with tax experts, personal advisors in and out of government, party officials, spokesmen of powerful interest groups, and above all with House and Senate leaders whose support may be indispensable to assure budgetary recommendation a favorable legislative reception.

The formal legislative phase of the budget cycle is initiated by the governor's budget message, usually delivered within a few days of the opening of the session. It is only natural that a governor will seek to present the fiscal plan of his administration in as attractive a light as possible. Spending requests are justified in terms of population growth and critical institutional needs, and special emphasis is given to savings and cutbacks already accomplished within the executive branch.

Where new taxes may be called for, assurances are provided that the business climate of the state will not be impaired competitively. Occasionally, invidious comparisons as to fiscal responsibility and morality will be drawn between a previous administration (when the opposition was in power) and the current one.

Possible failure of the legislature to adopt the budgetary recommendations may be anticipated with visions of major financial dislocations and widespread human suffering.

How a governor's budget will fare in the legislature is difficult to predict. Much depends upon the support that his party can give, upon his personal political power (as well as upon his ability to cajole, plead, beg, threaten, and persuade), upon public reactions to his recommendations, and on the degree of competence and strength with which department heads defend their expenditure requests to appropriations committees of House and Senate as they probe for padding, waste, and weakness. Important variables also are the political effectiveness of interest groups that favor and oppose the governor's policies and whether or not the constitution of the state grants the governor the power of the item veto.

BUDGETS AS INSTRUMENTS OF EXECUTIVE MANAGEMENT
AND PLANNING

Ever since World War II, as state and local governments were forced to expand their activities, and as their financial operations became vastly more complex, administrative reforms were introduced furnishing governors and mayors with greater budget-making authority. Centralization of purchasing, departmental allotments, accounting, and property management and the introduction of electronic data processing equipment were among the most significant of these developments. Instead of mere fiscal restraints, budgets were becoming more and more instruments of managerial control and planning. (For the 1964–1965 budget of New York City, see Figure 7.)

FIGURE 7. NEW YORK CITY BUDGET, 1964–1965

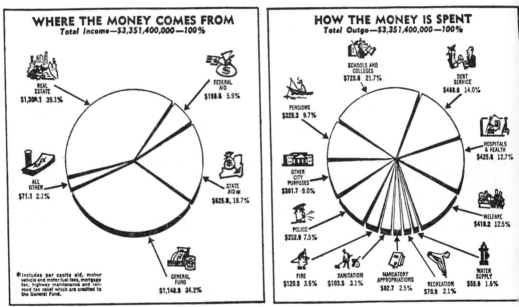

CITY BUDGET: Estimated 1964-65 revenues and expenditures in millions of dollars and percentages of the total

SOURCE: *The New York Times*, April 16, 1964, p. 29.

Performance and program budgeting, first made famous through the recommendations of the Hoover Commission (and strongly endorsed by many experts in public administration), have begun to leave their impact on quite a few state and local governments. Various reform-oriented public administrators criticized traditional cash budgets for their alleged failure to provide an adequate basis upon which legislators and the public could arrive at informed judgments. Performance and program budgets on the other hand seemed preferable over cash budgets because of their ability to focus attention not on mere dollar allocations to agencies or departments, but on levels of service and objectives towards which governmental activities should be primarily directed.

> If a Cincinnati councilman wants to cut the board of health budget, for example, he has before him enough information to decide whether he will cut out the health statistician at $6,500 a year, the alcoholism clinic at $11,567 . . .

or some part of the school or clinic health services. . . . At the top of each page are written explanations of what each division does, what its work program will be for the year and why the program matters. . . .[33]

Related to these more descriptive types of budgets is the effort of local governments to develop capital budgets which employ long-range objectives of capital construction and improvements. By setting careful building priorities, cities hope to plan more intelligently for their revenue needs and expenditures and thus reduce crisis financing, excessive debt charges, and an unstable tax climate.

Some critics of performance budgeting suggest that this approach has a tendency to camouflage hard dollar figures with appealing descriptions which are aimed more at justifying increased governmental spending than at helping government save money.

Other critics maintain that there may be considerable value in the "partial," "uncoordinated," "specialized," "incremental," and "fragmented" process which characterizes so much of governmental budget-making.

> The partial approach is more efficient for resolving conflicts, a process that lies at the heart of democratic politics. Because the approach is partial, it does not require its practitioners to discover all or most possible conflicts and to work out answers to problems that may never materialize. . . . A partial adversary system in which the various interests compete for control of policy (under agreed-upon rules) seems more likely to result in reasonable decisions—that is, decisions that take account of the multiplicity of values involved—than one in which the best policy is assumed to be discoverable by a well-intentioned search for the public interest for all by everyone.[34]

The kind of reforms which this theory of budget-making might tend to oppose would likely be those that would effectively reduce the range of opportunities through which diverse interests can hammer out their colliding perceptions of community needs.

---

[33] Thomas Talburt, "City Solved Problem by 1-Man Rule," *The Cincinnati Post and Times Star*, August 7, 1959, cited by Vernon E. Koch in "Progress in the Budgeting Process During the Past Decade," a paper delivered at the 54th Annual Conference of Municipal Finance Officers, August 1, 1960, pp. 4–5.

For a similar view see T. W. Fletcher, "A New Look at Budgeting," *Public Management*, February, 1964, pp. 26–28 (program budgeting in San Diego); note also Charles M. Tiebout and David B. Houston, "Metropolitan Finance Reconsidered: Budget Functions and Multi-Level Governments," *The Review of Economics and Statistics*, November, 1962, pp. 412–417; on another related aspect of local finances see Advisory Commission on Intergovernmental Relations, *Investment of Idle Cash Balances By State and Local Governments* (Washington, 1961); a questionnaire sent out in 1957 by the International City Managers Association to 813 cities with populations of over 10,000 (with 792 replying) showed that capital budgeting was used by 198 cities or 25 per cent of those replying. Of cities with over 1 million population, Los Angeles was the only city not using a capital budget. In the 500,000 to 1 million classification, Houston, Texas and Minneapolis, Minnesota were the only exceptions. In the 10,000 to 250,000 category, capital budgets were used by only 156 out of 709 cities; for further information, see *American Federationist*, March, 1962, cited in *Congressional Record*, March 5, 1962, p. A1665.

[34] Aaron Wildavsky, *The Politics of the Budgetary Process* (Boston, 1964), pp. 166–167.

CASE PROBLEMS FOR CLASS DISCUSSION

1. You are staff director of the state AFL-CIO Legislative Research Committee. Your committee has asked you to prepare a publication attacking a proposed statewide sales tax pending before the House Tax Committee. In the course of preparing this publication, what would be the sources that you would consult, what statistical information and tables would you prepare, and what would be the general nature of your argument?

2. You are the legislative representative (lobbyist) for the state chamber of commerce. The chamber has decided to support the adoption of a sales tax on the grounds that income tax rates (already high) would otherwise have to be raised even further in view of the general fiscal setting of the state. You are now preparing the testimony that you wish to present before the House Tax Committee. The committee is controlled by a group of powerful rural legislators. How would you argue your case and what type of exhibits would you bring along?

3. The chairman of the state tax equalization board has asked you, as board secretary, to prepare the agenda and summarize the various cases that are to be submitted to the board at its next meeting. What kind of background information and professional assistance would the board want in connection with its deliberations?

4. As a member of a city council in a community with a population of 5,000 and a 10% unemployment rate, you and the council are visited by a representative of a plastic manufacturing concern who informs you that the company is interested in establishing a new plant in your city, and that it expects to employ 500 people when fully operative. It quickly becomes apparent that the company, by way of inducement, would like to obtain immunity from the local property tax for a period of at least five years. What types of problems does this request raise, and what considerations would your council have to explore before accepting or rejecting these terms?

SELECTED BIBLIOGRAPHY

Advisory Commission on Intergovernmental Relations, *The Role of the States in Strengthening the Property Tax* (Washington, 1963).

Advisory Commission on Intergovernmental Relations, *State and Local Taxation of Privately Owned Property Located on Federal Areas: Proposed Amendment to the Buck Act* (Washington, 1961).

Advisory Commission on Intergovernmental Relations, *Tax Overlapping in the United States* (Washington, 1961).

VANCE Q. ALVIS, *The West Virginia Gross Sales Tax* (Morgantown, 1960).

R. B. ANDREWS and JEROME J. DASSO, "The Influence of Annexation on Property Tax Burdens," *National Tax Journal,* March, 1961, pp. 88–97.

ARTHUR B. BARBER, " 'Nonapportionable Income' under a Uniform State Net Income Tax Law Imposed by Congress," *National Tax Journal,* June, 1963, pp. 147–158.

ARTHUR B. BARBER, "State Income Tax Uniformity Concerning Taxable Units," *National Tax Journal,* December, 1963, pp. 354–364.

FREDERICK BIRD, *The General Property Tax* (Chicago, 1960).

CLARENCE A. BLACK, *Capital Budgeting in the Missouri State Highway Department* (Columbia, 1963).

JOSEPH L. BOWER, "Investment in United States Government Securities by State Governments," *National Tax Journal,* June, 1960, pp. 127–140.

HARVEY E. BRAZER, *Taxation in Michigan: An Appraisal* (Ann Arbor, 1961).

HARVEY E. BRAZER, DANIEL B. SUITS, and MURIEL W. CONVERSE, "Municipal Bond Yields: The Market's Reaction to Michigan's Fiscal Crisis," *National Tax Journal,* March, 1962, pp. 66–70.

JOHN F. BRIGGS, *A Refined Program Budget for State Governments* (Washington, 1962).

LEONARD D. BRONDER, "Michigan's First Local Income Tax," *National Tax Journal*, December, 1962, pp. 423-431.

GORDON K. BRYAN, *Trends in County Revenues and Expenditures in Mississippi, 1950-1959* (State College, 1963).

JESSE BURKHEAD, "Uniformity in Governmental Expenditures and Resources in a Metropolitan Area: Cuyahoga County," *National Tax Journal*, December, 1961, pp. 337-348.

CARL H. CHATTERS, "New Money for Cities," *National Civic Review*, June, 1961, pp. 298-303.

HARLAN CLEVELAND, "Are the Cities Broke," *National Civic Review*, March, 1961, pp. 126-130.

CHARLES F. CONLON, "Some Tax and Revenue Problems of the States," *State Government*, Spring, 1960, pp. 114-121.

HAROLD A. CONROY, "Municipal Sharing in State Revenues," *Municipal Finance*, August, 1962, pp. 60-66.

Constitutional Earmarking of Tax Revenues (Detroit, 1962).

KENNETH E. DAANE, "Some Empirical Data on the Gross Receipts and Property Factors of the Colorado Corporate Apportionment Formula," *National Tax Journal*, September, 1963, pp. 256-266.

CLAUDE J. DAVIS, EUGENE R. ELKINS, and PAUL E. KIDD, *Municipal and County Budgets in West Virginia, 1958-1960* (Morgantown, 1960).

MALCOLM M. DAVISSON, *Financing Local Governments in the San Francisco Bay Area* (Berkeley, 1963).

ELIZABETH Y. DERAN, *Financing Capital Improvements: The "Pay-As-You-Go" Approach* (Berkeley, 1961).

JOHN F. DUE, *State Sales Tax Administration* (Chicago, 1963).

JOHN F. DUE, "Studies of State-Local Tax Influences on Location of Industry," *National Tax Journal*, June, 1961, pp. 163-173.

DEAN ELLIS, "The Battle for Income Tax Simplification—The Oregon Story," *National Tax Journal*, September, 1962, pp. 246-259.

Financing State and Local Governments in Pennsylvania (University Park, 1961).

GLENN W. FISHER, "Determinants of State and Local Government Expenditures: A Preliminary Analysis," *National Tax Journal*, December, 1961, pp. 349-355.

GLENN W. FISHER, *Financing Illinois Government* (Urbana, 1960).

GLENN W. FISHER, "Interstate Variation in State and Local Government Expenditure," *National Tax Journal*, March, 1964, pp. 57-74.

GLENN W. FISHER, "Revenue and Expenditure Patterns in Five Large Cities," *Quarterly Review of Economics and Business*, Autumn, 1963, pp. 61-72.

WAYLAND D. GARDNER, "The Usefulness of Comparative Studies of State Tax Systems," *National Tax Journal*, December, 1961, pp. 388-393.

EDWIN A. GERE, JR., *Some Aspects of Massachusetts Public Finance: A Survey of Intergovernmental Fiscal Relations in the Commonwealth* (Amherst, 1961).

RALPH GRAY, "Raising State Income Tax Yields Through Equity Reforms," *National Tax Journal*, March, 1960, pp. 69-96.

WALTER T. GREANEY, JR., *The Massachusetts Budget Process* (Amherst, 1962).

WILLIAM M. GRIFFIN, *Tax Rates in Virginia Cities* (Charlottesville, 1963).

HAROLD M. GROVES and JOHN RIEW, "The Impact of Industry on Local Taxes—A Simple Model," *National Tax Journal*, June, 1963, pp. 137-146.

THOMAS F. HADY, "The Incidence of the Personal Property Tax," *National Tax Journal*, December, 1962, pp. 368-384.

JOHN T. HATCHETT and T. NOEL STERN, *Revenue Estimating in Indiana* (Bloomington, 1962).

CHARLES T. HENRY, "Financial Comparisons for City Governments," *Public Management*, May, 1961, pp. 105-107.

A. M. HILLHOUSE and S. KENNETH HOWARD, *State Capital Budgeting* (Chicago, 1963).

IRVING HOWARDS, "Property Tax Rate Limits in Illinois and Their Effect Upon Local Government," *National Tax Journal*, September, 1963, pp. 285-293.

ROBERT J. HUCKSHORN, *Municipal Finance in Idaho* (Moscow, 1960).

"Inequality in Property Tax Assessments: New Cures for an Old Ill," *Harvard Law Review*, May, 1962, pp. 1374-1395.

JACOB M. JAFFE, "The 1962 Census of Governments Report on Taxable Property Values," *National Tax Journal*, September, 1963, pp. 267-276.

ERNEST KURNOW, "Determinants of State and Local Government Expenditures Reexamined," *National Tax Journal*, September, 1963, pp. 252-255.

ERNEST KURNOW, "The Nonguaranteed Debt of State and Local Governments," *National Tax Journal*, September, 1962, pp. 239-245.

Y. S. LEONG and ROBERT M. KAMINS, "Hawaii's General Excise after a Quarter of a Century," *National Tax Journal,* December, 1963, pp. 365–388.

Y. S. LEONG and ROBERT M. KAMINS, "Property Taxation in the 50th State," *National Tax Journal,* March, 1961, pp. 59–69.

CHARLES S. LIEBMAN, HAROLD HERMAN, OLIVER P. WILLIAMS, and THOMAS R. DYE, "Social Status, Tax Resources, and Metropolitan Cooperation," *National Tax Journal,* March, 1963, pp. 56–62.

LOUIS K. LOEWENSTEIN, "The Impact of New Industry on the Fiscal Revenues and Expenditures of Suburban Communities," *National Tax Journal,* June, 1963, pp. 113–136.

HARRY E. MCALLISTER, "The Border Tax Problem in Washington," *National Tax Journal,* December, 1961, pp. 362–374.

JAMES T. MCDONALD, *Municipal Finance in Kansas, 1948–1959: A Study of Selected Cities of the Third Class* (Lawrence, 1961).

R. JOSEPH MONSEN and GARTH R. MANGUM, "Alternative Investment Outlets for Idle State Operating Funds," *State Government,* Summer, 1963, pp. 189–197.

DICK NETZER, "Paying for Services," *National Civic Review,* April, 1962, pp. 195–199.

JOHN L. O'DONNELL, "The Tax Cost of Constitutional Debt Limitation in Indiana," *National Tax Journal,* December, 1962, pp. 406–412.

JAMES A. PAPKE, "Michigan's Value-Added Tax After Seven Years," *National Tax Journal,* December, 1960, pp. 350–363.

CLARA PENNIMAN, "Property Tax Equalization in Wisconsin," *National Tax Journal,* June, 1961, pp. 182–189.

CLARA PENNIMAN and WALTER W. HELLER, *State Income Tax Administration* (Chicago, 1960).

CLARA PENNIMAN and H. RUPERT THEOBOLD, "The Wisconsin Income Tax and Erosion," *National Tax Journal,* December, 1962, pp. 413–422.

Property Taxation and the Wisconsin Tax System (Madison, 1960).

KENNETH E. QUINDRY and DON M. SOULE, "Adaptability of Local Government Revenue to Economic Differential in Kentucky," *National Tax Journal,* September, 1963, pp. 277–284.

CHARLES E. RATLIFF, JR., "Interstate Apportionment of Business Income," *National Tax Journal,* September, 1962, pp. 260–267.

CHARLES E. RATLIFF, JR., *Interstate Apportionment of Business Income for State* Income Tax Purposes (Chapel Hill, 1962).

JACK E. ROBERTSON, "Comparative Tax Burdens for a Midwestern City," *National Tax Journal,* September, 1962, pp. 308–313.

WILLIAM D. ROSS and JOSEPH M. BONIN, "A Proposed New System of Non-Highway Bond Financing for Louisiana," *National Tax Journal,* December, 1960, pp. 364–368.

GERHARD N. ROSTVOLD, "Property Tax Payments in Relation to Household Income: A Case Study of Los Angeles County," *National Tax Journal,* June, 1963, pp. 197–199.

LEON ROTHENBERG, "State Budgets—1960," *State Government,* Spring, 1960, pp. 89–95.

LEON ROTHENBERG, "State Budgets—1961," *State Government,* Spring, 1961, pp. 93–99.

LEON ROTHENBERG, "State Budgets—1962," *State Government,* Spring, 1962, pp. 89–95.

LEON ROTHENBERG, "State Budgets—1963," *State Government,* Spring, 1963, pp. 84–93.

SEYMOUR SACKS and ROBERT HARRIS, "The Determinants of State and Local Government Expenditures and Intergovernmental Flows of Funds," *National Tax Journal,* March, 1964, pp. 75–85.

LLOYD SAVILLE, "Regional Contrasts in the Development of Local Public Finance," *National Tax Journal,* June, 1962, pp. 155–169.

LYLE E. SCHALLER, "The Balance Sheet on Capital Budgeting," *National Tax Journal,* June, 1960, pp. 163–167.

WALTER F. SCHEFFER, "Problems in Municipal Finance," *Western Political Quarterly,* September, 1962, pp. 522–535.

HENRY J. SCHMANDT and G. ROSS STEPHENS, "Measuring Municipal Output," *National Tax Journal,* December, 1960, pp. 369–375.

ARLENE T. SHADOAN, "Developments in State Budget Administration," *Public Administration Review,* December, 1963, pp. 227–231.

ALAN H. SMITH, "State Payments to Local Governments in Wisconsin," *National Tax Journal,* September, 1962, pp. 297–307.

RICHARD SPANGLER, "The Effect of Population Growth upon State and Local Government Expenditures," *National Tax Journal,* June, 1963, pp. 193–196.

FRANCES L. STARNER *et al.,* General Obliga-

tion Bond Financing by Local Governments: A Survey of State Controls (Berkeley, 1961).

J. A STOCKFISCH, "Fees and Service Charges as a Source of City Revenues: A Case Study of Los Angeles," *National Tax Journal,* June, 1960, pp. 97–121.

MILTON C. TAYLOR, "Local Income Taxes after Twenty-One Years," *National Tax Journal,* June, 1962, pp. 113–124.

MILTON C. TAYLOR, *Local Income Taxes as a Source of Revenue for Michigan Communities* (East Lansing, 1961).

ROGER C. VAN TASSEL, *State Regulation of Boston's Financial Administration* (Amherst, 1961).

JOHN A. VIEG (ed.), *California Local Finance* (Stanford, 1960).

W. PAUL WALKER, *Taxation in Maryland with Special Reference to State-County Fiscal Relations* (College Park, 1962).

PAUL H. WILEDEN, "Earmarking: Good or Bad?" *State Government,* Autumn, 1960, pp. 251–255.

DEIL S. WRIGHT, ROBERT W. MARKER, and GARLYN H. WESSEL, *A Half-Century of Local Government Finances: The Case of Iowa—1910–1960* (Iowa City, 1963).

REUBEN A. ZUBROW, "Recent Trends and Developments in Municipal Finance," *Public Management,* November, 1963, pp. 247–254.

REUBEN A. ZUBROW and ROBERT L. DECKER, "The Taxation of Legalized Gambling in Nevada," *National Tax Journal,* March, 1962, pp. 71–81.

GENERAL BIBLIOGRAPHY

INDEX

TABLE OF CASES

↩ GENERAL BIBLIOGRAPHY

CHARLES R. ADRIAN, *Governing Our Fifty States and Their Communities* (New York, 1963).

HENRY M. ALEXANDER, *Government in Arkansas: Organization and Function at State, County, and Municipal Levels,* rev. ed. (Little Rock, 1959).

TOTTEN J. ANDERSEN, "California: Enigma of National Politics," in Frank H. Jonas (ed.), *Western Politics* (Salt Lake City, 1961), pp. 69–112.

WILLIAM ANDERSON, CLARA PENNIMAN, and EDWARD W. WEIDNER, *Government in the Fifty States,* rev. ed. (New York, 1960).

ROBERT S. BABCOCK, *State and Local Government and Politics,* 2nd ed. (New York, 1963).

CHARLES P. BEALL, "Wyoming: The Equality State," in Frank H. Jonas (ed.), *Western Politics* (Salt Lake City, 1961), pp. 335–356.

WILBOURN E. BENTON, *Texas: Its Government and Politics* (Englewood Cliffs, N. J., 1961).

PAULINE BETH (comp.), "Selected New York City and New York State Dissertations and Theses," *Municipal Reference Library Notes,* November, 1961, pp. 133–142.

Bibliography on State and Local Government in New England (Boston, 1952).

PENELOPE BILLACK (comp.), *Michigan Bibliographies and Indexes* (Ypsilanti, 1960).

GEORGE S. BLAIR, *American Local Government* (New York, 1964).

EUGENE J. BOCKMAN (comp.), "The Basic Literature for Political Campaigning in New York City," *Municipal Reference Library Notes,* September, 1962, pp. 117–122.

HUGH A. BONE, "Washington: Free Style Politics," in Frank H. Jonas (ed.), *Western Politics* (Salt Lake City, 1961), pp. 303–334.

DAVID A. BOOTH, *A Guide to Local Politics* (East Lansing, 1961).

ALAN CLEM, *South Dakota Political Almanac* (Vermillion, 1962).

WINSTON W. CROUCH and JOHN C. BOLLENS, *Your California Government in Action,* 2nd ed. (Berkeley, 1960).

WINSTON W. CROUCH, DEAN McHENRY, JOHN C. BOLLENS, and STANLEY SCOTT, *California Government and Politics,* 3rd ed. (Englewood Cliffs, N. J., 1964).

JAMES R. DONOGHUE, *How Wisconsin Voted, 1848–1960* (Madison, 1962).

J. C. DOYLE, "Alaska: On Its Way," *State Government,* Winter, 1960, pp. 2–10.

JAMES W. DRURY and ASSOCIATES, *The Government of Kansas* (Lawrence, 1961).

ROBERT W. DURRENBERGER (comp.), *Sources of Information about California* (Northridge, 1961).

W. O. FARBER, T. C. GEARY and W. H. CAPE, *Government of South Dakota* (Sioux Falls, 1962).

THOMAS A. FLINN, "The Outline of Ohio Politics," *Western Political Quarterly,* September, 1960, pp. 702–721.

Florida Legislative Council, Committee on Governmental Organization (comp.), *Bibliography of Florida Government, 1960* (Tallahassee, 1960).

CHARLES N. FORTENBERRY, *A Handbook for Mississippi Legislators, 1960* (University, Miss., 1960).

625

WAYNE L. FRANCIS and SHARRON E. DOERNER (eds.), *Indiana Votes* (Bloomington, 1962).

RICHARD T. FROST (ed.), *Cases in State and Local Government* (Englewood Cliffs, N. J., 1961).

DANIEL R. GRANT and H. C. NIXON, *State and Local Government in America* (Boston, 1963).

W. BROOKE GRAVES, *Centralization of Government in Hawaii* (Washington, D. C., 1962).

ALEXANDER GREENE, *Ohio Government* (Englewood Cliffs, N. J., 1961).

LEROY C. HARDY, *California Government* (New York, 1964).

JOSEPH P. HARRIS, *California Politics*, 3rd ed. (Stanford, 1961).

ANNIE MARY HARTSFIELD and ELSTON E. ROADY, *Florida Vote, 1920–1962* (Tallahassee, 1963).

JAMES HERNDON, CHARLES PRESS, and OLIVER P. WILLIAMS (comps.), *A Selected Bibliography of Materials in State Government and Politics* (Lexington, Ky., 1963).

W. EUGENE HOLLON, "Politics and Politicians: New Mexico and Arizona," in *The Southwest: Old and New* (New York, 1961), pp. 390–412.

W. EUGENE HOLLON, "Politics and Politicians: Texas and Oklahoma," in *The Southwest: Old and New* (New York, 1961), pp. 360–389.

HENRY F. HOWE, *Massachusetts: There She Is, Behold Her* (New York, 1960).

BERNARD L. HYINK, SEYOM BROWN, ERNEST W. THACKER, *Politics and Government in California* (New York, 1963).

FREDERICK C. IRION, "New Mexico: The Political State," in Frank H. Jonas (ed.), *Western Politics* (Salt Lake City, 1961), pp. 223–246.

MALCOLM E. JEWELL, *Kentucky Votes*, 2 vols. (Lexington, 1963).

FRANK H. JONAS, "Utah: Cross Roads of the West," in Frank H. Jonas (ed.), *Western Politics* (Salt Lake City, 1961), pp. 272–302.

ROBERT F. KARSCH, *The Government of Missouri*, 7th ed. (Columbia, 1961).

HERBERT KAUFMAN, *Politics and Policies in State and Local Governments* (Englewood Cliffs, N. J., 1963).

JOE W. KRAUS, *Notes on Virginia State Bibliography*, 2nd ed. (Richmond, 1960).

JOSEPH G. LAPALOMBARA, *Guide to Michigan Politics* (East Lansing, 1960).

EARL LATHAM and GEORGE GOODWIN, JR., *Massachusetts Politics*, rev. ed. (Medford, 1960).

League of Women Voters of Nebraska, *Nebraska State Government* (Lincoln, 1961).

DUANE LOCKARD, "Connecticut: The Politics of Competition," and "Connecticut: Legislative Politics and Party Competition," in *New England State Politics* (Princeton, 1959), pp. 228–269 and 270–304.

DUANE LOCKARD, "Maine: Pine, Power, and Politics," in *New England State Politics* (Princeton, 1959), pp. 79–118.

DUANE LOCKARD, "Massachusetts: The Standing Order Under Attack," and "Lawmaking in Massachusetts: Traditional Pomp and Political Circumstance," in *New England State Politics* (Princeton, 1959), pp. 119–147 and 148–171.

DUANE LOCKARD, "New Hampshire Politics: Triumph of Conservatism," in *New England State Politics* (Princeton, 1959), pp. 46–78.

DUANE LOCKARD, *The Politics of State and Local Government* (New York, 1963).

DUANE LOCKARD, "Rhode Island: One Party Facade and Two Party Reality?" and "Rhode Island: Politics on the Seamy Side," in *New England State Politics* (Princeton, 1959), pp. 172–208 and 209–277.

DUANE LOCKARD, "Vermont: Political Paradox," in *New England State Politics* (Princeton, 1959), pp. 8–45.

CLIFTON MCCLESKY et al., *The Government and Politics of Texas* (Boston, 1963).

STUART A. MACCORKLE and DICK SMITH, *Texas Government*, 4th ed. (New York, 1960).

RUSSELL W. MADDOX, JR., and ROBERT F. FUQUAY, *State and Local Governments* (Princeton, 1966).

ARTHUR F. MANN, *Hawaii: The Fiftieth State: Government and Economy* (Honolulu, 1960).

ELWYN E. MARINER, *This Is Your Massachusetts Government: A Description of the Structure and Functions of the State and Local Governments of the People of the Commonwealth of Massachusetts*, 3rd ed. (Arlington Heights, 1962).

BOYD A. MARTIN, "Idaho: The Sectional State," in Frank H. Jonas (ed.), *Western Politics* (Salt Lake City, 1961), pp. 161–180.

CURTIS MARTIN, "Colorado: The Highest State," in Frank H. Jonas (ed.), *Western Politics* (Salt Lake City, 1961), pp. 113–136.

CURTIS MARTIN, *Colorado Politics* (Denver, 1962).

BRUCE B. MASON, *Arizona General Election Results, 1911–1960* (Tempe, 1961).

GEORGE B. MATHER, *Voting in Iowa* (Iowa City, 1960).

DONALD R. MATTHEWS (comp.), *North Carolina Votes* (Chapel Hill, 1962).

NORMAN MELLER, "Hawaii and Honolulu Revamp Governments," *National Civic Review*, November, 1960, pp. 551–552.

NORMAN MELLER and DANIEL W. TUTTLE, JR., "Hawaii: The Aloha State," in Frank H. Jonas (ed.), *Western Politics* (Salt Lake City, 1961), pp. 137–160.

G. THEODORE MITAU, *Politics in Minnesota* (Minneapolis, 1960).

G. THEODORE MITAU, *A Selected Bibliography of Minnesota Government, Politics and Public Finance Since 1900* (Saint Paul, 1960).

G. THEODORE MITAU and HAROLD W. CHASE (eds.), *Insoluble Problems: Case-Problems on the Functions of State and Local Government* (New York, 1964).

G. THEODORE MITAU and HAROLD W. CHASE (eds.) *Proximate Solutions: Case-Problems in State and Local Government* (New York, 1964).

FRANK MUNGER and RALPH STRAETZ, *New York Politics* (New York, 1960).

North Dakota Legislative Research Committee, *Legislative Handbook on State Governmental Agencies and Their Principal Duties* (Bismarck, 1960).

DANIEL M. OGDEN, JR. and HUGH A. BONE, *Washington Politics* (New York, 1960).

STAN OPOTOWSKY, *The Longs of Louisiana* (New York, 1960).

JAMES S. OTTENBERG (comp.), "Political Reform, 'Machines' and Big City Politics, 1950–1962: A Selected and Annotated Bibliography," *Municipal Reference Library Notes*, November, 1962, pp. 153–159.

RALPH E. OWINGS, *Montana Directory of Public Affairs, 1804–1960* (Hamilton, 1960).

GERTRUDE PARMELEE (comp.), *A South Dakota Bibliography* (Rapid City, 1960).

THOMAS PAYNE, "Under the Copper Dome: Politics in Montana," in Frank H. Jonas (ed.), *Western Politics* (Salt Lake City, 1961), pp. 181–206.

ROBERT J. PITCHELL (ed.), *Indiana Votes* (Bloomington, 1960).

CHARLES PRESS (comp.), *Selected Bibliography, Michigan Government and Politics* (East Lansing, 1963).

CHARLES PRESS and OLIVER WILLIAMS, *State Manuals, Blue Books, and Election Results* (Berkeley, 1962).

HUGH D. PRICE and BRUCE B. MASON, *Florida Voters' Guide*, rev. ed. (Gainesville, 1960).

"Problems of Iowa Government," *Iowa Business Digest*, August, 1960, pp. 3–35.

AUSTIN RANNEY, *Illinois Politics* (New York, 1960).

JOHN E. REEVES, *Kentucky Government*, 4th ed. (Lexington, 1960).

ROSS R. RICE, "Amazing Arizona: Politics in Transition," in Frank H. Jonas (ed.), *Western Politics* (Salt Lake City, 1961), pp. 41–68.

PHILIP J. SCHLESSINGER and RICHARD WRIGHT, *Elements of Government in California* (New York, 1962).

HERMAN E. SLOTNICK, "Alaska: Empire of the North," in Frank H. Jonas (ed.), *Western Politics* (Salt Lake City, 1961), pp. 21–40.

JOHN O. STITELY, *An Outline of Rhode Island State Government* (Kingston, 1961).

JOHN M. SWARTHOUT, "Oregon: Political Experiment Station," in Frank H. Jonas (ed.), *Western Politics* (Salt Lake City, 1961), pp. 247–272.

H. V. THORNTON and GENE ALDRICH, *The Government of Oklahoma* (Oklahoma City, 1960), pp. 366.

HENRY A. TURNER and JOHN A. VIEG, *The*

Government and Politics of California (New York, 1960).

University of Hawaii, *The Structure of the Hawaii State Government* (Honolulu, 1960).

University of Hawaii, *Guide to Government in Hawaii* (Honolulu, 1961).

ROBERT S. WALKER and SAMUEL C. PATTERSON, *Oklahoma Goes Wet: The Repeal of Prohibition* (New York, 1962).

DONALD H. WEBSTER et al., *Washington State Government: Administrative, Organization and Functions,* revised by David W. Stevens (Seattle, 1962).

JOHN P. WHITE, *Michigan Votes: Election Statistics, 1928–1956* (Ann Arbor, 1958). Supplements for 1960 and 1962 elections.

JOSEPH F. ZIMMERMANN, *State and Local Government* (New York, 1962).

INDEX

TABLE OF CASES

ACKNOWLEDGMENTS

Bureau of the Census, *The 1960 Census of Population:* p. 404

Copyright 1964 *Congressional Quarterly,* Inc.: p. 114

© 1957 by The New York Times Company: p. 613
© 1962 by The New York Times Company: p. 517
© 1963 by The New York Times Company: p. 467
© 1964 by The New York Times Company: pp. 96, 240, 547, 616
All reprinted by permission.

Courtesy of The Register and Tribune Syndicate, Des Moines, Iowa: p. 107

Reprinted by permission of The University of Texas: p. 168